The Maastricht Collection

Europa Law Publishing, Amsterdam 2019

The Maastricht Collection (Sixth Edition)

Edited by Sascha Hardt & Nicole Kornet

Volume IV: Comparative Private Law

Europa Law Publishing is a publishing company
specializing in European Union law, international trade
law, public international law, environmental law and
comparative national law.
For further information please contact Europa Law
Publishing via email: info@europalawpublishing.com
or visit our website at: www.europalawpublishing.com.

© Europa Law Publishing, S. Hardt, N. Kornet, 2019

Typeset in Scala and Scala Sans, Graphic design by
G2K Designers, Groningen/Amsterdam

NUR 822
ISBN 9789089522115 (volumes I-IV)
ISBN 9789089522153 (volume I)
ISBN 9789089522160 (volume II)
ISBN 9789089522177 (volume III)
ISBN 9789089522146 (volume IV)

Preface to the sixth edition

The Faculty of Law of Maastricht University attaches great importance to the study of European and comparative law. Its curriculum includes several internationally oriented Master programmes and the *European Law School* bachelor programme, in which law is taught from a European and comparative perspective from the very first day. These four volumes, *The Maastricht Collection*, are based on the Maastricht Law Faculty's expertise and experience in teaching European, international, and comparative law.

The Maastricht Collection comprises a selection of legal instruments and provisions which have proven to be particularly relevant and useful to students and practitioners of European and comparative law. It includes constitutions, codes and statutory legislation from France, Germany, the Netherlands, and the United Kingdom, international treaties, and instruments of international organisations, as well as legal instruments of the European Union.

The content of the present sixth edition of *The Maastricht Collection* is divided into four volumes, corresponding to different areas of the law. Volume I contains selected international treaties and protocols, important resolutions of international organisations, international and European fundamental rights instruments, as well as the Treaties and selected secondary legislation of the European Union; Volume II contains national instruments from France, Germany, the Netherlands, and the United Kingdom in the areas of constitutional law (where the US constitution is also included as one of the standard points of reference of comparative constitutional law), administrative law, as well as criminal law and procedure; Volume III contains instruments from international and European private law, including international treaties and secondary EU legislation on international business law, private international law, European company law, European private law and civil procedure, as well as tax law; Volume IV contains national legislation from France, Germany, the Netherlands, and the United Kingdom in the area of private law and civil procedure.

Next to a comprehensive update and revision of all the instruments in *The Maastricht Collection*, this sixth edition also contains a number of useful additions, such as legislation relating to Brexit and statutory legislation from France, Germany, the Netherlands, and the United Kingdom in the area of criminal procedure. With these updates and additions, *The Maastricht Collection* now presents itself as an even more comprehensive resource for students of European, international, and comparative law.

While many of the materials included in these four volumes are reproduced in the original English, *The Maastricht Collection* remains true to its original aim of facilitating the study of comparative law by offering fresh translations of legal instruments from different national legal traditions. Many existing translations of written law, including officious translations available on government websites, are significantly out of date and not sufficiently faithful to the original. They often seek to turn old-fashioned or ambiguous original texts into modern and elegant English. Or, instead of translating, they seek to *explain* how certain terms or formulations are interpreted in practice. The translations contained in *The Maastricht Collection* remain true to the content, style, and syntax of the original as far as possible, allowing the reader to appreciate not only the substance but also the authentic form of legal sources.

Formatting styles, such as the use of §§ ('Paragraphs') rather than 'Articles' in most German statutes, and 'Sections' in UK legislation, or the absence of paragraph numbering in French legislation, are preserved. In the interest of consistency of style, the headings of individual articles are suppressed in translated materials. Enactment formulas are omitted; preambles are retained unless indicated otherwise. For easy reference within translated texts, key legal terms and proper names are added in the original language as in-text citations between square brackets.

The idea to create *The Maastricht Collection* came about during a conversation between Philipp Kiiver and Nicole Kornet about the need for English language learning resources for students following a programme on European and comparative law taught entirely in English. Just like students who follow a curriculum oriented on national law, these students also need a compilation of legislation relevant to their studies. Since the publication of the second edition, the editorship of the Maastricht Collection has since been continued by Sascha Hardt and Nicole Kornet. We are more than grateful to Philipp for being such a driving force behind the idea of *The Maastricht Collection*.

We would in particular like to thank Sarah Sørensen, a student of the *European Law School* and assistant to the editors, without whose meticulous hard work and dedication this edition of *The Maastricht Collection* and its publication in keeping with the regular two-year interval would not have been possible.

We would further like to thank the following people for their contributions and input to this and the previous editions: Dr. Bram Akkermans, Prof. Chris Backes, Dr. Anna Berlee, Stephanie Blom, Claire Boost, Caroline Calomme, Sylvain Caris, Prof. Fons Coomans, Merel Dekker, Prof. Mariolina Eliantonio, Prof. Sjef van Erp, Dr. Catalina Goanta, Dr. Franziska Grashof, Dr. Nicola Gundt, Prof. René de Groot, Heike Hauröder, Prof. Aalt-Willem Heringa, Dr. Sander Jansen, Prof. Anselm Kamperman Sanders, Prof. André Klip, Maartje Krabbe, Giesela Kristoferitsch, Prof. Raymond Luja, Prof. Gerrit van Maanen, Prof. Mieke Olaerts, Dr. Christina Peristeridou, Dr. Eveline Ramaekers, Dr. Stephan Rammeloo, Prof. Remco van Rhee, Dr. David Roef, Gereon Roetering, Dr. Kees Saarloos, Dr. René Seerden, Prof. Jan Smits, Prof. Taru Spronken, Dr. Ilse van den Driessche, Dr. Jacob van der Velde, Prof. Luc Verhey, Dr. Remme Verkerk, Yvonne Walhof, Dr. Stefan Weishaar, Dr. Daniëlle Wenders, Rob van de Westelaken, Irene Wieczorek and Prof. Jan Willems.

Maastricht, June 2019,

Dr. Sascha Hardt, Assistant Professor of Comparative Constitutional Law
Dr. Nicole Kornet, Senior Lecturer in Commercial Law and programme coordinator of the *European Law School*

Preface to the sixth edition
Contents

VOLUME IV: COMPARATIVE PRIVATE LAW

France

Civil Code

Civil Code [Code Civil]. Selected provisions from the Preliminary Title and Books I, II, III and IV. As last amended by the Act of 20 April 2018, LOI n° 2018-287, JORF n° 0093, 21 April 2018.*

Preliminary Title. Of the publication, effects and application of laws in general

[Articles 1 and 2 are omitted.]

Article 3. Laws of public order and security [les lois de police et de sûreté] bind all those residing in the territory.
Immovables, even those owned by foreigners, are governed by French law.
Laws concerning the status and capacity of persons govern the French, even while residing in foreign countries.

[Articles 4 is omitted.]

Article 5. The courts shall be prohibited from issuing rules which take the form of general and binding decisions on those cases which are submitted to them.

Article 6. One cannot derogate by private agreements from laws which concern public policy and good morals.

[Article 6-1 is omitted.]

Book I. Of persons

Title I. Of civil rights

[Article 7 is omitted.]

Article. 8. Every French person enjoys civil rights.

Article. 9. Everyone has the right to respect for his family life.

[The remainder of Article 9 and Article 9-1 is omitted.]

Article 10. Each person is obliged to assist in the judicial process to reveal the truth.
The person who without a lawful reason evades this obligation after having been legally obliged to assist may be forced to comply, if necessary by means of a penalty [astreinte] or a civil fine [amende], without prejudice to damages.

[Articles 11 – 15 are omitted.]

Chapter II. Of respect for the human body

[Articles 16 – 16-6 are omitted.]

Article 16-7. All agreements relating to procreation or gestation for the sake of a third party are void.

[The remainder of Title I and Titles I bis – IV are omitted.]

Title VI. Of divorce

[Chapters I-IV are omitted.]

Chapter V. Of divorce and judicial separation

Article 309. Divorce and judicial separation [le divorce et la séparation de corps] are governed by French law:
- where one and the other spouse have the French nationality;
- where both spouses have their domicile on French territory;
- where no foreign law considers itself applicable, whereas French courts have jurisdiction to adjudicate a case of divorce or judicial separation.

---

*   Translation by Sascha Hardt, Bram Akkermans, Eveline Ramaekers & Anna Berlee.

Title VII. Of parent and child

Article 310. All children whose parentage has been legally established have the same rights and the same duties in relation to their father and mother. They are taken into the family of each of them.

Chapter I. General provisions

[Articles 310-1 – 310-2 and Section 1 are omitted.]

Section 2. Of the conflict of laws relating to parentage

Article 311-14. Parentage is governed by the personal law of the mother on the day of birth of the child; if the mother is unknown, by the personal law of the child.

Article 311-15. Nevertheless, if the child and his father and mother or either one of them has their habitual residence in France, together or separately, the apparent status produces all the effects according to French law, even if the other elements of parentage would depend on a foreign law.

Article 311-17. Voluntary acknowledgement of paternity or maternity is valid if it has been made in accordance with either the personal law of the person who acts, or with the personal law of the child.

Article 311-18. (Repealed.)

[The remainder of Title VII and Titles VIII and IX are omitted.]

Title X. Minority, Guardianship, and Emancipation

Chapter I. Minority

Article 388. A minor is the individual of one or the other sex who has not yet reached the age of eighteen years.
Radiological bone examinations for the purpose of establishing the age of an individual in the absence of valid identity documents and where the stated age appears unlikely may only be carried out upon a judicial decision and with the consent of the person concerned.
The conclusions of such examinations, which must state their margin of error, may not constitute the sole basis for determining whether the person concerned is a minor. The person concerned has the benefit of the doubt.
In case of doubt as to the minority of the person concerned, the age may not be evaluated on the basis of an examination of the pubertal development of the primary and secondary sexual characteristics of the person concerned.

Article 388-1. In any proceedings concerning him, a minor capable of discernment may, without prejudice to any provisions prescribing his intervention or his consent, be heard by the judge or, where the interest of the minor demands it, by the person designated by the judge for this purpose. Such a hearing must take place where the minor requests it. Where the he refuses to be heard, the judge assesses the reasons for this refusal. He may be heard alone, with a lawyer, or with a person of his choice. If this choice does not appear in conformity with the interest of the minor, the judge may move to designate another person.
The hearing of a minor does not make him a party to the proceedings.
The judge ensures that the minor has been informed of his right to by heard and to be assisted by a lawyer.

Article 388-1-1. The legal administrator represents the minor in all acts of civil life, except in case where the law or usage authorise the minors to act themselves.

[The remainder of Title X is omitted.]

Title XI. Age of Majority and Adults Protected by Law

Chapter 1. General Provisions

Section 1. Provisions independent of measures of protection

Article 414. Majority is fixed at having completed eighteen years; at this age, everyone has capacity to exercise the rights he enjoys.

Article 414-1. In order to enter into a valid transaction, it is necessary to be of sound mind. But it is for those who seek annulment on that ground to prove the existence of a mental disorder at the time of the transaction.

[The remainder of Section 1 and Section 2 are omitted.]

Chapter II: Judicial Measures for the Protection of Adults

Section 1. General Provisions

Article 425. Any person who is unable to safeguard his own interests by reason of a medically established change in mental faculties or physical abilities which prevents the expression his will, can benefit from a measure of legal protection provided for in this Chapter.
If it is not otherwise provided, the measure is intended to protect both the person and the patrimonial interests of the person. It may, however, be expressly limited to one of these two purposes.

[The remainder of Section 1 is omitted.]

Section 2. Provisions Common to Judicial Measures

Article 428. A judicial measure of protection may only be ordered by the judge in case of necessity and where there interests of the person concerned cannot be sufficiently provided for by the implementation of a power of attorney [mandate de protection future] granted by the person concerned, by the application of the rules of general law governing representation, of those relating to the respective rights and duties of spouses and the rules governing marriage, in particular those laid down in articles 217, 219, 1426, and 1429, or by another less constraining measure of protection. The measure of protection is individualised in proportion to the degree of alteration of the personal capacities of the person concerned.

[The remainder of section 2 and Section 3 are omitted.]

Section 4. Curatorship and Guardianship

Article 440. The person who, without being unable to act himself, is in need, is in need of permanent assistance or supervision in important transactions of civil life for one of the reasons mentioned in Article 425, can be placed under curatorship [curatelle].
Curatorship is ordered only if it is shown that judicial protection cannot assure sufficient protection. The person who, for one of the causes mentioned in Article 425, must be represented in a continual manner in the acts of civil life, may be placed under guardianship [tutelle].
Guardianship is declared only if it is shown that neither judicial protective supervision nor curatorship can guarantee a sufficient protection.

[The remainder of Book I is omitted.]

Book II. Of things and the different modifications of the right of ownership

Title I. Of the classification of things

Article 516. All things [biens] are movable or immovable.

Chapter 1. Of immovables

Article 517. Things [biens] are immovable, by their nature, by their purpose, or through the object [objet] to which they apply.

Article 518. Land and buildings are immovable by their nature.

[Articles 519 – 525 are omitted.]

Article 526. Immovable are, through the object [objet] to which they apply:
The right of usufruct of immovable objects [choses];
Servitudes or easements [services fanciers];
Actions to revindicate an immovable.

Chapter II. Of movables

Article 527. Things are movable by their nature or by operation of law.

Article 528. Movable are by their nature such goods as can be transported from one place to another.

[The remainder of Chapter II is omitted.]

Chapter III. Of things in their relation to those who possess them

Article 537. Private persons have free disposition over the things [biens] that belong to them, within the boundaries established by law.

Things which do not belong to private persons are administered and may not be disposed of other than in the forms and following the rules that apply in particular to them.

Article 539. The things [biens] of persons who have died without any heirs or whose things are abandoned, belong to the State.

[Article 542 is omitted.]

Article 543. One may have in respect to things either a right of ownership, or a simple right of enjoyment, or a servitude.

Title II. Of ownership

Article 544. Ownership is the right to enjoy and dispose of objects [choses] in the most absolute manner, provided they are not used in a way prohibited by statutes or regulations.

Article 545. No one may be compelled to yield his ownership, unless for public purposes and for a fair and previous indemnity.

Article 546. Ownership of an object [chose], whether movable or immovable, gives right to all it produces and to that which is accessory to it, whether naturally or artificially.

This right is called "accession" [droit d'accession].

[Chapter I is omitted.]

Chapter II. On accession of things that unite or incorporate with a thing

Article 552. The ownership of land encompasses the ownership of what is on and below it. The owner may place any plants or constructions that he deems fit on it, except for those exceptions laid down in the title 'on servitudes and land services'. He may place any constructions and conduct any excavations under his land that he deems fit and draw from those excavations all products that they may provide, except for the amendments resulting from statutes and regulations concerning mines, and of statutes and policing measures [règlements de police].

[The remainder of Title II is omitted.]

Title III. Of usufruct, use and habitation

Chapter I. Of usufruct

Article 578. The right of usufruct is the right to use and enjoy an object [chose] of another in the same way as an owner himself, but on condition that the substance of the object is preserved.

[Articles 579 – 580 are omitted.]

Article 581. It may be created on any kind of movable and immovable things [biens meubles ou immeubles].

Section 1. Of the rights of the usufructuary

Article 582. The usufructuary has the right to enjoy every kind of fruit, whether natural, industrial or civil, which may be produced by the object [objet] in relation to which he has a right of usufruct.

[Articles 583 – 586 are omitted.]

Article 587. Where a right of usufruct is created on objects [choses] which cannot be used without being consumed, such as money, grain, liquors, the usufructuary has a right to use them, but with the obligation to, at the end of the usufruct, return either objects of the same quantity and quality or their value estimated at the date or return.

[The remainder of Section 1 is omitted.]

Section 2. Of obligations of the usufructuary

Article 600. The usufructuary takes the objects [choses] in the way they are, but he may not commence his enjoyment before, in the presence of the owner, drafting an inventory of the movables and an inventory of immovables that are subject to the right of usufruct.

Article 601. He shall guarantee to enjoy reasonably, if this is not dispensed with by the instrument creating the usufruct; however, the father and mother who have the legal usufruct of their children's property, a seller or donor, under the condition of the usufruct, are not obliged to give security.

[The remainder of Section 2 is omitted.]

Section 3. Of the ways a usufruct comes to an end

Article 617. A usufruct is destroyed:
By the death of the usufructuary;
By the expiry of the time for which it was granted;
By the consolidation or vesting in the same person of the two capacities of usufructuary and of owner;
By non-use of the right for thirty years;
By the total loss of the object [chose] on which the usufruct was created.

[Article 618 is omitted.]

Article 619. The right of usufruct which is not granted to private persons lasts no longer than thirty years.

[Articles 620 – 622 are omitted.]

Article 623. Where only a part of an object [chose] subject to the right of usufruct is destroyed, the right of usufruct is preserved on that what remains.

Article 624. Where a right of usufruct is created on a building only, and that building is destroyed by fire or by another accident, or collapses from decay, the usufructuary does not have a right to use and enjoy the land or on the materials.
Where the right of usufruct was created on an area of which the building was a part only, the usufructuary has the right to use and enjoy the land and the materials.

Chapter II. Of use and habitation

Article 625. Rights of use and habitation are created and destroyed in the same manner as the right of usufruct.

[Article 626 is omitted.]

Article 627. The user and he who has a right to reside must enjoy it reasonably.

[Articles 628 – 630 are omitted.]

Article 631. The user may not assign nor lease his right to another.

[The remainder of Title III is omitted.]

Title IV. Of servitudes and land services

Article 637. A right of servitude is a burden imposed on a piece of land for the use of that land on behalf of another owner.

[Articles 638 – 639 are omitted.]

Chapter I. Of servitudes that arise from a specific factual situation

Article 640. Lower pieces of land are subjected to those pieces of land that are situated higher, to receive waters that flow naturally from them without the hand of man having contributed thereto.
An owner of a lower piece of land may not raise dams that prevent that flow.
An owner of an upper piece of land may not do anything that worsens the servitude of the lower piece of land.

[Articles 641 – 648 are omitted.]

Chapter II. Of servitudes that arise by operation of law

Article 649. Servitudes created by operation of law [établies par la loi] are for the purpose of public or municipal use, or for use by private individuals.

Article 650. Those created for public or municipal use have as their objects towing-paths along public waterways [marchepied de long des cours d'eau dominiaux], the construction or repair of roads, and other public or municipal works.

All that relates to that kind of servitudes is determined by statutes or specific regulations.

[Articles 651 – 652 and Sections 1 – 4 are omitted.]

Section 5. Of the right of way

Article 682. An owner whose land is enclosed and who has no way out to the public road, or only one which is insufficient either due to an agricultural, industrial or commercial exploitation of his land, or due to operations of construction or development that are being carried out, is entitled to claim on his neighbour's land a right of way sufficient for complete access to his own land, provided he pays a compensation in proportion to the damage he may cause.

[Articles 683 – 685-1 are omitted.]

Chapter III. Of servitudes created by an act of man

Section 1. Of the different classes of servitudes that may be created in respect to things

Article 686. Owners are permitted to create in respect to their things, or in favour of their things, such servitudes as they deem fit, provided however that the servitudes created are imposed neither on a person, nor in favour of a person, but only on a piece of land and for a piece of land, and provided that those servitudes are not in any way contrary to public policy.

The use and extent of the servitudes so created are regulated by the instrument that creates them; by lack of an instrument, by the following rules.

[Articles 687 – 689 are omitted.]

Section 2: How servitudes are established

Article 690. Continuous and apparent servitudes are acquired on title, or by possession of thirty years.

[Articles 691 – 695 are omitted.]

Article 696. If one creates a servitude, one is obliged to provide all that is necessary to use it.

Thus, a servitude to tap water from another's fountain necessarily implies a right of passage.

Section 3. Of the rights of the owner of the piece land on which the servitude runs

Article 697. A person whose land is burdened with a right of servitude has the right to make all works necessary to use and maintain the right.

[Article 698 is omitted.]

Article 699. Even in the case where the owner of the land on which the right of servitude runs is compelled under the instrument of creation to make the works necessary for the use or preservation of a right of servitude at his own expense, he may always exempt himself from that burden by abandoning the servient land to the owner of the land that benefits from the existence of the right of servitude.

[Articles 700 – 702 are omitted.]

Section 4. On how servitudes cease to exist

Article 703. Rights of servitude are destroyed when the things are in such a condition that they can no longer be used.

Article 704. They revive when things are restored in such a manner that they can be continued to be used; unless so much time has already passed to give rise to the presumption that the right of servitude is destroyed, as is stated in Article 707.

Article 705. A right of servitude is destroyed when the ownership of the servient land and the ownership of the dominant land are united in the same hands.

Article 706. A right of servitude is destroyed by non-use for a period of thirty years.

Article 707. The thirty years begin to run, according to the different kinds of servitudes, either from the day a holder of right ceased to enjoy them, with respect to discontinuous servitudes, or from the day when an act contrary to the right of servitude has been performed, with respect to continuous servitudes.

[The remainder of Book II is omitted.]

Book III. Of the various ways in which ownership is acquired

General Provisions

Article 711. Ownership of things [biens] is acquired and transferred through succession, through a donation during life or by testament, and as a result of obligations.

Article 712. Ownership is also acquired through accession or incorporation, and through prescription.

Article 713. Things [biens] that have no master belong to the community on whose territory the things are situated. By means of a decision of the municipal council, the community may renounce the exercise of its rights on all or part of its territory, for the benefit of a public institution of inter-communal cooperation endowed with budgetary autonomy of which it is a member. In this case, the things without master are deemed to belong to the public institution of inter-communal cooperation endowed with budgetary autonomy.
If the community or the public institution of inter-communal cooperation endowed with budgetary autonomy renounces the exercise of its rights, ownership is transferred by operation of the law:
1° for things situated in the zones defined in article L. 322-1 of the Environmental Code [Code de l'Environnement], to the coastal and lake shores conservation authority [conservatoire de l'espace littoral et des rivages lacustres] where it makes a request to that effect or, failing that, to the regional conservation authority for natural spaces [conservatoire régional d'espaces naturels] certified pursuant to article L. 414-11 of the same Code or, failing that, to the State;
2° for other things, to the State.

Article 714. There are objects [choses] that do not belong to anyone and whose usage is common to all.
Public order statutes regulate the manner in which these are to be enjoyed.

[Articles 715 – 717 are omitted.]

Title I. Of succession

[Chapters I – IV are omitted.]

Chapter VII. Of legal regime of co-entitlement [régime légal de l'indivision]

Article 815. Nothing may be restricted to remain in a situation of co-entitlement [indivision] and a division may always be initiated, unless this has been postponed by a judgment or an agreement.

Article 815-1. Persons who are co-entitled [indivisaires] may conclude agreements relating to the exercise of their common rights, in conformity with Articles 1873-1 to 1873-18.

[The remainder of Title I is omitted.]

Title II. Of gifts inter vivos and of wills [liberalités]

Chapter I. General provisions

[Articles 893 – 900 are omitted.]

Art. 900-1. Non-transferability clauses concerning a thing donated or bequeathed are valid only where they are temporary and justified by a serious and legitimate aim. Even in that case, a donee or legatee may be judicially authorized to dispose of the thing if the aim which justified the clause has disappeared or if it happens that a more important interest so requires.
The provisions of this Article do not prejudice gratuitous transfers granted to legal persons or even to natural persons responsible for forming legal persons.

[The remainder of Chapter I and Chapters II – III are omitted.]

Chapter IV. Of inter vivos gifts

Section 1. Of the form of inter vivos gifts

Article 931. All acts containing a gift among living persons shall be passed before a notary in the ordinary form of contracts; and the original shall remain, under penalty of annulment.

[The remainder of Chapter IV is omitted.]

Chapter V. Of testamentary provisions

[Section 1 is omitted.]

Section 2. General provisions on the form of wills

[Articles 967 – 969 are omitted.]

Article 970. A holographic will is not valid unless it is entirely written, dated and signed by the hand of the testator: it is not subject to any other form.

Article 971. A will by public instrument shall be received by two notaries or by one notary attended by two witnesses.

[The remainder of Title II is omitted.]

Title III: Of the sources of obligations

Article 1100. Obligations arise from legal acts, legal facts, or the authority of the law alone.
They can result from the voluntary performance or promise to perform a duty of conscience toward each other.

Article 1100-1. Legal acts are manifestations of will intended to produce legal effects. They can be contractual [*conventionnel*] or unilateral.
With regard to their validity and their effects, they are governed, as far as it is reasonable, by the rules that govern contracts.

Article 1100-2. Legal facts are acts or events to which the law attaches legal effects.
Obligations arising from a legal fact are governed, as the case may be, by the sub-title relating to extra-contractual liability or the sub-title relating to other sources of obligations.

Sub-title I: Of Contracts

Chapter 1: Introductory provisions

Article 1101. A contract is an agreement of will between two or more persons that is intended to create, modify, or extinguish obligations.

Article 1102. Everyone is free to contract or not to contract, to choose his contracting partner, and to determine the content and form of a contract within the limits set by the law.
The freedom of contract does not allow for a derogation from rules of public order [ordre public].

Article 1103. Contracts lawfully entered into operate as law for those who entered into them.

Article 1104. Contracts must be negotiated, entered into, and performed in good faith.

This provision is of public order [ordre public].

Article 1105. Contracts, whether or not specifically named, are subject to the general rules laid down in the present sub-title.
The specific rules for certain contracts are laid down in the provisions specific to each of them.
The general rules apply subject to these specific rules.

Article 1106. The contract is synallagmatic where the contracting parties oblige themselves reciprocally towards each other.
It is unilateral where one or several persons oblige themselves towards one or several others without there being a reciprocal commitment on the part of the latter.

Article 1107. The contract is for pecuniary interest [à titre onéreux] where each party receives from the other a benefit in return for the one it provides.
It is without pecuniary interest [à titre gratuit] where one of the parties provides to the other a benefit without expecting or receiving one in return.

Article 1108. The contract is commutative where each party agrees to provide to the other a benefit which is deemed equivalent to the one it receives.
It is aleatory where the parties agree to make the effects of the contract, with regard to the benefits and losses resulting from it, dependent on an uncertain event.

Article 1109. The contract is consensual where it is entered into by mutual consent, regardless of the way in which it is expressed.

The contract is formal [solennel] where its validity is subject to formalities prescribed by law.

The contract is real where its formation is subject to the delivery of a thing.

Article 1110. An individually negotiated contract [contrat de gré à gré] is one whose terms are negotiable between parties.

A standard-term contract [contrat d'adhésion] is one that contains a set of non-negotiable terms, determined in advance by one of the parties.

Article 1111. A framework contract [contrat cadre] is an agreement by which parties agree to the general characteristics of their future contractual relations. Implementation contracts specify the modalities of the performance of framework contracts.

Article 1111-1. A contract of instant execution is one whose obligations can be executed in one single performance.

A contract of successive execution is one in which the obligations of at least one party are executed in several performances staggered in time.

Chapter II: Contract formation

Section I: The conclusion of a contract

Sub-section 1: Negotiations

Article 1112. The initiation, carrying-out, and termination of pre-contractual negotiations are free. They must in any event fulfil the requirements of good faith.

In case of a wrongful act [faute] committed in the negotiations, the remedy for the damage resulting therefrom may neither have as its object to compensate for the loss of benefits expected from a contract that was not concluded, nor the loss of the chance to obtain these benefits.

Article 1112-1. The party who has knowledge of information whose importance is decisive for the consent of the other party must inform that other party thereof, as far as the latter is legitimately ignorant of that information or relies on his contractual partner.

Nevertheless, this duty of information does not affect the assessment of the value of the performance. Information is of decisive importance where is has a direct and necessary link with the content of the contract or to the nature of the parties.

It is for the party who claims that a certain information was due to him to prove that the other party was under a duty to provide it to him, while it is for the other party to prove that he has provided this information.

Parties may neither limit nor exclude this duty.

In addition to liability of the relevant party, failure to fulfil this duty of information can lead to the annulment of the contract under the conditions laid down in article 1130 and following.

Article 1112-2. He who uses or disseminates, without authorisation, a piece of confidential information obtained during negotiations is held liable under the conditions of general law.

Sub-section 2: Offer and acceptance

Article 1113. A contract is formed by the meeting of an offer and an acceptance through which the parties express their will to be bound.

This will can emanate from a statement or from unambiguous behaviour.

Article 1114. The offer, made to a specific person or to anyone or indeterminately, comprises the essential elements of the envisaged contract and expresses the will of its author to be bound in case of acceptance. Otherwise, there is only an invitation to enter into negotiations.

Article 1115. It can be withdrawn freely as long as it has not reached its addressee.

Article 1116. It cannot be withdrawn before the expiry of a period of time set by its author or, failing that, before the expiry of a reasonable period.

The withdrawal of the offer in breach of this prohibition prevents the conclusion of the contract.

It leads to extra-contractual liability of the offeror under the conditions of general law without obliging him to compensate for the loss of the benefits expected from the contract.

Article 1117. The offer lapses upon the expiry of the period of time set by its author or, failing that, after a reasonable period.

It also lapses in case of incapacity or death of its author, or death of its addressee.

Article 1118. The acceptance is the expression of the will of its author to be bound under the terms of the offer.

As long as the acceptance has not yet reached the offeror, it can be withdrawn freely, provided that the withdrawal reaches the offeror before the acceptance.

An acceptance that does not conform to the offer is without effect, except that it constitutes a new offer.

Article 1119. The general conditions invoked by one party do not take effect with regard to the other party unless the latter has been made aware of them and had accepted them.

In case of discrepancy between the general conditions invoked by one party and those invoked by the other, the incompatible clauses are without effect.

In case of discrepancy between general conditions and specific conditions, the latter take precedence over the former.

Article 1120. Silence does not amount to acceptance, unless otherwise follows from the law, custom, business relations, or special circumstances.

Article 1121. The contract is concluded as soon as the acceptance reaches the offeror. It is deemed to be located at the place where the acceptance is received.

Article 1122. The law or the contract may provide for a period of reflection, which is the time limit before the expiry of which the offeree cannot express his acceptance, or a withdrawal period, which is the time limit before the expiry of which its beneficiary can withdraw its consent.

Sub-section 3: Preference pact and unilateral promise

Article 1123. A preference pact is a contract by which one party commits to making an offer to the beneficiary of the pact with priority, in case the former party will decide to contract.

Where a contract is concluded with a third party in breach of a preference pact, the beneficiary is entitled to compensation of the damaged he incurred. Where the third party knew of the existence of the preference pact and of the intention of the beneficiary to make use of it, the latter may also bring an action for nullity or request the court to instate him, instead of the third party, as a party to the contract that has been concluded.

The third party may make a written request to the beneficiary to confirm, within a period of time that is to be set by the third party and must be reasonable, the existence of a preference pact and whether the beneficiary intends to make use of it.

The document shall mention that in the absence of a response within the period of time set, the beneficiary will no longer be able to request his instatement as a substitute party to the contract concluded with the third party or to apply for nullity of the contract.

Article 1124. A unilateral promise is a contract by which one party, the promisor, grants the other, the beneficiary, the right to opt for the conclusion of a contract whose essential elements are specified and whose formation only the consent of the beneficiary is still required.

The revocation of the promise during the time granted to the beneficiary to opt does not preclude the formation of the promised contract.

A contract concluded in violation of the promise with a third party who knew of the existence of the promise is void.

Sub-section 4: Provisions specific to contracts concluded by electronic means

Article 1125. Electronic means may be used to make available contractual terms or information regarding goods or services.

Article 1126. Information requested for the conclusion of a contract or sent in the course of its performance may be sent by e-mail if their addressee has accepted the use of this means of communication.

Article 1127. Information intended for a professional may be sent to him by e-mail once he has communicated his electronic address.

If the information must be entered into a form, the latter is made available electronically to the person who needs to fill it in.

Article 1127-1. Whoever offers in a professional capacity, by electronic means, the supply of goods or the provision of services makes available the applicable contractual terms in such a way as to allow for their storage and reproduction.

The author of an offer remains bound by it as long as it is accessible by such electronic means as he has created.

The offer further states:

1° The different steps to follow to conclude the contract electronically;

2° Technical means enabling the addressee of the offer, before the conclusion of the contract, to identify possible mistakes made in the entry of date and to correct them;

3° The languages proposed for the conclusion of the contract, one of which must be the French language;

4° Where applicable, the archiving method used by the offeror to store the contract and the conditions for accessing the stored contract;

5° Means of consulting electronically the professional and commercial regulations by which, where applicable, the offeror is bound.

Article 1127-2. The contract is only validly concluded if the addressee of the offer has had the opportunity to verify the details of his order as well as its total price and to correct any errors before confirming it in order to express his definite acceptance.

The offeror must acknowledge, by electronic means, the receipt of the order sent to him without undue delay.

The order, the confirmation of the acceptance of the offer, as well as the acknowledgement of receipt are considered received once the parties to whom they are addressed are able to access them.

Article 1127-3. An exception is made to the obligations referred to in nos. 1° to 5° of article 1127-1 and the first two paragraphs of Article 1127-2 with regard contracts for the supply of goods or the provision of services that are concluded exclusively by exchange of e-mails.

Moreover, derogations may be made from the provisions of nos. 1° to 5° of Article 1127-1 and of Article 1127-2 in contracts concluded between professionals.

Article 1127-4. Except in the cases provided for in Articles 1125 and 1126, the delivery of an electronic document is effective where the addressee, after having been able to view it, has acknowledged its receipt.

If a term provides that a document must be read by the addressee, the delivery of the electronic document to the party concerned under the conditions laid down in the first paragraph implies that it has been read.

Section 2: Validity of the contract

Article 1128. Necessary for the validity of the contract are:

1° The consent of the parties;

2° Their capacity to contract;

3° A legal and certain content.

Sub-section 1: Consent

Paragraph 1: The existence of consent

Article 1129. In conformity with article 414-1, one must be of a sane mind in order to validly consent to a contract.

Paragraph 2: Defects of consent

Article 1130. Error, fraud, and duress vitiate consent where their nature is such that, without them, one of the parties would not have entered into the contract or would have entered into it under substantially different conditions.

Their specific character is assessed having regard to the persons involved and to the circumstances under which consent has been given.

Article 1131. Defects of consent constitute a cause for relative nullity of the contract.

Article 1132. Error or law or of fact, unless it is inexcusable, is a cause for nullity of the contract where it affects the essential characteristics of the performance due or those of the other contracting party.

Article 1133. The essential characteristics of the performance are those which have been explicitly or tacitly agreed upon and in consideration of which the parties have entered into the contract.
Error is a cause for nullity where it affects the performance of one of the parties.
The acceptance of a risk with regard to a characteristic of the performance excludes error with regard to that characteristic.

Article 1134. Error with regard to the characteristics of the other contracting party only constitutes a cause for nullity in the case of contracts concluded in consideration of the person.

Article 1135. A minor error [erreur sur un simple motif], unrelated to the essential characteristics of the performance due or of the other party, does not constitute a cause for nullity, unless the parties have explicitly made it a specific element of their consent.
Nevertheless, an error with regard to a gift which the donor would not have been made in the absence of the error, does constitute a cause for nullity.

Article 1136. An error with regard to the value by which, without being mistaken about the essential characteristics of the performance, a contracting party merely makes an incorrect economic assessment of the latter, does not constitute a cause for nullity.

Article 1137. Fraud is the act, by a contracting party, of obtaining the other party's consent through intrigue or lies.
Fraud is also constituted by the intentional concealment, by one of the contracting parties, of information of which the latter knows that it is decisive to the other party.
Nevertheless, no fraud is present where one party fails to reveal its estimation of the value of performance to the other.

Article 1138. Fraud is equally present where it originates from the representative, business manager, employee, or guarantor of a contracting party.
It is also present where it originates from a third party in connivance.

Article 1139. An error resulting from fraud is always excusable; it constitutes a cause for nullity even where it relates to the value of the performance or to a minor element of the contract.

Article 1140. Duress is present where one party enters into a contract under the pressure of the fear that his person, his property, or the person or property of those close to him be exposed to considerable harm.

Article 1141. The threat of legal action does not constitute duress. This is different where the legal action is diverted from its purpose or where it is invoked or exercised in order to obtain a manifestly excessive advantage.

Article 1142. Duress is a cause for nullity, whether it has been exerted by a contracting party or by a third party.

Article 1143. Duress is also present where one contracting party abuses the state of dependency of the other party on the former, thereby obtaining a commitment the latter would not have made in the absence of such a constraint and procuring a manifestly excessive advantage.

Article 1144. The period of time during which an action for nullity may be broad start, in case of error or fraud, on the day on which they are discovered and, in the case of duress, on the day on which the duress ceases.

Sub-section 2: Capacity and representation

Paragraph 1: Capacity

Article 1145. Any natural person may enter into a contract, except in case of incapacity provided by law.
The capacity of legal persons is limited by the rules applicable to each of them.

Article 1146. Unable to contract, to the extent defines by law, are:
1° Non-emancipated minors;
2° Adults protected within the meaning of article 425.

Article 1147. Inability to contract constitutes a cause for relative nullity.

Article 1148. Persons who lack the capacity to contract may nevertheless conduct common transactions authorised by law or custom, provided that they are concluded under normal conditions.

Article 1149. Common transactions conducted by a minor may be annulled in case of an economic disadvantage [lésion]. However, nullity does not occur where the economic disadvantage results from an unforeseeable event.

The mere declaration of majority made by a minor does not constitute an obstacle to the annulment. A minor may not evade commitments he has made in the exercise of his profession.

Article 1150. Acts performed by protected adults are governed by articles 435, 465, and 494-9 without prejudice to articles 1148, 1151, and 1352-4.

Article 1151. The contracting party with capacity may bar an action for nullity against him by establishing that the act was useful for the protected person and without an economic disadvantage, or that the protected person has profited from it.

He may also hold against the action for nullity the confirmation of the transaction, given by the other party after having gained or re-gained capacity.

Article 1152. The prescription period for the action begins:

1° With regard to acts of a minor, on the day on which he reaches the age of majority or on the day of emancipation;

2° With regard to acts of a protected adult, on the day he becomes aware of it while in a situation in which he can validly repeat such acts.

3° With regard to the heirs of a person under tutelage or guardianship or a person subject to family fosterage [habilitation familiale], on the day of death, if it did not begin at an earlier moment.

Paragraph 2: Representation

Article 1153. A legal, judicial or conventional representative is entitled to act only within the limits of the powers which have been conferred on him.

Article 1154. Where a representative acts within the limit of his powers in name and on behalf of the principal, only the latter is bound by the contractual commitment thus created.

Where a representative acts on behalf of another but enters into a contract in his own name, only he is bound as against the other party.

Article 1155. Where the power of the representative is defined in general terms, it only covers conservatory and administrative acts.

Where the power has been specifically determined, the representative may only perform acts for which he is empowered, as well as ancillary acts.

Article 1156. An act performed by a representative without authority or outside the scope of his power cannot be enforced against the principal, except where the third contracting party has legitimately believed that the representative was actually authorised, in particular on the basis of the behaviour or statements of the principal.

Where he did not know that the act was performed by a representative without authority or outside the scope of his powers, the third contracting party may invoke the nullity of the act.

Both the unenforceability as the nullity of the act may no longer be invoked once the principal has ratified the act.

Article 1157. Where the representative abused his powers to the detriment of the principal, the latter may invoke the nullity of the act performed if the third party had knowledge of the abuse or could not have been ignorant of it.

Article 1158. A third party who is in doubt about the scope of the authority of a representative with regard to an act he is about to perform may make a written request to the principal to confirm to him, within a period of time which the third party determines and which must be reasonable, that the representative is authorised to perform this act.

The document mentions that, failing a response within this period of time, the representative shall be deemed authorised to perform this act.

Article 1159. The establishment of a legal or judicial representation deprives, for the time of its duration, the principal of the powers transferred to the representative.

In case of conventional representation, the principal remains entitled to exercise his rights.

Article 1160. The powers of the representative cease if he becomes incapacitated or subject to a ban.

Article 1161. Regarding the representation of natural persons, a representative may not act on behalf

of several parties to the contract with opposing interests, nor enter into a contract in his own name with the person represented.
In these cases, the performed act is void, unless the law authorises it or unless the principal has authorised or ratified it.

Sub-section 3: Content of the contract

Article 1162. A contract may not derogate from public order [ordre public] either by its terms or by its aim, regardless of whether or not the latter was known to all parties.

Article 1163. An obligation relates to a present or future performance.
The latter must be possible and determined or determinable.
The performance is determinable where it can be deduced from the contract or by reference to custom or to prior relations of the parties, without the need for a new agreement between the parties.

Article 1164. In framework contracts, it may be agreed that the price will be fixed unilaterally by one of the parties, whereby it is for that party to justify the amount in case of a dispute.
In case of abuse in fixing the price, the court may be requested to order the payment of damages with interest and, as the case may be, rescission of the contract.

Article 1165. In contracts relating to the provision of services, in the absence of an agreement between parties prior to performance, the price may be fixed by the creditor, whereby it is for him to justify the amount in case of a dispute.
In case of abuse in fixing the price, the court may be requested to order the payment of damages with interest and, as the case may be, the termination of the contract.

Article 1166. Where the quality of the performance is not determined or determinable under the contract, the debtor must offer a performance of such quality as may be legitimately expected by parties in light of its nature, custom, and the amount of the consideration.

Article 1167. Where the price or any other element of the contract must be determined by reference to an index that does not exist or has ceased to exist or is no longer accessible, the latter is replaced by the most similar index.

Article 1168. In synallagmatic contracts, the lack of equivalence of the performances does not constitute a cause for nullity of the contract, unless the law provides otherwise.

Article 1169. A contract for pecuniary interest [à titre onéreux] is void where, at the moment of its formation, the agreed consideration for the one who enters into it is illusory or derisory.

Article 1170. Any clause which deprives the essential obligation of the debtor of its substance is deemed not to exist.

Article 1171. In a standard-term contract [contrat d'adhésion], any non-negotiable clause, determined in advance by one of the parties, which creates a significant imbalance between the rights and obligations of the parties is deemed not to exist.
The assessment of the significant imbalance does not concern the main purpose of the contract or the appropriateness of the price to the performance.

Section 3: The form of the contract

Sub-section 1: General provisions

Article 1172. Contracts are in principle consensual.
By way of exception, the validity of formal contracts [contrats solennels] is subject to the observance of formal requirements determined by law, in the absence of which the contract is void, except in case of possible legal recognition [régularisation].
Moreover, the law makes the formation of certain contracts subject to the delivery of a thing.

Article 1173. Formal requirements for the purpose of evidence or opposability have no effect on the validity of contracts.

Sub-section 2: Provisions specific to contracts concluded by electronic means

Article 1174. Where a written document is required for the validity of a contract, it may be drawn up and saved in electronic form under the conditions provided for in articles 1366 and 1367 and, where a deed is required, in the second paragraph of article 1369.

Where the handwritten signature of the person obliging himself is required, the latter may attach it in electronic form if the conditions of this attachment are of such a kind as to guarantee that it cannot be done by anyone other than the signatory himself.

Article 1175. An exception to the provisions of the preceding article applies to:
1° Private deeds relating to family law and succession;
2° Private deeds relating to personal security or security in rem, civil or commercial, save if they are provided by a person for the purpose of his profession.

Article 1176. Where the written document on paper is submitted under specific conditions of readability or format, the electronic document must fulfil equivalent requirements.
The requirement of a detachable form is fulfilled by an electronic process which makes it possible to access the form and return it by the same means.

Article 1177. The requirement of sending several copies of a document is deemed fulfilled electronically if the document can be printed by the addressee.

Section 4: Sanctions

Sub-section 1: Nullity

Article 1178. A contract which does not meet the requirements for its validity is null and void.
Nullity must be pronounced by a court, unless the parties establish it in a mutual agreement.
An annulled contract is deemed never to have existed.
Performances already executed give rise to restitution under the conditions provided for in articles 1352 to 1352-9.
Independent of the annulment of the contract, the injured party may demand compensation for damage incurred under the conditions of general law on extra-contractual liability.

Article 1179. Nullity is absolute where the violated rule serves purpose of protecting public interest.
It is relative where the violated rule serves the sole purpose of protecting a private interest.

Article 1180. Absolute nullity may be claimed by any person with a justified interest, as well as by the public prosecutor.
It cannot be overturned by confirmation of the contract.

Article 1181. Relative nullity may only be claimed by the party that the law intends to protect.
It may be overturned by confirmation.
If several parties are entitled to bring an action for relative nullity, the waiver of one party does not prevent the others from bringing the action.

Article 1182. Confirmation is the act by which the one who could avail himself of nullity waives this right. This act mentions the object of the obligation as well as the defect that affects the contract.
Confirmation can only take place after the conclusion of the contract.
The voluntary performance of the contract, knowing of the cause for nullity, implies confirmation. In the event of duress, the confirmation may only take place only once the duress has ceased.
Confirmation constitutes a waiver of remedies and exceptions which could be held against the contract, without prejudice, however, to the rights of third parties.

Article 1183. Any party may make a written request to the party that could claim nullity to either confirm the contract or bring an action in nullity within a period of six months, on pain of foreclosure. The cause for nullity must have ceased.
The document explicitly states that, in the absence of an action for nullity brought before the expiry of the period of six months, the contract shall be deemed confirmed.

Article 1184. Where the cause for nullity only affects one or several clauses of the contact, it only leads to nullity of the entire contract if this clause or these clauses constitute a decisive element of the commitment of the parties or of one of them.
The contract is maintained where the law deems the clause non-existent, or where the aims of the infringed legal rule require its maintenance.

Article 1185. The objection of nullity does not become time-barred if it relates to a contract which has not been executed.

Sub-section 2: Lapse

Article 1186. A validly formed contract lapses if one of its essential elements disappears.

Where the execution of several contracts is necessary for the same operation and one of them disappears, the contracts whose execution becomes impossibly by such disappearance, as well as those for which the execution of the disappeared contract was a decisive condition for the consent of a party, shall lapse.
However, the lapse only occurs if the contracting party against whom it is invoked knew of the existence of the overall transaction when he gave his consent.

Article 1187. The lapse terminates the contract.
It can give rise to a claim in restitution under the conditions provided for in Articles 1352 to 1352-9.

Chapter III: Contract interpretation

Article 1188. The contract is interpreted according to the common intention of the parties rather than in the literal sense of its terms.
Where this intention cannot be established, the contract shall be interpreted according to the meaning which a reasonable person would attribute to it in the same situation.

Article 1189. All the clauses of a contract are interpreted in relation to each other, giving each one the meaning which respects the coherence of the entire contract.
Where, according to the common intention of the parties, several contracts contribute to the same operation, they are interpreted accordingly.

Article 1190. When in doubt, an individually negotiated contract is interpreted against the creditor and in favour of the debtor, and the standard-term contract against the party who proposed it.

Article 1191. Where a clause has two possible meanings, the one that produces an effect is given preference over the one which produces none.

Article 1192. Clear and precise clauses must not be interpreted, so as to avoid distortion of the nature of the contract.

Chapter IV: Effects of the contract

Section 1: Effects of the contract as between parties

Sub-section 1: Binding force

Article 1193. Contracts may only be amended or revoked by mutual consent of the parties, or for reasons authorised by law.

Article 1194. Contracts do not only oblige parties to what is expressed in them, but also to everything that follows from them to fairness, custom, or law.

Article 1195. If a change of circumstances unforeseeable at the time of the conclusion of the contract renders its execution excessively onerous for a party that had not accepted to assume the risk that this would happen, that party may demand a renegotiation of the contract from the other party. The party continues to perform its obligations during the renegotiation.
In the event of refusal or failure of the renegotiation, the parties may agree to rescind the contract on the date and under the conditions they determine or, by mutual agreement, request the court to adjust the contract.
Failing agreement within a reasonable time, the court may, at the request of one party, revise or terminate the contract, on the date and under the conditions he sets.

Sub-section 2: Transfer effect [effet translatif]

Article 1196. In contracts for the disposal of property or the cession of another right, the transfer takes place at the moment the contract is concluded.
This transfer may be delayed by the will of the parties, the nature of the things concerned, or by operation of law.
The transfer of ownership entails transfer of the risks of the thing. However, this burden returns to the debtor of the obligation to deliver as of the moment of formal notice of default, in accordance with Article 1344-2 and subject to the rules provided for by article 1351-1.

Article 1197. The obligation to deliver a thing entails the obligation to preserve it until delivery, applying to it the care of a reasonable person.

Article 1198. Where two successive acquirers of the same movable corporeal object [meuble corporel] derive their right from the same person, the one who takes possession of that movable first takes precedence, even if his right has arisen later, provided that he is in good faith.

Where two successive acquirers of rights pertaining to the same movable object obtain their rights from the same person, the one who has first published his duly certified [passé en la forme authentique] title in the land register [fichier immobilier] takes precedence, even if his right has arisen later, provided that he is in good faith.

Section 2: Effectiveness of a contract against third parties

Sub-section 1: General provisions

Article 1199. A contract only creates obligations between parties.

Third parties may neither demand the performance of a contract nor be obliged to perform it, subject to the provisions of the present section and those of chapter III of title IV.

Article 1200. Third parties must observe the legal situation created by a contract.

In particular, they may rely on it as evidence.

Article 1201. Where parties have concluded an apparent contract [contrat apparent] which conceals a secret contract [contrat occulte], the latter one, also referred to as counter letter [contre-lettre] is effective between parties. It may not be invoked against third parties, who may nevertheless rely on it.

Article 1202. Any counter letter intended to increase the price stipulated in the treaty of cession of a public office [office ministériel] is void.

Equally void is any contract aimed to conceal a part of the price, where it relates to the sale of immovables, the transfer of business or client capital, the transfer of a right to lease or of the benefit of a promise to lease relating to a building or part thereof, or aimed to conceal the entirety or a part of the adjustment payment [soulte] of an exchange or a partition containing immovable goods, a business asset, or customers.

Sub-section 2: Guarantee and stipulation for the benefit of others.

Article 1203. One may bind oneself in one's own name only for oneself.

Article 1204. One may provide a guarantee by promising an act of a third party.

The promisor is released from any obligation if the third party performs the promised act. In the contrary case, he may be ordered to damages and interest.

Where the guarantee has as its object the ratification of a commitment, the latter is retroactively validated as from the date on which the guarantee was signed.

Article 1205. One may stipulate for the benefit of others.

One of the contracting parties, the stipulator, may require a commitment from the other, the promisor, to do something for the benefit of a third party, the beneficiary. The latter may be a future person but must be specifically designated or determinable throughout the performance of the promise.

Article 1206. The beneficiary is invested with a direct right to the performance against the promisor as from the time of the stipulation.

Nevertheless, the stipulator may freely revoke the stipulation as long as the beneficiary has not accepted it.

The stipulation becomes irrevocable at the moment that the acceptance reaches the stipulator or the promisor.

Article 1207. The revocation may be effected only by the stipulator or, after his death, by his heirs. The latter may only do so after the expiry of a period of three months, starting on the day he put the beneficiary on notice to accept.

If it is not accompanied by the designation of a new beneficiary, the revocation benefits, as the case may be, the stipulator or his heirs.

The revocation takes effect as soon as the third party beneficiary or the promisor become aware of it. Where it is made by testament, it becomes effective at the moment of death.

The third party initially designated is deemed never to have benefited from the stipulation made in his favour.

Article 1208. The acceptance may be effected by the beneficiary or, after his death, by his heirs. It may be explicit or tacit.

It may be effected even after the death of the stipulator or promisor.

Article 1209. The stipulator may himself demand from the promisor the performance of his commitment to the beneficiary.

Section 3: The duration of the contract

Article 1210. Perpetual obligations are prohibited.
Each contracting party may terminate under the conditions laid down for contracts concluded for an indefinite period.

Article 1211. Where a contract has been concluded for an indefinite period, each party may terminate it at any moment, subject to observance of the contractually provided period of notice or, failing that, a reasonable period.

Article 1212. Where a contract has been concluded for a fixed period, each party must perform it until its end.
No one may require the renewal of the contract.

Article 1213. The contract may be extended if the contracting parties manifest the will to do so before it expires. The extension may not affect the rights of third parties.

Article 1214. Fixed-term contracts may be renewed by operation of law or by agreement of the parties.
The renewal gives rise to a new contract whose content is identical to that of its predecessor but whose duration is indefinite.

Article 1215. Where the contracting parties, upon the expiry of a fixed-term contract, continue to perform the obligations emanating from it, this constitutes tacit renewal. The latter produces the same effects as the explicit renewal of the contract.

Section 4: Assignment of contract

Article 1216. One contracting party, the assignor [cédant], may transfer his quality of being a party to the contract to a third person, the assignee [cessionaire], with the consent of his co-contracting party, the assigned debtor [cédé].
This consent may be given in advance, in particular in the contract concluded between the future assignor and assigned debtor, in which case the cession becomes effective with regard to the assigned debtor as soon as the contract concluded between the assignor and the assignee is notified to the assigned debtor or as soon as he takes note of it.
The assignment must be declared in writing, on pain of nullity.

Article 1216-1. With the explicit consent of the assigned debtor, the assignment of the contract releases the assignor from his obligations for the future.
By default, and unless otherwise agreed, the assignor is held jointly and severally liable for the performance of the contract.

Article 1216-2. The assignee may invoke against the assigned debtor any defences inherent in the debt, such as nullity, non-performance, rescission, or the set-off of connected debts. He may not invoke any defences specific to the person of the assignor.
The assigned debtor may invoke against the assignee any defences which he could invoke against the assignor.

Article 1216-3. If the assignor is not released by the assigned debtor, any securities that have been granted remain in place. In the opposite case, securities granted by the assignor or by third parties only remain in place with their consent.
If the assignor is released, his joint and several co-debtors remain bound with the exception of the assignor's share of the debt.

Section 5: Non-performance of the contract

Article 1217. The party against whom a contractual obligation has not been performed, or has been performed imperfectly, may:
- refuse to perform or suspend the performance of his own obligation;
- seek specific enforcement of the obligation;
- obtain a reduction of the price;

- seek the termination of the contract;
- demand compensation for damages resulting from the non-performance.

Sanctions that are not incompatible may be combined; damages and interest may always be added.

Article 1218. In contractual matters, force majeure is present where an event beyond the debtor's control, which could not have been reasonably foreseen at the time the contract was concluded and whose effects cannot be prevented by appropriate measures, prevents the debtor from performing his obligation.

If the impediment is temporary, the performance of the obligation is suspended, unless the resulting delay justifies the rescission of the contract. If the impediment is permanent, the contract is rescinded by operation of law and the parties are resealed from their obligations under the conditions laid down in articles 1351 and 1351-1.

Sub-section 1: The defence of non-performance

Article 1219. A party may refuse to perform his obligation even though the latter is due, if the other party fails to fulfil his own obligation and if this non-performance is sufficiently severe.

Article 1220. A party may suspend the performance of his obligation when it is clear that the other party will not perform in due time and that the consequences of this non-performance for the suspending party are sufficiently severe.

This suspension must be notified as soon as possible.

Sub-section 2: Specific enforcement

Article 1221. The creditor of an obligation may, after formal notice, seek specific performance unless such performance is impossible or unless the cost of such performance for the debtor in good faith is manifestly disproportionate to the interest of the creditor.

Article 1222. After formal notice, the creditor may also, within a reasonable time and at reasonable cost, bring about the performance of the obligation himself or, with prior permission of the court, destroy what has been made in violation of the obligation. He may demand reimbursement of the expenses made for this purpose from the debtor.

He may also request the court to order the debtor to advance the amount required for such performance or such destruction.

Sub-section 3: Reduction of the price

Article 1223. In case of imperfect execution of the performance, the creditor may, after formal notice, and if he has not yet payed all or part of the performance, notify the debtor without undue delay of his decision to reduce the price proportionally. The acceptance of the creditor's decision to reduce the price by the debtor must be drawn up in writing.

If the creditor has already paid, failing agreement between parties, he may request a reduction of the price from the judge.

Sub-section 4: Termination

Article 1224. The termination either results from the application of a termination clause or, in case of sufficiently severe non-performance, from a notice of the creditor to the debtor, or from a judicial decision.

Article 1225. The termination clause specifies the obligations whose non-performance entail the termination of the contract.

The termination is subject to an unsuccessful formal notice, unless it has been agreed that non-performance will lead to it automatically. The formal notice is only effective if it mentions the termination clause explicitly.

Article 1226. The creditor may, at his own risk, terminate the contract by way of notification. Except in case of urgency, he must first give formal notice to the defaulting debtor to perform his obligation within a reasonable time.

This formal notice mentions explicitly that, in case of failure of the debtor to perform his obligation, the creditor will have the right to terminate the contract.

Where the non-performance continues, the creditor notifies the debtor of the termination of the contract and of the reasons for it.

The debtor may at any time apply to the court to challenge the termination. The creditor must prove the severity of the non-performance.

Article 1227. The termination may in any event be requested from the court.

Article 1228. The court may, as appropriate, establish or pronounce the termination, or order the performance of the contract, possibly granting the debtor a period of time, or only order the payment of damages and interest.

Article 1229. The termination puts an end to the contract.
The termination takes effect, as appropriate, under the conditions laid down in the termination clause, or on the date of receipt by the debtor of the notification of the creditor, or on the date set by the court, or,
Failing that, on the date of the writ [assignation en justice].
Where the performances exchanged between parties are only useful in case of complete execution of the terminated contract, the parties must restore all they have procured from one another. Where the performances exchanged have found their usefulness with the reciprocal performance of the contract, no such restitution must take place with regard to the period prior to the last performance for which no counterpart has been received; in this case, the termination qualifies as a cancellation [résiliation]. The restitution take place in accordance with Articles 1352 to 1352-9.

Article 1230. The termination does not affect clauses relating to the settlement of disputes, clauses intended to remain effective in case of termination, as well as confidentiality and non-competition clauses.

Sub-section 5: Compensation of damages resulting from non-performance of the contract

Article 1231. Unless the non-performance is permanent, damages and interest are only due if the debtor has previously been given formal notice to perform within a reasonable time.

Article 1231-1. The debtor is ordered, if applicable, to pay damages and interest for non-performance or delayed performance of his obligation, if he fails to show that his performance has been prevented by force majeure.

Article 1231-2. In general, the creditor is entitled to damages for the loss he has incurred and for the profits he missed, subject to the exceptions and qualifications laid down in the following articles.

Article 1231-3. The debtor is only liable for damages and interest which had been or could have been anticipated at the time of conclusion of the contract, unless where the non-performance is due to a gross fault or wrongful act [faute lourde ou dolosive].

Article 1231-4. Even where the non-performance of the contract results from a gross fault or wrongful act, the damages and interest only comprise the immediate consequences of the non-performance.

Article 1231-5. Where the contract stipulates that the one who fails to perform shall pay a certain sum in damages and interest, the other party may not be allocated a higher or lower sum.
Nevertheless, the court may, also on its own motion, moderate or increase the agreed penalty if it is manifestly excessive or derisory.
Where an obligation has been performed in part, the agreed penalty may be reduced by the court, also on its own motion, in proportion to the benefit which the partial performance has provided to the creditor, without prejudice to the foregoing paragraph.
Any contractual term contrary to two preceding paragraphs is deemed not to have been written.
Except in case of permanent non-performance, the penalty is only due after formal notice to the debtor.

Article 1231-6. The damages and interest due for a delay in the performance of an obligation to pay an amount of money consist of the interest at the legal rate as from the date of formal notice of default.
These damages and interest are due without the creditor having to show any loss.
The creditor to whom his debtor, in bad faith, has caused a loss independent of this delay, may obtain damages and interest distinct from the interest due on account of the delay.

Article 1231-7. In any matter, a sentence to pay damages includes interest at the legal rate, even in the absence of a request or special provisions of in the judgement. Except where statute provides otherwise, such interest is payable from the day on which the judgement is pronounced, unless the court decides otherwise.
In case of an outright confirmation by the court of appeals of a court judgement ordering the

compensation of damage, such a ruling entails, by operation of law, interest payable as from the day of the judgement in first instance.

In other cases, damages awarded on appeal entail interest payable as from the day of the judgement on appeal. The court of appeals may always derogate from the provisions of the present paragraph.

Sub-title II: Extra-contractual liability

Chapter 1: Extra-contractual liability in general

Article 1240. Any act whatever of a person, which causes damage to another, obliges the one by whose fault it occurred to compensate for the damage.

Article 1241. Everyone is liable for the damage he causes not only by his act, but also by his negligence or by his imprudence.

Article 1242. A person is liable not only for the damage caused by his own acts, but also for damage caused by the acts of persons for whom he is responsible, or by things he has in his custody.

However, he who holds, under whichever title, an immovable thing or part thereof, or any movable goods, in which a fire has originated, shall only be liable against third parties for the damage caused by that fire if it is proven that it must be attributed to its fault or to the fault of any person for whom he is responsible.

This provision does not apply to the relationship between landlords and tenants, which remains governed by articles 1733 and 1734 of the Civil Code.

The father and the mother, as far as they exercise parental authority, are jointly and severally liable for damage caused by their minor children living with them.

Masters and employers [maîtres et commettants] are liable for damage caused by their domestic workers and employees [domestiques et préposés] in the functions for which they have employed them.

Teachers and craftspeople [instituteurs et artisans] are liable for damage caused by their students and apprentices while under their surveillance.

The liability aforementioned liability arises, unless the father and mother or craftspeople prove that they could not have prevented the act giving rise to this liability.

With regard to teachers, the faults, recklessness, or negligence [fautes, imprudences ou négligences] relied upon against them as having caused the damaging act must be proven by the applicant in legal proceedings.

Article 1243. The owner of an animal, or he who uses it, while it is in his usage, is liable for damage caused by the animal, regardless of whether the animal was in his custody or whether it had gone astray or escaped.

Article 1244. The owner of a building is liable for damage caused by its ruin where the latter is the consequence of a defect in its maintenance or construction.

Chapter II: Product liability

Article 1245. The producer is liable for damage caused by a defect in his product, regardless of whether or not he is in a contractual relationship with the victim.

Article 1245-1. The provisions of the present chapter apply to the compensation of damage resulting from personal injury.

They also apply to the compensation of damage, greater than an amount determined by decree, inflicted on a good other than the defective product itself.

Article 1245-2. A product is any movable good, even if incorporated into an immovable, including products of the soil, of livestock breeding, of hunting, and of fishery. Electricity is considered a product.

Article 1245-3. A product is defective within the meaning of the present chapter where it does not offer the safety that may legitimately be expected from it.

In the assessment of the safety that may legitimately be expected, all circumstances must be taken into account, in particular the presentation of the product, the use which may be reasonably expected from it, as well as the time of its release into circulation.

A product may not be considered defective for the sole reason that another, better product has subsequently been released into circulation.

Article 1245-4. A product is released into circulation when the producer relinquishes it voluntarily. A product is only released into circulation once.

Article 1245-5. A producer is the manufacturer of a finished product, the maker of a raw material, or the manufacturer of a component part, where he acts in a professional capacity.
For the purposes of this chapter, any person acting in a professional capacity is equated to a producer, if:
1° He presents himself as a producer by affixing his name, brand, or other distinctive sign on the product;
2° He imports a product into the European Community [Communauté Européenne] for the purpose of its sale or rent, with or without an agreement to sell, or any other form of distribution.
Persons liable on the basis of articles 1792 to 1792-6 and 1646-1 are not considered producers within the meaning of the present chapter.

Article 1245-6. If the producer cannot be identified, the seller, the lessor, with the exception of a financial lessor [crédit-bailleur] or a lessor who can be equated to a financial lessor, or any other professional provider, is liable for defects to the safety of a product under the same conditions as the producer, unless he designates his own provider or the producer within a period of three months from the date on which the claim of the victim has been notified to him.
The legal recourse of the provider against the producer is governed by the same rules as the claim of the immediate victim of the defect. However, he must act within one year after the date of the judicial summons [citation en justice].

Article 1245-7. In case of damage caused by the defect of a product incorporated into another, the producer of the component part and the one who has effected the incorporation are jointly and severally liable.

Article 1245-8. The applicant must prove the damage, the defect, and the causal relationship between defect and damage.

Article 1245-9. The producer may be held liable for the defect even though the product has been manufactured in accordance with the rules of the art or existing norms, or despite having been granted an administrative authorisation.

Article 1245-10. The producer is liable by operation of law unless he proves:
1° That he did not release the product into circulation;
2° That, considering the circumstances, the defect must be deemed not to have existed at the time the product was released into circulation by him, or that the defect has arisen thereafter.
3° That the product was not intended for sale or any other any other form of distribution;
4° That the state of scientific and technical knowledge at the time when he released the product into circulation did not permit the detection of the existence of the defect;
5° Or that the defect is due to compliance of the product with mandatory rules of statute or regulation [règles d'ordre législatif ou réglementaire].
The producer of a component part is no longer liable if he establishes that the defect is attributable to the design of the product in which this part has been incorporated, or to the instructions given by the producer of that product.

Article 1245-11. The producer may not invoke the ground for exemption laid down in article 1245-10 where the damage has been caused by a part of the human body or by the products of the latter.

Article 1245-12. The liability of the producer may be reduced or eliminated, considering all circumstances, where the damage is caused both by a defect of the product and by a fault of the victim or of a person for whom the victim is responsible.

Article 1245-13. The liability of the producer as against the victim is not reduced by the act of a third party having contributed towards bringing about the damage.

Article 1245-14. Contractual clauses that seek to exclude or limit liability for defective products are prohibited and deemed not written.
However, with regard to damage caused to goods that are not primarily used by the victim for his private usage or consumption, such clauses, agreed upon between professionals, are valid.

Article 1245-15. Except in case of fault of the producer, the liability of the latter, based on the provisions of the present chapter, ceases ten years after the release into circulation of the product which caused the damage, unless the victim has taken legal action during this period.

Article 1245-16. The action for damages based on the provisions of the present chapter lapses upon the expiry of a period of three years from the date on which the applicant has or ought to have become aware of the damage, the defect, and the identity of the producer.

Article 1245-17. The provisions of the present chapter do not affect the rights to which a victim of damage is legally entitled by virtue of contractual or extra-contractual liability or by virtue of a special liability system [régime spécial de responsabilité].
The producer remains liable for the consequences of his fault and of the fault of persons for whom he is responsible.

Chapter III: Repair of ecological damage

Article 1246. Any person responsible for ecological damage is required to repair it.

Article 1247. Under the conditions provided for in the present title, any ecological damage consisting of significant harm [atteinte non négligeable] to the elements or functions of ecosystems or to the collective benefits derived by human beings from the environment must be repaired.

Article 1248. Legal action for the repair of ecological damage may be taken by any person with the capacity and interest to act, such as the State, the French Agency for Biodiversity, the territorial authorities [collectivités territoriales], and their groupings, whose territory is concerned, as well as any public institutions and associations, approved or created no less than five years prior to the initiation of proceedings, whose object is the protection of nature and the defence of the environment.

Article 1249. The repair of ecological damage is to be effected by priority in kind.

In case of legal or factual impossibility, or if the measures taken are insufficient, the court orders the responsible party to pay damages and interest, assigned to the repair of the environment, to the applicant or, if the latter is unable to take useful measures to that end, to the State.
The evaluation of the damage takes into account, as the case may be, any measures of repair already taken, in particular in the context of the implementation of Title VI of Book I of the Environmental Code.

Article 1250. In case of a penalty payment, the latter is liquidated by the court in favour of the applicant, who assigns it to the repair of the environment, or, if the applicant is unable to take useful measures to that end, in favour of the State, which assigns it to the same purpose.
The court retains the power to liquidate the penalty payment.

Article 1251. Expenses incurred in order to prevent the imminent occurrence of damage, to prevent its aggravation, or to mitigate its consequences constitute repairable harm.

Article 1252. Independently of the repair of ecological damage, the court may, upon an application made by a person referred to in article 1248, prescribe reasonable measures to prevent or bring an end to the damage.

Sub-title III: Other sources of obligations

Article 1300. Quasi-contracts are purely voluntary acts which result in an obligation of the one who benefits from them without entitlement, and at times in an obligation of their author towards others.
The quasi-contracts governed by the present sub-section are management of the affair of another person without authority [gestation daffier], undue payment, and unjustified enrichment.

Chapter I: Acting for another person without authority

Article 1301. He who, without being required to do so, knowingly and expediently manages the affair of another person without the knowledge of or without opposition from that person is, in the performance of juridical and factual acts in the course of such management, subject to all the obligations of an authorised agent.

Article 1301-1. He is obliged to manage the affair with the care of a reasonable person; he must continue this management until such time as the principal of the affair or his successor is able to provide for it. The court may moderate the compensation payable to the principal of the affair due to the fault or negligence of the manager in accordance with the circumstances.

Article 1301-2. He whose affair has been expediently managed must perform the obligations entered into in his interest by the manager.

He reimburses the manager for any expenses incurred in the interest of the principal and compensates the manager for damage suffered due to his management.

Any amount advanced by the manager bears interest from the date of payment.

Article 1301-3. The ratification of the management by the principal constitutes its authorisation.

Article 1301-4. Personal interest of the manager in taking charge of the affair of another does not exclude the application of the rules governing the unauthorised management of the affair of another. In this case, the burden of the obligations, costs, and damages is shared in proportion with the interest of every party involved in the common affair.

Article 1301-5. If the action of the manager does not meet the conditions of unauthorised management of the affair of another but benefits the principal of the affair nevertheless, the latter must compensate the manager in accordance the rules governing unjustified enrichment.

Chapter II: Undue payments

Article 1302. Every payment presumes a debt; that which has been received without being due is subject to restitution. A claim for restitution is not permitted with respect to natural obligations [*obligations naturalles*] which have been fulfilled voluntarily.

Article 1302-1. He who receives, by error or knowingly, that which is not due to him must restore it to the one from whom he has unduly received it.

Article 1302-2. He who has paid, by error or under duress, the debt of another may bring an action for restitution against the creditor. Nevertheless, this right ceases in case the creditor, following the payment, has destroyed his title or abandoned the security rights that guaranteed his claim. Restitution may also be claimed from the one whose debt has been paid by error.

Article 1302-3. Restitution is subject to the rules laid down in articles 1352 to 1352-9. It may be reduced if the payment results from a wrongful act [*faute*].

Chapter III: Unjustified enrichment

Article 1303. Apart from cases of unauthorised agency and undue payment, he who benefits from unjustified enrichment at the expense of another must pay, to the one who has thereby incurred a loss, compensation equal to the lesser of the two values of the enrichment and the loss.

Article 1303-1. The enrichment is unjustified where it follows neither from the performance of an obligation of the one who has incurred the loss nor from his intention to make a gratuitous gift.

Article 1303-2. No compensation must be paid where the loss results from an act performed by the one who has incurred the loss for the purpose of a personal gain.

The compensation may be moderated by the court if the loss results from a wrongful act [*fate*] of the one who has incurred the loss.

Article 1303-3. The one who has incurred the loss may not bring legal action on this basis where another legal action is open to him or meets a legal obstacle, such as the statute of limitations.

Article 1303-4. The loss as established on the day of the expenditure and the enrichment as it persists on the day of the claim are assessed on the day of the judgment. In case of bad faith of the enriched party, the compensation due is equal to the higher of the two values.

Title IV: Of the general regime of obligations

Chapter I: The terms of an obligation

Section 1: Conditional obligations

Article 1304. An obligation is conditional where it depends on a future and uncertain event.

The condition is suspensive where its fulfilment renders the obligation pure and simple.

It is resolutory where its fulfilment entails the annulment of the obligation.

Article 1304-1. The condition must be lawful. Otherwise, the obligation is null and void.

Article 1304-2. Any obligation agreed under a condition whose fulfilment depends solely on the on the will of the debtor is null and void.

This nullity may not be invoked where the obligation has been performed in the knowledge thereof.

Article 1304-3. A suspensive condition is deemed fulfilled if the one who had an interest therein has prevented its fulfilment.

A resolutory condition is deemed not fulfilled if its fulfilment has been provoked by the party who had an interest in doing so.

Article 1304-4. Any party is free to waive a condition stipulated in the sole interest of that party, as long as that condition has not been fulfilled or non-fulfilment has not been formally notified [n'a pas défailli].

Article 1304-5. Before a suspensive condition has been fulfilled, the debtor must abstain from any act that would prevent the proper performance of the obligation; the creditor may perform any conservatory act and impugn any acts of the debtor performed in violation of the rights of the creditor.

Any payment already made may be reclaimed, as long as the suspensive condition has not been fulfilled.

Article 1304-6 An obligation becomes pure and simple as from the fulfilment of a suspensive condition.

However, parties may stipulate that the fulfilment of the condition shall have retroactive effect as from the day of the contract. The thing that constitutes the object of the obligation remains subject to the risk of the debtor, who remains responsible for its administration and entitled to its fruits until the fulfilment of the condition.

In case of non-fulfilment of a suspensive condition, the obligation is deemed never to have existed.

Article 1304-7 The fulfilment of a resolutory conditions annuls the obligation retroactively, without jeopardising, as the case may be, any conservatory and administrative acts.

Such retroactivity does not arise if parties have agreed accordingly or if the performances already exchanged amount to an incremental reciprocal execution of the contract.

Section 2: Forward obligations [obligation à terme]

Article 1305. An obligation is forward [à terme] where its due date is deferred until the occurrence of a future and certain event, although the date on which it will occur is uncertain.

Article 1305-1. The term may be explicit or tacit.

In the absence of an agreement, the court may fix the term, taking into account the nature of the obligation and the situation of the parties.

Article 1305-2. That which only becomes due upon the arrival of a term cannot be claimed before the arrival of this term; but what has been paid in advance may not be recovered.

Article 1305-3. The term benefits the debtor if it does not follow from the law, from the will of the parties, or from circumstances that it has been established in favour of the creditor or both parties. The party for whose exclusive benefit the term has been established may waive it without the consent of the other party.

Article 1305-4. The debtor may not claim the benefit of the term if he does not provide the securities promised to the creditor or if he reduces the securities that guarantee the obligation.

Article 1305-5. The forfeiture of the term incurred by a debtor cannot be relied on against other co-obligated parties, even if they are jointly and severally liable, or against his sureties.

Section 3: Plural obligations

Sub-section 1: Plurality of objects

Paragraph 1: Cumulative obligations

Article 1306. An obligation is cumulative where its object consists of several performances and only the execution of all of them releases the debtor.

Paragraph 2: Alternative obligations

Article 1307. An obligation is alternative where its object consists of several performances and the execution of one of them releases the debtor.

Article 1307-1. The choice between the performances belongs to the debtor.

If that choice is not made within the agreed time or within a reasonable period, the other party may, after formal notice, make the choice or rescind the contract.

The choice made is definite and causes the obligation to lose its alternative nature.

Article 1307-2. Where it is the result of force majeure, the impossibility of executing the chosen performance releases the debtor.

Article 1307-3. The debtor who has not announced his choice must, if one of the alternative performances becomes impossible, execute one of the others.

Article 1307-4. The creditor who has not announced his choice must, if one of the alternative performances becomes impossible to execute as a result of force majeure, content himself with one of the others.

Article 1307-5. Where the performances become impossible, the debtor is only released if the impossibility of each of them results from force majeure.

Paragraph 3: Discretionary obligations

Article 1308. An obligation is discretionary where its object consists of a certain performance but the debtor has the option to release himself by providing another.

A discretionary obligation is extinguished if the execution of the performance initially agreed becomes impossible due to force majeure.

Sub-section 2: Plurality of subjects

Article 1309. An obligation that binds several creditors or debtors is divided between them by operation of law. This division also takes place between their successors, even where it concerns a joint and several obligation. If not otherwise regulated by law or contract, the division takes place in equal parts.

Each of the creditors is only entitled to his parts of the common claim; each of the debtors is only liable for his part of the common debt.

With regard to the relations between creditors and debtors, it can only be otherwise if the obligation is joint and several or if the performance is indivisible.

Paragraph 1: Joint and several obligations

Article 1310. Jointness and severalty [solidarité] is legal or contractual; it is not presumptive.

Article 1311. Jointness and severalty among creditors permits each of them to claim and to receive the entire debt.

Payment to one of them, who then owes it to the others, releases the debtor from his obligation against all creditors.

The debtor may make his payment to any of the joint and several creditors, as long none of them has initiated legal proceedings against him.

Article 1312. Any which interrupts or suspends the period of limitation with regard to one of the joint and several creditors mutually benefits the other creditors.

Article 1313. Jointness and severalty among debtors obliges each of them to the entire debt. Payment by one of them releases all the debtors from their obligation against the creditor.

The creditor may claim payment from the joint and several debtor of his choice. Legal proceedings against one of the joint and several debtors do not prevent the creditor from initiating proceedings against the others.

Article 1314. An interest claim [demande d'intérêts] that has arisen against one of the joint and several debtors causes interest to run against all.

Article 1315. A joint and several debtor who is sued by the creditor may invoke the defences that are common to all the co-debtors, such as nullity or termination, as well as personal defences. He may not invoke defences that are personal to other co-debtors, such as the granting of a term for payment. However, where a defence that is personal to another co-debtor extinguishes the latter's share in the debt, in particular in case of a set-off or debt remission, he may invoke that defence to deduct this share from the total of the debt.

Article 1316. The creditor who receives payment from one of the joint and several debtors and releases him from joint liability retains his claim against the others, less the share of the debtor he has discharged.

Article 1317. Between themselves, the joint and several so-debtors are only liable for their respective share.

He who has paid more than his share has a right of legal recourse against the others in proportion to their own share.

If one of them becomes insolvent, his share is divided pro rata between the solvent co-debtors, including any co-debtor who has made his payment or has been released from joint liability by the creditor.

Article 1318. If the debt arises from a matter which only concerns one of the joint and several co-debtors, only the latter is liable for the debt as against the others.

If he has paid the debt, he does not have any right of recourse against his co-debtors.

If the co-debtors have paid the debt, they have a right of recourse against him.

Article 1319. Joint and several co-debtors are jointly and severally liable for the non-performance of the obligation. Final responsibility for the non-performance is borne by those to whom the non-performance is attributable.

Paragraph 2: Indivisible obligations

Article 1320. Each of the creditors of an obligation that is indivisible, by nature or contract, may claim and receive its integral performance and is only accountable to the other creditors; but he may not, alone, dispose of the claim or receive the price instead of the thing.

Each of the debtors of such an obligation is liable for the whole of it; but he has a claim pro rata against the other debtors.

The same applies for each of the successors of the creditors and debtors.

Chapter II: Bond transactions

Section 1: Voluntary assignment

Article 1321. Voluntary assignment is a contract by which the assigning creditor [créancier cédent], transmits, for consideration or free of charge, all or part of his claim against the debtor to a third party, called the assignee [cessionaire].

It may relate to one or more claims that are present or future, determined or determinable.

It extends to the accessories of the claim.

The consent of the debtor is not required, unless the claim has been stipulated as non-assignable.

Article 1322. Assignment of debt must be done in writing, on pain of nullity.

Article 1323. Between the parties, the transfer of the claim takes place on the date of the act.

It is effective against third parties as of that moment. In case of a dispute, the burden of proof with regard to the date of the assignment rests with the assignee, who may establish it by any means.

However, the transfer of a future claim only takes place on the day the claim arises, both between the parties and with regard to third parties.

Article 1324. The assignment is only enforceable against the debtor, unless he has already consented to it, if it has been notified to him or if he has taken notice of it.

The debtor may invoke against the assignee any defence that is inherent in the debt, such as nullity, non-performance, termination, or the set-off of related debts. He may also invoke defences that have arisen from his relations with the assignor before the assignment became enforceable against the debtor, such as the granting of a term, debt remission, or the set-off of unrelated debts.

The assignor and the assignee are jointly and severally liable for all additional costs caused by the assignment which the debtor does not have to bear. Unless otherwise stipulated, these costs are borne by the assignee.

Article 1325. In case of several successive assignees of the same claim, the one to whom it was assigned first takes precedence, he enjoys a right of recourse against any person to whom the debtor has made a payment.

Article 1326. He who assigns a claim for consideration guarantees the existence of the claim and its accessories, unless the assignee acquires it at his own risk or was aware of the uncertainty of the claim.

The assignor is only liable for the solvency of the debtor where he has obliged himself to that effect, and up the price he has been able to procure from the assignment of his claim.

Where the assignor has guaranteed the solvency of the debtor, this guarantee is limited to his current solvency; it may however extend to solvency at the time of maturity of the claim, on condition that this is explicitly specified by the assignor.

Section 2: Assignment of debt

Article 1327. A debtor may, with the consent of the creditor, assign his debt.
The assignment must be drawn up in writing, on pain of nullity.

Article 1327-1. The creditor, if he has given his consent to the assignment in advance and has not intervened, may not oppose it or rely on it until it has been notified to him or until he has taken notice of it.

Article 1327-2. If the creditor explicitly consents with the assignment, the original debtor is released for the future. Otherwise, and unless provided for by the contract, he is joint and severally liable for the payment of the debt.

Article 1328. The substituted debtor, and the original debtor if he remains liable, may invoke against the creditor any defence inherent in the debt, such as nullity, non-performance, termination, or the set-off of connected debts. Each of them may also invoke defences that are personal to him.

Article 1328-1. Where the original debtor has not been discharged by the creditor, any securities that have been provided remain in place. In the contrary case, securities provided by the original debtor or by third parties only remain in place with their consent.
If the assignor is discharged, his joint co-debtors remain liable, less his share in the debt.

Section 3: Novation

Article 1329. Novation is a contract with the purpose of substituting for an obligation, which it extinguishes, a new obligation, which it creates.
It may take place by substitution of obligations between the same parties, by a change of debtor, or by a change of creditor.

Article 1330. Novation is not presumptive; the will to effect it must emanate clearly from the act.

Article 1331. Novation only takes place if the old and the new obligations are both valid, unless its declared purpose is to substitute a valid obligation for a flawed one.

Article 1332. Novation by change of debtor may be effected without the cooperation of the first debtor.

Article 1333. Novation by change of creditor requires the consent of the debtor. The latter may, beforehand, accept that the new creditor be designated by the first one.
The novation is enforceable against third parties as from the date of the act. In the event of a dispute concerning the date of novation, the burden of proof rests with the new creditor, who may establish it by any means.

Article 1334. The extinction of the old obligation extends to all its accessories.
By way of exception, any original securities may, with the consent of the third party guarantors, be retained for the guarantee of the new obligation.

Article 1335. A novation agreed upon between the creditor and one of the joint and several co-debtors releases the others.
A novation agreed upon between the creditor and a surety does not release the principal debtor. It does release the other sureties to the extent of the contributory share of the surety whose obligation was the object of the novation.

Section 4: Delegation

Article 1336. Delegation is an operation whereby one person, the delegator, procures from another, the delegate, that the latter obliges himself against a third, the delegatee, who accepts the delegate as a new debtor.
The delegate may not, unless stipulated otherwise, invoke against the delegatee any defence arising from his relations with the delegator or the relations between the latter and the delegatee.

Article 1337. Where the delegator is the debtor of the delegatee and the willingness of the delegatee to discharge the delegator emanates explicitly from the act, the delegation leads to novation.
However, the delegator remains bound if he has explicitly undertaken to guarantee the future

solvency of the delegate or if the latter is subject to a debt clearing procedure at the time of the delegation.

Article 1338. Where the delegator is a debtor of the delegatee but the latter has not discharged him from his debt, the delegation provides the delegatee with a second debtor.
Payment made by one of the two debtors releases the other to a proportional extent.

Article 1339. Where the delegator is the creditor of the delegate, his claim is extinguished only by the performance of the obligation of the delegate against the delegatee, and in proportion to that performance.
Until then, the delegator may claim or receive payment only for the part which exceeds the obligation of the delegate. He only regains his rights by executing his own obligation against the delegatee.
The assignment or seizure of the delegator's claim is effective only under the same limitations.
However, if the delegatee has released the delegator, the delegate is thereby himself released with regard to the delegator, to the extent of the amount of his commitment to the delegatee.

Article 1340. The mere indication, given by the debtor, of a person designated to pay in his place does not imply novation or delegation.
The same applies to the mere indication, given by the creditor, of a person designated to receive payment for him.

Chapter III: Legal actions open to the creditor

Article 1341. The creditor is entitled to the performance of the obligation; he may compel the debtor under the conditions provided for by law.

Article 1341-1. Where the failure of the debtor to exercise his proprietary rights and legal actions compromises the rights of his creditor, the latter may exercise them on behalf of his debtor, with the exception of those that are exclusively attached to his person.

Article 1341-2. The creditor may also act in his own name in order to have any acts performed by his debtor in violation of his rights declared unenforceable against him, subject to the burden of proving, where it concerns an act for consideration, that the third contracting party had knowledge of the violation.

Article 1341-3. In the cases determined by law, the creditor may directly bring an action for payment of his claim by a debtor of his debtor.

Chapter IV: The extinction of the obligation

Section 1: Payment

Sub-section 1: General provisions

Article 1342. Payment is the voluntary execution of a due performance.
It must be effected as soon as the debt becomes enforceable.
It releases the debtor with regard to the creditor and extinguishes the debt, except where law or contract provides for subrogation to the rights of the creditor.

Article 1342-1. Payment may be made even by a person who is not obliged, except where the creditor legitimately refuses it.

Article 1342-2. Payment must be made to the creditor or the person designated to receive it.
Payment made to a person who was not entitled to receive it is nevertheless valid if the creditor ratifies it or has benefited from it.
Payment made to a creditor who is unable to contract is invalid if he has not benefited from it.

Article 1342-3. Payment made in good faith to an apparent creditor is valid.

Article 1342-4. The creditor may refuse a partial payment even if the performance is divisible.
He may accept to receive in payment something other than what is due to him.

Article 1342-5. The debtor of an obligation to surrender a certain object is released from his obligation upon surrendering it to the creditor in its current condition, unless it is proven, in case of deterioration, that the latter is due to him or to persons for whom he is responsible.

Article 1342-6. Unless otherwise is provided by law, contract, or the court, payment must be made at the residence of the debtor.

Article 1342-7. The costs of payment are borne by the debtor.

Article 1342-8. Payment is proven by any means.

Article 1342-9. The voluntary surrender by the creditor to the debtor of the original private deed or the executive copy of the title of his claim gives rise to a simple presumption of discharge.
Such surrender to one of the joint and several co-debtors has the same effect with regard to all.

Article 1342-10. The debtor of several debts may indicate, when he pays, that which he intends to pay.
Failing such an indication by the debtor, the following allocation takes place: first, to debts which are due; among the latter, to those debts which the debtor had the greatest interest in paying.
In case of equal interest, the payment is allocated to the oldest debt; where everything is equal, the payment is allocated proportionally.

Sub-section 2: Special provisions relating to monetary obligations

Article 1343. The debtor of a monetary obligation is released by payment of its nominal amount.
The amount of the amount of the sum due may vary as a result of index variation [jeu de l'indexation].
The debtor of a debt of value is released by payment of the sum of money resulting from its liquidation.

Article 1343-1. Where the obligation to pay a sum of money bears interest, the debtor is released by paying the main sum as well as the interest. Partial payment is first allocated to the interest.
The interest is granted by law or stipulated in the contract.
The contractual interest rate must be stipulated in writing. The interest is deemed annual by default.

Article 1343-2. The interest due, for at least one entire year, accrues interest itself if the contract so provides or if a judicial decision determines it.

Article 1343-3. In France, the payment of a monetary obligation is effected in Euros.
However, payment may take place in another currency if the obligation thus worded arises from an international contract or from a foreign judgment. Parties may agree that the payment shall be made in another currency [en devise] if it takes place between professionals, where the use of a foreign currency is generally permitted for the operation concerned.

Article 1343-4. In the absence of any other designation by law, contract, or the court, the place of payment of a monetary obligation is the place of residence of the creditor.

Article 1343-5. Taking into account the situation of the debtor and the needs of the creditor, the court may postpone or stagger, within a limit of two years, the payment of sums due.
By a special and reasoned decision, it may order that the sums corresponding to the deferred terms accrues interest at a reduced rate at least equal to the legal rate, or that payments will first be allocated to the capital.
It may make such measures subject to the performance, by the debtor, of appropriate acts to facilitate or guarantee payment of the debt.
The decision of the court suspends any enforcement proceedings initiated by the creditor.
The interest charges or penalties provided for in the event of delayed payment are not incurred during the period specified by the court.
Any provision to the contrary is deemed unwritten.
The provisions of this article do not apply to debts of alimony.

Sub-section 3: Giving formal notice of default

Paragraph 1: Giving formal notice of default to the debtor

Article 1344. The debtor is given formal notice of default of payment by an exhortation or a document that gives sufficient warning, or, if the contract so provides, automatically when the obligation becomes due.

Article 1344-1. Formal notice of default of payment of a monetary obligation gives rise to moratory interest, at the legal rate, without the creditor being required to prove any disadvantage.

Article 1344-2. Formal notice of default of delivering a thing places the risk on the debtor, if he does not bear it already.

Paragraph 2: Giving formal notice of default to the creditor

Article 1345. Where the creditor, at the due date and without legitimate reason, refuses to receive payment due to him, or where he prevents it by his act, the debtor may give him formal notice of default of accepting payment or permitting its execution.

Formal notice of default of the creditor stops the accrual of interest owed by the debtor and places the risk of the thing on the creditor, if he does not bear it already, except in case of gross negligence or intentional unlawful act [faute lourde ou dolosive] on the part of the debtor.

It does not interrupt prescription.

Article 1345-1. If the obstruction does not end within two months after formal notice of default, the debtor may, where the obligation concerns a sum of money, deposit it with the Deposits and Consignments Fund [Caisse des dépôts et consignations] or, where the obligation concerns the delivery of a thing, sequester it with a professional guardian.

Where the sequestration of the thing is impossible or too costly, the court may authorize its amicable sale or public auction.

The proceeds are deposited with the Deposits and Consignments fund, less the costs of the sale.

The consignment or sequestration releases the debtor as soon as they are notified to the creditor.

Article 1345-2. Where the obligation relates to another object, the debtor is released if the obstruction has not ceased within two months of the formal notice of default.

Article 1345-3. The costs of the formal notice of default and of the consignment or the sequestration are borne by the creditor.

Sub-section 4: Payment with subrogation

Article 1346. Subrogation takes place by operation of law for the benefit of the person who, having a legitimate interest therein, pays the debt in order to release, as against the creditor, the person who is finally liable for all or part of the debt.

Article 1346-1. Contractual subrogation takes place on the initiative of the creditor where he, receiving his payment from a third person, subrogates the latter in his rights against the debtor.

This subrogation must be explicit.

It must take place at the same time as the payment, unless, in a prior act, the subrogator has expressed the will that his co-contracting party will be subrogated to him at the time of payment.

The concomitance of the subrogation and the payment may be proven by any means.

Article 1346-2. Subrogation also takes place when the debtor, borrowing an amount to pay its debt, subrogates the lender in the rights of the creditor with the consent of the latter.

In this case, the subrogation must be explicit and the receipt provided by the creditor must indicate the origin of the funds.

Subrogation may be granted without the consent of the creditor, but on condition that the debt is due or that the term is in favour of the debtor.

It is then required that the deed of lending and the receipt are signed before a notary, that it is declared in the lending deed that the sum is borrowed for the purpose of making the payment, and that it is declared on the receipt that the payment has been made out of the sum provided for the purpose by the new creditor.

Article 1346-3. The subrogation may not harm the creditor where he has only been paid in part; in this case, he may exercise his rights, with regard to what is still owed to him, by preference against the person from who he has received only a partial payment.

Article 1346-4. Subrogation transmits to its beneficiary, to the extent of what he has paid, the claim and its accessories, with the exception of rights attached exclusively to the person of the creditor.

However, the subrogee is only entitled to the legal interest as from the time of formal notice of default, if he has not agreed upon a new interest with the debtor.

The interest is guaranteed by the securities attached to the claim, to the extent, where these securities have been provided by third parties, of their initial commitment, unless they agree to oblige themselves again.

Article 1346-5. The debtor may invoke the subrogation as soon as he becomes aware of it, but it may only be invoked against him if it has been notified to him or if he has taken notice of it.

Subrogation is enforceable against third parties upon payment.

The debtor may invoke any defences against the subrogee creditor that are inherent in the debt; such as nullity, non-performance, rescission or the set-off of connected debts.

The debtor may also invoke any defences against the subrogee creditor that have arisen from his relations with the subrogator before the subrogation became effective against him, such as the granting of a term, debt remission or the set-off of unconnected debts.

Section 2: Set-off

Sub-section 1: General rules

Article 1347. A set-off is the simultaneous extinction of reciprocal obligations between two persons. It takes place, subject to being invoked, on the date on which its conditions are met.

Article 1347-1. Subject to the provisions of the following sub-section, a set-off only takes place between two fungible, certain, liquid, and payable obligations.

Obligations are fungible where they concern sums of money, even in different currencies, provided that they are convertible, or where concern a quantity of things of the same kind.

Article 1347-2. Unseizable claims and obligations to return a deposit, of loan for use, or of a thing whose owner has been unlawfully deprived of it can only be the object of a set-off with the consent of the creditor.

Article 1347-3. A grace period does not stand in the way of a set-off.

Article 1347-4. If there are several debts eligible for a set-off, the rules regarding the allocating payments apply mutatis mutandis.

Article 1347-5. A debtor who has accepted the assignment of the claim without reservations may not invoke the set-off, which he was able to invoke against the assignor, against the assignee.

Article 1347-6. A surety may set-off any debt the creditor owes to the principal debtor.

A joint and several co-debtor may avail himself of a set-off of any debt the creditor owes to one of his co-debtors in order to deduct the share of the latter in the debt from its total.

Article 1347-7. A set-off does not prejudice rights acquired by third parties.

Sub-section 2: Special rules

Article 1348. A set-off may be awarded in court, even if one of the obligations, though certain, is not yet liquid or payable. Unless otherwise decided, the set-off takes effect on the date of the decision.

Article 1348-1. The court may not deny the set-off of connected debts for the sole reason that one of the obligations is not liquid or payable.

In that case, the set-off is deemed to be effective on the day on which the first of the obligations becomes payable.

In the same case, the acquisition of rights by a third party with regard to one of the obligations does not prevent its debtor from invoking the set-off.

Article 1348-2. Parties may freely agree to extinguish all reciprocal obligations, present or future, by way of a set-off; the latter takes effect on the date of their agreement or, if it concerns future obligations, on that of their co-existence.

Section 3: Confusion

Article 1349. Confusion arises from the combination of the qualities of creditor and debtor of the same obligation in the same person.

It extinguishes the claim and its accessories, subject to the rights acquired by or against third parties.

Article 1349-1. Where there is jointness and severalty between several debtors or several creditors, and where the confusion only concerns one of them, the extinction only takes place, as against the others, with regard to his share in the debt or claim.

Where the confusion concerns an obligation secured by suretyship, the surety, even if joint and several, is released.

Where the confusion concerns the obligation of one of the sureties, the principal debtor is not released. the other joint and several sureties are released to the extent of the share of that surety.

Section 4: Debt remission

Article 1350. Debt remission is a contract by which the creditor releases the debtor from his obligation.

Article 1350-1. Debt remission granted to one of the joint and several co-debtors releases the others to the extent of his share in the debt.

Debt remission granted by only one of the joint and several creditors only released the debtor from his obligation to the extent of the share of that creditor in the claim.

Article 1350-2. Debt remission granted to the principal debtor releases the sureties, even if they are joint and several.

Remission granted to one of the joint and several sureties does not release the principal debtor, but it does release the others to the extent of his share.

That which a creditor receives from a surety for the discharge of his bond must be allocated to the debt and must discharge the principal debtor proportionately.

The other sureties only remain bound for what remains of the debt after deduction of the share of the released surety of the value provided, if it exceeds that share.

Section 5: Impossibility of execution

Article 1351. The impossibility of executing the performance due releases the debtor to the extent that it constitutes a case of force majeure and to the extent that the impossibility is definite, unless he has agreed to be liable for it or unless he has been given prior formal notice of default.

Article 1351-1. Where the impossibility of performance results from the loss of the thing due, the debtor who has been given formal notice of default is nevertheless released if he proves that the loss would have likewise taken place if the obligation had been executed.

However, he is obliged to assign the rights and legal actions attached to the thing to his creditor.

Chapter V: Restitution

Article 1352. Restitution of a thing other than a sum of money takes place in kind or, where that is impossible, in value, estimated on the day of the restitution.

Article 1352-1. The person who restores the thing is responsible for its decay or deterioration that has depleted its value, unless he is in good faith and the decay or deterioration is not attributable to him.

Article 1352-2. He who, having received it in good faith, has sold a thing must only restore the proceeds of the sale.

If he has received it in bad faith, he must restore the value of the thing on the day of the restitution, if that value exceeds the proceeds of the sale.

Article 1352-3. Restitution includes the fruits and the value of the enjoyment which the thing has procured.

The value of the enjoyment is evaluated by the court on the day of the judgment.

Unless otherwise provided, the restitution of the fruits of a thing, if not possible in kind, takes place on the basis of a value estimated on the day of the reimbursement according to the state of the thing on the day of performance of the obligation.

Article 1352-4. Any restitution owed by a non-emancipated minor by a protected adult is reduced by the amount of the benefit he has procured from the annulled act.

Article 1352-5. In order to determine the amount of the restitution, any necessary expenses made for the conservation of the thing, as well as expenses which have enhanced its value, are taken into account, up to the estimated added value on the day of the restitution, in favour of the person who must restore the thing.

Article 1352-6. The restitution of a sum of money includes interest at the legal rate, as well as taxes paid by the person who has received it.

Article 1352-7. He who has received in bad faith owes interest, the fruits he has taken, or the value of the enjoyment as from the time of payment.

He who has received in good faith shall only owes such interest, fruits, and value as from the day of the claim.

Article 1352-8. The restitution of the performance of a service takes place in value.

The latter is assessed on the date on which the service was provided.

Article 1352-9. Any securities provided for the payment of an obligation are, by operation of law, extended to the obligation of restitution, however without depriving a surety of the benefit of the term.

Title IV bis: Proof of obligations

Chapter I: General provisions

Article 1353. He who demands the performance of an obligation must prove its existence.
Reciprocally, he who claims to be released from an obligation must show its payment or the fact that has caused the extinction of his obligation.

Article 1354. A legal presumption that the law attaches to certain acts or to certain facts in, taking them for granted, dispenses him in whose favour the presumption exists from proving them.
It is called a simple presumption where the law reserves proof of the contrary and where it can thus be reversed by any means of proof; it is called a mixed presumption where the law limits the means by which or the object with regard to which it can be reversed; it is called an irrebuttable presumption where it cannot be reversed.

Article 1355. The authority of res judicata only applies to that which was the object of a judgment. The thing claimed must be the same; that the claim be based on the same cause; that the claim be between the same parties and brought by them and against them acting in the same qualities.

Article 1356. Contracts on evidence are valid where they relate to rights of which parties dispose freely.
Nevertheless, they may not contradict any irrebuttable legal presumptions, nor modify the right to rely on an avowal [aveu] or oath.
Further, they may not establish an irrebuttable presumption for the benefit of one of the parties.

Article 1357. The judicial administration of evidence and of disputed relating to it are governed by the Code of Civil Procedure.

Chapter II: Admissibility of evidence and means of proof

Article 1358. Except where otherwise provided by law, evidence may be furnished by any means.

Article 1359. Any legal act relating to a sum or value exceeding an amount fixed by decree must be proven in writing by a private deed or an authentic act.
Evidence against a written document establishing a legal act, even if the sum or value does not exceed the amount mentioned above, may only consist of another document under private or authentic act.
He whose claim exceeds the threshold mentioned in the first subparagraph may not be exempted from written proof, even by reducing his claim.
The same applies to him whose claim, though lower than this threshold, relates to the balance or to a part of a claim exceeding the threshold.

Article 1360. The rules provided for in the preceding article may be derogated from in case of material or moral impossibility of procuring a written document, if it is customary not to draft a document, or where the document has been lost by force majeure.

Article 1361. A judicial avowal [aveu judiciaire], a decisive oath [serment décisoire], or a commencement of written evidence corroborated by another means of proof may be substituted to the written document.

Article 1362. A commencement of written evidence is constituted by any piece of writing which, coming from the person who challenges an act or from the person representing him, renders plausible what is alleged.
The court may consider as equivalent to a commencement of written evidence any declarations made by a person during his personal appearance in court, his refusal to answer, as well as his absence from the hearing.
The reference to an authentic or private act in a public register constitutes a commencement of written evidence.

Chapter III: Different means of proof

Section 1: Written proof

Sub-section 1: General provisions

Article 1363. No one may provide title to himself.

Article 1364. A written document in authentic form or as a private deed constitutes prima facie evidence of a legal act.

Article 1365. A written document consists of a series of letters, characters, numbers, or any other signs or symbols endowed with an intelligible meaning, regardless of their medium.

Article 1366. An electronic document has the same evidential value as a document on paper, Provided that the person from whom it emanates can be clearly identified and that it is drafted and saved in such a manner as guarantee its integrity.

Article 1367. The signature necessary for the perfection of a legal act identifies its author. It shows his consent to the obligations arising from the act.
When it is affixed by a public officer, it confers authenticity on the act.
Where it is electronic, it must consist of the use of a reliable identification process that guarantees its link with the act to which it is attached.
The reliability of this process is presumed, subject to proof of the contrary, where the electronic signature is created and where the identity of the signatory and the integrity of the act are guaranteed under the conditions determined by the Council of State.

Article 1368. In the absence of provisions or contractual stipulations to the contrary, the court resolves conflicts between pieces of written evidence by determining by any means the most plausible title

Sub-section 2: Authentic acts

Article 1369. An authentic act is that which has been received, with the necessary solemnities, by a public official who has the competence and capacity to certify.
It may be drawn up in electronic form if it is drafted and saved under the conditions laid down by decree of the Council of State.
Where it is received by a notary, it is exempt from any legal requirement of handwriting.

Article 1370. An act which is not authentic due to the lack of competence or capacity of the official, or due to a formal error, constitutes a private act if it has been signed by parties.

Article 1371. An authentic act is authoritative until an allegation of forgery is raised against that which the public official claims to have personally performed or witnessed.
In case of an allegation of forgery, the court may suspend the execution.

Sub-section 3: Private deeds

Article 1372. A private deed, recognised by the party against whom it is invoked or legally deemed to be recognised with regard to that party, is authoritative as between those who have signed it and with regard to their heirs and successors.

Article 1373. The party against whom it is invoked may disavow his handwriting or signature.
The heirs or successors of a party may likewise disavow the writing or signature of its author, or declare that they do not know it. In these cases, the writing must be verified.

Article 1374. A private deed countersigned by the lawyers of each party or by the lawyer of all the parties provides authority to the writing and signature of the parties, both with regard to them and to their heirs or successors.
The procedure for the establishment of forgery laid down in the Code of Civil Procedure is applicable.
Such an act is exempt from any legal requirement of handwriting.

Article 1375. The private deed which establishes a synallagmatic contract only has force of evidence where it has been made in as many original copies as there are parties with a distinct interest, unless the parties have agreed to deposit the only original copy with a third party.
Each original must indicate the number of originals made.
He who has performed the contract, even partially, may not invoke the lack of plurality of originals or of the indication of their number.

The requirement of a plurality of originals is be deemed to be satisfied, in case of electronic contracts, where the act is drawn up and saved in accordance with article 1366 and 1367, and where the process used permits each party to keep a copy on a durable medium or to have access to one.

Article 1376. A private deed by which a single party incurs an obligation against another to pay the latter a sum of money or to deliver to him a fungible good only has force of evidence if it bears the signature of the one who thus obliges himself and if it indicates, in his own writing, the sum or quantity both in letters and numbers.
In case of a difference, the private deed has force of evidence with regard to the sum or quantity indicated in letters.

Article 1377. A private deed only acquires a definite date [date certaine] with regard to third parties as from the day when it is registered, from the day of the death of a signatory, or from the day that its content is laid down in an authentic act.

Sub-section 4: Other documents

Article 1378. The registers and records which professionals must keep or establish have, against their author, the same evidential value as private deeds; but the one who relies on them may not split up the entries so as to only retain those that are favourable to him.

Article 1378-1. Private registers and papers do not constitute evidence in favour of the person who has written them.
They do constitute evidence against him:
1° In all cases where they formally declare a payment received;
2° Where they contain an explicit statement that the document has been written in order to
Remedy the defect of title in in favour of the person for whose benefit they state an obligation.

Article 1378-2. A reference to a payment or to another cause for release, made by the creditor on an original title which has always remained in his possession gives rise to a simple presumption of the debtor's release.
The same holds for such a reference on the duplicate of a title or receipt, provided that this duplicate is in the hands of the debtor.

Sub-section 5: Copies

Article 1379. A reliable copy has the same probative force as the original. Reliability is left to the discretion of the court.
Nevertheless, an executive or authentic copy of an authentic document is deemed reliable.
Any copy that results from an identical reproduction of the form and content of an act, and whose lasting integrity is guaranteed by a process that is in conformity with the conditions laid down in a decree of the Council of State, is deemed reliable.
Where the original still exists, its presentation may be required.

Sub-section 6: Acknowledgement

Article 1380. Formal acknowledgement does not dispense with the requirement to present the original title, except where its content is set out specifically in the acknowledgement.
Any content of the acknowledgement that differs from or adds to that of the original title does not have any effect.

Section 2: Testimonial evidence

Article 1381. The probative force of declarations made by a third party under the conditions of the Code of Civil Procedure is left to the discretion of the court.

Section 3: Presumptive evidence

Article 1382. Presumptions not established by law are left to the discretion of the court, which must only admit them if they are serious, precise, and concordant, and only in cases where the law permits proof by any means.

Section 4: Avowal

Article 1383. An avowal is a declaration by which a person recognises as true a fact which entails legal consequences for him.
It may be judicial or extra-judicial.

Article 1383-1. A purely verbal extra-judicial avowal is only admissible in cases where the law permits proof by any means.

Its probative value is left to the discretion of the court.

Article 1383-2. A judicial avowal is a declaration made in court by a party or by the specially appointed representative of a party.

It can be relied upon against the person who has made it.

It cannot be divided against its author.

It is irrevocable, except in case of a factual error.

Section 5: Oath

Article 1384. A decisive oath [serment à titre décisoire] may be required from one party by the other in order to make the judgment of the case depend on it.

It may also be required from one of the parties by the court ex officio.

Sub-section 1: The decisive oath

Article 1385. The decisive oath may be required on any matter in dispute and at any stage of proceedings.

Article 1385-1. It may only be required with regard to a fact that is personal to the party from whom it is required.

It may be turned over by the latter to the other party, unless the fact which constitutes its object is personal exclusively to him.

Article 1385-2. He from whom the oath is required and who refuses it or does not want to turn it over, or to whom it has been turned over and who refuses it, loses his claim.

Article 1385-3. The party who has required or turned over the oath may no longer retract it when the other party has declared to be willing to take the oath.

Where the oath that has been required or turned over has been taken, the other party is not allowed to prove its falsehood.

Article 1385-4. The oath only has probative force in favour of the one who has required it and his heirs or successors, or against them.

The oath required by one of the joint and several creditors from the debtor only releases the latter with regard to the share of that creditor in the claim.

The oath required from the principal debtor also releases the sureties.

The oath required from one of the joint and several debtors benefits the other co-debtors.

The oath required from a surety benefits the principal debtor.

In the two latter cases, the oath of the joint and several co-debtors or the surety benefits the other co-debtors or the principal debtor only where it has been required with regard to the debt, and not to the fact of joint and several liability or suretyship.

Sub-section 2: The oath required ex officio

Article 1386. The court may require an oath from one of the parties ex officio.

That oath may not be turned over to the other party.

Its probative value is left to the discretion of the court.

Article 1386-1. The judge may only require the oath ex officio, with regard to the claim or to the defence invoked against it, if it is not either fully justified or totally devoid of evidence.

[Title V is omitted.]

Title VI. Of sales

Chapter I. Of the nature and the form of sale

Article 1582. Sale is an agreement whereby on party obliges himself to deliver an object [chose], and the other to pay for it.

It may be made by authentic instrument or by an instrument with a private signature.

Article 1583. It is performed between the parties, and ownership is acquired by the buyer as against the seller the moment they have agreed about the object [chose] and the price, even if the object has not yet been delivered or the price not yet been paid.

[The remainder of Chapter I and Chapter II are omitted.]

Chapter III. Of objects that may be sold

[Article 1598 is omitted.]

Article 1599. The sale of an object [chose] of someone else is void: it may give rise to damages where the buyer did not know that the thing belonged to another.

[The remainder of Chapter III is omitted.]

Chapter IV. Of the obligations of the seller

Section 1. General provisions

Article 1602. The seller is obliged to explain clearly what he binds himself to.
Any obscure or ambiguous agreement shall be interpreted against the seller.

[The remainder of Sections 1 is omitted.]

Section 2. Of delivery

[Articles 1604-1611 are omitted.]

Article 1612. The seller is not obliged to deliver the thing where the buyer does not pay the price of it unless the seller has granted him time for the payment.

[The remainder of Section 2 is omitted.]

Section 3. Of warranty

Paragraph 2. Of warranty against the defects of the object sold

Article 1641. The seller is held to stand guarantee for latent defects of the object sold which render it unfit for its intended use, or which diminish that use so much that the buyer would not have acquired it, or would only have paid a smaller price for it, if he would have known them.

Article 1642. The seller is not held responsible for apparent defects [vices apparents] and which the buyer could ascertain for himself.

Article 1643. He is held responsible for latent defects [vices cachés], even where he could not have known them, unless, in that case, he has stipulated that he shall not be bound to any guarantee.

Article 1644. In the case of Articles 1641 and 1643, the buyer has the choice to return the object and to have the price repaid to him, or to keep the object and get part of the price back.

Article 1645. If the seller knew about the defects of the object, he is held, besides restitution of the price which he has received for it, as against the buyer to pay all the damages.

Article 1646. If the seller did not know the defects of the object, he shall only be held to pay restitution of the price, and to reimburse the buyer for all the costs caused by the sale.

Article 1647. If the object which had defects has perished as a consequence of its bad quality, the loss is for the seller, who will be held as against the buyer to pay restitution of the price and of other indemnities as provided for in the two preceding articles.
However, a loss that occurred due to a fortuitous event shall be for the account of the buyer.

Article 1648. An action resulting from irreparable defects must be initiated by the buyer within a period of two years counting from the discovery of the defect.
In the case foreseen by Article 1642-1, the action must be initiated, upon penalty of foreclosure, in the year which follows the date at which the seller may be discharged from apparent defects [vices] and defects in conformity [défauts de conformité].

[The remainder of Chapter IV and Chapter V are omitted.]

Chapter VI. Of nullity and cancellation of the sale

[Article 1658 and Section 1 are omitted.]

Section 2. Of the rescission of the sale for reason of injury

Article 1674. Where a seller has suffered a loss greater than seven-twelfths of the price of an immovable, he is entitled to apply for the rescission of the sale, even though he may have expressly renounced in the contract the faculty of applying for that rescission and have declared to donate the surplus.

[The remainder of Chapter VI is omitted.]

Chapter VIII. Of assignment of claims and of other incorporeal rights

[Article 1689 is omitted.]

Article 1690. An assignee [cessionnaire] is vested with regard to third parties only by notice of the assignment to debtor. Nevertheless, the assignee may likewise be vested if he accepts the assignment given by the debtor in an authentic act.

Article 1691. Where, before the debtor has been given notice by the assignor or the assignee, the debtor has paid the assignor, he is lawfully discharged.

Article 1692. The sale or assignment of a claim includes the accessories of the claim, such as the surety, priority right and hypothec.

[The remainder of Title VI and Title VII are omitted.]

Title VIII. Of the contract of lease

[Chapter I is omitted.]

Chapter II. Of the lease of objects [louage des choses]

[Article 1713 is omitted.]

Section 1. General provisions in respect to the lease of houses and agricultural leases

[Articles 1714 – 1718 are omitted.]

Article 1719. A lessor is bound, by the nature of the contract, and without need of any particular stipulation:
1° To deliver the thing leased to the lessee and, where the main dwelling of the latter is concerned, a decent lodging. In case a residential dwelling is not fit for this use, the lessor cannot claim the nullity of the lease or its termination in order to evict the resident;
2° To maintain that thing in order so that it can serve the use for which it has been let;
3° To secure to the lessee a peaceful enjoyment for the duration of the lease;
4° To secure also the permanence and quality of plantings.

[Articles 1720 – 1742 are omitted.]

Article 1743. If the lessor sells the object [chose] that is leased, the acquirer may not evict the tenant-farmer, share-tenant [colon partiaire] or tenant who has an authentic lease or one the date of which is certain.
He may, however, evict a tenant of non-rural things [biens non ruraux] where he has reserved that right in the contract of lease.

[The remainder of Title VIII and Titles VIII bis and IX are omitted.]

Title IXbis. Of agreements in respect to the exercise of undivided rights [droits indivis]

Chapter 1. Of agreements in respect to the exercise of undivided rights in the absence of a right of usufruct

[Article 1873-2 is omitted.]

Article 1873-3. The agreement may be concluded for a determined duration which may not exceed five years. It may be renewed by an express decision of the parties. A division [partage] may be instigated before the agreed term only where there are proper reasons for it.
The agreement may equally be concluded for an indeterminate duration. In that case, a division may be instigated at any time, provided it is not in bad faith or at an inappropriate time.
It may be decided that an agreement for a determined duration will be renewed by tacit extension, for a determined or indeterminate duration. For lack of such an agreement, the co-entitlement

[l'indivision] shall be governed by Articles 815 and following at the expiry of the agreement for a determined duration.

[The remainder of Title IXbis is omitted.]

Title X. Of loans

[Article 1874 is omitted.]

Chapter I. Of loans for use

[Section 1 and 2 are omitted.]

Section 3. Of the obligations of the one who lends

[Articles 1888 – 1890 are omitted.]

Article 1891. Where the thing loaned has such defects that it may cause harm to the person who uses it, the lender is liable, where he knew of the defects and did not warn the borrower.

[The remainder of Title X and Titles XI – XII are omitted.]

Title XIII. Mandate

Chapter I. Nature and form of mandate

Article 1984. Mandate or power of attorney is an act by which a person gives to another the authority to do something for the principal [mandant] and in his name.
The contract is formed only through acceptance of the agent [mandataire].

[The remainder of Title XIII is omitted.]

Title XIV. Of trusts [fiducie]

Article 2011. The trust [fiducie] is a transaction through which one or more constituents transfer things [biens], rights or securities, or a collection of things, rights or securities, to one or more fiduciaries [fiduciaires] , keeping them segregated from their own patrimony, act so as to further a particular purpose for the benefit of one or more beneficiaries.

Article 2012. The trust is created by law or by contract. It must be express.

If the things [biens], rights or securities transferred to the trust patrimony depend on the community of property between the spouses or on undivided ownership, the contract of trust is created by an instrument drawn up by a notary on the penalty of annulment.

Article 2013. A contract of trust is void if it is made with the intention of conferring wealth upon a beneficiary. This nullity is public policy.

Article 2014. (Repealed.)

Article 2015. Only credit institutions within the meaning of Article L. 511-1 of the Monetary and Financial Code, institutions or agencies referred to in Article L. 518-1 of that Code, investment enterprises referred to in Article L. 531-4 of that Code, portfolio management firms, or insurance companies regulated by Article L. 310-1 of the Insurance Code may be fiduciaries.
Lawyers [membres de la profession de l'avocat] may also be fiduciaries.

Article 2016. The constituant or the fiduciary may be the beneficiary or one of the beneficiaries of a contract of trust.

Article 2017. Subject to provision to the contrary in the contract of trust, the constituant may at any time appoint a third party to protect his interests in the context of carrying out the contract. Such third party may exercise any of the powers conferred by law on the constituant.
When the constituant is a natural person, he cannot renounce this power.

Article 2018. The contract shall provide, upon penalty of nullity:
(1) the things [biens], rights or securities transferred. If they are future things, rights or securities, they must be identifiable;
(2) the period for which they have been transferred, which must not exceed ninety nine years dating from the execution of the contract;
(3) the constituant or constituants;

(4) the fiduciary or fiduciaries;
(5) the beneficiary or beneficiaries, or at least provides for their ascertainment;
(6) the purpose which the fiduciary or fiduciaries have undertaken, and the extent of their powers, both administrative and dispositive.

[Article 2018-1 and Article 2018-2 are omitted]

Article 2019. Upon penalty of nullity, a contract of trust and its variation shall be registered within one month of its date with the tax office of the place where the fiduciary has its seat or, where the fiduciary has no domicile in France, with the tax office for non-residents.
Where it deals with immovable things [immeubles] or immovable property rights [droits réels immobiliers], it is, subject to the same penalty, unless it receives the publicity required by Articles 647 and 657 of the General Tax Code [Code général des impôts].
The transfer of rights resulting from a contract of trust, and, if the beneficiary is not named in the contract, his subsequent designation, upon penalty of nullity, shall give rise to an instrument in writing, to be registered under the same conditions.

Article 2020. A national register of trusts will be constituted in accordance with the requirements of a decree of the Council of State [Conseil d'État].

[Articles 2021 – 2023 are omitted.]

Article 2024. The institution of any safeguard procedure [procédure de sauvegarde], administration [redressement judiciaire], compulsory sale [liquidation judiciaire] for the benefit of the fiduciary has no effect on the trust patrimony.

Article 2025. Without prejudice to the rights of any creditors of the constituants who have a right of recourse against a security, notified before the contract of trust, and except in the case of fraud on the creditors of the constituant, the trust patrimony is subject to execution only for debts arising from the keeping or the management of this patrimony. *[The remainder of this Article is omitted.]*

Article 2026. The fiduciary is personally liable for any wrongs that he commits whilst carrying out his functions.

[Article 2027 is omitted.]

Article 2028. The contract of trust may be revoked by the constituant at any time before it has been accepted by the beneficiary.
After such acceptance, the contract may only be modified or revoked with the consent of the beneficiary or by a decision of the court.

Article 2029. A contract of trust ends if the constituant who is a natural person dies, with the occurrence of its expiry date, or with the achievement of its object before the expiration.
When all the beneficiaries abandon the trust, it will also end automatically, unless terms of the contract provide circumstances in which it is to continue. Subject to the same exception, it will end if the fiduciary becomes subject to compulsory sale [liquidation judiciaire] or dissolution, or ceases to exist as a result of an assignment or a merger and, if he is a lawyer, in case of temporary suspension, disbarment or omission from the bar.

Article 2030. If the contract of trust ends at a time when there are no beneficiaries, the rights, things or securities forming part of the trust patrimony automatically revert to the constituant.
If it ends due to the death of the constituant, the trust patrimony automatically reverts to the succession.

[Titles XV – XIX are omitted.]

Title XX. Of extinctive prescription

Chapter I. General provisions

Article 2219. Extinctive prescription is a way in which rights can be destroyed as a result of their non-use by the holder of the right after a certain period of time.

[Article 2220 is omitted.]

Article 2221. The extinctive prescription is subject to the provisions that are applicable to the right it concerns.

[Articles 2222 – 2223 are omitted.]

Chapter II. Of the prescription period and the start of the prescription period for extinctive prescription

Section 1. Of the common rules on the prescription period and its start

Article 2224. Personal or movable claims are lost through the completion of a prescription period of five years to be calculated from the day that the holder of a right knew or should have known the facts that entitle him to exercise the right.

Section 2. Of some prescription periods and specific starting points

[Articles 2225 – 2226 are omitted.]

Article 2227. The right of ownership cannot be lost through prescription. Taking that into account, real immovable claims prescribe after a period of thirty years to be calculated from the day that the holder of a right knew or should have known the facts that entitle him to exercise the right.

Chapter III. Of the running of the prescription period

Section 1. General provisions

Article 2228. The prescription period is calculated in days, not in hours.

Article 2229. It is completed when the last day of the period has passed.

Article 2230. The suspension of the prescription period brings the running of the prescription period to a temporary halt.

Article 2231. The interruption ends the prescription period that has passed. A new period of the same time as the old one will start to run.

Article 2232. The changing of the starting point of the prescription period as a result of a suspension or interruption may not have the effect of making the prescription period longer than twenty years, to be calculated from the day the right was created. The first paragraph is not applicable in cases mentioned in Articles 2226, 2227, 2233, 2236, first paragraph and Article 2241 until 2244. It does not apply to claims on the state of persons.

[The remainder of Title XX is omitted.]

Title XXI. Of possession and acquisitive prescription

Chapter I. General provisions

Article 2255. Possession is the holding [detention] or the enjoyment of an object [chose] or of a right that we have or hold for ourselves, or by another that has or holds it for us.

Article 2256. One is always presumed to possess for oneself, and in the capacity as owner, where it is not proved that one has started by possessing for another.

Article 2257. Where one has started by possessing for another, one is always presumed to possess in the same capacity, unless there is proof to the contrary.

Chapter II. Of acquisitive prescription

Article 2258. Acquisitive prescription is a way to acquire a thing [bien] or a right through possession without requiring him to show a title for the thing or without opposing him the exception following bad faith.

Article 2259. Articles 2221 and 2222 are applicable to acquisitive prescription, as well as Chapters III and IV of Title XX of this book, except if the provisions in this chapter provide otherwise.

Section 1. Of the requirements for acquisitive prescription

Article 2260. One cannot acquire through prescription things [biens] or rights which are not commercial.

Article 2261. In order to complete the prescription uninterrupted and continuous possession, peaceful, public, unambiguous, and with the title as owner is needed.

Article 2262. Acts which are merely allowed or simply tolerated may not give rise to possession or prescription.

Article 2263. Acts of duress may not give rise to a possession capable of bringing about prescription either.
Possession begins to produce effects only from the time the duress has ceased.

Article 2264. A present possessor who proves that he has formerly possessed, is presumed to have possessed during the intervening time, unless there is proof to the contrary.

Article 2265. To complete a prescription, one may join to one's possession that of one's predecessor, in whatever manner one may have succeeded to him, whether by virtue of a universal or specific title, or for value or gratuitously.

Article 2266. Those who possess for another never acquire ownership by prescription, whatever the time elapsed may be.
Thus, a farm tenant, a depositary, a usufructuary, and all those who precariously hold the thing of an owner, may not prescribe it.

[Articles 2267 – 2269 are omitted.]

Article 2270. Prescription cannot have effect against the title, in that regard it is not possible to change, by yourself, the cause and the basis of possession.

Article 2271. Acquisitive prescription is interrupted when the possessor of a thing [bien] is deprived, during more than one year, of the enjoyment of that thing, either by the owner, or even by a third person.

Section 2. Of acquisitive prescription in respect to immovable things

Article 2272. The period required to acquire the ownership in respect to immovables through acquisitive prescription is thirty years. However, he who acquires an immovable in good faith and with a legal title [juste titre] acquires ownership in ten years.

[Article 2273 is omitted.]

Article 2274. Good faith [bonne foi] is always presumed, it is for the person who argues bad faith to prove this.

Article 2275. It is sufficient if good faith exists at the moment of acquisition.

Section 3. Of acquisitive prescription in respect to movable things

Article 2276. As regards movables, possession counts as title.
Nevertheless, the person who has lost an object [chose] or from whom an object has been stolen is, during three years from the day of the loss or theft, able to revindicate the object from the person in whose hands he finds it. This does not exclude the latter's remedy against the person from whom he got the object.

Article 2277. Where the current possessor of an object that is lost or is stolen has bought it at a fair or on a market, or at a public sale, or from a merchant selling similar objects, the original owner may have it returned to him only by reimbursing the possessor for the price that the object has cost him.
A lessor who revindicates, under Article 2332, the movables that have been displaced without his consent and which have been bought in the same conditions, must likewise reimburse the buyer for the price which that the things have cost him.

Chapter III. Of protection of possession

Article 2278. Possession is protected, regardless of the substance of the right, against disturbance which affects or threatens it.
Protection of possession is also granted to a person who holds a thing for another [detenteur] against any other person than the one from whom he derives his rights.

Article 2279. Claims for the protection of possession may be brought under the conditions provided by the Code of Civil Procedure by those who possess or hold for another peacefully.

Book IV. Of Securities

Article 2284. He who is obliged to something is liable for the performance of that obligation with all his movables and immovables, present and future.

Article 2285. The things [biens] of the debtor are pledge to all the creditors; the value is divided among them according to their contribution, if no rights of preference exist among the creditors.

Article 2286. May claim a right of retention to a thing:
1o The person to whom the object [chose] was handed over until payment of his debt;
2o The person whose outstanding debt results from the contract which binds him to deliver it;
3o The person whose outstanding debt arose at the moment that the object [chose] came in his power [détention].
4 o The person who benefits from a right of non-possessory pledge.
A right of retention is lost through voluntary relinquishment.

[Article 2287 is omitted.]

Title I. Of personal security rights

Article 2287-1. The personal security rights dealt with in this title are suretyships [cautionnement], the independent guarantee [garantie autonome] and the letter of intention [lettre d'intention].

Chapter I. Of suretyship

[Articles 2288 – 2291 are omitted.]

Article 2292. Suretyship is not presumed; it must be explicit, and one may not extend it beyond the limits within which it was contracted.

[The remainder of Title I is omitted.]

Title II. Of property security rights

Sub-title I. General provisions

Article 2323. Lawful causes of preference are priority rights and hypothecs.

Article 2324. A priority right is a right of a creditor of a claim that arises due to the nature of that claim to have preference over other creditors, even holders of a right of hypothec.

[Articles 2325 – 2328-1 are omitted.]

Sub-title II. Of security rights in respect to movable things

Article 2329. Securities on movables are:
1o Movable priority rights [privileges mobiliers];
2o A right of pledge [gage] on corporeal movables;
3o A right of pledge [nantissement] on incorporeal movables;
4o Retained ownership or ownership transferred for security purposes.

Chapter I. Of prior charges over movables

[Section 1 is omitted.]

Section 2. Of special prior charges

Article 2332. Debts which have precedence over particular movables are:

[nos. 1-3 are omitted]

4. The price of unpaid movable effects, where they are still in the possession of the debtor, whether he has bought on credit or not.
Where the sale was not made on credit, the seller may even revendicate those effects as long as they are in the possession of the buyer, and prevent a re-sale, provided the claim is made within eight days after the delivery, and the effects are in the same condition in which the delivery was made.

[The remainder of the article is omitted.]

[The remainder of Chapter I is omitted.]

Chapter II. Of pledge on movable things

Section 1. Of common rules on the right of pledge [gage]

Article 2333. A right of pledge is an agreement by which the pledgor grants a creditor the right to be paid in preference to his other creditors out of a movable thing [bien mobilier] or a set of corporeal things, present or future.
The claims secured may be present or future; in the latter case, they must be determinable.

[Article 2334 – 2336 are omitted.]

Article 2337. A pledge is enforceable against third parties due to the publicity attached to it.
It is likewise so by surrendering possession of the thing [bien] which it concerns into the hands of the creditor or an agreed third party.
Where a pledge has been duly disclosed to the public, the particular successors of the pledgor may not invoke Article 2276.

[Articles 2338 – 2341 are omitted.]

Article 2342. Where a non-possessory pledge attaches to fungible objects [choses fongibles], the pledgor may dispose of them if the agreement so provides, on the condition that they be replaced by the same quantity of equivalent objects.

[Articles 2343 – 2345 are omitted.]

Article 2346. In case of failure to pay the secured debt, a creditor may acquire a court order for the sale of the pledged thing [bien gagé]. That sale shall take place following the rules on enforcement proceedings from which a contract of pledge may not derogate.

Article 2347. A creditor may also acquire a court order that the thing [bien] will remain with him by way of satisfaction.
Where the value of the thing exceeds the amount of the secured debt, the sum which is equal to the difference shall be paid to the debtor or, if there are other pledgee creditors [créanciers gagistes], shall be deposited.

Article 2348. When creating the pledge or afterwards, it may be agreed that in case of failure to perform the secured obligation, the creditor will become owner of the pledged thing [bien gagé].
The value of the thing shall be determined on the day of the transfer by an expert designated by amicable arrangement or judicially, in the absence of an official quotation of the thing on a regulated market within the meaning of the Monetary and Financial Code [code monétaire et financier]. Any clause to the contrary is deemed not written.
Where that value exceeds the amount of the secured debt, the sum equal to the difference shall be paid to the debtor or, if there are other pledgee creditors, shall be deposited.

[The remainder of Chapter II is omitted.]

Chapter III. Of pledge on incorporeal movable things [nantissement]

Article 2355. The pledge [nantissement] on an incorporeal movable thing [bien meubles incorporel] is the connection, in order to secure an obligation, of a movable incorporeal thing or a group of movable incorporeal things, present or future.
It is created by agreement or by court decision.
The pledge created by court decision is regulated by the provisions applicable to the procedure of realization [exécution].
The pledge created by agreement that is created in respect to claims is regulated, in the absence of any particular provisions, by the current chapter.
He who takes incorporeal things is subject, in the absence of any special provisions, by the provisions on the pledge of movable corporeal things.

[The remainder of Chapter III is omitted.]

Chapter IV. Of the right of ownership reserved for security purposes

Article 2367. Ownership of a thing [bien] may be retained as security through a clause of retention of title [clause de réserve de propriété] that withholds the transferring effect of a contract until payment in full of the obligation which compensates for it.
Ownership so retained is the accessory of the debt the payment of which it secures.

Article 2368. A retention of title shall be agreed upon in writing.

Article 2369. The retention of title of a fungible thing [bien fongible], up to the amount of the debt remaining due, attaches to things of the same nature and quality detained by the debtor or on his behalf.

[Articles 2370 – 2372 are omitted.]

Sub-title III. Of security rights in respect to immovable things

Article 2373. Property security rights in respect to immovables are priority rights, the *antichresis* [le gage immobilier] and rights of hypothec.
The right of ownership in respect to immovable things can also be reserved for security purposes.

[Chapter I is omitted.]

Chapter II. Of the right of antichresis **[du gage immobilier]**

Article 2387. The right of *antichresis* is the connection of an immovable thing in order to secure an obligation. It brings the dispossession of him who creates the right.

[Articles 2388 – 2391 are omitted.]

Article 2392. The rights of a creditor by way of *antichresis* are destroyed in particular:
1° Through the extinguishment of the principal obligation;
2° Through anticipated restoration of the immovable to his owner.

Chapter III. Of the right of hypothec

Section 1. General provisions

Article 2393. A hypothec is a property right on immovables allocated to the discharge of an obligation.
It is, by its nature, indivisible and remains in existence in its entirety on all the immovables concerned, on each one and on each part of those immovables.
It follows them in whatever hands they may pass.

[Articles 2394 – 2396 are omitted.]

Article 2397. Can only be susceptible to a hypothec:
1° Immovable things [biens immobiliers] which may be the subject matter of legal transactions, and their accessories deemed immovable;
2° The usufruct on the same thing and accessories for the time of its duration.
A hypothec covers the improvements which are made to the immovable.

[The remainder of Section 1 and Sections 2 – 3 are omitted.]

Section 4. Hypothecs created by agreement [hypothèques conventionelles]

Article 2413. Rights of hypothec by agreement [hypothèques conventionelles] can only be consented to by those who have the power to alienate [aliéner] the immovables they burden.

[Articles 2414 – 2415 are omitted.]

Article 2416. A hypothec created by agreement may only be granted by an instrument drawn up by a notary.

[Articles 2417 – 2418 are omitted.]

Article 2419. As a rule, a hypothec may be granted only in respect to existing immovables.

Article 2420. By derogation from the preceding article, a hypothec may be granted with regard to future immovables in the following circumstances and subject to the following conditions:
1° He who does not possess existing and unburdened immovables or who does not possess a sufficient quantity of them to secure the claim may agree that each one which he may subsequently acquire be allocated to the payment of the latter as the acquisitions proceed;
2° He whose existing immovable burdened with a hypothec has perished or suffered deteriorations so that it has become insufficient for the security of the claim may likewise do so, without prejudice to the right of the creditor to enforce at once his reimbursement;

3° He who possesses an existing right which allows him to build for his benefit on another's tenement may burden the buildings whose construction has been started or merely planned with a hypothec; in case of destruction of the latter, the hypothec burdens as of right new buildings erected on the same place.

Article 2421. A hypothec may be granted for security of one or several debts, present or future. Where they are future, they must be determinable.
Their grounds shall be determined in the instrument.

[Article 2422 is omitted.]

Article 2423. A right of hypothec is always created, as regards the capital, up to a fixed sum that the notarial instrument shall specify, on the penalty of annulment. Where appropriate, the parties shall estimate for that purpose the annuities, benefits and undetermined, contingent or conditional rights. Where the debt is subject to an index-linking clause, the guarantee extends to the revalued debt, provided the instrument so specifies.
A hypothec extends, by operation of the law, to interest and other accessories.
Where it is granted for security of one or several future debts and for an undetermined duration, the holder of the right of hypothec may at any time terminate the right subject to him giving a three month notice. Once terminated, the right still exists for security of pre-existing claims.

Article 2424. A hypothec is transferred with the secured debt by operation of law. The mortgagee may subrogate another creditor to the hypothec and retain his debt.
He may also, by a ranking agreement, assign his rank of registration to a creditor of a lower rank, with whom he changes places.

Section 5. Classification of hypothecs

Article 2425. As between creditors, a hypothec, either statutory, or judicial, or conventional, ranks only from the day of the registration made by the creditor at the land registry, in the form and manner prescribed by law.
Where several registrations are required on the same day as regards the same immovable, that which is required by virtue of the instrument of title bearing the least recent date shall be deemed of prior rank, whatever the order resulting from the register provided for in Article 2453 may be.
However, the registrations of separations of patrimony provided for by Article 2283, in the case referred to in Article 2386, second paragraph, as well as those of the statutory hypothecs provided for in Article 2400, 1°, 2° and 3°, shall be deemed of a rank prior to the one of any registration of judicial or conventional hypothecs made on the same day.
Where several registrations are made on the same day as regards the same immovable, either by virtue of instruments of title provided for in the second paragraph but bearing the same date, or for the benefit of requiring parties vested with the prior claim or the hypothecs referred to in the third paragraph, the registrations rank equally whatever the order of the above mentioned register may be.
The registration of a statutory hypothec of the Exchequer [l'hypothèque légale du Trésor] or a conservatory judicial hypothec [hypothèque judiciaire conservatoire] shall be deemed of an earlier rank than that conferred to an agreement for the coverage of new claims where the registration of the aforesaid agreement is subsequent to the registration of that hypothec.
The provisions of the fifth paragraph apply to the registration of the statutory hypothec of administrative organs of an obligatory regime of social protection.
The order of priority between creditors having a prior claim or hypothec and holders of warrants, insofar as the latter are secured on assets deemed immovable, is determined by the dates on which the respective instruments have been published, the publicity of warrants remaining subject to the special statutes which regulate them.

[Chapter IV is omitted.]

Chapter V. Of the effect of priority rights and hypothecs

Article 2458. Unless one takes action to sell the thing [bien] burdened with a hypothec under the terms provided for by the laws which apply to enforcement proceedings, from which a contract of hypothec may not derogate, an unpaid hypothecee may request the court that the immovable remain with him.

Article 2459. It may be agreed in an agreement of hypothec that the creditor shall become owner of the immovable burdened by the hypothec. However, that clause is ineffective in respect to an immovable that is the principal residence of the debtor.

[The remainder of Chapter V is omitted.]

Chapter VI. Of the realization [purge] of priority rights and hypothecs

Article 2475. Where, on the occasion of a sale of an immovable that is burdened with a right of hypothec, all creditors notify to the debtor that the proceeds of the sale is affected completely or partially by their claims or some of these, they exercise their right of preference on the price and they may oppose this right to any acquirer or creditor of the claim to the proceeds of the sale.
By payment, the immovable is relieved from the right to follow that is connected to the right of hypothec.
In absence of an agreement foreseen in the first paragraph, the formalities of realization [purge] apply in conformity with the articles that follow.

[The remainder of Chapter VI is omitted.]

Chapter VII. The destruction of priority rights and hypothecs

Article 2488. Prior charges and hypothecs are destroyed:
1° By extinguishment of the principal obligation except for the case provided for in Article 2422;
2° By the creditor's abandonment of the right of hypothec under the same exception;
3° By the fulfilment of the formalities and conditions prescribed to third parties in possession to redeem the thing that they have acquired;
4° By prescription.
Prescription is acquired to a debtor, as to the things [biens] that are in his hands, by the time prescribed by the statute of limitations in respect of the claims provided by a hypothec or a priority right.
As to the things which are in the hands of a third party in possession, they are acquired by him at the moment regulated for prescription periods of ownership for his benefit: in case where prescription depends upon a title, the prescription period begins to run only from the day when that title has been registered in the land register of the situation of the immovables.
Registrations made by a creditor do not interrupt the running of the prescription period established by law in favour of the debtor or of the third party in possession.
5° By the termination allowed by Article 2423, last paragraph, and as far as provided for by this provision.

[The remainder of the Civil Code is omitted.]

Miscellaneous Private Law Codes and Statutes*

Code on Civil Execution Procedures (Code des procédures civiles d'exécution). Consolidated version of 19 July 2017. Selected provision: Article L 111-1, paragraph (1).

Article L111-1. Each creditor can, under the conditions laid down by law, compel his defaulting debtor to perform his obligations towards him.

[The remainder of the article is omitted.]

Commercial Code (Code de Commerce). Consolidated version at 4 July 2015, Selected provisions : Articles L 110-3; L 142-1; L142-1 ; L223-18, L223-22, L225-35; L225-56; L225-57; L225-64, L225-66; L225-251; L225-252, L446-II(c), L624-14, L624-16 and L624-18.

Article L110-3. With regard to traders, commercial instruments may be proven by any means unless the law specifies otherwise.

Article L142-1. Businesses may be the subject of a security, without conditions and formalities other than those specified by the present chapter and Chapter III below.
A security on a business does not give the secured creditor the right to have the business allotted to him in payment up to the full amount due.

Article L142-2. The security subject to the provisions of this chapter may cover the following items only as forming part of a business: style and trademark, leasing rights, clientele and custom, company building, equipment or materials used for the operation of the business, patents, licences, trademarks, industrial drawings and designs, and in general the intellectual property rights attached thereto.
A certificate of addition subsequent to the security, which includes the patent to which it applies shall follow the fate of this patent and, as shall it, be part of the security as constituted.
For lack of an explicit and precise designation in the instrument creating it, the security shall cover only the style and trademark, leasing rights, clientele and custom.
If the security relates to a business and its branches, then these must be designated by the precise indication of their seat.

Article L223-18. A limited liability company is managed by one or more natural persons.
The managers [gérants] may be chosen from outside of the members [associés]. They are appointed by the members, in the articles of association [statuts] or by an ordinary decision, according to the conditions laid down in Article L223-29. Under the same conditions, the reference to the name of a manager in the articles of association can, in the case of the cessation of the functions of this manager for whatever cause, be repealed by way of decision of the shareholders.
In the absence of provisions in the articles of association, they are appointed for the duration of the company.
In his dealings with the shareholders, the powers of the managers are determined by the articles of association, and in case of their silence, according to Article L.221-4.
In his dealings with third parties, the manager is invested with the most extensive powers to act in all circumstances in the name of the company, unless the powers are expressly attributed by the law to the members. The company is bound in the same way by the acts of the manager which are not covered by the company's purpose, unless it can prove that the third party knew that the act exceeded this purpose or that he could not have been ignorant thereof given the circumstances, excluding that the mere publication of the articles of association suffices to constitute such proof.
Provisions in the articles of association restricting the powers of the managers which result from the present article are inapplicable towards third parties.
In the case of a plurality of managers, they exercise power separately as laid down in the present article. Opposition formed by one manager against the acts of another manager does not have effect in respect of third parties, unless it can be established that they had knowledge thereof.

Article L223-22. Managers are jointly or severally liable, depending on the case, to the company or to third parties for infringements of the legislative or regulatory provisions applicable to limited

---

*   Translations by Eveline Ramaekers, Heike Hauröder, and Sascha Hardt.

liability companies, for violations of the articles of association, and for errors committed in their management.

Should more than one manager have participated in the same facts, the court is to determine the contributory share of each to the compensation of damage.

Besides the proceedings for compensation of loss suffered personally, the member can bring proceedings for civil liability against the managers, either individually or as a group in accordance with the conditions laid down in a decree of the Council of State [Conseil d'État]. The claimants are authorized to pursue compensation for the entirety of the loss suffered by the company to which, if the case arises, damages can be awarded.

Any clause in the articles of association is deemed not written that have the effect of subordinating the exercise of civil proceedings to prior notice to or authorization of the meeting [assemblée], or which entails in advance a waiver of the exercise of these proceedings.

No decision by the meeting may have the effect of extinguishing civil liability proceedings against the managers for errors committed in the performance of their office.

Article L225-35. The board of directors [conseil d'administration] determines the orientation of the activities of the company and ensures their implementation. Without prejudice to the powers expressly attributed to the shareholders' meetings [assemblée d'actionnaires], and within the limits of the company's purpose, it deals with all matters relevant to the good conduct of the company's business and decides through its deliberations the matters that concern it.

In its dealings with third parties, the company is bound even by acts of its board of directors which are not covered by the company's purpose, unless it can prove that the third party knew that the act exceeded that purpose or that he could not have been ignorant thereof given the circumstances, excluding that the mere publication of the articles of association suffices to constitute such proof.

The board of directors carries out the inspections and verifications which it considers appropriate.

The chairman [président] or general manager [directeur général] of the company is required to communicate to each director [adminstrateur] all the documents and information necessary to perform its task.

Securities [cautions], avals and guarantees given by companies other than banking or financial institutions are the subject of an authorization by the board under the conditions laid down in a decree by the Council of State [Conseil d'État]. That decree also lays down the conditions under which the overstepping of that authorization can be raised against third parties.

Article L225-56. I. - The general manager is invested with the most extensive powers to act in the name of the company in all circumstances. He is to exercise these powers within the limits of the company's purpose and those that the law expressly attributes to shareholders' meetings and to the board of directors.

He represents the company in its dealings with third parties. The company is bound even by those acts of the general manager that do not relate to the company's purpose, unless it can prove that the third party knew that the act exceeded that purpose or that he could not have been ignorant thereof given the circumstances, excluding that the mere publication of the articles of association suffices to constitute such proof.

Provisions in the articles of association and decisions of the board of directors limiting the powers of the general manager are inapplicable towards third parties.

II. - In agreement with the general manager, the board of directors shall determine the scope and the duration of the powers conferred upon the assistant general managers [directeurs généraux délégués]. The assistant general managers have the same powers as the general manager with respect to third parties.

Article L225-57. It can be stipulated in the articles of association of any public limited company that it shall be governed by the provisions of this sub-section. In that case, the company remains subject to all rules applicable to public limited companies, with the exception of those contained in Articles L225-17 to L225-56.

The introduction of this stipulation, or its deletion, can be decided during the existence of the company.

Article L225-64. The management board [directoire] is invested with the most extensive powers to act in the name of the company behalf in any circumstances. It exercises them within the limits of the company's purpose and subject to those expressly attributed by the law to the supervisory board and shareholders' meetings.

In dealings with third parties, the company is bound even by acts of the management board that do not relate to the company's purpose, unless it can prove that the third party knew that the act exceeded that purpose or that he could not have been ignorant thereof given the circumstances, excluding that the mere publication of the articles of association suffices to constitute such proof. Provisions of the articles of association limiting the powers of the management board are inapplicable towards third parties.

The management board considers and takes its decisions in accordance with the conditions laid down by the articles of association.

Article L225-66 The chairman of the management board [président du directoire] or if the case arises the sole general manager [directeur général unique], represents the company in its dealings with third parties.

Nevertheless, the articles of association may empower the supervisory board to attribute the same power of representation to one or more other members of the management board, who will then carry the title of general manager.

Provisions of the articles of association limiting the powers of representation of the company are inapplicable towards third parties.

Article L225-251. The directors [administrateurs] and general manager [directeur général] are individually or jointly liable, depending on the case, to the company or to third parties either for infringements of legislative or regulatory provisions applicable to public limited companies, for violations of the articles of association, or for faults committed in their management.

If more than one director, or more than one director and the general manager, have participated in the same acts, the Court determines the contributory share of each to the reparation of damage.

Article L225-252. Besides the proceedings for compensation of loss personally, the shareholders may either individually or in an association fulfilling the conditions laid down in Article L.225-120, or as a group in accordance with conditions to be laid down in a decree of the Council of State [Conseil d'Etat], bring proceedings for civil liability against the directors or general manager. The claimants are authorized to pursue compensation for the entirety of the loss suffered by the company to which, if the case arises, damages can be awarded.

Article L442-6. *[Paragraph I is omitted.]* II. – Clauses or contracts are void when providing a producer, a trader, a manufacturer or a person registered in the index of craftsmen with the possibility:

[Subparagraphs (a) and (b) are omitted.]

(c) to prohibit the fellow contracting party from assigning to third parties claims which he himself has.

[The remainder of this provision is omitted.]

Article L624-14. The seller may retain goods [marchandises] that have not been delivered or dispatched to the debtor or to a third party acting on his behalf.

Article L624-16. Movable things delivered precariously [à titre précaire] to the debtor or those transferred to a patrimony of a fiducie [patrimoine fiduciaire] of which the debtor remains to have the right to use or the right to enjoy in his capacity of constituant, may be claimed if they still exist in kind.

Things [biens] sold under a retention of title clause may equally be claimed if they still exist in kind at the time proceedings are opened. This clause must have been agreed upon by the parties in writing at the latest at the time of delivery. It may be laid down in a document governing a number of commercial operations entered into by the parties.

The recovery claim in kind may be brought under the same conditions with respect to movable things incorporated in another thing where they may be removed without damaging them. A recovery claim in kind may also be made in relation to fungible things where things of the same nature and the same quality are in the possession of the debtor or any person keeping them on his behalf has.

In every instance, the thing may not be recovered if, by decision of the supervisory judge [juge-commissaire], the price is paid immediately. The supervisory judge may also, with the consent of the petitioning creditor, grant a moratorium [délai de règlement]. The payment of the price shall thus be considered equivalent to [the payment] of debts referred to under Article L 622-17 (I).

Article L624-18. The price or a part of the price of the things [biens] as meant in Article L 624-16, which was not paid nor settled in valuables or set off between the debtor and the purchaser at the date of the order opening the proceedings, may be claimed. Insurance payouts subrogated for the property may be claimed under the same conditions.

Consumer Code (Code de la Consommation). Selected provisions: Article L 132-1 (1)-(3); Article L211-1 (1) and (2); Article L212-1 – L212-3; Article L224-90 - L224-91; Article L312-17; Article L341-3; Article L 421-6; Article L621-7 – L621-8; Article R212-1 – R212-2, as last amended by Ordinance no. 2016-301 of 16 March 2016. *

Article L132-1. In contracts concluded between a business and a non-business or consumers, clauses which aim to create or result in the creation, to the detriment of the non-professional or the consumer, of a significant imbalance between the rights and obligations of the parties to the contract, are unfair. Decrees of the Council of State [Conseil d'Etat] issued upon the advice of the committee set up as per article L 132-2, may determine the types of clauses that must be regarded as unfair in the sense of the first paragraph.
An annex to this code includes an illustrative and non-exhaustive list of clauses that may be regarded as unfair if they satisfy the conditions posed in the first paragraph.

[The remainder of this article is omitted.]

Art. L211-1. Contract terms proposed by professionals to consumers must be presented and written in a clear and comprehensible manner.
In the event of doubt, they are interpreted in the sense which is most favourable to the consumer.

[The remainder of this article is omitted]

Art. L212-1. In contracts concluded between a business and a a non-business or consumers, clauses which aim to create or result in the creation, to the detriment of the non-professional or the consumer, of a significant imbalance between the rights and obligations of the parties to the contract, are unfair. Without prejudice to the rules of interpretation in Articles 1156 to 1161, 1163 and 1164 of the Civil Code, the abusive nature of a clause is assessed by referring at the moment of conclusion of the contract to all the circumstances surrounding its conclusion, as well as all the other terms of the contract. It also includes those contained in another contract when the two contracts are legally bound in their conclusion or implementation.
The assessment of the abusive nature of clauses in the sense of the first paragraph does not include the definition of the main object of the contract or the adequacy of the price or the remuneration of the good sold or the service offered as long as the clauses are drafted in a clear and comprehensible manner.
A Council of State decree issued upon the advice of the commission for abusive clauses, may determine the types of clauses that must be regarded as unfair in the sense of the first section.
A decree under the same conditions determines a list of clauses presumed to be abusive; in case of dispute regarding a contract containing such a clause, the professional must provide evidence of the non-abusive nature of the disputed clause.
These provisions are applicable regardless of the form or the medium of the contract. It includes purchase orders, invoices, guarantees, delivery notes or orders, tickets or receipts, whether or not containing freely negotiated stipulations or references to the pre-formulated general conditions.

Article L212-2. The provisions of article L212-1 are also applicable to contracts concluded between professionals and non-professionals.

Article L212-3. The provisions of this chapter are of public order.

Article L224-90. The offer of meetings for the realization of a marriage or a stable union, proposed by a professional, is the subject of a written contract, written in readable characters, a copy of which is given to the co-contracting party of the professional at the time of its conclusion.
The contract mentions the name of the professional, his address or that of its headquarters, the nature of services provided, as well as the amount and terms of payment of the price. Attached to the contract is the indication of the qualities of the person sought by the co-contracting party of the professional.
These contracts are established for a fixed term, which shall not be more than one year; they may not be renewed by tacit agreement. They provide an ability to cancel for a legitimate reason for cause for the benefit of both parties.

Article L224-91. Without prejudice to the provisions of Article L221-18, within a period of seven days from the signing of the contract, the co-contracting party of the professional mentioned in

---

* Translation by Nicole Kornet & Sascha Hardt.

Article L224-90 can go back on its commitment without being bound to the payment of an indemnity. Before the expiry of this period, he may not receive the payment or the deposit in any form whatsoever.

Article L312-17. When credit transactions are concluded at the place of sale or using a distance communication method, a separate information sheet on the form referred to in Article L312-12 is provided by the lender or through a credit intermediary to the borrower.

This sheet, established on paper or on another durable medium, contains in particular information relating to resources and expenses of the borrower as well, where appropriate, to the current loans taken out by the latter.

The fact sheet is signed and its contents confirmed electronically by the borrower and contributes to the assessment of solvency of the borrower. The information featured on the fact sheet is subject to a declaration certifying on their honour its accuracy.

This sheet is kept by the lender for the duration of the loan.

If the amount of the credit granted is higher than a threshold defined by Decree, the sheet is supported by documentary evidence, the list of which is defined by Decree.

Article L341-3. The lender who grants a credit without submitting and having electronic signature or validation of the sheet referred to in Article L. 312-17 shall forfeit the right to interest.

Article L 421-6. A product is deemed to satisfy the general safety obligation laid down in article L. 421-3 with regard to the risks and categories of risk covered by the norms applicable to it if it complies with the non-obligatory national norms transposing the European norms to which the European Commission makes reference in its publication in the Official Journal of the European Union in application of article 4 of directive 2001/95/EC of 3 December 2001 on general product safety.

Article L621-7. The associations referred to in article L621-1 and the bodies justifying their inclusion on the list published in the Official Journal of the European Union in application of article 4 of Directive 2009/22/EC of the European Parliament and of the Council of 23 April 2009 amended relating to injunctions for the protection of the interests of consumers, can act before the civil court to stop or prohibit any unlawful act under the provisions transposing the Directive referred to in the first article of the above-mentioned directive.

Article L621-8. When it is seized pursuant to article L621-7, the judge may order, if necessary under penalty, the removal of a clause unlawful or abusive in any contract or contract type proposed or intended for the consumer or in any contract being performed.

The associations and bodies referred to in Article L621-7 can also ask the judge to declare that this clause is deemed unwritten in identical contracts concluded by the same professional with consumers, and order him to inform consumers concerned by all appropriate means at his expense.

Article R212-1. In contracts concluded between professionals and consumers, always presumed abusive in the sense of sections 1 and 4 of article L. 212-1, and therefore prohibited, are clauses with the aim or effect of:

1. Recognizing the adhesion of the consumer to clause that are not in the written form he accepts or that are reproduced in another document to which reference is not expressly made when concluding the contract and which he has no knowledge of prior to its conclusion;
2. Restricting the obligation of the professional to respect the commitments made by his employees or agents;
3. Reserving the right for the professional to unilaterally modify the terms of the contract relating to its duration, the characteristics or the price of the goods to be delivered or the service to be provided;
4. Granting the professional the sole right to determine whether the goods or services supplied are in conformity with the terms of the contract, or giving him the exclusive right to interpret any term of the contract;
5. Compelling the consumer to perform its obligations while conversely the professional does not perform its obligation to deliver or guarantee a good or his obligation to supply a service;
6. Removing or reducing the right to compensation for the damage suffered by the consumer in case of breach by the professional of any of its obligations;
7. Not allowing the consumer the right to request the termination or cancellation of the contract in case of non-performance by the professional of his obligations to deliver or guarantee the good or his obligation to supply a service;
8. Recognizing for the professional the right to cancel the contract discretionarily without recognizing

the same right for the consumer;
9. Allowing the professional to retain payments in respect of performances not made by him, when he himself cancelled the contract discretionarily;
10. Subjecting, in contracts of indeterminate duration, the cancellation to a longer notice period for the consumer than for the professional;
11. Subordinating, in contracts of indeterminate duration, the cancellation by the consumer to the payment of compensation for the benefit of the professional;
12. Imposing on the consumer the burden of proof, which in application of the applicable law, should normally be the responsibility of the other party to the contract.

Article R212-2. In contracts concluded between businesses and consumers, presumed abusive in the sense of sections 1 and 5 of article L. 212-1, except in case the professional proves differently, are clauses with the aim or effect of:
1. making an agreement binding on the consumer whereas the fulfilment of the performances of the professional are subject to a condition whose realization depends on his own will alone;
2. Authorising the professional to retain sums paid by the consumer when he renounces to conclude or perform the contract, without providing reciprocally the right to the consumer to receive compensation for an equivalent amount, or equal to the double in case of a deposit within the meaning of article L214-1, if it is the professional who renounces;
3. Requiring the consumer who fails to fulfil his obligation to pay a manifestly disproportionate sum in compensation;
4. Recognising for the professional the ability to cancel the contract without providing a reasonable time;
5. Allowing the professional to proceed with the transfer of his contract without the consent of the consumer and when this assignment is likely to lead to a reduction in the rights of the consumer;
6. Reserving to the professional the right to unilaterally modify the terms of the contract relating to the rights and obligations of the parties, other than those allowed by paragraph 3 of Article R212-1;
7. Stipulating an indicative date for the performance of the contract, except where permitted by law;
8. Subjecting the termination or the cancellation of the contract to the conditions or terms more stringent for the consumer than for the professional;
9. Limiting unduly the means of proof available to the consumer;
10. Removing or impeding the taking of legal action or remedies by the consumer, in particular by requiring the consumer to refer exclusively to arbitration not covered by legal provisions or to go exclusively through an alternative means of dispute settlement.

Construction and Housing Code [Code de la Construction et d l'Habitation]. Version in force from 01 July 2015. Selected provision: Article L 251-3.

Article L251-3. The construction lease confers upon the lessee an immovable property right [droit réel immobilier].
This right may be burdened with a hypothec, just as the constructions built on the rented land; it can be seized through the prescribed forms for seizure of immovable things [saisie immobilière].
The lessee may assign all or part of his rights or contribute them to a company. The assignees or the company are held to the same obligations as the assignor who remains liable for them until the completion of the whole of the constructions that the lessee has undertaken to build, by application of Article L. 251-1.
The lessee may assign the passive servitudes indispensable to the realization of the constructions provided for by the lease.

Insurance Code [Code des assurances]. Version of 26 June 2017. Selected provision: Article L132-5(1).

Article L132-5. (1). The life insurance contract and the capitalisation contract must contain clauses that aim, for the security of the parties and the clarity of the contract, to define the purpose of the contract and the respective obligations of the parties, based on information specified by decree of the Conseil d'Etat.

Rural and Sea Fishing Code [Code Rural]. Version in force at 06 July 2015. Selected provision:

Article 451-1.

Article L451-1. The right of emphyteusis [bail emphytéotique] of immovable things gives the holder a property right which is susceptible to a hypothec; this right may be assigned and seized in the forms as prescribed for seizure of immovable things [saisie immobilière].
This right must be created for more than eighteen years and may not exceed ninety-nine years; it cannot be tacitly renewed.

Monetary and Financial Code [Code Monétaire et Financier]. Consolidated version of 15 July 2017. Selected provision: Article L 313-23.

Article L313-23. Any credit which a credit institution, an alternative investment fund [fonds d'investissement alternative, FIA] pursuant to paragraph 2 of sub-section 3 or of sub-section 5 of section II of chapter IV of the first title of book II, or a financing company grants to a private-law or public-law legal entity, or to a natural person for use in the exercise of this person's business activities, may give rise to the assignment or pledge [nantissement] by the beneficiary of the credit of any claim which he may have as against a third party, private-law or public-law legal entity, or natural person, if it relates to his business activities, for the benefit of that institution, alternative investment fund, or company by the simple submission of a list of claims [bordereau].
Claims which are due and payable may be assigned or pledged, even for the future. Claims resulting from an instrument that has already been executed, or which is yet to be executed but the amount and due date of which have not yet been determined, may equally be assigned or pledged.
The invoice must include the following elements:
1. The designation "deed of assignment of receivables" or "deed of pledge of receivables", as applicable;
2. An indication that the document is subject to the provisions of Articles L 313-23 to L 313-34;
3. The name of the credit institution, of the alternative investment fund mentioned in the first paragraph, or of the financing company which is the beneficiary;
4. The designation or individualization of the claims assigned or pledged, or of the elements likely to create that designation or that individualization, particularly by indication of the debtor, the place of payment, the amount of the claims or of their valuation and, if applicable, their due date.
However, when the transfer of the claims assigned or pledged is effected via an electronic process which makes it possible to identify them, the invoice may merely indicate, in addition to the elements indicated in 1, 2 and 3 above, the means through which they are transferred, their number and their overall amount.
In the event of a dispute being raised concerning the existence or transfer of one of the claims, the assignee may prove, by any means possible, that the claim which is the object of the dispute is included in the overall amount shown on the invoice.
A document from which one of the above indications is missing does not constitute a valid deed of assignment or pledge of claims within the meaning of Articles L 313-23 to L 313-34.

Law [Loi] No. 85-677 of 5 July 1985 concerning the improvement of the situation of victims of traffic accidents and the facilitation of the compensation procedure. Version in force of 28 April 2012 (Loi Badinter).*

Article 1. The provisions of the present chapter apply, even when they are carried by virtue of a contract, to the victims of traffic accidents in which a motorized vehicle or its trailer or semi-trailer is involved, with the exception of trains and trams circulating on their own tracks.

Section 1. Provisions concerning the right to compensation

Article 2. The victims, including the driver, cannot have force majeure or the act of a third party invoked against them as a defence by the driver or the keeper of a vehicle mentioned in the first article.

---

*   Translation by Caroline Calomme.

Article 3. The victims, except for the drivers of motorized vehicles, are compensated for damages resulting from injury to the person which they have suffered, without their own fault being invoked against them except for their inexcusable fault if it is the sole cause of the accident.

The victims mentioned in the previous paragraph, when they are younger than sixteen years or older than seventy years, or if, whatever their age, they are in possession, at the moment of the accident, of a title recognizing their permanent incapacity or invalidity at least equal to 80 per cent, are in all cases compensated for damages resulting from the injury to the person which they have suffered. Nonetheless, in the situations envisaged in the two previous paragraphs, the victim is not compensated from the person responsible for the accident for damages resulting from the injury to his person when he has voluntarily sought the damage which he has suffered.

Article 4. The fault committed by the driver of the motorized vehicle has the effect to limit or exclude the compensation for damages that he has suffered.

Article 5. The fault committed by the victim has the effect to limit or exclude the compensation that he could claim for damages to his property. Nonetheless, supplies and devices medically prescribed may give rise to compensation under the rules concerning the reparation for injury to the person. When the driver of a motorized vehicle is not the owner, the fault of this driver can be claimed against the owner for compensation of damages caused to his vehicle. The owner has a right of recourse against the driver.

Article 6. The harm suffered by a third person due to the damage caused to the direct victim of a traffic accident is remedied by taking into account.

Germany

Civil Code

Civil Code of Germany [Bürgerliches Gesetzbuch (BGB)] of 18 August 1896, in the version promulgated on 2 January 2002 (BGBl I p. 42, 2909; 2003 I p. 738), last amended by Article 7 of the statute of 31 January 2019 (BGBl. I p. 54). Selected provisions from Books 1, 2, 3, 4, and 5.*

Book 1. General Part

Division 1. Persons

Title 1. Natural persons, consumers, entrepreneurs

§ 1. The legal personality [Rechtsfähigkeit] of a human being begins on the completion of birth.

§ 2. Majority [Volljährigkeit] begins on the completion of the eighteenth year of age.

§§ 3 – 6. (Repealed.)

[§§ 7 – 9 are omitted.]

§10. (Repealed.)

[§§ 11 – 12 are omitted.]

§ 13. A consumer [Verbraucher] is any natural person who concludes a legal transaction for a purpose that can neither be attributed to his business nor his independent professional activities.

§ 14. (1) An entrepreneur [Unternehmer] is a natural or legal person or a partnership with legal personality who or which, for the conclusion of a legal transaction, acts in exercise of his business or independent professional activity.
(2) A partnership with legal personality is a partnership that has the capacity to acquire rights and to assume liabilities.

§§ 15 – 20. (Repealed.)

[The remainder of Division 1 is omitted.]

Division 2. Objects and animals

§ 90. For the purpose of this Code, objects [Sachen] can only be corporeal objects [körperliche Gegenstände].

[The remainder of Division 2 is omitted.]

Division 3. Legal transactions [Rechtsgeschäfte]

Title 1. Legal Capacity [Geschäftsfähigkeit]

§ 104. Lacking legal capacity is
1. a person who has not yet completed his seventh year of age,
2. a person who is in a state of mental disturbance caused by disease that excludes the free determination of will [die freie Willensbestimmung ausschließenden Zustand krankhafter Störung der Geistestätigkeit], unless the state by its nature is a temporary one.

§ 105. (1) The declaration of intent [Willenserklärung] of a person lacking legal capacity is void.
(2) A declaration of intent that is made in a state of unconsciousness or temporary mental disturbance is also void.

§ 105a. Where a person of full age incapable of contracting enters into an everyday transaction that can be effected with funds of low value, the contract he enters into is regarded as effective with regard to performance and, if agreed, counter performance, as soon as performance has been effected and counter performance rendered. Sentence 1 does not apply in the case of considerable danger to the person or the property of the person incapable of contracting.

---

*   Translations by Bram Akkermans, Anna Berlee, Sascha Hardt, Heike Hauröder, Nicole Kornet and Stefan Weishaar.

§ 106. A minor who has completed his seventh year of age has, in accordance with the requirements §§107 to 113 limited legal capacity.

§ 107. A minor requires the consent [Einwilligung] of his legal representative for a declaration of intent through which he receives not only a legal benefit.

§ 108 (1) If the minor concludes a contract without the necessary consent of the legal representative, the effectiveness of the contract is subject to the ratification [Genehmigung] of the legal representative.
(2) If the other party requests the representative give a declaration regarding his ratification, the declaration can only be made to the other party; a declaration or refusal of ratification made to the minor before the request is ineffective. The ratification can only be declared before the expiry of two weeks after receipt of the request; if it is not declared, it is held to have been refused.
(3) If the minor has attained full legal capacity, his ratification takes the place of the ratification of the representative.

§ 109. (1) Until the ratification of the contract, the other party is entitled to withdrawal [Widerruf]. The withdrawal may also be made to the minor.
(2) If the other party knew of the minority, he may only withdraw if the minor contrary to the truth claimed the consent of the legal representative; he may not withdraw in this case either if, when the contract was concluded, he knew of the lack of consent.

§ 110. A contract concluded by the minor without the approval [Zustimmung] of the legal representative is held to be effective from the beginning if the minor effects performance under the contract with means that were given to him for this purpose or for free disposal by the legal representative or with his approval by a third party.

§ 111. A unilateral legal transaction undertaken by a minor without the necessary consent of the legal representative is ineffective. If the minor undertakes such a legal transaction with regard to another person with this consent, the legal transaction is ineffective if the minor does not present the consent in writing and the other person rejects the legal transaction for this reason without undue delay. Rejection is excluded if the representative had given the other person notice of the consent

[§ 112 is omitted.]

§ 113. (1) If the legal representative authorises the minor to enter service or employment, the minor has unlimited capacity to perform legal acts that relate to entering or leaving service or employment of the permitted nature or performing the duties arising from such a relationship. Contracts for which the representative requires the approval of the family court are excepted.
(2) The authorisation may be withdrawn or limited by the representative.
(3) Where the legal representative is a legal guardian [Vormund], the authorisation may, if he refuses it, be substituted by the family court upon request by the minor. The family court has the authority to substitute where this is in the interest of the minor under guardianship.
(4) In cases of doubt, the authorisation provided for an individual case is deemed a general authorisation to enter relationships of the same kind.

§§ 114 – 115. (Repealed.)

Title 2. Declaration of intent [Willenserklärung]

§ 116. A declaration of intent is not void because the declarant has made a mental reservation that he does not intend the declaration made. The declaration is void if it is to be made to another person and this person knows of the reservation.

§ 117. (1) Where a declaration of intent that is to be made to another person is only made for the sake of appearance, with that person's consent, it is void.
(2) If a sham transaction conceals another legal transaction, the provisions applicable to the concealed transaction apply.

§ 118. A declaration of intent that is not seriously intended, which is made in the expectation that the lack of seriousness will not be mistaken, is void.

§ 119. (1) A person who, when making a declaration of intent, was mistaken about its contents or had no intention of making a declaration with this content at all, may avoid [anfechten] the declaration if it is to be assumed that he would not have made the declaration with knowledge of the factual situation and with a rational appreciation of the circumstances.

(2) Also held to be a mistake about the content of the declaration is a mistake about such characteristics of a person or a thing as are commonly [im Verkehr] regarded as essential is.

§ 120. A declaration of intent that has been incorrectly transmitted by the person or apparatus used for its transmission may be avoided subject to the same condition as a mistakenly given declaration of intent under § 119.

§ 121. (1) Avoidance [Anfechtung] must take place, in the cases set out in §§ 119 and 120, without culpable delay (without undue delay) after the person entitled to avoid has obtained knowledge of the ground for avoidance. Avoidance made to an absent person is held to take place in due time if the declaration of avoidance is dispatched without undue delay.

(2) Avoidance is excluded if ten years have elapsed since the declaration of intent was made.

§ 122. (1) If a declaration of intent is void under § 118, or avoided under §§ 119 and 120, the declarant must, if the declaration was to be made to another person, compensate this person, or failing this any third party, for the damage that the other or the third party suffers as a result of relying on the validity of the declaration; but not in excess of the total amount of the interest which the other or the third party has in the validity of the declaration.

(2) A duty to compensate for damage does not arise if the injured person knew the reason for the nullity or the voidability or did not know it as a result of his negligence [Fahrlässigkeit] (ought to have known it).

§ 123. (1) A person who has been induced to make a declaration of intent by wilful deceit [arglistige Täuschung] or unlawfully by threat [widerrechtlich durch Drohung] may avoid the declaration.

(2) Where a third party carried out this deceit, a declaration that had to be made to another may be avoided only if the latter knew or ought to have known of the deceit. In so far as a person other than the person to whom the declaration was to be made has acquired a right directly under the declaration, the declaration made to him may be avoided if he knew or ought to have known of the deceit.

§ 124. (1) The avoidance of a declaration of intent that is voidable under § 123 may only take place within one year.

(2) The period commences in the case of wilful deceit at the point in time when the person entitled to avoid discovers the deceit, and in case of threat, from the point in time when the predicament ceases. With respect to the course of time, the provisions in §§ 206, 210 and 211 applicable to the limitation period apply mutatis mutandis.

(3) Avoidance is excluded, if ten years have passed since the declaration of intent was made.

§ 125. A legal transaction [Rechtsgeschäft] that lacks the form prescribed by law is void. Lack of the form specified by the legal transaction, in case of doubt, also results in nullity.

§ 126. (1) If written form is prescribed by law, the document must be signed by the creator with his name in his own hand, or by way of his notarially certified mark.

(2) In the case of a contract, the signature of the parties must be made on the same document. Where several identical documents of the contract are drawn up, it suffices if each party signs the document intended for the other party.

(3) Written form may be replaced by electronic form, unless a different consequence follows from the law.

(4) Notarial authentication [Beurkundung] takes the place of the written form.

§ 126a. (1) If the written form prescribed by law is replaced by electronic form, the issuer of the declaration must add his name to it and provide the electronic document with a qualified electronic.

(2) In the case of a contract, the parties must each sign an identical document with an electronic signature as described in sub-paragraph (1).

§ 126b. If text form is prescribed by law, a readable declaration, in which the person making the declaration is named, must be made on a permanent medium. A permanent medium is any medium that

1. Allows the recipient to store or save the declaration on the data carrier addressed to him personally so that it is accessible to him during a period appropriate for his purpose, and

2. Is suitable to keep the declaration unchanged.

[§§ 127 – 129 are omitted.]

§130. (1) A declaration of intent that is to be made to another, if made in that person's absence, becomes effective at the point in time at which the declaration reaches him. It does not become effective if a withdrawal [Widerruf] reaches the other person previously or at the same time.
(2) The effectiveness of a declaration of intent is not affected if the declarant dies or becomes legally incapable after it is made.
(3) These provisions apply even if the declaration of intent is to be made to an authority.

[§§ 131 – 132 are omitted.]

§ 133. When interpreting a declaration of intent, the actual intention is to be ascertained rather than adhering to the literal meaning of the expression.

§134. A legal transaction that violates a statutory prohibition is void, unless a different consequence follows from the law.

[§§ 135 – 136 are omitted.]

§ 137. The power to dispose [Befugnis zur Verfügung] over a transferable right cannot be excluded or limited by a legal transaction. The effectiveness of an obligation not to dispose over such a right is unaffected by this provision.

§ 138. (1) A legal transaction that violates good morals [guten Sitten] is void.
(2) In particular, a legal transaction is void by which a person, by exploiting the predicament, inexperience, lack of sound judgment or considerable weakness of will of another, causes to be promised or granted to himself or a third party, in return for a performance, pecuniary advantages which are clearly disproportionate to the performance.

§ 139. If a part of a legal transaction is void, then the whole legal transaction is void, unless it is to be assumed that it would have been undertaken even without the void part.

§ 140. Where a void legal transaction fulfils the requirements of another legal transaction, then the latter is held to be valid, if it is to be assumed that its validity would be intended if there were knowledge of the nullity.

[§ 141 is omitted.]

§ 142. (1) If a voidable legal transaction is avoided, it is to be regarded as having been void from the beginning.
(2) A person who knew or ought to have known of the possibility of avoidance is treated, in case of avoidance, as if he had known or ought to have known of the nullity of the legal transaction.

§ 143. (1) Avoidance occurs by declaration to the opposing party.
(2) The opposing party is, in the case of a contract, the other party to the contract and, in the case of § 123, sub-paragraph (2) sentence 2, the person who has acquired a right directly under the contract.
(3) In the case of a unilateral legal transaction that was to be undertaken in relation to another person, the other person is the opposing party. The same applies to a legal transaction that is required to be undertaken in relation to another person or to an authority, even if the legal transaction has already been undertaken as against the authority.
(4) In the case of any other kind of unilateral legal transaction, any person who has received a legal advantage directly on the basis of the legal transaction is an opposing party. The avoidance may, however, if the declaration of intent was to be made to an authority, be made by declaration to the authority; the authority shall inform the person who was directly affected by the legal transaction of the avoidance.

§ 144. (1) Avoidance is excluded, if the voidable legal transaction is confirmed by the person entitled to avoid.
(2) The confirmation is not required to have the form prescribed for the legal transaction.

Title 3. Contract [Vertrag]

§ 145. A person who offers to another to conclude a contract is bound by the offer [Antrag], unless he has excluded this binding effect.

§ 146. An offer lapses if it is rejected as against the offeror, or if it is not accepted in due time as against this person in accordance with §§ **147** to 149.

§ 147. (1) An offer made to a person who is present may only be accepted immediately. This also applies to an offer made by one person to another using a telephone or another technical apparatus. (2) An offer made to an absent person may only be accepted up to the point in time when the offeror may expect receipt of the answer under ordinary circumstances.

§ 148. Where the offeror has fixed a period of time for the acceptance of an offer, the acceptance may only occur within this period.

§ 149. Where a declaration of acceptance that reaches the offeror belatedly was sent in such a way that it would have reached him in time if it had been sent by regular delivery, and if the offeror ought to have recognized this, he must notify the acceptor without undue delay after the receipt of the declaration of the delay, unless this has already been done. If he delays in sending the notification, the acceptance is held not to be late.

§ 150. (1) The late acceptance of an offer is held to be a new offer. (2) An acceptance with additions, limitations or other modifications is held to be a rejection combined with a new offer.

§ 151. A contract is formed by the acceptance of an offer without the offeror needing to be notified of acceptance, if such a declaration is not to be expected according to common practice [Verkehrssitte], or if the offeror has waived it. The point in time at which the offer lapses, is determined in accordance with the intention of the offeror, which is to be inferred from the offer or the circumstances.

§ 152. If a contract is notarially authenticated without both parties being present at the same time, the contract is formed, unless otherwise provided, on the authentication of acceptance effected in accordance with § 128. The provision of § 151 sentence 2 applies.

§ 153. The formation of the contract is not prevented by the offeror dying or becoming legally incapable before acceptance, unless a different intention of the offeror is to be assumed.

§ 154. (1) As long as the parties have not yet agreed on all points of a contract about which an agreement is to be reached according to the declaration of even only one party, the contract is, in case of doubt, not concluded. Agreement on individual points is not legally binding even if a record has been made. (2) If authentication of the proposed contract has been arranged, the contract is, in case of doubt, not concluded until authentication has taken place.

§ 155. If the parties to a contract which they consider having been concluded have, in fact, not agreed on a point on which agreement was required, whatever is agreed applies in so far as it is to be assumed that the contract would have been concluded even without a provision concerning this point.

[§ 156 is omitted.]

§ 157. Contracts are to be interpreted in accordance with good faith [Treu und Glauben], taking common practice [Verkehrssitte] into consideration.

[Title 4 is omitted.]

Title 5. Representation [Vertretung] and Mandate [Vollmacht]

§ 164. (1) A declaration of intent which a person makes within the scope of his own power of representation in the name of a principal takes effect directly in favour of and against the principal. It is irrelevant whether the declaration is made explicitly in the name of the principal, or whether the circumstances indicate that it is to be made in his name.

[The remainder of §164 and §165 are omitted.]

§ 166. (1) Insofar as the legal consequences of a declaration of intent are influenced by an absence of intent or by knowledge or by constructive knowledge of certain circumstances, it is not the person of the principal, but that of the agent, that is taken into account. (2) If, in the case of a power of representation granted by a legal transaction [Vollmacht], the agent has acted in compliance with certain instructions given by the principal, then the latter may not invoke the lack of knowledge of the agent with regard to circumstances of which the principal himself knew. The same applies to circumstances which the principal ought to have known, insofar as constructive knowledge is equivalent to knowledge.

[The remainder of Title 5 is omitted.]

Title 6. Consent and ratification

§ 182. (1) If the effectiveness of a contract, or of a unilateral legal transaction which is to be undertaken as against another, depends on the approval of a third party, the grant and refusal of approval may be declared either to one party or to the other.
(2) The approval is not required to have the form prescribed for the legal transaction.
(3) If a unilateral legal transaction, the effectiveness of which depends on the approval of a third party, is undertaken with the consent of the third party, then the provisions of § 111 sentences 2 and 3 apply mutatis mutandis.

[§ 183 is omitted.]

§ 184. (1) Subsequent approval (ratification) takes effect retroactively from the point in time when the legal transaction was undertaken, unless otherwise provided.
(2) The retroactive effect does not cancel the effectiveness of dispositions made by the ratifying person before the ratification of the subject matter of the legal transaction or made by execution or attachment or by the administrator in insolvency proceedings.

[§ 185 is omitted.]

Division 4. Periods of time [Fristen, Termine]

[§ 186 is omitted.]

§ 187. (1) If an event [Ereignis] or a certain moment during a day is decisive for the start of a period of time, for the calculation of the period time, the day on which the event or moment occurs is not included.
(2) If the start of a day is decisive for the start of a period of time, this day is included in the calculation of the period of time. The same applies for the day of birth in case of calculation of age.

[The remainder of Division 4 is omitted.]

Division 5. Prescription [Verjährung]

Title 1. Subject matter and duration of prescription

§ 194. (1) The right of one person to require an act or forbearance of another (claim) [Anspruch] is subject to prescription.
(2) Claims based on a family-law relationship are not subject to limitation to the extent that they are directed towards creating a situation appropriate for the relationship for the future or towards consent to a genetic test to clarify biological descent.

§ 195. The regular prescription period [regelmäßige Verjährungsfrist] is three years.

§ 196. Claims for the transfer of ownership in respect to a piece of land, as well as in respect to creation, assignment or termination of a right in respect to a piece of land or for the alteration of the content of such a right as well as the claims for the counter-performance of such prescribe after a period of ten years.

§ 197. (1) In so far as is not determined otherwise, the following claims prescribe after a period of 30 years:
1. Claims for the revindication of the right of ownership and other property rights

[The remainder of §197 is omitted]

[§ 198 is omitted.]

§ 199. (1) The regular prescription period starts to run at the end of the year, in which
1. the claim has arisen, and
2. the creditor acquires or, in the absence of gross negligence, should have acquired, knowledge of the circumstances giving rise to the claim and the identity of the debtor.
[Sub-paragraphs (2), (3) and (3a) are omitted.]
(4) Other claims, such as claims for compensation for damage, prescribe without regard to the knowledge or grossly negligent knowledge after a period of ten years after they have arisen.
[Sub-paragraph (5) is omitted.]

§ 200. The prescription period that is applicable to claims that are not subject to the regular prescription period, starts at the moment the claim arises, in so far as another commencement of the prescription period is not provided. § 199 sub-paragraph (5) applies mutatis mutandis.

[The remainder of Book 1 is omitted.]

Book 2. Law of Obligation Relationships [Recht der Schuldverhältnisse]

Division 1. Subject matter of obligation relationships

Title 1. Duty of performance

§ 241. (1) By virtue of an obligation relationship the creditor [Gläubiger] is entitled to claim performance from the debtor [Schuldner]. The performance may also consist in a forbearance.
(2) An obligation relationship may also, depending on its contents, oblige each party to take into account the rights, legal interests and other interests of the other party.

[§241a is omitted.]

§ 242. A debtor has a duty to perform according to the requirements of good faith [Treu und Glauben], taking common practice [Verkehrssitte] into consideration.

§ 243. (1) A person who is obliged to provide an object defined only according to its class must provide an object of average kind and quality.
(2) If the debtor has done what is necessary on his part to provide such an object, the obligation relationship is restricted to that object.

[§§ 244 – 248 are omitted.]

§ 249. (1) A person who is obliged to compensate for damage [Schadensersatz] must restore the state of affairs that would have existed if the circumstance obliging him to compensate had not occurred.
(2) Where compensation for damage is to be provided due to injury to a person or damage to a thing, the creditor may instead of restoration [Herstellung] demand the required monetary amount. Where a thing is damaged, the monetary amount required under sentence 1 only includes value-added tax if and to the extent that it is actually incurred.

§ 250. The creditor may fix an appropriate period of time [angemessene Frist] for restoration by the person obliged to compensate through a declaration that he will reject restoration after expiry of this period. After the expiry of the period of time, the creditor may demand compensation in money, if restoration does not occur in due time; the claim to restoration is excluded.

§ 251 (1) To the extent that restoration is not possible or is not sufficient for the indemnification [Entschädigung] of the creditor, the person obliged to compensate must compensate the creditor in money.
(2) The person obliged to compensate may indemnify the creditor in money if restoration is only possible with disproportionate expenditure. Expenditure incurred as a result of the medical treatment of an injured animal is not disproportionate simply because it significantly exceeds its value.

§ 252. The damage to be compensated also encompasses lost profits. Profits that are deemed to be lost are those that in the normal course of events or in the special circumstances, in particular due to the measures and precautions taken, could with probability be expected.

§ 253. (1) For damage that is not pecuniary loss [immaterieller Schaden], indemnification in money may only be demanded in those cases determined by law.
(2) Where compensation for damage is to be made for an injury to body, health, freedom or sexual self-determination, fair indemnification in money may also be demanded for any damage that is not pecuniary loss.

§ 254. (1) If fault on the part of the injured person contributed to the occurrence of the damage, the duty to compensate as well as the extent of compensation to be made will depend on the circumstances, in particular to what extent the damage is caused predominantly by one or the other party.
(2) This also applies if the fault of the injured person is limited to the fact that he failed to draw to the attention of the debtor to the risk of unusually extensive damage, where the debtor neither was nor ought to have been aware of the risk, or he failed to avert or reduce the damage. The provision of § 278 applies mutatis mutandis.

§ 255. A person who must compensate for damage for the loss of a thing or a right is only obliged to compensate in return for the assignment of the claims [Abtretung der Ansprüche] which the person entitled to the compensation holds against third parties on the basis of ownership of the thing or on the basis of the right.

[§§ 256 – 265 are omitted.]

§ 266. The debtor is not entitled to render partial performance.

§ 267. (1) If the debtor does not have to perform in person, a third party may also render performance. The consent of the debtor is not required.
(2) The creditor may reject the performance if the debtor objects.

§ 268. (1) If the creditor carries out compulsory execution [Zwangsvollstreckung] against an object belonging to the debtor, anyone who risks losing a right in the object due to execution is entitled to satisfy the creditor. The possessor of a thing is entitled to the same right if he risks losing possession due to the execution.
(2) The satisfaction may also take place by deposit [Hinterlegung] or by set-off [Aufrechnung].
(3) To the extent that the third party satisfies the creditor the claim passes to him. The passing of ownership may not be asserted to the disadvantage of the creditor.

§ 269. (1) If the place of performance is neither specified nor evident from the circumstances, in particular from the nature of the obligation relationship, performance must be made in the place where the debtor had his residence at the time when the obligation relationship arose.
(2) If the obligation arose in the course of business of the debtor, the place of establishment takes the place of the residence if the debtor had his business establishment at another place.
(3) It may not be concluded from the circumstance alone that the debtor has assumed shipping costs that the place to which the shipment is to be made is to be the place of performance.

§ 270. (1) In case of doubt, the debtor must transmit money at his own risk and his own expense to the creditor at the residence of the latter.
(2) If the claim [Forderung] arose in the course of business of the creditor, then, if the creditor has his business establishment in another place, the place of establishment takes the place of the residence.
(3) Where, as the result of a change in the place of residence or business establishment of the creditor occurring after the obligation arises, the costs or risk of transmission increase, the creditor must in the former case bear the additional costs and in the latter case the risk.
(4) The provisions on the place of performance remain unaffected.

[§ 270a is omitted.]

§ 271. (1) If the time for performance is neither specified nor evident from the circumstances, the creditor may demand performance immediately, and the debtor may effect it immediately.
(2) If a time has been specified, then in case of doubt it must be assumed that the creditor may not demand performance prior to that time, but the debtor may effect it earlier.

[§§ 271a and 272 are omitted.]

§ 273. (1) If the debtor has a claim that is due against the creditor under the same legal relationship as that from which his obligation arises, he may, unless another consequence follows from the obligation relationship, refuse the performance owed by him, until the performance owed to him is effected (right of retention) [Zurückbehaltungsrecht].
(2) The person who is obliged to return an object has the same right, if he is entitled to a claim that is due for expenditure on the object or because of damage caused to him by the object, unless he obtained the object by means of an intentionally committed wrongful act [unerlaubte Handlung].
(3) The creditor may avert the exercise of the right of retention by providing security. The provision of security by guarantors is excluded.

§ 274 (1) As against the legal action by the creditor, assertion of the right to of retention only has the effect that the debtor is to be ordered to effect performance in return for receiving the performance owed to him (concurrent performance) [Erfüllung Zug um Zug].
(2) On the basis of such an order the creditor may pursue his claim by way of compulsory execution, without effecting the performance he owes, if the debtor is in delay of acceptance.

§ 275. (1) A claim to performance is excluded in so far as that performance is impossible for the debtor or for any other person.

(2) The debtor may refuse performance to the extent it requires expenditure which, taking into account the content of the obligation relationship and the requirements of good faith, is grossly disproportionate to the interest of the creditor in performance. When determining what efforts may be expected of the debtor, it must also be considered whether he is responsible for the obstacle to performance.

(3) The debtor may further refuse performance if he is to effect the performance in person and, when the obstacle to his performance is weighed against the interest of the creditor in performance, performance cannot be expected of him.

(4) The rights of the creditor are governed by §§ 280, 283 to 285, 311a and 326.

§ 276. (1) The debtor is responsible for intention and negligence, if a stricter or more lenient degree of liability is neither laid down nor to be inferred from the other content of the obligation relationship, in particular from the giving of a guarantee or the assumption of a procurement risk. The provisions of §§ 827 and 828 apply mutatis mutandis.

(2) A person acts negligently if he fails to exercise due and necessary care [im Verkehr erforderliche Sorgfalt].

(3) The debtor may not be released in advance from liability for intention.

§ 277. A person who owes only such standard of care that he has to exercise in his own affairs is not released from liability for gross negligence [grober Fahrlässigkeit].

§ 278. The debtor is responsible for fault on the part of his legal representative, and of persons whom he uses to perform his obligation, to the same extent as for his own fault. The provision of § 276 sub-paragraph (3) does not apply.

§ 279. (Repealed.)

§ 280. (1) If the debtor violates a duty arising from the obligation relationship, the creditor may demand compensation for the damage caused thereby. This does not apply if the debtor is not responsible for the violation of duty.

(2) Compensation for delay in performance may be demanded by the creditor only subject to the additional prerequisites of § 286.

(3) Compensation instead of performance may be demanded by the creditor only under the additional prerequisites of §§ 281, 282, or 283.

§ 281. (1) To the extent that the debtor does not effect performance when it is due or does not effect performance as owed, the creditor may, subject to the prerequisites of § 280 sub-paragraph (1), demand compensation instead of performance, if he has set a reasonable period of time for the debtor for performance or subsequent fulfilment, but without result. If the debtor has effected a partial performance, the creditor may only demand compensation instead of whole performance if he has no interest in the partial performance. If the debtor has not effected performance as owed, the creditor may not demand compensation instead of the whole performance if the violation of duty is immaterial.

(2) The setting of a period of time for performance can be dispensed if the debtor seriously and definitively refuses performance or if there are special circumstances which, on weighing the interests of both parties, justify the immediate assertion of a claim to compensation.

(3) If the nature of the violation of duty is such that setting a period of time is out of the question, a warning notice will take its place.

(4) The claim for performance is excluded as soon as the creditor has demanded compensation instead of performance.

(5) If the creditor demands compensation instead of whole performance, the debtor is entitled to claim the return of his performance under §§ 346 to 348.

§ 282. If the debtor violates a duty under § 241 sub-paragraph (2), the creditor may, subject to the prerequisites of § 280 sub-paragraph (1), demand compensation instead of performance, if allowing performance by the debtor can no longer reasonably be expected of him.

§ 283. If the debtor is not obliged to perform pursuant to § 275 sub-paragraphs (1) to (3), the creditor may, subject to the prerequisites of § 280 sub-paragraph (1), demand compensation instead of performance. § 281 sub-paragraph (1) sentences 2 and 3 and sub-paragraph (5) apply mutatis mutandis.

§ 284. In the place of compensation instead of performance, the creditor may demand reimbursement of expenditure which, in reliance on receiving performance, he has made and was fairly [billigerweise] entitled to make, unless its purpose would not have been achieved, even if the debtor had not violated his duty.

§ 285. (1) If the debtor, as a result of the circumstance by reason of which, according to § 275 sub-paragraph (1) to (3), he has no duty of performance, obtains a replacement or a claim to replacement for the object owed, the creditor may demand return of what has been received in replacement or an assignment of the claim to replacement.
(2) If the creditor may demand compensation instead of performance, this will be reduced, if he exercises the right provided for in sub-paragraph (1), by the value of the replacement or the claim to replacement he has obtained.

§ 286. (1) If the debtor fails to perform, following a warning notice from the creditor that is made after performance has become due, he is in delay as a result of the warning notice. Bringing an action for performance as well as the service of default summons in collection proceedings are equivalent to a warning notice.
(2) There is no need for a warning notice if
1. a period of time has been determined for performance according to the calendar,
2. performance must be preceded by an event and a reasonable time for performance has been determined in such a way that it can be calculated, starting from the event, according to the calendar,
3. the debtor seriously and definitively refuses performance,
4. for special reasons, on weighing the interests of both parties, the immediate commencement of the delay is justified.
(3) The debtor of a claim for payment is in delay at the latest if he does not perform within thirty days after the due date and receipt of an invoice or equivalent statement of payment; this only applies to a debtor who is a consumer if these consequences are specifically referred to in the invoice or statement of payment. If the point of time at which the invoice or payment statement is received by the debtor is uncertain, a debtor who is not a consumer is in delay at the latest thirty days after the due date and receipt of the counter-performance.
(4) The debtor is not in delay for as long as performance is not made as the result of a circumstance for which he is not responsible.
(5) § 271a applies mutatis mutandis to an agreement on the commencement of delay that deviates from sub-paragraphs (1) – (3).

§ 287. While he is in delay, the debtor is responsible for all negligence. He is liable for performance even in the case of chance events, unless the damage would also have occurred if performance had been made in due time.

[The remainder of Title 1 and Division 2 are omitted.]

Division 2. Drafting contractual obligations by means of standard business terms

§ 305. (1) Standard business terms are all contract terms pre-formulated for more than two contracts which one party to the contract (the user) presents to the other party upon the entering into of the contract. It is irrelevant whether the provisions take the form of a physically separate part of a contract or are made part of the contractual document itself, what their volume is, what typeface or font is used for them and what form the contract takes. Contract terms do not become standard business terms to the extent that they have been negotiated in detail between the parties.
(2) Standard business terms only become a part of a contract if the user, when entering into the contract,
1. refers the other party to the contract to them explicitly or, where explicit reference, due to the way in which the contract is entered into, is possible only with disproportionate difficulty, by posting a clearly visible notice at the place where the contract is entered into, and
2. gives the other party to the contract, in an acceptable manner, which also takes into reasonable account any physical handicap of the other party to the contract that is discernible to the user, the opportunity to take notice of their contents,
and if the other party to the contract agrees to their applying.
(3) The parties to the contract may, while complying with the requirements set out in sub-paragraph (2) above, agree in advance that specific standard business terms are to govern a specific type of legal transaction.

[§ 305a is omitted.]

§ 305b. Individually agreed terms take priority over standard business terms.

§ 305c. (1) Provisions in standard business terms which in the circumstances, in particular with regard to the outward appearance of the contract, are so unusual that the other party to the contract with the user need not expect to encounter them, do not form part of the contract.

(2) Any doubts in the interpretation of standard business terms are resolved against the user.

[§§ 306 and 306a are omitted.]

§ 307. (1) Provisions in standard business terms are ineffective if, contrary to the requirement of good faith, they unreasonably disadvantage the other party to the contract with the user. An unreasonable disadvantage may also arise from the provision not being clear and comprehensible.

(2) An unreasonable disadvantage is, in case of doubt, to be assumed to exist if a provision
1. is not compatible with essential principles of the statutory provision from which it deviates, or
2. limits essential rights or duties inherent in the nature of the contract to such an extent that attainment of the purpose of the contract is jeopardised.

(3) Sub-paragraphs (1) and (2), as well as §§ 308 and 309, apply only to provisions in standard business terms on the basis of which arrangements derogating from legal provisions, or arrangements supplementing those legal provisions, are agreed. Other provisions may be ineffective under sub-paragraph (1) sentence 2 in conjunction with sub-paragraph (1) sentence 1.

§ 308. In standard business terms the following are in particular ineffective
(1) (Period of time for acceptance and performance) a provision by which the user reserves to himself the right to unreasonably long or insufficiently specific periods of time for acceptance or rejection of an offer or for rendering performance; this does not include the reservation of the right not to perform until after the end of the period of time for revocation or return under §§ 355 (1) to (3) and 356;

(2) (Additional period of time) a provision by which the user, contrary to legal provisions, reserves to himself the right to an unreasonably long or insufficiently specific additional period of time for the performance he is to render;

(3) (Reservation of the right to terminate) the agreement of a right of the user to free himself from his obligation to perform without any objectively justified reason indicated in the contract; this does not apply to continuing obligations;

(4) (Reservation of the right to modify) the agreement of a right of the user to modify the performance promised or deviate from it, unless the agreement of the modification or deviation can reasonably be expected of the other party to the contract when the interests of the user are taken into account;

(5) (Fictitious declarations) a provision by which a declaration by the other party to the contract with the user, made when undertaking or omitting a specific act, is deemed to have been made or not made by the user unless
(a) the other party to the contract is granted a reasonable period of time to make an express declaration, and
(b) the user agrees to especially draw the attention of the other party to the contract to the intended significance of his behaviour at the beginning of the period of time;

(6) (Fictitious receipt) a provision providing that a declaration by the user that is of special importance is deemed to have been received by the other party to the contract;

(7) (Reversal of contracts) a provision by which the user, to provide for the event that a party to the contract terminates the contract or gives notice of termination of the contract, may demand
(a) unreasonably high remuneration for enjoyment or use of a thing or a right or for performance rendered, or
(b) unreasonably high reimbursement of expenses;

(8) (Unavailability of performance) the agreement, admissible under no. 3, of the reservation by the user of a right to free himself from the duty to perform the contract in the absence of availability of performance, if the user does not agree to
(a) inform the other party to the contract without undue delay, of the unavailability, and
(b) reimburse the other party to the contract for consideration, without undue delay.

§ 309. Even to the extent that a deviation from the statutory provisions is permissible, the following are ineffective in standard business terms:
(1) (Price increases at short notice) a provision providing for an increase in payment for goods or services that are to be delivered or rendered within four months of the entering into of the contract; this does not apply to goods or services delivered or rendered in connection with continuing obligations;

(2) (Right to refuse performance) a provision by which
(a) the right to refuse performance to which the other party to the contract with the user is entitled

under § 320, is excluded or restricted, or

(b) a right of retention to which the other party to the contract with the user is entitled to the extent that it is based on the same contractual relationship, is excluded or restricted, in particular made dependent upon acknowledgement of defects by the user;

(3) (Prohibition of set-off) a provision by which the other party to the contract with the user is deprived of the right to set off a claim that is uncontested or has been finally and non-appealably established;

(4) (Warning notice, setting of a period of time) a provision by which the user is exempted from the statutory requirement of giving the other party to the contract a warning notice or setting a period of time for the latter to perform or cure;

(5) (Lump-sum claims for damages) the agreement of a lump-sum claim by the user for damages or for compensation of a decrease in value if

(a) the lump sum, in the cases covered, exceeds the damage expected under normal circumstances or the customarily occurring decrease in value, or

(b) the other party to the contract is not expressly permitted to show that damage or decrease in value has either not occurred or is substantially less than the lump sum;

(6) (Contractual penalty) a provision by which the user is promised the payment of a contractual penalty in the event of non-acceptance or late acceptance of the performance, payment default or in the event that the other party to the contract frees himself from the contract;

(7) (Exclusion of liability for injury to life, body or health and in case of gross fault)

(a) (Injury to life, body or health) any exclusion or limitation of liability for damage from injury to life, body or health due to negligent breach of duty by the user or intentional or negligent breach of duty by a legal representative or a person used to perform an obligation of the user;

(b) (Gross fault) any exclusion or limitation of liability for other damage arising from a grossly negligent breach of duty by the user or from an intentional or grossly negligent breach of duty by a legal representative of the user or a person used to perform an obligation of the user;

letters (a) and (b) do not apply to limitations of liability in terms of transport and tariff rules, authorised in accordance with the Passenger Transport Act, of trams, trolley buses and motor vehicles in regular public transport services, to the extent that they do not deviate to the disadvantage of the passenger from the Order on Standard Transport Terms for Tram and Trolley Bus Transport and Regular Public Transport Services with Motor Vehicles; letter (b) does not apply to limitations on liability for state-approved lotteries and gaming contracts;

(8) (Other exclusions of liability for breaches of duty)

(a) (Exclusion of the right to free oneself from the contract) a provision which, where there is a breach of duty for which the user is responsible and which does not consist in a defect of the thing sold or the work, excludes or restricts the right of the other party to free himself from the contract; this does not apply to the terms of transport and tariff rules referred to in no. 7 under the conditions set out there;

(b) (Defects) a provision by which in contracts relating to the supply of newly produced things and relating to the performance of work

(aa) (Exclusion and referral to third parties) the claims against the user due to defects in their entirety or in regard to individual parts are excluded,

(bb) (Limitation to cure) the claims against the user are limited in whole or in regard to individual parts to a right to cure, to the extent that the right is not expressly reserved for the other party to the contract to reduce the purchase price, if the cure should fail or, except where building work is the object of liability for defects, at its option to terminate the contract;

(cc) (Expenses for cure) the duty of the user to bear or compensate for the expenses necessary for the purpose of cure pursuant to §439 (2) and (3) or §635 (2) is excluded or limited;

(dd) (Withholding cure) the user makes cure dependent upon prior payment of the entire fee or a portion of the fee that is disproportionate taking the defect into account;

(ee) (Cut-off period for notice of defects) the user sets a cut-off period for the other party to the contract to give notice of non-obvious defects which is shorter than the permissible period of time under double letter (ff) below;

(ff) (Making limitation easier) the limitation of claims against the user due to defects in the cases cited in § 438 (1) no. 2 and § 634a (1) no. 2 is made easier, or in other cases a limitation period of less than one year reckoned from the beginning of the statutory limitation period is attained;

(9) (Duration of continuing obligations) in a contractual relationship the subject matter of which is the regular supply of goods or the regular rendering of services or work performance by the user,

(a) a duration of the contract binding the other party to the contract for more than two years,

(b) a tacit extension of the contractual relationship by more than one year in each case that is binding on the other party to the contract, or

(c) a notice period longer than three months prior to the expiry of the duration of the contract as originally agreed or tacitly extended at the expense of the other party to the contract; this does not apply to contracts relating to the supply of things sold as belonging together, to insurance contracts or to contracts between the holders of copyright rights and claims and copyright collecting societies within the meaning of the Act on the Administration of Copyright and Neighbouring Rights;

(10) (Change of other party to contract) a provision according to which in the case of purchase, loan or service agreements or agreements to produce a result a third party enters into, or may enter into, the rights and duties under the contract in place of the user, unless, in that provision,

(a) the third party is identified by name, or

(b) the other party to the contract is granted the right to free himself from the contract;

(11) (Liability of an agent with power to enter into a contract) a provision by which the user imposes on an agent who enters into a contract for the other party to the contract

(a) a liability or duty of responsibility for the principal on the part of the agent himself, without any explicit and separate declaration to this effect, or

(b) in the case of agency without authority, liability going beyond § 179;

(12) (Burden of proof) a provision by which the user modifies the burden of proof to the disadvantage of the other party to the contract, in particular by

(a) imposing on the latter the burden of proof for circumstances lying in the sphere of responsibility of the user, or

(b) having the other party to the contract confirm certain facts;

letter (b) does not apply to acknowledgements of receipt that are signed separately or provided with a separate qualified electronic signature;

(13). (Form of notices and declarations) a provision by which notices or declarations that are to be made to the user or a third party are tied to a more stringent form than written form or tied to special receipt requirements;

(14) (Waiver of litigation) a provision pursuant to which the other contractual partner may only bring a judicial claim after having sought an amicable settlement in extra-judicial dispute settlement proceedings;

(15) (Payment on account and security) a provision, pursuant to which the user, in case of a service contract [Werksvertrag]

(a) may demand payments on account for partial performances that are significantly larger than the payments on account due pursuant to §632a (1) and §650m (1), or

(b) does not have to make the security payment pursuant to §650m, or must only pay a smaller amount.

§ 310. (1) § 305 (2) and (3) and §§ 308 and 309 do not apply to standard business terms which are used in contracts with an entrepreneur, a legal person under public law or a special fund under public law. § 307 (1) and (2) nevertheless apply to these cases in sentence 1 to the extent that this leads to the ineffectiveness of the contract provisions set out in §§ 308 and 309; reasonable account must be taken of the practices and customs that apply in business dealings. In cases coming under sentence 1, § 307 (1) and (2) do not apply to contracts in which the entire Award Rules for Building Works, Part B [Vergabe- und Vertragsordnung für Bauleistungen Teil B - VOB/B] in the version applicable at the time of conclusion of the contract are included without deviation as to their content, relating to an examination of the content of individual provisions.

(2) §§ 308 and 309 do not apply to contracts of electricity, gas, district heating or water suppliers for the supply of electricity, gas, district heating or water from the supply grid to special customers to the extent that the conditions of supply do not derogate, to the disadvantage of the customer, from orders on general conditions for the supply of standard-rate customers with electricity, gas, district heating and water. Sentence 1 applies with the necessary modifications to contracts for the disposal of sewage.

(3) In the case of contracts between an entrepreneur and a consumer (consumer contracts) the rules in this division apply with the following provisos:

1. Standard business terms are deemed to have been presented by the entrepreneur, unless they were introduced into the contract by the consumer;

2. § 305c (2) and §§ 306 and 307 to 309 of this Code and Article 46b of the Introductory Act to the Civil Code [Einführungsgesetz zum Bürgerlichen Gesetzbuch] apply to pre-formulated contract terms even if the latter are intended only for non-recurrent use on one occasion, and to the extent that the consumer, by reason of the pre-formulation, had no influence on their contents;

3. in judging an unreasonable disadvantage under § 307 (1) and (2), the other circumstances attending the entering into of the contract must also be taken into account.

(4) This division does not apply to contracts in the field of the law of succession, family law and company law or to collective agreements and private-sector works agreements or public-sector establishment agreements. When it is applied to employment contracts, reasonable account must be taken of the special features that apply in labour law; § 305 (2) and (3) must not be applied. Collective agreements and private-sector works agreements or public-sector establishment agreements are equivalent to legal provisions within the meaning of § 307 (3).

Division 3. Contractual obligation relationships [Schuldverhältnisse aus Verträgen]

Title 1. Creation, content and termination

Sub-title 1. Creation

§ 311. (1) In order to create an obligation relationship [Schuldverhältnis] by legal transaction [Rechtsgeschäft] as well as to alter the contents of an obligation relationship, a contract [Vertrag] between the parties is necessary, unless otherwise provided by law.

(2) An obligation relationship with duties under § 241 sub-paragraph (2) also arises by
1. the commencement of contractual negotiations
2. the initiation of a contract where one party, with regard to a potential contractual relationship, grants the other party the possibility of affecting his rights, legal interests and other interests, or entrusts these to him, or
3. similar business contacts.

(3) An obligation relationship with duties under § 241 sub-paragraph (2) may also arise in relation to persons who are not themselves to be contracting parties. Such an obligation arises in particular where the third party, by claiming to have been given a special degree of reliance, substantially influences the contractual negotiations or the conclusion of the contract.

§ 311a. (1) It does not stand in the way of the effectiveness of a contract that according to § 275 sub-paragraphs (1) to (3) the debtor does not need to perform and the obstacle to performance already exists at the conclusion of the contract.

(2) The creditor may, at his option, demand compensation instead of performance or reimbursement of his expenditure to the extent specified in § 284. This does not apply if the debtor did not know of the obstacle to performance at the conclusion of the contract and is also not responsible for his lack of knowledge. § 281 sub-paragraph (1) sentences 2 and 3 and sub-paragraph (5) apply mutatis mutandis.

§ 311b. (1) A contract by which one party agrees to transfer or acquire ownership of a plot of land must be recorded by a notary. A contract not entered into in this form becomes valid with all its contents if a declaration of conveyance and registration in the Land Register are effected.

(2) A contract by which one party agrees to transfer his future property or a fraction of his future property or to charge it with a usufruct is void.

(3) A contract by which one party agrees to transfer his present property or a fraction of his present property or to charge it with a usufruct must be recorded by a notary.

(4) A contract relating to the estate of a third party who is still living is void. The same applies to a contract relating to a compulsory portion or a legacy from the estate of a third party who is still living.

(5) Sub-paragraph (4) does not apply to a contract entered into between future heirs on intestacy relating to the hereditary share on intestacy or the compulsory portion of one of them. Such a contract must be recorded by a notary.

[§ 311c and Sub-title 2 are omitted.]

Sub-title 3. Adaptation and termination of contracts

§ 313. (1) If the circumstances which have become the foundation of the contract have significantly changed after the conclusion of the contract and if the parties would not have concluded the contract or would have concluded it with different contents if they had foreseen this change, adaptation of the contract may be demanded in so far as, taking account of all the circumstances of the individual case, in particular the contractual or statutory distribution of risk, adherence to the unadapted contract cannot be expected of one of the parties [Störung des Geschäftsgrundlage].

(2) It is equivalent to a change of circumstances if material preconceptions that have become the foundation of the contract are found to be incorrect.

(3) If adaptation of the contract is not possible or cannot be expected of one of the parties, the

disadvantaged party may withdraw from the contract. For long term obligation relationships, a right to cancel [Recht zur Kündigung] takes the place of right of withdrawal [Rücktrittsrecht].

§ 314. (1) Long term obligation relationships can be cancelled by each contracting party for a significant reason without the observance of a notice period. A significant reason arises if the continuation of the contractual relationship until the agreed termination [Beendigung] or until the expiry of a notice period cannot be expected of the cancelling party, taking account of all the circumstances of the individual case and weighing the interests of both parties.
(2) If the significant reason consists of a violation of a duty under the contract, the cancellation is allowed only after the expiry without result of a period specified for relief or after a warning notice without result. With regard to the dispensability of specifying a period for relief and to the dispensability of a warning notice, §323 sub-paragraph (2) no. 1 and 2 applies mutatis mutandis. The specification of a period for relief and a warning notice are also dispensable where special circumstances exist which, under consideration of the interests of both parties, justify the immediate cancellation.
(3) The person so entitled may only cancel within a reasonable period after he has obtained knowledge of the reason for cancellation.
(4) The right to demand compensation for damage is not excluded by the cancellation.

[Sub-title 4 is omitted.]

Title 2. Synallagmatic contracts [Gegenseitige Verträge]

§ 320. (1) A person who is bound by a synallagmatic contract may refuse the performance incumbent upon him until the effectuation of the counter-performance, unless he is obliged to perform beforehand. If the performance is to be made to several persons, an individual person can be refused the part due to him until the effectuation of the whole counter-performance. The provision of § 273 sub-paragraph (3) is not applicable.
(2) If one party has partially performed, the counter-performance cannot be refused in so far as the refusal in the circumstances, in particular due to the relative triviality the part in arrears, is contrary to good faith.

§ 321. (1) A person who is obliged to perform in advance under a reciprocal contract may refuse to render his performance if, after the contract is entered into, it becomes apparent that his entitlement to consideration is jeopardised by the inability to perform of the other party. The right to refuse performance is not applicable if consideration is rendered or security is given for it.
(2) The person required to perform in advance may specify a reasonable period in which the other party must, at his choice, render consideration or provide security reciprocally and simultaneously against performance. If the period ends without result, the person required to perform in advance may revoke the contract. § 323 applies mutatis mutandis.

[§ 322 is omitted.]

§ 323. (1) If the debtor, in the case of a synallagmatic contract, does not render the performance which is due, or does not render it in conformity with the contract, the creditor may withdraw from the contract [zurücktreten], if he has determined for the debtor without result, an appropriate period of time for performance or subsequent fulfilment [Nacherfüllung].
(2) The setting of a period of time can be dispensed with if
1. the debtor seriously and definitively refuses performance,
2. the debtor does not render performance until a date specified in the contract or within a period specified in the contract even though performance on the due date or in due time is essential pursuant to information provided to the debtor by the creditor before the conclusion of the contract or pursuant to other circumstances attendant to the conclusion of the contract, or
3. special circumstances exist in the case of performance not in accordance with the contract, which, the interests of both parties considered, justify immediate withdrawal [Rücktritt].
(3) If in view of the nature of the violation of duty the setting a period of time does not come into consideration, a warning notice takes its place.
(4) The creditor may withdraw already before the occurrence of the due date for performance if it is obvious that the prerequisites for withdrawal will be met.
(5) If the debtor has effected partial performance, the creditor may only withdraw from the whole contract if he has no interest in partial performance. If the debtor has not effected performance in conformity with the contract, the creditor cannot withdraw from the contract if the violation of duty is trivial.

(6) Withdrawal is excluded if the creditor is solely or very predominantly responsible for the circumstance that would entitle him to withdraw or if the circumstance for which the debtor is not responsible occurs at a time when the creditor is in default of acceptance.

§ 324. If the debtor, in the case of a synallagmatic contract, violates a duty under § 241 sub-paragraph (2), the creditor can withdraw if adherence to the contract can no longer be expected of him.

§ 325. The right to demand compensation for damage in case of a synallagmatic contract is not excluded by withdrawal.

§ 326. (1) If the debtor is not required to perform under § 275 sub-paragraphs (1) to (3), the claim counter-performance is inapplicable; in the case of partial performance, § 441 sub-paragraph (3) applies mutatis mutandis. sentence 1 does not apply if the debtor, in the case of failure to perform in conformity with the contract, does not have to effect subsequent fulfilment under § 275 sub-paragraphs (1) to (3).
(2) If the creditor is solely or predominantly responsible for the circumstance due to which the debtor does not have to effect subsequent fulfilment under § 275 sub-paragraphs (1) to (3), or if this circumstance for which the debtor is not responsible occurs at a time when the creditor is in default of acceptance, the debtor retains the right to counter-performance. He must, however, allow to be credited against him what he saves as a result of the release from performance or through other use of his labour acquires or wilfully refrains from acquiring.
(3) If the creditor demands under § 285 the return of the replacement obtained for the object owed or assignment of the claim to replacement under § 285, he remains obliged to render counter-performance. The latter is reduced, however, under the requirement of § 441 sub-paragraph (3) in so far as the value of the replacement or of the claim to replacement falls short of the value of the performance owed.
(4) In so far as the counter-performance that is not owed under this provision is effected, what has been performed can be demanded back under §§ 346 to 348.
(5) If the debtor does not have to perform under § 275 sub-paragraphs (1) to (3), the creditor may withdraw; § 323 applies mutatis mutandis to the withdrawal, with the proviso that setting of a period of time is unnecessary.

Title 3. Promise of a performance to a third party

§ 328. (1) Performance to a third party may be agreed by contract with the effect that the third party acquires the right to demand the performance directly.

[The remainder of §328 and Title 3 is omitted.]

Title 4. Earnest, contractual penalty

[§§ 336 – 338 are omitted.]

§ 339. Where the debtor promises the creditor, in the event that he fails to perform his obligation or fails to do so properly, payment of an amount of money as a penalty, the penalty is payable if he is in default. If the performance owed consists in forbearance, the penalty is payable on breach.

§ 340. (1) If the obligor has promised the penalty in the event that he fails to perform his obligation, the obligee may demand the penalty that is payable in lieu of fulfilment. If the obligee declares to the obligor that he is demanding the penalty, the claim to performance is excluded.
(2) If the obligee is entitled to a claim to damages for non-performance, he may demand the penalty payable as the minimum amount of the damage. Assertion of additional damage is not excluded.

§ 341. (1) If the obligor has promised the penalty in the event that he fails to perform his obligation properly, including without limitation performance at the specified time, the obligee may demand the payable penalty in addition to performance.
(2) If the obligee has a claim to damages for the improper performance, the provisions of § 340 (2) apply.
(3) If the obligee accepts performance, he may demand the penalty only if he reserved the right to do so on acceptance.

[§ 342 is omitted]

§ 343. (1) If a payable penalty is disproportionately high, it may on the application of the obligor be reduced to a reasonable amount by judicial decision. In judging the appropriateness, every legitimate interest of the obligee, not merely his financial interest, must be taken into account. Once the penalty is paid, reduction is excluded.

(2) The same also applies, except in the cases of §§ 339 and 342, if someone promises a penalty in the event that he undertakes or omits an action.

[The remainder of Title 4 is omitted.]

Title 5. Right of Termination; the right of termination and right to return in consumer contracts

Sub-title 1. Termination [Rücktritt]

§ 346. (1) Where a contracting party has contractually reserved the right to terminate or the party has a statutory right to terminate, in case of termination, the performances received are to be returned and the benefits derived are to be restored.

(2) Instead of the return or restoration, the creditor is to provide compensation for value, in so far as
1. the return or the restoration of that which was obtained is precluded by its nature,
2. he used up, disposed of, burdened, processed or transformed the received object,
3. the received object has deteriorated or is lost; however, the deterioration that occurred through the designated use of the object is not to be taken into account.

If the contract determines a counter-performance, the calculation of compensation for value is to be based on it; if the compensation for value for the benefit of use of a loan is to be made, it can be shown that the value of the benefit of use was lower.

(3) The obligation to compensate for value does not apply,
1. if the defect entitling the termination only become apparent during the processing or transformation of the object,
2. in so far as the creditor is responsible for the deterioration or loss or the damage would also have occurred to him,
3. if in the case of a statutory right to terminate the deterioration or loss has occurred to the person entitled, even though he used the care that he tends to apply to his own affairs.

A remaining enrichment is to be restored.

(4) The creditor can demand compensation for damage according to the standards of §§280 to 283 for a violation of a duty under sub-paragraph (1).

[§ 347 is omitted.]

§ 348. The duties of the parties deriving from the termination are to be performed concurrently. The provisions of §§ 320 and 322 apply mutatis mutandis.

§ 349. The termination occurs by declaration to the other party.

§ 350. If no time limit is fixed for the exercise of a contractual right of termination, the other party can fix for the person entitled an appropriate period of time for the exercise. The right to withdraw extinguishes when the withdrawal is not declared before the expiry of the period of time.

[The remainder of Division 3 and Division 4 are omitted.]

Division 5. Assignment of a claim

§ 398. The creditor of a claim [Forderung] can, by contract with another, transfer that claim to this other (assignment) [Abtretung]. The new creditor takes the place of the old creditor with the conclusion of the contract.

§ 399. A claim cannot be assigned if the performance to another person than the original creditor cannot take place without alteration of its content or if the assignment has been excluded by agreement with the debtor.

[§§ 400 – 406 are omitted.]

§ 407. (1) The new creditor must, after the assignment, allow a performance that the debtor makes to the previous creditor, as well as any legal transaction undertaken after the assignment between the debtor and the previous creditor in respect to the claim, allow it to be asserted against him, unless the debtor is aware of the assignment at the moment of performance or the undertaking of the legal transaction.

(2) If, in a legal dispute between the debtor and the previous creditor that has become pending at a court after the assignment, a final and non-appealable judgment in respect to the claim has been

made, the new creditor must allow the judgment to be asserted against him, unless the debtor was aware of the assignment when the legal proceedings became pending.

[§ 408 is omitted.]

§ 409. (1) If the creditor notifies the debtor that he has assigned the claim, the debtor must allow the notified assignment to be asserted against him, also if it does not take place or has no effect. It is equivalent to a notice that the creditor creates a deed [Urkunde] relating to the assignment to the new creditor identified in the deed and the latter presents it to the debtor.
(2) The notice can only be revoked with the permission of the person who is identified as the new creditor.

[The remainder of Division 5 and Divisions 6 – 7 are omitted.]

Division 8. Particular types of obligation relationships

Title 1. Sale, exchange

Sub-title 1. General provisions

§ 433. (1) By a contract of sale [Kaufvertrag], the seller of an object is obliged to deliver the object to the buyer and to provide ownership of the object. The seller must provide the object to the buyer free from physical and legal defects [Sach- und Rechtsmängeln].
(2) The buyer is obliged to pay the seller the agreed purchase price and to take delivery of the purchased object.

§ 434. (1) The object is free from physical defects [Sachmangel] if it possesses the agreed upon properties [Beschaffenheit] when the risk passes [Gefahrübergang]. In so far as that the properties are not agreed, the object is free of physical defects
1. if it is suitable for the intended use under the contract, or otherwise
2. if it is suitable for the customary use and possesses the properties that are usual in objects of the same kind and which the buyer may expect given the nature of the object.
Properties under sentence 2 no. 2 includes characteristics which the buyer can expect from the public statements by the seller, the producer (§ 4 sub-paragraphs (1) and (2) of the Product Liability Act [Produkthaftungsgesetz]) or his assistant, in particular in advertising or labelling about the specific characteristics of the object, unless the seller was not aware and did not have to be aware of the statement, or at the point in time of the conclusion of the contract it had been corrected in an equivalent manner, or it could not have influenced the decision to purchase.
(2) It is also a physical defect if the agreed installation by the seller or his assistants has been carried out improperly. A physical defect further exists in an object that is to be installed if the installation instructions are defective, unless the object has been installed correctly.
(3) It is equivalent to a physical defect if the seller supplies a different object or too small a quantity.

§ 435. The object is free of legal defects [Rechtsmängeln] if third parties cannot enforce any rights against the buyer in relation to the object, or only those that have been taken over in the contract of sale. It is equivalent to a legal defect if a right that does not exist is registered in the Land Register.

[§ 436 is omitted.]

§ 437. If the object is defective, the buyer may, provided the prerequisites of the following provisions are met and unless otherwise specified,
1. under § 439, demand subsequent fulfilment [Nacherfüllung],
2. under §§ 440, 323, and 326 sub-paragraph (5) withdraw from the agreement or under § 441 reduce the purchase price, and
3. under §§ 440, 280, 281, 283, and 311a, demand compensation for damage, or under § 284, compensation for futile expenditure.

§ 438. (1) The claims cited in § 437 nos. 1 and 3 become prescribed
1. in thirty years, if the defect consists of
a) a property right [dingliches Recht] of a third party on the basis of which return of the purchased object may be demanded, or
b) some other right which is registered in the Land Register,
2. in five years
a) in relation to a construction, and
b) in relation to an object that has been used for a construction in accordance with its usual manner it

is used and has caused the defectiveness of the building, and

3. otherwise in two years.

(2) In the case of a piece of land the prescription period commences upon the delivery of possession, in other cases upon delivery of the object.

(3) Contrary to sub-paragraph (1) nos. 2 and 3 and sub-paragraph (2), claims become prescribed after the regular prescription period, if the seller wilfully kept silent about the defect. In the case of sub-paragraph (1) no. 2, however, the prescription period does not take effect before the expiry of the period determined there.

(4) §218 applies to the right of withdrawal referred to in § 437. Notwithstanding the ineffectiveness of a withdrawal under § 218 sub-paragraph (1), the buyer may refuse payment of the purchase price in so far as he would be entitled to do so on the basis of withdrawal. If he makes use of this right, the seller may withdraw from the contract.

(5) § 218 and sub-paragraph (4) sentence 2 above apply correspondingly to the right to reduction referred to in § 437.

§ 439. (1) The buyer may, as subsequent fulfilment, at his option, demand the removal of the defect or delivery of an object free of defects.

(2) The seller must bear all the necessary expenditure for the purpose of subsequent fulfilment, in particular transport, road tolls, labour and materials costs.

(3) Where the buyer has installed the defective object into another object or mounted it onto another object in accordance with its nature and purpose, the seller is obliged, in the context of subsequent fulfilment, to reimburse the expenses necessary for the removal of the defective object and the installation or mounting of the repaired or replaced defect-free object to the buyer. §442 (1) is to be applied with the proviso that, with regard to the knowledge of the buyer, the installation or mounting of the defective thing by the buyer takes the place of the conclusion of the contract.

(4) Notwithstanding §275 (2) and (3), the seller may refuse the means of subsequent fulfilment chosen by the buyer if it is only possible at a disproportional cost. In this respect, the value of the object in its defect-free state, the significance of the defect, as well as the question whether another means of subsequent fulfilment could be resorted to without significant disadvantages to the buyer must be taken into particular account. Where the latter is the case, the claim of the buyer is limited to the other means of subsequent fulfilment; the right of the seller to also refuse this means of subsequent fulfilment subject to the conditions of clause 1 remains unaffected.

(5) If the seller delivers an object free from defects for the purpose of subsequent fulfilment, he may demand from the buyer the retransfer [Rückgewähr] of the defective object in accordance with §§ 346 to 348.

§ 440. Except in the cases of § 281 sub-paragraph (2) and § 323 sub-paragraph (2), the setting of a period of time is also not necessary when the seller refuses both kinds of subsequent fulfilment pursuant to § 439 sub-paragraph (3) or when the kind of subsequent fulfilment due to the buyer has failed or cannot be expected of him. A subsequent improvement [Nachbesserung] is regarded as failed after the second unsuccessful attempt, unless something else results in particular from the nature of the object or the defect or other circumstances.

§ 441. (1) Instead of withdrawing the buyer can r-educe the purchase price by a declaration to the seller. The ground for exclusion in § 323 sub-paragraph (5) sentence 2 does not apply.

(2) Where on the side of the buyer or on the side of seller several take part, the reduction can only be declared by all or to all.

(3) In the case of reduction, the purchase price is to be reduced in the proportion in which the value of the object in a defect free state at the time of the conclusion of the contract would have stood to the actual value. The reduction is, to the extent necessary, to be determined by appraisal.

(4) Where the buyer paid more than the reduced purchase price, the surplus amount is to be reimbursed by the seller. § 346 sub-paragraph (1) and § 347 sub-paragraph (1) apply mutatis mutandis.

§ 442. (1) The rights of the buyer concerning a defect are excluded if he knew of the defect at the conclusion of the contract. Where the defect remains unknown to the buyer due to gross negligence, the buyer can only assert his rights arising out of the defect if the seller fraudulently concealed the defect or gave a guarantee concerning the properties of the object.

(2) A right that is registered in the land register is to be rectified by the seller, also if the buyer is aware of it.

§ 443. (1) If the seller, the producer, or another third party commits, in a declaration or pertinent

advertising that was available prior to the conclusion of the contract of sale, in excess of legal liability for defects, to reimburse the purchase price, replace the thing, mend it, or provide services in relation to the thing if it is not of the quality described in the advertisement or does not satisfy any other requirements, not relating to the absence of defects, described in the advertisement (guarantee), then the buyer is entitled, in case of a guarantee claim, without prejudice to statutory claims, to the rights arising from the guarantee, on the terms provided by the declaration of guarantee and the relevant advertising against the person who granted the guarantee (guarantor).
(2) In so far as the guarantor has given the guarantee that the thing will maintain a certain quality for a certain period of time (guarantee of durability), it is presumed that a physical defect occurring during its validity period gives rise to the rights under the guarantee.

§ 444. The seller cannot invoke an agreement by which the rights of the buyer arising from a defect are excluded or limited, in so far as he fraudulently concealed the defect or gave a guarantee concerning the properties of the object.

[§ 445 is omitted.]

§ 446. With the delivery of the object sold, the risk of accidental loss or accidental deterioration passes to the buyer. From the delivery, the buyer is entitled to the benefits and he bears the burdens of the object. It is equivalent to delivery, when the buyer is in default of acceptance.

§ 447. (1) Where the seller, at request of the buyer, ships the object sold to another place than the place of performance, the risk passes to the buyer as soon as the seller hands the object over to the freight forwarder, carrier or any other person or body, responsible for the performance of shipment.
(2) Where the buyer gave a particular instruction concerning the manner of shipment, and the seller without good reason derogates from the instruction, the seller is responsible to the buyer for the resulting damage.

§ 448. (1) The seller bears the costs of delivery of the object, the buyer the costs of acceptance and the shipment of the object to another place than the place of performance.
(2) The buyer of a piece of land bears the costs of authentication of the sales contract and the deed, the registration in the land register and the declarations required for the registration.

§ 449. (1) If the seller of a movable object has reserved his right of ownership until payment of the purchase price, in case of doubt, it is presumed that the right of ownership is transferred under the suspensive condition [aufschiebende Bedingung] of full payment of the purchase price.
(2) On the basis of the reservation of ownership [Eigentumsvorbehalt], the seller of the object can only claim back the object if he has withdrawn from the contract.
(3) The agreement on a reservation of ownership is void in so far as the transfer of ownership is made dependent on the payment of claims to a third person, in particular one to a business connected to the seller.

[The remainder of Title 2 is omitted.]

Title 3. Loan contract; financing assistance and contracts for delivery by instalments between an entrepreneur and a consumer

Sub-title 1. Loan contract

[Chapter 1 is omitted.]

Chapter 2. Special provisions concerning consumer loan contracts

[§§ 491 – 493 are omitted.]

§ 494. (1) The consumer loan contract and the power of attorney given by the consumer to enter into such a contract are void if written form is not complied with at all or if any of the items of information specified in Article 247, §§ 6 and 9 to 13 of the Introductory Act to the Civil Code [Einführungsgesetz zum Bürgerlichen Gesetzbuch, EGBGB] for the consumer loan contract is lacking.
(2) Irrespective of a defect under sub-paragraph (1), the consumer loan contract is valid to the extent that the borrower receives the loan or draws on it. However, the lending rate on which the consumer loan contract is based is reduced to the statutory rate of interest if there is no information on the lending rate, on the effective annual rate of interest or on the total amount.
(3) If the effective rate of interest is stated at a rate that is too low, the lending rate on which the

consumer loan contract is based is reduced by the percentage by which the effective rate of interest is too low.

(4) Costs not stated are not owed by the borrower. If the contract does not state under what preconditions costs or interest can be adjusted, the possibility to adjust these to the disadvantage of the borrower ceases to apply.

(5) If instalments have been agreed, their amount is to be re-calculated by the lender, taking account of the reduced interest or costs.

(6) If the contract does not contain information on the term or on the right of termination, the borrower is entitled to terminate at any time. If information on securities is missing, they cannot be demanded. Sentence 2 does not apply if the net loan amount is more than €75,000.

(7) The lender must provide to the borrower a copy of the contract in which the contractual amendments are considered as revealed by sub-paragraphs (2) to (6).

[The remainder of Title 3 is omitted.]

Title 4. Gift

§ 516. (1) A donation [Zuwendung] by means of which someone enriches another person from his own patrimony [Vermögen] is a gift [Schenkung] if both parties are in agreement that the donation occurs gratuitously.

(2) If the donation occurs without the intention of the other party, the donor may request him to make a declaration as to acceptance specifying an appropriate period of time. After expiry of the period of time, the gift is deemed to be accepted if the other party has not previously rejected it. In the case of rejection, return of what has been donated may be demanded according to the provisions on the return of unjust enrichment.

[§ 517 is omitted.]

§ 518. (1) For the validity of a contract by which a performance is promised as a gift, the notarial authentication of the promise is required. The same applies to a promise or a declaration of acknowledgement when a promise to fulfil an obligation or the acknowledgement of an obligation in the manner referred to in §§ **780** and 781 is made as a gift.

(2) A defect of form is cured by the effectuation of the performance promised.

[The remainder of Title 4 is omitted.]

Title 5. Lease contract [Mietvertrag], agricultural lease contract [Pachtvertrag]

Sub-title 1. General provisions for lease contracts

[§ 535 is omitted.]

§ 536. (1) If the leased property at the time of surrender to the lessee has a defect which removes its suitability for the contractually agreed use, or if such a defect arises during the lease period, then the lessee is exempted for the period when suitability is removed from paying the rent. For the period of time when suitability is reduced, he need only pay reasonably reduced rent. A trivial reduction of suitability is not taken into account.

(1a) A reduction of suitability will not be considered for the duration of three months insofar as this takes place because of a measure which serves the purpose of energy efficiency modernisation in accordance with § 555b, no. 1.

(2) Sentences 1 and 2 of sub-paragraph (1) also apply if a warranted characteristic is lacking or later ceases.

(3) If the lessee is fully or partially deprived by a third-party right of use of the leased property, then sub-paragraphs (1) and (2) apply mutatis mutandis.

(4) With regard to a lease for residential space, a deviating agreement to the disadvantage of the lessee is ineffective.

[The remainder of Sub-title 1 is omitted.]

Sub-title 2. Lease for living space

Chapter 1. General provisions

[§ 549 is omitted.]

§ 550. If a lease agreement for a longer period of time than one year is not entered into in written form, then it applies for an indefinite period of time. However, termination is only allowed at the earliest at the end of one year after use of the residential space has been permitted.

[The remainder of Chapter 1 and Chapter 1a are omitted.]

Chapter 2. The rent

Subchapter 1. Agreements on the rent

§ 556. (1) The parties to the contract may agree that the lessee is to bear operating costs. Operating costs are the costs that are incurred from day to day by the owner or the holder of the heritable building right as a result of the ownership of or the heritable building right to the plot of land or as a result of the intended use of the building, the outbuildings, facilities, installations and the land. The drawing up of the statement of operating costs continues to be governed by the Operating Costs Order [Betriebskostenverordnung] of 25 November 2003 (Federal Law Gazette I pp. 2346, 2347). The Federal Government is authorised to pass provisions on the drawing up of the statement of operating costs by statutory order without the approval of the Bundesrat.
(2) The parties to the contract may agree, subject to other provisions, that operating costs may be reported as a lump sum or as an advance payment. Advance payments for operating costs may only be agreed in a reasonable amount.
(3) Advance payments for operating costs are to be invoiced once per year, and when this is done the principle of economic efficiency is to be observed. The lessee is to be notified of the statement of operating costs at the latest by the end of the twelfth month subsequent to the accounting period. After this period, assertion of a subsequent demand by the lessor is excluded unless the lessor is not responsible for the lateness of the assertion. The lessor is not obliged to provide interim invoicing. The lessor must be informed by the lessee of any objections to invoicing at the latest by the end of the twelfth month after receipt of the invoice. After expiry of this period, objections may no longer be asserted unless the lessee is not responsible for the lateness of the assertion.
(4) An agreement deviating to the disadvantage of the lessee from sub-paragraphs (1) and (2) sentence 2, or sub-paragraph (3) is ineffective.

[§ 556a is omitted.]

§ 556b. (1) Rent is to be paid at the commencement of the periods of time according to which it is computed but at the latest by the third working day of each such period.

(2) The lessee may, notwithstanding a contract provision to the contrary, set off a claim based on §§ 536a and 539 or a claim for unjust enrichment for excess payment of rent against a claim for rent, or may exercise a right of retention in relation to such a claim if he has notified the lessor in text form of his intention to do so at least one month prior to the due date of the rent. A deviating agreement to the disadvantage of the lessee is ineffective.

[The remainder of Chapter 2 and Chapter 3 are omitted.]

Chapter 4. Change of contracting parties

[§§ 563 – 565 are omitted.]

§ 566. (1) If the leased living space, after the lessee has taken up the lease, is transferred to a third party, the acquirer will take the place of the lessor in respect to the rights and obligations that follow from the lease for the duration of his ownership.
(2) If the acquirer does not fulfil his obligations, the lessor is liable in the same was as a surety who has waived the defence of unexhausted remedies [Einrede der Vorausklage] for the damage to be compensated for by the acquirer. If the lessee obtains knowledge of the transfer of ownership through a notification by the lessor, the lessor is released from liability, unless the lessee cancels the lease at the earliest date at which cancellation is permitted.

[The remainder of Chapter 2 and Chapters 3 and 4 are omitted.]

Chapter 5. Termination of the lease

Subchapter 1. General provisions

§ 568. (1) The notice of termination of the lease must be in written form.
(2) The lessor should, in good time, draw the attention of the lessee to the possibility of an objection and the form and period for the objection under §§ 574 to 574b.

[The remainder of Title 5 and Titles 6 - 7 are omitted.]

Title 8. Employment contract and similar contracts

Sub-title 1. Employment Contract

[§611 – 622 are omitted.]

§623 Termination of employment by notice of termination or agreement requires written form to be effective; electronic form is excluded.

[The remainder of Title 8 and Titles 9 - 10 are omitted.]

Title 11. Offer of a reward [Auslobung]

§ 657. Anyone offering by means of public announcement a reward for undertaking an act, including without limitation for producing an outcome, is obliged to pay the reward to the person who has undertaken the act, even if that person did not act with a view to the promise of a reward.

§ 658. (1) The promise of a reward may be revoked until the act is undertaken. Revocation is only effective if it is announced in the same way as the promise of a reward was or if it occurs by means of a special announcement.

[The remainder of Title 11 is omitted.]

Title 12. Mandate and contract for the management of the affairs of another [Auftrag und Geschäftsbesorgungsvertrag]

[§§ 662 – 666 are omitted.]

§ 667. The mandatary [Beauftragte] is obliged to return to the mandator [Auftraggeber] everything he receives to perform the mandate [Auftrag] and that which he obtains from carrying out the transaction.

[§§ 668 – 672 are omitted.]

§ 673. In case of doubt, the mandate is extinguished on the death of the mandatary. If the mandate is extinguished, the heir of the mandatary must notify the mandator of the death without undue delay and, if postponement entails risk, must continue carrying out the transaction entrusted to him until the mandator can make other arrangements; the mandate is to this extent deemed to continue.

[The remainder of Title 12 and Titles 13 – 19 are omitted.]

Title 20. Suretyship

§ 765. (1) By a contract of suretyship, the surety puts himself under a duty to the creditor of a third party to be responsible for discharging that third party's obligation.
(2) Suretyship may also be assumed for a future or contingent obligation.

§ 766. For the contract of suretyship to be valid, the declaration of suretyship must be issued in writing. The declaration of suretyship may not be made in electronic form. If the surety discharges the main obligation, the defect of form is remedied.

[The remainder of Title 20 and Titles 21 – 25 are omitted.]

Title 26. Unjustified enrichment

§ 812. (1) A person who obtains something as a result of the performance of another person or otherwise at his expense without legal grounds for doing so is under a duty to make restitution to him. This duty also exists if the legal grounds later lapse or if the result intended to be achieved by those efforts in accordance with the contents of the legal transaction does not occur.
(2) Performance also includes the acknowledgement of the existence or non-existence of an obligation.

[§§ 813 – 816 are omitted.]

§ 817. If the purpose of performance was determined in such a way that that the recipient, in accepting it, was violating a statutory prohibition or public policy, then the recipient is obliged to make restitution. A claim for return is excluded if the person who rendered performance was likewise guilty of such a breach, unless the performance consisted in entering into an obligation; restitution may not be demanded of any performance rendered in fulfilment of such an obligation.

[The remainder of Title 26 is omitted.]

Title 27. Wrongful acts [Unerlaubte Handlungen]

§ 823. (1) A person who intentionally [vorsätzlich] or negligently [fahrlässig], unlawfully injures the life, body, health, freedom, property or another right of another person is obliged to compensate the other party for the damage arising there from.

(2) The same duty arises for a person who infringes a law intended to protect another. If, according to the contents of the law, an infringement is possible even without fault [Verschulden], the duty to compensate only arises in the case of fault.

§ 824. (1) A person who contrary to the truth asserts or disseminates a fact that is capable of endangering the credit of another or to lead to other disadvantages for his income or advancement shall compensate the other for the damage arising there from, even if he does not know that the fact is untrue but should have known of it.

(2) A communication, the untruth of which is unknown to the person making it, will not oblige a person to compensate for damage if he or the recipient of the communication has a justified interest in it.

§ 825. A person who by deceitfulness, threat or abuse of a relationship of dependence, induces another person to undertake or tolerate sexual acts, is obliged to compensate him for the damage caused.

§ 826. A person who, in a manner that infringes good morals [guten Sitten], intentionally inflicts damage on another person, is obliged to compensate the other for damage.

§ 827. A person who, in a state of unconsciousness or in a state of pathological mental disturbance that excludes the free determination of will, inflicts damage on another is not responsible for that damage. Where he has temporarily brought himself in such a state through spirituous beverages or similar means, he is responsible for any damage that he unlawfully causes in this condition in the same manner as if negligence [Fahrlässigkeit] were imputable to him; the responsibility does not arise if he came into this state without fault.

§ 828. (1) A person who has not completed his seventh year of age is not responsible for the damage that he inflicts on another.

(2) A person who has completed his seventh, but not his tenth, year of age is not responsible for the damage that he inflicts on another in an accident involving a motor vehicle, railway or a cable railway. This does not apply if he intentionally caused the injury.

(3) A person who has not yet completed his eighteenth year is, in so far as his responsibility is not excluded according to sub-paragraph (1) or (2) not responsible for damage that he inflicts on another if, when committing the damaging act, he did not possess the insight necessary to understand his responsibility.

§ 829. A person who, in one of the cases specified in §§ 823 to 826, is not responsible for damage caused by him on the basis of §§ 827 and 828, must nevertheless, in so far as compensation cannot be claimed from a third party with a duty of supervision, compensate for the damage to the extent that fairness requires according to the circumstances, and in particular the position of the parties, and he is not deprived of the means which he needs for his own reasonable subsistence as well as for the fulfilment of his statutory maintenance duties.

§ 830. (1) Where several persons, through a jointly committed wrongful act, have caused damage, each is responsible for the damage. The same applies if it is not possible to establish who of the several persons involved caused the damage through his action.

(2) Instigators and assistants are equivalent to joint actors.

§ 831. A person who appoints another to perform a task is obliged to compensate for damage which the other in the performance of his tasks unlawfully causes to a third party. The duty to compensate does not arise if the principal [Geschäftsherr], in selecting the person appointed and, in so far as he has to procure devices or equipment or to supervise the execution of the performance, observed due and necessary care [im Verkehr erforderliche Sorgfalt] in the procurement or supervision, or if the damage would have arisen notwithstanding the exercise of such care.

(2) The same responsibility arises for any person who undertakes the performance of one of the transactions specified in sub-paragraph (1) sentence 2 for the principal by contract.

§ 832. (1) A person who is obliged by law to exercise supervision over a person who requires supervision by reason of minority or his mental or physical condition is obliged to compensate for the damage that this person unlawfully inflicts on a third party. The duty to compensate does not arise if he fulfils his duty to supervise or if the damage would even have arisen in the case of proper exercise of supervision.

(2) The same responsibility arises for a person who assumes the exercise of supervision by contract.

§ 833. If a human being is killed by an animal, or the body or health of a human being is injured, or a thing is damaged, the person who keeps the animal is obliged to compensate the injured person for the damage arising there from. The duty to compensate does not arise if the damage is caused by a domestic animal intended to serve the profession, economic activity or subsistence of the keeper of the animal and either the keeper of the animal in supervising the animal has exercised due and necessary care or the damage would also have arisen even if this care had been exercised.

§ 834. A person who undertakes under contract to exercise supervision of an animal for a person who keeps the animal is responsible for the damage inflicted by the animal on a third party in the manner specified in § 833. The responsibility does not arise if he exercises due and necessary care or if the damage would also have arisen even if such care had been exercised.

§ 835. *(Repealed.)*

§ 836. (1) If, by the collapse of a building or any other structure attached to a piece of land or by the dislocation of parts of the building or structure, a human being is killed, the body or health of a human being is injured or a thing is damaged, the possessor of the piece of land is, to the extent that the collapse or dislocation is a consequence of defective construction or inadequate maintenance, obliged to compensate the injured person for damage arising there from. The duty to compensate does not arise if the possessor has observed due and necessary care for the purpose of averting the danger.

(2) A previous possessor of the piece of land is responsible for the damage if the collapse or dislocation arises within one year after the termination of his possession, unless during his period of possession he exercised due and necessary care or a later possessor would have been able to avert the danger by the exercise of such care.

(3) The possessor within the meaning of these provisions is the possessor for his own benefit [Eigenbesitzer].

§ 837. If a person possesses, in the exercise of a right, on the piece of land of another, a building or another structure, the responsibility specified in § 836 applies to him instead of the possessor of the piece of land.

§ 838. A person who undertakes for the possessor the maintenance of a building or of a structure attached to a piece of land, or has to maintain the building or the other structure by virtue of a right of use to which he is entitled, is responsible for the damage caused by the collapse or the dislocation of parts in the same way as the possessor.

§ 839. (1) If an official intentionally or negligently violates the official duty incumbent upon him as against a third party, he shall compensate the third party for damage arising there from. Where only negligence is imputable to the official, he may only be held liable if the injured person is unable to obtain compensation in another way.

(2) If an official violates his official duties in a judgment in a legal matter, he is only responsible for any damage arising there from if the violation of duty consists in a criminal offence. This provision is not applicable to a breach of duty that consists of refusal or delay in the exercise of the public function.

(3) The duty to compensate does not arise if the injured person has intentionally or negligently failed to avert the damage by making use of a legal remedy.

§ 839a. (1) If an expert appointed by the court intentionally or by gross negligence provides a false expert opinion, he is liable to compensate for the damage incurred by a party to the proceedings as a result of a court decision based on this expert opinion.

(2) § 839 sub-paragraph (3) applies mutatis mutandis.

[§§ 840 – 843 are omitted.]

§ 844. (1) In cases where death is caused, the person under the duty to compensate shall reimburse the costs of a funeral to the person under a duty to bear such costs.

(2) If the person killed, at the time of the injury, stood in a relationship to a third party on the basis of which he was obliged or might become obliged by law to provide maintenance for that person and if

the third party has as a result of the death been deprived of his right to maintenance, the person under the duty to compensate shall compensate the third party for damages by payment of an annuity to the extent that the person killed would have been obliged to provide maintenance for the presumed duration of his life; the provisions of § 843 sub-paragraphs (2) to (4) apply mutatis mutandis. The duty to compensate also arises where the third party at the time of injury had been conceived but not yet born.

(3) The person under the duty to compensate must pay to a survivor [Hinterbliebener] who stood in a relationship of particular personal proximity to the person killed an appropriate compensation in money for the emotional suffering caused to that survivor. A relationship of particular personal proximity is deemed to exist where the survivor was the spouse, the life partner, a parent, or a child of the person killed.

[The remainder of Book 2 is omitted.]

Book 3. Property law [Sachenrecht]

Division 1. Possession [Besitz]

§ 854. (1) Possession of an object is acquired by obtaining actual control of the object.
(2) Agreement between the previous possessor and the acquirer is sufficient for acquisition if the acquirer is in a position to exercise control over the object.

§ 855. If a person exercises actual control over an object for another in the other's household or business or in a similar relationship, by virtue of which he has to follow the other's instructions relating to the object, only the other is possessor.

§ 856. (1) Possession is terminated as a result of the possessor giving up, or losing in another way, actual control of the object.
(2) Possession is not terminated as a result of a, by its nature, temporary prevention to exercise control.

§ 857. Possession devolves on the heir.

§ 858. (1) A person who deprives the possessor against his will of the possession or interferes with the possession acts, except where the deprivation or interference is permitted by law, unlawfully (unlawful interference) [verbotene Eigenmacht].
(2) The possession obtained as a result of unlawful interference is defective. The successor in possession must allow the defectiveness to be asserted against him if he is the heir of the possessor or if he knows when he acquires possession of the defectiveness of his predecessor's possession.

§ 859. (1) The possessor may ward off unlawful interference by use of force.
(2) If a moveable object is taken away from the possessor by means of unlawful interference, the possessor may use force to remove the object from the perpetrator caught in the act or pursued.
(3) If the possessor of a piece of land is deprived of possession by unlawful interference, he may recover possession immediately after the deprivation by dispossession of the perpetrator.
(4) The possessor has the same rights against a person who under § 858 sub-paragraph (2) must allow the defectiveness of the possession to be asserted against him.

§ 860. The rights to which the possessor is entitled under § 859 may also be exercised by the person who exercises actual control for the possessor under § 855.

§ 861. (1) If the possessor is deprived of possession by unlawful interference, he may request the person who in relation to him possesses defectively to restore possession.
(2) The claim is excluded if the removed possession was defective as against the current possessor or his predecessor and if the possession was obtained in the last year before the deprivation of possession.

§ 862. (1) If the possessor is disturbed in his possession by unlawful interference, he may request the disturber [Störer] to remove the disturbance. If further disturbances are to be feared, the possessor may apply for an injunction.
(2) The claim is excluded if the possessor possesses defectively as against the interferer or his predecessor and if the possession was obtained in the last year before the disturbance.

§ 863. Against the claims set out in §§ 861 and 862, a right to possession or to undertake the interfering act may be put forward only to establish the assertion that the deprivation or disturbance of the possession is not unlawful interference.

§ 864. (1) A claim founded on §§ 861, 862 extinguishes upon the expiry of one year after the perpetration of the unlawful interference, except where the claim is asserted by way of legal action before this date.
(2) Extinction also occurs if it is established after the perpetration of the unlawful act by a final and non-appealable judgment that the interferer holds a right to the object by virtue of which he may claim the establishment of a possessory status that corresponds to his course of action.

§ 865. The provisions of §§ 858 to 864 apply also in favour of a person who possesses only part of an object, in particular separate living spaces or other rooms.

§ 866. If several persons possess an object collectively, in their relationship to each other no protection of possession takes place insofar as it concerns the limits of the use to which each of them is entitled.

§ 867. If an object in the control of the possessor gets on a piece of land in the possession of another, the possessor of the piece of land must permit the possessor of the object to locate and remove the object, except where the object has meanwhile been taken into possession. The possessor of the piece of land may claim compensation for the damage caused by the locating and removal. He may refuse permission, if causation of damage is to be feared, until he is given security; the refusal is not permitted if delay entails danger.

§ 868. If a person possesses an object as a usufructuary [Nießgebraucher], pledgee [Pfandgläubiger], lessee [Pächter], tenant [Mieter], depositary [Verwahrer] or in a similar relationship, by virtue of which he is as against another entitled or obliged, to have possession for a period of time, the other person is also a possessor (indirect possession) [mittelbarer Besitz].

§ 869. If unlawful interference is perpetrated against a possessor, the claims set out under § 861, 862 also apply to the indirect possessor. In case of deprivation of possession, the indirect possessor is entitled to claim that restoration of possession to the previous possessor; if the latter cannot or does not wish to retake possession, the indirect possessor may require that possession is restored to him. Under the same prerequisites he may, in the case of § 867, require that he is permitted to locate and remove the object.

§ 870. Indirect possession may be transferred to another by assigning to the other the claim to return the object.

§ 871. If the indirect possessor is in a relationship with a third party as set out in § 868, the third party is also indirect possessor.

§ 872. A person who possesses an object as belonging to him is a possessor for his own benefit [Eigenbesitzer].

Division 2. General Provisions on rights in respect to pieces of land

§ 873. (1) The transfer of the ownership of a piece of land [Grundstück], the burdening of a piece of land with a right, as well as the transfer or burdening of such a right requires, in so far as the law does not otherwise provide, the agreement of the person entitled and the other party on the occurrence of the change of title and the registration of the change of title in the Land Register [Grundbuch].
(2) Before the registration, the parties are bound by the agreement only if the declarations are notarially recorded or made before the land registration office [Grundbuchamt] or filed with the same, or if the person entitled has handed over to the other party an authorization for registration [Eintragungsbewilligung] that is in accordance with the provisions of the Land Register Code [Grundbuchordnung].

[§ 874 is omitted.]

§ 875. (1) The abandonment of a right in respect of a piece of land requires, in so far as the law does not provide otherwise, the declaration of the person holding the right that he abandons his right and the cancellation [Löschung] of the right in the land register. The declaration must be made to the land registration office or to the person for whose benefit it is made.
(2) Before the cancellation the person holding the right is only bound to his declaration if it has been made to the land registry office or the person, for whose benefit it is made, has handed over an authorization of cancellation in accordance with the provisions of the Land Register Code.

§ 876. If a right in respect to a piece of land is burdened with the right of a third party, the abandonment of the right that burdens the land requires the permission of that third party. If the right that is to be abandoned belongs to the owner of another piece of land and that piece of land is burdened with a right of a third party, the permission of that third party is needed, unless the right is not affected by the abandonment. The permission must be declared to the land registration office or to the person for whose benefit the declaration is made; it cannot be withdrawn.

[§§ 877 – 878 are omitted.]

§ 879. (1) The ranking of several rights that burden a piece of land are determined according to the sequence of the entries, if the rights are entered in the same section of the land register. If the rights are registered in different sections, the right entered by indicating an earlier day has priority; rights that are entered by indicating the same date have the same priority.
(2) The entry is also decisive for the order of priority, if the agreement, which is according to § 873 necessary for the acquisition of the right, was concluded only after the entry.
(3) A deviating determination of the ranking must be registered in the land register.

[§§ 880 – 882 are omitted.]

§ 883. (1) To secure a claim to the granting or abolition [Aufhebung] of a right in a piece of land or in a right burdening a piece of land or the alteration of the content or the priority of such a right, a priority notice [Vormerkung] may be entered in the land register. The registration of a priority notice is also admissible to secure a future or a conditional claim.
(2) A disposition that is made after the registration of the priority notice on the piece of land or the right is ineffective to the extent that it would defeat or adversely affect the claim. This also applies, if the disposition is made by way of compulsory execution or enforcement of an attachment or by the insolvency administrator.
(3) The priority of the right to the granting of which the claim relates is determined according to the registration of the priority notice.

[§§ 884 – 888 are omitted.]

§ 889. A right on another piece of land does not cease to exist when the owner of the land acquires the right or the holder of the right acquires ownership.

[§ 890 is omitted.]

§ 891. (1) If a right has been registered in the land register for a person, it is presumed that he is entitled to the right.
(2) If a registered right is cancelled in the land register, it is presumed that the right does not exist.

§ 892. (1) In favour of the person who acquires a right in a piece of land or a right in such a right by legal transaction, the contents of the land register are presumed to be accurate, unless an objection to the accuracy is registered or the inaccuracy is known to the acquirer. If the person entitled is restricted in favour of a particular person in his disposition of a right entered in the land register, the restriction is effective as against the acquirer only if it is apparent from the land register or known to the acquirer.
(2) If registration is necessary for the acquisition of the right, the knowledge of the acquirer at the date when the application for registration is made or, if the agreement required under § 873 is reached only later, the date of agreement, is conclusive.

§ 893. The provisions of § 892 apply mutatis mutandis if, on the basis of this right, performance is made to the person for whom a right is registered in the land register, or if, on the basis of this right, between this person and another person a legal transaction that does not fall under the provision of § 892 is made which contains a disposition of the right.

[§§ 894 – 899 are omitted.]

§ 900. (1) A person who has been registered in the land registry as owner of a piece of land, without having obtained the right of ownership, acquires the right of ownership when the registration has existed for 30 years and he has been in possession of the land for his own benefit for that time. The thirty-year period is calculated in the same way as the period for prescription of a movable object. The running of the prescription period is interrupted as long as an objection to the accuracy of the registration in the land register is registered.
(2) These provisions apply mutatis mutandis when a right has been registered in the land register for a person who is not entitled to it, that gives a right to possession or the exercise of which is protected by the provisions on possession. The order of registration is decisive for the priority of the right.

§ 901. If a right to another piece of land has been unlawfully cancelled in the land register, the right ceases to exist when the claim of the holder of the right against the owner has prescribed. The same applies, when a right that was created by operation of law on another piece of land was not registered in the land register.

§ 902. (1) The claims arising out of the registered rights are not subject to prescription. This does not apply to claims for recurrent performances in arrears or for compensation for damage.
(2) A right, against which an objection to accuracy has been registered in the land register, is equal to the right that is registered.

Division 3. Ownership [Eigentum]

Title 1. Content of ownership

§ 903. The owner of an object can, when this is not contrary to the law or the rights of third parties, do with the object what he wishes and exclude others from exercising influence. The owner of an animal must, in the exercise of his powers, observe the special provisions for the protection of animals.

[§§ 904 – 916 are omitted.]

§ 917. (1) If a piece of land lacks the connection to a public road necessary for the due use, the owner may require of the neighbours that until the defect is removed, they tolerate the use of their pieces of land to establish the necessary connection. The direction of the road of necessity [Notweg] and the scope of the right of use are, if necessary, determined by judicial decision.
(2) The neighbours, over whose pieces of land the road of necessity goes, are to be compensated by periodical payments. The provisions of §912(2) sentence 2 and §§913,914, 916 apply mutatis mutandis.

[The remainder of Title 1 is omitted]

Title 2. Acquisition and loss of ownership in respect to a piece of land

§ 925. (1) The agreement between the disposer and the acquirer required for the transfer of ownership of a piece of land under § 873 (conveyance agreement) [Auflassung] must be declared in the simultaneous presence of both parties before a competent authority. Any notary is, without prejudice to the competence of other authorities, competent to receive the conveyance agreement. A conveyance agreement may also be stipulated in a judicial settlement or in a finally confirmed insolvency plan.
(2) A conveyance agreement subjected to a condition or time stipulation is ineffective.

§ 925a. The conveyance agreement shall be accepted only if the document relating to the contract required under § 311b first sentence is submitted or simultaneously drawn up.

[§§ 926 – 927 are omitted.]

§ 928. (1) The ownership of a piece of land can be abandoned by the owner declaring his abandonment [Verzicht] to the land registration office and by registering the abandonment in the land register.
(2) The right to appropriate the relinquished plot of land belongs to the fiscal authority of the Land in which the plot of land is situated. The fiscal authority acquires ownership by having itself registered in the Land Register as owner.

Title 3. Acquisition and loss of ownership in respect to movable objects

Sub-title 1. Transfer [Übertragung]

§ 929. For the transfer of ownership of a movable object it is necessary that the owner of the object hands it over to the acquirer and that both agree that the ownership is to be transferred. If the acquirer is in possession of the object, agreement about the transfer of ownership is sufficient.

[§ 929a is omitted]

§ 930. If the owner is in possession of the object, the handing over of the object can be replaced by a legal relationship agreed upon between him and the acquirer by virtue of which the acquirer demands indirect possession.

§ 931. If a third party is in possession of the object, the handing over of the object can be replaced by the owner assigning the acquirer the claim to return of the object. [Anspruch auf Herausgabe].

§ 932. (1) As a result of a transfer under § 929 the acquirer becomes owner even when the object did not belong to the transferor, unless he was not in good faith [in gutem Glauben] at the time he would acquire ownership under these provisions. In the case of § 929 second sentence, this applies only if the acquirer has acquired possession from the transferor.
(2) The acquirer is not in good faith if he knew or due to gross negligence did not know that the object did not belong to the transferor.

[§ 932a is omitted]

§ 933. If an object that is transferred under § 930 does not belong to the transferor, the acquirer will become owner when the object is handed over to him by the transferor, unless he is not in good faith at that moment.

§ 934. If an object that is transferred under § 931 does not belong to the transferor, the acquirer will become owner with the assignment of the claim, if the transferor is indirect possessor of the object, or else if he demands possession of the object from a third party, unless he is not in good faith at the time of the assignment of the claim or at the time of the acquisition of possession.

§ 935. (1) The acquisition of ownership on the basis of §§ 932 to 934 does not have effect, when the object was stolen from the owner, was lost or otherwise went astray. The same applies, if the owner was only indirect possessor, when the possessor lost the object.
(2) These provisions do not apply to money or bearer documents [Inhaberpapiere] or to objects that are transferred by way of a public auction.

[§ 936 is omitted.]

Sub-title 2. Acquisitive possession [Ersitzung]

§ 937. (1) A person who possesses a movable object for ten years for himself acquires the ownership of that object (acquisitive possession) [Ersitzung].
(2) Acquisitive possession is excluded, if the acquirer is not in good faith or if he later discovers the right of ownership does not belong to him.

[The remainder of Sub-title 2 and Subtitles 3 – 4 are omitted.]

Sub-title 5. Occupation/Taking of objects [Aneignung]

[§ 958 is omitted.]

§ 959. A movable object becomes without a master, when the owner gives up possession of the object with the intention to lose the right of ownership.

[Remainder of Sub-title 5 and Sub-title 6 are omitted.]

Title 4. Claims arising from ownership

§ 985. The owner may claim from the possessor return of the object [Herausgabeanspruch].

§ 986. (1) The possessor may refuse the return of the object, if he or the indirect possessor from whom he derives a right to possession is entitled to possession as against the owner. If the indirect possessor is not authorized as against the owner to grant possession to the possessor, the owner may require the possessor to return the object to the indirect possessor or, if he cannot or does not wish to resume possession, to himself.
(2) The possessor of an object that has been transferred under § 931 by assignment of the claim may raise against the new owner any defence available to him against the assigned claim.

[§§ 987 – 1003 are omitted.]

§ 1004. (1) If the ownership is interfered with in another way than by removal or retention of possession, the owner may require the removal of the interference from the interferer. If further interferences are to be feared, the owner may ask for injunction.

(2) The claim is excluded if the owner is obliged to tolerate the interference.

[§1005 is omitted.]

§ 1006. (1) In favour of the possessor of a movable object, it is presumed that he is the owner of the object. This does not apply, however, as against a former possessor from whom the object was stolen, or lost otherwise went astray, unless it concerns money or bearer documents.

(2) In favour of a former possessor, it is presumed that during the period of his possession he was the owner of the object.

(3) In the case of indirect possession, the presumption applies to the indirect possessor.

§ 1007. (1) A person who has had a movable object in his possession may require the return of the object from possessor if he was not in good faith in the acquisition of possession.

(2) If the object was stolen from the former possessor, or was lost or otherwise went astray, he may require return even from a possessor in good faith, unless the latter is the owner of the object or has lost possession before the former owner acquired possession. This provision does not apply to money and bearer documents.

(3) The claim is excluded if the former possessor was not in good faith on the acquisition of possession or if he has given up possession. Apart from this, the provisions of §§ 986 to 1003 apply mutatis mutandis.

[Title 5 is omitted.]

Division 4. Servitudes [Dienstbarkeiten]

Title 1. Real servitudes [Grunddienstbarkeiten]

§ 1018. A piece of land can, for the benefit of an owner of another piece of land, be burdened in such a way, that the owner may use this piece of land for specific purposes or that on the piece of land certain actions cannot be undertaken or that the exercise of a certain right which follows from the ownership of the burdened piece of land as against the other piece of land is excluded.

[The remainder of Title 1 is omitted.]

Title 2. Usufruct [Nießbrauch]

Sub-title 1. Usufruct of objects

§ 1030. (1) An object can be burdened in such a way, that the person for whose benefit this burdening occurs is entitled to the use of the object and to take the fruits (Usufruct) [Nießbrauch].

(2) The usufruct can be restricted by the exclusion of certain powers of use.

[§§ 1031 – 1035 are omitted.]

§ 1036. (1) The usufructuary [Nießbraucher] is entitled to possession of the object.

(2) In the exercise of his right of usufruct he must maintain the economic purpose of the object and must act according to the ordinary rules of business.

§ 1037. (1) The usufructuary is not entitled to transform [umzugestalten] the object or to change its nature.

(2) The usufructuary of a plot of land may erect new facilities to extract stone, gravel, sand, loam, clay, marl, peat and other components of the ground, except where the economic purpose of the plot of land is materially altered as a result.

[§§ 1038 – 1060 are omitted.]

§ 1061. The right of usufruct ceases to exist with the death of the usufructuary. When the right of usufruct is created for a legal person or a partnership with legal personality, it ceases to exist with these.

[§ 1062 is omitted.]

§ 1063. (1) The right of usufruct on a movable object ceases to exist, when it falls together with the right of ownership in the same person.

(2) The right of usufruct does not cease to exist in so far as the owner has a legal interest in the continuation of the usufruct.

§ 1064. In order to end a right of usufruct on a movable object by legal transaction, a declaration of the usufructuary to the owner or the person creating the right that he ends suffices.

[§§ 1065 – 1066 are omitted.]

§ **1067**. (1) If the right of usufruct is created on consumable objects, the usufructuary becomes the owner of those objects; after the termination of the right of usufruct, he must pay the creator of the right [Besteller] the value that the objects had at the time of creation of the right. Both the person creating the right and the holder of the right of usufruct can, at their own costs, ask an expert to determine the value of the object.
(2) The person creating the right can demand security when the claim for compensation of the value is endangered.

Sub-title 2. Usufruct of rights

§ **1068**. (1) The object on which the right of usufruct is created can also be a right.
(2) In so far as §§ 1069 to 1084 do not provide otherwise, the provisions on the right of usufruct on objects are applicable mutatis mutandis to the right of usufruct on rights.

§ **1069**. (1) The creation of a right of usufruct on a right occurs in accordance with the provisions applicable to the transfer of that right.
(2). A right of usufruct cannot be created on a right that cannot be transferred.

[§§ 1070 – 1073 are omitted.]

§ **1074**. The usufructuary on a claim is entitled to seize the claim and to cancellation, if the due date of a cancellation [Kündigung] depends on the creditor. He has to secure the orderly seizure. He is not entitled to dispose over the claim in any other way.

§ **1075**. (1) With the performance by the debtor to the usufructuary, the creditor receives the provided object and the usufructuary receives the usufruct on the object.
(2) If consumable objects are provided, the usufructuary acquires the right of ownership; the provision of § 1067 applies mutatis mutandis.

§ **1076**. If an outstanding debt receiving interest is the subject of the right of usufruct, the provisions of §§ **1077** to 1079 apply.

§ **1077**. (1) The debtor can only pay the capital to the usufructuary [Nießbraucher] and the creditor together. Each of them may request, that they will be paid together; each may demand instead of the payment a deposit for both.
(2) The usufructuary and the creditor can only cancel together. The cancellation of the debtor is only effective if it is declared to the usufructuary and the creditor.

§ **1078**. When the claim has become due, the usufructuary and the creditor are obliged to each other to cooperate with the payment of the claim. If the due date of the claim is dependent on a cancellation, each of them may require the cooperation of the other to the cancellation, if the payment of the claim is needed because, following the rules of normal management of assets [ordnungsmäßige Vermögensverwaltung], their security is endangered.

§ **1079**. The usufructuary and the creditor are obligated to each other to cooperate to ensure that the seized capital is invested to receive interest in accordance with the provisions applicable to the investment of ward money [Mündelgeld] and at the same time that the usufructuary receives his usufruct. The nature of the investment is determined by the usufructuary.

[§§ 1080 – 1089 are omitted.]

Title 3. Limited personal servitudes

§ **1090**. (1) A piece of land can be burdened in such a way, that the person, for whose benefit the right is created, is entitled to a specific use of the land or which grants him a power which can constitute the subject matter of a real servitude (limited personal servitude) [beschränkte persönliche Dienstbarkeit].

[The remainder of Title 3 is omitted.]

Division 5. Option to purchase [Vorkaufsrecht]

§ **1094**. (1) A piece of land can be burdened in such a way that the person, for whose benefit the right is created, is entitled as against the owner to an option to purchase.
(2) The right of pre-emption may also be created in favour of the respective owner of another piece of land.

[The remainder of Division 5 is omitted.]

Division 6. Real burdens [Reallasten]

§ **1105.** (1) A piece of land can be burdened in such a way that the person, for whose benefit the right is created, is entitled to receive recurrent performances from the piece of land (Real Burden) [Reallast]. As a part of the real burden, it can also be agreed that the performances that must be conducted on the land will, when on the basis of the contents of the agreement the nature and size of the burden on the land can be established, adapt itself, without further agreement, to changing circumstances.

[The remainder of Division 6 is omitted.]

Division 7. Hypothec, Land Charge [Grundschuld], and Annuity Charge [Rentenschuld]

Title 1. Hypothec

§ **1113.** (1) A piece of land can be burdened in such a way that the person, for whose benefit the right is created, is entitled to be paid a specific sum of money out of the land for satisfaction of a claim to which he is entitled (Hypothec) [Hypothek].
(2) The right of hypothec can also be created for a future or conditional claim [künftige oder bedingte Forderung].

§ **1114.** A share in a piece of land can, with the exception of the cases mentioned in § 3 sub-paragraph (6) of the Land Register Code, only be burdened with a right of hypothec, if it concerns a share in a co-ownership.

[§§ 1115 – 1146 are omitted.]

§ **1147.** The satisfaction of the creditor out of the land and its belongings [Gegenständen] to which the right of hypothec applies, occurs by way of compulsory execution.

[§§ 1148 – 1152 are omitted.]

§ **1153.** (1) With the assignment of the claim, the right of hypothec is transferred to the new creditor.
(2). The claim cannot be assigned without the right of hypothec, the right of hypothec cannot be assigned without the claim.

[§§ 1154 – 1161 are omitted.]

§ **1162.** If the hypothec-document [Hypothekenbrief] is lost or destroyed, it can, under the cancellation proceedings [Aufgebotverfahrens], be declared to be without effect.

[§§ 1163 – 1180 are omitted.]

§ **1181.** (1) If the creditor is satisfied from the piece of land, the right of hypothec ceases to exist.
(2) If the satisfaction of the creditor is made from one of the pieces of land that is burdened with a co-entitled hypothec [Gesamthypothec], the other pieces of land are also freed.
(3) The satisfaction out of the piece of land is equal to the satisfaction out of the belongings to which the right of hypothec applies.

[§ 1182 is omitted.]

§ **1183.** The permission of the owner is needed for the ending [Aufhebung] by a legal transaction of a right of hypothec. The permission must be declared to the land registration office or to the creditor; it cannot be withdrawn.]

[The remainder of Title 1 is omitted.]

Title 2. Land Charge [Grundschuld], Annuity Charge [Rentenschuld]

Sub-title 1. Grundschuld

§ **1191.** (1) A piece of land can be burdened in such a way, that the person for whose benefit the right is created is entitled to receive a specific sum of money out of the piece of land (Grundschuld).
(2) The right can also be created in such a way that interest from the sum of money or other secondary performances are to be paid arising from the piece of land.

§ **1192.** (1) The provisions on the right of hypothec are applicable mutatis mutandis to the *Grundschuld*, unless otherwise follows from the fact that the *Grundschuld* does not require a claim.

(1a) If the *Grundschuld* has been procured so as to provide security for a claim [Sicherungsgrundschuld], defences which are available to the owner on the basis of the security agreement with the previous creditor or which arise from the security agreement may also be opposed to any purchaser of the *Grundschuld*; § 1157 sentence 2 does not apply in this respect. For the remainder, § 1157 remains unaffected.
(2) The provisions on interest on the claim arising from the right of hypothec are applicable to interest on the *Grundschuld*.

[§§ 1193 – 1198 are omitted.]

Sub-title 2. Rentenschuld

§ 1199. (1) A *Grundschuld* can be created in such a way that on regular and recurrent dates a certain sum of money arising from the piece of land must be paid [Rentenschuld].
(2) When the *Rentenschuld* is created, the amount of money by which the *Rentenschuld* can be redeemed must be determined. This redemption sum must be entered into the land registry.

[The remainder of Sub-title 2 is omitted.]

Division 8. Right of pledge on movable objects and on rights

Title. 1. Right of pledge on movable objects

§ 1204. (1) In order to secure a claim, a movable object can be burdened in such a way that the creditor is entitled to satisfaction of his claim from the object (right of pledge) [Pfandrecht].
(2) The right of pledge can also be created for a future claim or conditional claim.

§ 1205. (1) To create a right of pledge it is necessary that the owner hands over the object to the creditor and both must agree, that the creditor will have a right of pledge. If the creditor is in possession of the object, it suffices that the parties agree on the creation of a right of pledge.
(2) The transfer of an object in the indirect possession of the owner can be replaced in such a way that the owner transfers indirect possession to the creditor of the pledge and notifies the possessor of taking away the existence of the pledge.

[§§ 1206 – 1227 are omitted.]

§ 1228. (1) The satisfaction of the creditor of the pledge is effected through a sale.

(2) The creditor of the pledge is entitled to sell, as soon as the claim has become completely or partially due. If the secured object is not money, the sale is only allowed once the claim is transformed into a monetary claim.

§ 1229. An agreement reached before the occurrence of the right to sell, according to which ownership of the object devolves on or will be transferred to the creditor of the pledge, if he is not satisfied or not satisfied on time, is void.

[§§ 1230 – 1249 are omitted.]

§ 1250. (1) With the assignment of the claim, the right of pledge is transferred to the new creditor. The right of pledge cannot be transferred without the claim.
(2) If the assignment of the claim excludes the transfer of the right pledge, the right pledge ceases to exist.

[§ 1251 is omitted.]

§ 1252. The right of pledge ceases to exist with the claim for which it was created.

§ 1253. (1) The right of pledge ceases to exist if the creditor of the pledge returns the object to the pledgor or to the owner. A stipulation that the right of pledge will continue to exist is ineffective.
(2) If the object under pledge is in possession of the pledgor or of the owner, it is presumed that the object was returned to him by the creditor of the pledge. The presumption also applies, if the object under pledge is in possession of a third party who demanded possession of the object from the pledgor or the owner after the creation of the right of pledge.

[§ 1254 is omitted.]

§ 1255. (1) For the ending [Aufhebung] by legal transaction of a right of pledge, a declaration by the creditor of the pledge to the pledgor or to the owner that he abandons his right, suffices.

(2) If the right of pledge is burdened with a right of a third party, the permission of that third party is required. The permission is to be declared to the person, for whose benefit it is made; it cannot be withdrawn.

§ 1256. (1) The right of pledge ceases to exist when it falls together with the right of ownership into the same hands. The right does not cease to exist as long as the claim, for which the right of pledge exists, is burdened with a right of a third party.
(2) The right of pledge is considered not to have ceased to exist, in so far as the owner has a legal interest in the continuation of the right.

[The remainder of Title 1 is omitted.]

Title 2. Right of Pledge on rights

[§ 1273 is omitted.]

§ 1274. (1) The creation of a right of pledge on a right is effected according to the provisions applicable to the transfer of rights. If the handing over of the object is necessary for the transfer of the right, the provisions of §§ 1205, 1206 apply.
(2) To the extent a right cannot be transferred, a right of pledge cannot be created on that right.

[The remainder of Title 2 and Titles 3 – 5 are omitted.]

Title 6. Matrimonial Property Rights

[Sub-title 1 is omitted.]

Sub-title 2. Contractual Property Rights

Chapter 1. General provisions

§ 1408. (1) The spouses may provide for their matrimonial property arrangements by contract (marriage contract), and in particular even after entering into marriage terminate or alter the matrimonial property regime.
(2) If the spouses conclude agreements on the equalisation of pension rights in a marriage contract, §§ 6 and 8 of the Equalisation of Pension Rights Act are applicable in this respect.

[§ 1409 is omitted.]

§ 1410. The marriage contract must be recorded by a notary in the presence of both parties.

[The remainder of Book 3 is omitted.]

Book 4. Family Law

[Division 1 is omitted.]

Division 2. Relationship

[Title 1 is omitted.]

Title 2. Descent

§ 1591. The mother of a child is the woman who has given birth to it.

[The remainder of Division 2 is omitted.]

Division 3. Guardianship, legal curatorship, custodianship

[Title 1 is omitted.]

Title 2. Legal custodianship

§ 1896. (1) If a person of full age, by reason of a mental illness or a physical, mental or psychological handicap, cannot in whole or in part take care of his affairs, the custodianship court, on his application or of its own motion, appoints a custodian for him. The application may also be made by a person incapable of contracting. To the extent that the person of full age cannot take care of his affairs by reason of a physical handicap, the custodian may be appointed only on the application of the person of full age, unless the person is unable to make his will known.
(1a) A custodian may not be appointed against the free will of the person of full age.

(2) A custodian may be appointed only for groups of tasks in which the custodianship is necessary. The custodianship is not necessary to the extent that the affairs of a person of full age may be taken care of by an authorised person who is not one of the persons set out in § 1897 (3), or by other assistants for whom no legal representative is appointed, just as well as by a custodian.

(3) The assertion of rights of the person under custodianship vis-à-vis the person authorised by him may also be defined as a group of tasks.

(4) The decision on the telecommunications of the person under custodianship and on the receipt, opening and withholding of his post are included in the group of tasks of the custodian only if the court has expressly ordered this.

[§§ 1897 – 1902 are omitted.]

§ 1903. (1) To the extent that this is necessary to prevent a substantial danger for the person or the property of the person under custodianship, the custodianship court orders that the person under custodianship requires the consent of the custodian for a declaration of intent that relates to the group of tasks of the custodian (reservation of consent). §§ 108 - 113, 131 (2), and section 210 apply mutatis mutandis.

(2) A reservation of consent may not extend to

1. declarations of intent directed towards the entering into a marriage or life partnership,

2. dispositions upon death,

3. the contestation of a contract of inheritance,

4. the rescission of a contract of inheritance by contract, and

5. to declarations of intent for which a person of limited legal capacity does not require the consent of his legal representative pursuant to books 4 and 5.

(3) Where a reservation of consent is ordered, the custodian nevertheless does not require the consent of his custodian if the declaration of intent merely confers a legal advantage on the person under custodianship. To the extent that the court does not order otherwise, this also applies if the declaration of intent relates to a trivial matter of everyday life.

(4) §1901 (5) applies mutatis mutandis.

[The remainder of Book 4 is omitted.]

Book 5. Law of succession

[Divisions 1 and 2 are omitted.]

Division 3. Will

[Titles 1 – 6 are omitted.]

Title 7. The drafting and revocation of a will

[§ 2229 is omitted.]

§ 2230. (Repealed)

§ 2231. A will may be made in regular form

1. by declaration for record to a notary,

2. by a declaration made by the testator in accordance with § 2247.

§ 2232. A will made by declaration to a notary is made by the testator declaring his last will to the notary or handing the notary a document with the statement that the document contains his last will. The testator may hand over the document either unsealed or sealed; it is not required to be written by him.

§§ 2234 – 2346. (Repealed)

§ 2247. (1) The testator may make a will by a declaration written and signed in his own hand.

(2) The testator should state in the declaration the time when (day, month and year) and the place where he wrote it down.

(3) The signature should contain the first name and the last name of the testator. If the testator signs in another manner and this signature suffices to establish the identity of the testator and the seriousness of his declaration, such a signature does not invalidate the will.

(4) A person who is a minor or is incapable of reading text may not make a will in accordance with foregoing.

(5) Where a will made under sub-paragraph (1) does not contain any information about the time when

it was made and where this causes doubt as to its validity, the will is to be deemed valid only if the necessary ascertainment about the time when it was made can be established in some other manner. The same applies with the necessary modifications to a will that does not contain any information about the place where it was made.

[The remainder of the BGB is omitted.]

Miscellaneous Private Law Statutes and Codes*

Authentication Act [Beurkundungsgesetz (BeurkG)] of 28 August 1969 (BGBl. I p. 1513), as amended by article 10 of the statute of 18 December 2018 (BGBl. I p. 2639). Selected provision: § 17.

§ 17. (1) The notary must ascertain the will of the parties involved, clarify the facts, inform the parties involved of the legal consequences of the transaction and record their statements in a clear and unequivocal manner in writing. In doing so, he must take care that errors and doubts are avoided, and that inexperienced and inexpert parties are not disadvantaged.

(2) Where there is doubt whether the transaction is in conformity with the law or with the true will of the parties involved, these concerns must be discussed with parties. Where the notary is in doubt as to the effectiveness of the transaction and the parties involved insist on authentication, he must make a note of having informed parties, and of their statements in response, in the written record.

(2a) The notary must conduct the authentication procedure in such a way that the observance of the duties pursuant to sub-paragraphs (1) and (2) is warranted. In case of consumer contracts, the notary must seek to ensure that

1. the legally relevant statements of the consumer are made by the latter personally or by a person of trust in the presence of the notary, and

2. the consumer has sufficient opportunity to look into the subject of authentication in advance; in case of consumer contract subject to the obligation of authentication pursuant to § 311b sub-paragraph (1) sentence 1 and sub-paragraph (3) of the Civil Code [BGB], the consumer must be provided with the intended text of the transaction by the authenticating notary or by a notary with whom the authenticating notary has entered a professional association. As a rule, this must be effected two weeks prior to authentication. Where it is effected less than two weeks prior to authentication, the reasons for this must be stated in the written record.

Further official duties of the notary remain unaffected.

(3) Where foreign law must be applied or where this is a matter of uncertainty, the notary must bring this to the intention of the parties involved and make a note thereof in the written record. He is not obliged to inform parties of the content of foreign legal orders.

Code of Civil Procedure [Zivilprozessordnung (ZPO)] of 12 September 1950, as last amended by Article 11 of the statute of 18 December 2018 (BGBl. I p. 2639). Selected provisions: §§ 851, 869, 883(1), 887 and 888.

§ 851. (1) A claim is, in the absence of special provisions, only subject to a right of pledge if it can be assigned.

(2) A claim that cannot be assigned according to §399 of the Civil Code can in so far be subject to a right of pledge and to forced payment [Einziehung] if the subject matter of the claim [geschuldeter Gegenstand] is subject of the pledge.

§ 869. The compulsory auction [Zwangsversteigerung] and the forced administration [Zwangsverwaltung] are regulated by special laws.

§ 887. (1) If the debtor does not fulfil the duty to perform an act, the performance of which can be effected by a third party, the creditor can, on authority of the court of first instance [Prozessgericht des ersten Rechtszuges], granted on request, have the act performed at the expense of the debtor.

(2) The creditor can request at the same time that the debtor be ordered to pay in advance the costs that will accrue from the performance of the act, without prejudice to the right to claim extra payment, if the performance of the act leads to greater expenditure.

(3) These provisions do not apply to the compulsory enforcement [Zwangsvollstreckung] for the return or provision of objects.

§ 888. (1) If an act cannot be carried out by a third party, where it exclusively depends on the will of the debtor, on application to be recognized by the court of first instance [Prozessgericht des ersten Rechtszuges], the debtor can be exhorted to perform the act through a fine and, in the situation that

---

* Translations by Nicole Kornet, Sascha Hardt, Bram Akkermans, Heike Hauröder, and Anna Berlee.

this cannot be collected, by imprisonment or by imprisonment. A single fine may not exceed 25.000 Euros. The provisions of the fourth section on detention apply mutatis mutandis to the imprisonment.
(2) A threat of the sanctions does not take place.
(3) These provisions do not apply in the case of an order to perform services under an employment contract.

Superficies Act [Gesetz über das Erbbaurecht (ErbbauRG)] of 15 January 1919, as last amended by Article 4 (7) of the statute of 1 October 2013 (BGBl. I p. 3719). Selected provision: § 1.

§ 1. A piece of land can be burdened in such a way that the person, for whose benefit the land is burdened, reserves the right to have a building on or under the surface of a piece of land, which can be transferred and passed on by succession (superficies) [Erbbaurecht].

Ownership of an Apartment and Long Term Tenancy Act [Gesetz über das Wohnungseigentum und das Dauerwohnrecht [Wohnungseigentumsgesetz (WoEigG)] of 15 March 1951, last amended by Article 4 of the statute of 05 December 2014 (BGBl. I p. 1962), selected provision: § 1.

§ 1. (1) Under this act, apartments can be burdened with a right of ownership of apartment, parts of a building that are not suitable for habitation, can be burdened with a right of co-ownership of a part.
(2) The ownership of an apartment is the exclusive ownership of an apartment in combination with a co-ownership share in the common ownership, to which it belongs.

Commercial Code [Handelsgesetzbuch (HGB)] of 10 May 1897, as last amended by Article 3 of the statute of 10 July 2018 (BGBl. I p. 1102). Selected provision: §§ 348, 350, 354a, and 369.

§ 348. A contractual penalty, promised by a merchant in the operation of his commercial business, cannot be reduced on the basis of § 343 of the Civil Code [BGB].

§ 350. With regard to a suretyship, a promise of debt [Schuldversprechen], or an acknowledgement of debt [Schuldanerkenntnis], the formal requirements of § 766 sentence 1 and 2, § 780 and § 781 sentence 1 and 2 of the Civil Code [BGB] do not apply as far as the surety on the part of the guarantor, the promise or acknowledgement on the part of the debtor, is a commercial transaction.

§ 354a. (1) If the transfer of a monetary claim has been excluded by agreement with the debtor under § 399 of the German Civil Code and the legal transaction that created this claim is a commercial transaction for both parties, or the debtor is a public legal person [juristische Person des öffentlichen Rechts] or a public separated set of assets and debt [öffentlich-rechtliches Sondervermögen], the transfer is nevertheless valid. The debtor may however satisfy the claim to the previous creditor. Agreements to the contrary are ineffective.
(2) Sub-paragraph (1) does not apply to a claim from a loan agreement whose creditor is a bank [Kreditinstitut] within the meaning of the Banking Act [Kreditwesengesetz].

§ 369. (1) A merchant has a right of lien, in respect of claims against another merchant due and owing to him arising out of their mutual commercial dealings, over movable goods and securities belonging to the debtor which have come into his possession with the debtor's consent in connection with commercial transactions, as far as they are still in his possession, in particular by virtue of a right of disposal under a bill of lading or warehouse receipt. The right of lien also exists where title to the article in question has passed from the debtor to the creditor or has been transferred to the creditor by a third party on the debtor's behalf but is subject to an obligation to transfer title back to the debtor.
(2) The right of lien is effective against a third party insofar as the grounds upon which the debtor's claim to recover possession of the article is denied can also be relied upon against that third party.
(3) The right of lien is excluded if retention of possession of the object is contrary to an instruction given by the debtor before or upon transferring possession or an obligation entered into by the creditor to deal with the article in a particular manner.
(4) The debtor can avoid the exercise of the right of lien by giving security for his debt. Security for this purpose shall not include a surety by a third party.

Compulsory Auction and Compulsory Administration Act [Gesetz über die Zwangsversteigerung und die Zwangsverwaltung (ZVG)] of 24 March 1897, as last amended by Article 9 of the statute of 24 May 2016 (BGBl. I p. 1217). Selected provision: § 15.

§ 15. The compulsory auction [Zwangsversteigerung] of a piece of land is ordered by the insolvency court upon request.

Insolvency Code [Insolvenzordnung (InsO)] of 5 October 1994, as last amended by Article 3 of the statute of 23 June 2007 (BGBl. I p. 1693). Selected provisions: §§ 47, 51, 115 and 116.

§ 47. A person who on the basis of a right in rem or in personam is entitled to claim that an object does not belong to the assets involved in the insolvency proceedings [Insolvenzmasse], is not a creditor of the insolvency proceedings. His claim to separation of the object is governed by the laws that apply outside the insolvency proceedings.

§ 51. The creditors mentioned in § 50 are equal to:
1. creditors, to whom a debtor, to secure the performance of a claim, transferred a movable object or a assigned a right;
2. creditors, who are entitled to a right of retention to an object, because they have used something for the benefit of the object, in so far as their claim for that use does not supersede the benefit.
3. creditors, who are entitled to a right of retention under the commercial code [Handelsgesetz]
4. The Federation [Bund], States [Länder], municipalities and associations thereof [Gemeindeverbände], in so far as objects subject to custom duties and taxation serve them as security for public dues in accordance with statutory provisions.

§ 115. (1) Any mandate ordered by the debtor referring to the property forming part of the assets involved in the insolvency proceedings shall expire upon the opening of the insolvency proceedings.
(2) If suspension of such mandate would cause a risk, the mandatory shall continue to perform the mandated transaction until the insolvency administrator is able to otherwise take care of any such transaction himself. For this purpose, the mandate shall be deemed to continue. The mandatory may claim reimbursement of his expenses incurred for such continuation as a creditor of the assets involved in the insolvency proceedings.
(3) As long as the mandatory is not at fault in being unaware of the opening of insolvency proceedings, he shall benefit from the presumption that the mandate continues. The mandatory shall rank among the creditors of the insolvency proceedings with his reimbursement claims arising from such continuation.

§ 116. If anyone is obligated under a service or work contract with the debtor to manage a business transaction for the latter, § 115 shall apply mutatis mutandis. The provision governing reimbursement claims arising from a continuation of such management contract shall also apply to claims to remuneration. Sentence 1 is not applicable to payment orders, as well as to orders between payment service providers or intermediate bodies and to orders for the transfer of securities [Wertpapiere]; these continue to have effect on the estate [Masse].

Road Traffic Act [Straßenverkehrsgesetz (StVG)] of 5 March 2003, as last amended by Article 3 of the statute of 4 December 2018 (BGBl. I p. 2251). Selected provisions: Division II (§§ 7 – 20)

II. Liability

§ 7. (1) If in the course of the operation of a motor vehicle or a trailer that is meant to go with a vehicle, a person is killed, the body or the health of a person injured, or an object damaged, the keeper is obliged to compensate the injured person for the damage resulting therefrom.
(2) The duty to compensate is excluded if the accident is caused by force majeure [höhere Gewalt].
(3) If somebody uses the vehicle without the knowledge and consent of the keeper of the vehicle, then the user is obliged to compensate the damage in the place of the keeper; in addition, the keeper remains obliged to compensate the damage if the use of the vehicle was made possible by his fault. The first sentence does not apply if the user was employed by the keeper of vehicle to operate the motor vehicle or if the keeper entrusted him with the vehicle. Sentences 1 and 2 are to be applied mutatis mutandis to the use of a trailer.

§ 8. The provisions of § 7 do not apply,

1. if the accident was caused by a motor vehicle that cannot travel on level ground at a speed higher than twenty kilometres per hour, or by a trailer connected to such a vehicle at the time of the accident,

2. if the injured person was involved in the operation the motor vehicle or the trailer, or

3. if an object has been damaged which was being transported by the motor vehicle or by a trailer connected to it, unless a person who is being transported is carrying the object on him or has it with him.

§ 8a. In case of remunerated commercial transport of persons, the duty of the keeper to pay compensation under § 7 for the death or injury of persons transported can be neither excluded nor limited. The commercial character of a transport of persons is not excluded by the fact that the transport is performed by a corporation or institution under public law.

§ 9. If a fault of the injured party contributed to the causation of the damage, the provisions of § 254 BGB apply providing that in case of damage to an object the fault of that person who exercises actual control over the object is the equivalent of the fault of the injured party.

§ 10. (1) In the case of death, the damages to be paid comprise compensation for the expenses of an attempted cure as well as the economic loss [Vermögensnachteil] which the deceased has suffered because during the illness his earning capacity was destroyed or reduced or because his needs were increased. The person liable to pay damages must also reimburse the cost of the burial to the person with whom the duty lies to bear these costs.

(2) If at the time of the injury the deceased stood in a relationship to a third person by virtue of which he was bound by law to maintain this person, or might become so bound, and if as a result of the death the third person has lost the right to maintenance, the person liable to pay compensation must pay damages to the third person to the extent that the deceased would have been obliged to pay maintenance during the probable duration of his life. The duty to compensate also arises if the third person was conceived at the time of the injury but had not yet been born.

(3) The person under the duty to compensate must pay to a survivor [Hinterbliebener] who stood in a relationship of particular personal proximity to the person killed an appropriate compensation in money for the emotional suffering caused to that survivor. A relationship of particular personal proximity is deemed to exist where the survivor was the spouse, the life partner, a parent, or a child of the person killed.

§ 11. In the case of injury to the body or to health, the damages to be paid comprise compensation for the expenses of the cure and for the economic loss which the injured party suffered because as a result of the injury his earning capacity was temporarily or permanently destroyed or reduced or because his needs were increased. For the damage which is not economic loss, an equitable compensation in money may also be claimed.

§ 12. (1) The person under a duty to compensate is liable to pay

1. in case of the death or injury of one or more persons in the same event, a total amount of no more than five million Euro, in case of causation of the damage by the use of a highly or fully automatized driving function within the meaning of § 1a a total amount of no more than ten million Euro; in case of a remunerated commercial transport of persons this amount increases for the keeper of the transporting motor vehicle or trailer who is under a duty to compensate in case of death or injury of more than eight transported persons with 600,000 Euro for each further person killed or injured who was transported;

2. in case of damage to an object, even if several objects are damaged in the same event, a total amount of no more than one million Euro, in case of causation of the damage by the use of a highly or fully automatized driving function within the meaning of § 1a a total amount of no more than two million Euro.

The maximum amounts in the first sentence under 1 also apply to the capital value of an annuity [Geldrente] to be paid as compensation.

(2) If the compensation to be paid to several claimants on the basis of the same event exceeds in total the maximum amount enumerated in paragraph 1, the damages payable to each individual are reduced in proportion of the total in relation to the maximum amount.

§ 12a. (1) If dangerous goods are transported, the person bound to pay compensation is liable to pay

1. in case of the death or injury of one or more persons a total sum of no more than ten million Euros,

2. in case of damage to immovable objects, even if several objects are damaged in the same event, a total sum of no more than ten million Euros,

in so far as the damage is caused by the characteristics which make the transported goods dangerous. In other respects, § 12 paragraph 1 remains unaffected.

(2) Dangerous goods within the meaning of this act are substances and objects [Gegenstände] the transportation of which on the road is forbidden, or allowed only under certain conditions, in accordance with Annexes A and B to the European Convention of 30 September 1957 on the International Carriage of Dangerous Goods by Road (ADR) (reference omitted) in the version applying at that time.

(3) Paragraph 1 is not to be applied in the case of exempted transports of dangerous goods or transports in limited quantities within in the limits laid down in table 1.1.3.6 to the in paragraph 2 mentioned Convention.

(4) Paragraph 1 is not to be applied when the damage occurred during transport within a business in which dangerous goods are produced, treated, processed, stored, used or destroyed, in so far as the transport takes place on a self-contained site.

(5) § 12 para 2 applies mutatis mutandis.

§ 12b. §§ 12 and 12a are not to be applied when damage is caused by the operation of an armoured caterpillar vehicle.

§ 13. (1) Damages in respect of the loss or the reduction of earning capacity or because the needs of the injured person have increased as well as the damages due to a third person under **§ 10**, paragraph 2 is for the future to be made by way of payment of an annuity [Geldrente].

(2) The provisions of § 843 paragraphs 2 to 4 of the BGB apply mutatis mutandis.

(3) If at the time when the judgment ordering the obligor to pay an annuity the provision of security was not ordered, the person entitled to the payment may demand security nevertheless, if the financial circumstances of the obligor have worsened considerably; under the same circumstances he can demand an increase of the security fixed by the judgment.

§ 14. For prescription, the provisions in the Civil Code concerning the prescription in case of wrongful acts apply mutatis mutandis.

§ 15. The person entitled to damages forfeits the rights granted by the provisions of this act, if he does not give notice of the accident to the person bound to pay compensation within two months after having ascertained the damage and the identity of the person bound to pay compensation. Forfeiture does not take place if the failure to give notice was due to circumstances for which the person entitled to damages is not responsible or if the person bound to pay compensation has knowledge of the accident through other means within the designated period.

§ 16. Any Federal provisions according to which the keeper of the vehicle is more extensively liable for damage caused by the vehicle than according to the provisions of this act or according to which another person is responsible for the damage remain unaffected.

§ 17. (1) If damage is caused by several motor vehicles and if the keepers of the vehicles involved are bound by law to pay compensation to a third party, the duty of the keepers of the vehicles to pay compensation and the extent of the compensation to be paid as between themselves depends upon the circumstances, especially whether the damage has been caused predominantly by one or the other of the parties.

(2) If one of the keepers of the vehicles involved suffers the damage, paragraph (1) also applies to the liability among the keepers of the vehicles.

(3) The duty to compensate according to paragraphs (1) and (2) is excluded if the accident was caused by an unavoidable event which is neither due to a defect in the construction of the vehicle nor to the failure of its equipment. An event is only deemed unavoidable if the keeper as well as the driver of the vehicle each observed the necessary care in the circumstances of the case. The exclusion also applies to the duty to compensate as against the owner of a motor vehicle who is not a keeper.

(4) The provisions of paragraphs (1) to (3) apply mutatis mutandis if the damage is caused by a motor vehicle and a trailer, by a motor vehicle and an animal, or by a motor vehicle and a train.

§ 18. (1) In the situations covered by § 7 paragraph 1, the driver of the motor vehicle or the trailer is also bound to pay compensation for the damage in accordance with the provisions of §§ 8 to 15. The duty to compensate is excluded if the damage was not caused by a fault of the driver.

(2) The provisions of § 16 apply mutatis mutandis.

(3) If in the situations covered by § 17 the driver of a motor vehicle or trailer is also bound to pay compensation for the damage, the provisions of § 17 are to be applied mutatis mutandis to this duty in his relationship with the keepers and drivers of the other motor vehicles involved, with the

keepers and drivers of the other trailers involved, with the keeper of the animal or with the railway undertaking.

§ 19. (Repealed.)

§ 20. Claims based on this act also fall within the jurisdiction of the court of the district in which the event occurred which caused the damage.

Limited Liability Company Act [Gesetz betreffend die Gesellschaften mit beschränkter Haftung (GmbHG)] of 20 April 1892, as amended by Article 10 of the statute of 17 July 2017 (BGBl. I p. 2446). Selected provisions: §§ 6, 35, 37, 43 (1) and (2), 64, and 84.

§ 6. (1) The company must have one or more managing directors [Geschäftsführer].
(2) The managing director can only be a natural person being of unrestricted legal capacity. Managing director cannot be he who
1. as a person under guardianship is entirely or partially subject to a reservation of consent [Einwillingungsvorbehalt] (§1903 Civil Code) in providing for his financial matters,
2. on the basis of a court order or an executable decision of an administrative authority, is not permitted to exercise a profession, a professional sector, a trade, or a branch of trade, in so far as the object of the business coincides entirely or partially with the object of the prohibition.
3. has been convicted of one or more intentionally committed criminal offences
a. of failure to file an application for the opening of insolvency proceedings [Insolvenzverschleppung],
b. pursuant to §§283 to 283d of the Criminal Code (insolvency crimes),
c. of making false statements pursuant to §82 of this act or §399 of the Stock Corporations Act [Aktiengesetz].
d. of misrepresentation pursuant to §400 of the Stock Corporations Act [Aktiengesetz], §331 of the Commercial Code [Handelsgesetzbuch, HGB], §313 of the Act on the Transformation of Companies [Umwandlungsgesetz], or §17 of the Disclosure Act [Publizitätsgesetz], or
e. pursuant to §§263 to 264a or §265b to §266a of the Criminal Code
and given a custodial sentence of at least one year; this exclusion applies for a period of five years from the judgment becoming legally effective, not including the time during which the offender has been kept in custody upon an official order.
Sentence 2 no. 3 applies mutatis mutandis to a conviction abroad of an offence which is comparable to the offences mentioned in sentence 2 no. 3.
(3) Shareholders [Gesellschafter] or other persons can be appointed as managing directors. The appointment is effected either in the articles of association [Gesellschaftsvertrag] or in compliance with the provisions of the third division [§§35-52].
(4) If the articles of association [Gesellschaftsvertrag] stipulate that all shareholders should be entitled to direct the company, then only those individuals who belong to the company at the time of this stipulation are deemed appointed directors.
(5) Shareholders who intentionally or grossly negligently leave the management to a person, who cannot be a director, are jointly [solidarisch] liable for the damage caused by any violation by this person of the obligations towards the company.

§ 35. (1) The company is represented judicially and extra-judicially by the managing directors. If a company does not have a managing director (lack of leadership) [Führungslosigkeit], the company is, in the event that declarations of intent are made or documents are served to it, represented by the shareholders.
(2) If several managing directors have been appointed, they are all only jointly competent to represent the company, unless the articles of association stipulate otherwise. If a declaration of intent is to be made to the company, making it to one of the representatives of the company pursuant to sub-paragraph (1) is sufficient. Declarations of intent can be made and written documents for the company can be served to the representatives of the company pursuant to sub-paragraph (1) at the business address registered with the Commercial Register [Handelsregister]. Irrespective thereof, the making of declarations of intent and the serving of documents can also take place at the registered address of the person authorized to receive pursuant to §10 sub-paragraph (2) sentence 2.
(3) If all shares of the company are in the hands of one shareholder or besides him in the hands of the company and if, at the same time, he is the sole managing director, §181 of the Civil Code applies to his legal transactions with the company. Legal transactions between him and the company which he represents must, without delay after their performance, recorded in writing.

§ 37. (1) The managing directors are obliged vis-à-vis the company to observe any restrictions of the scope of their competence to represent the company that have been stipulated by the articles of association or, in so far as the latter do not provide otherwise, by the decisions of the shareholders.
(2) A restriction of the competence of the managing director to represent the company does not have legal effect against third persons. This applies in particular in the case that the representation only extends to certain transactions or types of transactions or should only take place under certain circumstances or for a certain time or in particular places, or that the consent of the shareholders or of an organ of the company is required for individual transactions.

§ 43. (1) The managing directors must exercise the due care of a prudent businessman [ordentilcher Geschäftsmann] in matters concerning the company.
(2) Managing directors who violate their obligations are held severally liable to the company for the damage caused.

[sub-paragraphs 3 and 4 are omitted.]

§ 64. The managing directors are obliged to compensate the company for payments made after the occurrence of the inability to pay [Zahlungsunfähigkeit] of the company or after the declaration of its insolvency [Überschuldung]. This does not apply to payments which, even after this point in time, are compatible with the care of a prudent businessman. The same obligation applies to the managing directors regarding payments made to shareholders, in so far as these payments had to lead to the company's inability to pay, unless this was unforeseeable despite observance of the due care referred to in sentence 2. The provisions of §43 sub-paragraph (3) and (4) apply mutatis mutandis to the claim for compensation.

§84. (1) He who, as a managing director, fails to notify the shareholders of a loss amount to half of the share capital is punished with imprisonment of up to three years or a fine.
(2) If the offender acts negligently, the punishment is imprisonment of up to one year or a fine.

Public Company Act [Aktiengesetz (AktG)] of 6 September 1965 (BGBl. I p. 1089), as last amended by art 9 of the statute of 17 July 2017 (BGBl. I p. 2446). Selected provisions: §§ 76 – 78, 82, 93, and 148.

§ 76. (1) The management board [Vorstand] is to manage [leiten] the company under its own responsibility.
(2) The management board may be composed of one or more persons. For corporations with an initial capital of more than three million Euros, it must be composed of at least two persons, unless the articles of association [Satzung] provide that it consists of one person. The provisions regarding the appointment of an labour relations director [Arbeitsdirektor] remain unaffected.
(3) Member of the management board can only be a natural person of unrestricted legal capacity. Member of the management board cannot be he who,
1. as a person under guardianship is entirely or partially subject to a reservation of consent [Einwillingungsvorbehalt] (§1903 Civil Code) in providing for his financial matters,
2. on the basis of a court order or an executable decision of an administrative authority, is not permitted to exercise a profession, a professional sector, a trade, or a branch of trade, in so far as the object of the business coincides entirely or partially with the object of the prohibition.
3. has been convicted of one or more intentionally committed criminal offences
a. of failure to file an application for the opening of insolvency proceedings [Insolvenzverschleppung],
b. pursuant to §§283 to 283d of the Criminal Code (insolvency crimes),
c. of making false statements pursuant to §82 of this act or §399 of the Stock Corporations Act [Aktiengesetz].
d. of misrepresentation pursuant to §400 of the Stock Corporations Act [Aktiengesetz], §331 of the Commercial Code [Handelsgesetzbuch, HGB], §313 of the Act on the Transformation of Companies [Umwandlungsgesetz], or §17 of the Disclosure Act [Publizitätsgesetz], or
e. pursuant to §§263 to 264a or §265b to §266a of the Criminal Code
and given a custodial sentence of at least one year; this exclusion applies for a period of five years from the judgment becoming legally effective, not including the time during which the offender has been kept in custody upon an official order.
Sentence 2 no. 3 applies mutatis mutandis to a conviction abroad of an offence which is comparable

to the offences mentioned in sentence 2 no. 3.

(4) The management board of companies that are listed on the stock exchange or subject to workers' participation sets targets for the proportion of women in the two levels of management below the management board. Where the proportion of women is lower than 30 per cent at the time of setting the targets, the targets may no longer fall short of the proportion achieved respectively. At the same time, periods of time must be set within which the targets are to be met. These periods of time may not be longer than five years respectively.

§ 77. (1) If the management board is composed of several persons, all members of the management board are only jointly competent to manage the corporation. The articles of association or the rules of procedure of the management board may provide otherwise; it may not be stipulated, however, that one or more members of the management board settle disagreements in the management board against the majority of its members.

(2) The management board may adopt rules of procedure for itself, provided that the articles of association did not confer the task of issuing the rules of procedure to the supervisory board [Aufsichtsrat] and that the supervisory board has not issued rules of procedure for the management board. The articles of association may govern individual questions regarding the rules of procedure in a binding way. Decisions of the management board about the rules of procedure must be taken unanimously.

§ 78. (1) The management board represents the corporation judicially and extra-judicially. If a corporation does not have a management board (lack of leadership) [Führungslosigkeit], the corporation is, in the event that declarations of intent are made or documents are served to it, represented by the supervisory board.

(2) If the management board is composed of several persons, they are all only jointly competent to represent the corporation, unless the articles of association stipulate otherwise. If a declaration of intent is to be made to the corporation, making it to one of the members of the management board or, in the case of sub-paragraph (1) sentence 2, to one of the members of the supervisory board is sufficient. Declarations of intent can be made and written documents for the corporation can be served to the representatives of the corporation pursuant to sub-paragraph (1) at the business address registered with the Commercial Register [Handelsregister]. Irrespective thereof, the making of declarations of intent and the serving of documents can also take place at the registered address of the person authorized to receive pursuant to §39 sub-paragraph (1)sentence 2.

(3) The articles of association may also determine that individual members of the management board, alone or in conjunction with an officer with statutory authority [Prokurist], are competent to represent the corporation. The same may be determined by the supervisory board, if the articles of association have authorized it to do so. Sub-paragraph (2) sentence 2 applies mutatis mutandis in these cases.

(4) Members of the management board competent to joint representation can entitle individual members to conduct certain transactions or certain types of transaction. This applies mutatis mutandis where an individual member of the management board in conjunction with an officer with statutory authority is competent to represent the corporation.

§ 82. (1) The management board's competence to represent cannot be restricted.

(2) In the relationship of the members of the management board with the corporation, the former are obliged to observe the restrictions concerning the competence to manage the corporation [Geschäftsführungsbefugnis] which, within the framework of the provisions governing the stock corporation, have been adopted by the articles of association, the supervisory board, the general meeting, and the rules of procedure of the management board and the supervisory board.

§ 93. (1) The members of the management board must apply the duty of care of a conscientious and prudent business manager. A violation of this duty is not at hand where the member of the management board, in an entrepreneurial decision, could reasonably assume on the basis of appropriate information to be acting in the interest of the corporation. With regard to confidential information and secrets of the corporation, namely company or business secrets, which became known to the members of the management board through their activity in the management board, they must maintain secrecy. The duty of sentence 3 does not apply vis-à-vis a recognized inspection body pursuant to §342b of the Commercial Code within the context of an inspection conducted by this body.

(2) Members of the management board who violate their duties are liable vis-à-vis the corporation to compensate as joint debtors [Gesamtschuldner] for the damage caused by the violation. In case of a dispute as to whether they exercised the care of a conscientious and prudent business manager, the burden of proof rests with them. If the corporation takes out an insurance to safeguard a member

of the management board against risks arising from his professional activity for the corporation, a deductible of at least ten per cent of the damage up to the amount of at least one and a half times the fixed yearly remuneration of the member of the management board must be provided for.

(3) The members of the management board are, in particular, obliged to compensate, if, contrary to this act,

1. contributed capital [Einlagen] is refunded to the shareholders,
2. the shareholders are paid interests or shares of profit,
3. own shares of the corporation or of another corporation are subscribed for, acquired, or taken as pledge or are redeemed,
4. shares are issued prior to the full performance of the face value,
5. assets of the corporation are distributed,
6. payments are made contrary to §92 sub-paragraph (2),
7. remunerations are granted to members of the supervisory board,
8. credit is granted,
9. pre-emptive shares [Bezugsaktien] are issued through the contingent increase of the share capital outside of the determined purpose or prior to the full performance of the equivalent value.

(4) The duty vis-à-vis the corporation to compensate does not arise, where the act is based on a lawful decision of the general meeting. The duty to compensate is not excluded by the fact that the supervisory board has approved the act. The corporation may only waive or settle claims to compensation after at least three years, and then only if the general meeting consents and if a minority, whose shares together attain the tenth part of the share capital, does not file an objection in writing. The temporal limit does not apply, where the one who is obliged to compensate is unable to pay and settles with his creditors in order to avert insolvency proceedings or if the duty to compensate is regulated by an insolvency plan.

(5) The claim to compensation of the corporation may also be asserted by the creditors of the corporation, where the latter cannot obtain satisfaction from the corporation. However, in cases other than one of sub-paragraph (3), this only applies if the members of the management board have grossly violated the care of a conscientious and prudent business manager; sub-paragraph (2) sentence 2 applies mutatis mutandis. With regard to the creditors, the duty to compensate is nullified neither by a waiver or settlement by the corporation, nor by the fact that the act is based on a decision of the general meeting. If insolvency proceedings have been opened regarding the assets [Vermögen] of the corporation, the insolvency administrator [Insolvenzverwalter] or the private attorney [Sachverwalter] exercises the right of the creditors against the members of the management board for the duration of these proceedings.

§ 148. (1) Shareholders [Aktionäre], whose shares together equal the 100th part of the share capital or a proportionate amount of 100,000 Euro at the time of filing the application, may apply for admission to assert in their own name the claims for compensation of the corporation specified in §147 sub-paragraph (1) sentence 1. The court will allow the proceedings, if

1. the shareholders prove that they acquired the shares prior to the point in time at which they or, in the case of universal succession [Gesamtsrechtsnachfolge], their predecessors had to obtain knowledge of the alleged violations of duty or the alleged damage on the basis of a publication.
2. the shareholders prove that they requested the corporation in vain, setting a reasonable time, to start proceedings itself.
3. facts exist which justify the suspicion that the corporation has, by way of impropriety [Unredlichkeit] or gross violation of the law or the articles of association, sustained damage, and
4. no prevailing reasons of corporate interest oppose the enforcement of the claim for compensation.

[sub-paragraphs (2)-(5) are omitted.]

(6) The costs of the derivative action [Zulassungsverfahrens] are to be borne by the applicant, in so far as his application is dismissed. If the dismissal rests on opposing grounds of the corporate interest, which the corporation could have made known prior to the application but did not make known, it must reimburse the applicant for the costs. Apart from that, bearing of the costs is to be decided upon in the final judgment. If the corporation brings proceedings itself or if it takes over pending proceedings from the shareholders, it bears any costs of the applicants which accrued up until the point in time of its initiation of proceedings or its taking-over of the proceedings and may only withdraw the action subject to the prerequisites of §93 sub-paragraph (4) sentence 3 and 4, with the exception of the blocking period [Sperrfrist]. If the action is entirely or partially dismissed, the corporation must reimburse the costs borne by the claimants, provided the claimant did not obtain the admittance by an intentional or grossly negligent false submission. Shareholders who jointly

act as applicant or as joined party [Streitgenossen] are only reimbursed, jointly, for the costs of one authorized representative, unless another authorized representative was indispensable in bringing the action.

The Netherlands

Civil Code*

Civil Code of the Netherlands [Burgerlijk Wetboek], as last amended by Article 3 of the Act of 28 November 2018 (*Stb*. 2018, 489). Selected provisions from Books 1, 2, 3, 4, 5, 6, 7 and 7A.

Book 1. Law of persons and family law

[Titles 1 – 9 are omitted.]

Title 8. Marriage Conditions

Article 1:114. Marriage conditions [huwelijkse voorwaarden] may be made by both future spouses prior to entry into marriage as well as by spouses during their marriage.

Art. 1:115. (1) Marriage conditions must be entered into by notarial deed upon penalty of invalidity.

[The remainder of Title 8 and Titles 9 – 12 are omitted.]

Title 13. Age of minority

Article 1:233. Minors are those persons who have not reached the age of eighteen, or been declared of age through application of Article 253ha.

Article 1:234. (1) A minor is, as far as he acts with the approval of his legal representative, capable of performing legal acts, unless statute provides otherwise.
(2) Approval can only be given for a specific legal act or for a specific purpose.
(3) Approval is deemed to have been given to the minor where it concerns a legal act of which it is generally accepted practice that minors of his age perform it independently.

[The remainder of 13 and Titles 14 and 15 are omitted.]

Title 16. Guardianship

Article 1:378. (1) An adult may be placed under guardianship by the local court [kantonrechter] if he temporarily or permanently fails to look after his own interests properly or if he endangers his own security or that of others as a result of
a. his physical or mental state, or
b. habitual abuse of alcohol or drugs,
and an appropriate safeguard for these interests cannot be achieved by means of a less far-reaching measure.
(2) Where it is to be expected that, with regard to a minor, one of the grounds for guardianship referred to in the previous paragraph shall exist at the moment he becomes an adult, the guardianship may already be ordered prior to adulthood.
(3) The court before which a request to grant a provisional or conditional authorisation, an authorisation for medical observation, an authorisation for continued abode within the meaning of the Special Receptions in Psychiatric Hospitals Act [Wet bijzondere opnemingen in psychiatrische ziekenhuizen], or an authorisation within the meaning of article 33 (1) of that Act is pending is also competent to hear a request for placement under guardianship.

[Articles 1:379 and 1:380 are omitted.]

Article 1:381. (1) Guardianship takes effect as of the day it is ordered. In the case referred to in article 1:378 (2), guardianship takes effect at the time that the person placed under guardianship reaches the age of majority.
(2) From these points in time onwards, the person placed under guardianship is incapable of performing legal acts insofar as statute does not provide otherwise.
(3) A person placed under guardianship is capable of performing legal acts with the approval of his guardian insofar as the latter is competent to perform these legal acts for the person placed under guardianship. Authorisation may only be given for a specific legal act or for a specific purpose. Authorisation for a specific purpose must be given in writing.
(4) With regard matters concerning grooming, care, treatment, and supervision of a person placed under guardianship, articles 453 and 454 of this Book apply mutatis mutandis.
(5) In accordance with this provision, he is competent to dispose of money made available to him by

---

*   Translation by Bram Akkermans, Anna Berlee, Sascha Hardt, Heike Hauröder and Nicole Kornet.

his guardian for the purpose of his sustenance.

(6) In matters relating to guardianship, the person whose guardianship is at issue is competent to be a party in legal proceedings and to appeal a judgment.

[Article 1:382 is omitted.]

Article 1:383. (1) The judge ordering guardianship appoints, at the time of ordering guardianship or as soon as possible thereafter, a guardian. He ascertains the readiness and makes an assessment of the suitability of the person to be appointed.

(2) In appointing a guardian, the judge follows the explicit preference of the person to be placed under guardianship, unless there are substantiated reasons against such appointment.

(3) Unless the previous paragraph is applied, if the person placed under guardianship is married, has entered into a registered partnership or otherwise has a life partner, the spouse, registered partner or other life partner is appointed as guardian by preference. Where the previous sentence does not apply, one of his parents, children, brothers or sisters is appointed as guardian by preference. Where the person placed under guardianship marries, enters into a registered partnership or otherwise acquires a life partner, each of them may request that the spouse who is not under guardianship, the registered partner, or other life partner be appointed instead of the present guardian.

(4) Legal persons with complete legal competence may be appointed as guardians.

[The remainder of this article is omitted.]

[The remainder of Book 1 is omitted.]

Book 2. Legal Persons [Rechtspersonen]

Title 1. General provisions

[Articles 2:1 – 2:8 are omitted.]

Article 2:9. (1) Each director [bestuurder] is responsible to the legal person [rechtspersoon] for a proper performance of his task. To the task of the director belong all management tasks that are not attributed to one or more other directors according to the law or the articles of association [statute].

(2) Each director bears the responsibility for the general state of affairs. He is wholly liable in case of improper management, unless also in light of the tasks attributed to the others no serious blame can be given to him and he was not negligent in taking measures to avert the consequences of improper management.

[The remainder of Title 1 and Titles 2 – 3 are omitted.]

Title 4. Public companies [naamloze vennootschappen]

[Divisions 1 – 4 are omitted.]

Division 5. The management of a public company and the supervision of the management board

Article 2:129. (1) Except for limitations according to the articles of association [statuten], the management board [bestuur] is responsible for managing the company.

(2) The articles of association may determine that a director, referred to by name or function, is granted more than one vote. A director cannot cast more votes than the other directors together.

(3) Decisions of the management board by or pursuant to the articles of association can only be subject to the consent of an organ of the company.

(4) The articles of association can determine that the management board is required to conduct itself according to the instructions of an organ of the company which relate to the general lines of the policy to be pursued in fields further specified in the articles of association.

(5) In the performance of their task, the directors conform to the interest of the company and the business connected with it.

(6) A director does not take part in the deliberation and decision making if he has a direct or indirect personal interest in it that is in conflict with the interest referred to in paragraph (5). If no managerial decision can be taken as a result, the decision is taken by the supervisory board. In the absence of a supervisory board, the decision is taken by the general assembly, unless the articles of association provide otherwise.

Article 2:129a. (1) In the articles of association it may be laid down that the management tasks are divided over one or more non-executive directors and one or more executive directors. The task of supervising the performance of tasks by directors may not be taken away from non-executive directors by way of a distribution of tasks. The chairmanship of the management board, the task of nominating candidates for appointment as a director, and that determining the remuneration of executive directors may not be assigned to an executive director. Non-executive directors are natural persons.

(2) The executive directors do not take part in deliberations and decision-making concerning the determination of the remuneration of executive directors or the granting of the assignment to examine the annual accounts to an external accountant as meant in Article 27 of the Statute on Oversight of Accountant Organisations if the general meeting has not proceeded to grant the assignment.

(3) In or by virtue of the articles of association it may be stipulated that one or more directors can take legally valid decisions on matters that belong to his or their task, respectively. Stipulation by virtue of the articles of association is done in writing.

Article 2:130. (1) The management board represents the company, in so far as something else does not stem from the law.

(2) The competence of representation is granted to each director. The articles of association may nevertheless determine that, it is granted to only one or more directors in addition to the management board. They can further determine that a director is only allowed to represent the company with the cooperation of one or more others.

(3) Competence of representation granted to the management board or to a director is unrestricted and unconditional, in so far as something else does not stem from the law. A restriction or condition allowed or prescribed by law for the competence of representation can only be invoked by the company.

(4) The articles of association can also grant the competence of representation to individuals other than directors.

Article 2:138. (1) In the event of bankruptcy of the public company, every director is jointly and severally liable to the estate [boedel] for the amount of the debts, in so far as these cannot be satisfied through settlement of the other benefits, if the management board performed its task in an obviously improper way and it can be assumed that this is an important cause of the bankruptcy.

(2) Where the management board has not fulfilled its duties under Articles 10 or 394, it has not performed its task properly and it is presumed that improper performance of the task is an important cause for the bankruptcy. The same applies if the company is a wholly liable partner of a general partnership [vennootschap onder firma] or a limited partnership [commanditaire vennootschap] and the tasks under Article 15i of book 3 are not fulfilled. An insignificant default will not be taken into account.

(3) Not liable is the director who proves that the improper performance of the task by the management board cannot be attributed to him and that he was not negligent in taking measures to avert the consequences thereof.

[Paragraphs (4) and (5) are omitted.]

(6) The claim can only be set up on the basis of improper performance of the task in the period of three years preceding the bankruptcy. A discharge [kwijting] granted to the director does not stand in the way of setting up the claim.

(7) For the application of this article, any person who determined or contributed to determining the policy of the company will be treated equal to a director, as if he were a director. The claim may not be set up against the administrator [bewindvoerder] appointed by the judge.

(8) This article does not impede the competence of the (official) receiver [curator] to set up a claim by virtue of the contract with the director or by virtue of Article 9.

[Paragraphs 9 and 10 are omitted.]

[The remainder of Title 4 is omitted.]

Title 5. Private limited liability companies [besloten vennootschappen met beperkte aansprakelijkheid]
[Divisions 1 – 4 are omitted.]

Division 5. The management of the company and the supervision of the management board

Article 2:239. (1) Except for limitations according to the articles of association [statuten], the management board [bestuur] is responsible for managing the company.

(2) The articles of association may determine that a director, referred to by name or function, is granted more than one vote. A director cannot cast more votes than the other directors together.

(3) Decisions of the management board by or pursuant to the articles of association can only be subject to the consent of an organ of the company.

(4) The articles of association can determine that the management board is required to conduct itself according to the instructions of another organ of the company. The management board is bound to follow the instructions, unless these are contrary to the interest of the company and the business connected with it.

(5) In the performance of their tasks the directors conform to the interests of the company and with business connected with it.

(6) A director does not take part in the deliberation and decision making if he has a direct or indirect personal interest in it that is in conflict with the interest referred to in paragraph (5). If no managerial decision can be taken as a result, the decision is taken by the supervisory board. In the absence of a supervisory board, the decision is taken by the general assembly, unless the articles of association provide otherwise.

Article 2:239a. (1) In the articles of association it may be laid down that the management tasks are divided over one or more non-executive directors and one or more executive directors. The task of supervising the performance of tasks by directors may not be taken away from non-executive directors by way of a distribution of tasks. The chairmanship of the management board, the task of nominating candidates for appointment as a director, and that determining the remuneration of executive directors may not be assigned to an executive director. Non-executive directors are natural persons.

(2) The executive directors do not take part in deliberations and decision-making concerning the determination of the remuneration of executive directors or the granting of the assignment to examine the annual accounts to an external accountant as meant in Article 27 of the Statute on Oversight of Accountant Organisations if the general meeting has not proceeded to grant the assignment.

(3) In or by virtue of the articles of association it may be stipulated that one or more directors can take legally valid decisions on matters that belong to his or their task, respectively. Stipulation by virtue of the articles of association is done in writing.

Article 2:240. (1) The management board represents the company, in so far as something else does not stem from the law.

(2) The competence of representation is granted to each director. The articles of association may nevertheless determine that, it is granted to only one or more directors in addition to the management board. They can further determine that a director is only allowed to represent the company with the cooperation of one or more others.

(3) Competence of representation granted to the management board or to a director is unrestricted and unconditional, in so far as something else does not stem from the law. A restriction or condition allowed or prescribed by law for the competence of representation can only be invoked by the company.

(4) The articles of association can also grant the competence of representation to individuals other than directors.

[Articles 2:241 – 2:247 are omitted.]

Article 2:248. (1) In the event of bankruptcy of the company, every director is jointly and severally liable to the estate [boedel] for the amount of the debts, in so far as these cannot be satisfied through settlement of the other benefits, if the management board performed its task in an obviously improper way and it can be assumed that this is an important cause of the bankruptcy.

(2) Where the management board has not fulfilled its duties under Articles 10 or 394, it has not performed its task properly and it is presumed that improper performance of the task is an important cause for the bankruptcy. The same applies if the company is a wholly liable partner of a general partnership [vennootschap onder firma] or a limited partnership [commanditaire vennootschap] and the duties under Article 15i of book 3 are not fulfilled. An insignificant default will not be taken into account.

(3) Not liable is the director who proves that the improper performance of the task by the management board cannot be attributed to him and that he was not negligent in taking measures to avert the consequences thereof.

[Paragraphs (4) and (5) are omitted.]

(6) The claim can only be set up on the basis of improper performance of the duty in the period of three years preceding the bankruptcy. A discharge [kwijting] granted to the director does not stand in

the way of setting up the claim.

(7) For the application of this article, any person who determined or contributed to determining the policy of the company will be treated equal to a director, as if he were a director. The claim may not be set up against the administrator [bewindvoerder] appointed by the judge.

(8) This article does not impede the competence of the (official) receiver [curator] to set up a claim by virtue of the contract with the director or by virtue of Article 9.

[Paragraphs (9) and (10) are omitted.]

[The remainder of Book 2 is omitted.]

Book 3. Patrimonial law in general [Vermogensrecht in het algemeen]

Title 1. General provisions

Division 1. Definitions

Article 3:1. Things are all objects and all patrimonial rights.

Article 3:2. Things are corporeal objects capable of human control.

Article 3:2a. (1) Animals are not things.
(2) Provisions relating to things are applicable to animals, with due regard for the limitations, duties and legal principles based on legislative provisions and rules of unwritten law as well as public policy and good morals.

Article 3:3. (1) Immovable are the land, not yet extracted minerals, plantings connected to the land, as well as the buildings and constructions that are permanently connected to the land, either directly or through combination with other buildings or constructions.
(2) Movable are all objects that are not immovable.

Article 3:4. (1) All that according to common opinion constitutes part of an object, is a component of that object.
(2) An object that is connected with a principal object in such a way that it cannot be separated without significant damage being done to one of the objects, becomes a component of the principal object.

Article 3:5. Household effects [inboedel] is the whole of from household goods and to upholstery and furnishings of a home serving movable objects, with the exception of libraries and collections of objects of art, science or historical nature.

Article 3:6. Rights that, either separately or together with another right, are transferable, or that provide the right holder with material advantage, or which are acquired in exchange for or in anticipation of material advantage, are patrimonial rights.

Article 3:7. A dependent right is a right that is connected to another right in such a way that it cannot exit without that other right.

Article 3:8. A limited right is a right that is derived from a more comprehensive right, which is burdened by the limited right.

Article 3:9. (1) Natural fruits are objects that according to common opinion are regarded as fruits of other objects.
(2) Civil fruits are rights that according to common opinion are regarded as fruits of things.
(3) The separate terms of an annuity shall be construed as fruits of the right on the annuity.
(4) A natural fruit becomes an independent right through its separation, a civil fruit an independent right by it becoming due.

Article 3:10. Registered objects are things for the transfer or creation of which registration in the relevant public registers is necessary.

Article 3:11. Good faith of a person, required for any legal effect, is not only lacking if he knew facts or the right to which his good faith shall relate, but also if he, in the given circumstances should have known of them. Impossibility of investigation does not prevent that the person who had good reason to doubt is regarded as someone who should have known the facts or the right.

Article 3:12. In determining what reasonableness and fairness require, account must be taken of generally recognized principles of law, the convictions with respect to the law in the Netherlands and the societal and individual interests that are involved in the given case.

Article 3:13. (1) The person to whom a power is conferred, may not invoke it, as far as he has abused it.
(2) A power can among others be abused by exercising it with no other purpose than to harm another or with another purpose than for which it is given or in case one in reasonableness should not have exercised it, taking account of the disproportionality between the interest in the exercise and the interest that is harmed thereby.
(3) From the nature of the power may arise that it cannot be abused.

Article 3:14. A power that someone has pursuant to civil law, may not be exercised contrary to written or unwritten rules of public law.

Article 3:15. Articles 11 - 14 shall apply outside patrimonial law as far as this is not contrary to the nature of the legal relationship.

[Divisions 1A and 1B are omitted.]

Division 2. Registration of Registered Things

Article 3:16. (1) Public registers are held in which facts that are important for the legal situation of registered things are registered.
(2) What these public registers are, where and how an entry in the registers can be made, what documents have to be offered to the registrar for this purpose, how the register are organized, how the registration occur, and how the registers can be consulted, is regulated by law.

Article 3:17. (1) Apart from those facts for which registration is possible under other legislative provisions, the following facts can be registered in these registers:
a. legal acts which bring about a change in the legal status of registered objects or are in any other way of significance for that legal status;
b. successions that concern registered objects, including the succession by the State under Articles 189 and 226 paragraph (4) of Book 4, and the granting of registered objects to the State under Article 226 paragraphs (1) and (2) of Book 4;
c. fulfilment of the condition, laid down in a registered conditional legal act, and the appearance of an uncertain point in time, indicated in the stipulation as to time connected to a registered legal act, as well as the death of a usufructuary of a registered thing;
d. regulations and other arrangements that have been established between co-entitled persons in registered objects;
e. court judgments that concern the legal status of registered objects or the power to dispose over them, provided they are immediately enforceable or a declaration of the clerk of court is produced, stating either that recourse by way of an ordinary legal remedy is no longer possible or that it is unapparent to him three months after the rendering of the judgment to him that an ordinary legal remedy has been instituted, besides the instituted legal remedies against the abovementioned judgments;
f. bringing of legal claims and filing of petitions to obtain a court judgment that concerns the legal status of a registered object;
g. executorial and prejudgment attachments on registered things;
h. name changes concerning persons entitled to registered things;
i. prescription that leads to acquisition of a registered object or destruction of a limited right that is a registered thing;
j. orders and judgments, by which an order registered by virtue of a special legislative provision is destroyed, withdrawn or altered;
k. the installation and removal of a network, comprising one or more cables or pipes, designed for the transportation of solid, liquid or gaseous materials, of energy or of information.
(2) Rental and lease contracts and other facts that only provide for or rescind personal rights, can only be registered, if allowed by a specific legislative provision.

Article 3:18. If documents are presented to the registrar of public registers for registration, he shall provide the presenter a proof of receipt stating the nature of those documents as well as the day, time and minute of the presentation.

Article 3:19. (1) If the necessary documents are presented for registration, the documents provided satisfy the legal requirements and other legal requirements for registration are met, then the registration shall take place immediately after the presentation.

(2) The time of presentation of the required documents for registration is deemed to be the time of registration.

(3) On the request of the presenter, the registrar shall note the rendered registration effect on the receipt or in those cases and in a manner by or pursuant to the law referred to in Article 16, paragraph 2 give the presenter notice thereof.

(4) If the registrar suspects that the characteristics set out in the offered documents do not correspond to those that should be mentioned for the registered thing, or that the legal act to be registered is carried out by an unauthorised person or is incompatible with another legal act, for registration of which the necessary documents are presented to him, he is authorised to notify the presenter and another stakeholder.

Article 3:20. (1) The registrar of public registers refuses to enter a registration if the requirements referred to in Article 19 paragraph 1 are not met. He enters the presentation in the register of preliminary records mentioning the raised reservations.

(2) If the refusal has been wrongly done, the interim relief judge of the District Court shall order, in summary proceedings, on application by the stakeholder the registrar to complete the registration, without prejudice to the competence of the ordinary courts. The interim relief judge can order the summons of other stakeholders designated by him. The order of the interim relief judge is *legally enforceable.*

(3) If the rejected registration is ordered, the registrar shall enter it immediately after the plaintiff has requested it again.

(4) If the stakeholder has issued a subpoena in summary proceedings to obtain the order referred to in paragraph 2 within two weeks after the original presentation to the registrar and the initially refused registration has been recorded pursuant to a renewed offer of the same documents, done within a week after a lawful order at first instance, the registration is deemed to have occurred at the time when the original listing took place. The same applies if the registrar on a renewed offer proceeds to enter the registration within two weeks either after the original *listing* or after a timely issued subpoena pending the proceedings in first instance.

(5) A fact which only is apparent from a document referred to in paragraph 1 second sentence is deemed not to be known by consulting the registers, unless it shall be deemed to have been registered at the time of consultation pursuant to the previous paragraph.

(6) A preliminary note shall be cancelled by the registrar once it is shown that the conditions for applying the fourth paragraph can no longer be fulfilled, or the registration has taken place taking into account the time of original listing.

Article 3:21. (1) The rank of registrations in respect to the same registered thing is determined by the order of registration, unless another ranking follows by law.

(2) If two registrations are made at the same time and if these lead to two incompatible rights being held by two different persons on that thing, the ranking is determined:

(a) in case the deeds that are offered for registration are passed ondifferent dates, by the order of those dates;

(b) in case both deeds have been passed on the same day and the deeds are notarial deeds, including notarial statements, by the order of the time at which the deeds or statements have been passed.

Article 3:22. When a fact is registered in the registers, then the validity of the registration can no longer be disputed on the ground that the formalities required for the registration were not taken into account.

Article 3:23. The claim of a transferee of a registered thing on good faith is not accepted if the claim includes a claim on ignorance of facts that would be known by consulting the registers.

Article 3:24. (1) If at the time when a legal act to obtain a right to a registered thing under special title is entered in the registers, a likewise for entry in the registers susceptible fact in relation to that registered thing was not entered, that fact cannot be invoked against the transferee, unless he knew it.

(2) The first paragraph shall not apply in respect of

(a) facts which by their nature are susceptible for registration in a register of civil status, a register for matrimonial property or an estate register, also if the fact in a given case could not be registered in it because the law of the Netherlands does not apply to it;

(b). in the guardianship and administratorship register registered guardianship and removal of guardianship;

(c) in the insolvency register, the suspension of payments [surseance] register and the debt restructuring scheme for natural persons register registered court judgments;

(d) acceptance and rejection of an estate;

(e) prescription.

(3) The first paragraph also does not apply in respect of successions and wills that were not registered at the time of registration of the legal act, but are registered in the registers thereafter within three months of the death of the testator.

Article 3:25. If at the time when a legal act to obtain a right to a registered thing under special title is registered, a fact relating to that registered thing is registered in the registers under an authentic deed in which the fact is established by an official with power of authenticity, the inaccuracy of this fact cannot be invoked against to the transferee unless he knew of this inaccuracy or by consulting the registers could have known of the possibility thereof.

Article 3:26. If at the time at which a legal act to obtain a right to a registered thing under special title is entered, with respect to that registered thing an incorrect fact is entered in the registers, the inaccuracy of that fact cannot be invoked against the transferee by the person who could reasonably have cared for conformity of the registers with reality, unless he knew of the inaccuracy or by consulting the registers could have known of the possibility thereof.

Article 3:27. (1) He who claims to have any right to a register thing, may in a public notice subpoena all stakeholders, and in addition those who are entered as right holder or judgment creditor to that thing, each by name to declare that he has the right that he claims accrues to him. Before such a claim is awarded, the court may order the measures and make order evidence, which he considers useful in the interest of any non-appearing right holders. A declaration obtained under this Article shall not be registered before the judgment has become res judicata.

(2) No objection is permitted against the judgment. Appeal and cassation are open according to the normal rules, subject to the following exceptions. Article 335 of the Code of Civil Procedure is not applicable. The subpoena whereby the appeal is brought, shall under penalty of inadmissibility be entered in the register referred to in Article 433 of the Code of Civil Procedure within eight days. The time for appeal starts to run for non-appearing stakeholders from the notification of the decision to them by name, so far as they were entered, or by public summons, where they were not registered. Cassation is open only to appeared stakeholders.

(3) The under paragraph 1 registered declaration is presumed to be correct with respect to not-appearing stakeholders who were not subpoenaed by name, as long as the contrary is not proved. No appeal can be made concerning the inaccuracy to the detriment of those unfamiliar with it, who succeeded the transferee of the judgment under special title.

(4) A public notice referred to in paragraph 1 shall occur in accordance with Article 54, second and third paragraph of the Code of Civil Procedure. A public summons referred to in paragraph 2 occurs in the same manner, unless the court orders measures as referred to in paragraph (1) The measures referred to in paragraph 1 may include prescribing of repeated or non-repeated announcements with content determined by the court in one or more domestic or foreign newspapers.

Article 3:28. (1) If a registration is worthless, they for whose benefit it otherwise would have served, required to provide a written statement of the worthlessness to he who has an immediate interest, upon his request. The statements indicate the facts on which the worthlessness is based, unless the registration concerns a mortgage or a seizure.

(2) Statements referred to in paragraph 1 may be entered in the registers. If the registration concerns a mortgage or a seizure, these statements authorise the registrar after registration to cancellation thereof.

Article 3:29. (1) If the required statements are not issued, the district court declares the registration worthless on the request of the direct stakeholder. If for the acquisition of this order someone is subpoenaed who is registered in the registers, thereby also all his legal successors, who have not taken a new registration, are subpoenaed.

(2) Before such a claim is awarded, the court may order the measures and order evidence, which he considers useful in the interest of any non-appearing right holders.

(3) Objection, appeal, and cassation must, under penalty of inadmissibility, be entered in the registers referred to in Article 433 of the Code of Civil Procedure within eight days of lodging the respective remedy [rechtsmiddel]. If no objection, but appeal is open to a registered defendant, the same applies for his legal successors who have not taken a new registration. Contrary to Article 143 of that Code, the time for objection in any case starts to run from the service of the judgment to the registered defendant, even if service is not made to him in person, so also with respect to all his legal successors who have not taken a new registration, unless the court has ordered further measures to this end and

that order is not met. Cassation is open only to stakeholders who appeared.

(4) The judgment containing the declaration cannot be registered before it has become res judicata. If the worthless registration concerns a mortgage or a seizure, the judgment authorises the registrar after its registration to cancellation thereof.

Article 3:30. Without prejudice to the liabilities of the Cadastre and Public Registers Agency and the public registers, referred to in Article 117, first and second paragraph of the Land Registry Act, the State is liable, if someone as a result of circumstances that according to reasonableness and fairness he is not accountable for, loses his right through application of one of the Articles 24, 25 or 27.

Article 3:31. Where a legislative provision relating to registered things, requires a notarial deed or a notarial declaration, a deed or declaration from a Dutch notary is required.

Title 2. Legal Acts

Article 3:32. (1) Every natural person is capable of performing legal acts, unless the law provides otherwise.

(2) A legal act by an incapable person is voidable. A unilateral act of an incapable person, that is not directed at one or more specific persons is however void.

Article 3:33. A legal act requires a will directed towards a legal effect which has been manifested by a declaration.

Article 3:34. (1) If someone whose mental capabilities have been permanently or temporarily disturbed, has declared something, a will corresponding to the declaration is deemed to be lacking, if the disturbance prevented a reasonable evaluation of the interests involved with the act, or if the declaration is made under the influence of the disturbance. A declaration is presumed to be made under the influence of the disturbance, if the legal act was disadvantageous for the mentally disturbed person, unless the disadvantage was not reasonably foreseeable at the time of the legal act.

(2) Such lack of will renders the legal act voidable. A unilateral legal act that was not directed at one or more specific persons becomes void for lack of will however.

Article 3:35 Against he who has interpreted another's declaration or conduct, in accordance with the sense that he could reasonably have attributed to it in the given circumstances, as a declaration of a particular scope directed towards him by that other, the lack of a will corresponding to this declaration cannot be invoked.

Article 3:36. Against he who as a third party on the basis of a declaration or conduct, in accordance with the sense that he in the given circumstances could reasonably attribute to it, has assumed the creation, existence or extinction of a specific legal relationship and acted in reasonable reliance on the accuracy of that assumption, the inaccuracy of that assumption cannot be invoked with respect to this act by those whose declaration or conduct is concerned.

Article 3:37. (1) Unless otherwise provided, declarations, including notices, may be made in any form, and may be contained in one or more acts.

(2) If it is provided that a declaration shall be made in writing, it may also be made by bailiff's notification, to the extent that the scope of that provision does not suggest otherwise.

(3) A declaration that is directed at a particular person must have reached that person, in order to have effect. Nevertheless, a declaration that has not reached the person to whom it was directed in time or not at all, also has effect, if the untimely arrival or lack of arrival is the consequence of his own conduct, of the conduct of persons for whom he is liable, or of other circumstances concerning his person that justify that he bears the disadvantage.

(4) Where a declaration that is directed to another person has been improperly conveyed by the person or means that was chosen thereto by the sender, the information received by the recipient counts as the sender's declaration, unless the means of conveyance that was used, was determined by the recipient.

(5) Withdrawal of a declaration that is directed to a particular person must, in order to have effect, reach that person before or at the same time as the declaration that is withdrawn.

Article 3:38. (1) Unless something else stems from the law or from the nature of the legal act, a legal act can be performed under a time-limit or a condition.

(2) The fulfilment of a condition does not have retroactive effect.

Article 3:39. Unless otherwise provided by law, legal acts which have not been performed in the prescribed form, are void.

Article 3:40. (1) A legal act that through its content or purpose is contrary to good morals or public order, is void.

(2) Violation of a mandatory legislative provision renders the legal act void, however, if the provision only serves to protect one of the parties to a multilateral legal act, it is only voidable, all this to the extent that nothing else results from the purpose of the provision.

(3) The previous paragraph does not apply to provisions that are not intended to affect the validity of legal acts which are in conflict therewith.

Article 3:41. If a ground for nullity only relates to part of a legal act, then the remaining part will stay intact, to the extent that this part, given the content and purpose of the act, is not inextricably linked to the part that is void.

Article 3:42. Where the purpose of a void legal act is to such an extent in conformity with another valid legal act, that one must assume that the latter would have been performed, had the former been abandoned for reason of its invalidity, then the effect of the latter is granted to the former, unless this would be unreasonable towards an interested third party who has not participated in the legal act as a party.

Article 3:43. (1) Legal acts which, either directly, or through persons who intervene, have as their purpose the acquisition by:

(a) judges, members of the public prosecution service, assistant judges, court clerks, advocates, bailiffs, and notaries, of things which are the subject of a dispute before the court in whose jurisdiction they exercise their profession;

(b) civil servants, of things which are sold by them or before them, or

(c) persons holding public office, of things that belong to the State, provinces, municipalities or other public institutions and that have been left in their care,

are void and oblige the recipients to pay damages.

(2) Paragraph (1) under (a) does not relate to testamentary provisions, made by a testator for the benefit of his legal heirs, nor to legal acts by which these heirs acquire goods of the estate.

(3) In the situation referred to in the first paragraph under (c) the act is valid if it is performed with Our consent or if it concerns a sale in public. If the legal act has as its purpose the acquisition by the member of a municipal council or an alderman [wethouder], or by the mayor [burgemeester], the competence to give consent mentioned in the previous sentence falls to the Provincial Executive [Gedeputeerde Staten] or the King's Commissioner.

Article 3:44. (1) A legal act is voidable, where it has been brought about by threat [bedreiging], by deceit [bedrog] or by abuse of circumstances.

(2) A threat consists of a person inducing another to perform a certain legal act by wrongfully threatening this or a third party with any disadvantage to person or property. The threat must be such, that a reasonable human being could be influenced thereby.

(3) Deceit consists of a person inducing another to perform a certain legal act by an intentionally incorrect statement made for that purpose, or by intentionally withholding any fact for that purpose, which he who withheld it was obligated to disclose, or by another ruse. Recommendations generally phrased, even if they are untrue, do not in themselves constitute deceit.

(4) Abuse of circumstances consists of a person, who knows or ought to understand that another is induced to perform a legal act because of special circumstances, such as an emergency situation, dependence, thoughtlessness [lichtzinnigheid], abnormal mental condition or inexperience, having facilitated that legal act, although what he knows or ought to understand should prevent him from doing so.

(5) If a declaration is brought about by threat, deceit or abuse of circumstances on the part of someone who is not a party to the legal act, one cannot rely on this defect as against the other party who had no reason to assume its existence.

Article 3:45. (1) If a debtor, while performing a voluntary legal act, knew or ought to know that a consequence thereof would be to prejudice one or more creditors' possibilities for redress, the legal act is voidable and the ground for annulment may be relied upon by each creditor whose possibilities for redress have been prejudiced because of the legal act, regardless of whether his claim arose before or after the legal act.

(2) A legal act other than a gratuitous one, which is either multilateral or unilateral and directed to one or several specified persons, can only be avoided because of a prejudicial act, if those with whom or towards whom the debtor performed the legal act also knew or ought to have known that a consequence thereof would be to prejudice one or more creditors.

(3) Where a gratuitous legal act is avoided because of a prejudicial act, the avoidance has no effect with regard to he who benefited and neither knew nor ought to have known that the legal act would prejudice one or more creditors, to the extent that he can show that he did not benefit from the legal act at the time of the declaration or the commencement of the action for avoidance.

(4) A creditor who opposes a legal act because he has been prejudiced, shall only avoid it in his own interest and no more than is necessary in order to remove the prejudice experienced by him.

(5) Rights to things, acquired by third parties in good faith and not gratuitously, which were the subject of an avoided legal act, shall be respected. As regards the third party who acquired gratuitously in good faith, the avoidance has no effect to the extent that he can show that he did not benefit from the legal act at the moment that the good is demanded from him.

Article 3:46. (1) If the legal act whereby one or more creditors are disadvantaged is performed within one year prior to invoking the ground for nullity and the debtor had not already committed to the legal act prior to the commencement of that period, it is presumed that both sides knew or ought to have known that such a disadvantage would be the result of the legal act:

10 in contracts where the value of the obligation on the side of the debtor substantially outweighs the obligation on the other side;

20 in legal acts in settlement of security for a debt not due;

30 in legal acts performed by a debtor who is a natural person with or towards

a. his spouse, his foster child or a blood relative by blood or marriage up to the third degree;

b. a legal person in which he, his spouse, his foster child or relative by blood or marriage up to the third degree who is director or supervisory board member, or in which these persons, separately or together, participate as shareholder directly or indirectly for at least half of the issued capital;

40 in legal acts performed by the debtor who is a legal person with or towards a natural person:

a. who is director or supervisory board member of the legal person, or with or for his spouse, foster child or relative by blood or marriage up to the third degree;

b. who with or without his spouse, his fostered and his relative by blood or marriage up to the third degree, participates as shareholder directly or indirectly to at least one half of the capital;

c. whose spouse, foster child or relative by blood or marriage up to the third degree, separately or together, participate as shareholder directly or indirectly to at least half of the capital;

50 in legal acts performed by the debtor who is a legal person with or towards another legal person, if

a. one of these legal persons is director of the other;

b. a director, natural person, of one of these legal persons, or his spouse, foster child or relative by blood or marriage up to the third degree, is director of the other;

c. a director, natural person or supervisory board member of one of these legal persons, or his spouse, foster child or relative by blood or marriage up to the third degree, separately or together, participate as shareholder directly or indirectly to at least half of the capital;

d. the same legal person participates in both legal persons for at least half of the capital directly or indirectly, or the same natural person, with or without his spouse foster child or relative by blood or marriage up to the third degree,

60 in legal acts, performed by the debtor who is a legal person, with or towards a group company.

(2) A registered partner is equated with a spouse.

(3) Foster child means the person who is durably cared for and raised as an own child.

(4) Director, supervisory board member or shareholder also means he who has been director, supervisory board member or shareholder for less than a year prior to the legal act.

(5) If the director of a legal person-director is himself a legal person, this legal person is equated to the legal person-director.

Article 3:47. In case of a disadvantage by a gratuitous legal act, which the debtor performed within one year prior to invoking the ground for nullity, it is presumed that he knew or ought to have known that disadvantaging one or more creditors would be the consequence of the legal act.

Article 3:48. Debtor in the sense of the three previous Articles means he who against whose thing recourse for a debt can be taken.

Article 3:49. A voidable legal act may be avoided, either by an extrajudicial declaration, or by a judicial decision.

Article 3:50. (1) An extrajudicial declaration which avoids a legal act is directed to those who are party to the legal act, by him in whose interest the ground for avoidance exists.

(2) An extrajudicial declaration can only avoid a legal act with regard to a registered thing, which has led to a registration in the public registers or to an instrument meant for transfer of a registered thing, if all parties accept the avoidance.

Article 3:51. (1) A judicial decision avoids a legal act by upholding a ground for avoidance which has been invoked at law.
(2) A legal action for avoidance of a legal act is instituted as against those who are party to the legal act.
(3) An appeal in law based on a ground for avoidance can be made at all times to repeal a claim based on the legal act or any other judicial measure. He who makes this appeal is obliged to notify it as soon as possible to the parties to the legal act who did not appear during the proceedings.

Article 3:52. (1) Legal actions for avoidance will become prescribed:
(a) in case of incapacity: three years after the incapacity ended, or, if the incapable person has a legal representative, three years after the legal representative became aware of the act;
(b) in case of threat or abuse of circumstances: three years after this influence ceased to exist;
(c) in case of deceit, mistake or prejudice: three years after the deceit, the mistake or the prejudice has been discovered;
(d) in case of another ground for avoidance: three years after the right to invoke this ground for avoidance has come to benefit him who has this right.
(2) After the period of prescription of the action for avoidance of the legal act, it can no longer be annulled on the same ground for avoidance by an extrajudicial declaration.

Article 3:53. (1) The avoidance has retroactive effect to the time at which the legal act was performed.
(2) If the consequences of a legal act which have already manifested can only be undone with difficulty, the court, if so requested, can wholly or partially deny the avoidance its effect. It can oblige a party who is thereby unfairly benefited to pay a monetary compensation to the party who has been disadvantaged.

Article 3:54. (1) The right to invoke abuse of circumstances for the avoidance of a multilateral legal act lapses where the other party suggests a timely amendment to the consequences of the legal act, which adequately brings an end to the disadvantage.
(2) The court can, at the request of one of the parties, moreover alter the consequences of the legal act in order to lift this disadvantage, instead of pronouncing an avoidance on grounds of abuse of circumstances.

Article 3:55. (1) The right to invoke a ground for avoidance to avoid a legal act lapses, where he who has this right has confirmed the legal act, after the period of prescription relating to the action for avoidance on that ground has commenced.
(2) The right to invoke a ground for avoidance also lapses, where a person with a direct interest has set a reasonable time at the onset of the period of prescription for him who has this competence, to choose between confirmation and avoidance and where he has not made a choice within this time.

Article 3:56. For the application of Articles 50-55 the following also count as party:
(a) in case of a unilateral legal act directed at one or more specific individuals targeted: those persons;
(b) in case of another unilateral legal acts: those who are directly stakeholders are in the maintenance of that act.

Article 3:57. If a legal act requires consent, authorisation, permit or another form of permission from a public body or of any other person to have its intended effect, none of whom is a party to the legal act, every direct stakeholder may notify those who have been party to the legal act that, unless permission is obtained within a reasonable time period fixed in that notification, the act will have no consequence with regard to them.

Article 3:58. (1) If a legal requirement required for the validity of a legal act is only satisfied after the performance of a legal act, but all direct stakeholders who could have invoked this defect in the period between the act and the fulfilment of the requirement regarded the act as valid, the legal act is thereby ratified.
(2) The previous paragraph is not applicable to the case that a legal act is void as a result of incapacity of the person who performed it and this person subsequently becomes competent.
(3) Rights acquired in the meantime by third parties do not stand in the way of ratification, provided they are respected.

Article 3:59. The provisions in this Title are applied mutatis mutandis outside patrimonial law to the extent that this is not contrary to the nature of the legal act or the legal relationship.

Title 3. Representation

Article 3:60. (1) Representation is the power a principal gives to another, the authorised representative, to perform legal acts in his name.
(2) Where this Title speaks of legal act, this includes receipt of a declaration.

Article 3:61. (1) A mandate can be given explicitly or silently.
(2) If a legal act is performed in the name of another, it cannot be invoked against the other party, if he assumed on the basis of a declaration or conduct of the other and in the given circumstances he could reasonably assume that sufficient authorisation was given.
(3) If a mandate given by law or usage made in public has limitations that are so unusual that the other party need not have expected them, these cannot be invoked against him, unless he knew them.

Article 3:62. (1) A general mandate only extends to acts of disposal if it is determined in writing and unequivocally that it also extents to these acts. General mandate means the mandate that includes all the objects of the principal and all legal acts, with the exception of that which is unequivocally excluded.
(2) A special mandate that is given in general terms only extends to acts of disposal if this is unequivocally determined. Nevertheless a mandate that is given for a specific purpose extends to all acts of management and of disposal that can be useful for achieving this purpose.

Article 3:63. (1) The circumstance that someone is incompetent to perform legal acts for himself does not make him incompetent to act as an agent.
(2) If a mandate is granted by an incompetent person, a legal act performed pursuant to that mandate by the authorised representative is valid, void or voidable in the same manner as if it would have been performed by the incompetent himself.

Article 3:64. Unless it is otherwise provided, an authorised representative is only competent to grant the authorisation granted to him to another in the following cases:
(a) to the extent the competence to do so necessarily stems from the nature of the legal acts to be performed or in accordance with usage;
(b) to the extent the granting of the mandate to another person is necessary on the interest of the principal and he is not able to arrange this himself;
(c) to the extent the mandate concerns things, that are located outside the country in which the authorised representative has his place of residence.

Article 3:65. If a mandate is granted to two or more persons together, each of them is competent to act independently, unless otherwise determined.

Article 3:66. (1) A legal act performed by the authorised representative within the limits of his competence in the name of the principal binds in its effects the principal.
(2) To the extent that the existence of a will or of defect of consent, as well as knowledge or ignorance of facts is relevant to the validity or the effects of a legal act, for the evaluation thereof, both the principal and the authorised representative are both to be considered, depending on the share that each of them has had in bringing about the legal act and in the determination of its content.

Article 3:67. He who enters a contract in the name of still to be named principal, shall name the name within the time period laid down by the law, the contract or usage, or, in the absence thereof, within a reasonable time.
(2) If he does not name the name of the principal within the time period, he is deemed to have entered the contract for himself, unless something else stems from the contract.

Article 3:68. Unless otherwise provided, an authorised representative can only act as the other party of the principal, if the content of the legal act to be performed is so accurately determined, that conflict between both interests is excluded.

Article 3:69. (1) If someone without being authorised there to as authorised representative acts in the name of another, the latter may ratify the legal act and thereby provide it with the same effect as it would have had if it had been performed pursuant to a mandate.
(2) If a certain form is required for granting a mandate, the same requirement applies for ratification.
(3) A ratification has no effect, if at the time when it takes place, the other party has already made known that she regards the act as invalid due to a lack of mandate, unless the other party at the time that she acted understood or in the given circumstances reasonably should have understood that no sufficient mandate had been granted.

(4) A direct stakeholder may determine a reasonable period of time acted for the ratification to the person in whose name was acted. He does not need to be satisfied with a partial or a conditional ratification.
(5) Rights granted to third parties by the principal before the ratification remain intact.

Article 3:70. He who acted as authorised representative, is responsible for the existence and the scope of the mandate against the other party, unless the other party knows or ought to understand that a sufficient mandate is lacking or the authorised representative has notified the other party of the content of the mandate completely.

Article 3:71. (1) Declarations made by an authorised representative, may be rejected as invalid by the other party if she immediately asked the authorised principal for proof of the mandate and she did not immediately either hand over a document from which the mandate follows or the mandate was not confirmed by the principal.
(2) Proof of mandate cannot be required if the mandate is brought to the attention of the other party by the principal, if it is made known in a certain way by law or usage, or if it stems from a position which is known to the other party.

Article 3:72. The mandate ends:
(a)upon death, guardianship, or insolvency of the principal or the application in respect of him of a debt restructuring scheme natural persons;
(b) upon death, guardianship, or insolvency of the authorised representative or the application in respect of him of a debt restructuring scheme natural persons, unless otherwise specified;
(c) by withdrawal by the principal;
(d) by cancellation by the authorised representative.

Article 3:73. (1) Notwithstanding the death of or the appointment of a guardian for the principal, the authorised representative remains competent to perform legal act that are necessary for the management of a company
(2) Notwithstanding the death of or the appointment of a guardian for the principal, the authorised representative remains competent to perform legal act that cannot be postponed without disadvantage. The same applies if the authorised principal has cancelled the authorisation.
(3) The competence mentioned in the previous paragraphs ends one year after the death, the guardianship or the cancellation.

Article 3:74. (1) To the extent an authorisation extends to the performance of a legal in the interest of the authorised representative or of a third party, it may be provided that it is irrevocable, or that it does not end due to the death of or the appointment of a guardian for the principal. The first provision encompasses the second, unless it turns out otherwise.
(2) If the authorisation includes a provision as meant in the previous paragraph, the other party may assume that the requirement laid down for the validity of that provision is fulfilled, unless the contrary is clear for her.
(3) Unless otherwise provided, the authorised representative may grant the irrevocably granted authorisation in accordance with the first paragraph to another even outside the cases referred to in Article 64.
(4) The district court may at the request of the principal or of an heir or the administrator of the principal amend or not give effect to a provision as meant in the first paragraph due to important reasons.

Article 3:75. (1) After then end of the authorisation the authorised representative shall, if asked, return writings from which the authorisation appears or allow the principal to write on it that the authorisation has ended. In case of an authorisation granted by notarial deed, the notary who has the deed in his charge at the request of the principal write the end of the authorisation on it.
(2) If it is feared that an authorised representative of an authorisation will make use of it despite its end, the principal can refer to the interim relief judge of the District Court with a request to determine the manner of publication of the end of the authorisation, which will have the effect that it can be invoked against any person. No higher appeal is permitted against a decision pursuant to this paragraph.

Article 3:76
(1) A cause that has ended the authorisation can only be invoked against the other party who did not know of the end of the authorisation, nor had knowledge of the cause:
(a) if the end of the authorisation or the cause that ended it was notified to the other party or was

made known in a manner that according to law or common practice brings with it that the principal can invoke the end of the authorisation against the other party;
(b) if the death of the principal was commonly known;
(c) if the position or employment from which the authorisation stems, ended in a manner recognisable to third parties;
(d) if the other party had acquired knowledge of the authorisation in no other way than through the statement of the authorised representative.
(2) In the cases mentioned in the previous paragraph, the authorised representative who continues to act in the name of the principal is liable for damages against the other party who did not know of the end of the authorisation. He is not liable if he neither knew nor ought to have known that the authorisation had ended.

Article 3:77. If despite the death of the principal a legal act is performed pursuant to the authorisation, the heirs of the principal and the other party are bound as if the act had been performed during the life of the principal.

Article 3:78. If someone acts as a representative on another basis than authorisation, Article 63 paragraph 1, 66 paragraph 1, 67, 69, 70, 71 and 75 paragraph 2 are applied mutatis mutandis to the extent that something else does not stem from the law.

Article 3:79. The provisions in this Title are applied mutatis mutandis outside patrimonial law to the extent that this is not contrary to the nature of the legal act or the legal relationship.

Title 4. Acquisition and Loss of Things

Division 1. General Provisions

Article 3:80. (1) A person can acquire things under general and under special title.
(2) (2) A person acquires things under general title through succession, mixing of estates, merger as meant in Article 309 of Book 2, through separation as meant in Article 334a of Book 2, and through application of a settlement instrument as meant in Articles 3A:1, parts a, b, and c, and 3A:77, parts b, c and d, of the Financial Supervision Law.
(3) A person acquires things under special title through transfer, through prescription and through expropriation, and further in the other ways of acquisition specified by the law for each kind.
(4) A person loses things in the ways specified by the law for each kind.

Article 3:81. (1) He who is entitled to an independent and transferable right may, within the limits of that right, create the limited rights that are mentioned in the law. He may also transfer his right subject to such limited right, provided he takes into account the provisions for the transfer of such a thing as well as for the creation of such a limited right.
(2) Limited rights are destroyed by:
a. the destruction of the right from which the limited right is derived;
b. the expiry of time for which, or the fulfilment of a resolutive condition under which the limited right was created;
c. abandonment;
d. renunciation, if the right thereto has been granted by law or has been granted upon the creation of the right to the holder of the principal right, to the holder of the limited right, or to both persons;
e. mixing of rights (confusio); and further in any other manner of destruction as provided for by law according to each type of destruction.
(3) Abandonment and mixing do not apply to the detriment of those who have in turn a limited right on the destructed limited right. Neither does mixing apply in favour of those who have a limited right on the burdened thing and should have respected the destructed right.

Article 3:82. Dependant rights follow the right to which they are connected.

Division 2. Transfer of Things and Abandonment of Limited Rights

Article 3:83. (1) The right of ownership, limited rights, and claims are transferrable, unless the law or the nature of the right resists the transferability.
(2) The transfer of claims can also be excluded by agreement between the creditor and the debtor.
(3) All other rights are only transferrable when the law provides this.

Article 3:84. (1) The transfer of a thing requires a delivery by virtue of a valid title, made by him who has the power of disposal over that thing.

(2) The title must describe the thing with sufficient certainty.

(3) A legal act that aims to transfer the thing for security purposes, or that lacks the objective to bring the thing into the patrimony of the acquirer after the transfer, is no valid title for the transfer of that thing.

(4) If transfer takes place under a conditional obligation, only a right is acquired that is subject to that same condition as the obligation.

Article 3:85. (1) An obligation for the transfer of a thing for a determined time is regarded as an obligation for the creation of a right of usufruct on the thing for the stipulated time.

(2) An obligation for the transfer of a thing under a suspensive time provision is regarded as an obligation for immediate transfer of the thing with the simultaneous creation of a right of usufruct for the transferor on the thing for the stipulated time.

Article 3:86. (1) Regardless of the lack of power of the transferor to dispose, a transfer made in accordance with Article 90, 91, or 93 of a movable object that is not a registered thing, or of a bearer or an order right, is valid, if the transfer was made for value and the acquirer was in good faith.

(2) Where a thing, referred to in the previous paragraph, which is transferred for value in accordance with Article 90, 91, or 93, is burdened with a limited right of which the acquirer neither knew nor ought to have known at that point in time, then this right ceases to exist, in case of transfer in accordance with Article 91 subject to the same suspensive condition as applied to the delivery.

(3) Nevertheless, the owner of a movable object, who has lost possession thereof through theft, may, for the duration of three years, to be calculated from the day of the theft, reclaim his ownership, unless:

(a) the object has been acquired by a natural person, who did not act in the exercise of a profession or a business, from a transferor whose business it is to deal with the public in similar objects, other than as an auctioneer, on business premises that are intended for such a purpose, being an immovable object or a part thereof with the land that belongs thereto, and provided that the transferor acted in the normal course of his business; or

(b) it concerns money or bearer or order documents.

(4) Articles 316, 318 and 319 regarding the interruption of the prescription period of a claim apply to the period mentioned in the last paragraph mutatis mutandis.

Article 3:86a. Article 86 may not be invoked against a member state of the European Union or against another state that is party to the Agreement on the European Economic Area that demands a movable thing that pursuant to Article 2(1) of Directive 2014/60/EU of the European Parliament and of the Council of 15 May 2014 on the return of cultural objects unlawfully removed from the territory of a Member State and amending Regulation (EU) No 1024/2012 (OJ 2014, L159), provided the thing in the sense of that directive was removed from the territory of that state in an unlawful manner.

(2) Article 86 may also not be invoked against the person who as owner demands a movable thing which at the time at which he lost possession therefore, pursuant to the Cultural Property Law was identified as protected cultural property or for which bringing it outside the Netherlands is forbidden on the basis of Article 4.22 of that law. The person who at that time in the register, referred to in Article 3.11 of that law or on an inventory list meant in Article 4.22, second paragraph, of that law, was mentioned as owner, is presumed to have been owner of the thing at that time.

(3) The court who grants a claim referred to in paragraph 1, grants the possessor a fair compensation established in accordance with the circumstances, if he when acquiring the thing exercised due care. The same applies if the court grants a claim as referred to in paragraph 2, unless reclaiming without compensation through application of Article 86 paragraph 3 would have been possible.

(4) The compensation encompasses in any case that which is owed to the possessor pursuant to Articles 120 and 121. It is paid with the return of the thing.

Article 3:86b. (1) Article 86 may not be invoked against a contracting state of the Convention on the means of prohibiting and preventing the illicit import, export and transfer or ownership of cultural property signed in Paris on 14 November 1970, nor against the right holders if on the basis of Article 6.7 of the Cultural Property Law they have initiated a legal claim as meant in Article 1011a of the Code of Civil Procedure to the return of a movable thing as meant in that Article 3.

(2) The court who grants a claim referred to in the previous paragraph, grants the possessor a fair compensation established in accordance with the circumstances, if he when acquiring the thing exercised due care, unless reclaiming without compensation through application of Article 86 paragraph 3 would have been possible.

(3) The compensation encompasses in any case that which is owed to the possessor pursuant to Articles 120 and 121. It is paid with the return of the thing.

Article 3:87. (1) An acquirer who, within three years after his acquisition, is asked who transferred the thing to him, must without delay provide the information that is needed to find this person or which he at the time of acquisition, could consider sufficient for that purpose. If he does not fulfil this obligation, he may not invoke the protection of Articles 86 and 86a against a transferee in good faith.
(2) The previous paragraph does not apply to money.

Article 3:87a. (1) To establish whether the possessor when acquiring cultural property as meant in Articles 86a paragraph 1 or Article 6.1 under c of the Cultural Property Law exercised due care, all the circumstances surrounding the acquisition will be taken into account, in particular
(a) the documentation over the origin of the thing
(b). the permits required according to the law of the requesting Member State or the law of the Contracting State from which the thing originates to take the thing outside the territory of that Member State or Contracting State;
(c) the nature of the parties;
(d) the price actually paid;
(e) whether the possessor consulted every reasonably accessible register in relation to stole cultural property and every other relevant information and documentation that he could reasonably have acquired, and whether the possessor consulted accessible bodies;
(f) whether the possessor took all other steps that a reasonable person in the circumstances would have taken.
(2) A trade as referred to in Article 437 of the Criminal Code does not exercise the due care when acquiring cultural property according to Article 86a paragraph 2 if he neglected to
(a) inform himself about the identity of the seller;
(b) demand a written statement from the seller that he is competent to dispose of the object;
(c) record in the register he keeps the origin of the cultural property, the names and the address of the seller, the purchase price paid to the seller and a description of the cultural property;
(d) consult the registers relating to stolen cultural property that in the given circumstances in light of the nature of the cultural property are eligible for consultation.
(3) An auction holder who did not fulfil the due diligence requirements under paragraphs 1 and 2 when receiving cultural property for public sale or who returns the cultural property to the person who offered it for public sale without fulfilling these due diligence requirements acts unlawfully towards those who can initiate a demand for return as meant in Article 86b.

Article 3:88. (1) Regardless of the lack of power of the transferor to dispose, the transfer of a registered thing, a non-documentary claim, or of another thing to which Article 86 does not apply, is valid, if the acquirer was in good faith and the lack of power to dispose was not the result of an invalid earlier transfer, that was not the consequence of a lack of the power to dispose of the transferor at that time.
(2) Paragraph (1) cannot be invoked against a claim meant in Articles 86a paragraphs (1) and (2) and 86b paragraph (1).

Article 3:89. (1) The delivery, required for a transfer of immovable objects, is effected by a notarial deed, drafted between the parties, followed by the registration of that deed in the appropriate public register. Both the acquirer as well as the transferor may ask for the registration.
(2) The deed of delivery must specifically mention the title of transfer; additional conditions, which do not concern the transfer, can be left out of the deed.
(3) When someone is acting as am authorised representative for another in the deed, the deed must specifically mention the mandate.
(4) This Article is applicable mutatis mutandis to the delivery required for the transfer of other registered things.

Article 3:90. (1) The delivery required for the transfer of movable objects, not registered things, that are in the power of the acquirer, is made by providing the acquirer with possession of the object.
(2) If the object remains in the hands of the transferor after the transfer, the transfer has effect against a third party with an older right to the object only from the moment that the object comes into the hands of the acquirer, unless the holder of the older right agreed to the transfer.

Article 3:91. (1) The delivery of the objects meant in the previous Article for the performance of an obligation to transfer under a suspensive condition occurs by providing the acquirer with the power over the object.

Article 3:92. (1) Where a contract has as its object that the right of ownership of an object is brought

into the power of another, but only once a performance that is due by the other party is completed, it is assumed that the right of ownership is transferred under the suspensive condition of completion of that performance.
(2) A reservation of ownership can only be validly made in respect to claims for counter-performance based on a contract for the object delivered, or to be delivered, by the transferor to the transferee, or based on a contract for work to be performed for the transferee, as well as for claims for deficiencies of performance of such contracts. To the extent that a condition is void on this basis, it is deemed not to have been written.
(3) A condition as meant in paragraph (1) is presumed to be fulfilled, when the transferor is satisfied in any other way than by performance, if the acquirer is freed from his obligation under Article 60 of Book 6, or if the prescription period in respect to the claim for performance has expired. Except for a stipulation stating otherwise, the same applies for the abandonment of the right to a counter-performance.

Article 3:92a. (Repealed.)

Article 3:93. The delivery, required for the transfer of a bearer right of which the bearer document is in the power of the transferor, is made by the delivery of that document in the way and with the effects as set forth in Articles 90, 91 and 92. For the transfer of a right to order, of which the order document is in the power of the transferor, the same applies, in so far as delivery also requires an endorsement.

Article 3:94. (1) Besides the cases dealt with in the previous Article, rights that can be exercised against one or more persons are delivered by a deed for that purpose, and notice to these persons by the transferor and acquirer.
(2) The delivery of a right that can be exercised against a certain, however on the date the deed is passed unknown person, that belongs on that day to the transferor, has retroactive effect, provided notice is given as soon as reasonably possible, after that person has become known.
(3) These rights can also be delivered by authentic deed or registered deed to that purpose, without notice to those persons against whom the right can be exercised, if these rights, already exist at the moment of delivery or will be acquired directly from an already existing legal relationship. The delivery cannot be invoked against those persons against whom it can be exercised until notice of the delivery has been made to them by the transferor or acquirer. For the acquirer of a right that is delivered according to the first sentence, Article 88 paragraph (1) only applies if he was in good faith at the point in time mentioned in the second sentence.
(4) Persons, against whom the right can be exercised, may demand to receive a summary of the deed and its title certified by the transferor. Stipulations that are irrelevant to these persons, do not have to be included in it. Where a deed has not been made of the title, the content of the title should, in so far as it is relevant to them, be notified in writing.

Article 3:95. Apart from the situations regulated in Article 89-94 and subject to what is laid down in Articles 96 and 98, things are delivered by a deed for that purpose.

Article 3:96. The delivery of a share in a thing occurs in the corresponding way and with the corresponding consequences as is provided with respect to the delivery of that thing.

Article 3:97. (1) Future things can be delivered in advance, unless it is forbidden to make these the subject of a contract or if they are registered things.
(2) A delivery in advance of a future thing does not work against someone who acquired the thing pursuant to an earlier delivery in advance. If it concerns a movable object, it works against him from the time that the object came in the hands of the acquirer.

Article 3:98. Unless the law provides otherwise, everything that this division provides on the transfer of things, is applicable mutatis mutandis to the creation, the transfer and the abandonment of a property right on such a thing.

Division 3. Acquisition and Loss through Prescription

Article 3:99. (1) Rights to movable objects that are not registered things, and bearer rights or order rights are acquired by a possessor in good faith through uninterrupted possession of three years, other things though uninterrupted possession of ten years.
(2) Paragraph 1 does not apply to movable objects that pursuant to the Cultural Property Law are regarded as protected cultural object.
(3) Paragraph 1 cannot be invoked against a claim referred to in Articles 86a paragraph 1 and 86b paragraph 1.

Article 3:100. He who has taken possession of a succession patrimony, cannot acquire the succession patrimony and the things belonging to it sooner through prescription to the detriment of the right holder that after his legal claim to demand the succession patrimony has prescribed.

Article 3:101. Prescription [verjaring] begins to run on the commencement of the day after the start of the possession.

[Articles 3:102-3:104 are omitted.]

Article 3:105. (1) He who possesses a thing at the point in time when the period of prescription of the claim aimed at ending that possession is completed, acquires that thing, even if his possession was not in good faith.
(2) Where a person has lost possession involuntarily prior to that point in time, but regains it after that point in time, provided within the year after the loss of possession or on the basis of a claim brought within that year, he is regarded to be the possessor at the point in time stated in the aforementioned paragraph.

[Article 3:106 is omitted.]

Title 5. Possession and holding [Bezit en houderschap]

Article 3:107. (1) Possession is holding a thing for oneself.
(2) Possession is direct when a person is in possession, without another holding the thing for him.
(3) Possession is indirect when a person is in possession through another person holding the thing for him.
(4) Holding is mutatis mutandis direct or indirect.

Article 3:108. Whether a person holds a thing and whether he does this for himself or for another, is assessed according to the common opinion [verkeersopvatting], taking into account the following rules and otherwise on the basis of external facts.

Article 3:109. A person who holds a thing, is presumed to hold it for himself.

[Articles 3:110 – 3:111 are omitted.]

Article 3:112. Possession is acquired by taking possession [inbezitneming], by transfer or by succession under general title [opvolging onder algemene titel].

Article 3:113. (1) A person takes possession of a thing by furnishing oneself with the actual power [feitelijke macht] over it.
(2) When a thing is in the possession of another, singular and independent acts of actual power are insufficient for taking possession.

Article 3:114. A possessor transfers his possession by putting the acquirer in a position to exercise the actual power that he himself could exercise over the thing.

Article 3:115. A bilateral declaration without any actual conduct is sufficient for the transfer of possession:
a. when the transferor possesses the object and in accordance with a stipulation made at the delivery he henceforth holds it for the acquirer;
b. when the acquirer was holder [houder] of the object for the transferor;
c. when a third party held the object for the transferor, and after the transfer of the object holds it for the acquirer. In that case, possession does not pass until that third party has recognized the transfer, or otherwise the transferor or acquirer notified him of the transfer. In dit geval gaat het bezit niet over voordat de derde de overdracht heeft erkend, dan wel de vervreemder de verkrijger de overdracht aan hem heeft medegedeeld.

Article 3:116. He who succeeds another under general title, thereby succeeds that other in his possession and holding, with all the qualities and deficiencies thereof.

Article 3:117. (1) A possessor of a thing loses possession when he apparently relinquishes the thing, or when another acquires possession of the thing.
(2) As long as the conditions for the loss of possession mentioned in the previous paragraph are not met, possession that has commenced continues.

Article 3:118. (1) A possessor is in good faith when he considers himself to be the right holder

[rechthebbende] and could reasonably consider himself so such.
(2) Once a possessor is in good faith, he is deemed to remain so.
(3) Good faith is presumed to be present; the lack of good faith must be proven.

Article 3:119. (1) The possessor of a thing is presumed to be the right holder.
(2) In respect to registered things this presumption yields, when it is established that the other party or his predecessor in title [rechtsvoorganger] was at any time the right holder and that the possessor cannot base his claim on subsequent acquisition under special title for which registration in the registers is required.

Article 3:120. (1) A possessor in good faith is entitled to the natural fruits and the civil fruits that can be claimed.
(2) The right holder to a thing who demands its return from a possessor in good faith or who has received the thing from such possessor is obliged to compensate the costs made on behalf of the thing as well as the damage for which the possessor is liable against third parties on the basis of Title 3 of Book 6 following from his possession, in as far as the possessor was not compensated by another for the fruits he enjoyed and other advantages. A court may limit the amount of compensation that is due when a complete compensation would lead to an unfair advantage for the possessor in relation to the right holder
(3) As long as the possessor has not received the compensation that is due to him, he is entitled to suspend the handing over of the thing.
(4) This Article also applies to he who assumes or he who may assume that he obtained possession in a lawful manner, even if he knows that the acts that are required for the delivery of the right, have not taken place.

Article 3:121. (1) A possessor who is not in good faith is obliged towards the right holder, apart from returning the thing, to also return the natural fruits and the civil fruits that can be claimed, regardless of his liability on the basis of that which is determined in Title 3 of Book 6 on the damage suffered by the right holder.
(2) He only has a claim against right holder for the compensation of costs that he has made in respect of the thing to obtain the fruits, in so far as he may claim such compensation from the right holder on the basis of what is determined regarding unjustified enrichment.
(3) This Article also applies to the possessor in good faith from the moment that the right holder invokes his right against him.

Article 3:122. In case the right holder wishes to transfer the thing to the possessor at his expense to release himself from the compensation owed by him pursuant to the two previous Articles, the possessor must cooperate with this.

Article 3:123. If the possessor of an object made alterations or additions to that object, he is entitled, instead of claiming the compensation due to him pursuant to Articles 120 and 121, to remove these alterations and additions, provided he returns the object to its original state.

Article 3:124. When someone holds a thing for another and a third party that claims to be the right holder demands the thing, that which is provided in the previous four Articles relating to the possessor applies, taking into account the legal relation that he had to the other.

Article 3:125.
(1) He who obtained possession of a thing may, in case of subsequent loss of possession or interference with his possession, use the same legal claims against a third person for the return of the thing or the cessation of the interference that the right holder of the thing has. of the right holder. Nevertheless, the legal claim must be initiated within one year after the loss or interference.
(2)The claim is denied if the defendant had a better right to hold the thing or performed the interference pursuant to a better right, than the claimant, unless the defendant took away the claimant's possession or interfered with possession by using force or in a secretive manner.
(3) The provisions in this Article leaves open the possibility for the possessor, also when the year mentioned in the first paragraph has passed, and for the holder to initiate a claim on the basis of wrongful act, when there is reason to do so.

Title 6. Administratorship [Bewind]

Article 3:126 (Reserved.)

Title 7. Community [Gemeenschap]

Division 1. General Provisions

Article 3:166. (1) Community [Gemeenschap] arises when one or more things jointly belong to two or more shareholders [deelgenoten].
(2) The shares in the community of the shareholders are equal, unless something else follows from their legal relation.
(3) Article 2 of Book 6 is applicable mutatis mutandis to the legal relations between the shareholders.

Article 3:167. Things that must be considered to replace a community thing belong to the community.

Article 3:168. (1) The shareholders may arrange the enjoyment, use and management of the community things by agreement.
(2) To the extent that an agreement is missing, the local court [kantonrechter] may, on the request of the party most ready, order any arrangement, if necessary with administratorship of the things. In doing so, he will consider in fairness the interests of the parties as well as the general interest.
(3) An existing arrangement may, at the request of the party most ready, be altered or set aside by the court on the basis of unforeseen circumstances.
(4) An arrangement also binds those that acquire a right from the shareholder.
(5) In so far as the local court [kantonrechter] does not decide otherwise, Articles 154, 158 to 168, 172, 173 and 174 of book 4, apply mutatis mutandis to an administratorship mentioned in paragraph 2, provided that the local court [kantonrechter] may also arrange the remuneration mentioned in Article 159 of Book 4 differently, as well as that he may demand the security mentioned in Article 160 of Book 4 at any moment. This may be cancelled by a joint decision of the shareholders or on the request of any one of them by the local court [kantonrechter].

Article 3:169. Unless a provision determines otherwise, every shareholder is entitled to the use of a community thing, provided the use can be aligned with the rights of the other shareholders.

Article 3:170. (1) Acts for the ordinary maintenance or preservation of a community thing, and in general acts that cannot be postponed, can be made by any of the shareholders where necessary independently. Every one of them is entitled to stop a prescription period on behalf of the community
(2) For the rest, the management is done by the shareholders together, unless a provision provides otherwise. Management includes all acts that are can be useful for the normal operation of the thing, as well as accepting performances due to the community.
(3) Other acts relating to a community thing than those mentioned in the previous paragraphs can only be made by the shareholders together.

Article 3:171. Unless a provision determines otherwise, every shareholder is entitled to initiate legal claims and make submit requests to obtain a court decision on behalf of the community. A provision that allocates the management to one or more of the shareholders excludes, unless it provides otherwise, this power for the others.

Article 3:172. Unless a regulation prescribes otherwise, the shareholders share in proportionality to their share in the fruits and other benefits that the community thing provides, and must contribute in the same proportion to the expenses that follow from acts that are competently done on behalf of the community.

Article 3:173. Each of the shareholders can demand from the person amongst them who has managed on their behalf, to annually and in any event at the end of the management account and justification.

Article 3:174. (1) The court that would be competent in relation to a claim for division or to whom such a claim has already been brought can authorise a shareholder, upon his request, for the payment of a debt that is owed by the community or for other serious grounds to liquidate a community thing. If a shareholder for whom the thing to be sold has special value, is prepared to take over the thing against compensation for the estimated value, the aforementioned court may order this acquisition.
(2) The court referred to in paragraph 1 may authorise a shareholder upon his request to burden a community thing with a right of pledge or hypothec for security of the payment of a debt owed by the community that already exists or which is appropriate to make for the preservation of a community thing.

Article 3:175. (1) Unless it follows otherwise from the legal relation between the shareholders, each of them may have at its disposal his share in a community thing.

(2) If it follows from the legal relation between the shareholders that they are not competent to have their share at their disposal, unless with the permission of all, paragraphs 3 and 4 of Article 168 apply mutatis mutandis.

(3) The creditors of a shareholder can exercise a right to sell against a share in the community thing. After the exercise of the right to sell [uitwinning] on a share, the limitations of the power to dispose over the share cannot be invoked between the acquirer of the share and the other shareholders.

Article 3:176. (1) The acquirer of a share of a limited property right thereon must immediately give notice to the other shareholders or to the person who has been given the task of management over the thing by the shareholders or by the court.

(2) A share that has been transferred is acquired with the burden to compensate to the community for that which the transferor owed. Transferor and acquirer are jointly and severally liable for this compensation. The acquirer can relieve himself of this duty by assigning his share, at his own expense to the other shareholders; they are obliged to cooperate with such assignment.

(3) The previous paragraphs do not apply to the exercise of a right to sell the joint shares in a community thing.

Article 3:177. (1) If a community thing is divided or transferred while a limited property right rests on a share of a shareholder, then that right will rest on the thing in so far as this is acquired by that shareholder, and the thing is freed from that right otherwise, notwithstanding that which the holder of the limited property right or the shareholder on whose share the right rests, may claim pursuant to the mutual relationship from the other for the surplus value of the thing this person has received.

(2) A division, as well as a transfer to which the shareholders have obliged themselves after creation of the limited property right, requires the cooperation of the holder of the limited property right.

(3) A right of pledge or hypothec stipulated when allocating the thing to the shareholder mentioned in the first paragraph to guarantee that which he owes or could owe to one or more of the shareholders as a result of the division, has, provided it is created at the same time as the delivery of that which is allocated to him, priority over a limited property right that a shareholder had created previously on his share.

Article 3:178. (1) Each of the shareholders, as well as he who has a limited property right on a share, may at all times claim a division of a community thing, unless something else follows from the nature of the community or the following paragraphs.

(2) On the request of a shareholder the court to which the claim for division has been made, may decide that all or some debts that are due and payable and for the account of the community, must be satisfied before a division can be made.

(3) If the interests of one or more of the shareholders in case of an immediate division are significantly larger than the interests that are served by the division, the court before which the claim for division has been made may, on the request of a shareholder one or more times, each for a period of a maximum of three years, exclude the claim for divide.

(4) If a claim for division has not been made, a decision as meant in paragraphs 2 and 3, may be made on the request of each of the shareholders by the court that would be competent had the claim for division been brought.

(5) Those who have the power to claim the division can exclude their power, once or several times, by contract, each time for a period of a maximum of five years. Paragraphs 3 and 4 of Article 169 apply to such contract mutatis mutandis.

Article 3:179. (1) If a claim for the division of a community thing is made, each of the shareholders may demand that all things belonging to the community and the debts that are owed by the community are included in the division, unless there are important reasons for a partial division. Those things that must remain undivided following one of the grounds mentioned in Article 178, are excluded from the division.

(2) The circumstance that one or more things are omitted in a division, only has the consequence that a further division thereof can be claimed.

(3) Division 3 of Title 2 of Book 6 applies to the allocation of a debt.

Article 3:180. (1) A creditor who has a due and payable claim on a shareholder, may claim division of the community, but no further than is necessary for the recovery of his debt. Article 178 paragraph 3 applies.

(2) If a creditor has obtained an order of division of the community, the division requires his cooperation.

Article 3:181. (1) In case shareholders or persons whose cooperation is required not cooperate with a division after this was ordered by a court decision, the judge who has taken notice of the claim to division in first instance appoints, in case this appointment has not already been made in that decision, on the request of the party the most ready, an impartial person who represents them in the division and looks after their interests following his own best judgement. If the persons who do not cooperate have conflicting interests, an impartial person will be appointed for each of them.
(2) An impartial person is obliged to receive that what is due to the person he represents in relation to the division, and until the release of this to the right holder hold the administratorship over it on the basis of Article 410 of Book 1.
(3) The reward that is due to the impartial person for the burden of the right holder, will be determined at his request by the court who appointed him.

Article 3:182. A division is regarded as any legal act to which all shareholders, either in person, or represented, cooperate and pursuant to which one or more of them acquire one or more things from the community with the exclusion of the other shareholders. The act is not a division if it is made to fulfil a debt of the community to one or more shareholders that does not stem from a legal act as meant in the previous sentence.

Article 3:183. (1) The division may take place in the manner and in the form that the parties see fit, provided that the shareholder and those persons whose cooperation is required all have the free disposal over their things and cooperate in person or through a legal representative appointed by them, or, in case of administratorship of their right, are represented by their administrator who was the appropriate permission or mandate to do so.
(2) In other cases, unless the court decides otherwise, the division must be made by notarial deed and be approved by the local court [kantonrechter] that is competent to authorise acts of disposal by the legal representative of the person who does not have the free disposal over his things.

Article 3:184. (1) Every one of the shareholders can request that that which is owed by another shareholder to the community is allocated to the share of that other in the division. The allocation is made irrespective of the financial status of the debtor. If it is a debt subject to a time provision, it is allocated for its actual value at the moment of division.
(2) The previous paragraph does not apply to debts under suspensive condition that have not been fulfilled.

Article 3:185. (1) To the extent that the shareholders and those persons whose cooperation is required cannot reach agreement on the division, the court at the request of the party most ready orders the manner in which division is made or it decides on the division itself, taking into account in accordance with fairness the interests of the parties as well as the general interest.
(2) Ways in which a division can be made include:
(a) The allocation of a part of thing to each of the shareholders;
(b) The over-allocation [overbedeling] of one or more of the shareholders against compensation of the surplus value;
(c) The distribution of the net-profit of a thing or a part thereof, after this is sold in a manner decided by the court.
(3) If necessary, the court can decide that the person who is over-allocated, may pay the surplus value in whole or in part in instalments. It can make a condition that security is provided for a certain amount established by and of a certain nature established by it.

Article 3:186. (1) A delivery in the same manner than as is prescribed for transfer is required for the passing of that what is allocated to each of the shareholders.
(2) That which a shareholder acquires, is held under the same title as it was held by the shareholders together before the division.

Article 3:187. (1) The documents and evidence of ownership that belong to the allocated things are given to him to whom the things are allocated.
(2) General inventory papers and documents as meant in paragraph 1 that relate to things allocated to one or more shareholders, remain with him who the majority of the involved shareholders have appointed thereto, under the duty to allow inspection to the other shareholders and, if someone requires, to provide copies or extracts at their expense.
(3) In the absence of a majority as meant in the previous paragraph, the appointment meant there is made at the request of a shareholder by the court that establishes the division, or in other cases at the request of a shareholder by the local court [kantonrechter]. Against the decision pursuant to this paragraph, no appeal is allowed.

Article 3:188. (1) Unless otherwise agreed, the shareholders are obliged to compensate each other in proportion to their share for damage that is the result of the exercise of a right to sell [uitwinning] or disturbance, stemming from a cause arising before the division, as well as, when the claim for the full sum is allocated, the damage that stems from a lack of financial means of the debtor at the moment of the division.

(2) If a shareholder is subject to exercise of a right to sell or disturbed due to his own fault, the other shareholders are not obliged to compensate his damage.

(3) A duty to compensate the damage that stems from a lack of financial means of the debtor ceases upon the expiry of three years after the division and after the allocated claim has become due payable.

(4) In case recourse to a shareholder for his share in compensation for damage that is due pursuant to the first paragraph, is impossible, the share of each of the other shareholders is increased proportionately.

Division 2. Some Specific Communities

Article 3:189. (1) The provisions of this Title do not apply to a marital community, community of registered partners, partnership [maatschap], company [vennootschap] or shipping company [rederij], for as long as these are not dissolved, nor for the community of a building divided into apartment rights, for as long as the division is not terminated.

(2) For the community of succession, for a dissolved marital community, dissolved community of registered partners, partnership, company or shipping company, and for a community of a building of which the division in apartment rights is terminated, the following provisions of this Division apply, as well as those in the first Division to the extent that these are not derogated from in this Division.

Article 3:190. (1) A shareholder does not have at his disposal his share in a thing belonging to the community separately, and his creditors cannot exercise a right to sell such a share without permission of the other shareholders.

(2) Nevertheless, a shareholder can create a right of pledge or hypthothec on such a share also without permission of the other shareholders. As long as the thing belongs to the community, the pledgor or hypothecor cannot proceed to sell, unless the other shareholders give permission to do so.

Article 3:191. (1) Unless it follows differently from the legal relations between the shareholders, each of the shareholder has at his disposal his share in the entire community and his creditors may exercise a right to sell on such a share.

(2) If it follows from the legal relation between the shareholders that they do not have the power to have their share at their disposal, unless with permission of all, paragraphs 3 and 4 of Article 168 apply mutatis mutandis.

Article 3:192. The debts belonging to the community may be recovered from the things belonging to the community.

Article 3:193. (1) A creditor whose claim on the community things can be recovered, may request a court to appoint a liquidator [vereffenaar] when the division of the community is made before the debts of the community that are due and payable are paid or when there is risk for him that the will not be paid in full or within a reasonable time, either because the community does not provide enough or is not managed or dissolved appropriately, or because a creditor will recover from one or more of the community things. Division 3 of Title 6 of Book 4 relating to the division of a succession patrimony applies mutatis mutandis.

(2) A creditor of a shareholder also may request the court to appoint a liquidator when his interests are severely damaged by the behaviour of the shareholders.

(3) Paragraphs 1 and 2 do not apply to the dissolved community of a partnership or company and instead the following sentences apply. A creditor whose claims can be recovered from community things is entitled to protest the division of the community. A division that was made after this protest is avoidable provided that the ground for avoidance can only be invoked by the creditor who protested and that he can only avoid the division to his needs and no further than is necessary to relieve the disadvantage that was suffered by him.

Article 3:194. (1) Each of the shareholders may claim that a division begins with description of assets [boedelbeschrijving].

(2) A shareholder who deliberately conceals, loses, keeps hidden community things forfeits his share in those things to the other shareholders.

Division 3. Void and Voidable Divisions

Article 3:195. (1) A division in which not all shareholders and all other persons whose cooperation is required have participated is void, unless it is made by notarial deed, in which case it only can be avoided upon the petition of the person who has not participated in the division. This legal claim prescribes on the expiration of one year after the division has come to his attention.
(2) If someone participated in the division who was not entitled to the community, or did a shareholder act in the division for a share larger than that was coming to him, the wrongly paid can be reclaimed on behalf of the community; for the remainder, the division remains in force.

Article 3:196. (1) Apart from the general grounds to avoid a legal act, a division van also voidable when a shareholder has made a mistake concerning the value or one or more of the things or debts to be divided and thereby has been disadvantaged by more than a quarter part.
(2) When the disadvantage of more than a quarter has been proven, the disadvantaged person is presumed to have made a mistake concerning the value of one or more of the things and debts.
(3) To determine whether disadvantage has taken place, the value of the things and debts of the community are estimated at the moment of division. Things and debts that are left undivided are not taken into account.
(4) A division cannot be avoided on the basis of a mistake in respect to the value of one or more of the things or debts to be divided if the disadvantaged person has accepted the allocation to his benefit or loss.

Article 3:197. The power to avoid a division based on disadvantage ceases when the other shareholders provide the disadvantaged person in money or in kind that which was missing from his share.

Article 3:198. If a request for the avoidance of a division is made in law, the court may, notwithstanding what is provided in Articles 53 and 54, at the request of one of the parties, change the division instead of ordering the avoidance.

Article 3:199. Articles 228-230 of Book 6 do not apply to a division.

Article 3:200. A legal claim for the avoidance of a division ceases upon expiration of three years after the division.

Title 8. Right of usufruct

Article 3:201. (1) The right of usufruct [vruchtgebruik] provides the right to use things that belong to another and to enjoy the fruits thereof.

Article 3:202. A right of usufruct is established by creation [vestiging] or by prescription [verjaring].

Article 3:203. (1) A right of usufruct can be created for one person, or for two or more persons either jointly or by succession. In the latter case those that will be entitled by succession must exist at the moment of creation.
(2) A right of usufruct cannot be created for a period longer than the life of the usufructuary. A right of usufruct for two or more persons will, upon the end of the right for one of them, accrue to that of the others, in equal parts relating to their share, and will end, unless otherwise provided, by the cessation of the right of the last right holder.
(3) If the usufructuary is a legal person, the right of usufruct ends with the dissolution of the legal person, and in any case after the passing of thirty years from the day of creation.

Article 3:204. [Repealed on 01-01-2003]

Article 3:205. (1) Unless an adminstratorship [bewind] has already led to a sufficient description of assets or obliges thereto, the usufructuary, in the presence of or after sufficient invitation by the principal right holder must make a notarial description of the things. The description can be made privately, if the principal right holder is present and the principal right holder and usufructuary have made provision for its keeping.
(2) Both the usufructuary and the principal right holder are entitled to include any specifics in the description that are useful to know the state of the objects subject to the right of usufruct.
(3) The principal right holder is entitled to suspend the delivery and handing over of things subject to the right of usufruct, if the usufructuary does not meet his obligation to describe in a timely manner.
(4) The usufructuary must send annually a signed and accurate report of which things are no longer present, which things have replaced these, and the advantages that the things have given rise to that are not fruits.

5. The usufructuary cannot be relieved of the responsibilities mentioned in the previous paragraphs.
6. Unless otherwise provided, the costs of the description and the annual report mentioned in paragraph 4 are for the usufructuary.

Article 3:206. (1) The usufructuary must provide security for the performance of his obligations towards the principal right holder, unless he is released from this responsibility or if the interests of the principal right holder are already sufficiently guaranteed by the creation of an administratorship.
(2) When the usufructuary is released from the obligation to provide security, the principal right holder may demand that the objects subject to the right of usufruct are shown to him on a yearly basis. In respect of value documents and money, except in special circumstance, the handing over of a declaration of a registered credit institution will suffice.

Article 3:207. (1) A usufructuary can use and use up the things under usufruct in accordance with the rules made upon creation of the usufruct, or where such rules are lacking, in accordance with the nature of the things and the local practice in respect to the use and using up.
(2) A usufructuary is moreover entitled to engage in all acts that can be useful for the good management of the things that are subject to the right of usufruct. With respect to all other acts concerning the things the person with the principal right holder and usufructuary are merely jointly competent.
(3) As against the principal right holder, the usufructuary is obliged with respect to the things subject to the right of usufruct and the management thereof to exercise the care of a good usufructuary.

Article 3:208. (1) The usufructuary may not alter the purpose that the objects subject to the right of usufruct had at the moment of creation of the right, without the permission of the principal right holder or authorisation from the local court [kantonrechter].
(2) Unless the deed of creation determines otherwise, the usufructuary of an object is entitled, both during the duration of his right as well as at the end of it, to remove alterations and additions made to the object, provided he returns the object to its original state.

Article 3:209. (1) The usufructuary is obliged to insure the subject matter of the right of usufruct on behalf of the principal right holder against those risks for which insurance is customary. In any case, the usufructuary is obliged, if a building is included in his right of usufruct, to insure this against fire.
(2)In so far as the usufructuary does not fulfil his obligations under the first paragraph, the principal right holder is entitled to take out insurance himself and the usufructuary is obliged to reimburse the costs made therefor.

Article 3:210. (1) Unless determined otherwise at the creation, the usufructuary is entitled to demand performance, both in and outside of court, of claims and to receive monetary payments under the right of usufruct.
(2) Unless determined otherwise at the creation, he is only entitled to dissolution and cancellation of contracts when this could be useful to a good management.
(3) The person with the principal entitlement is only entitled to exercise the powers mentioned in the previous paragraphs if he has obtained permission from the usufructuary or a mandate from the local court [kantonrechter]. No appeal is permitted against the mandate given by the local court by virtue of this paragraph.

Article 3:211. (1) Although the description or the annual report only describes one or more things that are subject to the right of usufruct by their type, the principal right holder keeps his right on these.
(2) The usufructuary is obliged to separate these things from the rest of his patrimony.

Article 3:212. (1) In so far as the things subject to the right of usufruct are destined to be transferred, the usufructuary is entitled to transfer these things in accordance with their purpose.
(2) The usufructuary may be given the power at the moment of creation to dispose of things other than those mentioned in the previous paragraph. In respect to these things, Articles 208, 210 paragraph 2 and 217 paragraphs 2 and 3, second sentence, and paragraph 4, are not applicable.
(3) In other cases, the usufructuary may only transfer or burden the things subject to the right of usufruct with permission of the principal right holder or with authorisation by the local court to do so. The authorisation will only be provided when the interest of the usufructuary or the principal right holder is served by the transfer or burdening and the interest of the other is not thereby harmed.

Article 3:213. (1) That which comes in the place of the things subject to the right of usufruct, through the exercise of the power to dispose over them, belongs to the principal right holder and is likewise subject to the right of usufruct. The same applies for that which is received through collection of claims subject to the right of usufruct, and claims for compensation that comes in the place of things subject to the right of usufruct, including claims in respect of the devaluation of those things.

(2) Also subject to the right of usufruct are those advantages that a thing yields during the existence of the right of usufruct and which are not fruits.

Article 3:214. (1) Unless otherwise determined at the creation of the right of usufruct, money that is subject to the right of usufruct must be, in consultation with the principal right holder fruitfully invested or spent for the benefit of the other things subject to the right of usufruct.

(2) In the case of a dispute concerning what is to happen to the money referred to in the first paragraph, the person who at the creation of the right of usufruct was appointed thereto decides on this matter, or in the absence of such an appointment, the local court [kantonrechter]. No appeal is permitted against the decision given by the local court by virtue of this paragraph.

Article 3:215. (1) Where upon creation of a right of usufruct, or after that, the power to partially or completely alienate or use up the things under usufruct is given to the usufructuary, the principal right holder may demand the retro-transfer of the things under usufruct or the things substituted for these, unless the usufructuary or acquirers of his right prove that the things were used up or vanished by coincidence.

(2) In granting such power to alienate or use up, one or more persons can be assigned whose permission is needed for the alienation or using up. If the right of usufruct is subject to administratorship, the alienation and using up are subject to cooperation of the administrator.

(3) If the usufructuary has been granted the power to alienate or use up, he may also use the things for ordinary small gifts.

Article 3:216. The usufructuary is entitled to all fruits that are separated or that can be claimed during the existence of the right of usufruct. What with respect to the right of usufruct can be regarded as a fruit can be further determined at the creation of the right of usufruct.

Article 3:217. (1) The usufructuary is entitled to rent [verhuren] or lease [verpachten] the object subject to the right of usufruct, in so far as nothing is determined otherwise at the moment of creation of the right.

(2) In case an immovable object was not rented or leased at the moment of creation of the right of usufruct, the usufructuary cannot rent out or lease the immovable without permission of the principal right holder or authorisation by the local court [kantonrechter], unless the power to do so was awarded to him at the moment of creation of the right.

(3) At the end of the right of usufruct, the principal right holder is obliged to uphold a rent or lease that was made in conformity with the right of usufruct. He may refuse to do so in so far as without his permission the time period of rent exceeded the time period that is locally customary, or a commercial premise, in the sense of the sixth division of Title 4 of Book 7, were rented out for a period longer than five years, unless the lease has been made for a longer duration than twelve years for farm buildings and six years for separate land, or the renting out or leasing has been made with unusual conditions disadvantage to him.

(4) The principal right holder loses the power to refuse to uphold when the tenant or lessee has given him a reasonable time period to declare himself on this matter, and he has not done so within that reasonable time.

(5) If the principal right holder is not obliged to uphold the rent of living space created during the existence of the right of usufruct in which the tenant has his principal residence at the end of the right of usufruct and to which Article 271 to 277 of Book 7 apply, he must nevertheless uphold the rental agreement with the tenant, taking into account that Article 269 paragraph 2 of Book 7 applies mutatis mutandis.

Article 3:218. Both usufructuary and principal right holder are entitled to initiate legal claims and request the court to make a decision that affects both the right of the usufructuary and the right of the principal right holder, provided he takes care that the other is involved in the proceedings in time.

Article 3:219. Outside of the situations dealt with in Articles 88 and 197 of Book 2 and Article 123 of Book 5 the use of the right to vote, connected to a thing that is subject to the right of usufruct, remains with the principal right holder, unless otherwise agreed at the moment of creation of the right. In case of a right of usufruct as meant in Articles 19 and 21 of Book 4, the voting right is also for the principal right holder, unless the parties at the moment of creation of the right of usufruct or the sub district court on the basis of Article 23 paragraph 4 of Book 4 decide otherwise.

Article 3:220. (1) Ordinary burdens and repairs are made by and paid for by the usufructuary. The usufructuary is obliged, when extraordinary repairs are needed, to inform the principal right holder of this necessity and to give him the opportunity to make these repairs. The principal right holder is not obliged to make any repairs.

(2) Nevertheless, a principal right holder who is, by limitation of the right to enjoyment of the usufructuary, entitled to a part of the fruits, is obliged to contribute proportionately in the burdens and costs that pursuant to the previous paragraph are borne by the usufructuary.

Article 3:221. (1) If the usufructuary seriously fails in the performance of his duties, the court may, at the request of the principal right holder, award him the management or place the right of usufruct under administratorship.

(2) The court may, during the proceedings, place the right of usufruct immediately under administratorship.

(3) The court may give the management or administratorship such conditions as it considers useful. Articles 154, 157 up to and including 166, 168, 170, 172, 173, 174 and 177 paragraph 1 of Book 4 apply mutatis mutandis to the administratorship, taking into account that the local court [kantonrechter] may also arrange the remuneration mentioned in Article 159 of Book 4 differently based on special circumstances, as well as that he may order the security mentioned in Article 160 of Book 4 at any time. The administratorship can be ended by a joint decision of the usufructuary and the principal right holder or by a court upon request of one of them.

Article 3:222. (1) If a succession, enterprise or any similar generality is given in usufruct, the principal right holder may require of the usufructuary that the debts belonging to that generality are paid from the things subject to the right of usufruct or, in so far as the principal right holder has paid these debts from his own funds, that he is compensated for the amount paid, increased with interest calculated from the day of payment, from the things that are subject of the right of usufruct. If the usufructuary pays the debt from his own patrimony, the principal right holder must repay him that amount only at the end of the right of usufruct.

(2) The previous paragraph also applies mutatis mutandis in case the right of usufruct is created on specific things on which extraordinary burdens exist.

Article 3:223. A usufructuary may transfer his right or burden it without that affecting the duration of the right. Apart from the acquirer, the original usufructuary is jointly and severally liable for all duties towards the principal right holder arising from the right of usufruct. If at the moment of creation, a wider power to alienate, use up or consume than the law prescribes was given to the usufructuary, later acquirers of the right of usufruct shall not have such wider power.

Article 3:224. If a usufructuary wishes to abandon his right at his own cost, due to the burdens and duties following from the right of usufruct, the person with the principal entitlement is obliged to cooperate herewith.

Article 3:225. After the end of the right of usufruct, the usufructuary or his successors are obliged to make the things available to the principal right holder.

Article 3:226. (1) The rules concerning the right of usufruct apply mutatis mutandis to the rights of use and a right of habitation, except the following provisions.

(2) Where only a right of use has been granted, the holder of the right has the power to use the objects that are subject to his right and to enjoy the fruits thereof, which he needs for himself and his family.

(3) Where only a right of habitation has been granted, the holder of the right has the power to live in the dwelling that is the subject of his right with his family.

(4) He who has one of the rights mentioned in this Article cannot transfer or burden his right, nor allow the use by another of the object, or allow the dwelling to be inhabited by another.

Title 9. Rights of Pledge and Hypothec

Division 1. General Provisions

Article 3:227. (1) The right of pledge [recht van pand] and the right of hypothec [recht van hypotheek] are limited rights aiming at recovering out of the things subject thereto a claim for the payment of a monetary sum with priority over other creditors. If the right is created on a registered thing, it is a right of hypothec; if the right is created on another thing, it is a right of pledge.

(2) A right of pledge or hypothec on an object extends to all that belongs to the ownership of that object.

Article 3:228. A right of pledge or hypothec can be created on all things that are capable of transfer.

Article 3:229. (1) The right of pledge or hypothec brings, by operation of law, a right of pledge on all claims for compensation that arise in the place of the thing that was subject to the right, including a claim for the devaluation of the thing.
(2) This right of pledge takes priority over any other right of pledge created on the claim.

Article 3:230. A right of pledge or hypothec is indivisible, even when the obligation for which it was created has two or more creditors or debtors and the obligation is divided between them.

Article 3:231. (1) A right of pledge or hypothec can be created for an existing as well as for a future claim. The claim can be non-documentary [op naam], to order [aan order] or to bearer [aan toonder]. It can be a claim on the pledgor or hypothecor as well as a claim on another.
(2) The claim for which a right of pledge or hypothec is given, must be sufficiently determinable.

Article 3:233. (1) The pledgor or hypothecor who is not also debtor, is liable for the devaluation of the thing, to the extent that the guarantee of the creditor is brought into danger thereby and the pledgor or hypothecor or a person for which these is liable, can be held responsible therefor.
(2) The costs he makes in respect of the thing other that for the maintenance thereof can be claimed from the pledgee or hypothecee, but only if he has sought recourse from the object and to the extent that the mentioned costs have led to a higher return of the object in his favour.

Article 3:234. (1) If, to secure the same claim, things of the debtor as well as things of a third party have been pledged or hypotheced, the third party, when the creditor executes his right, may request that the things of the debtor are also taken into the sale and be sold first.
(2) If to secure the same claim two or more things have been pledged or hypotheced and one of these is burdened with a limited property right that the creditor does not have to recognise in executing his right, the holder of the limited property right has the same power as mentioned in the first paragraph. When the creditor refuses to comply with the request made on the basis of paragraph 1 or paragraph 2, the injunction chamber of the court may, at the request of the party most ready, or in case of a hypothec, of the notary in front of who the sale shall be made, decide on this refusal. No appeal is allowed against a decision made pursuant to this paragraph.

Article 3:235. Every stipulation by which the pledgee or hypothecee is given the power to appropriate the thing subject of this right, is void.

Division 2. Right of Pledge

Article 3:236. (1) A right of pledge on a movable object, a right to bearer or order, or on the right of usufruct of such an object or right, is created by bringing the object, or the bearer or order document, within the power of the pledgee or of a third party on whom the parties have agreed. The creation of a right of pledge on a right to order or on the right of usufruct thereon also requires an endorsement.
(2) A right of pledge on other things is created in the same way as is determined for the delivery of the thing that is to be pledged.

Article 3:237. (1) A right of pledge on a movable object, on a bearer right, or on the right of usufruct on such an object or right, can also be created by authentic or registered deed, without bringing the object or bearer document into the power of the pledgee or of a third party.
(2) The pledgor is obliged to declare in the deed that he has the power to pledge the thing as well as that there are no limited property rights on the thing or which rights exist on the thing.
(3) When the pledgor or the debtor fails in his duties towards the pledgee or there are good reasons that make him fear that the pledgor or debtor will fail in these duties, the pledgee is entitled to claim that the object or bearer document is brought in the power of a third party. If there are more rights of pledge on the thing, each pledgee against which the pledgor or debtor fails his duties can exercise this power, provided that a pledgee other than the one with highest priority can only claim release of the thing from a pledgee or person on which all pledgees agree or who is designated by the court.
(4) When a pledgor or debtor fails in his obligations against the pledgee who has a right of pledge created in advance on fruits or plantings that are on the field, the local court [kantonrechter] may give the pledgee on his request authorisation to harvest these fruits or plantings that are on the field himself. If the pledgor is owner of the land or derives his right to the fruits and plantings from a limited property right on the land, the decision of the court that allows the request may be entered in the public registers.
(5) No appeal is allowed against the decision made pursuant to the previous paragraph.

Article 3:238. (1) Regardless of a lack of competence of the pledgor, the creation of a right of pledge on a movable object, a bearer right or right to order or a right of usufruct of such an object or right is valid, if the pledgor was in good faith at the moment the object or the bearer document or the endorsed order document were brought in his power or the power of a third party.

(2) If a limited property right exists on the object mentioned in paragraph 1 that he pledgee did not know about, nor ought to have known about, then the right of pledge will outrank that limited property right.

(3) If the right of pledge is created on a movable object of which the owner has lost possession by theft, or on a right of usufruct on such object, then paragraph 3, first sentence and under b, and paragraph 4 of Article 86 are applicable mutatis mutandis.

(4) This Article cannot be invoked against the person who claims the object, if pursuant to Article 86a, paragraphs 1 and 2 or Article 86b paragraph 1, or according to Article 6.15 of the Law on Cultural Property Article 86 also cannot be invoked against him.

[Articles 3:239 – 3:247 are omitted.]

Article 3:248. (1) When the debtor is in default of the performance for which the right of pledge was created as security [waarborg], the pledgee is entitled to sell the thing under pledge and to recover what is owed to him from the proceeds.

(2) The parties can stipulate that the sale can only take place after a court has determined, on the request of the pledgee, that the debtor is in default.

(3) A pledgee or seizor [beslaglegger] with a lower rank can only sell the thing under pledge while upholding the higher ranked rights of pledge.

Article 3:249. (1) Unless otherwise agreed, a pledgee who wishes to proceed to sale, in as far as this is reasonably possibly, is obliged to notify the creditor and the pledgor at least three days in advance of the proposed sale, mentioning date and time in a manner set forth by ordinance [algemene maatregel van Bestuur], as well as to those who have a limited property right or who placed the thing in seizure.

(2) The notification should mention the sum of money as accurately as possible, for which the pledge can be discharged. Discharge can occur until the moment of the sale, provided that the costs incurred in the execution procedure are also satisfied.

Article 3:250. (1) The sale takes place in public according to local customs and on the basis of the usual conditions.

(2) If the right of pledge is created on things that are tradable on a market or exchange, the sale may occur on a market through intervention of an intermediary in the trade or on the exchange through that of an authorised intermediary according to the rules and usages that apply there for a normal sale.

(3) The pledgor is allowed to bid in the sale.

[Articles 3:251 – 3:252 are omitted.]

Article 3:253. (1) The pledgor deducts, after payment of the costs of the execution procedure, from the net-profit the amount that is due to him on the basis of his right of pledge. The surplus is paid out to the pledgee. If there are pledgees or other right holders of a limited property right, whose right to the thing has ceased through the execution procedure, or have creditors seized the good or the proceeds of the sale, the pledgee must act in accordance with Article 490b of the Code of Civil Procedure.

(2) The pledgee cannot satisfy the amounts he must pay to the aforementioned stakeholders through set-off, unless this concerns a payment to the pledgor and this payment is not made during his insolvency, suspension of payment [surseance], the application to him of the debt-restructuring scheme natural persons or the completion of his succession patrimony. If the pledgor falls under the debt-restructuring scheme natural persons, a payment to the pledgor can nevertheless be made through set-off if the right of pledge was created after the ruling to apply the debt-restructuring scheme and both the claim as well as the debt have arisen after that ruling.

[Article 3:254 is omitted.]

Article 3:255. (1) If the pledge concerns money, the pledgee, as soon as his claim becomes due, may take the money without prior notice from the pledge in accordance with Article 253. He is obliged to do so, if the pledgor so demands and this person is competent to pay the claim in the relevant currency.

(2) Article 252 applies mutatis mutandis.

Article 3:256. If the right of pledge has ended, the pledgee is obliged to do whatever is necessary to restore the factual control over the thing to the pledgee, and if so required to provide evidence in writing that the right of pledge has ended. If the claim, for which the right of pledge was created is burdened with a limited property right, a similar duty rests on the right holder of such limited property right.

[Article 3:257 is omitted.]

Article 3:258. (1) When a thing that is subject to a right of pledge, as meant in Article 236 paragraph 1, comes into the power of the pledgor, the right of pledge is terminated, unless it was created in accordance with Article 237 paragraph (1).
(2) Abandonment of a right of pledge can be made by a simple contract, provided that the permission of the pledgee follows from a written or electronic declaration. In case the permission follows from an electronic declaration, Article 227a of Book 6 applies mutatis mutandis.
[Division 3 is omitted.]

Division 4. The right of hypothec

Article 3:260. (1) A right of hypothec is created by a notarial deed between the parties in which the hypothecor [hypotheekgever] grants a right of hypothec on a registered thing to the hypothecee [hypotheeknemer], followed by registration of the deed in the relevant public registers. The deed must contain a reference to the claim for which the right of hypothec provides security, or to the facts on the bases of which that claim can be determined. In addition, the amount of money for which the right of hypothec is created, or, when the amount of money is not yet determined, the maximum amount of money that can be claimed with the right of hypothec must be mentioned. The hypothecee must in the deed choose residence in the Netherlands.
(2) Unless agreed otherwise, the costs of the granting and creation are for the debtor.
(3) In order to conclude the deed mentioned in the first paragraph someone can only act for the hypthecor as authorised representative pursuant to a mandate granted by authentic deed.
(4) For all other matters the general provisions that apply for the creation of limited property rights on registered things also apply to the right of hypothec.

[Article 3:261 is omitted.]

Article 3:262. (1) It can be provided by notarial deed, which is entered into the registers, that a right of hypothec in relation of one or more rights of hypothec on the same thing has a higher rank than would follow from the moment of its registration, provided that it follows from the deed that the right holders of that other right or rights of hypothec consent to this.
(2) With corresponding application of the first paragraph, it can also be provided that a right of hypothec and another limited property right, in relation to each other, are deemed to have been created in a different order than actually occurred.

Article 3:263. (1) Unless provided otherwise in the deed of hypothec, the right of hypothec for the security of one or more specific claims also extends to secure three years of interest that is due thereon pursuant to law.
(2) A term that a right of hypothec for the security of one or more specific claims also extends to secure the interest for a period longer than three years, without mentioning a maximum amount, is void.

Article 3:264. (1) In case the deed of hypothec contains an explicit term in which the hypothecor is limited in his power, either to rent or lease the burdened thing without permission of the hypothecee, or in relation to the way in which or the time for which the thing may be rented or leased, or in relation to the advance payment of payments for rent or lease, or in relation to the right to transfer or pledge the right to payments for rent or lease, this term can not only be invoked against those that acquire the burdened thing later, but also against the tenant or lessee and against those to whom the right to payment for rent or lease was transferred or pledged, such by not only the hypothecee but also by the buyer after the exercise of a right to sell [uitwinning] of the burdened thing, the latter however only to the extent that this power still accrued to the hypothecee at the moment of the sale and he, following the conditions of sale, leaves the exercise thereof to the buyer. The hypothecee invokes the rent clause [huurbeding] prior to the public sale of an immovable object meant for habitation, a share in that, or a limited right therein, unless there are reasonable grounds to assume that:
(a) the continuation of the rent agreement is in the interest of the proceeds at the public sale; or

(b) also with the continuation of the rent agreement apparently sufficient proceeds will be obtained to satisfy all hypothecees who have made this stipulation and who can invoke it against the tenant; or

(c) there are no persons who pursuant to the rent agreement can use the burdened thing at the moment of announcement of the executory sale, meant in Article 516 of the Code of Civil Procedure.

(2) The term cannot be invoked before the writ of notification or underwriting [exploit van aanzegging of overneming] referred to in Article 544 of the Code of Civil Procedure has been made. The provisions relating to avoidability are applicable provided that the time period of Article 52 paragraph 1 runs from the moment of the aforementioned notification or underwriting and that a legal act that is in violation of the term will be avoided only in favour of he who invokes it, and no further than is in conformity with his right.

(3) If the term is made in relation to farms or separate land, it only has effect to the extent that it is not in violation of any mandatory statutory provision relating to lease [pacht]. Such a term does not have effect, to the extent that the land chamber has applied a content binding on the lease agreement that contradicts it, or that the term cannot be complied with because the land chamber annulled a modification agreement that meets the term. A term that obliges the hypothecor to lease farms for a shorter duration than twelve years and separate land for a shorter term than six years, is void.

(4) If the term is made in relation to the rent of living space or the rent of commercial space it only applies to the extent that it is not in violation of any mandatory statutory provision relating to such rent. The term that excludes the renting out of living space or commercial space, cannot be invoked against the tenant, to the extent that the living space or commercial space at the moment of creation of the right of hypothec was already rented out and the new renting out did not take place on unusual, for the hypothecee more detrimental conditions.

(5) To the extent that invoking term will have the consequence that the tenant must vacate a living space to which Articles 271 up to and including 277 of Book 7 are applicable, the term can only be invoked after the injunction chamber of the court, on request of the hypothecee, has granted permission to do so. Permission is not required in relation to a rent agreement, the avoidance of which the tenant agreed to in writing or that was made after the announcement, as meant in Article 516 of the Code of Civil Procedure.

(6) The injunction chamber of the court grants permission, unless also with the continuation of the rent agreement apparently sufficient proceeds will be obtained to satisfy all hypothecees who have made the term and who can invoke it against the tenant. If he grants permission, he also orders the tenants or sub-tenants who were invited or who appeared to vacate and he establishes a time period of no longer than six months after the decision is served for the tenant or sub-tenants, within which no vacation may take place. No appeal is possible against a decision pursuant to which permission is granted by the court.

(7) If the right of the tenant or lessee is lost due to avoidance pursuant to paragraph 2, a compensation will be paid from the net-profit obtained from the compulsory sale of the good with priority immediately after those against who he could not invoke his right, for the amount of the damage he suffered as a consequence of the avoidance. If the buyer is entitled to invoke the clause, a sum of money, corresponding to the damage, will be reserved, from the that which accrues to the creditors with a lower rank, until it is established that the buyer will not make use of his entitlement.

(8) Tenant in the sense of this Article means the person who is co-tenant under Article 266 paragraph 1 or Article 267 paragraph 1 of Book 7.

Article 3:265. If the deed of hypothec explicitly contains a clause according to which the hypothecor cannot change the organisation [inrichting] or appearance [gedaante] of the thing that was burdened without permission of the hypothecee, this clause cannot be invoked if the tenant has been granted authorisation to do so by the local court [kantonrechter] on the basis of the provisions relating to rent or to the lessor or lessee by the land chamber on the basis of the provisions relating to lease.

Article 3:266. When an object is the subject-matter of a right of hypothec and the hypothecor has, after the creation of the right, made alterations or additions without being obliged to do so in order to provide further objects for security of the right, he is entitled to remove these alterations and additions, provided he returns the object to its original state and, if requested, for the time that this was not done, provides security for the devaluation. The person who is entitled to fruits and plantings that are in the field, is entitled to harvest these; could this not happen before the executory sale, then he and the buyer are obliged to behave towards each other in accordance with the duties that the leaving and new lessee on the basis of the provisions on lease have towards each other.

[Articles 3:267 3:267a are omitted.]

Article 3:268. (1) Where a debtor is in default in respect of the performance for which the right of

hypothec is created as security, the hypothecee is entitled to have the object subject to the right of hypothec sold in public, in the presence of an authorized notary.
(2) On the request of the hypothecee, the hypothecor, the seizor or the limited property right holder, the court of provisionary measures [voorzieningenrechter] of the district court [rechtbank] may decide that the sale takes place through an informal sale by a contract that is presented to him for approval at the time of making the request. Where the hypothecor, hypothecee, seizor or holder of a limited right, who has an interest in higher proceeds from the sale of the object, is presented with a better offer before the proceedings dealing with the request to the court are completed, he may decide that the sale will proceed on the basis of this offer. If requested, the judge on provisionary measures also orders the hypothecor and his family to clear the property subject to hypothec by a specified point in time. Such clearing does not take place before the moment of inscription referred to in Article 89 of Book 3
(3) The request mentioned in paragraph 2 must be submitted by an advocate or notary within the period set by the Code of Civil Procedure. No appeal is possible against a decision of the court referred to in paragraph (2).
(4) An execution as referred to in the previous paragraphs is to be made in conformity with the pertinent formalities laid down in the Code of Civil Procedure.
(5) The hypothecee cannot exercise his recovery of the object subject to the right of hypothec in any other way. Any term seeking to achieve this is void.

[Articles 3:269 - 3:273 are omitted.]

Article 3:274. (1) When a right of hypothec has ended, the creditor is obliged to provide the right holder of the burdened thing at his request and at his costs, by authentic deed, a declaration that the right of hypothec has ended. In case the claim for which the right of hypothec was created is burdened with a limited property right, a similar duty rests on the right holder of that limited property right.
(2) These declarations can be entered into the registers. They authorise together authorise the registrar to strike out.
(3) In case the required declarations are not provided, Article 29 applies mutatis mutandis.
(4) If the right of hypothec ended through mixing, the registrar is authorised to strike out the right by a declaration to that effect, made by authentic deed by him to whom the thing belongs, unless a limited property right rests on the claim.

Article 3:275. A mandate to provide a declaration as meant in the previous Article, must be made in writing.

Title 10. Recourse to retrieval of things

Division 1. General Provisions

Article 3:276. Unless the law or an agreement provides otherwise, a creditor may satisfy his claim against all things of his debtor.

Article 3:277. (1) Creditors have an equal right amongst themselves, after payment of the costs of execution, to be paid from the net-proceeds of the things of their debtor proportionally to each person's claim, except for the reasons of priority recognized by the law.
(2) By a contract between a creditor and the debtor, it may be provided that his claim against all or specific other creditors takes a lower rank than the law grants him.

Article 3:278 (1) Priority stems from the right of pledge, the right of hypothec and preferential right [voorrecht] and from the other grounds provided in the law.
(2) Preferential rights arise by law only. They rest on specific things or on all things belonging to a patrimony.

Article 3:279. The rights of pledge and hypothec take priority over preferential rights, unless the law provides otherwise.

Article 3:280. Preferential rights on specific things have priority over those that rest on all things in a patrimony, unless the law provides otherwise.

Article 3:281. (1) Distinguishable preferential rights that rest on the same thing have equal rank, unless the law provides otherwise.
(2) The preferential rights on all things are exercised in the order in which the law positions them.

[Article 3:282 is omitted.]

Division 2. Preferential claims on specific things

Article 3:283. A preferential right on a specific thing includes claims for compensation that have come in place of that thing, including claims for the devaluation of the thing.

Article 3:284. (1) A claim for the payment of costs, made to preserve a thing, are preferential to the thing that has been maintained.
(2) The creditor may satisfy the claim on the thing without rights of third parties being invoked against him, unless these rights have arisen after the making of the costs to preserve the thing. A right of pledge created after those costs are incurred in accordance with Article 237 can only be invoked against the creditor, in case the object or the bearer document is brought in the power of the pledgee or a third party. A right that has arisen on the basis of Article 90 after these costs are incurred can only be invoked against the creditor if the requirements of paragraph 2 of that Article are fulfilled.
(3) The preferential right has priority over all other preferential rights, unless the claims to which these other preferential rights are connected arose after the costs of preservation were incurred.

Article 3:285. (1) The person who has a claim out of labour on an object arising from a labour contract [aanneming van werk], has thereby priority to that thing, provided he personally participates in the execution of labour undertaken in the course of his business or is a company or a legal person of which one or more managing partners or directors do so. The preferential right ceases after the expiry of two years after the claim arises.
(2) The preferential right has priority over a right of pledge created in accordance with Article 237 on the object, unless this right was created after the preferential claim and the object was brought in the power of the pledgee or a third party.

[Articles 3:286 - 3:287 are omitted.]

Division 3. Preferential claims on all things

Article 3:288. Preferential claims on all things are claims relating to:
(a) the costs for the application for a declaration of insolvency, although only in case of an insolvency that was granted upon request, as well as the costs, made by a creditor, to attain a settlement outside of the insolvency;
(b) the costs of burial of a deceased person, to the extent that they correspond to the circumstances of the deceased;
(c) that which an employee, a former employee and their heirs may claim in relation to pension payments that are already payable from the employer, to the extent that the claim is not older than one year;
(d) that which an employee, not being a director of a legal person by which he is employed, a former employee or their heirs may claim in relation to payment of future pension payments from the employer;
(e) all that an employee may claim in the current or previous calendar year in money on the basis of an employment contract from his employer, as well as the amounts of money that are payed by the employer to the employee in case of ending of the employment contract following the provisions of the Civil Code relating to the employment contract.

Article 3:289. (1) Also preferential on all things are claims that have arisen from the imposing of levies and increased payments for delay in payment of these levies on the basis of Articles 49 and 50 from the European Coal and Steal Treaty of 18 April 1951 (Trb. 1951, 82)
(2) This preferential right has the same rank as the preferential right on the basis of payment of sales taxes.

Division 4. Right of retention

Article 3:290. A right of retention [retentierecht] is the power that is granted to a creditor in those cases mentioned by law, to suspend performance of a duty of delivery of an object to his debtor until the claim is satisfied.

Article 3:291. (1). The creditor can invoke his right of retention also against third parties that have acquired a right to the object after his claim had arisen and the object came into his power.
(2) He can also invoke the right of retention against third parties with an older right, if his claim results from a contract that the debtor was entitled to enter into with respect to the object, or if he had no reason to doubt the power of the debtor.

(3) The creditor cannot invoke the right of retention against the Minister of Education, Culture and Science, who, on the basis of Article 7 of the Act on the restitution of cultural goods from occupied territory, initiates a claim.

Article 3:292. A creditor may claim from the object with preference over all against whom the right of retention may be invoked.

Article 3:293. The right of retention can also be exercised for the costs that the creditor has incurred for the care over the object to which he is obliged by law.

Article 3:294. The right of retention ends when the object comes into the power of the debtor or the right holder, unless the creditor regains the object based on the same legal relationship.

Article 3:295. If the object leaves the power of the creditor, he may demand the object under the same conditions as an owner.

Title 11. Legal claims [Rechtsvorderingen]

Article 3:296. (1) Unless otherwise provided by law, the nature of an obligation or a legal act, he who is obliged as against another to give, to do or not to do something, is held to do so by the court, at the request of he who has this right.
(2) He who is held to something under a condition or time-limit may be adjudicated under that condition or time limit.

[Article 3:297 -3:305d are omitted.]

Article 3:306. Unless the law determines otherwise, a claim is time-barred after the completion of a period of twenty years.

Article 3:307. (1) A claim for the performance of an obligation arising from a contract to do or to give something is time-barred after the completion of a period of five years after the day, following the day on which the claim became due.
(2) In case of an obligation to perform after an undetermined period of time, the prescription period mentioned in paragraph (1) will not commence until beginning of the day, following the day on which the creditor has notified to proceed to ,enforce the claim mentioned in paragraph (1) prescribes in any case after the completion of a period of twenty years after the beginning of the day, following the day on which the enforceability, if necessary after cancellation by the creditor, was at the earliest possible.

Article 3:308. Claims for the payment of interest and sums of money, life interest, dividends, lease payments, agricultural lease payments and anything else that must be paid within a year or a shorter period, prescribe after the completion of a period of five years after the day, following the day on which the claim became due.

[Articles 3:309 – 3:312 are omitted.]

Article 3:313. Unless the law provides otherwise, the prescription period for a claim for the performance of an obligation to give or to do something commences on the day, following the day on which immediate performance may be demanded.

[Articles 3:314 – 3:318 are omitted.]

Article 3:319. (1) By interruption of the prescription period of a claim, other than by initiating a demand that is followed by an award, a new prescription period commences from the following day. If a binding advice is requested and obtained, the new prescription period commences as of the beginning of the day following that on which the binding advice was rendered.
(2) The new prescription period is equal to the original one, but not longer than five years. Nevertheless, the prescription will in no case have effect earlier than the day on which the original prescription period would have expired without the interruption.
(3) In case of interruption of the prescription period of a claim pursuant to Article 3:316 (4), a new prescription period commences as of the beginning of the day following that of the final judicial ruling. The new prescription period is equal to the original one, but not longer than five years. Nevertheless, the prescription will in no case have effect earlier than the day on which the original prescription period would have expired without the interruption.

[Articles 3:320 – 3:222 are omitted.]

Article 3:323. (1) By completion of the prescription of a claim for the performance of an obligation, the rights of pledge and hypothec that secure it cease to exist.

(2) Neither does the prescription prevent that the right of pledge is exercised on the thing that is subject to the right, if this thing is a movable object, a bearer or order right or the bearer or order document was brought in the power of the pledgee or a third party.

(3) The claim for the performance of an obligation for which a right of hypothec was created, does not prescribe before twenty years have passed after the day following the day on which the right of hypothec was connected to the obligation.

[Articles 3:324 – 3:326 are omitted.]
Book 4. Law of Succession [Erfrecht]

Title 1. General Provisions

Article 4:1. (1) Succession [Erfopvolging] takes place intestate [versterf] or by last will [uiterste wilsbeschikking].

(2) A derogation can be made from the intestate succession regime by a last will that contains an appointment of heir or disinheritance.

Article 4:2. (1) When the order in which two or more persons have died cannot be established, these persons are assumed to have died at the same time and the one person cannot benefit from the succession patrimony [nalatenschap] of the other.

(2) If an interested party experiences difficulties, as a result of circumstances that cannot be attributed to him, to provide evidence of the order of death, the court can grant him a postponement once or several times, such to the extent that it can be reasonably assumed that the evidence can be provided within the period of the postponement.

Article 4:3. (1) Unworthy to obtain benefit from the succession patrimony [nalatenschap], by operation of law, are:

(a) he who has been irrevocably convicted for the death of the deceased, for attempting to kill him, for preparing such a fact or for participating therein;

(b) he who has been irrevocably convicted of an intentionally committed crime against the deceased [erflater] for which the legal description of the Netherlands prescribe imprisonment with a maximum of at least four years, or of an attempt thereto, preparation thereof, or participation in such a crime.

(c) he for whom is determined, by irrevocable court decision, that he brought a defamatory accusation of a crime against the deceased, for which the legal description in the Netherlands prescribe imprisonment with a maximum of at least four years;

(d) he who has forced or prevented the deceased from making a last will by a factual act or by threatening a factual act;

(e) he who has embezzled, destroyed or forged the last will of the deceased.

(2) Rights acquired by third parties in good faith before the unworthiness has been established are recognised. In case things have been acquired gratuitously, the court may order the payment of compensation established in accordance with fairness to the right holders, at the expense of he who has benefitted therefrom.

(3) Unworthiness ceases when the deceased has unambiguously forgiven the behaviours of the unworthy person.

Article 4:4. (1) A legal act carried out before the opening of the succession patrimony is void, to the extent that it seeks to limit a person in his freedom to exercise powers, which fall to him under this Book in relation to that succession patrimony.

(2) Contracts relating to the disposal of succession patrimonies that have not opened in their entirety or for a proportional part thereof, are void.

Article 4:5. (1) At the request of the creditor, a court can order that a sum of money that is owed pursuant to this Book or, in relation to the distribution of the succession patrimony pursuant to Title 7 of Book 3, only needs to be paid after a certain period of time, either immediately, or in instalments, whether or not increased with interest determined in the decision. In doing so, the court will consider the interests of both parties; a condition can be attached to the consent that within a determined time a proprietary or personal security approved by the court is provided for the payment of the principal sum and interest.

(2) The decision meant in the previous paragraph can, at the request of one of the parties, be amended by the court mentioned in the previous paragraph, on the basis of circumstances not foreseen at the time of the decision.

Article 4:6. In this Book, the value of the things in the succession patrimony means the value that those things have immediately after the death of the deceased, whereby the right of usufruct that could come to rest on these pursuant to Division 1 or 2 of Title 3 is not taken into account.

Article 4:7. Debts of the succession patrimony are:
(a) The debts of the deceased that do not cease with his death, in so far as not included under (i);
(b) the costs of burial, in so far as they are in accordance with the circumstances of the deceased;
(c) the costs of set-off of the succession patrimony, including the salary of the administrator;
(d) the costs of executorship, including the salary of the executor;
(e) the debts following from taxes that are levied following the opening of the succession patrimony, to the extent they rest on the heirs;
(f) The debts that arise by application of Division 2 of Title 3;
(g) debts made for the legitimate portions [legitieme porties] that are invoked pursuant to Article 80;
(h) debts from legacies that rest on one or more heirs;
(i) the debts from gifts and other acts that are considered legacies following Article 126.
(2) In satisfying the debts of the succession patrimony the following will be made with priority.
1st the debts meant in paragraph 1 under (a) to (e);
2nd the debts, meant in paragraph 1 under (f);
3rd the debts, meant in paragraph 1 under (g).
In case there are no debts as meant in paragraph 1 under (f), the debts meant in paragraph 1 under d, e, and g, are satisfied with priority.
(3) In the succession patrimony of the longest living parent, meant in Article 20, and the stepparent meant in Article 22, a duty to transfer things as meant in those Articles is equated with a debt as meant in paragraph 1 under a.

Article 4:8. (1) In this Book, registered partners are equated to spouses.
(2) For the application of paragraph 1, is included under:
(a) marriage: registered partnership
(b) married: registered as partner
(c) matrimonial property: community of the registered partnership
(d) wedding vows: vows made at the conclusion of a registered partnership
(e) divorce: termination of a registered partnership in the manner as meant in Article 80c under c or d of Book 1.
(3) Stepchild of the deceased in this Book means a child of the spouse or registered partner of the deceased, of which the deceased is not a parent himself. Such a child remains a stepchild when the marriage or registered partnership ends.

Title 2. Intestate succession

Article 4:9. To act as heir in an intestate succession, one must be alive at the moment of the opening of the succession patrimony.

Article 4:10. (1) The law calls the following persons as heirs to the succession patrimony on their own account in the following order:
(a) the spouse who is not in temporary separation together with his children;
(b) the parents of the deceased together with his brothers and sisters;
(c) the grandparents of the deceased;
(d) the great-grandparents of the deceased.
(2) The descendants of a child, brother, sister, grandparent or great-grandparent shall be called by substitution.
(3) Only those who were in a family relation to the deceased are considered, for the purpose of the previous paragraphs, as blood relatives.

Article 4:11. (1) The persons who are called together on their own account to the succession patrimony, inherit in equal shares.
(2) In derogation from paragraph 1, the share of a half-brother or half-sister is half of the share of a full brother, a full sister or a parent.
(3) When the share of a parent through application of paragraphs 1 and 2 would be less than a quarter, it is increased to a quarter and the shares of the other heirs are reduced proportionately.

Article 4:12. (1) Substitution occurs in relation to persons who at the moment of opening of the succession patrimony no longer exist, are unworthy, disinherited or reject or whose heirship has ceased.

(2) They who inherit by substitution are called per stirpes to the share of the person they substitute for.

(3) The persons who exist from the deceased further than in the sixth degree, do not inherit.

Title 3. The law of succession in case of intestate succession of non-separated spouses and of children as well as other legal rights

Division 1. Intestate succession of non-separated spouses and of the children

Article 4:13. (1) The succession patrimony of the deceased who leaves a spouse and one or more children as heirs is divided, unless the deceased has decided otherwise by last will that this part is not applicable, in accordance with the following paragraphs.

(2) The spouse acquires, by operation of law, the things of the succession patrimony. The payment of the debts of the succession patrimony are for his account. Debts of the succession patrimony include for this purpose the testamentary dues that are for the account of the joint heirs.

(3) Each of the children receives, by operation of a law, a monetary claim on the spouse, corresponding to the value of his share in the succession. This claim becomes due if:

(a) the spouse is declared in state of insolvency or when the special provisions of the debt-restructuring scheme natural persons apply;

(b) when the spouse has passed away.

The claim is also due in the situations mentioned by the deceased in his last will.

(4) The sum of money mentioned in paragraph 3, unless the deceased or the spouse and the child together decide otherwise, are increased with a percentage that corresponds to the statutory interest, to the extent that this percentage is higher than six, to be calculated annually from the day on which the succession patrimony opened, in which calculation only the principal sum will be taken into account.

(5) If the claim referred to in paragraph 3 has become due because the debt-restructuring scheme natural persons has become applicable to the spouse, the claim to the extent has not been paid, is once more not due through the cessation of the application of debt-restructuring scheme natural persons on the basis of Article 356 sub 2 of the Insolvency Law. Article 358 paragraph 1 of the Insolvency Law does not apply in relation to the claim.

(6) For the purpose of the Title, spouse does not include a separated spouse.

Article 4:14. (1) If the succession patrimony has been divided in accordance with Article 13, the spouse of the deceased is obliged towards the creditors and towards the children to pay the debts of the succession patrimony. In the internal relation of the spouse and the children, the debts of the succession patrimony are for the account of the spouse.

(2) For debts of the succession patrimony, as well as for debts of the deceased that can be claimed on the things of a community of which the spouse and the deceased where the shareholders, the creditor takes rank in his recourse on the things that following Article 13 paragraph 2 belong to the spouse before those that seek recourse for other debts of the spouse.

(3) For debts of the succession patrimony, the things of a child cannot subject to the exercise of a right to sell [uitgewonnen], with the exception of the monetary claim mentioned in Article 13 paragraph 3. Exercising the right to sell [uitwinning] of the things is possible to the extent that the monetary claim of the child is decreased by payment or by transfer of things, unless the child indicates things of the spouse that offer sufficient compensation.

(4) The duty to carry the debts of the spouse stemming from paragraph 1 second sentence also applies when the debts of the succession patrimony exceed the benefits, notwithstanding Article 184 paragraph 2.

Article 4:15. (1) To the extent the heirs cannot reach agreement on the size of the monetary claim meant in Article 13 paragraph 3, it will be determined by the court upon the request of the party that is the most ready. Articles 677 to 679 of the Code of Civil Procedure apply mutatis mutandis.

(2) If for the determination of the monetary claim meant in Article 13 paragraph 3:

(a) a mistake has been made about the value of the things and the debts of the succession patrimony and an heir has been disadvantaged for more than a fourth by that,

(b) the balance of the succession patrimony has been otherwise wrongly calculated, or

(c) the monetary claim has not been calculated in accordance to the share that the child could claim, the determination, upon the request of a child or the spouse, will be changed accordingly by the local court [kantonrechter]. That which is laid down in relation to division in Articles 196 paragraphs 2, 4, and 4, 199 and 200 of Book 3 apply mutatis mutandis to the determination.

(3) In determining the monetary claim Articles 229 to 233 apply mutatis mutandis.

(4) Articles 187 and 188 of Book 3 apply to the determination mutatis mutandis.

Article 4:16. (1) The spouse and each child may demand that a description of assets is made. The description of assets contains a valuation of the things and the debts of the succession patrimony.
(2) If the spouse or a child does not have the free disposition over his patrimony, his legal representative will deliver within a year after the death of the deceased a confirmation of the accuracy of the description of assets signed by him to the registry of the District Court [rechtbank] at the domicile of the spouse or the child. The local court [kantonrechter] can decide that the description of assets must be made by notarial deed.
(3) Articles 673 to 676 of the Code of Civil Procedure apply mutatis mutandis to the description of assets and the valuation. The spouse and each child are for the application of the provisions referred to in the previous sentence party to the description of assets.
(4) The spouse and each child have towards each other a right to access and a right to a copy of all documents and other data carriers, that they need in order to make their claims. The information for that purpose is provided to them at their request. They are bound towards each other to cooperate in the provision of information by third parties.

Article 4:17. (1) The spouse can, subject to that which is laid down in paragraphs 2 and 3, pay the monetary claim referred to in Article 13 paragraph 3 and the increased amount meant in paragraph 4 at any moment. A payment is set off in the first place against the principal sum, followed by the increase, unless the deceased, or the spouse and child together, have decided otherwise.
(2) If a child is entitled to make a request as meant in Article 19, 20, 21 or 22, the spouse or his heirs will not begin performance until they have acted in accordance with Article 25 paragraph 3.
(3) If the child referred to in paragraph 2 is a minor, or of but not with the free disposition over his patrimony, the performance must be approved by local court [kantonrechter]. The court decides according to the standard in Article 26 paragraph 1.

Article 4:18. (1) The spouse can, within three months from the day on which the succession patrimony opened, by declaration in a notarial deed, within that period, followed by registration in the asset register, undo the division made in accordance with Article 13. The declaration can only be made in the name of the spouse pursuant to an explicit written mandate given for this purpose.
(2) The declaration has retroactive effect until the moment of the opening of the succession patrimony. The rights of third parties referred to in paragraph 1, co-owners included, acquired before the passing of the time period mentioned in paragraph 1, will be upheld. If the spouse has made payments before the making of the declaration on the basis of Article 13 paragraph 2, these are set off between the spouse and the child.
(3) The circumstance that the spouse is under guardianship [curatele] or that the things that this person acquires from the succession patrimony are under administratorship, does not prevent the exercise of the power mentioned in paragraph 1. The power will then be exercised in accordance with the rules that apply for the guardianship or administratorship respectively. If the spouse is declared insolvent, or is made subject to the debt-restructuring scheme natural persons, or suspension of payment [surseance van betaling] has been granted, this power is exercised by the guardian, by the administrator, respectively by the spouse with cooperation of the administrator.
(4) If, in respect to the deceased, Division 2 of 3 of Title 18 of Book 1 is applied, the time period of three months mentioned in paragraph 1 will run from the day on which the decision, meant in Article 417 paragraph 1 or 427 paragraph 1 of Book 1, has become res judicata [kracht van gewijsde].

Article 4:19. If a child has acquired a monetary claim in accordance with Article 13 paragraph 3 on his longest living parent in respect to the succession patrimony of his first deceased parent, and that parent has given notice of his intention to conclude a marriage once more, this person is obliged to transfer things to the child at the child's request with a value of maximum that monetary claim, increased with the increase meant in paragraph 4 of that Article. The transfer takes place, unless the parent does not require so, subject to a right of usufruct on the things.

Article 4:20. If a child has acquired a monetary claim in accordance with Article 13 paragraph 3 on his longest living parent in respect to the succession patrimony of his first deceased parent and the longest living parent was married at the time of his death, the stepparent is obliged to transfer things to the child at the child's request with a value of maximum that monetary claim, increased with the increase mentioned in paragraph 4 of that Article. If the succession patrimony is not divided in accordance with Article 13, the duty referred to in the previous sentence rests on the heirs of the longest living parent.

Article 4:21. If a child has acquired a monetary claim in accordance with Article 13 paragraph 3 on his stepparent in respect to the succession patrimony of his deceased parent, the stepparent is obliged to transfer things to the child at the child's request with a value of maximum that monetary claim, increased with the increase mentioned in paragraph 4 of that Article. The transfer takes place, unless the stepparent does not require so, subject to a right of usufruct on the things.

Article 4:22. If a child has acquired a monetary claim in accordance with Article 13 paragraph 3 on his stepparent in respect to the succession patrimony of his deceased parent, and the stepparent has also died, the stepparent's heirs are obliged to transfer things to the child at the child's request with a value of maximum that monetary claim, increased with the increase mentioned in paragraph 4 of that Article.

Article 4:23. (1) The provisions of Title 8 of Book 3 apply to the right of usufruct mentioned in Articles 19 and 21, with the understanding that:
(a) the spouse is exempted from the annual report as meant in Article 205 paragraph 4 as well as to provide security as meant in Article 206 paragraph 1, and Article 206 paragraph 2 does not apply;
(b) a mandate as meant in Article 212 paragraph 3 can also be given to the extent that the care needs of the spouse or the performance of his duties under Article 13 paragraph 2 make this necessary.
(2) The local court [kantonrechter] can on the ground mentioned in paragraph 1 under b, at the request of the spouse, give him the power for full or partial alienation and using up as meant in Article 215 of Book 3. The principal right holder will be called to the proceedings. The court can make further arrangements in its decision.
(3) In derogation from the first sentence of Article 213 paragraph 1 of Book 3 and of Article 215 paragraph 1 of Book 3, the principal right holder acquires, unless he agrees otherwise with the spouse, at the time of alienation a claim on the spouse for the amount of the value that the thing had at that time. Paragraphs 3 and 4 of Article 13 and paragraph 15 are applicable to that claim mutatis mutandis, with the understanding that the increase referred to in Article 13 paragraph 4 is calculated from the moment of creation of the claim.
(4) At the creation of the right of usufruct, further arrangements can be made by the spouse and the principal right holder, or by the local court upon the request of one of them.
(5) The spouse is not entitled to transfer or burden the right of usufruct.
(6) The right of usufruct cannot be invoked against creditors who claim things subject to that right in recourse for the debts of the succession patrimony or for the debts of the spouse that could have been recovered from things in a community of which the spouse and the deceased where shareholders. In case of such an exercise of the right to sell [uitwinning] Article 282 of Book 3 does not apply.

Article 4:24. (1) The duty to transfer as meant by Articles 19, 20, 21 and 22, concerns things that have been part of the succession patrimony of the deceased or of a marital community of things that was dissolved by his death. In derogation from the first sentence, the duty to transfer meant in Articles 21 and 22 does not relate to things that have come into the marital community from the side of the stepparent.
(2) The duty to transfer as meant in Articles 19, 20, 21 and 22, also concerns the things that have come in place of the things meant in paragraph 1, first sentence. If a thing as been acquired with means that come for less than half from the succession patrimony or dissolved marital community meant in paragraph 1, it does not fall under the duty referred to in the first sentence. If a thing is acquired also from means that obtained from a loan, these means are not taken into account for the application of the second sentence.
(3) A thing that belongs to the patrimony of the person who is obliged to transfer or to the marital community within which he is married, it is presumed to have been part of the succession patrimony or dissolved marital community meant in paragraph 1, or to have taken the place of such a thing.

Article 4:25. (1) The value of a thing that is to be transferred, to be established at the moment of transfer, is in the first place deducted from the principal sum that is due to the child and subsequently to the increase, unless the deceased or by transfer determines otherwise. For the application of Articles 19 and 21, the value of the thing is established without taking the right of usufruct into account.
(2) A child that has the intention to make the request referred to in Articles 19, 20, 21 and 22, is bound to notify the other children that may make a similar request of his request at such a time that they can still make a timely decision to also make a request.
(3) The person that may be obliged to transfer this thing can give the child a reasonable time period within which the request mentioned in articles 19, 20, 21 and 22 can be made. If he does so, he also notifies that other children that may make such as request, thereof.

(4) If there is no agreement between the person obliged to transfer the things and the child, or between two or more children, on the transfer of a thing, the local court decides upon the request of one of them, taking into account in accordance with fairness the interests of each of them.
(5) To the extent that a child transfers the claim referred to in Article 13 paragraph 3 to another person, the power referred to in Articles 19, 20, 21 and 22 ceases.
(6) By last will, the deceased can extend, limit or remove the powers mentioned in Articles 19 to 22.

Article 4:26. (1) If a minor child has a power as meant in Articles 19, 20, 21 and 22, his statutory representative must, within three months after the power has arisen, notify the local court in writing of his intention to exercise that power. If the child has no statutory representative, this time period runs from the day of the appointment. The local grants its approval to the intention or withholds it, taking into account in accordance with fairness the interest of the child, the other children who also have the power and those against whom the power can be exercised. It can attach conditions to the approval. If necessary, the local court makes its own decision.
(2) The same applies if the child is of age but does not have the free disposition over his patrimony. If the monetary claim meant in Article 13 paragraph 3 is under administratorship, the power meant in paragraph 1 is exercised according to the rules that apply to the respective administratorship. If the child is declared insolvent or is subject to the debt-restructuring scheme natural persons or if suspension of payment [surseance van betaling] has been granted, the duty rests of the guardian, the administrator, respectively on the child with cooperation of the administrator.
(3) If, with the approval of the local court, a request as meant in Articles 19, 20, 21 and 22 is waived, such a request cannot still be made after that. The local court can decide otherwise when giving his approval.

Article 4:27. The deceased can provide by last will that a stepchild must be included in the division as meant in Article 13 as his own child. In that case this Division applies, except to the extent that the deceased has determined otherwise. The descendants of the stepchild are called in substitution.
[Division 2 is omitted.]

Title 4. Last Will

Division 1. Last will in general

Article 4:42. (1) A last will is a unilateral legal act by which the deceased [erflater] makes a disposition that is effective only after his death and that is regulated in this Book or in the law or recognized by law as such.
(2) The deceased can always unilaterally revoke a last will.
(3) A testamentary disposition can only be made by last will and only be made and revoked by the deceased personally.
[The remainder of Division 1 and Divisions 2 – 3 are omitted.]

Division 4. Form of Last Wills

Article 4:93. A last will that is made by two or more persons in the same deed is void.

Article 4:94. Except for what is provided for in the Articles 97-107, a last will can only be made by way of a notarial deed or by way of a private deed that is given in custody to a notary.

Article 4:95. (1) A person who has not been able to read his last will due to ignorance or another cause cannot make a valid last will by private deed.
(2) A last will made by private deed must be signed by the deceased. If the last will is written by a person other than the deceased or by mechanical means, and the will comprises more than one page, each page must be numbered and certified with the signature of the deceased.
(3) A last will made by private deed must be handed over to a notary by the deceased. The deceased must declare, when doing so, that the presented private deed contains his last will and that the requirements of the previous paragraph have been met. If the document is presented in a closed form, the deceased can also declare, when handing it over, that it may be opened only if specific conditions mentioned by him have been fulfilled on the day of his death.
(4) The notary draws up a deed of the declarations of the deceased and of their custody, to be signed by the deceased and the notary. [The remainder of Article 4:95 and Title 4 are omitted.]
Book 5. Property Rights in Respect to Objects [Zakelijke rechten]

Title 1. Ownership in general

Article 5:1. (1) Ownership [Eigendom] is the most comprehensive right that a person can have to an object.

(2) The owner is free to the exclusion of everyone else, to use the object, provided that this use is not in violation of the rights of others and the limitations based upon legislative provisions and rules of unwritten law are complied with.

(3) The owner of the object becomes, without prejudice to the rights of others, owner of the fruits the object produces once these are separated.

Article 5:2. The owner of an object is entitled to demand the object from everyone else who holds it without a right to it.

Article 5:3. In so far as the law does not prescribe otherwise, the owner of an object is the owner of all its components [bestanddelen].

Title 2. Ownership of movable objects

Article 5:4. He who takes possession of a movable object that belongs to no one, acquires ownership thereof.

Article 5:5. (1) He who finds an unattended object and takes it for himself, is obliged:

(a) as soon as possible, in accordance with paragraph 2, first sentence, to report the finding, unless he notified the person who he could consider owner or as entitled to receive it thereof immediately after finding it;

(b) as soon as possible, also in accordance with paragraph 2, second sentence, notifies the finding, in case this occurred in a house, a building or a transport vehicle; unless he, pursuant to subparagraph a final part, was not obliged to report the finding;

(c) to give the object into custody to the municipality that so requests.

(2.) The reporting mentioned in paragraph 1 under a can be made in any municipality to the relevant civil servant. The notification of paragraph 1 under b is made to the person who lives in the house or the building or who uses or operates the transport vehicle, or to the person who supervises there for him.

(3) The finder is entitled at any time to give the object into custody at the municipality. As long as he does not do so, he is obliged to take care of the custody and maintenance himself.

(4) The finder may request evidence of placing the object in custody from the civil servant meant in paragraph 2 first sentence.

[Articles 5:6 – 5:13 are omitted.]

Article 5:14. (1) Ownership of a movable object that becomes a component [bestanddeel] of another movable object that can be regarded as the principal object [hoofdzaak], passes to the owner of this principal object.

(2) Where neither of the objects can be regarded as the principal object and they belong to different owners, they become co-owners of the new object, each for a share equal to the value of the object.

(3) To be regarded as the principal object is the object of which the value substantially exceeds that of the other or which according to the common opinion [verkeersopvatting] is considered as such.

Article 5:15. If movable objects that belong to different owners are united into one object through merger [vermenging], the former article applies mutatis mutandis.

Article 5:16. (1) When a person creates a new object from one or more movable objects, they become property of the owner of the original objects. If these belonged to different owners, then the previous two articles apply mutatis mutandis.

(2) When a person creates an object for himself or has an object created from or partly from one or more movable objects that do not belong to him, he becomes owner of the new object, unless the costs of creation due to their limited amount do not justify this.

(3) The paragraphs above apply mutatis mutandis to the processing of substances into a new substance or the culture of plants.

Article 5:17. The person who is entitled to the fruits of an object pursuant to his right of use and enjoyment thereof, acquires the ownership of these fruits by their separation.

Article 5:18. Ownership of a movable object is lost, when the owner relinquishes possession with the intention to free himself of ownership.

Article 5:19. (1) The owner of domesticated animals loses the ownership of these, when he, after they have left his power, have become wild.

(2) The owner of other animals loses the ownership of these, when they gain freedom and the owner does not immediately attempt to catch them or ceases his attempts to do so.

Title 3. Ownership of immovable objects

Article 5:20. (1) Ownership of land includes, in as far as not otherwise determined by law:
a. the surface;
b. the layers of earth beneath it;
c. the underground water that has come to the surface through a source, a well or a pump;
d. the water that is on the land and which is not in connection with water on another's land;
e. buildings and constructions that are permanently connected to the land, either directly, or through incorporation with other buildings and constructions, in so far as they are not a component of another's immovable object;
f. plants connected to the land.

(2) In derogation from paragraph (1), the ownership of a network, consisting of one or more cables or pipelines, destined for transport of solid, fluid or gaseous materials, of energy or of information, which is or will be laid in, on or above the land of others, belongs to the person entitled to construct such a network or his successor in title.

Article 5:21. (1) The power of the owner of land to use the land, includes the power to use the space above and under the surface.

(2) The use of the space above and under the surface is granted to others, in case this is so high above or so deep below the surface, that the owner no longer has an interest to resist such use.

(3) The previous paragraphs do not apply to the authorisation to fly.

Article 5:22. In case a parcel is not closed off, everyone may enter it, unless the owner could suffer damage or nuisance from this or has made known, in a clear way, that it is prohibited to be on the parcel without his permission, notwithstanding that which is determined for public roads.

Article 5:23. (1) If an object [voorwerp] or an animal finds itself unintentionally or without gross negligence on the land of another, the owner of the land must allow him on his request to search for the object or the animal and to remove it.

(2) The owner of the object or the animal shall compensate the owner of the law for the damage caused by the search and removal. With respect to this claim, the latter has a right of retention over the object or the animal.

Article 5:24. Immovable objects that do not have another owner belong to the State.

Article 5:25. The bottom of the territorial sea and of the Wadden Sea [Waddenzee] is owned by the State.

Article 5:26. The beaches of the sea until the foot of the dunes are presumed to be owned by the State.

Article 5:27. (1) The ground on which public water ways exist, is presumed to be owned by the State.

(2) This presumption does not apply against a public body:
(a) that maintains the waters and has not taken over the maintenance from the State;
(b) that maintained the waters and from which the State or another public body has taken over the maintenance.

Article 5:28. (1) Immovable objects that are public are, with the exceptions of the beaches of the sea, when they are maintained by a public body, presumed to be owned by the public body.

(2) This presumption does not work against he who has taken over that maintenance.

Article 5:29. The border of a parcel situated alongside water will shift with the shoreline, except in case of intentional drainage of the land or temporary flood. A flood is not temporary if the land is still overflown with water after ten years after the flood and the drainage of water has not started.

Article 5:30. (1) A shifting of the shoreline no longer changes the border after it has been established, either by the owners of the land and water in accordance with Article 31, or by a court at the request of one of them against the other in accordance with Article 32. The establishment is valid against both.

(2) When, at the moment of establishment, instead of the actual owner, someone who was registered

in the public registers as such was a party, the former paragraph applies nonetheless, unless the actual owner resisted the registration of the deed or the ruling before registration was made.

Article 5:31. (1) The establishment of the border by the owners of land or water is made by a notarial deed for that purpose within fourteen days followed by the registration of that deed in the public registers.
(2) The registrar of the registers is entitled to notify anyone of that registration who is registered as rightholder or seizor on one of the parcels.
(3) To the extent that the border described in the deed deviates from the former shoreline, a third party who at the moment of registration has a right on one of the parcels, is a tenant or lessee thereof, or has registered a seizure on one of the parcels, may regard the former shoreline as the established border.

Article 5:32. (1) A claim for the establishment of the border is awarded only if its instatement is registered in the public registers and all parties that were registered as a right holder or seizor of one of the parcels were called to the proceedings on time.
(2) The court decides on the border in accordance with the shoreline at the moment of registration of the claim. Before awarding the demand, he may order measures or evidence to be gathered that he considers relevant for the benefit of stakeholders who have not appeared.
(3) The costs of the claim are for the claimant.
(4) An application to set aside, appeal and appeal in cassation shall, upon penalty of inadmissibility, be registered in the registers within eight days after the the action is taken, as meant in Article 433 of the Code of Civil Procedure. In derogation from Article 143 of that Code, the period for setting aside starts running from the service of the decision to the person registered, also if the service is not made to him in person, unless the court has ordered further measures in this respect that and that order has not been met.
(5) The establishment takes effect at the moment that the ruling that allows the claim is registered in the public registers. This registration is not made until the ruling has become res judicata.

Article 5:33. (1) If the shoreline of a public water shifts inland after the border has been established, the owner of the flooded parcel shall tolerate the use of the water in accordance with its purpose.
(2) If the shoreline of a water that the owner of the adjacent parcel may use for any purpose shifts, after the border has been established, in the direction of the water, the owner of that parcel may claim that one or more rights of servitude are granted to him on the dried up land, whereby he may continue to exercise his powers in relation to the water.
(3) The previous paragraph applies mutatis mutandis for the benefit of he who may use the water for any purpose and who has a right of servitude to that effect on the parcel adjacent to the water.
(4) In case of an establishment of the border in accordance with Article 32, the former paragraphs apply when the the shoreline shifts after the registration of the claim.

Article 5:34. The shoreline in the sense of the previous five Articles is determined by the normal water level, or, in case of waters of which the level changes periodically, by the normal high water level. Land on which plants other than those that usually grow in water are considered, however, to be on the landside of the shoreline, even if that land is flooded in case of high water level.

Article 5:35. (1) A new dune that forms on the beach belongs to the owner of dune that borders the beach when both dunes have become one and the same in such a manner that they can no longer be distinguished from each other.
(2) On the other hand, this owner loses the land that becomes part of the beach by diminuition of the dune.
(3) Expansion or diminuition of a dune as meant in paragraphs 1 and 2 does not change the ownership anymore after the border has been established, either by the owners of beach and dune, or by the court on the request of one of them against the other. Articles 30-32 apply mutatis mutandis.
(4) Outside of the situations mentioned in paragraphs 1 and 2 the expansion or diminuition of a dune does not bring a change in ownership.

Article 5:36. If a wall, fence, hedge or ditch, or non-navigable running water, a trench, canal or similar waterway, serves as the border between two parcels, the centre of this border is presumed to be the border between these parcels. This presumption does not apply in case the wall is supported by a building or construction on one side only.

Title 4. Powers and duties of owners of neighbouring parcels

Article 5:37. The owner of a parcel may not, in a manner that in any way according to Article 162 of Book 6 is wrongful, cause a nuisance to owners of other parcels by speading noise, vibrations, smell, smoke or gasses, by taking away light or air or by taking away support.

Article 5:38. Lower parcels must receive the water that comes from higher parcels by way of nature.

Article 5:39. The owner of a parcel may not, in a manner that in any way according to Article 162 of Book 6 is wrongful, cause nuisance to owners of other parcels by altering the course, quantity or quality or water that flows on his parcel or of the ground water on his parcel, or by the use of water that is on his parcel and is in direct connection to the water on another's parcel.

Article 5:40. (1) The owner of a parcel that borders on public or running water may use the water to irrigate, drench livestock or any similar purposes, provided he does not cause nuisance to the owners of other parcels in a way or manner that according to Article 162 of Book 6 is wrongful.
(2) If it concerns public water, the former paragraph applies only in so far as the purpose of the water does not precule this.

Article 5:41. Articles 38, 39 and 40 paragraph 1 can be derogated from by regulation.

Article 5:42. (1) It is not allowed to have trees, shrubs or hedges within a distance to the border of a parcel determined by paragraph 2, unless the owner has given permission thereto or that parcel is a public road or a public water.
(2) The distance mentioned in paragraph 1 is two meters for trees, to be calculated from the centre of the foot of the tree and for shrubs and hedges half a meter, unless a shorter distance is allowed on the basis of a regulation or local custom.
(3) The neighbour cannot object to the presence of trees, shrubs or hedges that are not higher than the partition wall between the parcels.
(4) In relation to the unauthorised situation following this article, compensation is due only for damage arising after the moment at which the removal of this situation has been demanded.

Article 5:43. Wall in this and the next title means every partition made of stone, wood or other suitable material.

Article 5:44. (1) If a neighbour whose plantings hang over the parcel of another, despite notices from the owner of that parcel, neglects to remove the overhanging pieces, the last-mentioned owner can cut away and appropriate the overhanging pieces himself.
(2) The person on whose parcel roots grow from another parcel, may cut away and appropriate these in so far as they extend on his parcel.

Article 5:45. Fruits that fall from trees of a parcel on a neighbouring parcel, belong to he who is entitled to the fruits of the latter parcel.

Article 5:46. The owner of a parcel can at any time, demand from the owner of a bordering parcel that visible demarcations are placed on the border between their parcels or that the existing demarcations are renewed if necessary. The owners share in the costs thereof in equal parts.

Article 5:47. (1) If the course of the border between two parcels is uncertain, each of the owners can, at any time, request that a court establishes the border.
(2) In case of uncertainty about where the border between two parcels runs, the legal presumption that the possessor is owner does not apply.
(3) In determining the border, the court can, depending on the circumstances, divide the area in respect to which uncertainty exists, in equal or unequal parts or award it to one of the parties in its entirety, with or without granting compensation for damage to one of the parties.

Article 5:48. The owner of a parcel is authorised to close off this parcel.

Article 5:49. (1) Each of the owners of neighbouring parcels in an area of a municipality with adjoining buildings can, at any moment, claim that the other owner cooperates to erect a partition wall of two metres high on the border of the parcels, to the extent a regulation or local custom does not provide differently for the manner or the height of the partition. The owners contribute to the costs of the partition in equal parts.
(2) The previous paragraph does not apply in case one of the parcels is a public road or public water.

Article 5:50. (1) Unless the owner of the neighbouring parcel has given permission, it is not allowed to have windows or other wall openings, or balconies or similar constructions within two metres of the border of this parcel, in so far as these provide a view to this parcel.

(2) The neighbour cannot object to the presence of such openings or constructions, in case his parcel is a public road or public water, in case there are public roads or public waters between the parcels or in case the view does not reach further than a wall within two meters of the opening or constructions. Permissible openings or constructions on this basis remain allowed, also after the parcels have lost their public purpose or the wall is demolished.

(3) The distance meant in this Article is measured squarely from the outside of the wall there where the opening is made, or from the outside of the edge that faces the neighbouring parcel of the protruding construction until the border between the parcels or the wall.

4. When the nighbour as a result of prescription can no longer claim removal of an opening or construction, he is prohibited to install buildings or constructions within two meters thereof that would unreasonably hinder the owner of the other parcel, unless such a building or construction was already there at the moment of completion of the prescription period.

(5) In relation to an unauthorised situation following this Article, compensation is due only for damage arising after the moment from which removal of this situation was demanded.

Article 5:51. In the walls that are within the distance mentioned in the previous Article, light openings may be made, provided that they are made of solid and non-transparent windows.

Article 5:52. (1) An owner is obliged to organise the covering of his buildings and constructions in such as way that the water does not flow from it onto another's parcel.

(2) Drainage of water onto the public road is authorised, unless this is prohibited by law or regulation.

Article 5:53. The owner is obliged to ensure that no water or garbage of his parcel enters the gutter of another's parcel.

Article 5:54. (1) Where part of a building or construction has been constructed on, above or under the land of another person and where removal of the protruding part would be disproportionately more prejudicial to the owner of the building or construction than its preservation would be to the owner of the land, the owner of the building or construction may at any time demand that, in return for compensation, a right of servitude [erfdienstbaarheid] be granted to him in order to preserve the existing situation or that, at the option of the owner of the land, the required part of the land is transferred to him.

(2) The preceding paragraph applies mutatis mutandis to a building or construction which over time has begun to lean over the land of another person.

(3) The preceding paragraphs do not apply if this is the result of an obligation, arising from the law or a legal act, to tolerate the existing situation or if the owner of the building or construction can be held to have been in bad faith or grossly negligent with respect to the construction or his acquisition of the building or construction.

Article 5:55. In case a neighbouring parcel is brought into danger by an imminent collapse of a building or construction, the owner of that parcel may claim, at any time, that measures are taken to remove such danger.

Article 5:56. When it is necessary for the carrying out of activities for the benefit of an immovable object to temporarily use another immovable object, the owner of this object is held to authorise this after proper notice and against compensation, unless there are serious considerations for this owner to refuse this use or postpone it to a later moment.

Article 5:57. (1) The owner of land who has no proper access to a public road or a public waterway, may at all times demand [vorderen] of the owners of the neighbouring land the designation of a road of necessity [noodweg] for the benefit of his land in exchange for compensation to be paid or secured in advance for the damage caused to them by the road of necessity.

(2) If after the designation of the road of necessity unforeseen circumstances arise, whereby the road causes the owner of the land a greater burden than was considered with when calculating the compensation referred to in paragraph (1), the judge may increase the amount of the compensation.

(3) When designating the road of necessity, the interests of the enclosed land are taken into account, that the public road or public waterway can be reached by that road as quickly as possible, and with the interest of the burdened lands to bear the least possible inconvenience from that road. If land has been closed off from a public road, because as a result of a legal act it has another owner than a former united part that bordered on the public road or had proper access to it, then this separated part is to be considered first for the burdening with a road of necessity.

(4) When a change in local circumstances makes this desirable, a road of necessity may be moved on

demand of an owner with a direct interest.

(5) A road of necessity lapses, however long it may have existed, as soon as it is no longer needed.

Article 5:58. (1) The owner of a parcel who wants to supply water, electricity, gas and heating available to him elsewhere, through a pipeline, may request, against paying compensation in advance or by securing such compensation for damage, from the owners of neighbouring parcels that they tolerate this pipeline goes through or over their parcels.

(2) The last four paragraphs of the previous Article are applicable to this mutatis mutandis.

Article 5:59. (1) When the border between two parcels runs, in the longitudinal direction, under non-navigable running water, a ditch, trench, canal or similar waterway, the owner of each of these parcels has in relation to that waterway in its entire width the same powers and duties as a co-owner. Each owner is obliged to maintain the side of the water, ditch, canal or waterway that is on his parcel.

(2) Each owner is entitled and obliged to receive that part that is taken from it by the maintenance thereof on his parcel.

(3) Any diverging arrangement made between the owners also binds their successors in title.

Title 5. Joint-ownership [mandeligheid]

Article 5:60. Joint-ownership [mandeligheid] arises when an immovable object is jointly owned by the owners of two or more parcels and is intended for the general use of those parcels by them through a notarial deed made between them, followed by registration thereof in the public registers.

Article 5:61. (1) Joint ownership that arises on the basis of the preceding article ends:
(a). when the community ends;
(b) when the purpose of the object for the general use of the parcels is removed by a notarial deed made between the co-owners, followed by registration thereof in the public registers;
(c) as soon as the use of the object for each of the parcels has ended.

(2) The fact that the use of the object for each of the parcels has ended, can be registered in the public registers.

Article 5:62. 1. A freestanding wall, a fence or a hedge is co-ownership and jointly held, in case the border of the parcels that belong to different owners, runs underneath it in the length.

(2) The separating wall that two buildings or constructions, that belong to different owners, have in common, is also co-owned and jointly-held.

Article 5:63. (1) The right to a joint object cannot be separated from the ownership of the parcels.

(2) A claim to divide the joint object is excluded.

Article 5:64. Joint ownership brings with it that each co-owner must grant access to the joint object to the other co-owners.

Article 5:65. Joint objects must be maintained, cleaned, and, if necessary, renewed at the costs of all co-owners.

Article 5:66. (1) A co-owner of a joint object can also transfer his share in that object separately from his parcel to the other co-owners.

(2) If a co-owner wants to do this at his own expense based on the burdens of maintenance, cleaning and renewal in the future, the other co-owners are bound to cooperate with that transfer, provided he provides them where necessary a right of superficies or servitude, that allows them to continue to exercise their rights in relation to the object.

(3) The previous paragraphs are not applicable to a wall that is common to two buildings or constructions, nor to a wall, fence or hedge by which two parcels in a connected part of a municipality are separated from each other.

Article 5:67. (1) Each co-owner may place build against the jointly-owned partition wall and until halfway the depth construct beams, ribs, anchors and other constructions, provided that he does not cause detriment to the wall and the authorised constructions connected to the wall.

(2) Except in case of emergency, a co-owner can demand that, before another co-owner begins to place constructions, experts determine in what way this can happen without detriment to the wall or for authorised constructions of the first mentioned owner.

Article 5:68. Each co-owner may construct a gutter on the jointly-owned partition wall until the half of its depth provided that the water does not end up on the parcel of the other co-owner.

Article 5:69. Articles 64, 65, 66 paragraph 2, 67 and 68 are not applicable in so far as an arrangement made in accordance with Article 168 of Book 3 determines otherwise.

Title 6. Right of servitude [Erfdienstbaarheid]

Article 5:70. (1) A right of servitude is a burden, whereby an immovable object, the servient land, is burdened for the benefit of another immovable object, the dominant land.
(2) In the deed of creation of a right of servitude, the owner of the dominant parcel can be given the duty to pay to the owner of the servient parcel, whether or not at regularly recurring moments, a sum of money - the retribution [retributie].

Article 5:71. (1) The burden that a right of servitude imposes on the servient land, consists of a duty to allow or refrain from doing something on, above or under one of the piece of land. It can be stipulated in the deed of creation that the burden also includes a duty to establish buildings, constructions or plantation that are required for the exercise of the right of servitude, provided these buildings, constructions or plantations are entirely or partly on the servient land.
(2) The burden that a right of servitude imposes on the servient land can also consist of a duty to maintain the servient land or the buildings, constructions or plantations that are, or will be, entirely or partly on the servient land.

Article 5:72. Rights of servitude can be created by creation [vestiging] or by prescription.

Article 5:73. (1) The content of a right of servitude and the manner in which it is exercised are determined by the deed of creation and, in so far as arrangements are missing in that deed, by the local custom. If the right of servitude has been exercised in good faith and without opposition in a certain way for a considerable period of time, then, in case of doubt, this exercise is decisive.
(2) Nonetheless, the owner of the servient parcel can designate another part of the parcel for the exercise of the right of servitude than that part on which the right of servitude must be exercised according to the previous paragraph, provided that this moving is possible without reduction of the enjoyment of the owner of the dominant parcel. Costs, necessary for such a change, are for the owner of the servient parcel.

Article 5:74. The exercise of the right of servitude must be made in the least burdening way for the servient land.

Article 5:75. (1) The owner of the dominant parcel is entitled, at his expense, to perform that which is necessary for the exercise of his right of servitude.
(2) He is also entitled, at his expense, to place buildings, constructions or plantings that are necessary for the exercise of his right of servitude.
(3) He is obliged to maintain that which he placed on the servient parcel, to the extent this is necessary in the interest of the servient parcel; he is entitled to remove it, provided he returns the parcel to its original condition.
(4) The owner of the servient parcel does not have a right to use the buildings, constructions or plantings, that have been lawfully placed on his parcel by the owner of the dominant parcel.
(5) The previous paragraphs can be derogated from in the deed of creation.
(6) In case of a forced co-ownership, instead of paragraphs 3 and 4, the relevant provisions apply respectively.

Article 5:76. (1) When the dominant parcel is divided, the right of servitude continues to exist for the benefit of each part for which it may provide a benefit.
(2) When the servient parcel is divided, the burden continues to rest on each part in relation to which an exercise of the right of servitude is possible in accordance with the deed of creation.
(3) The previous paragraphs can be derogated from in the deed of creation.

Article 5:77. (1) If the dominant or the servient parcel belongs to two or more persons, either as shareholders [deelgenoten], or as owners of different parts thereof, they are jointly and severally liable for the performance of the monetary duties that stem from the right of servitude that become due during their right, to the extent that these are not divided over their rights.
(2) After a transfer or allocation of the dominant or the servient land or of a part thereof or of a share therein, the acquirer and his predecessor in title are jointly and severally liable for the monetary duties mentioned in paragraph 1 that have become due in the previous two years.
(3) The previous paragraphs can be derogated from in the deed of creation, but from the second paragraph not to the detriment of the acquirer.

Article 5:78. A court may, on the request of the owner of the servient land modify or terminate a right of servitude:
(a) on the basis of unforeseen circumstances, which are of such a nature that following the requirements of reasonableness and fairness unaltered continuation of the right of servitude cannot be expected of the owner of the servient land;
(b) if at least twenty years after the creation of the right of servitude have passed and the unaltered continuation of the right of servitude is contrary to the general interest [algemeen belang].

Article 5:79. A court may, on the request of the owner of the servient land, terminate a right of servitude, if the exercise of that right has become impossible or the owner of the dominant land no longer has a reasonable interest in the exercise of the right, and it cannot be assumed that the possibility to exercise the right or the reasonable interest will return with that.

Article 5:80. A court can, on the request of the owner of the dominant parcel, change the content of a right of servitude if unforseen circumstances make the exercise of the right of servitude temporarily or permanently impossible or if the interest of the owner of the dominant land has significantly diminished, in such a way that the possibility of exercising the right of servitude is restored, provided that the changes, according to reasonableness and fairness, can be asked from the owner of the dominant parcel.

Article 5:81. (1) A court can allow a claim as meant in Articles 78-80 under conditions set forth by it.
(2) If a limited property right exists on one of the parcels, the claim is only allowed if the holder of the limited property right was summoned to the proceedings. In determining whether the requirementrs of Articles 78 under a, 79 and 80 have been met, his interests must be taken into account as well.

Article 5:82. (1) If the owner of the dominant land wishes to abandon his right at his own costs, due to the burdens and obligations arising from the right of servitude, the owner of the servient land is obliged to cooperate with this.
(2) The deed of creation may provide otherwise for the duration of the first twenty years.

Article 5:83. If at the moment that the dominant and the servient parcel acquire one owner, a third party rents or leases one of the parcels or uses the land on the basis of another personal right, the right of servitude only ceases to exist by mixing at the end of this right to use.

Article 5:84. (1) He who has a right of empyteusis, superficies or usufruct on an immovable object, can stipulate a right of servitude for the benefit of this object. He can also burden this with a right of servitude.
(2) Rights of servitude, stipulated by a holder of a limited property right on the object on which his right rests or, in case of a right of superficies, for the benefit of the building [opstal], only cease to exist with the limited property right if this is so determined in the deed of creation of the right of servitude. If the right of servitude continues to exist, a stipulation as meant in Article 82 paragraph 2 no longer prevents the abandonment of the right of servitude.
(3) Rights of servitude, created by a holder of a limited property right on the object on which his right rests or, in case of a right of superficies, for the benefit of the building, cease to exist at the end of the limited property right, unless this right ends by mixing or abandonment or the owner of the object on which the limited property rights rests has declared to agree with the creation of the right of servitude in a deed that is registered in the public registers.
(4) The lessee [erfpachter], holder of a right of superficies or usufructuary is designated as owner of the dominant or servient land respectively for the purpose of the other Articles in this Title.

Title 7. Right of emphyteusis [Erfpacht]

Article 5:85. (1) The right of emphyteusis is the property right that entitles the emphyteuticarius [erfpacher] the power to hold and use the immovable object that belongs to someone else.
(2) An obligation for the emphyteuticarius to pay, periodically or not, the owner a sum of money – the canon – can be imposed on him by the deed of creation of the right.

Article 5:86. Parties may agree on the duration of the right of emphyteusis in the deed of creation.

Article 5:87. (1) A right of emphyteusis can be terminated by the emphyteuticarius, unless the deed of creation provides otherwise.
(2) A right of emphyteusis can be terminated by the owner, if the emphyteuticarius is in default of payment of the canon for two consecutive years or fails to a serious extent in the performance of his

obligations. The termination shall, under the penalty of nullity, be notified to those who are registered as holder of a property right or as seizor in the public registers within eight days. After the end of the right of emphyteusis, the owner is obliged to compensate the emphyteuticarius for the value that the emphyteusis has at that time, set-off with the costs he may claim from the emphyteuticarius arising out of the right of emphyteusis.

(3) A stipulation that deviates from the previous paragraph to the disadvantage of the emphyteuticarius, is void. In the deed of creation, the owner may be granted the right to terminate, except on the basis of a deficiency in the performance of his obligations by emphyteuticarius.

Article 5:88. (1) Each termination is done by formal notice [exploit]. It is made at least a year before the moment it is terminated, in case of Article 87 paragraph 2 at least a month before that moment. (2) In case of Article 87 paragraph 2, the registrar refuses to register the termination if the evidence of notification of the persons who are registered in the public registers as rightholders of a limited property right or the seizor of the right of emphyteusis is not included.

Article 5:89. (1) Unless provided otherwise in the deed of creation, the emphyteuticarius will have the same power to enjoy the object as the owner.

(2) Without permission of the owner, he may not give another purpose to the object or act in violation of the purpose of the object.

(3) To the extent that it is not otherwise agreed in the deed of creation, the emphyteuticarius has, both during the existence of the right of emphyteusis as well as at its end, the power to remove buildings, constructions or plantings, that were placed by him or his predecessors in title without the obligation to do so, provided he returns the object under emphyteusis in its original state.

Article 5:90. (1) To the extent that it is not otherwise agreed in the deed of creation, fruits that have separated or which have become due during the existence of the right of emphyteusis, and benefits of a movable nature that the object provides, belong to the emphyteuticarius.

(2) Benefits of an immovable nature belong to the owner. They are also subject to the right of emphyteusis, unless otherwise determined in the deed of creation.

Article 5:91. (1) It can be stipulated in the deed of creation that the right of emphyteusis cannot be transferred or allocated without permission of the owner. Such a stipulation does not prevent execution by creditors.

(2) It can also be stipulated in the deed of creation that the emphyteuticarius cannot divide his right by transfer or allocation of the right of emphyteusis on a part of the object without permission of the owner.

(3) A stipulation as meant in the previous paragraphs can also be made in respect to the rights of appartment, in which a building is divided by the emphyteuticarius. It can only be invoked against an acquirer under special title of a right of appartment if it is described in the deed of separation.

(4) If the owner refuses the required permission without reasonable justification or does not explain himself, his permission can, at the request of the person who needs it be replaced by a mandate from the local court in the District court of the district in which the object or the largest part thereof is situated.

Article 5:92. (1) If the right of emphyteusis belongs to two or more people, either as shareholder or as emphyteuticarius of different parts of the object, they are jointly and severally liable for the entire canon that becomes due during the existence of their right, to the extent that it has not been divided over their rights.

(2) After the transfer or allocation of a right of emphyteusis on an object or a part thereof or of a share in the right of emphyteusis, the acquirer and his predecessor in title are jointly and severally liable for the payment of the aforementioned canon that has become due in the previous five years.

(3) The deed of creation can derogate from the previous paragraphs, but from the second paragraph not to the detriment of the acquirer.

Article 5:93. (1) The emphyteuticarius is entitled to create a right of sub-emphyteusis on the object on which his right is created, in so far as the deed of creation does not determine otherwise. The sub-emphyteuticarius has, in respect to the object, no more powers than the emphyteuticarius has against the owner.

(2) The right of sub-emphyteusis ceases to exist at the end of the right of emphyteusis, unless it ceases to exist through mixing or abandonment. The owner can exercise the right to sell [uitwinnen] the right of emphyteusis free from the right of sub-emphyteusis to satisfy his right to payment of the canon. That what is determined in the pervious sentences of this paragraph does not apply if the

owner declared in a notarial deed registered in the public registers that he agreed to the creation of the right of sub-emphyteusis.

(3) For the application of the other Articles of this Title, the empheuticarius in his relation to the sub-emphyteuticarius is regarded as owner.

Article 5:94. (1) The emphyteuticarius is authorised to rent or lease the object on which the right of emphyteusis is created, in so far as the deed of creation does not precribe otherwise.

(2) At the end of the right of emphyteusis the owner is obliged to uphold a rent or lease that was validly created. He can nonetheless refuse to uphold it in so far as without his permission the time period for rent was longer than the time period locally customary or commercial space in the sense of the sixth Division of Title 4 of Book 7 is rented out for longer period than five years, or the lease has been made for a time period longer than twelve years for farms and six years for separate land, or the renting out or lease has been made on the basis of conditions onerous for him.

(3) He loses the power to refuse to uphold when the tenant or lessee gives him a reasonable time period in which to declare himself with regard to the upholding and he has not made such declaration within this period.

(4) If the owner is not obliged, according to the previous paragraphs, to uphold a renting out of living space by the emphyteuticarius in which the tenant has, at the end of the rent period, his principal residence and to which Articles 271 to 277 of Book 7 are applicable, he must nevertheless continue the rent agreement with the tenant with the understanding that Article 269 paragraph 2 of book 7 applies mutatis mutandis.

Article 5:95. To initiate claims and making request to obtain a court decision that concerns both the right of the owner as well as that of the emphyteuticarius, each of them is authorised, provided he takes care that the other is summoned to the proceedings in a timely manner.

Article 5:96. (1) Ordinary burdens and repairs are made and paid for by the emphyteuticarius. The emphyteuticarius is obliged, when extraordinary repairs are necessary, to inform the owner of this necessity and to provide him with the opportunity to make these repairs. The owner is not obliged to make any repair.

(2) The emphyteuticarius is obliged to pay the extraordinary burdens that rest on the object.

(3) The previous paragraphs can be derogated from in the deed of creation.

Article 5:97. (1) If twenty-five years have passed since the creation of the right of emphyteusis, a court, on the request of the owner or the emphyteuticarius, may modify or terminate the right on the basis of changed circumstances, which are of such a nature that according to the requirements of reasonableness and fairness the unaltered continuation of the deed of creation can no longer be expected of the owner or the emphyteuticarius.

(2) A court may allow the request, subject to conditions determined by it.

(3) If a limited right is created on the right of emphyteusis or the object, the request can only be allowed, if the holder of the limited right is called to the procedure and the standard of paragraph (1) is also fulfilled in respect to him.

Article 5:98. (1) When the time for which the right of emphyteusis was created has passed and the empthyteuticarius has not vacated the object at that time, the right of emphyteusis continues to exist, unless the owner makes clear ultimately six months after that period, that he considers the right to have ended. The owner and the emphyteuticarius can terminate the prolonged right of emphyteusis in the manner and taking into account the time period mentioned in Article 88.

(2) Every stipulation that deviates from this Article to the detriment of the emphyteuticarius, is void.

Article 5:99. (1) After the end of the right of emphyteusis the former emphyteuticarius is entitled to compensation for the value of buildings, constructions and plantings that are still present that have been placed by himor one of his predecessors in title or by which have been taken over from the owner for compensation.

(2) The deed of creation can stiplulate that the emphyteuticarius is not entitled to compensation as mentioned in paragraph 1:

(a) if the land on which the right of emphyteusis was created did not have a residential purpose.

(b) if the emphyteuticarius did not pay for the buildings, constructions or plantings;

(c) if the right of emphyteusis ended by termination by the emphyteuticarius;

(d) to the extent that the buildings, constructions and plantings were placed without a duty to do so and he could remove them at the end of the right of emphyteusis.

(3) The owner is entitled to deduct from the payment he owes on the basis of this Article that which he may claim from the emphyteuticarius following from the right of emphyteusis.

Article 5:100. (1) The emphyteuticarius has a right of retention to the object on which the right of emphyteusis was created until the compensation owed him is paid.
(2) Every stipulation that derogates from the previous paragraph is void.
(3) The owner has a right of retention on that which the emphyteuticarius could have taken down until that what he can claim on the basis of the right of emphyteusis is paid to him

Title 8. Right of superficies [Opstal]

Article 5:101. (1) The right of superficies is a property right to have or acquire a right of ownership of buildings, constructions or plantations in, on or above an immovable object, that belongs to someone else.

Article 5:102. The powers of the right holder of the superficies to use, make or remove buildings, constructions and plantings, can be limited in the deed of creation.

Article 5:103. In the absence of a provision on this in the deed of creation, the rightholder of the right of superficies has the powers that are required for the full enjoyment of the object on which the right of superficies is created.

Article 5:104. (1) Articles 92 and 95 apply mutatis mutandis to the right of superficies.
(2) Articles 86, 87, 88, 91, 93, 94, 97 and 98 are applicable mutatis mutandis to an independent right of superficies.

Article 5:105. (1) When the right of superficies ends, the ownership of the buildings, constructions and plantings pass to the owner of the immovable object on which it rested by operation of law.
(2) To the extent it is not otherwise determined in the deed of creation, the right holder of the right of superficies is at the end of his right, entitled to remove the buildings, constructions and plantings made by him or by his predecessor in title without having the duty to do so, or which have been taken over from the owner for compensation, provided he returns the object to its original state.
(3) Articles 99 and 100 apply mutatis mutandis, with the understanding that the right holder of the right of superficie's right of retention only extends to the buildings, constructions and plantings.

Title 9. Rights of apartment [Appartementsrechten]

Article 5:106. (1) An owner, holder of a right of emphyteusis or of a right of superficies, is entitled to divide his right in respect to a building and its appurtenances and to the land that belongs to it and its appurtenances, into rights of apartment.
(2) An owner, holder of a right of emphyteusis or of a right of superficies is also entitled to divide his right in respect to a piece of land into rights of apartment.
(3) A right of apartment in its turn can be divided into rights of apartment. A holder of a right of apartment is entitled to this subdivision, in so far as the deed of creation does not provide otherwise.
(4) A right of apartment is a share in the things that are included in the division, that includes the power to exclusively use specific parts of the building that by their design are meant to be or will be used separately. The share can also include the power to exclusively use certain parts of the land that belongs to the building. In case of paragraph (2), the share includes the power to exclusively use those parts of the land that by their design or designation are meant to be or will be used as a separate part.
(5) An owner of an apartment shall be understood to be a holder of a right of apartment.
(6) As a building as referred to in this Title shall also be understood a group of buildings that are part of the same division into rights of apartment.
(7) A holder of a right of emphyteusis or right of superficies is only entitled to a division into rights of apartments after obtaining permission from the owner of the land. Where the necessary permission is not granted evidently without a reasonable foundation or the owner does not respond at all, the permission may be replaced upon a petition by the person that needs it with a mandate of the local court [kantonrechter] of the district court [arrondissementsrechtbank] in which the building or the largest part of the building is situated.

Article 5:107. The owner, emphyteuticarius or holder of the right of superficies is also entitled in relation to the intended creation or change in organisation of the building to divide the building with its belongings and also the land that belongs to that into apartment rigths. Also in case of such a division the rights of apartment are created at the moment of registation of a deed of division.

Article 5:108. (1) The apartment owners are obliged towards each other to effectuate and maintain the building, organisation of the building or indication [aanduiding] of the land in accordance with

that which is determined in this respect in the deed of division.
(2) The court can stay a decision on a claim based on the previous paragraph, when a request is made on the basis of Article 144 under c, d, or h.

Article 5:109. (1) A division is made by a notarial deed made for that purpose, followed by registration of that deed in the public registers.
(2) A drawing is attached to the original of the deed of division that describes the boundaries of the separate parts of the building and the land that are intended to be used separately and for which, according to the deed of division, the exclusive use will be included in a right of apartment. The drawing must comply with the requirements that pursuant to the law referred to in Article 16 paragraph 2 of Book 3 prescribes for the registration thereof.
(3) Where the provisions of this Title mention the deed of division, this includes the drawing, unless it follows differently from the provision.

Article 5:110. (1) Despite the lack of the power of the person who made the division to have a registered thing at his disposal, the division is valid if it is followed by a valid transfer of a right of apartment or creation of a limited property right on the right of apartment.
(2) An invalid division is considered valid as well, if a right of apartment is acquired by prescription.

Article 5:111. The deed of division must contain:
(a) state the factual location of the building or the land;
(b) a detailed description of the separate parts of the building or the land that are destined to be used as a separate part, which description can take place by referring to the drawing mentioned in Article 109 paragraph 2, as well as state, for each part, which power to use belongs to which right of apartment.
(c) the Cadastral indication [aanduiding] of the rights of apartment and state the apartment owner.
(d) a regulation, to which are considered to belong the provisions of an accurately identified model regulation that is registered in the public registers of the place where the deed must be registered.

Article 5:112. (1) The regulation must contain:
(a) which debts and costs are for the account of the joint apartment owners;
(b) an arrangement concerning an operating account to be drawn up annually, running over the past year, and the contributions to be made by the apartment owners.
(c) an arrangement concerning the use, the management and the maintenance of the parts that are not intended to be used as a separate part;
(d) for whose care and against which risks the building must be insured for the benefit of the joint apartment owners;
(e) the creation of an association of owners that has as its purpose looking after the joint interests of the apartment owners, and the statutes of the association.
(2) The statutes of the association of owners must contain:
(a) the name of the association and the municipality in which it has its seat. The name of the association must be preceded by the words: "Association of Owners", either written in full, or abbreviated to "AoO" [V.v.E.] and furthermore must make mention of the location of the building or the land;
(b) the purpose of the association;
(c) an arrangement on the contributions that are due to the association by the apartment owners periodically, at least annually.
(d) the manner in which the meeting of owners and the determination of the number of votes that each of the apartment owners can bring out in the meeting.
(3) The regulation can include an arrangement, pursuant to which all or certain rights of appartment bring with it the membership of another, to be further described in the regulation, association or cooperation, in so far as this membership is in accordance with the statutes of that association or cooperation.
(4) The regulation can contain an arrangement on the use, the management and the maintenance of the parts that have as their purpose to be used as a separate part. Such an arrangement can include that the meeting of owners is entitled to withhold an apartment owner or he who exercises his right, the use of these parts based on serious reasons, to be further provided in the regulation.

Article 5:113. (1) The shares that come into existence by division are equal, unless the deed of division prescribes another proportion. In the latter case, it follows from the deed on which basis this proportion is based.
(2) For the debts and costs that following the law or the regulation are for the account of the joint

apartment owners, they must amongst each other and towards the association of owners, contribute an equal share for each right of apartment, unless the regulation determines another proportion.

(3) If the apartment owners are jointly liable for the debt mentioned in the previous paragraph and the performance owed is divisible, they are each liable for a part, in the proportion mentioned in the previous paragraph.

(4) If the apartment owners are jointly liable for a debt mentioned in paragraph 2, the association is jointly and severally liable for that debt.

(5) Those persons who were apartment owner at the moment of creation of the debt, are jointly and severally liable with the association and in case the performance is divisible, each for the share in the proportion mentioned in paragraph 2, for the debts of the association.

(5) Those persons who were apartment owner at the moment of creation of the debt, are jointly and severally liable with the association and in case the performance is divisible, each for the share in the proportion mentioned in paragraph 2, for the debts of the association. If the debt is a monetary loan as meant in Article 126 paragraph 4, in case of transfer under special title or allocation of an apartment right, the apartment owner is discharged from his liability for that debt upon the transfer or allocation, in so far as with respect to that debt in accordance with Article 122 paragraph 5 a statement has been provided to the acquirer referred to there.

(6) For the application of paragraphs 2 and 3, the debt arising out of a monetary loan as meant in Article 126 paragraph 4 is divisible.

Article 5:114. (1) If at the moment of registration of the deed of division a right of hypothec, a seizure or a preferential right rests on all registered things involved in the division, then this burden, seizure or preferential right rests from that moment on each of the rights of apartment for the entire debt.

(2) If at the moment of registration of the deed of division a right of hypothec, a seizure of a preferential right rests on a part of the registered things only, the power to exercise the right to sell [uitwinning] this part continues to exist despite the division; the division is ended on that part with the exercise of the right to sell.

(3) A right of servitude, emphyteusis, superficies or usufruct that exists at the moment of the registration of the deed of division on the registered object or a part thereof, continues to exist unchanged after that.

Article 5:115. (1) When a right of emphyteusis or superficies is involved in the division, the canon or retribution that becomes due afterwards, is divided amongst the rights of apartment in a proportion as meant in Article 113 paragraph 2.

(2) The association of owners is jointly and severally liable for the canon or retribution that is owed by one or more of the apartment owners.

Article 5:116. (1) When a right of emphyteusis or superficies is involved in the division, in addition to Articles 87 paragraphs 2 and 3 and 88, the following paragraphs apply.

(2) Termination of the right due to default in the payment of the canon or retribution can only happen when the entire canon or retribution has not been paid for two consecutive years.

(3). If a limited property right or seizure rests on one or more rights of apartment, Article 87 paragraph 2 second sentence and Article 88 paragraph 2 apply mutatis mutandis in relation to this right or seizure as well.

(4) If the canon or retribution owed for a right of apartment has been unpaid for two consecutive years, this right of apartment can be allocated by the court to the land owner upon his demand. The summons [dagvaarding] must, upon penalty of inadmissibility, be served on those who are registered as holder of a limited property right or seizor in the public registers, within eight days.

(5) By registration in the public registers of the ruling in which the allocation is ordered, the right of apartment passes to the land owner and the limited property rights and seizures on it will cease to exist. This registration does not occur, before the decision has become res judicata [kracht van gewijsde]. After this registration, the land owner is obliged to compensate the value the right of apartment has at the moment of registration to the former apartment owner, after deduction of that which he had to claim from the former apartment owner in respect to the right of emphyteusis, including the costs.

(6) The manner in which the value as meant in the previous paragraph is established can be determined in the deed of creation.

(7) Every stipulation that derogates from this Article to the detriment of the apartment owner is void.

Article 5:117. (1) A right of apartment can be transferred, allocated, burdened and subjected to a right to sell [uitgewonnen] as an independent registered thing.

(2) Without prejudice to that which is laid down in Article 114 paragraph 2, things that are involved in the division cannot be transferred, allocated, burdened or subjected to a right to sell, partly or in their entirety.

(3) The cessation of the division in relation to a part of the registered things involved in the division can only happen through amendment of the deed of division.

4. In derogation from paragraph 2, the joint apartment owners can burden the immovable objects involved in the division with a right of servitude.

[The remainder of Book 5 is omitted.]

Book 6. General Part on the Law of Obligations

Title 1. Obligations in general

Division 1. General provisions

Article 6:1. Obligations [verbintenissen] can only arise if they follow from the law.

Article 6:2. (1) Creditor [schuldeiser] and debtor [schuldenaar] are obligated to behave as against each other in accordance with the requirements of reasonableness and fairness [redelijkheid en billijkheid].

(2) A rule which governs them on the basis of law, custom or a legal act is not applicable, as far as this would be unacceptable in the given circumstances according to the standards of reasonableness and fairness.

Article 6:3. (1) A natural obligation is a legally unenforceable obligation.

(2) A natural obligation exists:

(a) when the law or a legal act denies enforceability of the obligation;

(b) when someone has an urgent moral obligation towards another of such a nature that performance thereof, although not legally enforceable, following societal views must be regarded as satisfaction of a performance that accrues to the other.

Article 6:4. The legislative provisions relating to obligations apply mutatis mutandis to natural obligations, unless it follows from the law or its purpose that a provision may not be applied to an unenforceable obligation.

Article 6:5. (1) A natural obligation is converted into a legally enforceable one by a contract between the debtor and the creditor.

(2) An offer from the debtor directed at the creditor for such a gratuitous contract, is deemed to be accepted when the offer became known to the creditor and he did not immediately reject it.

(3) The provisions relating to donations and gifts do not apply to the contract.

Division 2. Plurality of debtors and Joint and Several Liability

Article 6:6. (1) If a performance is due from two or more debtors, they are each bound for an equal share, unless it follows from the law, custom or legal act that they are bound for unequal parts or jointly and severally liable.

(2) If the performance is indivisible or it stems from the law, custom or legal act that the debtors with respect to the same debt are each liable for the whole, then they are jointly and severally liable.

(3) It can follow from a contract between a debtor and his creditor that if the debt is transferred to two or more successors at law, they are liable for unequal parts or jointly and severally liable.

Article 6:7. (1) If two or more debtors are jointly and severally liable, the creditor has the right to performance of the whole from each of them.

2 (2) Performance by one of the debtors also discharges the fellow debtors towards the creditor. The same applies if the debt is paid by payment in kind or set-off, as well as when the court on the application of one of the debtors applies Article 60, unless he determines otherwise.

Article 6:8. Article 2 applies to the legal relations between the joint and several debtors.

Article 6:9. (1) Every joint and several debtor is authorized to accept an offer to waive the claim gratuitously on behalf of the other debtors, so far as the waiver also concerns the other debtors.

(2) Postponement of payment, granted by the creditor to a one of the debtors, also applies to his fellow debtors, so far as it appears that this is the intention of the creditor.

Article 6:10. (1) Joint and several debtors are, each for the part of the debt that concerns him in their mutual relationship, under a duty to contribute to the debt and the costs in accordance with the following paragraphs.

(2) The duty to contribute to the debt that is borne by one of the joint and several debtors for a larger part than for which he is responsible, comes to rest on every fellow debtor for the amount of this excess, each time to a maximum the portion of the debt that the fellow debtor is responsible for.

(3) Every fellow debtor must contribute to the costs reasonably incurred by a joint and several debtor in proportion to the portion of the debt that he is responsible for, unless the costs only affect the debtor personally.

Article 6:11. (1) A fellow debtor who is asked to contribute on the basis of the previous article can also invoke the defences that he had against the creditor at the time of the creation of the duty to contribute against the joint and several debtor who demands the contribution from him.

(2) Nevertheless he cannot invoke such a defence against this debtor if it arose after their respective obligation from a legal act that the creditor performed with or towards him.

(3) An appeal to prescription of the legal claim of the creditor only arises for the person asked to contribute if at the time of the creation of the duty to contribute both he and the person demanding the contribution could have invoked the completion of the prescription period against the creditor.

(4) The previous paragraphs are only applicable to the extent that contrary does not follow from the legal relationship between the debtors.

Article 6:12. (1) If the debt is paid at the expense of a joint and several debtor for more than the portion for which he is responsible, the rights of the creditor towards the fellow debtors and towards third parties pursuant to subrogation transfer to the debtor for this larger part, each time to the maximum the part that the fellow debtor or the third party is responsible for in his relationship to the debtor.

(2) Through subrogation the claim, if it concerns a performance other than money, is converted into a claim to money of equal value.

Article 6:13. (1) If recourse from a joint and several debtor for a claim as meant in Articles 10 and 12 appears to be wholly or partly impossible, the part that cannot be recovered is spread over al his fellow debtors in proportion to the part of the debt for which each is responsible in their mutual relationship.

(2) if the debt is wholly or partly paid at the expense of a joint and several debtor who did not himself enter the debt and if it appears that recourse from one of the fellow debtors who did enter the debt is not possible, the part that cannot be recovered is spread over all the fellow debtors who did not enter the debt in proportion to the amount for which each at the time of the payment of the debt towards the creditor was liable.

(3) Every person who is involved in the apportionment remains entitled to still claim back the contribution from the person who offered no recourse.

Article 6:14. A waiver by the creditor of his legal claim towards a joint and several debtor does not discharge him from his duty to contribute. The creditor can nevertheless discharge him from his duty to contribute towards a fellow debtor by committing to the latter that he will reduce his claim on him with the amount that could be claimed as contribution.

Division 3 Plurality of creditors

Article 6:15. (1) If a performance is owed to two or more creditors, each of them has a legal claim for an equal part, unless it follows from the law, custom or legal act that the performance is due to them in unequal parts or that they have one legal claim together.

(2) If the performance is indivisible or if the right thereto belongs to communal property, they have one legal claim together.

(3) It cannot be invoked against the debtor that the legal claim belongs to communal property if this right stems from a contract that he concluded with the participants, but he did not know nor ought he to have known that the right would become part of the communal property.

Article 6:16. If it is agreed with the debtor that two or more persons can claim the performance from him in whole as creditor, such that satisfaction towards one also discharges him towards the other, yet in the mutual relationship of the persons the performance does not accrue to them all together, the rules applicable to community property are correspondingly applicable to their legal relationship towards the debtor.

Division 4. Alternative obligations

Article 6:17. (1) An obligation is alternative when the debtor is under a duty to perform one of two or more different performances at his choice, or that of the creditor or a third party.
(2) The choice accrues to the debtor, unless something else follows from the law, custom or legal act.

Article 6:18. An alternative obligation becomes singular by the making of a choice by the person authorised thereto.

Article 6:19. (1) if the choice accrues to one of the parties, the power to choose transfers to the other party if he gives his counter-party a reasonable time for making the choice and this person does not make a choice within it.
(2) The power to choose does not transfer to the creditor however before he has the right to claim performance, nor to the debtor before he has the right to perform.
(3) If the claim is burdened with a pledge or seizure and the already initiated foreclosure cannot be continued due to a lack of choice, the pledgee or the seizer may set a reasonable time for both parties to make a choice in accordance with their mutual legal relationship. If a choice is not made within this period, the power to choose is transferred to the pledgee or seizer. They are bound not to make needless used of this power.

Article 6:20. (1) The impossibility to perform one or more of the performances does not diminish the power to choose.
(2) If the choice accrues to the debtor, he is not authorised to choose an impossible performance, however, unless the impossibility is a consequence of a cause that can be attributed to the creditor or if this person agrees with the choice.

Division 5. Conditional obligations

Article 6:21. An obligation is conditional [voorwaardelijk] if, according to the legal act, its effect has been made dependent on a future event.

Article 6:22. A suspensive [opschortende] condition renders the obligation effective only after the occurrence of the event; a resolutive [ontbindende] condition renders the obligation terminated.

Article 6:23. (1) When the party who had an interest in the non-fulfillment, prevented the fulfillment, the condition is treated as fulfilled if reasonableness and fairness demand this.
(2) When the party who had an interest in the fulfillment, made this happen, the condition is treated as not fulfilled, if reasonableness and fairness demand this.

Article 6:24. (1) After a resolutive condition has been fulfilled, the creditor is obliged to restore the performance already rendered, unless something else follows from the content or purpose of the legal act.
(2) If the duty to undo extends to return of a thing, the natural and due civil fruits that separated after the fulfilment of the condition belong to the debtor and Articles 120-124 of Book 3 are correspondingly applicable with respect to that which is laid down therein in relation to compensation of costs and damage, so far as those costs and the damage occurred after the fulfilment.

Article 6:25. If a performance pursuant to an obligation under suspensive condition is performed before the fulfilment of the condition, in accordance with division 2 of Title 4, restoration of the performance can be claimed as long as the condition has not been fulfilled.

Article 6:26. The provisions concerning unconditional obligations are applicable to conditional obligations, in so far as the conditional character of the relevant obligation does not stand in the way.

Division 6. Performance of obligations

Article 6:27. He who has to deliver an individually determined object is obliged to exercise care for delivery of this object in the manner that a careful debtor would do in the given circumstances.

Article 6:28. If the object or objects owed are only determined according to their sort, and within the mentioned sort differences in quality exist, that which the debtor delivers may not be below the good average quality.

Article 6:29. The debtor is not entitled, without the permission of the creditor, to fulfil that which is owed in parts.

Article 6:30. (1) An obligation may be performed by a person other than debtor, unless its nature or purpose oppose this.

(2) The creditor is not in default if he refuses a realization offered by a third party with the approval of the debtor.

Article 6:31. Payment to an incompetent creditor discharges the debtor to the extent that the payment led to a real advantage for the incompetent or came within the power of his legal representative.

Article 6:32. Payment to another than the creditor or the person who is authorised with him or in his place to receive it, discharges the debtor to the extent that the person who was to be paid ratified the payment or is advantaged by it.

Article 6:33. If the payment is made despite a seizure or while the creditor was not authorised to receive it due to a limited right, an administration of property or a similar impairment, and the debtor is required to make the payment again, he has a right of recourse against the creditor.

Article 6:34. (1) The debtor who has paid to someone who was not competent to receive the payment, can invoke against the person to whom he was required to pay, that his payment discharged him, if he assumed on reasonable grounds that the recipient of the payment was entitled to performance as creditor or that he had to be paid on some other ground.
(2) If someone loses his right to demand payment, so that with retroactive effect it accrues to another, the debtor can invoke a payment already made to the other, unless that which he could foresee in relation to this loss, should have prevented him from making payment.

Article 6:35. (1) If the requirement of one of the paragraphs of the previous articles is satisfied in case of a payment by a third person in his respect, he can invoke the discharging effect of the payment on his behalf.
(2) the debtor can invoke the discharging effect of the payment on his behalf, if the requirements would also be satisfied for him if he had paid.

Article 6:36. In the case meant in the two previous articles, the person truly entitled has a right of recourse against the person who received the payment without right.

Article 6:37. The debtor is authorised to suspend the performance of his obligation if he has reasonable grounds to doubt who he must pay.

Article 6:38. If no time has been determined for the performance, the obligation may be performed immediately, and performance may be demanded immediately.

Article 6:39. (1) If a time for performance has been determined, it is presumed that this only prevents the performance from being claimed earlier.
(2) Payment before the due date is not undue.

Article 6:40. The debtor can no longer invoke the time provision:
(a) when he has been declared bankrupt or in respect of him the debt restructuring arrangement natural persons has been declared applicable;
(b) when he fails to provide the security promised by him;
(c) when due to a cause attributable to him the security lodged security has diminished, unless the remainder still provides a sufficient guarantee for the satisfaction.

Article 6:41. If no place for performance is determined, delivery of the object owed shall occur:
(a) in case of an individually determined object: at the place where it was situated at the time of the creation of the obligation;
(b) in case of an object determined by sort: at the place where the debtor conducts his profession or business or, in the absence thereof, where he has his residence.

Article 6:42. He who delivers an object for the performance of an obligation over which he is not authorised to dispose, can claim that it be handed over to the person to whom it belongs, provided he simultaneously offers another object that corresponds to the obligation and the interest of the creditor does not stand in the way.

Article 6:43. (1) If the debtor makes a payment that could be allocated to two or more obligations towards one and the same creditor, it is allocated to the obligation that the creditor designates at payment.
(2) In the absence of such a designation it is allocated in the first place to the obligations that are due. If there are still more obligations to which the allocation could occur, it is allocated in the first place to the most burdensome and if the obligations are equally burdensome, to the oldest. If the obligations are also equally old, the allocation is made proportionately.

Article 6:44. (1) Payment of a monetary sum attributable to a particular obligation extends in the first place to reducing the costs, subsequently to reducing the incurred interest and lastly to reducing the principal sum and current interest.
(2) The creditor may, without being in default, refuse an offer for payment, if the debtor designates another order for the allocation.
(3) The creditor may refuse the full payment of the principal amount, if the accrued and current interest as well as the costs are not settled as well.

Article 6:45. Only with the consent of the creditor can a debtor be released from his obligation by another performance than that owed, even if it is of equal or higher value.

Article 6:46. (1) When the creditor receives a cheque, postal cheque, transfer order or another paper offered to him as means of payment, it is presumed that this takes place subject to a good outcome.
(2) if the creditor is authorised to suspend the performance of a duty resting with him until the moment of payment, he retains this right of suspension until a good outcome is certain or could have been obtained by him.

Article 6:47. (1) The costs of payment are borne by the person who performs the obligation.
(2) the costs of a receipt are borne by the person for whose benefit it is given.

Article 6:48. (1) The creditor is under a duty to give a receipt for every fulfilment, unless something else follows from the contract, custom or fairness.
(2) If the creditor has a piece of evidence given in respect of the debt, the debtor can claim handing over of the piece of evidence upon fulfilment, unless the creditor has a reasonable interest in keeping the piece and makes the necessary notation of proof of discharge of the debtor on it.
(3) the debtor can suspend the fulfilment of his obligation if the creditor does not meet the requirement of the first paragraph.

Article 6:49. (1) Upon fulfilment of a bearer or order claim, the debtor can demand that a acquittal on paper is made and that he is given the paper.
(2) If the fulfilment does not concern the whole claim or the creditor still needs the paper for the exercise of other rights, he can keep the paper, provided that he next to the acquittal that is made on paper, he also gives a separate acquittal.
(3) He can, irrespective of whether fully or partially is fulfilled, settle for the single handing over of an acquittal, provided that he shows at the request of the other party that the paper was destroyed or had become worthless, or provides security for twenty years or a much shorter period of time as can be expected that the other party could still be exposed to a claim based on the paper.
(4) The debtor can suspend the fulfilment of his obligation if the creditor does not satisfy the previous paragraphs.

Article 6:50. (1) If at consecutive intervals similar performances have to be made, the receipts of two consecutive terms raise the presumption that also the earlier terms have been met.
(2) If the creditor hands over a receipt for the principal sum, it is presumed that the interest and the costs have also been paid.

Article 6:51. (1) When it follows from the law that someone is under a duty to provide security or that providing security is a condition for the existence of any legal consequence, he who does so, has the choice between a personal and real security.
(2) The security offered must be such that the claim and if there are grounds thereto the interest and costs resting on it are covered sufficiently and that the creditor can exercise recourse against them without effort.
(3) If the security offered has become inadequate due to a cause that is not attributable to the creditor, the debtor is under a duty to supplement or substitute it.

Division 7. Rights of suspension [Opschortingsrechten]

Article 6:52. (1) A debtor who has a claim on his creditor which is due, is entitled to suspend performance of his obligation until his claim has been met, if there is sufficient connection between the claim and the obligation to justify this suspension.
(2) Such a connection can be assumed inter alia in case both obligations follow from the same legal relationship or from transactions frequently conducted by the parties.

Article 6:53. A right of suspension can also be invoked as against the creditors of the other party.

Article 6:54. No right to suspend exists:
(a) to the extent that performance of the obligation of the other party is prevented by default of the creditor;
(b) to the extent that performance of the obligation of the other party has become permanently impossible;
(c) to the extent that seizure of the other party's claim is not permitted.

Article 6:55. As soon as security has been provided for fulfilment of the obligation of the other party, the right to suspend lapses, unless that fulfilment would thereby unreasonably be delayed.

Article 6:56. The right to suspend remains even after prescription of the legal claim on the other party.

Article 6:57. If the power to suspend meets the description of a retention of title right in Article 290 of Book 3, the provisions of the subsequent division are applicable, to the extent Division 4 of Title 10 of Book 3 does not diverge from them.

Division 8. Creditor's Default

Article 6:58. The creditor is in default when fulfilment of the obligation is prevented because he did not provide the necessary cooperation thereto, or because another impediment of his side arises, unless the cause of the impediment cannot be attributed to him.

Article 6:59. The creditor is also in default when he as a result of circumstances attributable to him does not meet a duty on his part towards the debtor and this person on that ground competently suspends the fulfilment of his obligation towards the creditor.

Article 6:60. If the creditor is in default, the court based on a claim by the debtor can determine that he is discharged of his obligation, whether or not under conditions set by the court.

Article 6:61. (1) Default of the creditor ends the default of the debtor.
(2) As long as the creditor is in default, the debtor cannot be put in default.

Article 6:62. During the default of the creditor, he is not entitled to take enforcement measures.

Article 6:63. The debtor has, within the limitations of reasonableness, a right to compensation of the costs, of an offer or a safekeeping as meant in Articles 66-70 or made otherwise as a result of the default.

Article 6:64. If during the default of the creditor a circumstance arises that renders proper fulfilment wholly or partly impossible, it is not attributable to the debtor, unless he due to his fault or that of a subordinate failed in the care that in the given circumstances could be expected of him.

Article 6:65. When in the case of an obligation to deliver generic objects the debtor identifies certain objects for the delivery that conform to the obligation and the creditor has been notified thereof, he is in case of default of the creditor only under a duty to deliver these objects. He remains authorised however to deliver other objects that conform to the obligation.

Article 6:66. If the obligation is to pay a monetary sum or to delivery an object, in case of default of the creditor, the debtor is authorised to place that owed in safekeeping for the creditor.

Article 6:67. The safekeeping of a monetary sum is made by consignment in accordance with the law, that of an object to be delivered by giving it for safe keeping to someone whose business is to keep objects like the person concerned in the place where the delivery is to take place. The rules on judicial safekeeping are applicable to this safekeeping, to the extent something else does not follow from Articles 68-71.

Article 6:68. During the safekeeping, no interest is payable by the debtor over a sum of money held in keeping.

Article 6:69. (1) During the safekeeping, the credit can only clear his default by accepting that which was placed in safekeeping.
(2) As long as the creditor does not accept that which was placed in safekeeping, the person putting it in safekeeping has the power to take it out of safekeeping.

Article 6:70. The keeper may only hand over the object to the creditor if he pays all the costs of the safekeeping. After the handing over, he is under a duty to reimburse the person who placed it in safekeeping for what he had already paid. If the object is handed over, before the creditor pays all the costs, the rights to the object transfer to the keeper by payment to the person who put in safekeeping.

Article 6:71. The legal claim against the debtor becomes time-barred no later than the legal claim to delivery of that which was placed in safekeeping.

Article 6:72. In case of joint and several liability, the legal consequences of default of the creditor apply towards each of the debtors.

Article 6:73. If the creditor refuses an offer from a third party, articles 60, 62, 63 and 66-70 are correspondingly applicable for the benefit of the third party, provided the offer conformed to the obligation and the third party had a justified interest in the performance.

Division 9. The consequences of non-performance of an obligation
§1 General provisions

Article 6:74. (1) Every deficiency in the performance [tekortkoming in de nakoming] of an obligation obliges the debtor to compensate the creditor for the damage thereby caused to him, unless the deficiency cannot be attributed to the debtor.
(2) In as far as performance is not yet permanently impossible, paragraph (1) is only applicable having taken into account what has been provided in §2 concerning default of the debtor.

Article 6:75. A deficiency cannot be attributed to the debtor if it cannot be ascribed to his fault, or if it is not for his account pursuant to the law, a legal act or generally accepted views in society [in het verkeer geldende opvattingen].

Article 6:76. Where the debtor makes use of the help of other persons when fulfilling an obligation, he is liable for their conduct in the same manner as for his own.

Article 6:77. If, for the fulfilment of an obligation an object is used which is unsuitable to that end, then the resulting deficiency is attributed to the debtor, unless this would be unreasonable given the content and purpose of the legal act which gives rise to the obligation, generally accepted views in society and the other circumstances of the case.

Article 6:78. (1) If a deficiency cannot be attributed to the debtor, but he enjoys an advantage in connection to that deficiency that he would not otherwise have had in case of proper performance, the creditor has a right to compensation of his damage to a maximum amount of that benefit, under application of the rules concerning unjust enrichment.
(2) Where this benefit consists of a claim on a third party, the debtor can comply with the previous paragraph by transferring that claim.

Article 6:79. If a creditor, whose debtor is prevented from performing as a result of a cause that cannot be attributed to him, is nevertheless capable of providing for himself that which is due through execution or set-off, he is authorized to do so.

Article 6:80. (1) The consequences of non-performance ensue even before the claim is due:
(a) if it is certain that performance without deficiency will be impossible;
(b) if the creditor is to deduce from a statement of the debtor that there will be a deficiency in his performance; or
(c) if the creditor on good grounds fears that there will be a deficiency in the debtor's performance and the latter does not comply with a written notice which contains those grounds by declaring himself willing to honour his commitments within a reasonable time indicated in that notice.
(2) The original time at which the obligation became due remains valid with regard to damages owed due to delay and the attribution to the debtor of the fact that performance became impossible during the time that he was in default.
§2 Default of the debtor

Article 6:81. The debtor is in default [verzuim] during the time that performance is lacking after it has become due and the requirements of Articles 82 and 83 are met, except to the extent that the delay cannot be attributed to him or performance is already permanently impossible.

Article 6:82. (1) Default commences when the debtor has been given written notice of default whereby a reasonable time for performance is set, and there is no performance within this reasonable time.
(2) If the debtor temporarily cannot perform or it appears from his conduct that a notice would be

useless, the notice of default [ingebrekestelling] can be made by a written statement proclaiming that he is held liable for the failure to perform.

Article 6:83. Default commences without a notice of default:
(a) where a period of time set for fulfilment lapses without the obligation having been performed, unless it appears that the time period has a different purpose;
(b) where the obligation follows from a wrongful act or is meant as damages as provided in Article 74 paragraph (1) and the obligation is not immediately performed;
(c) where the creditor is to understand from a statement of the debtor that the latter will fail to perform the obligation.

Article 6:84. Every impossibility to perform that arises during the time that the debtor was in default and which cannot be attributed to the creditor, is attributed to the debtor; the latter shall compensate the resulting damage, unless the creditor would also have suffered the damage had performance been proper and timely.

Article 6:85. The debtor is only obliged to compensate damage resulting from delay in performance as regards the time during which he was in default.

Article 6:86. The creditor may refuse performance that is offered after commencement of the default, as long as payment of the damages that have in the meantime become due, and of the costs, is not offered as well.

Article 6:87. (1) To the extent that performance is not yet permanently impossible, the obligation is converted into one to pay substitutionary damages [vervangende schadevergoeding], when the debtor is in default and the creditor informs him in writing that he claims damages instead of performance.
(2) Conversion shall not take place if it is not justified by the deficiency, given its inferior nature.

§3 Further consequences of non-performance

Article 6:88. (1) The debtor who has fallen short in the performance of his obligation may set a reasonable time for the creditor within which he must inform him which of the measures available to him at the commencement of the time period he wishes to exercise on penalty of only being able to claim:
(a) the compensation which the deficiency in performance gives right to and, if the
obligation relates to the payment of a sum of money, to that sum of money;
(b) termination of the contract from which the obligation stems if the debtor claims that the deficiency in performance cannot be attributed to him.
(2) if the creditor has demanded performance, but it is not met within a reasonable period of time, he can assert all his rights once again; the preceding paragraph applies mutatis mutandis.

Article 6:89. The creditor may no longer assert a failure in performance if he has not protested to the debtor in this respect within a suitable time after he discovered the failure or reasonably should have discovered it.

Article 6:90. (1) In case of an impediment to delivery of an object that is susceptible to quick destruction or deterioration or which for another reason the ongoing custody is so burdensome that it cannot be expected of the debtor in the given circumstances, he is authorised to have the good sold in a suitable manner. The debtor is bound towards the creditor to such a sale when his interests unmistakably require this sale or the creditor indicates that he demands the sale.
(2) The net proceeds come in the place of the object, without prejudice to the rights of the creditor due to deficiencies in the performance of the obligation.

§4 Penalty clause

Article 6:91. A penalty clause is deemed to be every clause according to which it is stipulated that the debtor, if he falls short in the performance of his obligation is bound to a sum of money or another performance, regardless of whether this is for compensation of damage or simply to provide an incentive to perform.

Article 6:92. (1) The creditor cannot claim performance of the penalty clause and the obligation to which the penalty clause is bound.
(2) What is owed pursuant to a penalty clause replaces the compensation for damages due pursuant to the law.
(3) The creditor cannot claim performance of the penalty clause if the deficiency in performance is not attributable to the debtor.

Article 6:93. A notice or another declaration in advance is required to claim performance of the penalty clause in the same cases as is required for the claim to compensation for damages due pursuant to the law.

Article 6:94. (1) On request by the debtor, the court may, where fairness manifestly demands this, mitigate the contractual penalty, on the understanding that it may not grant the creditor less than the compensation for damages that is due pursuant to statute.
(2) On the request by the creditor, the court may, where fairness manifestly demands this, order additional compensation for damages in addition to a contractual penalty that is meant to take the place of the compensation for damages that is due pursuant to statute.
(3) Contractual clauses that derogate from paragraph (1) are null and void.

Division 10. Statutory duties to compensate

Article 6:95. (1) Damage that must be compensated on the basis of a legal obligation to pay damages consists of patrimonial damage [vermogensschade] and any other disadvantage, the latter to the extent that the law grants a right to compensation thereof.
(2) The right to compensation for a disadvantage that does not comprise patrimonial loss, is not subject to attachment. For transfer under general title, it is sufficient that the rightholder has notified the other party that he will claim compensation.

Article 6:96. (1) Patrimonial damage comprises both losses suffered as well as lost profits.
(2) Loss that can be compensated as damage to patrimony includes:
(a) reasonable costs to prevent or limit damage that was to be expected as a consequence of the event which gave rise to the liability;
(b) reasonable costs to determine damage and liability;
(c) reasonable costs to acquire extrajudicial compensation.
(3) Paragraph 2 under (b) and (c) are not to be applicable to the extent that in the given case , the rules relating to procedural costs are applicable on the basis of Article 241 of the Code of Civil Procedure.
(4) In case of a commercial contract as meant in Article 119b paragraph 1 the reimbursement of the costs referred to in paragraph 2 under c comprises at least an amount of 40 euro. This amount is payable without notice from the day following the day on which the statutory or agreed upon final day of payment has expired. This may not be derogated from to the detriment of the creditor.
(5) Pursuant to an order in Council further rules will be made for the reimbursement of the costs referred to in paragraph 2 under c. It is not permitted to derogate from these rules to the detriment of the debtor if the debtor is a natural person, who is not acting in the exercise of a profession or business. In this case, Article 241 first sentence of the Code of Civil Procedure is not applicable.
(6) The reimbursement pursuant the further rules only becomes due if the debtor is a natural person not acting in the exercise of a profession or business, once the debtor, after the commencement of default as meant in Article 81, under reference to the consequences of failure to pay, including the reimbursement that is claimed in accordance with the further rules, has been notified to no avail to pay within a time period of fourteen days, starting the day of the notice.
(7) if a debtor can be notified for more than one claim by a creditor as meant in paragraph 6, this must be carried out in one notice. For the calculation of the reimbursement, the principal amounts of these claims are added together.

Article 6:97. The court assesses the damage in a manner which is most in accordance with its nature. If the extent of the damage cannot be established accurately, it will be estimated.

Article 6:98. Only damage which is in such a way connected to the event which gave rise to the liability of the debtor, that it can be attributed to him as a consequence of this event, taking into consideration as well the nature of the liability and of the damage, can be compensated.

Article 6:99. Where the damage could be the consequence of two or more events for each of which another person is liable, and if it is certain that the damage has been caused by at least one of these events, then each of these persons is obliged to compensate the damage, unless he proves that this damage is not the consequence of an event for which he is liable.

Article 6:100. Where one and the same event has resulted in benefit as well as damage to the aggrieved party, then this benefit must be offset against the damage to be compensated when it is established, to the extent that this is reasonable.

Article 6:101. (1) Where the damage is partly a consequence of a circumstance that can be attributed to the prejudiced person [benadeelde], the duty to compensate is reduced by dividing the damage among the prejudiced person and he who has a duty to compensate in proportion to the extent to which the circumstances attributable to each have contributed to the damage, provided that a different division shall take place or the duty to compensate lapses or remains in its entirety, where fairness [billijkheid] so demands given the discrepancy between de severity of the errors made or other circumstances of the case.

(2) Where the duty to compensate concerns damage inflicted to an object which a third party kept for the aggrieved party, circumstances that can be attributed to the third party shall be attributed to the prejudiced person when applying the previous paragraph.

Article 6:102. (1) Where each of two or more persons are obliged to compensate the same damage, they are jointly and severally responsible. In order to establish what they are to contribute to each other in their mutual relationship in accordance with Article 10, the damage is divided amongst them in accordance with Article 101, unless another division follows from law or legal act.

(2) Where the damage is partly the consequence of a circumstance that can be attributed to the prejudiced person, Article 101 is applicable to the duty to compensate of each of the persons separately as meant in the previous paragraph, provided that the prejudiced person can in total not claim more from them than he would have been entitled to if only one person had been liable for the circumstances which gave rise to the duties to compensate. Where recovery from one of the persons held to contribute appears not to be entirely possible, the judge, at the request of one of them, can decide that, when applying Article 13, the part which has not been recovered will be apportioned to the prejudiced person.

Article 6:103. Damages are paid in money. Nevertheless, the court, at the request of the prejudiced person, mat award damages in another form than payment of a monetary sum. If such a decision is not complied with within a reasonable time, the prejudiced person regains his competence to demand damages in monetary form.

Article 6:104. If someone who is liable as against someone else on the basis of a wrongful act or a deficiency in the performance of an obligation has profited from that act or defect, the court may, at the request of the other person, establish the damage to the amount of that profit or to a part of it.

Article 6:105. (1) The calculation of damage that has not yet occurred can be wholly or partially postponed by the court or be carried out in advance after consideration of good and bad chances. In the last case, the court may condemn the debtor either to payment of an amount at once or to payment of periodically payable amounts, with or without the duty to provide security; this sentence may be carried out under conditions determined by the court.

2 (2) To the extent that the court condemns the debtor to pay to pay out amounts periodically, he can in his ruling determine that these can be amended on the request of each of the parties by the Court of first instance that dealt with the claim for compensation for damages, if circumstances arise after the ruling that are important for the scope of the duty to compensate and with the possibility of the occurrence thereof no account was taken.

Article 6:106. For disadvantage that is not in patrimonial damage, the disadvantaged has the right to compensation of damage established according to fairness:
(a) if the liable person had the intention to bring about such disadvantage;
(b) if the injured party has suffered physical injury, is harmed in his honour or good name or is affected in another way in his person;
(c) if the disadvantage lies in the violation of the memory of a deceased person and is inflicted on the non-separated spouse, the registered partner or a blood relative up to the second degree of the deceased, provided the violation took place in a manner that would give the deceased person, if he were still, a right to compensation for damage for harming his honour and good name.

Article 6:107. (1) If someone, as a result of an event for which another is liable, suffers physical or mental injury, the other is obliged to compensate not only the damage of the injured himself, but also to compensate:
(a) the costs that a third party makes for the benefit of the injured other than pursuant to an insurance and which the latter, would he have made them himself, could have claimed from the other; and
(b) an amount or amounts to be established by or pursuant to a general administrative order [algemene maateregel van bestuur] for the disadvantage that does not comprise patrimonial damage suffered by the loved ones of the injured with serious and permanent injury.

(2) The loved ones, referred to in paragraph 1 under b, are:

(a) the spouse who is not separated or divorced, or the registered partner of the injured at the time of the event;
(b) the life companion of the injured who at the time of the event run a joint household with him on a sustainable basis;
(c) the person who at the time of the event is the parent of the injured;
(d) the person who at the time of the event is the child of the injured;
(e) the person who at the time of the event cared for the injured in a family relationship on a sustainable basis;
(f) the person for whom at the time of the event the injured cared in a family relationship on a sustainable basis;
(g) another person who stands in such a close personal relationship to the injured that it stems from the requirements of reasonableness and fairness [redelijkheid en billijkheid] that for the application of paragraph 1 under b he is considered as a loved one.
(3) Rules can be made by general administrative order [algemene maatregel van bestuur] by which it is further determined when injury is considered serious and permanent injury as meant in paragraph 1 under b.
(4) Notwithstanding Article 6, paragraph 2 of the Motor Vehicle Liability Insurance Act, claims by third parties concerning damage suffered as a result of the injury cannot be exercised to the detriment of the right to compensation for damage of the injured.
(5) He who, pursuant to paragraph 1, is held liable for compensation for damage can invoke the same defence that would have been available to him against the injured.

Article 6:107a. (1) If a person as a result of an event for which another is liable, suffers physical or mental injury, the court in fixing the compensation for damage to which the injured can claim takes into consideration in the claim to wages that the injured has pursuant to Article 629 paragraph 1 of Book 7 or pursuant to an individual or collective employment contract.
(2) If an employer is obliged pursuant to Article 629 paragraph 1 of Book 7 or pursuant to an individual or collective employment contract to continue to pay the wages during illness or incapacity to work of the injured, he has, if the incapacity to work of the injured is the result of an event for which another is liable, towards that other a right compensation for damage to the amount of the wages he paid, but no more than the amount for which the liable person, in the absence of the duty to continue to pay wages would have been liable, less the amount equal to that of the compensation for damage of payment to which the person liable towards the injured is held.
(3) The liable person referred to in paragraph 2 is also obliged to pay compensation for the reasonable costs incurred by the employer in fulfilment of his duties under Article 658a of book 7. The liable person can invoke the same defence that would have been available to him against the injured person.
(4) If the liable person is an employee, the employer only has a right to compensation of damage if the incapacity to work is due to done intentionally or with conscious recklessness.

Article 6:108. (1) If someone as a result of an event for which another is liable towards him dies, the other is obliged to compensate the damage as a result of diminished livelihood:
(a) to the not-separated spouse, the registered partner and the under-age children of the deceased to at least an amount of the livelihood due them pursuant to the law;
(b) to other relatives by blood or marriage of the deceased, provided he already at the time of his death wholly or partly provided in their livelihood or was required to do so pursuant to a judicial ruling;
(c) to those who already before the event on which the liability rests, lived together with the deceased as a family and whose livelihood he wholly or partly provided for, to the extent that it is plausible is that this would have continued without the death and they cannot reasonably provide adequately for the own livelihood;
(d) to the person who was living with the deceased as a family and in whose livelihood the deceased contributed by doing the common housekeeping, to the extent that he suffers damage because after the death the housekeeping has to be taken care of in another way.
(2) In addition, the liable person is obliged to compensate the person who bears the undertaking costs these costs to the extent they correspond to the circumstances of the deceased.
(3) The liable person is further obliged to compensate an amount or amounts to be established by or pursuant to a general administrative order [algemene maateregel van bestuur] for disadvantage that does not comprise patrimonial damage suffered by the loved ones referred to in paragraph 4 as a result of the death.
(4) The loved ones referred to in paragraph 3 are:
(a) the spouse who is not separated or divorced, or the registered partner of the deceased at the time of the event;

(b) the life companion of the deceased who at the time of the event run a joint household with him on a sustainable basis;

(c) the person who at the time of the event is the parent of the deceased;

(d) the person who at the time of the event is the child of the deceased;

(e) the person who at the time of the event cared for the deceased in a family relationship on a sustainable basis;

(f) the person for whom at the time of the event the deceased cared in a family relationship on a sustainable basis;

(g) another person who stands in such a close personal relationship to the deceased that it stems from the requirements of reasonableness and fairness [redelijkheid en billijkheid] that for the application of paragraph 3 he is considered as a loved one.

(5) He who, pursuant to the previous paragraphs, is held liable for compensation for damage can invoke the same defence that would have been available to him against the deceased.

(6) There is no right to compensation of the damaged referred to in paragraph 3 in so far as the rightholder already received compensation for the same event on the basis of Article 107 paragraph 1 under b.

Article 6:109. (1) If granting full compensation in the given circumstances, including the nature of the liability, the legal relationship existing between the parties and their respective financial means, could lead to obviously unacceptable consequences, the court may modify the statutory duty to compensate for damage.

(2) The modification may not be made to a lower amount than for which the debtor is covered by insurance or was obliged to cover.

(3) Every clause contrary to paragraph 1 is void.

Article 6:110. To ensure that the liability that can arise in respect of damage does not exceed that which could be reasonably covered by insurance, amounts can be established by order in Council above which the liability does not extend. Separate amounts can be established according to among others the nature of the event, the nature of the damage, and the basis for liability.

Division 11. Obligations to pay a sum of money

Article 6:111. An obligation to pay a sum of money must be satisfied to its nominal amount, unless something else follows from the law, custom or legal act.

Article 6:112. The money that is paid to settle the obligation must be accepted in the country in whose currency the payment is made at the time of the payment.

Article 6:13. Withdrawn per 1-1-2002

Article 6:114. (1) If there is an account for non-cash payment in a country where the payment must or may be made in the name of the creditor, the debtor can fulfil the obligation by transferring the owed amount into that account, unless the creditor has validly excluded payment into that account.

(2) In the case of the previous paragraph, the payment is made at the moment in time at which the creditor's account is credited.

Article 6:115. The place where the payment must be made is determined by the Articles 116-118, unless it follows from the law, custom or legal act that payment must or may be paid in a different place.

Article 6:116. (1) The payment must be made at the habitual residence of the creditor at the time of payment.

(2) The creditor is authorised to designate another place for payment in the country of the habitual residence of the creditor at the time of the payment or at the moment in time of the creation of the obligation.

Article 6:117. If the payment in accordance with Article 116 must take place at another place than the habitual residence of the creditor at the time of payment or at the time of the creation of the obligation and the fulfilment of the obligation thereby becomes considerably more burdensome for the debtor, he is authorised to suspend the payment until the creditor designates another place for payment as meant in Article 116 paragraph 1 to which such an objection does not attach.

Article 6:118. If the obligation arose in the course of business or professional activities of the creditor, the habitual residence of the creditor of Articles 116 and 117 is the place of establishment where the activities are carried out.

Article 6:119. (1) The compensation for damage payable for delay in the payment of a sum of money comprises the statutory interest of that sum over the time that the debtor is in default with the payment thereof.

(2) Each time at the end of a year, the amount over which statutory interest is calculated, increased with the interest owed over that year.

(3) A negotiated interest that is higher than that which pursuant to the previous paragraphs would have been owed, continues in its place after the debtor is in default.

Article 6:119a. (1) The compensation for damage payable for delay in the payment of a sum of money comprises in the case of a commercial agreement the statutory interest of that sum with effect from the day following the day agreed as the deadline for payment until and including the day on which the debtor has paid the sum. Commercial agreement means the contract for benefit that obliges one or more of the parties to give or to do and which arose between one or more natural persons who are acting in the exercise of a profession or business or legal person.

(2) If no deadline for payment is agreed, the statutory interest is owed under law:

(a) from 30 days after the start of the day following that on which the debtor received the invoice, or

(b) if the date of receipt of the invoice is not established or if the debtor receives the invoice before he receives the performance, from 30 days after the start of the day following that on which the performance is received, or

(c) if the debtor stipulated a time limit within which he may accept the received performance or can assess whether it conforms to the contract, and if he receives the invoice before he has accepted the performance or assessed it, from 30 days after the start of the day following that on which the debtor has accepted performance or assessed it, or, if he does not communicate his approval or acceptance, from 30 days after the start of the day following that on which the time limit expires.

(3) Each time at the end of a year, the amount over which statutory interest is calculated, increased with the interest owed over that year.

(4) The time limit referred to in paragraph 2 under c does not exceed more than 30 days from the date of receipt of the performance, unless the parties expressly agree to a longer time limit and this time limit is not obviously unfair towards the creditor, in light of:

(a) the question whether the debtor has objective reasons to deviate from the 30-day time limit;

(b) the nature of the performance; and

(c) every significant deviation from good commercial practices.

(5) Parties may agree to a deadline for payment of up to 60 days, unless they expressly include a longer period for payment in the contract and this period is not obviously unfair towards the creditor, in light of:

(a) the question whether the debtor has objective reasons to deviate from the 60-day time limit;

(b) the nature of the performance; and

(c) every significant deviation from good commercial practices.

(6) No statutory interest is owed when the creditor is himself in default.

(7) The statutory interest is owed except to the extent that the delay cannot be attributed to the debtor.

(8) For the application of this Article, statutory interest is equated to another agreed upon interest.

Article 6:119b. (1) The compensation for damage payable by a government institution for delay in the payment of a sum of money comprises in the case of a commercial agreement with the governmental institution the statutory interest of that sum with effect from the day following the day agreed as the deadline for payment until and including the day on which the debtor has paid the sum.

(2) Governmental institution means the State, a province, a municipality, a water board or a public law institution or a consortium of these governments or public law institutions as meant in Article 2 paragraph 2 of directive 2011/7 of the European Parliament and the Council of 23 February 2011 on combating late payment in commercial transactions (OJ L48/11).

(2) If no deadline for payment is agreed, the statutory interest is owed under law:

(a) from 30 days after the start of the day following that on which the debtor received the invoice, or

(b) if the date of receipt of the invoice is not established or if the debtor receives the invoice before he receives the performance, from 30 days after the start of the day following that on which the performance is received, or

(c) if the debtor stipulated a time limit within which he may accept the received performance or can assess whether it conforms to the contract, and if he receives the invoice before he has accepted the performance or assessed it, from 30 days after the start of the day following that on which the debtor has accepted performance or assessed it, or, if he does not communicate his approval or acceptance, from 30 days after the start of the day following that on which the time limit expires.

(3) Each time at the end of a year, the amount over which statutory interest is calculated, increased

with the interest owed over that year.
(4) The time limit referred to in paragraph 2 under c does not exceed more than 30 days from the date of receipt of the performance, unless the parties expressly agree to a longer time limit in the contract and the procurement documents and this time limit is not obviously unfair towards the creditor, in light of:
(a) the question whether the debtor has objective reasons to deviate from the 30-day time limit;
(b) the nature of the performance; and
(c) every significant deviation from good commercial practices.
(5) The contract cannot deviate from the deadline for payment of up to 30 days in accordance with the second paragraph, unless the parties expressly include a longer period for payment in the contract and the special nature or the characteristics of the contract objectively justify this. The period for payment comprises in that case no more than 60 days.
(6) No statutory interest is owed when the creditor is himself in default.
(7) The statutory interest is owed except to the extent that the delay cannot be attributed to the debtor.
(8) For the application of this Article, statutory interest is equated to a higher agreed upon interest.

Article 6:120. (1) The statutory interest provided for in Article 119 shall be laid down by order in Council. Statutory interest accruing on the date of entry into force of a new interest rate set by Order in Council, is calculated in accordance with the new interest rate starting from that date.
(2) The statutory interest referred to in Article 119a and Article 119b is equal to the refinancing interest that is set by the European Central Bank for its most recent main refinancing operation that was carried out before the first calendar day of the relevant half-year, increased with eight percentage points. Statutory interest accruing on the first day of the relevant half-year is calculated for a half year in accordance with the new interest rate starting from that date.

Article 6:121. (1) If an obligation extends to payment in a currency other than that of the country in which the payment must be made, the debtor is entitled to fulfil the obligation in the currency of the place of payment.
(2) The previous paragraph does not apply if it follows from the law, custom or legal act that the debtor is obliged to pay effectively in the currency to which the payment obligation extends.

Article 6:122. (1) If an obligation extends to payment of currency other than that of the country in which the payment must be made and the debtor is not in a position or claims that he is not in a position to pay in this currency, the creditor can claim satisfaction in the currency of the place of payment.
(2) The previous paragraph does not apply if the debtor is obliged to pay effectively in the currency to which the payment obligation extends.

Article 6:123. (1) In case a legal claim is initiated in the Netherlands for the acquisition of a sum of money, expressed in foreign currency, the creditor can claim a ruling for payment at his choice in that foreign currency or in currency of the Netherlands.
(2) The creditor who can enforce in the Netherlands an executorial title designated in foreign currency can claim that due under this this execution in the currency of the Netherlands.
(2) The previous paragraphs do not apply if the debtor is obliged to pay effectively in the currency to which the payment obligation extends.

Article 6:124. If an obligation is fulfilled in another currency than that the payment of which it extends as a result of application of articles 121, 122 or 123 or by conversion to a claim for compensation for damage in accordance with the provisions of Division 9 of Title 1, the conversion is made according to the exchange rate on the day on which the payment is made.

Article 6:125. (1) Article 119 leaves intact the right of the creditor to compensation for the damage he suffered because after the commencement of default the exchange rate of the currency to which the payment obligation extends, has changed in respect of that of the currency of one or more other countries.
(2) The previous paragraph is not applicable if the obligation extends to payment in the currency of the Netherlands, the payment must take place in the Netherlands, and the creditor at the time of the creation of the obligation had his habitual residence in the Netherlands.

Article 6:126. For the application of this Division, the exchange rate is the exchange rate against which the creditor can without delay procure for himself the money, taking into consideration that which could follow from the law, custom and the content and purpose of the obligation.

Division 12. Set-off

Article 6:127. (1) If a debtor who is entitled to set-off, declares to his creditor that he settles his debt with a claim, both obligations are ended to their common course.
(2) A debtor is entitled to set-off if he has to claim a performance that meets his obligation towards the same other party and he is entitled to payment of the debt as well as to enforce the payment of the claim.
(3) The power to set-off does not exist with respect to a claim and a debt that fall into patrimonies separated from each other.

Article 6:128. (1) The creditor of a bearer or order claim sets these off by writing his set-off declaration on the paper and giving this to the other party.
(2) If the set-off does not concern the whole claim or if he still needs the paper for the exercise of other rights, he can keep the paper, provided that he not only writes the declaration on the paper, but also directs in writing to the other party.
(3) He can, irrespective of whether the set-off concerns the whole claim, with some, settle not on the paper written declaration, provided that he shows at the request of the other party that the paper was destroyed or had become worthless, or provides security for twenty years or a much shorter period of time as can be expected that the other party could still be exposed to a claim based on the paper.

Article 6: 129. (1) The set-off has retroactive effect to the time at which the power to set-off arose.
(2) If due and payable interest has already been paid over one or both of the claims, then the set-off does not have effect beyond the end of the last period for which interest was paid.
(3) If for the calculation of the effect of a set-off in case of money debts an exchange rate calculation is needed, this occurs following the same standards as if mutual payment had taken place on the day of the set-off.

Article 6:130. (1) If a claim under special title has been transferred, the debtor is entitled despite the transfer to also set off a counterclaim on the original creditor, provided this counterclaim stems from the same legal relationship as the transferred claim or it already accrued to him and became due prior to the transfer.
(2) The preceding paragraph applies where a claim has been seized or a limited right is established which has been notified to the debtor.
(3) The preceding paragraphs are not applicable if the transfer or the establishment of the limited right concerns a bearer or order claim and took place in accordance with Article 93 of Book 3.

Article 6:131. (1) The power to set-off does not end with the prescription of the legal claim.
(2) Deferred payment or execution, given by way of favour by the creditor, does not stand in the way of set-off by the creditor.

Article 6:132. If a declaration of set off is made by a person thereto entitled, the other party who had grounds to refuse to fulfil its obligation can nevertheless deprive the declaration of set off its effect by invoking the ground for refusal without delay after the declaration was made and he could invoke this ground.

Article 6:133. After one party has made a declaration of set off, the other party can, provided without delay, deprive the declaration its effect by nonetheless using its one power to set-off, but only if the latter set-off works back further.

Article 6:134. The debtor of a reciprocal contract, who is entitled to set off, can deprive the declaration of the other party seeking to terminate the contract due to non-performance, by making use of his power to set off without delay.

Article 6:135. A debtor is not entitled to set off:
(a) to the extent that seizure of the claim of the other party would not be valid;
(b) if his duty extends to compensation for damage he inflicted intentionally.

Article 6:135. The court may grant an application despite the defendant invoking set off, if the merits of this defence cannot be established simply and the claim is otherwise capable of being granted.

Article 6:137. (1) To the extent a declaration of set off insufficiently indicates which obligations the set off concerns, the order of allocation laid down in Articles 43 paragraph 2 and 44 paragraph 1 applies.
(2) The other party of the person who made the declaration to set off, can deprive the declaration of

its affect by making a protest without delay if in this declaration, the allocation of the principal sum, costs and the interest to be calculated taking Article 129 into account, follows a different order than that of Article 44 paragraph 1.

Article 6:138. (1) The circumstance that de place of performance of the obligations is not the same, does not rule out set off. He who sets off, is in this case obliged to compensate the other party for the damage he suffers because mutual performance does not take place in the same place.
(2) The other party of the person who despite a difference in the place of performance has set off, can by an immediate protest deprive the declaration to set off of its effect if he has a legitimate interest in ensuring that no set off, but performance takes place.

Article 6:139. (1) The surety and the person whose thing is attached for the debt of another, can invoke the suspension of their liability to the extent that the creditor is entitled to set off his claim with a debt due and payable to the debtor.
(2) They can invoke the release from their liability to the extent that the creditor has let go of power to set off against a debt to the debtor, unless he had a reasonable ground or no blame is attached to him.

Article 6:140. (1) If between two parties, pursuant to law, custom or legal act, monetary claims and monetary debts must be included in one account, they are actually set off by law in the order in which parties in the previous articles of this division or pursuant to their mutual legal relationship are entitled to set off, and at any time only the balance is due. Article 137 shall not apply.
(2) The party who administers the account, closes it annually and notifies the other party of the balance due at that time, stating the items that had not previously been communicated to him on which basis it is based.
(3) If the other party does not protest within a reasonable time against the balance communicated on the basis of the previous paragraph, it is deemed to be determined between the parties.
(4) After determination of the balance, no appeal can be made against the separate items with respect to the commencement of the prescription period or the expiration of a deadline. The legal claim to payment of the balance is time-barred after five years after the day following that on which the account was closed and the balance became due and payable.
(5) Something other than what is determined in the previous paragraphs can follow from the legal relationship between the parties.

Article 6:141. If an obligation wholly or partly is extinguished by offsetting, paragraphs 1 and 2 of Article 48 are correspondingly applicable.

[Title 2 is omitted.]

Title 3. Wrongful act

Division 1. General provisions

Article 6:162. (1) He who commits a wrongful act [onrechtmatige daad] as against another, which can be attributed to him, is obliged to compensate the damage suffered by that other as a consequence thereof.
(2) A wrongful act is considered to be a violation of a right and an act or omission [een doen of nalaten] contrary to a legal obligation or to what is socially acceptable according to unwritten law [hetgeen volgens ongeschreven recht in het maatschappelijk verkeer betaamt], all this subject to the availability of a ground for justification.
(3) A wrongful act can be attributed to the wrongdoer [dader], if it is due to his fault or to a cause that is attributed to him pursuant to the law or to generally accepted views in society [de in het verkeer geldende opvattingen].

Article 6:163. There is no obligation to pay damages where the violated norm does not extend to protect against the damage as it was suffered by the wronged person [benadeelde].

Article 6:164. Conduct [gedraging] of a child who has not yet reached the age of fourteen cannot be attributed to him as a wrongful act.

Article 6:165. (1) The circumstance that conduct by a person of fourteen years or older must be considered as an act occurring under the influence of a mental or physical deficiency is not an obstacle to attributing it as a wrongful act to the wrongdoer.
(2) If a third party is also liable as against the wronged person due to insufficient supervision, then

this third party is obliged as against the wrongdoer to contribute to the compensation to the full amount of his liability as against the wronged person.

Article 6:166. (1) Where a person belonging to a group wrongfully causes damage and the likelihood of so causing damage should have discouraged these persons from acting as a group, they are jointly and severally liable [hoofdelijk aansprakelijk] if these actions can be attributed to them.
(2) Among themselves, they each bear an equal share of the compensation, unless, given the circumstances of the case, fairness [billijkheid] requires a different division.

Article 6:167. (1) Where a person is liable as against another pursuant to this title as regards incorrect or, due to its incompleteness, misleading publication of data of a factual nature, a court may, at the request of that other person, order him to publish a rectification in a manner to be indicated by the court.
(2) The same applies where there is no liability because the publication cannot be attributed as a wrongful act to the wrongdoer since he was unfamiliar with the incorrectness or incompleteness.
(3) In the case of paragraph (2), the court granting the claim may determine that the costs of the proceedings and of the publication of the rectification must be borne wholly or partially by the person who initiated the claim. Each of the parties may recover his part in the costs of the proceedings and the publication of the rectification that he must bear as a result of the judgment from anyone who is liable for the damage resulting from the publication.

Article 6:168. (1) The court may reject a claim to prohibit a wrongful act on the basis that this act ought to be tolerated for imperative reasons of public interest. The wronged person retains his right to compensation of the damage in accordance with the present title.
(2) In the case as meant in Article 170, the subordinate is not liable for this damage.
(3) If a judgment to pay damages or to provide security is not complied with, the court may nonetheless prohibit the act.

Division 2. Liability for persons and objects

Article 6:169. (1) A person who exercises parental authority or custody over a child is liable for damage caused to a third party by conduct that is to be regarded as an act of a child who has not yet reached the age of fourteen years and to whom this conduct could be attributed as a wrongful act had his age not prevented it.
(2) A person who exercises parental authority or custody over a child is liable for damage caused to a third party by a fault of that child, who has reached the age of fourteen years but not yet that of sixteen years, unless he cannot be reproached for not preventing the conduct of the child.

Article 6:170. (1) The person in whose service a subordinate fulfils his task is liable for damage caused to a third party by a fault of that subordinate, if the likelihood of the fault is increased by the order to undertake the task and the person in whose service he was, due to the legal relationship, had control over the conduct resulting in the fault.
(2) If the subordinate was in the service of a natural person and was not employed for a profession or business of this person, then the latter is only liable if the subordinate, when making the mistake, was acting in fulfilment of the task assigned to him.
(3) If the subordinate and he in whose service he was are both liable for the damage, then the subordinate need not contribute to the compensation in their mutual relationship, unless the damage is the result of wilful misconduct or deliberate recklessness [opzet of bewuste roekeloosheid]. Something other than what is determined in the previous sentence may follow from the circumstances of the case, also taking into account the nature of their relationship.

Article 6:171. Where a non-subordinate carries out activities assigned by another in the course of that person's business is liable as against a third party for a fault committed during those activities, then that other is also liable as against the third party.

Article 6:172. Where an act by a representative in the exercise of the powers attributed to him amounts to a fault as against a third party, then the represented party is also liable as against the third party.

Article 6:173. (1) The possessor [bezitter] of a movable object of which it is known that it constitutes a serious danger to persons or objects, in case it does not meet the standards that may be set for such an object in the given circumstances,, is liable if this danger manifests itself, unless there would have been no liability on the basis of the previous division if he would have had known of this danger at the time it arose.

(2) If the object does not meet the standards as meant in the previous paragraph due to a defect as meant in Division 3 of Title 3, there is no liability on the basis of the previous paragraph for damage as meant in that division, unless
(a) taking all circumstances into account, it is likely that the defect did not exist at the time at which the product was brought into circulation or that the defect arose at a later time; or
(b) it concerns damage to the object itself [zaakschade] with regard to which, pursuant to Division 3 of Title 3, there is no right to compensation on the basis of the franchise regulated in that division.
(3) The previous paragraphs do not apply to animals, vessels and aircraft.

Article 6:174. (1) The possessor of a structure which does not meet the standards that may be set in the given circumstances and which thereby constitutes a danger for persons or objects, is liable if this danger manifests itself, unless there is no liability on the basis of the previous division if he would have known of this danger at the time it arose.
(2) As regards emphyteusis [erfpacht], liability lies with the possessor of the right of emphyteusis. As regards public roads, it lies with the public authority that must take care that the road is in good condition, as regards pipes, with the person managing them, except in as far as the pipe is in a building or construction and is meant for supply and drainage of that building or edifice.
(3) As regards underground structures, liability lies with the person who, at the moment that the damage becomes known, uses the structure in the exercise of his business. If, after the damage becomes known another person becomes the user, liability remains with the person who was user at the time this [damage] became known. If the damage has become known after the use of the underground construction ended, liability lies with the person who was the last user.
(4) In this article, a structure is considered to be a building or edifice that is permanently connected to the ground, either directly, or through a connection to other buildings or edifices.
(5) The person who is registered in the public registry as owner of the construction or of the ground is presumed to be the possessor of the construction.
(6) In applying this article, a public road is considered to be both the actual road, as well as the surrounding road fixtures.

[Articles 6:175 – 6:178 are omitted.]

Article 6:179. The possessor of an animal is liable for damage caused by the animal, unless there is no liability on the basis of the previous division if he would have had control over the conduct of the animal that caused the damage.

Article 6:180. (1) In the cases of Articles 173, 174 and 179, co-possessors are jointly and severally liable.
(2) In case of transfer of an object under the suspensive condition of fulfilment of a counter-performance, the liability that is imposed upon the possessor by Articles 173, 174 and 179 lies with the acquirer from the time of this transfer.

Article 6:181. (1) Where the objects, constructions or animals as meant in Articles 173, 174 and 179 are used in the course of business, then the liability stemming from Articles 173(1), 174 paragraphs (1) and (2), first sentence, and 179 lies with the person who carries out this business, unless it concerns a construction and the cause of the damage was not related to the carrying out of the business.
(2) Where the objects, constructions or animals are used in the course of business by making them available for use in the course of another's business, then that other is considered to be the person liable pursuant to the previous paragraph.
(3) Where a substance as meant in Article 175 is used in the course of business by making this substance available for use in the course of another's profession or business, that other is considered to be the person liable pursuant to Article 175 paragraph (1).

Article 6:182. Where in the cases of Articles 176 and 177 there are at the same time two or more operators, either acting jointly or not, then they are jointly and severally liable.

Article 6:183. (1) As regards liability on the basis of this Division, the person sued may not invoke his youthful age or a mental or physical deficiency.
(2) The person who exercises parental authority or custody over a child who has not yet reached the age of fourteen years, is liable in his place on the basis of Articles 173 and 179 for the objects and animals as meant therein, unless these are used in the course of business.

[Article 6:184 is omitted.]

Division 3. Product Liability

Article 6:185. (1) The producer is liable for damage caused by a defect in his product, unless:
(a) he did not put the product in circulation;
(b) that, having regard to the circumstances, it is probable that the defect that caused the damage did not exist at the time when he put the product into circulation, or that this defect arose later;
(c) the product was neither manufactured for sale or for any other form of distribution with economic purpose of the producer, nor manufactured or distributed in the course of the exercise of his profession or business;
(d) the defect is a consequence of the fact that the product is in compliance with mandatory regulations issued by the public authorities;
(e) on the basis of the state of scientific and technical knowledge at the time when the product was put into circulation, it was impossible to discover the existence of the defect;
(f) in relation to the producer of raw material or the manufacturer of a part, the defect is attributable to the design of the product of which the raw material or the part is a component of, or to the instructions that were provided by the manufacturer of the product.
(2) The liability of the producer is reduced or lifted having regard to all the circumstances, if the damage is caused both by a defect in the product and by the fault of the injured person or a person for whom the injured person is liable.
(3) The liability of the producer is not reduced, if the damage is caused by both a defect in the product and the behaviour of a third person.

Article 6:186. (1) A product is defective when it does not provide the safety which a person is entitled to expect, taking all circumstances into account and in particular
(a) the presentation of the product;
(b) the use to which the product could reasonably be expected to be put;
(c) the time when the product was put into circulation.
(2) A product shall not be considered as defective exclusively because subsequently a better product has been put into circulation.

Article 6:187. (1) For the application of this division, product means a movable object, even after it has become a component of another movable or immovable object, as well as electricity.
(2) For the application of Article 185 up to and including 193, producer means the manufacturer of a finished product, the producer of a raw material or the manufacturer of a part, as well as any person who presents himself as producer by putting his name, trade mark or other distinguishing feature on the product.
(3) Without prejudice to the liability of the producer, any person who imports a product in European Economic Area to sell, hire, lease or distribute in any other way in the course of his commercial activities is treated as producer; his liability is the same as that of the producer.
(4) If it cannot be established who is the producer of the product, each supplier is treated as producer, unless he informs the injured person within a reasonable time of the identity of the producer or the person who supplied him with the product. If it cannot be established who the importer of a product is in relation to a product imported into the European Economic Area, each supplier is also treated as producer thereof, unless he informs the injured person within a reasonable time of the identity of the importer into the European Economic Area or of the supplier within the European Economic Area who supplied him with the product.

Article 6:188. The injured person shall prove the damage, the defect and the causal link between the defect and the damage.

Article 6:189. Where different persons are liable for the same damage on the basis of Article 185, first paragraph, each is liable for the whole.

Article 6:190. (1) The liability referred to in Article 185 first paragraph exists for
(a) damage through death or physical injury;
(b) damage caused by the product to another object that is commonly intended for use or consumption in the private sphere and is also used or consumed by the injured person mainly in the private sphere with a lower threshold of €500.
(2) The amount referred to in the first paragraph shall be amended by order in Council if on the basis of Article 18, second paragraph of the EEC directive of 25 July 1985 (OJ L 210) the amounts mentioned in that directive are revised.

Article 6:191. (1) The legal claim to compensation for damage of the injured person against the producer pursuant to Article 185, first paragraph, is time-barred upon expiration of three years after the commencement of the day following that on which the injured person discovered or ought to have discovered the damage, the defect and the identity of the producer.

(2) The right to compensation for damage of the injured person towards the producer pursuant to Article 185, first paragraph lapses upon expiration of ten years after the commencement of the day following that on which the producer put the object that caused the damage into circulation. The same applies for the right of a third party who is also liable for the damage, in relation to recourse against the producer.

Article 6:192. The liability of the producer under this division cannot be excluded or limited towards the injured person.

If a third party who did not use the product in the exercise of a profession or business is also liable towards the injured person, the rules relating to recourse cannot be derogated from to the disadvantage of that third party.

Article 6:193. The injured party is entitled to the right to compensation for damage towards the producer under this division without prejudice to all other rights and claims.

Division 3A. Unfair Commercial Practices

Article 6:193a. (1) In this Division the following definitions apply:
(a) consumer: natural person not acting in the exercise of a profession or business;
(b) trader: natural or legal person acting in the exercise of a profession or business or the person who acts on his behalf;
(c) product: good, including electricity, or service;
(d) commercial practice: every act, omission, conduct, representation of affairs or commercial communication, including advertising and marketing, from the trader, that relates directly to the promotion of sales, sale or delivery of a product to consumers;
(e) decision about a contract: a decision taken by a consumer on the question whether, and, if so, how and on what terms he purchases a product, makes payment in whole or in part for, retains or disposes of, or exercises a contractual right in relation to the product, irrespective of whether the consumer decides to act;
(f) professional diligence: normal level of special skill and care that can reasonably be expected of a trader in respect of consumers, in accordance with the responsibility resting upon him, stemming from the professional standard applying to the trade and fair market practices;
(g) invitation to purchase: commercial communication which indicates characteristics of the product and the price in a manner appropriate to the used means and thereby enables the consumer to make a purchase;
(h) undue influence: exploiting a position of power in relation to the consumer so as to apply pressure, even without using or threatening to use physical force, in a way which significantly limits the consumer's ability to make an informed decision;
(i) code of conduct: rules that determine how traders are bound by the code, act in relation to one or more particular commercial practices or business sectors and which are not determined by or pursuant to legislative provisions;
(j) code owner: legal person or group of traders who are responsible for the formulation and revision of a code of conduct or for monitoring compliance with the code by those who have bound themselves to it;
(k) directive: directive 2005/29/EC of the European Parliament and of the Council of 11 May 2005 concerning unfair business-to-consumer commercial practices in the internal market (OJ L 149);
(2) In this Division, under the average consumer is also meant: the average member of a specific group on which the trader focuses or the average member of a specific group that the trader can reasonably foresee that the group because of their mental or physical disabilities, their age or credulity are particularly susceptible for the commercial practice or to the underlying product.
(3) This Division is not applicable to certification of goods of precious metals and the indication of the precious metal content for these goods.

Article 6:193b. (1) A trader acts wrongfully towards a consumer if he carries out a commercial practice that is unfair.
(2) A commercial practice is unfair if a trader deals:
(a) in contravention with the requirements of professional diligence, and
(b) the ability of the average consumer to make an informed decision is noticeably limited or could be limited;

whereby the average consumer takes or may take a decision about the contract that he otherwise would not have taken.

(3) A commercial practice is particularly unfair if a trader:

(a) carries out a misleading commercial practice as meant in Articles 193 c up to and including 193g, or

(b) carries out an aggressive commercial practice as meant in Articles 193 h and 193i.

(4) The common and legitimate advertising practice of making exaggerated statements or statements which are not meant to be taken literally, do not as such make an advertisement unfair.

Article 6:193c. (1) A commercial practice is misleading if information is provided that is factually incorrect or that misleads or could mislead the average consumer, whether or not by the general presentation of the information, for instance in relation to:

(a) the existence or nature of the product;

(b) the main characteristics of the product, such as its availability, benefits, risks, execution, composition, accessories, customer assistance and complaint handling, method and date of manufacture or provision, delivery, fitness for purpose, usage, quantity, specification, geographical or commercial origin, the results to be expected from its use, or the results and material features of tests or checks carried out on the product;

(c) the extent of the trader's duties, the motives for the commercial practice and the nature of the sales process, any statement or symbol in relation to direct or indirect sponsorship or approval of the trader or the product;

(d) the price or the manner in which the price is calculated, or the existence of a specific price advantage;

(e) the need for a service, part, replacement or repair;

(f) the nature, attributes and rights of the trader or his agent, such as his identity and assets, his qualifications, status, approval, affiliation or connection and ownership of industrial, commercial or intellectual property rights or his awards and distinctions;

(g) the rights of the consumer including the right of repair or replacement of the delivered object or the right to price reduction, or the risks the consumer may bear,

whereby the average consumer takes or may take a decision about the contract that he otherwise would not have taken.

(2) A commercial practice is also misleading if:

(a) through the marketing of the product including the use of comparative advertising confusion is created regarding products, trade names or other distinguishing marks of a competitor;

(b) the trade does not comply with a duty that is included in a code of conduct, to the extent that:

10 the duty is concrete and knowable, and

20 the trade indicates that is bound by the code of conduct,

whereby the average consumer takes or could take a decision about the contract that he otherwise would not have taken.

Article 6:193d. (1) A commercial practice is furthermore misleading if there is a case of a misleading omission.

(2) A misleading omission is every commercial practice whereby essential information which the average consumer needs to take an informed decision about a transaction, is omitted, whereby the average consumer takes or could take a decision about the contract that he otherwise would not have taken.

(3) There is also a misleading omission if essential information as meant in paragraph 2 is kept hidden or is provided in an unclear, unintelligible or ambiguous manner or too late, or the commercial purpose, if it is not already apparent from the context, does not appear, whereby the average consumer takes or could take a decision about the contract that he otherwise would not have taken.

(4) In determining whether essential information is left out or kept hidden, the factual context, the limitations of the communication medium as well as the measures that have been taken to provide the consumer with the information using other means, are to be considered.

Article 6:193e. In the case of an invitation to purchase, the following information, to the extent that it is not already apparent from the context, is essential as meant in Article 193d paragraph 2:

(a) the main characteristics of the product, to the extent that this appropriate in light of the medium and the product;

(b) the identity and geographical address of the trader, his trading name and, where appropriate, the identity and geographical address of the trader on whose behalf he is acting;

(c) the price, including taxes, or, if it concerns a product for which a reasonable price cannot be

calculated in advance, the manner in which the price will be calculated and, where appropriate, the extra freight, delivery or postal charges, or if these costs cannot reasonably be calculated in advance, the fact that these additional costs must be paid;
(d) the manner of payment, delivery, performance and the policy relating to complaint handling, if these differ from the requirements of professional diligence; and
(e) if there is a right of withdrawal or cancellation, the existence of this right.

Article 6:193f. If there is a commercial communication, including advertising or marketing, the information referred to in or pursuant to the following articles is in any event essential as meant in Article 193d paragraph 2:
(a) Article 15d paragraphs 1 and 2 and Article 15e paragraph 1 of Book 3;
(b) Articles 230m paragraph 1, under a, b and c, e up to and including h, o and p and 230v paragraphs 1 up to an including 3, 5 as well as paragraph 6 first sentence, and paragraph 7 of Book 6;
(c) Article 502 paragraphs 1 up to and including 3 of Book 7;
(d) Articles 73 up to and including 75 of the Pharmaceutical law;
(e) Articles 4:20, 4:73 and 5:13 of the Financial Supervision law;
(f) Article 2b of the Price law.

Article 6:193g. The following commercial practices are under all circumstances misleading:
(a) claiming to be bound by a code of conduct and acting in accordance with it, when this is not the case;
(b) displaying a trust mark, quality mark, or another similar label without having obtained the necessary authorisation;
(c) claiming that a code of contract is recognized by a public or other body when this is not the case;
(d) claiming that a trade or a produce has been recommended, endorsed or authorised by a public or private body when this is not the case, or making such a claim without complying with the terms of approval, endorsement or authorisation;
(e) offering products for sale at a specified price without the trader indicating that there a reasonable ground exists that he cannot deliver this product or a equivalent product at that price or procure the delivery from another trade during a period and in quantities that are reasonable, having regard to the product, the scale of the advertising of the product and the price offered;
(f) offering products for sale at a specified price and then:
10 refusing to show the offered item to the consumer, or
20 refusing to take an order or to deliver the product within a reasonable time, or
30 demonstrating a sample of the item with defects, with the intention of promoting another product;
(g) falsely claiming that the product will only be available for a very limited time or that it will only be available on particular terms for a very limited time in order to have the consumer decide immediately and not giving him the opportunity or sufficient time to make an informed decision;
(h) promising the consumer, with whom the trader communicated before the transaction in a language that is not an official language of the member state in which the trader is located, to provide a customer service and then only making this service available in another language without clearly informing the consumer before the consumer enters the contract;
(i) claiming or otherwise creating the impression that a product can be sold legally when this is not the case;
(j) presenting statutory rights of consumers as a distinguishing characteristic of the trader's offer;
(k) using editorial content in the media, for which the trader has paid, to promote the product, without making it clear from the content or from images or sounds clearly identifiable by the consumer;
(l) making factually incorrect claims relating to the nature and the extent of the risk that could threaten the personal safety of the consumer or his family if the consumer does not purchase the product;
(m) recommending a product that looks like a product manufactured by a particular producer in such a way that it intentionally raises the wrong impression for the consumer that the product is indeed manufactured by that producer, when this is not the case;
(n) establishing, operating or promoting a pyramid scheme whereby the consumer against payment has the chance to receive compensation that is primarily derived from the introduction of new consumers in the system rather than from the sale or use of goods;
(o) claiming that the trader is about to cease trading or move, if this is not the case;
(p) claiming that products can facilitate winning in games of chance;
(q) falsely claiming that a product can cure illnesses, dysfunction or malformations;
(r) providing factually incorrect information about market circumstances or the possibility of obtaining the product with the intention to have the consumer purchase the product on conditions less favourable than normal market conditions

(s) in the context of a commercial practice, claiming that there is a competition or offering prizes without actually awarding the prizes announced or a reasonable alternative;

(t) describing a product as gratis, free, without charge if the consumer has to pay something else than the unavoidable costs of responding to the offer and collecting the product of having it delivered;

(u) including an invoice or a similar document in which payment is sought with marketing material which gives the consumer the impression that he has already ordered the marketed product when this is not the case;

(v) claiming in a false manner or giving the impression that the trade does not act for the purpose of his trade, business, craft or profession, or representing himself in a false manner as a consumer;

(w) giving the impression in a false manner that after sale service is available for a particular product in another member state that that in which the product is sold.

Article 6:193h. (1) A commercial practice is in its factual context, taking all its features and circumstances into account, aggressive if by intimidation, coercion, including the use of physical force, or undue influence, the freedom of choice or freedom to act of the average consumer in relation to the product is significantly limited or could be limited whereby the average consumer takes or could take a decision about the contract that he otherwise would not have taken.

(2) In determining whether a commercial practice is aggressive, the following shall be taking into account:

(a) the time, the place, the nature and the persistence that is shown with the commercial practice;

(b) the use of threatening behaviour or threatening or coarse language;

(c) the exploitation by the trader of particular misfortune or circumstances that are so serious that they could impair the consumer's judgment, which is known to the trader, with the purpose of influencing the decision of the consumer with respect to the product;

(d) onerous or disproportionate non-contractual barriers that are imposed by the trade with respect to a consumer who wishes to exercise his rights under the contract including the right to terminate the contract or to choose another product;

(e) threatening with actions that cannot legally be taken.

Article 6:193g. The following commercial practices are under all circumstances aggressive:

(a) giving the impression that the consumer may not leave the premises before a contract has been formed;

(b) ignoring the request of the consumer to leave his house or not to return, except if, and to the extent legally justified, the aim is to have a contractual duty performed;

(c) persistent or unwanted solicitation by telephone, fax, email or other distant media, unless, to the extent legally justified, the aim is to have a contractual duty performed;

(d) requiring a consumer who submits a claim on the basis of an insurance policy to produce documents that cannot reasonably be considered relevant for the determining the validity of the claim, or refusing systematically to respond to pertinent correspondence with the intention to prevent the consumer from exercising his contractual rights;

(e) encouraging children directly in advertising to purchase advertised products or to persuade their parents or other adult to purchase the products for them;

(f) demanding immediate or deferred payment or the return or safe keeping of products delivered by the trader, but not solicited by the consumer;

(g) informing the consumer explicitly that if he does not purchase the product or service, the trader's job or livelihood will be in jeopardy;

(h) giving the false impression that the consumer has won or shall win a prize or will win a prize or another equivalent benefit if he performs a certain act, when in fact:

10 there is no prize or other equivalent benefit; or

20 taking steps to come into consideration for the prize or for another equivalent benefit is dependent on the payment of an amount by the consumer or if there are costs associated to it for him.

Article 6:193j. (1) If a claim is initiated or a petition as meant in Article 305d paragraph 1 under a of Book 3 is submitted pursuant to Articles 193b up to and including 193i, the burden of proof with respect to the material accuracy and completeness of the information he has provided lies with trader if that appears appropriate, considering the circumstances of the case and taking into account the lawful interests of the trader and each other party in the proceedings.

(2) if the trader acts unlawfully on the basis of Article 193b, he is liable for the damage that results as a consequence, unless he proves that it is not due to his fault or attributable to him on another basis.

(3) A contract that is concluded as a consequence of an unfair commercial practice is voidable.

[The Title 4 is omitted.]

Title 5. Contracts in general

Part 1. General provisions

Article 6:213. (1) A contract [overeenkomst] in the sense of this title is a multilateral legal act [meerzijdige rechtshandeling], whereby one or more parties undertake an obligation as against one or more others.
(2) The statutory provisions with regard to contracts do not apply to contracts between more than two parties to the extent that this is contrary to the purpose of the provisions concerned in relation to the nature of the contract.

Article 6:214. (1) A contract entered into by one of the parties in the exercise of his business or profession, is, apart from the statutory provisions, also subject to a standard regulation, where such a standard regulation is applicable with regard to such a contract to the branch to which the business belongs or to the profession. The special kinds of contract for which standard regulations may be established and the branch or profession to which each of these regulations is meant to apply are designated by ordinance.
(2) A standard regulation is established, altered and repealed by a committee to be appointed by Our Minister of Justice. Further rules will be laid down by law as regards the manner of assembling the committees and their method of working.
(3) The establishment, alteration or repeal of a standard regulation does not enter into force before it has been approved by Us and has been published in the Netherlands Government Gazette [Nederlandse Staatscourant] following Our endorsement order.
(4) In a standard regulation one may deviate from statutory provisions, to the extent that deviation is also permitted by contract, whether or not in compliance with a particular form. An exception is made to the previous sentence, where a statutory provision provides otherwise.
(5) Parties may deviate in their contract from a standard regulation. A standard regulation may however prescribe a particular form for deviation.

Article 6:215. Where a contract satisfies the description of two or more particular kinds of contracts regulated by law, then the provisions provided for each of these types are applicable simultaneously, except in as far as these provisions are not entirely compatible or if their purpose opposes application in relation to the nature of the contract.

Article 6:216. That which is laid down in this and the following five divisions is applicable mutatis mutandis to other multilateral patrimonial legal acts [meerzijdige vermogensrechtelijke rechtshandeling], to the extent that the purpose of the provisions concerned is not opposed thereto in the light of the nature of the legal act.

Division 2. The formation of contracts

Article 6:217. (1) A contract is formed through an offer and the acceptance thereof.
(2) Articles 219 – 225 are applicable, unless something else follows from the offer, from another legal act or from a custom.

Article 6:218. An offer is valid, void or voidable in accordance with the rules on multilateral legal acts.

Article 6:219. (1) An offer may be revoked [herroepen], unless it contains a time period for acceptance or if its irrevocability follows from the offer in another manner.
(2) The revocation may only occur, as long as the offer has not been accepted nor a statement containing the acceptance sent. If the offer contains a statement that it is made free of obligation [vrijblijvend], then the revocation may still be made without delay after the acceptance.
(3) A stipulation by which one of the parties binds himself, should the other party wish it, to conclude a particular contract with him, constitutes an irrevocable offer.

Article 6:220. (1) An offer of a reward [uitloving] for a given time may be revoked or altered for significant reasons.
(2) In case of revocation or alteration of a reward, the court may award a fair compensation to a person who has started with the preparation of the requested performance on the basis of the reward.

Article 6:221. (1) An oral offer lapses if it is not immediately accepted, a written offer if it is not accepted within a reasonable time.

(2) An offer lapses when it is rejected.

Article 6:222. An offer does not lapse due to death or loss of legal capacity of one of the parties, nor because one of the parties loses the competence to conclude the contract as a consequence of legal administration.

Article 6:223. (1) The offeror may regard a late acceptance as having been made in time, provided that he immediately informs the other party thereof.
(2) If an acceptance occurs too late, but the offeror understands or ought to understand that this was not clear to the other party, then the acceptance counts as having been made in time, unless he immediately informs the other party that he considers the offer to have lapsed.

Article 6:224. If an acceptance does not reach the offeror at all or not in time due to a circumstance on the basis of which it nevertheless has effect following Article 37 paragraph (3), second sentence, of Book 3, then the contract is deemed to have been formed at the time at which the declaration would have been received without the hindering circumstance.

Article 6:225. (1) An acceptance which deviates from the offer constitutes a new offer and as a rejection of the original.
(2) If a reply to an offer containing an acceptance deviates from that offer only on insignificant points, then this reply counts as acceptance and the contract is formed in conformity with this acceptance, unless the offeror instantaneously objects to the differences.
(3) If offer and acceptance refer to different sets of conditions, then the second reference does not have effect where the applicability of the set of conditions as indicated in the first reference is therein not also expressly rejected.

Article 6:226. If the law provides, for the formation of a contract, a pre-requisite concerning form, this pre-requisite is equally applicable to a contract whereby a party for whose benefit it is intended commits to conclude such a contract, unless the purpose of the pre-requisite suggests otherwise.

Article 6:227. The obligations which parties undertake must be determinable.

Article 6:227a. (1) Where, as a result of a statutory provision, a contract can only be formed validly and unchallengeably in writing, this requirement is also fulfilled if the contract has been formed by electronic means and
a. can be consulted by parties;
b. the authenticity of the contract is sufficiently warranted;
c. the moment of formation of the contract can be established with sufficient certainty; and
d. the identity of parties can be established with sufficient certainty.
(2) Paragraph (1) does not apply to contracts for which the law requires the intervention of a court, a public authority, or a profession exercising a public task.

Article 6:227b. (1) Before a contract by electronic means is concluded, the person who supplies a service for the information society service as meant in Article 15d paragraph 3 of book 3 shall provide the other party in a clear, understandable and unambiguous manner information on at least:
(a) the contract will be concluded and in particular what actions that requires;
(b) whether or not the contract will be archived after it is concluded, as well as, if the contract is archived, in what manner it can be consulted by the other party;
(c) the manner in which the other party can become informed about acts not wanted by him, as well as the manner in which he can recover these before the contract is concluded;
(d) the languages in which the contract can be concluded;
(e) the codes of conduct to which the he is subject and the manner in which the other party can consult these codes of conduct electronically.
(2) The service provider shall before or at the conclusion of the contract make available to the other party the conditions thereof, not being general conditions as meant in Article 231, in such a manner that they can be stored by him so that they are accessible for him for later information.
(3) Paragraph 1 shall not apply to contracts that are concluded exclusively by means of the exchange of electronic mail or a similar form of individual communication.
(4) A contract that has been concluded under the influence of non-compliance by the service provider of the duties mentioned in paragraph 1 under a, c or d, is voidable. If the service provider has not fulfilled the duty mentioned in paragraph under a or, it is presumed that a contract has been concluded under the influence thereof.
(5) During the time that the service provider does not supply the information referred to in paragraph

1 (b) and (e) and (2), the other party may terminate the contract.

(6) Between parties acting in the exercise of a profession or business, paragraph 1 may be derogated from.

Article 6:227c. (1) The person who provides a service referred to in article 15d paragraph 3 of Book 3, shall provide the other party with appropriate, effective and accessible resources with which the other party for the acceptance of the contract can become informed about acts not wanted by him and how he can recover these.

(2) If a counterparty of a service provider makes a statement by electronic means that may be construed by the service provider either as an acceptance of the offer made by him using electronic means, or as an offer in response to an invitation to enter negotiations made using electronic means, the service provider shall confirm the receipt of this statement as soon as possible using electronic means. The other party can terminate the contract as long as the receipt of the acceptance has not been confirmed. The non-timely confirmation of the receipt of an offer is regarded as a rejection thereof.

(3) A statement as meant in paragraph 2 and the confirmation of receipt are deemed to be received when they become accessible for the parties to whom they are addressed.

(4) Paragraphs 1 and 2 do not apply if the contract was concluded exclusively by means of the exchange of electronic mail or a similar form of individual communication.

(5) A contract that has been concluded under the influence of non-compliance by the service provider of the duties mentioned in paragraph 1 is voidable. If the service provider has not fulfilled the duty mentioned in paragraph 1, it is presumed that a contract has been concluded under the influence thereof.

(6) This article may only be deviated from between parties who are acting in the exercise of a profession or business.

Article 6:228. (1) A contract which has been concluded under the influence of mistake [dwaling] and would not have been concluded under a correct impression of the situation, is voidable:

(a) if the mistake is attributable to information from the other party, unless the latter was allowed to presume that the contract would also be concluded without this information;

(b) if the other party should have informed the mistaken person in relation to what he knew or should have known regarding the mistake;

(c) if the other party, when concluding the contract, has relied on the same wrong impression as the mistaken person, unless, even under a correct impression of the situation, he would not have had to understand that the mistaken person ought to have been deterred from concluding the contract.

(2) The avoidance may not be grounded on a mistake which only concerns an exclusively future circumstance or which, with regard to the nature of the contract, generally accepted views in society [de in het verkeer geldende opvattingen] or the circumstances of the case should remain for the account of the mistaken person.

Article 6:229. A contract that aims to build upon an existing legal relationship between the parties, is voidable, if this legal relationship does not exist, unless given the nature of the contract, generally accepted views in society or the circumstances of the case, this absence should remain for the account of the mistaken party.

Article 6:230. (1) The right to avoid on the basis of Articles 228 and 229 lapses, where the other party proposes in time an alteration of the consequences of the contract, which sufficiently eliminates the disadvantage suffered by the person entitled to avoid in case the agreement is maintained.

(2) Furthermore, the court may, at the request of one of the parties, instead of pronouncing the avoidance, alter the consequences of the agreement to eliminate this disadvantage.

Division 3. General conditions

Article 6:231. In this Division:

(a) general conditions [algemene voorwaarden] are: one or more terms drawn up in order to be included in a number of contracts, with the exception of terms that concern the essence of the performances, to the extent that the latter stipulations are clearly and understandably formulated;

(b) the user is: he who uses general conditions in a contract;

(c) the other party is: he who by signing a document or in another manner has accepted the application of general conditions.

Article 6:232. The other party is bound to the general conditions even if, at the time of conclusion of the contract, the user understood or ought to have understood that he did not know the content thereof.

Article 6:233. A term in general conditions is voidable
(a) if, given the nature and other content of the contract, the manner in which the general conditions have come about, the mutually identifiable interests of the parties and the other circumstances of the case, it is unreasonably onerous for the other party; or
(b) if the user has not offered the other party a reasonable opportunity to become acquainted with the general conditions.

Article 6:234. (1) The user has offered the other party the opportunity as meant in Article 233(b), if he has either provided the other party with the general terms and conditions before or at the time of conclusion of the contract, has provided the general terms and conditions in the manner referred to in Article 230c, or, where this is not reasonably possible, he has informed the other party before conclusion of the contract that the general terms and conditions are available for inspection with him or have been deposited at a Chamber of Commerce [Kamer van Koophandel en Fabrieken] or a registry of a court indicated by him, and that they will be sent upon request. If the general terms and conditions are not provided to the other party before or at the time of conclusion of the contract, the terms are also voidable if the user does not immediately and at his own expense send the general terms and conditions to the other party upon his request. What is laid down in relation to the duty to send does not apply in so far as such sending cannot be reasonably required of the user.
(2) The user has also offered the other party the opportunity as meant in Article 233(b) if he has provided the other party with the general terms and conditions electronically before or at the time of conclusion of the contract, in such a manner that they can be saved by her and are accessible to her for consultation at a later time, or, if this is not reasonably possible, has informed the other party before conclusion of the contract where she may consult the general terms and conditions electronically, and that they will be sent upon request, electronically or in another manner.
If the general terms and conditions have not been provided to the other party electronically before or at the time of conclusion of the contract, the terms are also voidable if the user does not immediately and at his own expense send the conditions electronically or in another manner upon request by the other party.
(3) Offering the reasonable opportunity, as meant in paragraph (2), to become acquainted with the general terms and conditions requires the explicit consent of the other party if the contract is not concluded electronically.

Article 6:235. (1) The grounds for avoidance as meant in Articles 233 and 234 may not be invoked by
(a) a legal person as meant in Article 360 of Book 2, that has at the time of conclusion of the agreement recently published its annual account, or with regard to which at that time Article 403 paragraph (1) of Book 2 was recently applied;
(b) a party to whom letter (a) does not apply, if at the aforementioned time he employs fifty or more persons or if at that time it follows from a report pursuant to the Trade Register Act 1996 [Handelsregisterwet 1996] that he employs fifty or more persons.
(2) The ground for avoidance as meant in Article 233 letter (a) may also be invoked by a party for whom the general conditions have been used by a representative, provided that the other party repeatedly concludes contracts to which the same or practically the same general conditions are applicable.
(3) The grounds for avoidance as meant in Articles 233 and 234 may not be invoked by a party that has repeatedly used the same or practically the same general conditions in his agreements.
(4) The time period as meant in Article 52 paragraph (1) under (d) of Book 3 starts at the beginning of the day, following that on which the term has been invoked.

Article 6:236. In a contract between a user and another party, who is a natural person not acting in the course of a profession or business, a term in the general conditions is considered to be unreasonably onerous
(a) where it deprives the other party entirely and unconditionally of the right to demand the performance promised by the user;
(b) where it excludes or restricts the other party's right to dissolve, as regulated in Division 5 of Title 5,
(c) where it excludes or restricts the other party's right, pursuant to the law, to suspend performance or grants the user a more far-reaching right to suspend than he is entitled to according to the law;
(d) where it leaves the assessment of the question whether the user has failed to fulfil one or more of his obligations to himself, or makes the exercise of the rights that the other party has according to the law with regard to such a deficiency dependent upon the condition that the latter has first brought a

legal action against a third party;

(e) where the other party grants the user permission in advance to pass his obligations stemming from the contract to a third party in one of the ways as meant in Division 3 of Title 2, unless the other party has at all times the right to dissolve the contract, or unless the user is liable as against the other party for performance by the third party, or unless the passing takes place in relation to the transfer of a company to which both these obligations as well as the rights acquired in exchange belong;

(f) where it, in case the rights of the user stemming from the contract are transferred to a third party, has as its purpose to exclude or restrict rights or defences which the other party could invoke against that third party according to the law;

(g) where it shortens a statutory period of prescription or expiry within which the other party must invoke a particular right to a period of prescription or expiry of less than a year;

(h) where it obliges the other party, in case during performance of the contract damage is caused to a third party by the user or by a person or object for which the latter is liable, to either compensate the third party for this damage, or to bear a larger part of it in his relation to the user than he would be obliged to according to the law;

(i) where it gives the user the right to raise the price stipulated by him within three months after conclusion of the contract, unless the other party has in that case the right to dissolve the contract;

(j) where it leads, in the case of a contract for the regular delivery of objects, including electricity, or for the regular provision of services, to tacit extension or renewal for more than a year;

(k) where it excludes or restricts the right of the other party to provide evidence, or where it alters the allocation of the burden of proof as follows from the law to the disadvantage of the other party, either by containing a declaration from the latter regarding the quality of the performance owed to him, or by placing upon him the burden of proving that a shortcoming of the user can be attributed to him;

(l) where it deviates from Article 37 of Book 3 to the disadvantage of the other party, unless it relates to the form of declarations to be made by the other party or determines that the user may continue to consider the address provided to him by the other party as such until he has been informed of a new address;

(m) as a result of which the other party who, at the time of conclusion of the contract has his habitual residence in a municipality in the Netherlands, chooses a residence for other reasons than in case he will at any time not have a known actual residence in that municipality, unless the contract relates to a registered object and a residence is chosen at the offices of a notary;

(n) where it provides for the adjudication of a dispute by a person other than the court that would be competent pursuant to the law, or one or more arbiters, unless it provides the other party with a time period of at least one month after the user has invoked the term in writing as against him, to choose a court that is competent pursuant to the law for adjudication of the dispute;

(o) where it excludes or limits the right of the other party to cancel a contract that has been concluded orally, in writing or electronically;

(p) where a contract for the regular delivery of daily, news or weekly periodicals or magazines leads to a tacit extension or renewal of the contract with a length that is longer than three months, or to the tacit extension or renewal of the contract with a length of maximum three months without the other party having the right to cancel each time at the end of the length of the extension or renewal with a cancellation period of a maximum of one month;

(q) where a contract for the regular delivery of daily, news or weekly periodicals or magazines leasd to a tacit continuation in a contract for undetermined duration without the other party having the right to cancel the continued contract at any time with a cancellation period of a maximum of one month or, in case the regular delivery takes place less than once a month, with a cancellation period of a maximum three months;

(r) where the other party is obliged to make the declaration of cancellation meant under (j), (p) or (q) at a certain moment in time;

(s) where a contract of limited duration for the regular introductory delivery of daily, news or weekly periodicals or magazines leads to continuation of the contract.

Article 6:237. In a contract between a user and another party, who is a natural person not acting in the exercise of a profession or business, a term in general conditions is presumed to be unreasonably onerous

(a) where, given the circumstances of the case, it gives the user an unusually long or insufficiently determined time period to react to an offer or other declaration of the other party;

(b) where it extensively restricts the content of the obligations of the user with regard to what the other party, taking into account the statutory rules that apply to the contract, could reasonably expect without this term;

(c) where it grants the user the right to provide a performance that deviates essentially from the promised performance, unless the other party has in that case the right to dissolve the contract;
(d) where it frees the user of being bound by the contract or grants him the right thereto on other grounds than those mentioned in the contract, which are of such a nature that he can no longer be required to be bound;
(e) where it gives the user an unusually long or insufficiently determined time period for performance;
(f) where it frees the user or a third party wholly or partially of a statutory obligation to pay damages;
(g) where it excludes or restricts the right to settle granted to the other party by law or grants the user a more extensive right to settle than he is entitled to pursuant to the law;
(h) where it imposes as a sanction on certain acts of the other party, including omission, the loss of rights to which he is entitled or of the right to invoke certain defences, except in as far as these acts justify the loss of these rights or defences;
(i) where, in case the contract is ended on grounds other than the fact that the other party has failed to perform his obligation, it obliges the other party to pay a sum of money, except in as far as it concerns a reasonable compensation for loss suffered by the user or profit of which he has been deprived;
(j) where it obliges the other party to conclude a contract with the user or with a third party, unless this, taking into account the connection of that contract with the contract as meant in this article, may reasonably be required of the other party;
(k) where it lays down a time period of more than one year for a contract as meant in Article 236 under (j), unless the other party has the right to cancel the contract after each year;
(l) where it binds the other party to a time period for cancellation that is longer than three months or longer than the time period for cancellation of the contract by the user;
(m) where it requires, for the validity of a declaration to be made by the other party, a stricter form than required for a private document [onderhandse akte];
(n) where it determines that a mandate granted by the other party is irrevocable or does not end at his death or his coming under legal guardianship [ondercuratelestelling], unless the mandate has as its purpose the delivery of a registered thing;
(o) where the other party by contracts, not being extended, renewed or continued contracts as meant in Article 236 under (j), (p) or (q) is bound to a cancellation period of longer than one month.

Article 6:238. In case of a contract as referred to in articles 6:236 and 6:237, the following facts may not be invoked against the counterparty:
a. the fact that the contract has been entered into in name of a third party, if this is solely based on the fact that a clause to that effect is part of the standard terms and conditions.
b. the fact that the standard terms and conditions contain limitations to the competence of an agent of the user that are so unusual that the counterparty, had it not been for the clause in the standard terms and conditions, would not have had to expect them unless he knew them.
(2) In case of a contract as referred to in articles 6:236 and 6:237, the contractual provisions must be drafted in a clear and understandable way. In case of uncertainty with regard to the meaning of a contractual provision, the interpretation most favourable to the counterparty prevails.

Article 6:239. (1) Sub-paragraphs a-n of Article 239 may be amended or their scope may be limited by ordinance [algemene maatregel van Bestuur].
(2) Before making a proposal to establish, amend or withdraw an order as meant in the first paragraph, Our Minister of Justice can hear the according to his judgment representative organisation of those who in the conclusion of the contracts to which the order relates are accustomed to using general conditions and from those who are accustomed to acting as the other party in those contracts.
(3) A decision as mean in the first paragraph shall be sent to the Presidents of both houses of the States General as soon as it is made. Such a decision does not entre into effect until after two months have passed since the date of issue of the Official Gazette in which it is placed.

Article 6:240. (1) On application of a legal person as meant in paragraph 3, certain terms in certain general conditions can be declared unreasonably onerous; Articles 233 under a, 236 and 237 apply mutatis mutandis. For the application of the preceding sentence, a term in general conditions that is contrary to a mandatory statutory provision, is regarded as unreasonably onerous. In the evaluation of a clause, the interpretation rule of Article 238 paragraph 2, second sentence, is not applicable.
(2) The claim can be brought against the user, as well as against a legal person with full legal capacity who has the objective of looking after the interests of persons who exercise a profession or business, if he facilitates the use of the general conditions by those persons.

(3) The application accrues to a legal persons with full legal capacity who has the objective of looking after the interests of persons who exercise a profession or business or of end user of goods or services not intended for a profession or business. It can only relate to general conditions that are used or intended to be used in contracts with persons on whose behalf the legal person acts.
(4) The claimant is not admissible if it not shown that, before making the application, he gave the user or, in the case referred to in article 1003 of the Code of Civil Procedure, the therein referred to association, the opportunity to amend the general conditions in mutual consultation in such a way that the objections that form the basis for the application would be removed. A deadline of two weeks after receipt of the invitation to consult including reference to the objections is in any case sufficient thereto.
(5) To the extent that a legal person has agreed to the use of terms in general conditions, no claim as meant in paragraph accrues to him.
(6) Equated to a legal person as meant in paragraph 3 is an organisation or public body with a seat outside the Netherlands which is placed on the list, meant in Article 4 paragraph 3 of directive 2009/22/EC of the European Parliament and the Council of the European Union of 23 April 2009 on injunctions for the protection of consumers' interests (OJ L 110), provided that the claim relates to general conditions that are used or intended to be used in contracts with persons who have their habitual residence in the country in which the organisation or the public body has its seat, and the organisation looks after the interests pursuant to its objective or the protection of these interests is entrusted to the public body..

Article 6:241. (1) The Court of Appeal in the Hague is exclusively competent to hear claims as referred to in the previous article.
(2) The legal persons referred to in the previous article have the powers, regulated in Articles 217 and 376 of the Code of Civil Procedure; Article 379 of that code does not apply.
(3) With respect to the claimant's claim, the judgment can attach
(a) a prohibition of the use of the terms affected by the ruling or the promotion thereof;
(b) an order to revoke a recommendation to the use of these terms;
(c) a ruling to make the judgment public or to have the judgment made public, in such a manner as determined by the court and at the expense of the party or parties indicated by the court.
(4) The court may indicate in its decision the manner in which the unreasonably onerous character of the terms to which the judgment relates can be removed.
(5) Disputes concerning the enforcement of the rulings referred to in paragraph 3, as well as the ruling to pay a penalty, if this is imposed, are exclusively decided by the Court of Appeal in the Hague.
(6) The summary proceedings court of the court in The Hague has exclusive jurisdiction to hear claims in summary proceedings relating to rulings as referred to in paragraph initiated by legal persons as meant in Article 240, paragraph 3. Paragraph 5, as well as Articles 62, 116 paragraph 2, 1003, 1005, 1006 of the Code of Civil Procedure apply mutatis mutandis.

Article 6:242. (1) On the application of one or more of those persons against whom a judgment as meant in Article 240 paragraph 1 is made, the court may amend or lift it on the ground that it is no longer justified as a result of a change in circumstances. The claim is brought against the legal person on whose application the judgment was made.
(2) If the legal person on whose application the judgment was made, has been dissolved, the case is initiated with a petition. For the application of Article 279 paragraph 1 of the Code of Civil Procedure, legal persons as meant in Article paragraph 3 are considered stakeholders.
(3) Article 241 paragraphs 1, 2, 3 under c and (5) apply mutatis mutandis.
(4) The previous paragraphs are not applicable to the extent the judgment was related to a term that is considered as unreasonably onerous by law.

Article 6:243. A term in general conditions that is incorporated in a contract by the person against whom a prohibition to use it has been pronounced, in contravention of the prohibition is voidable. Article 235 applies mutatis mutandis.

Article 6:244. (1) A person acting in the exercise of a profession or business, cannot rely on a term in a contract with a party who in respect of the goods or services to which the contract is related, concluded contracts with its suppliers making use of general conditions, to the extent that relying on the term would be unreasonable due to the close connection with a term arising in the general conditions that has been annulled pursuant to this Division or that is affected by a judgment as referred to in Article 240 paragraph 1.
(2) If a claim as meant in Article 240 paragraph is initiated against the user, he is competent to call

that person in the proceedings in order to hear declared in law that reliance on the term as meant in the previous paragraph would be unreasonable. Article 241 paragraphs 2, 3 under c, 4 and 5 as well as Articles 210, 211 and 215 of the Code of Civil Procedure apply mutatis mutandis.
(3) Article 242 applies to the judgment mutatis mutandis.
(4) Paragraphs 1 - 3 apply mutatis mutandis to earlier contracts relating to the above-mentioned goods and services.

Article 6:245. This Division is not applicable to employment contracts or collective employment contracts.

Article 6:246. Neither Articles 231 – 244, nor the provisions of the ordinances as meant in Article 239 paragraph (1) may be deviated from. The right to avoid a term pursuant to this division by an extrajudicial declaration cannot be excluded.

Article 6:247. (1) This division applies to contracts between parties acting in the exercise of a profession or business which are both established in the Netherlands, irrespective of the law governing the contract.
(2) This division does not apply to contracts between parties acting in the exercise of a profession or business that are not both established in the Netherlands, irrespective of the law governing the contract.
(3) A party is established in the Netherlands in the sense of paragraphs (1) and (2), if its central administration, or, where the performance is to be carried out according to the contract by a place of business other than the central administration, this other place of business is located in the Netherlands.
(4) This division applies to contracts between a user and another party, natural person, not acting in the exercise of a profession or business, if the other party has his habitual residence in the Netherlands, irrespective of the law governing the contract.

Division 4. Legal Consequences of Contracts

Article 6:248. (1) A contract does not only contain the legal consequences agreed upon by the parties, but also those which, in relation to the nature of the contract, stem from the law, custom or the requirements of reasonableness and fairness [redelijkheid en billijkheid].
(2) A provision which has effect as between the parties as a consequence of the contract is not applicable, to the extent that this would be unacceptable in the given circumstances according to the standards of reasonableness and fairness.

Article 6:249. The legal consequences of a contract also apply for the legal successors under general title, unless something else follows from the contract. In the case of division of an estate pursuant to Article 13 of Book 4 the legal consequences of the contract do not also to the children of the deceased, unless something else follows from the contract.

Article 6:250. This division may be derogated from by contract, with the exception of Articles 251 paragraph 3, 252 paragraph 2 as far as the requirement of a notarial deed is concerned, and paragraph 3, 253 paragraph 1, 257, 258, 259 and 260.

Article 6:251. (1) If a right stemming from a contract that is capable of transfer is so closely connected with a thing belonging to the creditor that he only has an interest in that right as long as he retains the thing, the right is transferred to the person who acquires the thing under special title.
(2) If a counterperformance has been agreed for the right, the duty to perform the counterperformance is also transferred, to the extent that it is related to the period after the transfer. The transferor remains liable next to the acquirer towards the other party, except to the extent that this person can release himself from the obligation after the transfer in case of failure of the counterperformance taking place through termination or cancellation of the contract.
(3) The provisions of the preceding paragraphs do not apply if the acquirer of the thing has directed a statement to the other party that he does not accept the transfer of the right.
(4) From the legal act by which the thing is transferred, it can follow that no transfer takes place.

Article 6:252. (1) It may be stipulated by contract that the duty of one of the parties to tolerate or not to do something in respect to a registered thing [registergoed] that belongs to that party, shall pass onto those that acquire the registered thing under specific title, and the persons who acquire a right to use the object from the holder of a right shall also be bound.
(2) To effect the stipulation mentioned in paragraph (1), the it is required that the parties draw up a notarial deed of their contract, followed by registration in the public land registers. The person who is

subject to the duty must choose residence in the Netherlands in the deed of creation.

(3) Also after registration, the stipulation will have no effect:

(a) against those that have acquired a right to the thing or a right to use the thing under specific title before registration.

(b) against the seizor of the thing or of a right on that thing, when the summons [proces-verbaal] for the seizure was registered before registration of the deed.

(c) against those who have acquired their right from a person that was not bound by the agreed upon duty under (a) or (b).

(4) If a counter-performance has been agreed upon for the duty, then with the passing of the duty, the right to the counter-performance will pass in so far as this relates to the period after the passing and this duty to perform has also been entered in the register.

(5) This article does not apply to those duties that limit a holder of a right in his powers to transfer or burden his right.

Article 6:253. (1) A contract creates for a third party the right to claim the performance of one of the parties or to rely on the contract in some other way if the contract contains a term to that effect and the third party accepted this term.

(2) The term may be revoked by the person who made it until the acceptance.

(3) An acceptance or revocation of the term occurs by a declaration directed at one of the two other parties involved.

(4) If the term is irrevocable and made gratuitously to the the third party, it is treated as accepted if it has come to the attention of the third party and it is not rejected immediately by him.

Article 6:254. (1) After the third party has accepted the term, he is considered a party to the contract.

(2) He can, if this is consistent with the scope of the term, also derive rights from it over the period before the acceptance.

Article 6:255. (1) if the term for the benefit of a third party has no consequence for that third party, the person who has made the term can designate either himself or another third party as right holder.

(2) He is deemed to have designated himself as rightholder, if he has been set a reasonable time by the person from whom the performance has been stipulated to make the designation and he has not made a designation within that time.

Article 6:256. The party who has made a term for the benefit of a third party, can claim performance against the third party, unless it opposes this.

Article 6:257. If a party to a contract can derive from the contract a defence against the other party to defend against its liability for the conduct of one of its subordinate, the subordinate can also, if he is held liable for this conduct by the other party, invoke this defence as if he were a party to the contract himself.

Article 6:258. (1) The court may, at the request of one of the parties, modify the consequences of a contract or terminate it wholly or partially on grounds of unforeseen circumstances which are of such a nature that the other party may not expect unaltered continuation of the contract according to the standards of reasonableness and fairness. The modification or termination may be granted retroactive effect.

(2) A modification or termination will not be pronounced to the extent that the circumstances are for the account of he who relies on them on the basis of the nature of the contract or public opinion.

(3) For the application of this article, he to whom a right or obligation from a contract has been transferred is equal to a party to that contract.

Article 6:259. (1) If a contract has the purpose as such to oblige a right holder to or a user of a registered thing to a performance that does not comprise of go together with the toleration of continuing holding, the court may on his request amend the consequences of the contract or wholly or partly terminate it:

(a) if at least ten years have passed since the conclusion of the contract and the unchanged continuation of the duty is contrary to the general interest;

(b) if the creditor no longer has a legitimate interest in the fulfilment of the duty and it is unlikely that this interest will return.

(2) The time period mentioned in paragraph 1 under a includes the whole period in which the right holder or the users of the thing were bound by a stipulation of the same scope. The time period does not apply in so far as the conflict with the public interest comprises that the stipulation forms an obstacle to the realisation of a valid zoning plan.

Article 6:260. (1) An amendment or termination as meant in Articles 258 and 259 can be pronounced under conditions set by the court.

(3) If the contract that has been amended or wholly or partly terminated on the basis of Articles 258 and 259, is registered in the public register, the judgment by which the amendment or termination took place can be registered in it, provided the judgment is res judicata gone or is provisionally enforceable.

(4) If someone is summoned in this respect at his chosen residence in accordance with Article 252 paragraph 2, first sentence, then all his successors who have not made a new registration are thereby also summoned. Article 29 paragraph 2 and paragraph 3 of Book 3 apply mutatis mutandis.

(5) Other legal facts that amend or end a registered contract are similarly capable of registration, to the extent that it relates to court judgments provided they are res judicata or provisionally enforceable.

Division 5. Synallagmatic Contracts [Wederkerige overeenkomsten]

Article 6:261. (1) A contract is synallagmatic if each of the parties assumes an obligation towards the other in order to acquire the performance to which the other party commits himself.

(2) The provisions regarding synallagmatic contracts are applicable mutatis mutandis to other legal relationships with the purpose of mutual execution of performances, in as far as the nature of those legal relationships is not opposed to it.

Article 6:262. (1) If one of the parties does not honour his commitment, then the other party is authorized to suspend his parallel obligations.

(2) In case of partial or improper performance, suspension is only allowed, to the extent that it is justified by the deficiency.

Article 6:263. (1) The party that is obliged to perform first, is nevertheless authorized to suspend performance of his obligation, if after the contract was concluded he gained knowledge of circumstances which give good grounds to fear that the other party will not perform his parallel obligations.

(2) In case there are good grounds to fear that performance will only be partial or improper, suspension is only allowed in as far as it is justified by the deficiency.

Article 6:264. In case of suspension on the basis of Articles 262 and 263, Articles 54 under (b) and (c) and 55 are not applicable.

Article 6:265. (1) Every deficiency in the performance of one of a party's obligations entitles the other party to terminate the contract wholly or partially, unless the deficiency, given its special nature or its insignificant meaning, does not justify this termination [ontbinding] and its consequences.

(2) To the extent that performance is not permanently or temporarily impossible, the right to termination only arises when the debtor is in default.

Article 6:266. (1) A termination cannot be based on a deficiency in the performance of an obligation with regard to which the creditor himself is in default.

(2) If, during the default of the creditor, however, proper performance becomes wholly or partially impossible, then the contract may be terminated, if through fault of the debtor or his subordinate there has been a lack of care which could have been required from him in the given circumstances.

Article 6:267. (1) The termination takes place by way of a written declaration of the person who is so entitled. If the contract was formed electronically, it can also be dissolved by a declaration brought about electronically. Article 227a paragraph (1) is applicable mutatis mutandis.

(2) It may also be pronounced by a court upon his request.

Article 6:268. The right to extrajudicial termination lapses through prescription of the legal claim for termination. The prescription does not impede a judicial or extrajudicial termination to avert a legal claim or other judicial measure which is based on the contract.

Article 6:269. The termination does not have retroactive effect, except where an offer to perform, made after the termination has been claimed, does not have effect, if the termination is pronounced.

Article 6:270. A partial termination contains an equal decrease of the mutual performances in quantity or quality.

Article 6:271. A termination releases the parties of the obligations affected thereby. In as far as these have already been performed, the legal ground for this performance remains intact, but an obligation arises for the parties to undo the performances already received by them.

Article 6:272. (1) If the nature of the contract excludes that it be undone, then compensation comes in its place to the amount of its value at the time of receipt.
(2) If the performance was not in conformity with the contract, then this compensation is limited to the amount of the value that the performance actually had for the recipient at that time in the given circumstances.

Article 6:273. A party who has received a performance, is, from the time at which he reasonably ought to take termination into account, obliged to take care as a careful debtor that the restoration [ongedaanmaking] of the owed performance as a consequence of that termination, will be possible. Article 78 applies mutatis mutandis.

Article 6:274. If a party has received a performance in bad faith in spite of an impending termination, he is deemed after the termination to have been in default from the receipt of the performance.

Article 6:275. Articles 120-124 of Book 3 apply mutatis mutandis in respect to that which is laid down therein relating to the handing over of fruits and the compensation of costs and damage.

Article 6:276. The duties described in this division apply to an incompetent person who has received a performance only to the extent that the what he received actually led to an advantage or came under the power of his statutory representative.

Article 6:277. (1) If a contract is wholly or partially terminated, the party whose deficiency gave rise to a ground for termination is obliged to compensate the other party for the damage he has suffered because no mutual performance or termination of the contract takes place.
(2) If the deficiency cannot be attributed to the debtor, the previous paragraph only applies within the limits of what is provided in Article 78.

Article 6:278. (1) The party who chooses termination of an already executed contract after the ratio in value between what mutually should occur through restoration [ongedaanmaking] has changed in its favour, is obliged to restore the original value ratio by additional payment, if it is likely that it would not have chosen for termination without this change.
(2) The previous paragraph is applicable mutatis mutandis in case the party in whose favour the change has occurred, initiates the restoration on a ground other than termination and it is likely that he would not have proceeded to do so without this change.

Article 6:279. (1) The provisions relating to synallagmatic contracts apply mutatis mutandis to contracts from which obligations arise between more than two parties, with due regard for the following paragraphs, to the extent that the nature of the contract does not contradict this.
(2) The party who has taken upon himself an obligation to acquire on the other hand a stipulated performance from one or more other parties, can base its right to terminate on a deficiency in the performance of the obligation towards himself.
If a party with related rights and duties himself fails in the performance of its obligation, the other parties can in any event terminate the contract.

Book 7. Special Types of Contract

Title 1. Sale and Exchange

Division 1. Sale: General Provisions

Article 7:1. Sale [koop] is a contract by which one person binds himself to give an object and the other party to pay a price in money therefor.

Article 7:2. (1) The purchase of an immovable object intended for habitation or of a part thereof must, where the buyer is a natural person not acting in the exercise of a profession or business, be concluded in writing.
(2) The deed drawn up between the parties or a copy thereof must be handed over to the buyer, in exchange for a dated receipt handed over to the seller if requested. During three days after this handing over, the buyer has the right to terminate the sale. If after the buyer has exercised this right, a new sale is entered within six months between the same parties in respect of the same object or the same part, then the right does not arise again.
(3) Paragraphs (1) and (2) apply mutatis mutandis to the sale of participation and membership rights that grant rights to the use of an immovable object intended for habitation or a part thereof.
(4) Paragraphs (1) – (3) cannot be derogated from to the disadvantage of the buyer, except in case of a standard regulation as meant in Article 214 of Book 6.

(5) Paragraphs (1) – (4) are not applicable to a hire purchase and to a public auction in the presence of a notary. Neither are they applicable if the contract also satisfies the description of a contract as meant in Article 50a under (c) or (f).

Article 7:3. (1) The sale of registered thing may be registered in the public registers referred to in Division 2 of Title 1 of Book 3, unless at the time of the registration, delivery of the thing by the seller is not yet possible because of the exclusion of delivery in advance of future registered things in Article 97 of Book 3. The previous sentence is not to derogated from to the detriment of the buyer in case of a sale of an immovable object intended as a dwelling or a component thereof, if the buyer is a natural person who is not acting in the exercise of a profession or business.
(2) During the cooling-off period referred to in Article 2 paragraph 2, the registration can only take place if the deed of sale is drawn up and countersigned by a notary located in the Netherlands.
(3) The following cannot be relied upon against the buyer whose sale is registered:
(a) an alienation or encumbrance arising after the registration of the sale, unless the alienation or encumbrance stems from an earlier registered sale or took place under a right to delivery that according to Article 298 of book 3 went before that of the buyer and that the buyer at the time of the registration knew of the sale or in relation to which at that time the minutes of a provisional attachment for delivery was registered;
(b) alienations or encumbrances that take place as a consequence to the alienation or encumbrances by the seller referred to in sub-paragraph (a);
(c) an administratorship that arose after the registration of the sale or which, in case it arose before, was not yet registered in the public registers, the latter unless the buyer knew of it at the time of the registration of the sale;
(d) a renting or leasing that arose after the registration of the sale;
(e) a stipulation as meant in Article 252 of Book 6 that is registered after the registration of the sale;
(f) a by way of execution or provisional attachment of which the minutes are registered after registration of the sale;
(g) insolvency or suspension of payment of the seller or the application of the debt restructuring scheme natural persons, pronounced after the day on which the sale is registered.
(4) The registration of the sale loses the retroactive effect referred to in paragraph 3 if the thing is not delivered to the buyer within six months after the registration. In that case, the sale is also deemed not to be known through consultation of the public registers.
(5) After the registration has lost its effect, no sale may be registered between the same parties with respect to the same thing during six months.
(6) Registration of the sale only takes place if a signed and dated statement of a notary is inserted under the deed, which contains his surname, given names, location and quality and in which it is stated that paragraphs 1, 2 and 5 do not impede a registration.

Article 7:4. When the sale is concluded without the price being determined, the buyer owes a reasonable one; for the determination of the price account is to be taken of the price the seller commonly demands at the time of the conclusion of the contract.

Article 7:5. (1) In this title a 'consumer sale' [consumentenkoop] means: the sale of a movable object, concluded by a seller acting in the exercise of his trade, business, craft, or profession, and a buyer, a natural person, acting for purposes outside his business or profession.
(2) If the object is sold by an authorised representative [gevolmachtigde] who acts in the exercise of a profession or a business, the sale will be regarded as a consumer sale, unless the buyer knows, at the time the contract is concluded that the principal [volmachtgever] does not act in exercise of a profession or a business.
(3) The previous paragraphs are not applicable if the contract concerns water that is delivered to the consumer by means of pipelines.
(4) If the movable object must yet be produced and the contract by virtue of which the object has to be delivered meets the description of Article 750, the contract will be regarded as a consumer sale, if the contract is concluded by a (building) contractor [aannemer] who acts in the exercise of a profession or business, and a customer [opdrachtgever], who is a natural person not acting in the exercise of a profession or a business. The provisions of this Title and of Division 1 of Title 12 apply simultaneously. In the case of conflict the provisions of this Title are applicable.
(5) With the exception of Articles 9, 11, and 19a, the provisions concerning consumer sales apply mutatis mutandis to the delivery of electricity, heat and cooling, and gas, as far as the latter have not been prepared for sale in limited volume or in a certain quantity, as well as to the delivery of central district heating, and of digital content which is not delivered on a physical storage device, but which

is individualised and can be subject to the exercise of factual power, to a natural person who acts for purposes outside the exercise of his trade, business, craft, or profession.

(6) For the application of Articles 9, 11, and 19a, a contract between any person acting in the exercise of his trade, business, craft, or profession, and the natural person acting for purposes outside the exercise of his business or profession, which concerns the delivery of movable things as well as the performance of services, is exclusively regarded as a consumer sale.

Article 7:6. (1) In a consumer sale, Divisions 1 – 7 of this Title cannot be derogated from to the disadvantage of the buyer and the rights and claims which the law accords to the buyer regarding a deficiency in the performance of the duties of the seller may not be limited or excluded.

(2) Paragraph (1) is not applicable to Articles 12, 13 first and second sentence, 26 and 35, but provisions in general terms and conditions whereby these Articles are derogated from to the disadvantage of the buyer, are deemed to be unreasonably burdensome.

(3) The applicability to the consumer sale of a right that does not or only partially offers the protection by way of directive 99/44/EC of the European Parliament and the Council of the European Union of 25 May1999 concerning certain aspects of consumer sales of and associated guarantees (O.J. L171), cannot result in the buyer losing the protection he is entitled to by virtue of this directive through the mandatory provisions of the law of the Member State of the European Union or another state which is party to the Agreement creating the European Economic Area, where he has his habitual residence.

Article 7:6a. (1) If in the case of a consumer sale, certain characteristics are promised by the seller or producer in a guarantee, in the absence whereof certain rights or claims are granted to the buyer, the buyer can exercise them notwithstanding all other rights or claims the law grants the buyer.

(2) In a guarantee, it must be specified in a clear and understandable manner which rights and claims referred to in paragraph (1) are granted to the buyer and it is to be stated that they are accorded to the buyer notwithstanding the rights and claims which he is entitled to by law. Furthermore, in a guarantee, the name and the address either of the seller or of the producer from whom the guarantee originated are to be stated as well as the duration and the territory for which the guarantee will have effect.

(3) The information referred to in paragraph (2) is to be provided to buyer on his demand. This occurs in writing or on another permanently accessible information medium at the disposal of the buyer.

(4) The rights and claims granted to the buyer by the seller or producer in a certificate of guarantee are also available to him if the object does not possess the characteristics which were promised by that seller or producer in an advertisement.

(5) In this Article the following means:

(a) Guarantee: a promise made in a certificate of guarantee or advertisement as meant in paragraph (1);

(b) Producer: the manufacturer of the object, the person who imports the object into the European Economic Area, as well as anyone else who presents himself to be the producer by placing his name, his trademark or any other distinguishing feature on the object.

Article 7:7. (1) The person to whom an object has been sent and who may reasonably assume that this sending occurred in order to induce him to purchase, is entitled, irrespective of any other contrary statement by the sender to him, to keep the object for free, unless it can be attributed to him that the sending occurred.

(2) No obligation of payment arises for a natural person acting for purposes outside the exercise of his business or profession, in case of the unsolicited delivery of objects, financial products, water, gas, electricity, central district heating, or digital content not delivered on a physical storage device, regardless of whether such digital content can be individualised and can be subject to the exercise of factual power, or the unsolicited rendering of services, referred to in Article 193i (f) of Book 6. The absence of a reaction of a natural person, acting outside the exercise of his business or profession, to an unsolicited delivery or rendering of services is not deemed an acceptance. If nonetheless an object as meant in the first sentence is sent, what is laid down in paragraph (1) regarding the right to keep the object for free applies mutatis mutandis. This paragraph applies regardless of whether the sender is represented.

(3) Where the receiver, in the cases referred to in paragraphs (1) and (2), returns the object, the sender bears the cost thereby incurred.

Article 7:8. If a newly built or to be built dwelling, comprising an immovable object or component thereof, is sold and the buyer is a natural person not acting in the exercise of a profession or business, Articles 767 and 768 apply mutatis mutandis. This may not be derogated from to the detriment of the buyer, unless by way of a standard regulation as meant in Article 214 of Book 6.

Division 2. Duties of the seller

Article 7:9. (1) The seller is obliged to transfer ownership of the sold object including any appurtenances and to deliver them. The appurtenances include the existing proofs of title and notices; in so far as the seller thereby retains an interest, he is only obliged to provide a copy or an excerpt to the buyer on the latter's demand and for the latter's account.
(2) To deliver means bringing the buyer into possession of the object.
(3) In the case of a sale with a reservation of title, delivery means putting the object under the control of the buyer.
(4) In case of a consumer sale, the seller delivers the objects to the buyer without delay and in any event within thirty days after concluding the contract. Parties may agree on a different period of time for delivery. With regard to the period of thirty days, Regulation 1182/71/EEC/Euratom (OJ L 124) of the Council of 3 June 1971, containing rules applicable to time periods, dates, as well as moments of commencement and expiry, is applicable mutatis mutandis.
(5) Where the consumer sale has been concluded through another person, acting in the exercise of his trade, business, craft, or profession, who, in concluding the contract, acts in name or on behalf of the seller, the consumer may also invoke the provisions of paragraphs (1) – (4) against this other person.

Article 7:10. (1) The object is at the risk of the buyer from the delivery, even if the ownership has not yet been transferred. Accordingly, he still owes the purchase price, notwithstanding the loss or deterioration of the object by a cause that cannot be attributed to the seller.
(2) The same applies from the moment at which the buyer is in default with the performance of an act with which he is to cooperate for the delivery. Depending on the sort of specific objects being sold, default of the buyer only causes the risk to pass to him once the seller has identified the objects destined for the performance of the contract and notified the buyer thereof.
(3) If the buyer on good grounds invokes his right to termination [ontbinding] of the sale or substitution of the object, these remain at the risk of the seller.
(4) When the object remained at the risk of the seller after delivery, the loss or deterioration thereof through the fault of the buyer will be likewise remains for the account of the seller. Nevertheless, the moment he must reasonably take into account the fact that he will have to return the object, the buyer has to care for the preservation thereof as a careful debtor; Article 78 of Book 6 applies mutatis mutandis.

Article 7:11. (1) Where in a consumer sale the object is delivered to the buyer, the object is only at the risk of the buyer as of the moment at which the buyer, or a third person designated by him, who is not the carrier, has received the object.
(2) Where the buyer designates a carrier and the choice for this carrier is not offered by the seller, the risk passes to the buyer as of the moment at which the carrier receives the object from the seller.
(3) Where the consumer sale has been concluded through another person, acting in the exercise of his trade, business, craft, or profession, who, in concluding the contract, acts in name or on behalf of the seller, the consumer may also invoke the provisions of paragraphs (1) and (2) against this other person.

Article 7:12. (1) The delivery costs, including those of weighting and count, are borne by the seller.
(2) Collection costs and costs of a deed of sale and of transfer are borne by the buyer.

Article 7:13. If in a consumer sale the object is delivered to the buyer by the seller or the carrier appointed by the latter, any costs thereby incurred may only be claimed if, in case of a contract concluded not at a distance or outside the sales space, referred to in Article 230g (1) (e) and (f), they have been specified separately by the seller, or if information was provided by the seller on the basis of which the costs were calculated by him. The same applies to costs owed for other activities which the seller performs for the buyer in relation to the sale. the costs therefor can only be claimed in so far as they were specified separately by the seller at the conclusion of the contract or information was provided by the seller on what basis they are calculated by him. The same applies to costs due for activities which the seller performs for the buyer in relation to the sale. For a consumer sale which meets the definition of a contract concluded at a distance or outside the sales space, no additional costs are owed either insofar as they have not been indicated previously, in conformity with Articles 230m (1) (e) and 230n (3) of Book 6.

Article 7:15. (1) The seller is obliged to transfer ownership of the object sold free from all special burdens and restrictions, with the exception of those which the buyer has explicitly accepted.
(2) Notwithstanding any provisions to the contrary, the seller warrants the absence of burdens and restrictions which might stem from facts that are capable of registration in the public register, but

which were not registered therein at the time of the conclusion of the contract.

Article 7:16. When a claim is brought against the buyer to exercise the right to sell [uitwinning] or for the recognition of a right with which the object should not have been burdened, the seller is obliged to appear in the proceedings in order to defend the interests of the buyer.

Article 7:17. (1) The delivered object must comply with the contract.
(2) An object does not comply with the contract if, in light of the nature of the object and the information that the seller gave about the object, it does not possess the characteristics which the buyer on the basis of the contract could have expected. The buyer may expect that the object has the characteristics which are necessary for ordinary use thereof and of which he did not need to doubt their presence, as well as the characteristics that are necessary for a particular use that is provided for in the contract.
(3) Another object than contracted for or an object of a different kind likewise does not comply with the contract. The same applies if the delivered object differs in number, size or weight from that which was contracted for.
(4) If the purchaser has been shown or was provided with a sample or model, then the object has to be identical to it, unless it was merely provided for the purpose of identification, without requiring the object to comply with it.
(5) The buyer cannot invoke that the object does not comply with the contract when he knew or reasonably could have known this at the time of the conclusion of the contract. The buyer can also not invoke that the object does not comply with the contract when this is attributable to defects or unsuitability of raw materials originating from the buyer, unless the seller should have warned him of these defects or unsuitability.
(6) In case of the sale of an immovable object, the reference to size is presumed to merely be meant as an indication without the object having to comply therewith.

Article 7:18. (1) When evaluating the question, whether an object delivered on the basis of a consumer sale complies with the contract, announcements made by or on behalf of a previous seller of the object, acting in the exercise of a profession or a business, which were made public with regards to the object count as notifications of the seller, except in so far as this person neither knew of a certain announcement nor ought to have known of it or ultimately at the time of the conclusion of the contract revoked the announcement in a for the buyer clear way, or the sale could not be influenced by that announcement.
(2) In a consumer contract, is presumed that the object did not comply with the contract at delivery, if the deviation from the agreed upon manifests itself within a period of six months after the delivery, unless the nature of the object or the nature of the deviation oppose this.
(3) If in a consumer sale, the seller is obliged to take care of the installation of the object and such installation was performed badly, this amounts to a lack of conformity of the object to the contract. The same applies if the installation by the buyer was executed badly by the buyer and this is to be attributed to the instruction sheet, which was given to the buyer with the delivery of the object.

Division 3. Special consequences of non-performance of the duties of the seller

Article 7:19a. (1) If the seller in a consumer sale is not forthcoming within the period fixed in Article 9 paragraph 4 or the agreed person, he is in default when he is put on notice by the buyer with a notice that fixes a reasonable period for the delivery and performance is not forthcoming within that period.
(2) The default of the seller starts without notice when:
(a) the seller has refused to deliver the objects;
(b) delivery within the agreed upon delivery time is essential, considering all the circumstances surrounding the conclusion of the contract; or
(d) the buyer has informed the seller before the conclusion of the contract that delivery before or on a specified date is essential.
(3) In case of the termination of a consumer sale due to a deficiency in the performance of the obligation referred to in Article 9 paragraph 4, the seller reimburses immediately all the payments received from the buyer.
(4) If the consumer sale has been formed via another person, acting in the course of his trade, business, craft or profession, who thereby acts on behalf of or for the account of the seller, the consumer can also invoke paragraphs 1-3 against that other person.

Article 7:20. If the object is tainted with a burden or restriction that should not have rested upon it, the buyer may demand the burden or restriction be removed, provided the seller can reasonably comply therewith.

Article 7:21. (1) If the delivered object does not comply with the contract, the buyer can demand:
(a) delivery of that which is lacking;
(b) repair of the delivered object, provided the seller can reasonably comply therewith.
(c) replacement of the delivered object, unless the deviation from that which was contracted for is too trivial to justify this, or that the object after the time that the buyer could reasonably take into consideration restoration [ongedaanmaking], is lost or has deteriorated because he did not care for the preservation thereof as a careful debtor.
(2) The costs of performance of the duties meant in paragraph (1) cannot be charged to the buyer.
(3) The seller is obliged to, also in light of the nature of the object and the particular use of the object which is provided for by the contract, within a reasonable time and without serious inconvenience to the buyer, fulfil his duties mentioned in paragraph (1).
(4) In a consumer sale, in derogation from paragraph (1), the buyer is only not entitled to repair or replacement of the delivered object, if repair or replacement is impossible or it cannot be required of the seller.
(5) Repair or replacement cannot be required of the seller, in a consumer sale, if the costs thereof are not in proportion to the costs of the exercise of another right or another claim which is accorded to the buyer, in light of the value of the object if it would conform with the contract, the extent of the deviation from that which was contracted for and the question whether the exercise of another right or another claim does not cause serious inconvenience to the buyer.
(6) If the seller did not, in a consumer sale, within a reasonable period of time after he was notified in writing by the buyer to do so, fulfil his duty to repair or replace the object, the buyer is authorized to have the repair take place by a third person and to claim the costs therefor from the seller.

Article 7:22. (1) If the delivered object does not comply with the contract, then in a consumer sale, the buyer is authorized to:
(a) terminate the contract, unless the deviation from that which was contracted for, in view of its trivial significance, would not justify such termination and its consequences.
(b) reduce the price in proportion to the degree of deviation from that which was contracted for.
(2) The competences referred to in paragraph (1) only arise where repair and replacement cannot be required of the seller, or the seller was deficient in performance of a duty meant in Article 21 paragraph (3).
(3) In so far as this Division did not derogate therefrom, the provisions of Division 5 of Title 5 of Book 6 in respect of termination of a contract apply mutatis mutandis to the powers referred to in paragraph (1) letter (b).
(4) The rights and powers mentioned in paragraph (1) and Articles 20 and 21 are accorded to the buyer without prejudice to all other rights and claims.

Article 7:23. (1) The buyer can no longer invoke that that which was delivered does not comply with the contract, if he does not notify the seller thereof within adequate time [bekwame tijd] after he has discovered it or reasonably ought to have discovered it. If it appears, however, that the object lacks a characteristic that according to the seller it possessed, or if the deviation is related to facts which he knew or ought to have known, but which he did not disclose, then the notification must take place within adequate time after the discovery. In a consumer sale, the notification has to occur within adequate time after the discovery, with a notification within a period of two months after the discovery being timely.
(2) Legal claims and defences grounded on facts that could justify the proposition that the delivered object does not comply with the contract, prescribe after a period of two years after the notification made in accordance with paragraph (1). However, the buyer retains the power to counter a claim for payment of the price with his right to reduction thereof or to damages.
(3) The period does not run as long as the buyer cannot exercise his right as a consequence of the intent of the seller.

Article 7:24. (1) If on the basis of a consumer sale an object has been delivered that does not possess the characteristics which the buyer could have expected on the basis of the contract, the buyer has against the seller the right to damages in accordance with Divisions 9 and 10 of Title 1 of Book 6.
(2) If the deficiency consists of a defect as meant in Division 3 of Title 3 of Book 6, the seller is not liable for damage as meant in that Division, unless
(a) he knew of the defect or ought to have known of it,
(b) he guaranteed the absence of the defect, or

(c) it concerns damage to the object with respect to which by virtue of Division 3 of Title 3 of Book 6, no right to compensation exists on the basis of the franchise regulated in that Division, notwithstanding his defences by virtue of Divisions 9 and 10 of Title 1 of Book 6.

(3) If the seller compensates the buyer's damage pursuant to paragraph 2 (a) or (b), the buyer is obliged to transfer his rights under Division 3 of Title 3 of Book 6 to the seller.

Article 7:25. (1) If the buyer, in the case of deficiency as meant in Article 24, has exercised one or more of his rights in respect of the deficiency against the seller, the seller has the right to damages from the person from whom he bought the object, provided this person also in the contract acted in the exercise of his profession or business. The costs of defence only will be compensated in so far as they were made reasonably by the seller.

(2) Paragraph (1) cannot be derogated from to the disadvantage of the seller.

(3) The right of damages by virtue of paragraph (1) is not accorded to the seller, if the deviation concerns facts which he knew or ought to have known, or its cause lies in a circumstance that occurred after the object had been delivered to him.

(4) If an object lacks a characteristic which according to the seller it possessed, the right of the seller to damages by virtue of paragraph (1) is restricted to the amount to which he could have been entitled if he had not made the promise.

(5) The previous paragraphs apply mutatis mutandis to recovery based on earlier contracts.

(6) The previous paragraphs are not applicable in so far as it concerns damage as meant in Article 24 paragraph (2).

Division 4. Duties of the buyer

Article 7:26. (1) The buyer is obliged to pay the price.

(2) The payment has to be made at the time and the place of delivery. In a consumer sale, the buyer can be obliged to pay in advance at most half of the purchase price

(3) If a notarial deed is required for the transfer of ownership, followed by registration thereof in the appropriate public registers, then that which is owed at the time of the signing of the deed must at least have been taken from the power of the buyer and it only needs to be brought in the power of the seller after the registration.

(4) In case of the sale of an immovable object intended for habitation or a component thereof, the buyer who is a natural person and not acting in the exercise of a profession or business cannot be obliged to pay the purchase price in advance, except that it can be stipulated that he deposits an amount not higher than 10% of the purchase price with the notary to secure the performance of his duties or that he provides an alternative security for this amount. The first sentence may not be derogated from to the detriment of the buyer, unless by way of a standard regulation as meant in Article 214 of Book 6. (6) The overpaid amounts are considered as unduly paid.

(5) Paragraph 4 applies mutandis to the sale of participation or membership rights that confer the right to use of an immovable object intended for habitation or a component thereof.

(6) The second sentence of paragraph 2 and paragraphs 4 – 5 are not applicable when the contract also meets the description of a contract as meant in Article 50a, sub-paragraphs c, d or f.

Article 7:27. When the buyer is disturbed or has good reason to fear that he will be disturbed by a claim to exercise the right to sell or for recognition of a right on the object that should not have rested on it, he can suspend the payment of the purchase price, unless the seller provides sufficient security to cover the detriment the buyer is likely to suffer.

Article 7:28. In a consumer sale, the claim for payment of the purchase price prescribes after a period of two years.

Article 7:29. (1) Where the buyer has received the object, but he intends to reject it, he must take charge of its preservation as a careful debtor; he has a right of retention to the object until he has been reimbursed by the seller for the costs reasonably made by him.

(2) The buyer who intends to reject an object that was sent to him and that was put at his disposal at the place of destination must in so far as this does not require the payment of the purchase price and without serious inconvenience or unreasonable expenses, take possession of it, unless the seller is present at the place of destination or someone else there who is authorized to be charged with the care of the object on his behalf.

Article 7:30. When in the situations of Article 29, the object is susceptible to loss or deterioration or when the safekeeping results in serious inconvenience or unreasonable expense, the buyer is bound to sell the object in an appropriate manner.

Division 5. Special consequence of default of the buyer

Article 7:31. If the contract gives the buyer the power to specify the object by indication of size or shape or in another manner and he is in default in this regard, the seller may himself proceed to do so, taking into account the needs of the buyer known to him.

Article 7:32. In case the buyer is in default with the taking receipt, Article 30 applies mutatis mutandis.

Division 6. Special cases of termination

Article 7:33. If the delivery of a movable good on a certain day is essential and on that day the buyer does not take possession, such conduct provides grounds to terminate as meant in Article 265 of Book 6.

Article 7:34. The seller can terminate the sale by way of written declaration, if the failure to take possession gives him good grounds to fear that the price will not be paid.

Article 7:35. (1) If the seller in a consumer sale, by virtue of a stipulation made in the contract, increases the purchase price after the conclusion of the contract, the buyer is authorized to terminate the contract by way of written declaration, unless it is stipulated that the delivery will take place more than three months after the purchase.
(2) For the application of paragraph (1), purchase price means the amount which at the conclusion of the contract subject to price changes was mentioned as the provisional purchase price.

Division 7. Damages

Article 7:36. (1) In the case of termination of the sale, if the object has a current price, the damages amounts to the difference between the price determined in the contract and the current price on the day of non-performance.
(2) In order to calculate these damages the current price to be taken into account is that of the market where the sale took place, or, if there is no such current price or it would be inconvenient to apply it, the price on the market which can reasonably replace it; with this differences in the costs for the carriage of the object are to be taken into consideration.

Article 7:37. Where the buyer or the seller concluded a cover purchase and in doing so he proceeded in a reasonable manner, he will be entitled to the difference between the agreed upon price and the price of the cover purchase.

Article 7:38. The provisions of the two previous Articles do not exclude the right to higher damages in case more damage is suffered.

Division 8. Right of reclamation

Article 7:39. (1) The seller who has transferred a movable thing, not being a registered good, to the buyer may, if the price has not been payed and, in connection with this, the requirements for termination as referred to in Article 265 of book 6 are fulfilled, reclaim it as his own property by means of a written declaration addressed to the buyer. Through this declaration, the sale is terminated and the right of ownership of the buyer or his legal successor comes to an end; Articles 271, 273, 275, and 276 of Book 6 apply mutatis mutandis.
(2) Where only the price of a certain part of the transferred thing has not been payed, the seller may only reclaim this part. Where, with regard to the whole thing, a part of the price has not been payed, the seller may reclaim a part of the transferred thing proportional to the part of the price not paid, insofar as the transferred thing is suitable for such Division. In both cases, the sale is only terminated with regard to the part of the transferred thing which is reclaimed.
(3) In all other cases of partial payment of the price, the seller may only reclaim the whole transferred thing in exchange for repayment of that which has already been payed.

Article 7:40. (1) If the buyer is declared bankrupt or has he been granted a suspension of payments, the reclamation has no effect, if the purchase price is paid by the receiver [curator] respectively the buyer and the administrator [bewindvoerder], within a reasonable time fixed for them for this purpose by the seller in his statement or security is provided for this payment.
(2) The first paragraph applies mutandis where the debt restructuring scheme natural persons has been declared applicable to the buyer, unless the sales contract is concluded after the judgment to apply the debt restructuring scheme.

Article 7:41. The power of reclamation may be exercised only to the extent that the delivered object is still in the same condition in which it was delivered.

Article 7:42. (1) Unless the object has remained in the hands of the buyer, the power of reclamation lapses when the object has been transferred non-gratuitously in accordance with Article 90 paragraph 1 or Article 91 of Book 3 to a third person who could not reasonably have expected that the right would be exercised.
(2) If the object is given in usufruct or pledged after the non-gratuitous delivery, paragraph 1 applies mutandis.

Article 7:43. The seller cannot exercise its power defined in Article 39 if the buyer has accepted a commercial paper for the full purchase price. Upon acceptance for part of the price, the seller can only exercise this power if it for the benefit of the buyer provides security for the compensation of what the buyer would have to pay based on his acceptance.

Article 7:44. The power defined in Article 39 lapses when both six weeks have passed after the claim for payment of the purchase price fell due and sixty days, to be calculated from the day on which the object was stored under the buyer or under someone for his sake.

Division 9. Sale on trial

Article 7:45. (1) Sale on trial [koop op proef] is deemed to have been concluded under the suspensive condition that the object satisfies the buyer.
(2) If he allows a period, long enough to evaluate the object, to go by without informing the seller of his decision, he can no longer reject the object.

Article 7:46. As long as the sale is not final, the seller bears the risk for the object.

Division 10. Sale of patrimonial rights

Article 7:47. A sale can also relate to a patrimonial right. In that case, the provisions of the previous Divisions are applicable to the extent that they consistent with the nature of the right.

Article 7:48. (1) He who sells an inheritance without stating its things piece by piece is only held to guarantee his status as heir.
(2) If the seller has already enjoyed fruits, collected a claim belonging to the estate or alienated things from the estate, he must compensate the buyer for them.
(3) The buyer must compensate the seller for that which this person has paid because of the debts and burdens of the estate and pay him that which he as creditor of the estate had to claim.

Division 12. Barter

Article 7:49. Barter is the contract whereby parties reciprocally commit to each other to give an object in exchange for another.

Article 7:50. The provisions concerning sale apply mutatis mutandis, it being understood that each party is regarded as seller for the performance that he owes, and each as buyer for that which accrues to him.

[Title 1A is omitted.]

Title 2a Consumer credit contracts

[Division 1 is omitted.]

Division 2. Information and acts preliminary to the conclusion of a credit contract

Article 7:59. (1) A lender who in advertising concerning credit contracts, not including credit concerning collateralised loan, does not comply with Article 4 of the Directive concerning the standard information in advertising, carries out an unfair commercial practice as meant in Article 193b of Book 6.
(2) A lender carries out an unfair commercial practice as meant in Article 193b of Book 6 if in advertising for contracts for securities credit:
(a) does not mention that a revolving credit is granted or promised against collateral of an investment portfolio, and the credit limit depends on the value thereof; or
(b) does not comply with Article 4 paragraphs 1, 2 (a), 3 or 4 of the Directive concerning standard information in advertising for credit contracts.

Article 7:60. (1) The creditor or, as the case may be, the credit intermediary provides to the consumer, in good time before the latter is bound by a credit contract or an offer, the pre-contractual information prescribed in Articles 5 and 6 of the Directive in the way required by these Articles.
(2) The creditor or, as the case may be, the credit intermediary provides to the consumer, in good time before the latter is bound by a contract or an offer relating to a collateralised loan, the pre-contractual information prescribed in Articles 6 of the Directive, with the exception of the information referred to in paragraph (1), letters c, d, f, h, and k of that Article, in the way required by that Article. In doing so, the creditor or, as the case may be, the credit intermediary, also informs the consumer
(a) that a revolving credit is granted or promised against a pledge on the portfolio of negotiable securities and that the credit limit depends on a certain coverage ratio and, if applicable, certain spreading requirements;
(b) which coverage ratio and which spreading requirements are used with regard to a pledged portfolio of negotiable securities, and
(c) in case the creditor applies different coverage ratios for different sorts of financial instruments, the coverage ratio that is used for each instrument.
(3) Where the creditor or, as the case may be, the credit intermediary does not observe paragraph (1) or (2), he engages in an unfair commercial practice as referred to in Article 193b of Book 6.

[The remainder of Title 2a and Title 3 are omitted.]

Title 4. Rent [Huur]

Division 1. General Provisions

Article 7:201. (1) Rent [huur] is the contract by which the one party, the lessor [verhuurder] commits himself to the other party, the lessee [huurder], to provide the use of an object or a part thereof and the lessee commits to a counter-performance.
(2) Rent can also relate to patrimonial rights. In that case, the provision of this Division and the Divisions 2-4 are applicable to the extent the scope of these provisions or the nature of the right do not contradict this.
(3) The lease contract [pachtovereenkomst] is not considered as rent.

Article 7:202. If the lessee has the right to the fruits of the object, this right is a right of enjoyment as meant in Article 17 of Book 5. The lessee acquires this right from the day on which the rent commenced with the understanding that civil fruits are calculated from day to day.

Article 7:203. The lessor is obliged to provide the object to the lessee and to leave it to the extent that is necessary for the agreed use.

Division 2. Obligations of the lessor

Article 7:204. (1) With regard to defects of the object, the lessor has the obligations described in this Division.
(2) A defect is a quality or characteristic of the object or another circumstance not attributable to the lessee, as a result of which the object cannot provide the lessee with the enjoyment that a lessee, when entering into the rental contract, may expect of a well-maintained object of the kind of that to which the lease agreement relates.
(3) A factual disturbance by a third party without a claim to the object as referred to in Article 211, as well as such a claim without a factual disturbance, do not constitute defects within the meaning of paragraph (2).

Article 7:205. The rights of the lessee stemming from this Division accrue to this person without prejudice to any other rights and claims.

Article 7: 206. (1) The lessor is obliged to remedy any defects on request by the lessee, unless this is impossible or requires expenses which, under the given circumstances, cannot reasonably be required of the lessor.
(2) This obligation does not exist with regard to the small repairs which the lessee is obliged to carry out by virtue of Article 217, and to defects for which the lessee is responsible towards the lessor.
(3) Where the lessor is in default of remedying any defects, the lessee may carry out the repair himself and may recover the costs thereby incurred, insofar as they were reasonable, from the lessor, if desired by deducting them from the rent. This provision may not be derogated from to the detriment of the lessee.

[The remainder of Division 2 and Division 3 are omitted.]

Division 4. The passing of rental on the transfer of the object and the cancellation of the rental

Article 7:226. (1) Transfer of ownership of an object in respect of which also a rental contract is made and creation or transfer of an independent right of usufruct, emphyteusis or superficies on the object in respect of which a lease contract is made, by the lessor, results in a passing of the rights and obligations of the lessor that pursuant to the rental contract become due after that time, to the acquirer.
(2) Transfer by a creditor of the lessor shall be equal to a transfer made by the lessor.
(3) The transferee shall only be bound by those stipulations in the rental contract that directly relate to granting the use of the object against a counter-performance to be paid by the lessee.
(4) No derogation can be made from the preceding paragraphs in case of the lease of a constructed immovable object or of a part of that object and of a caravan referred to in Article 235 and of a caravan site referred to in Article 236.

Article 7:227. In the case of creation or assignment of a limited right to a rented object does not fall under Article 226, paragraph (1), the holder must, as regards the lessee, refrain from exercising his right in a way that interferes with the lessee's use.

Article 7:228. (1) A rental entered into for a fixed period ends without the requirement of a cancellation when the term has expired.
(2) A rental entered into for an indefinite period or extended for an indefinite period ends through cancellation. If the rental relates to an immovable object that is neither a residential or business space, the cancellation must take place as of an agreed rental payment date at a period of at least one month.

[The remainder of Division 4 is omitted.]

Division 5. Rental of residential space

[Subdivisions 1 -3 are omitted.]

Subdivision 4. Cancellation of the rental

Article 7:271. (1) By way of derogation from Article 228 paragraph 1, a fixed period rental
(a) entered into for longer than two years in case of a residential space in so far as it is rented as an independent dwelling, or a caravan or a caravan site, or
(b) entered into for longer than five years in case of a residential space in so far as it is not rented as an independent dwelling,
does not end simply due to the lapse of the rental period; It may be cancelled by each of the parties as of an agreed rent payment date, not falling before the passage of the fixed period. Article 228 paragraph 1 is fully applicable to a rental entered into for a fixed period for the duration of two respectively five years or shorter, provided that the lessor informs the lessee not earlier than three months but not later than one month before the fixed period has expired of the day on which the rental expires. If the lessor does not fulfil the duty referred to in the second sentence, the rental contract is extended for an indefinite period after the expiry of the fixed period referred to in that sentence. The rental entered into for a fixed period referred to in the second sentence can be cancelled by the lessee before the expiry of the fixed period as of an agreed rent payment date. If after the end of a rental entered into for fixed period of two respectively five years or shorter a new rental contract is entered into with the same lessee, this later contract is treated as an extension for an indefinite period of the first rental contract.
(2) A rental contract entered into or continued for an indefinite period may be cancelled by either of both parties as of an agreed rent payment day.
(3) Cancellation must be effected by means of a bailiff's notification [exploot] or registered mail. Where, pursuant to Article 266, the spouse or registered partner of the lessee is a co-lessee, the notice of cancellation must be addressed to both spouses of registered partners separately.
(4) On pain of nullity, the notice of cancellation by the lessor must mention the grounds which have led to the cancellation. A cancellation by the lessor on other grounds than those mentioned in Article 274 (1) is void. At the time of cancellation, the lessee must be asked to inform the lessor within six weeks whether or not he agrees with the cancellation of the contract.
(5) In cancelling the rental contract, the following time periods must be observed:
(a) in case of cancellation by the lessee: a period equal to that which elapses between two consecutive rent payment days, but not shorter than one month and not longer than three months;
(b) in case of cancellation by the lessor: a period not shorter than three months, increased by one

month for each year that the lessee had the object continuously in use by virtue of the rental contract, up to a maximum of six months.

(6) A cancellation in violation of paragraph (1), (3), or (5) (a), as well as a cancellation effected on shorter notice than stipulated in paragraph (5) (b) is nevertheless valid but deemed to take effect no earlier than the day prescribed and to observe the required period.

(7) Any contractual term stipulating a longer cancellation period in violation of paragraph (5) (a), a shorter termination period in violation of paragraph (5) (b), or derogating from another provision of this Article, is void. Any contractual term with the effect of ending the lease without cancellation is equally void.

(8) This Article does not apply if termination is effected in mutual agreement after the lease period has begun.

[The remainder of Title 4 and Titles 5-9 are omitted.]

Title 10. Employment contract

Division 1. General provisions

Article 7:610. (1) The employment contract is the contract by which one party, the employee, obliges himself to perform work in service of the other party, the employer, for a certain amount of time in exchange for payment.

(2) Where a contract fulfils both the definition of paragraph (1) and that of another special kind of contract regulated by statute, the provisions of the present Title and those applicable to the other kind of contract apply alongside each other. In case of conflict, the provisions of the present Title apply.

[The remainder of Division 1 and Divisions 2-4 are omitted.]

Division 5. Some special terms in the employment contract

[Articles 7:650-7:652 are omitted.]

Article 7:653. (1) A contractual term between the employer and the employee with the effect of limiting the latter in his right to work in a certain way after the end of the employment contract is only valid if

(a) the employment contract is concluded for an indefinite time; and

(b) the employer and an adult employee have agreed on this contractual term in writing.

(2) By way of derogation from paragraph (1), opening sentence and under (a), a contractual term as referred to in paragraph (1) may be included in an employment contract concluded for a fixed term, if the employer's written statement of reasons attached to this contractual term shows that the term is necessary in the light of momentous operational or company interests [zwaarwegende dienst- of bedrijfsbelangen].

(3) With regard to a contractual term referred to in paragraph (1) and (2), the court may

(a) nullify the contractual term referred to in paragraph (2) is not necessary in the light of momentous operational or company interests; or

(b). nullify the contractual term entirely or partially, if, in view of the interest of the employer which is to be protected, the employee is unfairly disadvantaged.

(4) The employer may not derive any rights from a contractual term as referred to in paragraphs (1) or (2), if the termination or non-continuation of the employment contract is the result of a serious imputable act or omission on the part of the employer.

(5) Where a contractual term as referred to in paragraph (1) or (2) seriously impedes the employee's ability to work otherwise than in service of the employer, the court may at all times order that the employer must pay compensation to the employee for the duration of the limitation. The court sets the amount of this compensation with a view to fairness in the light of the circumstances of the case. No compensation is owed where the termination or non-continuation of the employment contract is the result of a serious imputable act or omission on the part of the employee.

Division 6. Some special obligations of the employer

[Article 7:654 and 7:655 are omitted.]

Article 7:656. (1) At the end of the employment contract, the employer is obliged to provide a job reference to the employee on his request.

(2) The job reference contains the following information:

(a) the kind of work performed by the employee and the daily or weekly working hours;

(b) the commencing date and the ending date of the employment;
(c) an indication of the way in which the employee has fulfilled his obligations;
(d) an indication of the way in which the employment contract has ended;
(e) in case the employer has terminated the employment contract, the reason for this.
(3) The information referred to in paragraph (2) (c), (d), and (e) are only included in the job reference on request by the employee.
(4) Where the employee has terminated the employment contract and has thereby become liable for damages to the employer, the employer has the right to mention this in the job reference.
(5) The employer who fails to provide the requested job reference, does not comply with a request as referred to in paragraph (3), deliberately or negligently includes false information in the job reference, or who marks the testimonial or drafts it in a specific way so as to make any statement which is not contained in the wording of the job reference is liable, both to the employee and to third parties, for the damage caused thereby.
(6) This article may not be derogated from to the detriment of the employee.

[The remainder of Title 10 and Title 11 are omitted.]

Title 12. Construction agreement

[Division 1 is omitted.]

Division 2. Special provisions for the construction of a dwelling on behalf of a natural person who does not act in the exercise of a profession or business

Article 7:765. This Division applies to construction agreements that relate to the construction of a dwelling, consisting of an immovable thing or a part thereof, on behalf of a natural person who does not act in the exercise of a profession or business.

Article 7:766. (1) An agreement as referred to in Article 765 is concluded in writing.
(2) The deed drawn up between parties, or a copy thereof, must be handed over to the principal, in exchange for a signed notice of receipt if this is requested by the constructer. During the three days following the handing-over of the deed, the principal has the right to rescind the construction agreement. Where, within six months after the principal has made use of this right, a new construction agreement is concluded between the same parties with regard to the same dwelling to be constructed, this right does not arise again.
(3) Paragraphs (1) and (2) do not apply where the construction agreement relates to the construction of a dwelling on land which the principal already owns and the construction agreement in not connected to the purchase of this land.

[The remainder Title 12 is omitted. Title 13 is not yet in force.]

Title 14. Suretyship

Division 1. General provisions

Article 7:850. (1) A surety agreement is a contract under which one party, the surety, obliges himself towards the other party, the creditor, to perform an obligation which a third party, the main debtor, has or will incur towards the creditor.
(2) For the validity of a surety agreement, it is not required that the main creditor is aware of the suretyship.
(3) The statutory provisions regarding joint and several obligations apply to suretyship for as far as this Title does not derogate from them.

[The remainder of Division 1 is omitted.]

Division 2. Suretyship accepted outside the course of a profession or business

[Articles 7:857 and 7:858 are omitted.]

Article 7:859. (1) Against the surety, suretyship is only proven by means of a written document signed by him.
(2) Suretyship may be proven by any means if it is established that the surety has fulfilled the obligation of the main debtor wholly or in part.
(3) The provisions of paragraphs (1) and (2) also apply to the proof of a contract which obliges a person to enter into a surety agreement.

[The remainder of the Civil Code is omitted.]

United Kingdom

Unfair Contract Terms Act

Unfair Contract Terms Act 1977 [An Act to impose further limits on the extent to which under the law of England and Wales and Northern Ireland civil liability for breach of contract, of for negligence or other breach of duty, can be avoided by means of contract terms and otherwise, and under the law of Scotland civil liability can be avoided by means of contract terms] (c. 50), as last amended by the Consumer Rights Act 2015 (c. 15).

Part I. Amendment of Law for England and Wales and Northern Ireland

Introductory

Section 1. (1) For the purposes of this Part of this Act, "negligence" means the breach—
(a) of any obligation, arising from the express or implied terms of a contract, to take reasonable care or exercise reasonable skill in the performance of the contract;
(b) of any common law duty to take reasonable care or exercise reasonable skill (but not any stricter duty);
(c) of the common duty of care imposed by the Occupiers' Liability Act 1957 or the Occupiers' Liability Act (Northern Ireland) 1957.
(2) This Part of this Act is subject to Part 111; and in relation to contracts, the operation of sections 2, 3 and 7 is subject to the exceptions made by Schedule 1.
(3) In the case of both contract and tort, sections 2 to 7 apply (except where the contrary is stated in section 6(4)) only to business liability, that is liability for breach of obligations or duties arising—
(a) from things done or to be done by a person in the course of a business (whether his own business or another's); or
(b) from the occupation of premises used for business purposes of the occupier;
and references to liability are to be read accordingly but liability of an occupier of premises for breach of an obligation or duty towards a person obtaining access to the premises for recreational or educational purposes, being liability for loss or damage suffered by reason of the dangerous state of the premises, is not a business liability of the occupier unless granting that person such access for the purposes concerned falls within the business purposes of the occupier.
(4) In relation to any breach of duty or obligation, it is immaterial for any purpose of this Part of this Act whether the breach was inadvertent or intentional, or whether liability for it arises directly or vicariously.

Avoidance of liability for negligence, breach of contract, etc.

Section 2. (1) A person cannot by reference to any contract term or to a notice given to persons generally or to particular persons exclude or restrict his liability for death or personal injury resulting from negligence.
(2) In the case of other loss or damage, a person cannot so exclude or restrict his liability for negligence except in so far as the term or notice satisfies the requirement of reasonableness.
(3) Where a contract term or notice purports to exclude or restrict liability for negligence a person's agreement to or awareness of it is not of itself to be taken as indicating his voluntary acceptance of any risk.
(4) This section does not apply to—
(a) a term in a consumer contract, or
(b) a notice to the extent that it is a consumer notice,
(but see the provision made about such contracts and notices in sections 62 and 65 of the Consumer Rights Act 2015).

Section 3. (1) This section applies as between contracting parties where one of them deals... on the other's written standard terms of business.
(2) As against that party, the other cannot by reference to any contract term—
(a) when himself in breach of contract, exclude or restrict any liability of his in respect of the breach; or
(b) claim to be entitled—
(i) to render a contractual performance substantially different from that which was reasonably expected of him, or
(ii) in respect of the whole or any part of his contractual obligation, to render no performance at all, except in so far as (in any of the cases mentioned above in this subsection) the contract term satisfies the requirement of reasonableness.

(3) This section does not apply to a term in a consumer contract (but see the provision made about such contracts in section 62 of the Consumer Rights Act 2015).

Section 4. (Repealed)

Liability arising from sale or supply of goods

Section 5. (Repealed)

Section 6. (1) Liability for breach of the obligations arising from—
(a) section 12 of the Sale of Goods Act 1979(seller's implied undertakings as to title, etc.);
(b) section 8 of the Supply of Goods (Implied Terms) Act 1973 (the corresponding thing in relation to hire-purchase),
cannot be excluded or restricted by reference to any contract term.
(1A) Liability for breach of the obligations arising from—
(a) section 13, 14 or 15 of the 1979 Act (seller's implied undertakings as to conformity of goods with description or sample, or as to their quality or fitness for a particular purpose);
(b) section 9, 10 or 11 of the 1973 Act (the corresponding things in relation to hire purchase),
cannot be excluded or restricted by reference to a contract term except in so far as the term satisfies the requirement of reasonableness.
(2)(Repealed)
(3)(Repealed)
(4) The liabilities referred to in this section are not only the business liabilities defined by section 1(3), but include those arising under any contract of sale of goods or hire-purchase agreement.
(5) This section does not apply to a consumer contract (but see the provision made about such contracts in section 31 of the Consumer Rights Act 2015).

Section 7. (1) Where the possession or ownership of goods passes under or in pursuance of a contract not governed by the law of sale of goods or hire-purchase, subsections (2) to (4) below apply as regards the effect (if any) to be given to contract terms excluding or restricting liability for breach of obligation arising by implication of law from the nature of the contract.
(1A) Liability in respect of the goods' correspondence with description or sample, or their quality or fitness for any particular purpose, cannot be excluded or restricted by reference to such a term except in so far as the term satisfies the requirement of reasonableness.
(2)(Repealed)
(3)(Repealed)
(3A) Liability for breach of the obligations arising under section 2 of the Supply of Goods and Services Act 1982 (implied terms about title etc. in certain contracts for the transfer of the property in goods) cannot be excluded or restricted by reference to any such term.
(4) Liability in respect of—
(a) the right to transfer ownership of the goods, or give possession; or
(b) the assurance of quiet possession to a person taking goods in pursuance of the contract,
cannot (in a case to which subsection (3A) above does not apply), be excluded or restricted by reference to any such term except in so far as the term satisfies the requirement of reasonableness.
(4A) This section does not apply to a consumer contract (but see the provision made about such contracts in section 31 of the Consumer Rights Act 2015).
(5)(Repealed)

Section 8. (1) In the Misrepresentation Act 1967, the following is substituted for section 3—

"3 Avoidance of provision excluding liability for misrepresentation.
If a contract contains a term which would exclude or restrict—
(a) any liability to which a party to a contract may be subject by reason of any misrepresentation made by him before the contract was made; or
(b) any remedy available to another party to the contract by reason of such a misrepresentation,
that term shall be of no effect except in so far as it satisfies the requirement of reasonableness as stated in section 11(1) of the Unfair Contract Terms Act 1977; and it is for those claiming that the term satisfies that requirement to show that it does.".
(2) The same section is substituted for section 3 of the Misrepresentation Act (Northern Ireland) 1967.

Section 9. (Repealed)

Section 10. A person is not bound by any contract term prejudicing or taking away rights of his which arise under, or in connection with the performance of, another contract, so far as those rights extend to the enforcement of another's liability which this Part of this Act prevents that other from excluding or restricting.

Explanatory provisions

Section 11. (1) In relation to a contract term, the requirement of reasonableness for the purposes of this Part of this Act, section 3 of the Misrepresentation Act 1967 and section 3 of the Misrepresentation Act (Northern Ireland) 1967 is that the term shall have been a fair and reasonable one to be included having regard to the circumstances which were, or ought reasonably to have been, known to or in the contemplation of the parties when the contract was made.
(2) In determining for the purposes of section 6 or 7 above whether a contract term satisfies the requirement of reasonableness, regard shall be had in particular to the matters specified in Schedule 2 to this Act; but this subsection does not prevent the court or arbitrator from holding, in accordance with any rule of law, that a term which purports to exclude or restrict any relevant liability is not a term of the contract.
(3) In relation to a notice (not being a notice having contractual effect), the requirement of reasonableness under this Act is that it should be fair and reasonable to allow reliance on it, having regard to all the circumstances obtaining when the liability arose or (but for the notice) would have arisen.
(4) Where by reference to a contract term or notice a person seeks to restrict liability to a specified sum of money, and the question arises (under this or any other Act) whether the term or notice satisfies the requirement of reasonableness, regard shall be had in particular (but without prejudice to subsection (2) above in the case of contract terms) to—
(a) the resources which he could expect to be available to him for the purpose of meeting the liability should it arise; and
(b) how far it was open to him to cover himself by insurance.
(5) It is for those claiming that a contract term or notice satisfies the requirement of reasonableness to show that it does.

Section 12. (Repealed)

Section 13. (1) To the extent that this Part of this Act prevents the exclusion or restriction of any liability it also prevents—
(a) making the liability or its enforcement subject to restrictive or onerous conditions;
(b) excluding or restricting any right or remedy in respect of the liability, or subjecting a person to any prejudice in consequence of his pursuing any such right or remedy;
(c) excluding or restricting rules of evidence or procedure;
and (to that extent) sections 2, 6 and 7 also prevent excluding or restricting liability by reference to terms and notices which exclude or restrict the relevant obligation or duty.
(2) But an agreement in writing to submit present or future differences to arbitration is not to be treated under this Part of this Act as excluding or restricting any liability.

Section 14. In this Part of this Act—
"business" includes a profession and the activities of any government department or local or public authority;
"consumer contract" has the same meaning as in the Consumer Rights Act 2015 (see section 61);
"consumer notice" has the same meaning as in the Consumer Rights Act 2015 (see section 61);
"goods" has the same meaning as in the Sale of Goods Act 1979;
"hire-purchase agreement" has the same meaning as in the Consumer Credit Act 1974;
"negligence" has the meaning given by section 1(1);
"notice" includes an announcement, whether or not in writing, and any other communication or pretended communication; and
"personal injury" includes any disease and any impairment of physical or mental condition.

Part II. Amendment of Law for Scotland

Section 15. (1) This Part of this Act... is subject to Part III of this Act and does not affect the validity, of any discharge or indemnity given by a person in consideration of the receipt by him of compensation in settlement of any claim which he has.
(2) Subject to subsection (3) below, sections 16 and 17 of this Act apply to any contract only to the extent that the contract—
(a) relates to the transfer of the ownership or possession of goods from one person to another (with or

without work having been done on them);

(b) constitutes a contract of service or apprenticeship;

(c) relates to services of whatever kind, including (without prejudice to the foregoing generality) carriage, deposit and pledge, care and custody, mandate, agency, loan and services relating to the use of land;

(d) relates to the liability of an occupier of land to persons entering upon or using that land;

(e) relates to a grant of any right or permission to enter upon or use land not amounting to an estate or interest in the land.

(3) Notwithstanding anything in subsection (2) above, sections 16 and 17 —

(a) do not apply to any contract to the extent that the contract—

(i) is a contract of insurance (including a contract to pay annuity on human life);

(ii) relates to the formation, constitution or dissolution of any body corporate or unincorporated association or partnership;

(b) apply to—

a contract of marine salvage or towage;

a charter party of a ship or hovercraft;

a contract for the carriage of goods by ship or hovercraft; or,

a contract to which subsection (4) below relates,

only to the extent that—

(i) both parties deal or hold themselves out as dealing in the course of a business (and then only in so far as the contract purports to exclude or restrict liability for breach of duty in respect of death or personal injury); or

(ii)(Repealed)

(4) This subsection relates to a contract in pursuance of which goods are carried by ship or hovercraft and which either—

(a) specifies ship or hovercraft as the means of carriage over part of the journey to be covered; or

(b) makes no provision as to the means of carriage and does not exclude ship or hovercraft as that means,

in so far as the contract operates for and in relation to the carriage of the goods by that means.

Section 16. (1) Subject to subsection (1A) below, Where a term of a contract, or a provision of a notice given to persons generally or to particular persons, purports to exclude or restrict liability for breach of duty arising in the course of any business or from the occupation of any premises used for business purposes of the occupier, that term or provision—

(a) shall be void in any case where such exclusion or restriction is in respect of death or personal injury;

(b) shall, in any other case, have no effect if it was not fair and reasonable to incorporate the term in the contract or, as the case may be, if it is not fair and reasonable to allow reliance on the provision.

(1A) Nothing in paragraph (b) of subsection (1) above shall be taken as implying that a provision of a notice has effect in circumstances where, apart from that paragraph, it would not have effect.

(2) Subsection (1) (*a*) above does not affect the validity of any discharge and indemnity given by a person, on or in connection with an award to him of compensation for pneumoconiosis attributable to employment in the coal industry, in respect of any further claim arising from his contracting that disease.

(3) Where under subsection (1) above a term of a contract or a provision of a notice is void or has no effect, the fact that a person agreed to, or was aware of, the term or provision shall not of itself be sufficient evidence that he knowingly and voluntarily assumed any risk.

(4) This section does not apply to—

(a) a term in a consumer contract, or

(b) a notice to the extent that it is a consumer notice,

(but see the provision made about such contracts and notices in sections 62 and 65 of the Consumer Rights Act 2015).

Section 17. (1) Any term of a contract which is... a standard form contract shall have no effect for the purpose of enabling a party to the contract—

(a) who is in breach of a contractual obligation, to exclude or restrict any liability of his to the... customer in respect of the breach;

(b) in respect of a contractual obligation, to render no performance, or to render a performance substantially different from that which the... customer reasonably expected from the contract;

if it was not fair and reasonable to incorporate the term in the contract.

(2) In this section "customer" means a party to a standard form contract who deals on the basis of

written standard terms of business of the other party to the contract who himself deals in the course of a business.

(3) This section does not apply to a term in a consumer contract (but see the provision made about such contracts in section 62 of the Consumer Rights Act 2015).

Section 18. (Repealed)

Section 19. (Repealed)

Section 20. (1) Any term of a contract which purports to exclude or restrict liability for breach of the obligations arising from—
(a) section 12 of the Sale of Goods Act 1979 (seller's implied undertakings as to title etc.);
(b) section 8 of the Supply of Goods (Implied Terms) Act 1973 (implied terms as to title in hire-purchase agreements),
shall be void.
(1A) Any term of a contract which purports to exclude or restrict liability for breach of the obligations arising from—
(a) section 13, 14 or 15 of the 1979 Act (seller's implied undertakings as to conformity of goods with description or sample, or as to their quality or fitness for a particular purpose);
(b) section 9, 10 or 11 of the 1973 Act (the corresponding things in relation to hire purchase),
shall have effect only if it was fair and reasonable to incorporate the term in the contract.
(1B) This section does not apply to a consumer contract (but see the provision made about such contracts in section 31 of the Consumer Rights Act 2015).
(2)(Repealed)

Section 21. (1) Any term of a contract to which this section applies purporting to exclude or restrict liability for breach of an obligation such as is referred to in subsection (3) below shall have no effect if it was not fair and reasonable to incorporate the term in the contract.
(2) This section applies to any contract to the extent that it relates to any such matter as is referred to in section 15(2) (*a*) of this Act, but does not apply to—
(a) a contract of sale of goods or a hire-purchase agreement; or
(b) a charter party of a ship or hovercraft....
(3) An obligation referred to in this subsection is an obligation incurred under a contract in the course of a business and arising by implication of law from the nature of the contract which relates—
(a) to the correspondence of goods with description or sample, or to the quality or fitness of goods for any particular purpose; or
(b) to any right to transfer ownership or possession of goods, or to the enjoyment of quiet possession of goods.
(3A) Notwithstanding anything in the foregoing provisions of this section, any term of a contract which purports to exclude or restrict liability for breach of the obligations arising under section 11B of the Supply of Goods and Services Act 1982 (implied terms about title, freedom from encumbrances and quiet possession in certain contracts for the transfer of property in goods) shall be void.
(3B) This section does not apply to a consumer contract (but see the provision made about such contracts in section 31 of the Consumer Rights Act 2015).
(4)(Repealed)

Section 22. (Repealed)

Section 23. Any term of any contract shall be void which purports to exclude or restrict, or has the effect of excluding or restricting—
(a) the exercise, by a party to any other contract, of any right or remedy which arises in respect of that other contract in consequence of breach of duty, or of obligation, liability for which could not by virtue of the provisions of this Part of this Act be excluded or restricted by a term of that other contract;
(b) the application of the provisions of this Part of this Act in respect of that or any other contract.

Section 24. (1) In determining for the purposes of this Part of this Act whether it was fair and reasonable to incorporate a term in a contract, regard shall be had only to the circumstances which were, or ought reasonably to have been, known to or in the contemplation of the parties to the contract at the time the contract was made.
(2) In determining for the purposes of section 20 or 21 of this Act whether it was fair and reasonable to incorporate a term in a contract, regard shall be had in particular to the matters specified in

Schedule 2 to this Act; but this subsection shall not prevent a court or arbiter from holding, in accordance with any rule of law, that a term which purports to exclude or restrict any relevant liability is not a term of the contract.

(2A) In determining for the purposes of this Part of this Act whether it is fair and reasonable to allow reliance on a provision of a notice (not being a notice having contractual effect), regard shall be had to all the circumstances obtaining when the liability arose or (but for the provision) would have arisen.

(3) Where a term in a contract or a provision of a notice purports to restrict liability to a specified sum of money, and the question arises for the purposes of this Part of this Act whether it was fair and reasonable to incorporate the term in the contract or whether it is fair and reasonable to allow reliance on the provision, then, without prejudice to subsection (2) above in the case of a term in a contract, regard shall be had in particular to—

(a) the resources which the party seeking to rely on that term or provision could expect to be available to him for the purpose of meeting the liability should it arise;

(b) how far it was open to that party to cover himself by insurance.

(4) The onus of proving that it was fair and reasonable to incorporate a term in a contract or that it is fair and reasonable to allow reliance on a provision of a notice shall lie on the party so contending.

Section 25. (1) In this Part of this Act—

"breach of duty" means the breach —

(a) of any obligation, arising from the express or implied terms of a contract, to take reasonable care or exercise reasonable skill in the performance of the contract;

(b) of any common law duty to take reasonable care or exercise reasonable skill;

(c) of the duty of reasonable care imposed by section 2(1) of the Occupiers' Liability (Scotland) Act 1960; "business" includes a profession and the activities of any government department or local or public authority;

"consumer contract" has the same meaning as in the Consumer Rights Act 2015 (see section 61);

"consumer notice "has the same meaning as in the Consumer Rights Act 2015 (see section 61);

"goods" has the same meaning as in the Sale of Goods Act 1979;

"hire-purchase agreement" has the same meaning as in section 189(1) of the Consumer Credit Act 1974; "notice "includes an announcement, whether or not in writing, and any other communication or pretended communication

"personal injury" includes any disease and any impairment of physical or mental condition.

(1A)(Repealed)

(1B)(Repealed)

(2) In relation to any breach of duty or obligation, it is immaterial for any purpose of this Part of this Act whether the act or omission giving rise to that breach was inadvertent or intentional, or whether liability for it arises directly or vicariously.

(3) In this Part of this Act, any reference to excluding or restricting any liability includes—

(a) making the liability or its enforcement subject to any restrictive or onerous conditions;

(b) excluding or restricting any right or remedy in respect of the liability, or subjecting a person to any prejudice in

consequence of his pursuing any such right or remedy;

(c) excluding or restricting any rule of evidence or procedure;

(d)(Repealed)

but does not include an agreement to submit any question to arbitration.

(4)(Repealed)

(5) In sections 15, 16, 20 and 21 of this Act, any reference to excluding or restricting liability for breach of an obligation or duty shall include a reference to excluding or restricting the obligation or duty itself.

Part III. Provisions Applying to Whole of United Kingdom

Miscellaneous

Section 26. (1) The limits imposed by this Act on the extent to which a person may exclude or restrict liability by reference to a contract term do not apply to liability arising under such a contract as is described in subsection (3) below.

(2) The terms of such a contract are not subject to any requirement of reasonableness under section 3...: and nothing in Part 11 of this Act shall require the incorporation of the terms of such a contract to be fair and reasonable for them to have effect.

(3) Subject to subsection (4), that description of contract is one whose characteristics are the following—

(a) either it is a contract of sale of goods or it is one under or in pursuance of which the possession or ownership of goods passes; and

(b) it is made by parties whose places of business (or, if they have none, habitual residences) are in the territories of different States (the Channel Islands and the Isle of Man being treated for this purpose as different States from the United Kingdom).

(4) A contract falls within subsection (3) above only if either—

(a) the goods in question are, at the time of the conclusion of the contract, in the course of carriage, or will be carried, from the territory of one State to the territory of another; or

(b) the acts constituting the offer and acceptance have been done in the territories of different States; or

(c) the contract provides for the goods to be delivered to the territory of a State other than that within whose territory those acts were done.

Section 27. (1) Where the law applicable to a contract is the law of any part of the United Kingdom only by choice of the parties (and apart from that choice would be the law of some country outside the United Kingdom) sections 2
to 7 and 16 to 21 of this Act do not operate as part of the law applicable to the contract.

(2) This Act has effect notwithstanding any contract term which applies or purports to apply the law of some country outside the United Kingdom, where...—

(a) the term appears to the court, or arbitrator or arbiter to have been imposed wholly or mainly for the purpose of enabling the party imposing it to evade the operation of this Act;...

(b)(Repealed)

(3)(Repealed)

Section 28. (Repealed)

Section 29. (1) Nothing in this Act removes or restricts the effect of, or prevents reliance upon, any contractual provision which—

(a) is authorised or required by the express terms or necessary implication of an enactment; or

(b) being made with a view to compliance with an international agreement to which the United Kingdom is a party, does not operate more restrictively than is contemplated by the agreement.

(2) A contract term is to be taken—

(a) for the purposes of Part I of this Act, as satisfying the requirement of reasonableness; and

(b) for those of Part 11, to have been fair and reasonable to incorporate,

if it is incorporated or approved by, or incorporated pursuant to a decision or ruling of, a competent authority acting in the exercise of any statutory jurisdiction or function and is not a term in a contract to which the competent authority is itself a party.

(3) In this section-

"competent authority" means any court, arbitrator or arbiter, government department or public authority; "enactment" means any legislation (including subordinate legislation) of the United Kingdom or Northern Ireland and any instrument having effect by virtue of such legislation; and "statutory" means conferred by an enactment.

Section 30. (Repealed)

General

Section 31. (1) This Act comes into force on 1st February 1978.

(2) Nothing in this Act applies to contracts made before the date on which it comes into force; but subject to this, it applies to liability for any loss or damage which is suffered on or after that date.

(3) The enactments specified in Schedule 3 to this Act are amended as there shown.

(4) The enactments specified in Schedule 4 to this Act are repealed to the extent specified in column 3 of that Schedule.

Section 32. (1) This Act may be cited as the Unfair Contract Terms Act 1977.

(2) Part I of this Act extends to England and Wales and to Northern Ireland; but it does not extend to Scotland.

(3) Part II of this Act extends to Scotland only.

(4) This Part of this Act extends to the whole of the United Kingdom.

Sale of Goods Act

Sale of Goods Act 1979 [An Act to consolidate the law relating to the sale of goods] (c. 54), as last amended by the Consumer Rights Act 2015 (c. 15).

Part I. Contracts to which Act Applies

Section 1. (1) This Act applies to contracts of sale of goods made on or after (but not to those made before) 1 January 1894.

(2) In relation to contracts made on certain dates, this Act applies subject to the modification of certain of its sections as mentioned in Schedule 1 below.

(3) Any such modification is indicated in the section concerned by a reference to Schedule 1 below.

(4) Accordingly, where a section does not contain such a reference, this Act applies in relation to the contract concerned without such modification of the section.

(5) Certain sections or subsections of this Act do not apply to a contract to which Chapter 2 of Part 1 of the Consumer Rights Act 2015 applies.

(6) Where that is the case it is indicated in the section concerned.

Part II. Formation of contract

Contract of sale

Section 2. (1) A contract of sale of goods is a contract by which the seller transfers or agrees to transfer the property in goods to the buyer for a money consideration, called the price.

(2) There may be a contract of sale between one part owner and another.

(3) A contract of sale may be absolute or conditional.

(4) Where under a contract of sale the property in the goods is transferred from the seller to the buyer the contract is called a sale.

(5) Where under a contract of sale the transfer of the property in the goods is to take place at a future time or subject to some condition later to be fulfilled the contract is called an agreement to sell.

(6) An agreement to sell becomes a sale when the time elapses or the conditions are fulfilled subject to which the property in the goods is to be transferred.

Section 3. (1) Capacity to buy and sell is regulated by the general law concerning capacity to contract and to transfer and acquire property.

(2) Where necessaries are sold and delivered to a minor or to a person who by reason of mental incapacity or drunkenness is incompetent to contract, he must pay a reasonable price for them.

(3) In subsection (2) above "necessaries" means goods suitable to the condition in life of the minor or other person concerned and to his actual requirements at the time of the sale and delivery.

Formalities of contract

Section 4. (1) Subject to this and any other Act, a contract of sale may be made in writing (either with or without seal), or by word of mouth, or partly in writing and partly by word of mouth, or may be implied from the conduct of the parties.

(2) Nothing in this section affects the law relating to corporations.

Subject matter of contract

Section 5. (1) The goods which form the subject of a contract of sale may be either existing goods, owned or possessed by the seller, or goods to be manufactured or acquired by him after the making of the contract of sale, in this Act called future goods.

(2) There may be a contract for the sale of goods the acquisition of which by the seller depends on a contingency which may or may not happen.

(3) Where by a contract of sale the seller purports to effect a present sale of future goods, the contract operates as an agreement to sell the goods.

Section 6. Where there is a contract for the sale of specific goods, and the goods without the knowledge of the seller have perished at the time when the contract is made, the contract is void.

Section 7. Where there is an agreement to sell specific goods and subsequently the goods, without any fault on the part of the seller or buyer, perish before the risk passes to the buyer, the agreement is avoided.

The price

Section 8. (1) The price in a contract of sale may be fixed by the contract, or may be left to be fixed in a manner agreed by the contract, or may be determined by the course of dealing between the parties.
(2) Where the price is not determined as mentioned in sub-section (1) above the buyer must pay a reasonable price.
(3) What is a reasonable price is a question of fact dependent on the circumstances of each particular case.

Section 9. (1) Where there is an agreement to sell goods on the terms that the price is to be fixed by the valuation of a third party, and he cannot or does not make the valuation, the agreement is avoided; but if the goods or any part of them have been delivered to and appropriated by the buyer he must pay a reasonable price for them.
(2) Where the third party is prevented from making the valuation by the fault of the seller or buyer, the party not at fault may maintain an action for damages against the party at fault.

Implied terms etc.

Section 10. (1) Unless a different intention appears from the terms of the contract, stipulations as to time of payment are not of the essence of a contract of sale.
(2) Whether any other stipulation as to time is or is not of the essence of the contract depends on the terms of the contract.
(3) In a contract of sale "month" prima facie means calendar month.

Section 11. (1) This section does not apply to Scotland.
(2) Where a contract of sale is subject to a condition to be fulfilled by the seller, the buyer may waive the condition, or may elect to treat the breach of the condition as a breach of warranty and not as a ground for treating the contract as repudiated.
(3) Whether a stipulation in a contract of sale is a condition, the breach of which may give rise to a right to treat the contract as repudiated, or a warranty, the breach of which may give rise to a claim for damages but not to a right to reject the goods and treat the contract as repudiated, depends in each case on the construction of the contract; and a stipulation may be a condition, though called a warranty in the contract.
(4) Subject to section 35A below Where a contract of sale is not severable and the buyer has accepted the goods or part of them, the breach of a condition to be fulfilled by the seller can only be treated as a breach of warranty, and not as a ground for rejecting the goods and treating the contract as repudiated, unless there is an express or implied term of the contract to that effect.
(4A) Subsection (4) does not apply to a contract to which Chapter 2 of Part 1 of the Consumer Rights Act 2015 applies (but see the provision made about such contracts in sections 19 to 22 of that Act).
(5)(Repealed)
(6) Nothing in this section affects a condition or warranty whose fulfilment is excused by law by reason of impossibility or otherwise.
(7) Paragraph (2) of Schedule 1 below applies in relation to a contract made before 22 April 1967 or (in the application of this Act to Northern Ireland) 28 July 1967.

Section 12. (1) In a contract of sale, other than one to which subsection (3) below applies, there is an implied term on the part of the seller that in the case of a sale he has a right to sell the goods, and in the case of an agreement to sell he will have such a right at the time when the property is to pass.
(2) In a contract of sale, other than one to which subsection (3) below applies, there is also an implied term that—
(a) the goods are free, and will remain free until the time when the property is to pass, from any charge or encumbrance not disclosed or known to the buyer before the contract is made, and
(b) the buyer will enjoy quiet possession of the goods except so far as it may be disturbed by the owner or other person entitled to the benefit of any charge or encumbrance so disclosed or known.
(3) This subsection applies to a contract of sale in the case of which there appears from the contract or is to be inferred from its circumstances an intention that the seller should transfer only such title as he or a third person may have.
(4) In a contract to which subsection (3) above applies there is an implied term that all charges or encumbrances known to the seller and not known to the buyer have been disclosed to the buyer before the contract is made.
(5) In a contract to which subsection (3) above applies there is also an implied term that none of the

following will disturb the buyer's quiet possession of the goods, namely—
(a) the seller;
(b) in a case where the parties to the contract intend that the seller should transfer only such title as a third person may have, that person;
(c) anyone claiming through or under the seller or that third person otherwise than under a charge or encumbrance disclosed or known to the buyer before the contract is made.
(5A) As regards England and Wales and Northern Ireland, the term implied by subsection (1) above is a condition and the terms implied by subsections (2), (4) and (5) above are warranties.
(6) Paragraph (3) of Schedule 1 below applies in relation to a contract made before 18 May 1973.
(7) This section does not apply to a contract to which Chapter 2 of Part 1 of the Consumer Rights Act 2015 applies (but see the provision made about such contracts in section 17 of that Act).

Section 13. (1) Where there is a contract for the sale of goods by description, there is an implied term that the goods will correspond with the description.
(1A) As regards England and Wales and Northern Ireland, the term implied by subsection (1) above is a condition.
(2) If the sale is by sample as well as by description it is not sufficient that the bulk of the goods corresponds with the sample if the goods do not also correspond with the description.
(3) A sale of goods is not prevented from being a sale by description by reason only that, being exposed for sale or hire, they are selected by the buyer.
(4) Paragraph (4) of Schedule 1 below applies in relation to a contract made before 18 May 1973.
(5) This section does not apply to a contract to which Chapter 2 of Part 1 of the Consumer Rights Act 2015 applies (but see the provision made about such contracts in section 11 of that Act).

Section 14. (1) Except as provided by this section and section 15 below and subject to any other enactment, there is no implied term about the quality or fitness for any particular purpose of goods supplied under a contract of sale.
(2) Where the seller sells goods in the course of a business, there is an implied term that the goods supplied under the contract are of satisfactory quality.
(2A) For the purposes of this Act, goods are of satisfactory quality if they meet the standard that a reasonable person would regard as satisfactory, taking account of any description of the goods, the price (if relevant) and all the other relevant circumstances.
(2B) For the purposes of this Act, the quality of goods includes their state and condition and the following (among others) are in appropriate cases aspects of the quality of goods—
(a) fitness for all the purposes for which goods of the kind in question are commonly supplied,
(b) appearance and finish,
(c) freedom from minor defects,
(d) safety, and
(e) durability.
(2C) The term implied by subsection (2) above does not extend to any matter making the quality of goods unsatisfactory—
(a) which is specifically drawn to the buyer's attention before the contract is made,
(b) where the buyer examines the goods before the contract is made, which that examination ought to reveal, or
(c) in the case of a contract for sale by sample, which would have been apparent on a reasonable examination of the sample.
(2D)(Repealed)
(2E)(Repealed)
(2F)(Repealed)
(3) Where the seller sells goods in the course of a business and the buyer, expressly or by implication, makes known—
(a) to the seller, or
(b) where the purchase price or part of it is payable by instalments and the goods were previously sold by a credit-broker to the seller, to that credit-broker, any particular purpose for which the goods are being bought, there is an implied term that the goods supplied under the contract are reasonably fit for that purpose, whether or not that is a purpose for which such goods are commonly supplied, except where the circumstances show that the buyer does not rely, or that it is unreasonable for him to rely, on the skill or judgment of the seller or credit-broker.
(4) An implied term about quality or fitness for a particular purpose may be annexed to a contract of sale by usage.
(5) The preceding provisions of this section apply to a sale by a person who in the course of a

business is acting as agent for another as they apply to a sale by a principal in the course of a business, except where that other is not selling in the course of a business and either the buyer knows that fact or reasonable steps are taken to bring it to the notice of the buyer before the contract is made.

(6) As regards England and Wales and Northern Ireland, the terms implied by subsections (2) and (3) above are conditions.

(7) Paragraph (5) of Schedule 1 below applies in relation to a contract made on or after 18 May 1973 and before the appointed day, and paragraph (6) in relation to one made before 18 May 1973.

(8) In subsection (7) above and paragraph (5) of Schedule 1 below references to the appointed day are to the day appointed for the purposes of those provisions by an order of the Secretary of State made by statutory instrument.

(9) This section does not apply to a contract to which Chapter 2 of Part 1 of the Consumer Rights Act 2015 applies (but see the provision made about such contracts in sections 9, 10 and 18 of that Act).

Sale by sample

Section 15. (1) A contract of sale is a contract for sale by sample where there is an express or implied term to that effect in the contract.

(2) In the case of a contract for sale by sample there is an implied term—

(a) that the bulk will correspond with the sample in quality;

(b)(Repealed)

(c) that the goods will be free from any defect, making their quality unsatisfactory, which would not be apparent on reasonable examination of the sample.

(3) As regards England and Wales and Northern Ireland, the term implied by subsection (2) above is a condition.

(4) Paragraph (7) of Schedule 1 below applies in relation to a contract made before 18 May 1973.

(5) This section does not apply to a contract to which Chapter 2 of Part 1 of the Consumer Rights Act 2015 applies (but see the provision made about such contracts in sections 13 and 18 of that Act).

Miscellaneous

Section 15A. (1) Where in the case of a contract of sale—

(a) the buyer would, apart from this subsection, have the right to reject goods by reason of a breach on the part of the seller of a term implied by section 13, 14 or 15 above, but

(b) the breach is so slight that it would be unreasonable for him to reject them,

... the breach is not to be treated as a breach of condition but may be treated as a breach of warranty.

(2) This section applies unless a contrary intention appears in, or is to be implied from, the contract.

(3) It is for the seller to show that a breach fell within subsection (1) (b) above.

(4) This section does not apply to Scotland.

Section 15B. (1) Where in a contract of sale the seller is in breach of any term of the contract (express or implied), the buyer shall be entitled—

(a) to claim damages, and

(b) if the breach is material, to reject any goods delivered under the contract and treat it as repudiated.

(1A) Subsection (1) does not apply to a contract to which Chapter 2 of Part 1 of the Consumer Rights Act 2015 applies (but see the provision made about such contracts in sections 19 to 22 of that Act).

(2)(Repealed)

(3) This section applies to Scotland only.

Part III. Effects of the Contract

Transfer of property as between seller and buyer

Section 16. Subject to section 20A below Where there is a contract for the sale of unascertained goods no property in the goods is transferred to the buyer unless and until the goods are ascertained.

Section 17. (1) Where there is a contract for the sale of specific or ascertained goods the property in them is transferred to the buyer at such time as the parties to the contract intend it to be transferred.

(2) For the purpose of ascertaining the intention of the parties regard shall be had to the terms of the contract, the conduct of the parties and the circumstances of the case.

Section 18. Unless a different intention appears, the following are rules for ascertaining the intention of the parties as to the time at which the property in the goods is to pass to the buyer.

Rule 1.—Where there is an unconditional contract for the sale of specific goods in a deliverable state the property in the goods passes to the buyer when the contract is made, and it is immaterial whether the time of payment or the time of delivery, or both, be postponed.

Rule 2.—Where there is a contract for the sale of specific goods and the seller is bound to do something to the goods for the purpose of putting them into a deliverable state, the property does not pass until the thing is done and the buyer has notice that it has been done.

Rule 3.—Where there is a contract for the sale of specific goods in a deliverable state but the seller is bound to weigh, measure, test, or do some other act or thing with reference to the goods for the purpose of ascertaining the price, the property does not pass until the act or thing is done and the buyer has notice that it has been done.

Rule 4.—When goods are delivered to the buyer on approval or on sale or return or other similar terms the property in the goods passes to the buyer:—

(a) when he signifies his approval or acceptance to the seller or does any other act adopting the transaction;

(b) if he does not signify his approval or acceptance to the seller but retains the goods without giving notice of rejection, then, if a time has been fixed for the return of the goods, on the expiration of that time, and, if no time has been fixed, on the expiration of a reasonable time.

Rule 5.(1) Where there is a contract for the sale of unascertained or future goods by description, and goods of that description and in a deliverable state are unconditionally appropriated to the contract, either by the seller with the assent of the buyer or by the buyer with the assent of the seller, the property in the goods then passes to the buyer; and the assent may be express or implied, and may be given either before or after the appropriation is made.

(2) Where, in pursuance of the contract, the seller delivers the goods to the buyer or to a carrier or other bailee or custodier (whether named by the buyer or not) for the purpose of transmission to the buyer, and does not reserve the right of disposal, he is to be taken to have unconditionally appropriated the goods to the contract.

(3) Where there is a contract for the sale of a specified quantity of unascertained goods in a deliverable state forming part of a bulk which is identified either in the contract or by subsequent agreement between the parties and the bulk is reduced to (or to less than) that quantity, then, if the buyer under that contract is the only buyer to whom goods are then due out of the bulk—

(a) the remaining goods are to be taken as appropriated to that contract at the time when the bulk is so reduced; and

(b) the property in those goods then passes to that buyer.

(4) Paragraph (3) above applies also (with the necessary modifications) where a bulk is reduced to (or to less than) the aggregate of the quantities due to a single buyer under separate contracts relating to that bulk and he is the only buyer to whom goods are then due out of that bulk.

Section 19. (1) Where there is a contract for the sale of specific goods or where goods are subsequently appropriated to the contract, the seller may, by the terms of the contract or appropriation, reserve the right of disposal of the goods until certain conditions are fulfilled; and in such a case, notwithstanding the delivery of the goods to the buyer, or to a carrier or other bailee or custodier for the purpose of transmission to the buyer, the property in the goods does not pass to the buyer until the conditions imposed by the seller are fulfilled.

(2) Where goods are shipped, and by the bill of lading the goods are deliverable to the order of the seller or his agent, the seller is prima facie to be taken to reserve the right of disposal.

(3) Where the seller of goods draws on the buyer for the price, and transmits the bill of exchange and bill of lading to the buyer together to secure acceptance or payment of the bill of exchange, the buyer is bound to return the bill of lading if he does not honour the bill of exchange, and if he wrongfully retains the bill of lading the property in the goods does not pass to him.

Section 20. (1) Unless otherwise agreed, the goods remain at the seller's risk until the property in them is transferred to the buyer, but when the property in them is transferred to the buyer the goods are at the buyer's risk whether delivery has been made or not.

(2) But where delivery has been delayed through the fault of either buyer or seller the goods are at the risk of the party at fault as regards any loss which might not have occurred but for such fault.

(3) Nothing in this section affects the duties or liabilities of either seller or buyer as a bailee or custodier of the goods of the other party.

(4) This section does not apply to a contract to which Chapter 2 of Part 1 of the Consumer Rights Act 2015 applies (but see the provision made about such contracts in section 29 of that Act).

Section 20A. (1) This section applies to a contract for the sale of a specified quantity of unascertained goods if the following conditions are met—

(a) the goods or some of them form part of a bulk which is identified either in the contract or by subsequent agreement between the parties; and

(b) the buyer has paid the price for some or all of the goods which are the subject of the contract and which form part of the bulk.

(2) Where this section applies, then (unless the parties agree otherwise), as soon as the conditions specified in paragraphs (a) and (b) of subsection (1) above are met or at such later time as the parties may agree—

(a) property in an undivided share in the bulk is transferred to the buyer, and

(b) the buyer becomes an owner in common of the bulk.

(3) Subject to subsection (4) below, for the purposes of this section, the undivided share of a buyer in a bulk at any time shall be such share as the quantity of goods paid for and due to the buyer out of the bulk bears to the quantity of goods in the bulk at that time.

(4) Where the aggregate of the undivided shares of buyers in a bulk determined under subsection (3) above would at any time exceed the whole of the bulk at that time, the undivided share in the bulk of each buyer shall be reduced proportionately so that the aggregate of the undivided shares is equal to the whole bulk.

(5) Where a buyer has paid the price for only some of the goods due to him out of a bulk, any delivery to the buyer out of the bulk shall, for the purposes of this section, be ascribed in the first place to the goods in respect of which payment has been made.

(6) For the purposes of this section payment of part of the price for any goods shall be treated as payment for a corresponding part of the goods.

Section 20B. (1) A person who has become an owner in common of a bulk by virtue of section 20A above shall be deemed to have consented to—

(a) any delivery of goods out of the bulk to any other owner in common of the bulk, being goods which are due to him under his contract;

(b) any dealing with or removal, delivery or disposal of goods in the bulk by any other person who is an owner in common of the bulk in so far as the goods fall within that co-owner's undivided share in the bulk at the time of the dealing, removal, delivery or disposal.

(2) No cause of action shall accrue to anyone against a person by reason of that person having acted in accordance with paragraph (a) or (b) of subsection (1) above in reliance on any consent deemed to have been given under that subsection.

(3) Nothing in this section or section 20A above shall—

(a) impose an obligation on a buyer of goods out of a bulk to compensate any other buyer of goods out of that bulk for any shortfall in the goods received by that other buyer;

(b) affect any contractual arrangement between buyers of goods out of a bulk for adjustments between themselves; or

(c) affect the rights of any buyer under his contract.

Transfer of title

Section 21. (1) Subject to this Act, where goods are sold by a person who is not their owner, and who does not sell them under the authority or with the consent of the owner, the buyer acquires no better title to the goods than the seller had, unless the owner of the goods is by his conduct precluded from denying the seller's authority to sell.

(2) Nothing in this Act affects—

(a) the provisions of the Factors Acts or any enactment enabling the apparent owner of goods to dispose of them as if he were their true owner;

(b) the validity of any contract of sale under any special common law or statutory power of sale or under the order of a court of competent jurisdiction.

Section 22. (1) (Repealed)

(2) This section does not apply to Scotland.

(3) Paragraph (8) of Schedule 1 below applies in relation to a contract under which goods were sold before 1 January 1968 or (in the application of this Act to Northern Ireland) 29 August 1967.

Section 23. When the seller of goods has a voidable title to them, but his title has not been avoided at the time of the sale, the buyer acquires a good title to the goods, provided he buys them in good faith and without notice of the seller's defect of title.

Section 24. Where a person having sold goods continues or is in possession of the goods, or of the documents of title to the goods, the delivery or transfer by that person, or by a mercantile agent acting for him, of the goods or documents of title under any sale, pledge, or other disposition thereof, to any person receiving the same in good faith and without notice of the previous sale, has the same effect as if the person making the delivery or transfer were expressly authorised by the owner of the goods to make the same.

Section 25. (1) Where a person having bought or agreed to buy goods obtains, with the consent of the seller, possession of the goods or the documents of title to the goods, the delivery or transfer by that person, or by a mercantile agent acting for him, of the goods or documents of title, under any sale, pledge, or other disposition thereof, to any person receiving the same in good faith and without notice of any lien or other right of the original seller in respect of the goods, has the same effect as if the person making the delivery or transfer were a mercantile agent in possession of the goods or documents of title with the consent of the owner.

(2) For the purposes of subsection (1) above—

(a) the buyer under a conditional sale agreement is to be taken not to be a person who has bought or agreed to buy goods, and

(b) "conditional sale agreement" means an agreement for the sale of goods which is a consumer credit agreement within the meaning of the Consumer Credit Act 1974 under which the purchase price or part of it is payable by instalments, and the property in the goods is to remain in the seller (notwithstanding that the buyer is to be in possession of the goods) until such conditions as to the payment of instalments or otherwise as may be specified in the agreement are fulfilled.

(3) Paragraph (9) of Schedule 1 below applies in relation to a contract under which a person buys or agrees to buy goods and which is made before the appointed day.

(4) In subsection (3) above and paragraph (9) of Schedule 1 below references to the appointed day are to the day appointed for the purposes of those provisions by an order of the Secretary of State made by statutory instrument.

Section 26. In sections 24 and 25 above "mercantile agent" means a mercantile agent having in the customary course of his business as such agent authority either—

(a) to sell goods, or

(b) to consign goods for the purpose of sale, or

(c) to buy goods, or

(d) to raise money on the security of goods.

Part IV. Performance of the Contract

Section 27. It is the duty of the seller to deliver the goods, and of the buyer to accept and pay for them, in accordance with the terms of the contract of sale.

Section 28. Unless otherwise agreed, delivery of the goods and payment of the price are concurrent conditions, that is to say, the seller must be ready and willing to give possession of the goods to the buyer in exchange for the price and the buyer must be ready and willing to pay the price in exchange for possession of the goods.

Section 29. (1) Whether it is for the buyer to take possession of the goods or for the seller to send them to the buyer is a question depending in each case on the contract, express or implied, between the parties.

(2) Apart from any such contract, express or implied, the place of delivery is the seller's place of business if he has one, and if not, his residence; except that, if the contract is for the sale of specific goods, which to the knowledge of the parties when the contract is made are in some other place, then that place is the place of delivery.

(3) Where under the contract of sale the seller is bound to send the goods to the buyer, but no time for sending them is fixed, the seller is bound to send them within a reasonable time.

(3A) Subsection (3) does not apply to a contract to which Chapter 2 of Part 1 of the Consumer Rights Act 2015 applies (but see the provision made about such contracts in section 28 of that Act).

(4) Where the goods at the time of sale are in the possession of a third person, there is no delivery by seller to buyer unless and until the third person acknowledges to the buyer that he holds the goods on his behalf; but nothing in this section affects the operation of the issue or transfer of any document of title to goods.

(5) Demand or tender of delivery may be treated as ineffectual unless made at a reasonable hour; and what is a reasonable hour is a question of fact.

(6) Unless otherwise agreed, the expenses of and incidental to putting the goods into a deliverable state must be borne by the seller.

Section 30. (1) Where the seller delivers to the buyer a quantity of goods less than he contracted to sell, the buyer may reject them, but if the buyer accepts the goods so delivered he must pay for them at the contract rate

(2) Where the seller delivers to the buyer a quantity of goods larger than he contracted to sell, the buyer may accept the goods included in the contract and reject the rest, or he may reject the whole.

(2A) A buyer... may not—

(a) where the seller delivers a quantity of goods less than he contracted to sell, reject the goods under subsection (1) above, or

(b) where the seller delivers a quantity of goods larger than he contracted to sell, reject the whole under subsection (2) above, if the shortfall or, as the case may be, excess is so slight that it would be unreasonable for him to do so.

(2B) It is for the seller to show that a shortfall or excess fell within subsection (2A) above.

(2C) Subsections (2A) and (2B) above do not apply to Scotland.

(2D) Where the seller delivers a quantity of goods—

(a) less than he contracted to sell, the buyer shall not be entitled to reject the goods under subsection (1) above,

(b) larger than he contracted to sell, the buyer shall not be entitled to reject the whole under subsection (2) above, unless the shortfall or excess is material.

(2E) Subsection (2D) above applies to Scotland only.

(3) Where the seller delivers to the buyer a quantity of goods larger than he contracted to sell and the buyer accepts the whole of the goods so delivered he must pay for them at the contract rate.

(4)(Repealed)

(5) This section is subject to any usage of trade, special agreement, or course of dealing between the parties.

(6) This section does not apply to a contract to which Chapter 2 of Part 1 of the Consumer Rights Act 2015 applies (but see the provision made about such contracts in section 25 of that Act).

Section 31. (1) Unless otherwise agreed, the buyer of goods is not bound to accept delivery of them by instalments.

(2) Where there is a contract for the sale of goods to be delivered by stated instalments, which are to be separately paid for, and the seller makes defective deliveries in respect of one or more instalments, or the buyer neglects or refuses to take delivery of or pay for one or more instalments, it is a question in each case depending on the terms of the contract and the circumstances of the case whether the breach of contract is a repudiation of the whole contract or whether it is a severable breach giving rise to a claim for compensation but not to a right to treat the whole contract as repudiated.

(3) This section does not apply to a contract to which Chapter 2 of Part 1 of the Consumer Rights Act 2015 applies (but see the provision made about such contracts in section 26 of that Act).

Section 32. (1) Where, in pursuance of a contract of sale, the seller is authorised or required to send the goods to the buyer, delivery of the goods to a carrier (whether named by the buyer or not) for the purpose of transmission to the buyer is prima facie deemed to be a delivery of the goods to the buyer.

(2) Unless otherwise authorised by the buyer, the seller must make such contract with the carrier on behalf of the buyer as may be reasonable having regard to the nature of the goods and the other circumstances of the case; and if the seller omits to do so, and the goods are lost or damaged in course of transit, the buyer may decline to treat the delivery to the carrier as a delivery to himself or may hold the seller responsible in damages.

(3) Unless otherwise agreed, where goods are sent by the seller to the buyer by a route involving sea transit, under circumstances in which it is usual to insure, the seller must give such notice to the buyer as may enable him to insure them during their sea transit; and if the seller fails to do so, the goods are at his risk during such sea transit.

(4) This section does not apply to a contract to which Chapter 2 of Part 1 of the Consumer Rights Act 2015 applies (but see the provision made about such contracts in section 29 of that Act).

Section 33. (1) Where the seller of goods agrees to deliver them at his own risk at a place other than that where they are when sold, the buyer must nevertheless (unless otherwise agreed) take any risk of deterioration in the goods necessarily incident to the course of transit.

(2) This section does not apply to a contract to which Chapter 2 of Part 1 of the Consumer Rights Act 2015 applies (but see the provision made about such contracts in section 29 of that Act).

Section 34. (1)...

Unless otherwise agreed, when the seller tenders delivery of goods to the buyer, he is bound on request to afford the buyer a reasonable opportunity of examining the goods for the purpose of ascertaining whether they are in conformity with the contract and, in the case of a contract for sale by sample, of comparing the bulk with the sample.

(2) Nothing in this section affects the operation of section 22 (time limit for short-term right to reject) of the Consumer Rights Act 2015.

Section 35. (1) The buyer is deemed to have accepted the goods subject to subsection (2) below—
(a) when he intimates to the seller that he has accepted them, or
(b) when the goods have been delivered to him and he does any act in relation to them which is inconsistent with the ownership of the seller.

(2) Where goods are delivered to the buyer, and he has not previously examined them, he is not deemed to have accepted them under subsection (1) above until he has had a reasonable opportunity of examining them for the purpose—
(a) of ascertaining whether they are in conformity with the contract, and
(b) in the case of a contract for sale by sample, of comparing the bulk with the sample.

(3)(Repealed)

(4) The buyer is also deemed to have accepted the goods when after the lapse of a reasonable time he retains the goods without intimating to the seller that he has rejected them.

(5) The questions that are material in determining for the purposes of subsection (4) above whether a reasonable time has elapsed include whether the buyer has had a reasonable opportunity of examining the goods for the purpose mentioned in subsection (2) above.

(6) The buyer is not by virtue of this section deemed to have accepted the goods merely because—
(a) he asks for, or agrees to, their repair by or under an arrangement with the seller, or
(b) the goods are delivered to another under a sub-sale or other disposition.

(7) Where the contract is for the sale of goods making one or more commercial units, a buyer accepting any goods included in a unit is deemed to have accepted all the goods making the unit; and in this subsection " commercial unit " means a unit division of which would materially impair the value of the goods or the character of the unit.

(8) Paragraph (10) of Schedule 1 below applies in relation to a contract made before 22 April 1967 or (in the application of this Act to Northern Ireland) 28 July 1967.

(9) This section does not apply to a contract to which Chapter 2 of Part 1 of the Consumer Rights Act 2015 applies (but see the provision made about such contracts in section 21 of that Act).

Section 35A. (1) If the buyer—
(a) has the right to reject the goods by reason of a breach on the part of the seller that affects some or all of them, but
(b) accepts some of the goods, including, where there are any goods unaffected by the breach, all such goods, he does not by accepting them lose his right to reject the rest.

(2) In the case of a buyer having the right to reject an instalment of goods, subsection (1) above applies as if references to the goods were references to the goods comprised in the instalment.

(3) For the purposes of subsection (1) above, goods are affected by a breach if by reason of the breach they are not in conformity with the contract.

(4) This section applies unless a contrary intention appears in, or is to be implied from, the contract.

(5) This section does not apply to a contract to which Chapter 2 of Part 1 of the Consumer Rights Act 2015 applies (but see the provision made about such contracts in section 21 of that Act).

Section 36. (1) Unless otherwise agreed, where goods are delivered to the buyer, and he refuses to accept them, having the right to do so, he is not bound to return them to the seller, but it is sufficient if he intimates to the seller that he refuses to accept them.

(2) This section does not apply to a contract to which Chapter 2 of Part 1 of the Consumer Rights Act 2015 applies (but see the provision made about such contracts in section 20 of that Act).

Section 37. (1) When the seller is ready and willing to deliver the goods, and requests the buyer to take delivery, and the buyer does not within a reasonable time after such request take delivery of the goods, he is liable to the seller for any loss occasioned by his neglect or refusal to take delivery, and also for a reasonable charge for the care and custody of the goods.

(2) Nothing in this section affects the rights of the seller where the neglect or refusal of the buyer to take delivery amounts to a repudiation of the contract.

Part V. Rights of Unpaid Seller Against the Goods

Preliminary

Section 38. (1) The seller of goods is an unpaid seller within the meaning of this Act—

(a) when the whole of the price has not been paid or tendered;

(b) when a bill of exchange or other negotiable instrument has been received as conditional payment, and the condition on which it was received has not been fulfilled by reason of the dishonour of the instrument or otherwise.

(2) In this Part of this Act "seller" includes any person who is in the position of a seller, as, for instance, an agent of the seller to whom the bill of lading has been indorsed, or a consignor or agent who has himself paid (or is directly responsible for) the price.

Section 39. (1) Subject to this and any other Act, notwithstanding that the property in the goods may have passed to the buyer, the unpaid seller of goods, as such, has by implication of law—

(a) a lien on the goods or right to retain them for the price while he is in possession of them;

(b) in case of the insolvency of the buyer, a right of stopping the goods in transit after he has parted with the possession of them;

(c) a right of re-sale as limited by this Act.

(2) Where the property in goods has not passed to the buyer, the unpaid seller has (in addition to his other remedies) a right of withholding delivery similar to and co-extensive with his rights of lien or retention and stoppage in transit where the property has passed to the buyer.

Section 40. In Scotland a seller of goods may attach them while in his own hands or possession by arrestment or poinding; and such arrestment or poinding shall have the same operation and effect in a competition or otherwise as an arrestment or poinding by a third party.

Unpaid seller's lien

Section 41. (1) Subject to this Act, the unpaid seller of goods who is in possession of them is entitled to retain possession of them until payment or tender of the price in the following cases:—

(a) where the goods have been sold without any stipulation as to credit;

(b) where the goods have been sold on credit but the term of credit has expired;

(c) where the buyer becomes insolvent.

(2) The seller may exercise his lien or right of retention notwithstanding that he is in possession of the goods as agent or bailee or custodier for the buyer.

Section 42. Where an unpaid seller has made part delivery of the goods, he may exercise his lien or right of retention on the remainder, unless such part delivery has been made under such circumstances as to show an agreement to waive the lien or right of retention.

Section 43. (1) The unpaid seller of goods loses his lien or right of retention in respect of them—

(a) when he delivers the goods to a carrier or other bailee or custodier for the purpose of transmission to the buyer without reserving the right of disposal of the goods;

(b) when the buyer or his agent lawfully obtains possession of the goods;

(c) by waiver of the lien or right of retention.

(2) An unpaid seller of goods who has a lien or right of retention in respect of them does not lose his lien or right of retention by reason only that he has obtained judgment or decree for the price of the goods.

Stoppage in transit

Section 44. Subject to this Act, when the buyer of goods becomes insolvent the unpaid seller who has parted with the possession of the goods has the right of stopping them in transit, that is to say, he may resume possession of the goods as long as they are in course of transit, and may retain them until payment or tender of the price.

Section 45. (1) Goods are deemed to be in course of transit from the time when they are delivered to a carrier or other bailee or custodier for the purpose of transmission to the buyer, until the buyer or his agent in that behalf takes delivery of them from the carrier or other bailee or custodier.

(2) If the buyer or his agent in that behalf obtains delivery of the goods before their arrival at the appointed destination, the transit is at an end.

(3) If, after the arrival of the goods at the appointed destination, the carrier or other bailee or custodier acknowledges to the buyer or his agent that he holds the goods on his behalf and continues in possession of them as bailee or custodier for the buyer or his agent, the transit is at an end, and it is immaterial that a further destination for the goods may have been indicated by the buyer.

(4) If the goods are rejected by the buyer, and the carrier or other bailee or custodier continues in possession of them, the transit is not deemed to be at an end, even if the seller has refused to receive them back.

(5) When goods are delivered to a ship chartered by the buyer it is a question depending on the circumstances of the particular case whether they are in the possession of the master as a carrier or as agent to the buyer.

(6) Where the carrier or other bailee or custodier wrongfully refuses to deliver the goods to the buyer or his agent in that behalf, the transit is deemed to be at an end.

(7) Where part delivery of the goods has been made to the buyer or his agent in that behalf, the remainder of the goods may be stopped in transit, unless such part delivery has been made under such circumstances as to show an agreement to give up possession of the whole of the goods.

Section 46. (1) The unpaid seller may exercise his right of stoppage in transit either by taking actual possession of the goods or by giving notice of his claim to the carrier or other bailee or custodier in whose possession the goods are.

(2) The notice may be given either to the person in actual possession of the goods or to his principal.

(3) If given to the principal, the notice is ineffective unless given at such time and under such circumstances that the principal, by the exercise of reasonable diligence, may communicate it to his servant or agent in time to prevent a delivery to the buyer.

(4) When notice of stoppage in transit is given by the seller to the carrier or other bailee or custodier in possession of the goods, he must re-deliver the goods to, or according to the directions of, the seller; and the expenses of the re-delivery must be borne by the seller.

Re-sale etc. by buyer

Section 47. (1) Subject to this Act, the unpaid seller's right of lien or retention or stoppage in transit is not affected by any sale or other disposition of the goods which the buyer may have made, unless the seller has assented to it.

(2) Where a document of title to goods has been lawfully transferred to any person as buyer or owner of the goods, and that person transfers the document to a person who take it in good faith and for valuable consideration, then—

(a) if the last-mentioned transfer was by way of sale the unpaid seller's right of lien or retention or stoppage in transit is defeated; and

(b) if the last-mentioned transfer was made by way of pledge or other disposition for value, the unpaid seller's right of lien or retention or stoppage in transit can only be exercised subject to the rights of the transferee.

Rescission: and re-sale by seller

Section 48. (1) Subject to this section, a contract of sale is not rescinded by the mere exercise by an unpaid seller of his right of lien or retention or stoppage in transit.

(2) Where an unpaid seller who has exercised his right of lien or retention or stoppage in transit re-sells the goods, the buyer acquires a good title to them as against the original buyer.

(3) Where the goods are of a perishable nature, or where the unpaid seller gives notice to the buyer of his intention to re-sell, and the buyer does not within a reasonable time pay or tender the price, the unpaid seller may re-sell the goods and recover from the original buyer damages for any loss occasioned by his breach of contract.

(4) Where the seller expressly reserves the right of re-sale in case the buyer should make default, and on the buyer making default re-sells the goods, the original contract of sale is rescinded but without prejudice to any claim the seller may have for damages.

Part 5A. Additional Rights of Buyer in Consumer Cases

......................................(Repealed.)

Part VI. Actions for Breach of the Contract
Seller's remedies

Section 49. (1) Where, under a contract of sale, the property in the goods has passed to the buyer and he wrongfully neglects or refuses to pay for the goods according to the terms of the contract, the seller may maintain an action against him for the price of the goods.

(2) Where, under a contract of sale, the price is payable on a day certain irrespective of delivery and the buyer wrongfully neglects or refuses to pay such price, the seller may maintain an action for the price, although the property in the goods has not passed and the goods have not been appropriated to the contract.

(3) Nothing in this section prejudices the right of the seller in Scotland to recover interest on the price from the date of tender of the goods, or from the date on which the price was payable, as the case may be.

Section 50. (1) Where the buyer wrongfully neglects or refuses to accept and pay for the goods, the seller may maintain an action against him for damages for non-acceptance.

(2) The measure of damages is the estimated loss directly and naturally resulting, in the ordinary course of events, from the buyer's breach of contract.

(3) Where there is an available market for the goods in question the measure of damages is prima facie to be ascertained by the difference between the contract price and the market or current price at the time or times when the goods ought to have been accepted or (if no time was fixed for acceptance) at the time of the refusal to accept.

Buyer's remedies

Section 51. (1) Where the seller wrongfully neglects or refuses to deliver the goods to the buyer, the buyer may maintain an action against the seller for damages for non-delivery.

(2) The measure of damages is the estimated loss directly and naturally resulting, in the ordinary course of events, from the seller's breach of contract.

(3) Where there is an available market for the goods in question the measure of damages is prima facie to be ascertained by the difference between the contract price and the market or current price of the goods at the time or times when they ought to have been delivered or (if no time was fixed) at the time of the refusal to deliver.

(4) This section does not apply to a contract to which Chapter 2 of Part 1 of the Consumer Rights Act 2015 applies (but see the provision made about such contracts in section 19 of that Act).

Section 52. (1) In any action for breach of contract to deliver specific or ascertained goods the court may, if it thinks fit, on the plaintiff's application, by its judgment or decree direct that the contract shall be performed specifically, without giving the defendant the option of retaining the goods on payment of damages.

(2) The plaintiff's application may be made at any time before judgment or decree.

(3) The judgment or decree may be unconditional, or on such terms and conditions as to damages, payment of the price and otherwise as seem just to the court.

(4) The provisions of this section shall be deemed to be supplementary to, and not in derogation of, the right of specific implement in Scotland.

(5) This section does not apply to a contract to which Chapter 2 of Part 1 of the Consumer Rights Act 2015 applies (but see the provision made about such contracts in section 19 of that Act).

Section 53. (1) Where there is a breach of warranty by the seller, or where the buyer elects (or is compelled) to treat any breach of a condition on the part of the seller as a breach of warranty, the buyer is not by reason only of such breach of warranty entitled to reject the goods; but he may—

(a) set up against the seller the breach of warranty in diminution or extinction of the price, or

(b) maintain an action against the seller for damages for the breach of warranty.

(2) The measure of damages for breach of warranty is the estimated loss directly and naturally resulting, in the ordinary course of events, from the breach of warranty.

(3) In the case of breach of warranty of quality such loss is prima facie the difference between the value of the goods at the time of delivery to the buyer and the value they would have had if they had fulfilled the warranty.

(4) The fact that the buyer has set up the breach of warranty in diminution or extinction of the price does not prevent him from maintaining an action for the same breach of warranty if he has suffered further damage.

(4A) This section does not apply to a contract to which Chapter 2 of Part 1 of the Consumer Rights Act 2015 applies (but see the provision made about such contracts in section 19 of that Act).

(5) This section does not apply to Scotland.

Section 53A. (1) The measure of damages for the seller's breach of contract is the estimated loss directly and naturally resulting, in the ordinary course of events, from the breach.

(2) Where the seller's breach consists of the delivery of goods which are not of the quality required by the contract and the buyer retains the goods, such loss as aforesaid is prima facie the difference between the value of the goods at the time of delivery to the buyer and the value they would have had if they had fulfilled the contract.

(2A) This section does not apply to a contract to which Chapter 2 of Part 1 of the Consumer Rights Act 2015 applies (but see the provision made about such contracts in section 19 of that Act).

(3) This section applies to Scotland only.

Interest, etc.

Section 54. (1) Nothing in this Act affects the right of the buyer or the seller to recover interest or special damages in any case where by law interest or special damages may be recoverable, or to recover money paid where the consideration for the payment of it has failed.

(2) This section does not apply to a contract to which Chapter 2 of Part 1 of the Consumer Rights Act 2015 applies (but see the provision made about such contracts in section 19 of that Act).

Part VII. Supplementary

Section 55. (1) Where a right, duty or liability would arise under a contract of sale of goods by implication of law, it may (subject to the Unfair Contract Terms Act 1977) be negatived or varied by express agreement, or by the course of dealing between the parties, or by such usage as binds both parties to the contract.

(1A) Subsection (1) does not apply to a contract to which Chapter 2 of Part 1 of the Consumer Rights Act 2015 applies (but see the provision made about such contracts in section 31 of that Act).

(2) An express term does not negative a term implied by this Act unless inconsistent with it.

(3) Paragraph (11) of Schedule 1 below applies in relation to a contract made on or after 18 May 1973 and before 1 February 1978, and paragraph (12) in relation to one made before 18 May 1973.

Section 56. Paragraph (13) of Schedule 1 below applies in relation to a contract made on or after 18 May 1973 and before 1 February 1978, so as to make provision about conflict of laws in relation to such a contract.

Section 57. (1) Where goods are put up for sale by auction in lots, each lot is prima facie deemed to be the subject of a separate contract of sale.

(2) A sale by auction is complete when the auctioneer announces its completion by the fall of the hammer, or in other customary manner; and until the announcement is made any bidder may retract his bid.

(3) A sale by auction may be notified to be subject to a reserve or upset price, and a right to bid may also be reserved expressly by or on behalf of the seller.

(4) Where a sale by auction is not notified to be subject to a right to bid by or on behalf of the seller, it is not lawful for the seller to bid himself or to employ any person to bid at the sale, or for the auctioneer knowingly to take any bid from the seller or any such person.

(5) A sale contravening subsection (4) above may be treated as fraudulent by the buyer.

(6) Where, in respect of a sale by auction, a right to bid is expressly reserved (but not otherwise) the seller or any one person on his behalf may bid at the auction.

Section 58. (1) In Scotland where a buyer has elected to accept goods which he might have rejected, and to treat a breach of contract as only giving rise to a claim for damages, he may, in an action by the seller for the price, be required, in the discretion of the court before which the action depends, to consign or pay into court the price of the goods, or part of the price, or to give other reasonable security for its due payment.

(2) This section does not apply to a contract to which Chapter 2 of Part 1 of the Consumer Rights Act 2015 applies (but see the provision made about such contracts in section 27 of that Act).

Section 59. Where a reference is made in this Act to a reasonable time the question what is a reasonable time is a question of fact.

Section 60. Where a right, duty or liability is declared by this Act, it may (unless otherwise provided by this Act) be enforced by action.

Section 61. (1) In this Act, unless the context or subject matter otherwise requires,—

"action" includes counterclaim and set-off, and in Scotland condescendence and claim and compensation;

" bulk " means a mass or collection of goods of the same kind which—

(a) is contained in a defined space or area; and

(b) is such that any goods in the bulk are interchangeable with any other goods therein of the same number or quantity; "business" includes a profession and the activities of any government department (including a Northern Ireland department) or local or public authority;

"buyer" means a person who buys or agrees to buy goods;

"contract of sale" includes an agreement to sell as well as a sale;

"credit-broker" means a person acting in the course of a business of credit brokerage carried on by him, that is a business of effecting introductions of individuals desiring to obtain credit—

(a) to persons carrying on any business so far as it relates to the provision of credit, or

(b) to other persons engaged in credit brokerage;

"defendant" includes in Scotland defender, respondent, and claimant in a multiplepoinding;

"delivery" means voluntary transfer of possession from one person to another; except that in relation to sections 20A and 20B above it includes such appropriation of goods to the contract as results in property in the goods being transferred to the buyer;

"document of title to goods" has the same meaning as it has in the Factors Acts;

"Factors Acts" means the Factors Act 1889, the Factors (Scotland) 1890, and any enactment amending or substituted for the same;

"fault" means wrongful act or default;

"future goods" means goods to be manufactured or acquired by the seller after the making of the contract of sale;

"goods" includes all personal chattels other than things in action and money, and in Scotland all corporeal moveables except money; and in particular "goods" includes emblements, industrial growing crops, and things attached to or forming part of the land which are agreed to be severed before sale or under the contract of sale; and includes an undivided share in goods;

"plaintiff" includes pursuer, complainer, claimant in a multiplepoinding and defendant or defender counter-claiming;

"property" means the general property in goods, and not merely a special property;

"sale" includes a bargain and sale as well as a sale and delivery;

"seller" means a person who sells or agrees to sell goods;

"specific goods" means goods identified and agreed on at the time a contract of sale is made and includes an undivided share, specified as a fraction or percentage, of goods identified and agreed on as aforesaid;

"warranty" (as regards England and Wales and Northern Ireland) means an agreement with reference to goods which are the subject of a contract of sale, but collateral to the main purpose of such contract, the breach of which gives rise to a claim for damages, but not to a right to reject the goods and treat the contract as repudiated.

(2)(Repealed)

(3) A thing is deemed to be done in good faith within the meaning of this Act when it is in fact done honestly, whether it is done negligently or not.

(4) A person is deemed to be insolvent within the meaning of this Act if he has either ceased to pay his debts in the ordinary
course of business or he cannot pay his debts as they become due, whether he has committed an act of bankruptcy or not, and whether he has become a notour bankrupt or not.

(5) Goods are in a deliverable state within the meaning of this Act when they are in such a state that the buyer would under the contract be bound to take delivery of them.

(5A)(Repealed)

(6) As regards the definition of "business" in subsection (1) above, paragraph (14) of Schedule 1 below applies in relation to a contract made on or after 18 May 1973 and before 1 February 1978, and paragraph (15) in relation to one made before 18 May 1973.

Section 62. (1) The rules in bankruptcy relating to contracts of sale apply to those contracts, notwithstanding anything in this Act.

(2) The rules of the common law, including the law merchant, except in so far as they are inconsistent with the provisions of legislation including this Act and the Consumer Rights Act 2015, and in particular the rules relating to the law of principal and agent and the effect of fraud, misrepresentation, duress or coercion, mistake, or other invalidating cause, apply to contracts for the sale of goods.

(3) Nothing in this Act or the Sale of Goods 1893 affects the enactments relating to bills of sale, or any enactment relating to the sale of goods which is not expressly repealed or amended by this Act or that.

(4) The provisions of this Act about contracts of sale do not apply to a transaction in the form of a contract of sale which is intended to operate by way of mortgage, pledge, charge, or other security.

(5) Nothing in this Act prejudices or affects the landlord's right of hypothec... in Scotland.

Section 63. (1) Without prejudice to section 17 of the Interpretation Act 1978 (repeal and re-enactment), the enactments mentioned in Schedule 2 below have effect subject to the amendments there specified (being amendments consequential on this Act).

(2) The enactments mentioned in Schedule 3 below are repealed to the extent specified in column 3, but subject to the savings in Schedule 4 below.

(3) The savings in Schedule 4 below have effect.

Section 64. (1) This Act may be cited as the Sale of Goods Act 1979.
(2) This Act comes into force on 1 January 1980.

Consumer Rights Act

Consumer Rights Act 2015 [An Act to amend the law relating to the rights of consumers and protection of their interests; to make provision about investigatory powers for enforcing the regulation of traders; to make provision about private actions in competition law and the Competition Appeal Tribunal; and for connected purposes] (c. 15), as last amended by the Digital Economy Act 2017 (c. 30).

Be it enacted by the Queen's most Excellent Majesty, by and with the advice and consent of the Lords Spiritual and Temporal, and Commons, in this present Parliament assembled, and by the authority of the same, as follows:—

Part I. Consumer Contracts for Goods, Digital Content and Services

Chapter 1. Introduction

Section 1. (1) This Part applies where there is an agreement between a trader and a consumer for the trader to supply goods, digital content or services, if the agreement is a contract.
(2) It applies whether the contract is written or oral or implied from the parties' conduct, or more than one of these combined.
(3) Any of Chapters 2, 3 and 4 may apply to a contract—
(a) if it is a contract for the trader to supply goods, see Chapter 2;
(b) if it is a contract for the trader to supply digital content, see Chapter 3 (also, subsection (6));
(c) if it is a contract for the trader to supply a service, see Chapter 4 (also, subsection (6)).
(4) In each case the Chapter applies even if the contract also covers something covered by another Chapter (a mixed contract).
(5) Two or all three of those Chapters may apply to a mixed contract.
(6) For provisions about particular mixed contracts, see—
(a) section 15 (goods and installation);
(b) section 16 (goods and digital content).
(7) For other provision applying to contracts to which this Part applies, see Part 2 (unfair terms).

Section 2. (1) These definitions apply in this Part (as well as the definitions in section 59).
(2) "Trader" means a person acting for purposes relating to that person's trade, business, craft or profession, whether acting personally or through another person acting in the trader's name or on the trader's behalf.
(3) "Consumer" means an individual acting for purposes that are wholly or mainly outside that individual's trade, business, craft or profession.
(4) A trader claiming that an individual was not acting for purposes wholly or mainly outside the individual's trade, business, craft or profession must prove it.
(5) For the purposes of Chapter 2, except to the extent mentioned in subsection (6), a person is not a consumer in relation to a sales contract if—
(a) the goods are second hand goods sold at public auction, and
(b) individuals have the opportunity of attending the sale in person.
(6) A person is a consumer in relation to such a contract for the purposes of—
(a) sections 11(4) and (5), 12, 28 and 29, and
(b) the other provisions of Chapter 2 as they apply in relation to those sections.
(7) "Business" includes the activities of any government department or local or public authority.
(8) "Goods" means any tangible moveable items, but that includes water, gas and electricity if and only if they are put up for supply in a limited volume or set quantity.
(9) "Digital content" means data which are produced and supplied in digital form.

Chapter 2. Goods

What goods contracts are covered?

Section 3. (1) This Chapter applies to a contract for a trader to supply goods to a consumer.
(2) It applies only if the contract is one of these (defined for the purposes of this Part in sections 5 to 8) —
(a) a sales contract;
(b) a contract for the hire of goods;

(c) a hire-purchase agreement;

(d) a contract for transfer of goods.

(3) It does not apply—

(a) to a contract for a trader to supply coins or notes to a consumer for use as currency;

(b) to a contract for goods to be sold by way of execution or otherwise by authority of law;

(c) to a contract intended to operate as a mortgage, pledge, charge or other security;

(d) in relation to England and Wales or Northern Ireland, to a contract made by deed and for which the only consideration is the presumed consideration imported by the deed;

(e) in relation to Scotland, to a gratuitous contract.

(4) A contract to which this Chapter applies is referred to in this Part as a "contract to supply goods".

(5) Contracts to supply goods include—

(a) contracts entered into between one part owner and another;

(b) contracts for the transfer of an undivided share in goods;

(c) contracts that are absolute and contracts that are conditional.

(6) Subsection (1) is subject to any provision of this Chapter that applies a section or part of a section to only some of the kinds of contracts listed in subsection (2).

(7) A mixed contract (see section 1(4)) may be a contract of any of those kinds.

Section 4. (1) In this Chapter ownership of goods means the general property in goods, not merely a special property.

(2) For the time when ownership of goods is transferred, see in particular the following provisions of the Sale of Goods Act 1979 (which relate to contracts of sale) —

section 16:	goods must be ascertained
section 17:	property passes when intended to pass
section 18:	rules for ascertaining intention
section 19:	reservation of right of disposal
section 20A:	undivided shares in goods forming part of a bulk
section 20B:	deemed consent by co-owner to dealings in bulk goods

Section 5. (1) A contract is a sales contract if under it—

(a) the trader transfers or agrees to transfer ownership of goods to the consumer, and

(b) the consumer pays or agrees to pay the price.

(2) A contract is a sales contract (whether or not it would be one under subsection (1)) if under the contract—

(a) goods are to be manufactured or produced and the trader agrees to supply them to the consumer,

(b) on being supplied, the goods will be owned by the consumer, and

(c) the consumer pays or agrees to pay the price.

(3) A sales contract may be conditional (see section 3(5)), but in this Part "conditional sales contract" means a sales contract under which—

(a) the price for the goods or part of it is payable by instalments, and

(b) the trader retains ownership of the goods until the conditions specified in the contract (for the payment of instalments or otherwise) are met;

and it makes no difference whether or not the consumer possesses the goods.

Section 6. (1) A contract is for the hire of goods if under it the trader gives or agrees to give the consumer possession of the goods with the right to use them, subject to the terms of the contract, for a period determined in accordance with the contract.

(2) But a contract is not for the hire of goods if it is a hire-purchase agreement.

Section 7. (1) A contract is a hire-purchase agreement if it meets the two conditions set out below.

(2) The first condition is that under the contract goods are hired by the trader in return for periodical payments by the consumer (and "hired" is to be read in accordance with section 6(1)).

(3) The second condition is that under the contract ownership of the goods will transfer to the consumer if the terms of the contract are complied with and—

(a) the consumer exercises an option to buy the goods,

(b) any party to the contract does an act specified in it, or

(c) an event specified in the contract occurs.

(4) But a contract is not a hire-purchase agreement if it is a conditional sales contract.

Section 8. A contract to supply goods is a contract for transfer of goods if under it the trader transfers or agrees to transfer ownership of the goods to the consumer and—

(a) the consumer provides or agrees to provide consideration otherwise than by paying a price, or

(b) the contract is, for any other reason, not a sales contract or a hire-purchase agreement.

What statutory rights are there under a goods contract?

Section 9. (1) Every contract to supply goods is to be treated as including a term that the quality of the goods is satisfactory.
(2) The quality of goods is satisfactory if they meet the standard that a reasonable person would consider satisfactory, taking account of—
(a) any description of the goods,(b) the price or other consideration for the goods (if relevant), and
(c) all the other relevant circumstances (see subsection (5)).
(3) The quality of goods includes their state and condition; and the following aspects (among others) are in appropriate cases aspects of the quality of goods—
(a) fitness for all the purposes for which goods of that kind are usually supplied;
(b) appearance and finish;
(c) freedom from minor defects;
(d) safety;
(e) durability.
(4) The term mentioned in subsection (1) does not cover anything which makes the quality of the goods unsatisfactory—
(a) which is specifically drawn to the consumer's attention before the contract is made,
(b) where the consumer examines the goods before the contract is made, which that examination ought to reveal, or
(c) in the case of a contract to supply goods by sample, which would have been apparent on a reasonable examination of the sample.
(5) The relevant circumstances mentioned in subsection (2) (c) include any public statement about the specific characteristics of the goods made by the trader, the producer or any representative of the trader or the producer.
(6) That includes, in particular, any public statement made in advertising or labelling.
(7) But a public statement is not a relevant circumstance for the purposes of subsection (2) (c) if the trader shows that—
(a) when the contract was made, the trader was not, and could not reasonably have been, aware of the statement,
(b) before the contract was made, the statement had been publicly withdrawn or, to the extent that it contained anything which was incorrect or misleading, it had been publicly corrected, or
(c) the consumer's decision to contract for the goods could not have been influenced by the statement.
(8) In a contract to supply goods a term about the quality of the goods may be treated as included as a matter of custom.
(9) See section 19 for a consumer's rights if the trader is in breach of a term that this section requires to be treated as included in a contract.

Section 10. (1) Subsection (3) applies to a contract to supply goods if before the contract is made the consumer makes known to the trader (expressly or by implication) any particular purpose for which the consumer is contracting for the goods.
(2) Subsection (3) also applies to a contract to supply goods if—
(a) the goods were previously sold by a credit-broker to the trader,
(b) in the case of a sales contract or contract for transfer of goods, the consideration or part of it is a sum payable by instalments, and
(c) before the contract is made, the consumer makes known to the credit-broker (expressly or by implication) any particular purpose for which the consumer is contracting for the goods.
(3) The contract is to be treated as including a term that the goods are reasonably fit for that purpose, whether or not that is a purpose for which goods of that kind are usually supplied.
(4) Subsection (3) does not apply if the circumstances show that the consumer does not rely, or it is unreasonable for the consumer to rely, on the skill or judgment of the trader or credit-broker.
(5) In a contract to supply goods a term about the fitness of the goods for a particular purpose may be treated as included as a matter of custom.
(6) See section 19 for a consumer's rights if the trader is in breach of a term that this section requires to be treated as included in a contract.

Section 11. (1) Every contract to supply goods by description is to be treated as including a term that the goods will match the description.
(2) If the supply is by sample as well as by description, it is not sufficient that the bulk of the goods matches the sample if the goods do not also match the description.
(3) A supply of goods is not prevented from being a supply by description just because—

(a) the goods are exposed for supply, and

(b) they are selected by the consumer.

(4) Any information that is provided by the trader about the goods and is information mentioned in paragraph (a) of Schedule 1 or 2 to the Consumer Contracts (Information, Cancellation and Additional Charges) Regulations 2013 (SI 2013/3134) (main characteristics of goods) is to be treated as included as a term of the contract.

(5) A change to any of that information, made before entering into the contract or later, is not effective unless expressly agreed between the consumer and the trader.

(6) See section 2(5) and (6) for the application of subsections (4) and (5) where goods are sold at public auction.

(7) See section 19 for a consumer's rights if the trader is in breach of a term that this section requires to be treated as included in a contract.

Section 12. (1) This section applies to any contract to supply goods.

(2) Where regulation 9, 10 or 13 of the Consumer Contracts (Information, Cancellation and Additional Charges) Regulations 2013 (SI 2013/3134) required the trader to provide information to the consumer before the contract became binding, any of that information that was provided by the trader other than information about the goods and mentioned in paragraph (a) of Schedule 1 or 2 to the Regulations (main characteristics of goods) is to be treated as included as a term of the contract.

(3) A change to any of that information, made before entering into the contract or later, is not effective unless expressly agreed between the consumer and the trader.

(4) See section 2(5) and (6) for the application of this section where goods are sold at public auction.

(5) See section 19 for a consumer's rights if the trader is in breach of a term that this section requires to be treated as included in the contract.

Section 13. (1) This section applies to a contract to supply goods by reference to a sample of the goods that is seen or examined by the consumer before the contract is made.

(2) Every contract to which this section applies is to be treated as including a term that—

(a) the goods will match the sample except to the extent that any differences between the sample and the goods are brought to the consumer's attention before the contract is made, and

(b) the goods will be free from any defect that makes their quality unsatisfactory and that would not be apparent on a reasonable examination of the sample.

(3) See section 19 for a consumer's rights if the trader is in breach of a term that this section requires to be treated as included in a contract.

Section 14. (1) This section applies to a contract to supply goods by reference to a model of the goods that is seen or examined by the consumer before entering into the contract.

(2) Every contract to which this section applies is to be treated as including a term that the goods will match the model except to the extent that any differences between the model and the goods are brought to the consumer's attention before the consumer enters into the contract.

(3) See section 19 for a consumer's rights if the trader is in breach of a term that this section requires to be treated as included in a contract.

Section 15. (1) Goods do not conform to a contract to supply goods if—

(a) installation of the goods forms part of the contract,

(b) the goods are installed by the trader or under the trader's responsibility, and

(c) the goods are installed incorrectly.

(2) See section 19 for the effect of goods not conforming to the contract.

Section 16. (1) Goods (whether or not they conform otherwise to a contract to supply goods) do not conform to it if—

(a) the goods are an item that includes digital content, and

(b) the digital content does not conform to the contract to supply that content (for which see section 42(1)).

(2) See section 19 for the effect of goods not conforming to the contract.

Section 17. (1) Every contract to supply goods, except one within subsection (4), is to be treated as including a term—

(a) in the case of a contract for the hire of goods, that at the beginning of the period of hire the trader must have the right to transfer possession of the goods by way of hire for that period,

(b) in any other case, that the trader must have the right to sell or transfer the goods at the time when ownership of the goods is to be transferred.

(2) Every contract to supply goods, except a contract for the hire of goods or a contract within subsection (4), is to be treated as including a term that—

(a) the goods are free from any charge or encumbrance not disclosed or known to the consumer before entering into the contract,

(b) the goods will remain free from any such charge or encumbrance until ownership of them is to be transferred, and

(c) the consumer will enjoy quiet possession of the goods except so far as it may be disturbed by the owner or other person entitled to the benefit of any charge or encumbrance so disclosed or known.

(3) Every contract for the hire of goods is to be treated as including a term that the consumer will enjoy quiet possession of the goods for the period of the hire except so far as the possession may be disturbed by the owner or other person entitled to the benefit of any charge or encumbrance disclosed or known to the consumer before entering into the contract.

(4) This subsection applies to a contract if the contract shows, or the circumstances when they enter into the contract imply, that the trader and the consumer intend the trader to transfer only—

(a) whatever title the trader has, even if it is limited, or

(b) whatever title a third person has, even if it is limited.

(5) Every contract within subsection (4) is to be treated as including a term that all charges or encumbrances known to the trader and not known to the consumer were disclosed to the consumer before entering into the contract.

(6) Every contract within subsection (4) is to be treated as including a term that the consumer's quiet possession of the goods—

(a) will not be disturbed by the trader, and

(b) will not be disturbed by a person claiming through or under the trader, unless that person is claiming under a charge or encumbrance that was disclosed or known to the consumer before entering into the contract.

(7) If subsection (4) (b) applies (transfer of title that a third person has), the contract is also to be treated as including a term that the consumer's quiet possession of the goods—

(a) will not be disturbed by the third person, and

(b) will not be disturbed by a person claiming through or under the third person, unless the claim is under a charge or encumbrance that was disclosed or known to the consumer before entering into the contract.

(8) In the case of a contract for the hire of goods, this section does not affect the right of the trader to repossess the goods where the contract provides or is to be treated as providing for this.

(9) See section 19 for a consumer's rights if the trader is in breach of a term that this section requires to be treated as included in a contract.

Section 18. (1) Except as provided by sections 9, 10, 13 and 16, a contract to supply goods is not to be treated as including any term about the quality of the goods or their fitness for any particular purpose, unless the term is expressly included in the contract.

(2) Subsection (1) is subject to provision made by any other enactment (whenever passed or made).

What remedies are there if statutory rights under a goods contract are not met?

Section 19. (1) In this section and sections 22 to 24 references to goods conforming to a contract are references to—

(a) the goods conforming to the terms described in sections 9, 10, 11, 13 and 14,

(b) the goods not failing to conform to the contract under section 15 or 16, and

(c) the goods conforming to requirements that are stated in the contract.

(2) But, for the purposes of this section and sections 22 to 24, a failure to conform as mentioned in subsection (1) (a) to (c) is not a failure to conform to the contract if it has its origin in materials supplied by the consumer.

(3) If the goods do not conform to the contract because of a breach of any of the terms described in sections 9, 10, 11, 13 and 14, or if they do not conform to the contract under section 16, the consumer's rights (and the provisions about them and when they are available) are—

(a) the short-term right to reject (sections 20 and 22);

(b) the right to repair or replacement (section 23); and

(c) the right to a price reduction or the final right to reject (sections 20 and 24).

(4) If the goods do not conform to the contract under section 15 or because of a breach of requirements that are stated in the contract, the consumer's rights (and the provisions about them and when they are available) are—

(a) the right to repair or replacement (section 23); and

(b) the right to a price reduction or the final right to reject (sections 20 and 24).

(5) If the trader is in breach of a term that section 12 requires to be treated as included in the contract, the consumer has the right to recover from the trader the amount of any costs incurred by the consumer as a result of the breach, up to the amount of the price paid or the value of other consideration given for the goods.

(6) If the trader is in breach of the term that section 17(1) (right to supply etc) requires to be treated as included in the contract, the consumer has a right to reject (see section 20 for provisions about that right and when it is available).

(7) Subsections (3) to (6) are subject to section 25 and subsections (3) (a) and (6) are subject to section 26.

(8) Section 28 makes provision about remedies for breach of a term about the time for delivery of goods.

(9) This Chapter does not prevent the consumer seeking other remedies—

(a) for a breach of a term that this Chapter requires to be treated as included in the contract,

(b) on the grounds that, under section 15 or 16, goods do not conform to the contract, or

(c) for a breach of a requirement stated in the contract.

(10) Those other remedies may be ones—

(a) in addition to a remedy referred to in subsections (3) to (6) (but not so as to recover twice for the same loss), or

(b) instead of such a remedy, or

(c) where no such remedy is provided for.

(11) Those other remedies include any of the following that is open to the consumer in the circumstances—

(a) claiming damages;

(b) seeking specific performance;

(c) seeking an order for specific implement;

(d) relying on the breach against a claim by the trader for the price;

(e) for breach of an express term, exercising a right to treat the contract as at an end.

(12) It is not open to the consumer to treat the contract as at an end for breach of a term that this Chapter requires to be treated as included in the contract, or on the grounds that, under section 15 or 16, goods do not conform to the contract, except as provided by subsections (3), (4) and (6).

(13) In this Part, treating a contract as at an end means treating it as repudiated.

(14) For the purposes of subsections (3) (b) and (c) and (4), goods which do not conform to the contract at any time within the period of six months beginning with the day on which the goods were delivered to the consumer must be taken not to have conformed to it on that day.

(15) Subsection (14) does not apply if—

(a) it is established that the goods did conform to the contract on that day, or

(b) its application is incompatible with the nature of the goods or with how they fail to conform to the contract.

Section 20. (1) The short-term right to reject is subject to section 22.

(2) The final right to reject is subject to section 24.

(3) The right to reject under section 19(6) is not limited by those sections.

(4) Each of these rights entitles the consumer to reject the goods and treat the contract as at an end, subject to subsections (20) and (21).

(5) The right is exercised if the consumer indicates to the trader that the consumer is rejecting the goods and treating the contract as at an end.

(6) The indication may be something the consumer says or does, but it must be clear enough to be understood by the trader.

(7) From the time when the right is exercised—

(a) the trader has a duty to give the consumer a refund, subject to subsection (18), and

(b) the consumer has a duty to make the goods available for collection by the trader or (if there is an agreement for the consumer to return rejected goods) to return them as agreed.

(8) Whether or not the consumer has a duty to return the rejected goods, the trader must bear any reasonable costs of returning them, other than any costs incurred by the consumer in returning the goods in person to the place where the consumer took physical possession of them.

(9) The consumer's entitlement to receive a refund works as follows.

(10) To the extent that the consumer paid money under the contract, the consumer is entitled to receive back the same amount of money.

(11) To the extent that the consumer transferred anything else under the contract, the consumer is

entitled to receive back the same amount of what the consumer transferred, unless subsection (12) applies.

(12) To the extent that the consumer transferred under the contract something for which the same amount of the same thing cannot be substituted, the consumer is entitled to receive back in its original state whatever the consumer transferred.

(13) If the contract is for the hire of goods, the entitlement to a refund extends only to anything paid or otherwise transferred for a period of hire that the consumer does not get because the contract is treated as at an end.

(14) If the contract is a hire-purchase agreement or a conditional sales contract and the contract is treated as at an end before the whole of the price has been paid, the entitlement to a refund extends only to the part of the price paid.

(15) A refund under this section must be given without undue delay, and in any event within 14 days beginning with the day on which the trader agrees that the consumer is entitled to a refund.

(16) If the consumer paid money under the contract, the trader must give the refund using the same means of payment as the consumer used, unless the consumer expressly agrees otherwise.

(17) The trader must not impose any fee on the consumer in respect of the refund.

(18) There is no entitlement to receive a refund—

(a) if none of subsections (10) to (12) applies,

(b) to the extent that anything to which subsection (12) applies cannot be given back in its original state, or

(c) where subsection (13) applies, to the extent that anything the consumer transferred under the contract cannot be divided so as to give back only the amount, or part of the amount, to which the consumer is entitled.

(19) It may be open to a consumer to claim damages where there is no entitlement to receive a refund, or because of the limits of the entitlement, or instead of a refund.

(20) Subsection (21) qualifies the application in relation to England and Wales and Northern Ireland of the rights mentioned in subsections (1) to (3) where—

(a) the contract is a severable contract,

(b) in relation to the final right to reject, the contract is a contract for the hire of goods, a hire-purchase agreement or a contract for transfer of goods, and

(c) section 26(3) does not apply.

(21) The consumer is entitled, depending on the terms of the contract and the circumstances of the case—

(a) to reject the goods to which a severable obligation relates and treat that obligation as at an end (so that the entitlement to a refund relates only to what the consumer paid or transferred in relation to that obligation), or

(b) to exercise any of the rights mentioned in subsections (1) to (3) in respect of the whole contract.

Section 21. (1) If the consumer has any of the rights mentioned in section 20(1) to (3), but does not reject all of the goods and treat the contract as at an end, the consumer—

(a) may reject some or all of the goods that do not conform to the contract, but

(b) may not reject any goods that do conform to the contract.

(2) If the consumer is entitled to reject the goods in an instalment, but does not reject all of those goods, the consumer—

(a) may reject some or all of the goods in the instalment that do not conform to the contract, but

(b) may not reject any goods in the instalment that do conform to the contract.

(3) If any of the goods form a commercial unit, the consumer cannot reject some of those goods without also rejecting the rest of them.

(4) A unit is a "commercial unit" if division of the unit would materially impair the value of the goods or the character of the unit.

(5) The consumer rejects goods under this section by indicating to the trader that the consumer is rejecting the goods.

(6) The indication may be something the consumer says or does, but it must be clear enough to be understood by the trader.

(7) From the time when a consumer rejects goods under this section—

(a) the trader has a duty to give the consumer a refund in respect of those goods (subject to subsection (10)), and

(b) the consumer has a duty to make those goods available for collection by the trader or (if there is an agreement for the consumer to return rejected goods) to return them as agreed.

(8) Whether or not the consumer has a duty to return the rejected goods, the trader must bear any

reasonable costs of returning them, other than any costs incurred by the consumer in returning those goods in person to the place where the consumer took physical possession of them.

(9) Section 20(10) to (17) apply to a consumer's right to receive a refund under this section (and in section 20(13) and (14) references to the contract being treated as at an end are to be read as references to goods being rejected).

(10) That right does not apply—

(a) if none of section 20(10) to (12) applies,

(b) to the extent that anything to which section 20(12) applies cannot be given back in its original state, or

(c) to the extent that anything the consumer transferred under the contract cannot be divided so as to give back only the amount, or part of the amount, to which the consumer is entitled.

(11) It may be open to a consumer to claim damages where there is no right to receive a refund, or because of the limits of the right, or instead of a refund.

(12) References in this section to goods conforming to a contract are to be read in accordance with section 19(1) and (2), but they also include the goods conforming to the terms described in section 17.

(13) Where section 20(21) (a) applies the reference in subsection (1) to the consumer treating the contract as at an end is to be read as a reference to the consumer treating the severable obligation as at an end.

Section 22. (1) A consumer who has the short-term right to reject loses it if the time limit for exercising it passes without the consumer exercising it, unless the trader and the consumer agree that it may be exercised later.

(2) An agreement under which the short-term right to reject would be lost before the time limit passes is not binding on the consumer.

(3) The time limit for exercising the short-term right to reject (unless subsection (4) applies) is the end of 30 days beginning with the first day after these have all happened—

(a) ownership or (in the case of a contract for the hire of goods, a hire-purchase agreement or a conditional sales contract) possession of the goods has been transferred to the consumer,

(b) the goods have been delivered, and

(c) where the contract requires the trader to install the goods or take other action to enable the consumer to use them, the trader has notified the consumer that the action has been taken.

(4) If any of the goods are of a kind that can reasonably be expected to perish after a shorter period, the time limit for exercising the short-term right to reject in relation to those goods is the end of that shorter period (but without affecting the time limit in relation to goods that are not of that kind).

(5) Subsections (3) and (4) do not prevent the consumer exercising the short-term right to reject before something mentioned in subsection (3) (a), (b) or (c) has happened.

(6) If the consumer requests or agrees to the repair or replacement of goods, the period mentioned in subsection (3) or (4) stops running for the length of the waiting period.

(7) If goods supplied by the trader in response to that request or agreement do not conform to the contract, the time limit for exercising the short-term right to reject is then either—

(a) 7 days after the waiting period ends, or

(b) if later, the original time limit for exercising that right, extended by the waiting period.

(8) The waiting period—

(a) begins with the day the consumer requests or agrees to the repair or replacement of the goods, and

(b) ends with the day on which the consumer receives goods supplied by the trader in response to the request or agreement.

Section 23. (1) This section applies if the consumer has the right to repair or replacement (see section 19(3) and (4)).

(2) If the consumer requires the trader to repair or replace the goods, the trader must—

(a) do so within a reasonable time and without significant inconvenience to the consumer, and

(b) bear any necessary costs incurred in doing so (including in particular the cost of any labour, materials or postage).

(3) The consumer cannot require the trader to repair or replace the goods if that remedy (the repair or the replacement) —

(a) is impossible, or

(b) is disproportionate compared to the other of those remedies.

(4) Either of those remedies is disproportionate compared to the other if it imposes costs on the trader which, compared to those imposed by the other, are unreasonable, taking into account—

(a) the value which the goods would have if they conformed to the contract,

(b) the significance of the lack of conformity, and

(c) whether the other remedy could be effected without significant inconvenience to the consumer.

(5) Any question as to what is a reasonable time or significant inconvenience is to be determined taking account of—

(a) the nature of the goods, and

(b) the purpose for which the goods were acquired.

(6) A consumer who requires or agrees to the repair of goods cannot require the trader to replace them, or exercise the short-term right to reject, without giving the trader a reasonable time to repair them (unless giving the trader that time would cause significant inconvenience to the consumer).

(7) A consumer who requires or agrees to the replacement of goods cannot require the trader to repair them, or exercise the short-term right to reject, without giving the trader a reasonable time to replace them (unless giving the trader that time would cause significant inconvenience to the consumer).

(8) In this Chapter, "repair" in relation to goods that do not conform to a contract, means making them conform.

Section 24. (1) The right to a price reduction is the right—

(a) to require the trader to reduce by an appropriate amount the price the consumer is required to pay under the contract, or anything else the consumer is required to transfer under the contract, and

(b) to receive a refund from the trader for anything already paid or otherwise transferred by the consumer above the reduced amount.

(2) The amount of the reduction may, where appropriate, be the full amount of the price or whatever the consumer is required to transfer.

(3) Section 20(10) to (17) applies to a consumer's right to receive a refund under subsection (1) (b).

(4) The right to a price reduction does not apply—

(a) if what the consumer is (before the reduction) required to transfer under the contract, whether or not already transferred, cannot be divided up so as to enable the trader to receive or retain only the reduced amount, or

(b) if anything to which section 20(12) applies cannot be given back in its original state.

(5) A consumer who has the right to a price reduction and the final right to reject may only exercise one (not both), and may only do so in one of these situations—

(a) after one repair or one replacement, the goods do not conform to the contract;

(b) because of section 23(3) the consumer can require neither repair nor replacement of the goods; or

(c) the consumer has required the trader to repair or replace the goods, but the trader is in breach of the requirement of section 23(2) (a) to do so within a reasonable time and without significant inconvenience to the consumer.

(6) There has been a repair or replacement for the purposes of subsection (5) (a) if—

(a) the consumer has requested or agreed to repair or replacement of the goods (whether in relation to one fault or more than one), and

(b) the trader has delivered goods to the consumer, or made goods available to the consumer, in response to the request or agreement.

(7) For the purposes of subsection (6) goods that the trader arranges to repair at the consumer's premises are made available when the trader indicates that the repairs are finished.

(8) If the consumer exercises the final right to reject, any refund to the consumer may be reduced by a deduction for use, to take account of the use the consumer has had of the goods in the period since they were delivered, but this is subject to subsections (9) and (10).

(9) No deduction may be made to take account of use in any period when the consumer had the goods only because the trader failed to collect them at an agreed time.

(10) No deduction may be made if the final right to reject is exercised in the first 6 months (see subsection (11)), unless—

(a) the goods consist of a motor vehicle, or

(b) the goods are of a description specified by order made by the Secretary of State by statutory instrument.

(11) In subsection (10) the first 6 months means 6 months beginning with the first day after these have all happened—

(a) ownership or (in the case of a contract for the hire of goods, a hire-purchase agreement or a conditional sales contract) possession of the goods has been transferred to the consumer,

(b) the goods have been delivered, and

(c) where the contract requires the trader to install the goods or take other action to enable the consumer to use them, the trader has notified the consumer that the action has been taken.

(12) In subsection (10) (a) "motor vehicle"—

(a) in relation to Great Britain, has the same meaning as in the Road Traffic Act 1988 (see sections 185 to 194 of that Act);

(b) in relation to Northern Ireland, has the same meaning as in the Road Traffic (Northern Ireland) Order 1995 (SI 1995/2994 (NI 18)) (see Parts I and V of that Order).

(13) But a vehicle is not a motor vehicle for the purposes of subsection (10) (a) if it is constructed or adapted—

(a) for the use of a person suffering from some physical defect or disability, and

(b) so that it may only be used by one such person at any one time.

(14) An order under subsection (10) (b) —

(a) may be made only if the Secretary of State is satisfied that it is appropriate to do so because of significant detriment caused to traders as a result of the application of subsection (10) in relation to goods of the description specified by the order;

(b) may contain transitional or transitory provision or savings.

(15) No order may be made under subsection (10) (b) unless a draft of the statutory instrument containing it has been laid before, and approved by a resolution of, each House of Parliament.

Other rules about remedies under goods contracts

Section 25. (1) Where the trader delivers to the consumer a quantity of goods less than the trader contracted to supply, the consumer may reject them, but if the consumer accepts them the consumer must pay for them at the contract rate.

(2) Where the trader delivers to the consumer a quantity of goods larger than the trader contracted to supply, the consumer may accept the goods included in the contract and reject the rest, or may reject all of the goods.

(3) Where the trader delivers to the consumer a quantity of goods larger than the trader contracted to supply and the consumer accepts all of the goods delivered, the consumer must pay for them at the contract rate.

(4) Where the consumer is entitled to reject goods under this section, any entitlement for the consumer to treat the contract as at an end depends on the terms of the contract and the circumstances of the case.

(5) The consumer rejects goods under this section by indicating to the trader that the consumer is rejecting the goods.

(6) The indication may be something the consumer says or does, but it must be clear enough to be understood by the trader.

(7) Subsections (1) to (3) do not prevent the consumer claiming damages, where it is open to the consumer to do so.

(8) This section is subject to any usage of trade, special agreement, or course of dealing between the parties.

Section 26. (1) Under a contract to supply goods, the consumer is not bound to accept delivery of the goods by instalments, unless that has been agreed between the consumer and the trader.

(2) The following provisions apply if the contract provides for the goods to be delivered by stated instalments, which are to be separately paid for.

(3) If the trader makes defective deliveries in respect of one or more instalments, the consumer, apart from any entitlement to claim damages, may be (but is not necessarily) entitled—

(a) to exercise the short-term right to reject or the right to reject under section 19(6) (as applicable) in respect of the whole contract, or

(b) to reject the goods in an instalment.

(4) Whether paragraph (a) or (b) of subsection (3) (or neither) applies to a consumer depends on the terms of the contract and the circumstances of the case.

(5) In subsection (3), making defective deliveries does not include failing to make a delivery in accordance with section 28.

(6) If the consumer neglects or refuses to take delivery of or pay for one or more instalments, the trader may—

(a) be entitled to treat the whole contract as at an end, or

(b) if it is a severable breach, have a claim for damages but not a right to treat the whole contract as at an end.

(7) Whether paragraph (a) or (b) of subsection (6) (or neither) applies to a trader depends on the terms of the contract and the circumstances of the case.

Section 27. (1) Subsection (2) applies where—

(a) a consumer has not rejected goods which the consumer could have rejected for breach of a term mentioned in section 19(3) or (6),

(b) the consumer has chosen to treat the breach as giving rise only to a claim for damages or to a right to rely on the breach against a claim by the trader for the price of the goods, and

(c) the trader has begun proceedings in court to recover the price or has brought a counter-claim for the price.

(2) The court may require the consumer—

(a) to consign, or pay into court, the price of the goods, or part of the price, or

(b) to provide some other reasonable security for payment of the price.

Other rules about goods contracts

Section 28. (1) This section applies to any sales contract.

(2) Unless the trader and the consumer have agreed otherwise, the contract is to be treated as including a term that the trader must deliver the goods to the consumer.

(3) Unless there is an agreed time or period, the contract is to be treated as including a term that the trader must deliver the goods—

(a) without undue delay, and

(b) in any event, not more than 30 days after the day on which the contract is entered into.

(4) In this section—

(a) an "agreed" time or period means a time or period agreed by the trader and the consumer for delivery of the
goods;

(b) if there is an obligation to deliver the goods at the time the contract is entered into, that time counts as the "agreed" time.

(5) Subsections (6) and (7) apply if the trader does not deliver the goods in accordance with subsection (3) or at the agreed time or within the agreed period.

(6) If the circumstances are that—

(a) the trader has refused to deliver the goods,

(b) delivery of the goods at the agreed time or within the agreed period is essential taking into account all the relevant circumstances at the time the contract was entered into, or

(c) the consumer told the trader before the contract was entered into that delivery in accordance with subsection (3), or at the agreed time or within the agreed period, was essential,

then the consumer may treat the contract as at an end.

(7) In any other circumstances, the consumer may specify a period that is appropriate in the circumstances and require the trader to deliver the goods before the end of that period.

(8) If the consumer specifies a period under subsection (7) but the goods are not delivered within that period, then the consumer may treat the contract as at an end.

(9) If the consumer treats the contract as at an end under subsection (6) or (8), the trader must without undue delay reimburse all payments made under the contract.

(10) If subsection (6) or (8) applies but the consumer does not treat the contract as at an end—

(a) that does not prevent the consumer from cancelling the order for any of the goods or rejecting goods that have been delivered, and

(b) the trader must without undue delay reimburse all payments made under the contract in respect of any goods for which the consumer cancels the order or which the consumer rejects.

(11) If any of the goods form a commercial unit, the consumer cannot reject or cancel the order for some of those goods without also rejecting or cancelling the order for the rest of them.

(12) A unit is a "commercial unit" if division of the unit would materially impair the value of the goods or the character of the unit.

(13) This section does not prevent the consumer seeking other remedies where it is open to the consumer to do so.

(14) See section 2(5) and (6) for the application of this section where goods are sold at public auction.

Section 29. (1) A sales contract is to be treated as including the following provisions as terms.

(2) The goods remain at the trader's risk until they come into the physical possession of—

(a) the consumer, or

(b) a person identified by the consumer to take possession of the goods.

(3) Subsection (2) does not apply if the goods are delivered to a carrier who—

(a) is commissioned by the consumer to deliver the goods, and

(b) is not a carrier the trader named as an option for the consumer.

(4) In that case the goods are at the consumer's risk on and after delivery to the carrier.

(5) Subsection (4) does not affect any liability of the carrier to the consumer in respect of the goods.

(6) See section 2(5) and (6) for the application of this section where goods are sold at public auction.

Section 30. (1) This section applies where—

(a) there is a contract to supply goods, and

(b) there is a guarantee in relation to the goods.

(2) "Guarantee" here means an undertaking to the consumer given without extra charge by a person acting in the course of the person's business (the "guarantor") that, if the goods do not meet the specifications set out in the guarantee statement or in any associated advertising—

(a) the consumer will be reimbursed for the price paid for the goods, or

(b) the goods will be repaired, replaced or handled in any way.

(3) The guarantee takes effect, at the time the goods are delivered, as a contractual obligation owed by the guarantor under the conditions set out in the guarantee statement and in any associated advertising.

(4) The guarantor must ensure that—

(a) the guarantee sets out in plain and intelligible language the contents of the guarantee and the essential particulars for making claims under the guarantee,

(b) the guarantee states that the consumer has statutory rights in relation to the goods and that those rights are not affected by the guarantee, and

(c) where the goods are offered within the territory of the United Kingdom, the guarantee is written in English.

(5) The contents of the guarantee to be set out in it include, in particular—

(a) the name and address of the guarantor, and

(b) the duration and territorial scope of the guarantee.

(6) The guarantor and any other person who offers to supply to consumers the goods which are the subject of the guarantee must, on request by the consumer, make the guarantee available to the consumer within a reasonable time, in writing and in a form accessible to the consumer.

(7) What is a reasonable time is a question of fact.

(8) If a person fails to comply with a requirement of this section, the enforcement authority may apply to the court for an injunction or (in Scotland) an order of specific implement against that person requiring that person to comply.

(9) On an application the court may grant an injunction or (in Scotland) an order of specific implement on such terms as it thinks appropriate.

(10) In this section—

"court" means—

(a) in relation to England and Wales, the High Court or the county court,

(b) in relation to Northern Ireland, the High Court or a county court, and

(c) in relation to Scotland, the Court of Session or the sheriff;

"enforcement authority" means—

(a) the Competition and Markets Authority,

(b) a local weights and measures authority in Great Britain, and

(c) the Department of Enterprise, Trade and Investment in Northern Ireland.

Can a trader contract out of statutory rights and remedies under a goods contract?

Section 31. (1) A term of a contract to supply goods is not binding on the consumer to the extent that it would exclude or restrict the trader's liability arising under any of these provisions—

(a) section 9 (goods to be of satisfactory quality);

(b) section 10 (goods to be fit for particular purpose);

(c) section 11 (goods to be as described);

(d) section 12 (other pre-contract information included in contract);

(e) section 13 (goods to match a sample);

(f) section 14 (goods to match a model seen or examined);

(g) section 15 (installation as part of conformity of the goods with the contract);

(h) section 16 (goods not conforming to contract if digital content does not conform);

(i) section 17 (trader to have right to supply the goods etc);

(j) section 28 (delivery of goods);

(k) section 29 (passing of risk).

(2) That also means that a term of a contract to supply goods is not binding on the consumer to the extent that it would—

(a) exclude or restrict a right or remedy in respect of a liability under a provision listed in subsection (1),

(b) make such a right or remedy or its enforcement subject to a restrictive or onerous condition,

(c) allow a trader to put a person at a disadvantage as a result of pursuing such a right or remedy, or

(d) exclude or restrict rules of evidence or procedure.

(3) The reference in subsection (1) to excluding or restricting a liability also includes preventing an obligation or duty arising or limiting its extent.

(4) An agreement in writing to submit present or future differences to arbitration is not to be regarded as excluding or restricting any liability for the purposes of this section.

(5) Subsection (1) (i), and subsection (2) so far as it relates to liability under section 17, do not apply to a term of a contract for the hire of goods.

(6) But an express term of a contract for the hire of goods is not binding on the consumer to the extent that it would exclude or restrict a term that section 17 requires to be treated as included in the contract, unless it is inconsistent with that term (and see also section 62 (requirement for terms to be fair)).

(7) See Schedule 3 for provision about the enforcement of this section.

Section 32. (1) If—

(a) the law of a country or territory other than an EEA State is chosen by the parties to be applicable to a sales contract, but

(b) the sales contract has a close connection with the United Kingdom, this Chapter, except the provisions in subsection (2), applies despite that choice.

(2) The exceptions are—

(a) sections 11(4) and (5) and 12;

(b) sections 28 and 29;

(c) section 31(1) (d), (j) and (k).

(3) For cases where those provisions apply, or where the law applicable has not been chosen or the law of an EEA State is chosen, see Regulation (EC) No.593/2008 of the European Parliament and of the Council of 17 June 2008 on the law applicable to contractual obligations.

Chapter 3. Digital Content

What digital content contracts are covered?

Section 33. (1) This Chapter applies to a contract for a trader to supply digital content to a consumer, if it is supplied or to be supplied for a price paid by the consumer.

(2) This Chapter also applies to a contract for a trader to supply digital content to a consumer, if—

(a) it is supplied free with goods or services or other digital content for which the consumer pays a price, and

(b) it is not generally available to consumers unless they have paid a price for it or for goods or services or other digital content.

(3) The references in subsections (1) and (2) to the consumer paying a price include references to the consumer using, by way of payment, any facility for which money has been paid.

(4) A trader does not supply digital content to a consumer for the purposes of this Part merely because the trader supplies a service by which digital content reaches the consumer.

(5) The Secretary of State may by order provide for this Chapter to apply to other contracts for a trader to supply digital content to a consumer, if the Secretary of State is satisfied that it is appropriate to do so because of significant detriment caused to consumers under contracts of the kind to which the order relates.

(6) An order under subsection (5) —

(a) may, in particular, amend this Act;

(b) may contain transitional or transitory provision or savings.

(7) A contract to which this Chapter applies is referred to in this Part as a "contract to supply digital content".

(8) This section, other than subsection (4), does not limit the application of section 46.

(9) The power to make an order under subsection (5) is exercisable by statutory instrument.

(10) No order may be made under subsection (5) unless a draft of the statutory instrument containing it has been laid before, and approved by a resolution of, each House of Parliament.

What statutory rights are there under a digital content contract?

Section 34. (1) Every contract to supply digital content is to be treated as including a term that the quality of the digital content is satisfactory.

(2) The quality of digital content is satisfactory if it meets the standard that a reasonable person

would consider satisfactory, taking account of—

(a) any description of the digital content,

(b) the price mentioned in section 33(1) or (2) (b) (if relevant), and

(c) all the other relevant circumstances (see subsection (5)).

(3) The quality of digital content includes its state and condition; and the following aspects (among others) are in appropriate cases aspects of the quality of digital content—

(a) fitness for all the purposes for which digital content of that kind is usually supplied;

(b) freedom from minor defects;

(c) safety;

(d) durability.

(4) The term mentioned in subsection (1) does not cover anything which makes the quality of the digital content unsatisfactory—

(a) which is specifically drawn to the consumer's attention before the contract is made,

(b) where the consumer examines the digital content before the contract is made, which that examination ought to reveal, or

(c) where the consumer examines a trial version before the contract is made, which would have been apparent on a reasonable examination of the trial version.

(5) The relevant circumstances mentioned in subsection (2) (c) include any public statement about the specific characteristics of the digital content made by the trader, the producer or any representative of the trader or the producer.

(6) That includes, in particular, any public statement made in advertising or labelling.

(7) But a public statement is not a relevant circumstance for the purposes of subsection (2) (c) if the trader shows that—

(a) when the contract was made, the trader was not, and could not reasonably have been, aware of the statement,

(b) before the contract was made, the statement had been publicly withdrawn or, to the extent that it contained anything which was incorrect or misleading, it had been publicly corrected, or

(c) the consumer's decision to contract for the digital content could not have been influenced by the statement.

(8) In a contract to supply digital content a term about the quality of the digital content may be treated as included as a matter of custom.

(9) See section 42 for a consumer's rights if the trader is in breach of a term that this section requires to be treated as included in a contract.

Section 35. (1) Subsection (3) applies to a contract to supply digital content if before the contract is made the consumer makes known to the trader (expressly or by implication) any particular purpose for which the consumer is contracting for the digital content.

(2) Subsection (3) also applies to a contract to supply digital content if—

(a) the digital content was previously sold by a credit-broker to the trader,

(b) the consideration or part of it is a sum payable by instalments, and

(c) before the contract is made, the consumer makes known to the credit-broker (expressly or by implication) any particular purpose for which the consumer is contracting for the digital content.

(3) The contract is to be treated as including a term that the digital content is reasonably fit for that purpose, whether or not that is a purpose for which digital content of that kind is usually supplied.

(4) Subsection (3) does not apply if the circumstances show that the consumer does not rely, or it is unreasonable for the consumer to rely, on the skill or judgment of the trader or credit-broker.

(5) A contract to supply digital content may be treated as making provision about the fitness of the digital content for a particular purpose as a matter of custom.

(6) See section 42 for a consumer's rights if the trader is in breach of a term that this section requires to be treated as included in a contract.

Section 36. (1) Every contract to supply digital content is to be treated as including a term that the digital content will match any description of it given by the trader to the consumer.

(2) Where the consumer examines a trial version before the contract is made, it is not sufficient that the digital content matches (or is better than) the trial version if the digital content does not also match any description of it given by the trader to the consumer.

(3) Any information that is provided by the trader about the digital content that is information mentioned in paragraph (a), (j) or (k) of Schedule 1 or paragraph (a), (v) or (w) of Schedule 2 (main characteristics, functionality and compatibility) to the Consumer Contracts (Information, Cancellation and Additional Charges) Regulations 2013 (SI 2013/3134) is to be treated as included as a term of the contract.

(4) A change to any of that information, made before entering into the contract or later, is not effective unless expressly agreed between the consumer and the trader.
(5) See section 42 for a consumer's rights if the trader is in breach of a term that this section requires to be treated as included in a contract.

Section 37. (1) This section applies to any contract to supply digital content.
(2) Where regulation 9, 10 or 13 of the Consumer Contracts (Information, Cancellation and Additional Charges) Regulations 2013 (SI 2013/3134) required the trader to provide information to the consumer before the contract became binding, any of that information that was provided by the trader other than information about the digital content and mentioned in paragraph (a), (j) or (k) of Schedule 1 or paragraph (a), (v) or (w) of Schedule 2 to the Regulations (main characteristics, functionality and compatibility) is to be treated as included as a term of the contract.
(3) A change to any of that information, made before entering into the contract or later, is not effective unless expressly agreed between the consumer and the trader.
(4) See section 42 for a consumer's rights if the trader is in breach of a term that this section requires to be treated as included in a contract.

Section 38. (1) Except as provided by sections 34 and 35, a contract to supply digital content is not to be treated as including any term about the quality of the digital content or its fitness for any particular purpose, unless the term is expressly included in the contract.
(2) Subsection (1) is subject to provision made by any other enactment, whenever passed or made.

Section 39. (1) Subsection (2) applies where there is a contract to supply digital content and the consumer's access to the content on a device requires its transmission to the device under arrangements initiated by the trader.
(2) For the purposes of this Chapter, the digital content is supplied—
(a) when the content reaches the device, or
(b) if earlier, when the content reaches another trader chosen by the consumer to supply, under a contract with the consumer, a service by which digital content reaches the device.
(3) Subsections (5) to (7) apply where—
(a) there is a contract to supply digital content, and
(b) after the trader (T) has supplied the digital content, the consumer is to have access under the contract to a processing facility under arrangements made by T.
(4) A processing facility is a facility by which T or another trader will receive digital content from the consumer and transmit digital content to the consumer (whether or not other features are to be included under the contract).
(5) The contract is to be treated as including a term that the processing facility (with any feature that the facility is to include under the contract) must be available to the consumer for a reasonable time, unless a time is specified in the contract.
(6) The following provisions apply to all digital content transmitted to the consumer on each occasion under the facility, while it is provided under the contract, as they apply to the digital content first supplied—
(a) section 34 (quality);
(b) section 35 (fitness for a particular purpose);
(c) section 36 (description).
(7) Breach of a term treated as included under subsection (5) has the same effect as breach of a term treated as included under those sections (see section 42).

Section 40. (1) Where under a contract a trader supplies digital content to a consumer subject to the right of the trader or a third party to modify the digital content, the following provisions apply in relation to the digital content as modified as they apply in relation to the digital content as supplied under the contract—
(a) section 34 (quality);
(b) section 35 (fitness for a particular purpose);
(c) section 36 (description).
(2) Subsection (1) (c) does not prevent the trader from improving the features of, or adding new features to, the digital content, as long as—
(a) the digital content continues to match the description of it given by the trader to the consumer, and
(b) the digital content continues to conform to the information provided by the trader as mentioned in subsection (3) of section 36, subject to any change to that information that has been agreed in accordance with subsection (4) of that section.
(3) A claim on the grounds that digital content does not conform to a term described in any of the

sections listed in subsection (1) as applied by that subsection is to be treated as arising at the time when the digital content was supplied under the contract and not the time when it is modified.

Section 41. (1) Every contract to supply digital content is to be treated as including a term—
(a) in relation to any digital content which is supplied under the contract and which the consumer has paid for, that the trader has the right to supply that content to the consumer;
(b) in relation to any digital content which the trader agrees to supply under the contract and which the consumer has paid for, that the trader will have the right to supply it to the consumer at the time when it is to be supplied.
(2) See section 42 for a consumer's rights if the trader is in breach of a term that this section requires to be treated as included in a contract.

What remedies are there if statutory rights under a digital content contract are not met?

Section 42. (1) In this section and section 43 references to digital content conforming to a contract are references to the digital content conforming to the terms described in sections 34, 35 and 36.
(2) If the digital content does not conform to the contract, the consumer's rights (and the provisions about them and when they are available) are—
(a) the right to repair or replacement (see section 43);
(b) the right to a price reduction (see section 44).
(3) Section 16 also applies if an item including the digital content is supplied.
(4) If the trader is in breach of a term that section 37 requires to be treated as included in the contract, the consumer has the right to recover from the trader the amount of any costs incurred by the consumer as a result of the breach, up to the amount of the price paid for the digital content or for any facility within section 33(3) used by the consumer.
(5) If the trader is in breach of the term that section 41(1) (right to supply the content) requires to be treated as included in the contract, the consumer has the right to a refund (see section 45 for provisions about that right and when it is available).
(6) This Chapter does not prevent the consumer seeking other remedies for a breach of a term to which any of subsections (2), (4) or (5) applies, instead of or in addition to a remedy referred to there (but not so as to recover twice for the same loss).
(7) Those other remedies include any of the following that is open to the consumer in the circumstances—
(a) claiming damages;
(b) seeking to recover money paid where the consideration for payment of the money has failed;
(c) seeking specific performance;
(d) seeking an order for specific implement;
(e) relying on the breach against a claim by the trader for the price.
(8) It is not open to the consumer to treat the contract as at an end for breach of a term to which any of subsections (2), (4) or (5) applies.
(9) For the purposes of subsection (2), digital content which does not conform to the contract at any time within the period of six months beginning with the day on which it was supplied must be taken not to have conformed to the contract when it was supplied.
(10) Subsection (9) does not apply if—
(a) it is established that the digital content did conform to the contract when it was supplied, or
(b) its application is incompatible with the nature of the digital content or with how it fails to conform to the contract.

Section 43. (1) This section applies if the consumer has the right to repair or replacement.
(2) If the consumer requires the trader to repair or replace the digital content, the trader must—
(a) do so within a reasonable time and without significant inconvenience to the consumer; and
(b) bear any necessary costs incurred in doing so (including in particular the cost of any labour, materials or postage).
(3) The consumer cannot require the trader to repair or replace the digital content if that remedy (the repair or the replacement) —
(a) is impossible, or
(b) is disproportionate compared to the other of those remedies.
(4) Either of those remedies is disproportionate compared to the other if it imposes costs on the trader which, compared to those imposed by the other, are unreasonable, taking into account—
(a) the value which the digital content would have if it conformed to the contract,
(b) the significance of the lack of conformity, and
(c) whether the other remedy could be effected without significant inconvenience to the consumer.

(5) Any question as to what is a reasonable time or significant inconvenience is to be determined taking account of—

(a) the nature of the digital content, and

(b) the purpose for which the digital content was obtained or accessed.

(6) A consumer who requires or agrees to the repair of digital content cannot require the trader to replace it without giving the trader a reasonable time to repair it (unless giving the trader that time would cause significant inconvenience to the consumer).

(7) A consumer who requires or agrees to the replacement of digital content cannot require the trader to repair it without giving the trader a reasonable time to replace it (unless giving the trader that time would cause significant inconvenience to the consumer).

(8) In this Chapter, "repair" in relation to digital content that does not conform to a contract, means making it conform.

Section 44. (1) The right to a price reduction is the right to require the trader to reduce the price to the consumer by an appropriate amount (including the right to receive a refund for anything already paid above the reduced amount).

(2) The amount of the reduction may, where appropriate, be the full amount of the price.

(3) A consumer who has that right may only exercise it in one of these situations—

(a) because of section 43(3) (a) the consumer can require neither repair nor replacement of the digital content, or

(b) the consumer has required the trader to repair or replace the digital content, but the trader is in breach of the requirement of section 43(2) (a) to do so within a reasonable time and without significant inconvenience to the consumer.

(4) A refund under this section must be given without undue delay, and in any event within 14 days beginning with the day on which the trader agrees that the consumer is entitled to a refund.

(5) The trader must give the refund using the same means of payment as the consumer used to pay for the digital content, unless the consumer expressly agrees otherwise.

(6) The trader must not impose any fee on the consumer in respect of the refund.

Section 45. (1) The right to a refund gives the consumer the right to receive a refund from the trader of all money paid by the consumer for the digital content (subject to subsection (2)).

(2) If the breach giving the consumer the right to a refund affects only some of the digital content supplied under the contract, the right to a refund does not extend to any part of the price attributable to digital content that is not affected by the breach.

(3) A refund must be given without undue delay, and in any event within 14 days beginning with the day on which the trader agrees that the consumer is entitled to a refund.

(4) The trader must give the refund using the same means of payment as the consumer used to pay for the digital content, unless the consumer expressly agrees otherwise.

(5) The trader must not impose any fee on the consumer in respect of the refund.

Compensation for damage to device or to other digital content

Section 46. (1) This section applies if—

(a) a trader supplies digital content to a consumer under a contract,

(b) the digital content causes damage to a device or to other digital content,

(c) the device or digital content that is damaged belongs to the consumer, and

(d) the damage is of a kind that would not have occurred if the trader had exercised reasonable care and skill.

(2) If the consumer requires the trader to provide a remedy under this section, the trader must either—

(a) repair the damage in accordance with subsection (3), or

(b) compensate the consumer for the damage with an appropriate payment.

(3) To repair the damage in accordance with this subsection, the trader must—

(a) repair the damage within a reasonable time and without significant inconvenience to the consumer, and

(b) bear any necessary costs incurred in repairing the damage (including in particular the cost of any labour, materials or postage).

(4) Any question as to what is a reasonable time or significant inconvenience is to be determined taking account of—

(a) the nature of the device or digital content that is damaged, and

(b) the purpose for which it is used by the consumer.

(5) A compensation payment under this section must be made without undue delay, and in any event

within 14 days beginning with the day on which the trader agrees that the consumer is entitled to the payment.

(6) The trader must not impose any fee on the consumer in respect of the payment.

(7) A consumer with a right to a remedy under this section may bring a claim in civil proceedings to enforce that right.

(8) The Limitation Act 1980 and the Limitation (Northern Ireland) Order 1989 (SI 1989/1339 (NI 11)) apply to a claim under this section as if it were an action founded on simple contract.

(9) The Prescription and Limitation (Scotland) Act 1973 applies to a right to a remedy under this section as if it were an obligation to which section 6 of that Act applies.

Can a trader contract out of statutory rights and remedies under a digital content contract?

Section 47. (1) A term of a contract to supply digital content is not binding on the consumer to the extent that it would exclude or restrict the trader's liability arising under any of these provisions—

(a) section 34 (digital content to be of satisfactory quality),

(b) section 35 (digital content to be fit for particular purpose),

(c) section 36 (digital content to be as described),

(d) section 37 (other pre-contract information included in contract), or

(e) section 41 (trader's right to supply digital content).

(2) That also means that a term of a contract to supply digital content is not binding on the consumer to the extent that it would—

(a) exclude or restrict a right or remedy in respect of a liability under a provision listed in subsection (1),

(b) make such a right or remedy or its enforcement subject to a restrictive or onerous condition,

(c) allow a trader to put a person at a disadvantage as a result of pursuing such a right or remedy, or

(d) exclude or restrict rules of evidence or procedure.

(3) The reference in subsection (1) to excluding or restricting a liability also includes preventing an obligation or duty arising or limiting its extent.

(4) An agreement in writing to submit present or future differences to arbitration is not to be regarded as excluding or restricting any liability for the purposes of this section.

(5) See Schedule 3 for provision about the enforcement of this section.

(6) For provision limiting the ability of a trader under a contract within section 46 to exclude or restrict the trader's liability under that section, see section 62.

Chapter 4. Services

What services contracts are covered?

Section 48. (1) This Chapter applies to a contract for a trader to supply a service to a consumer.

(2) That does not include a contract of employment or apprenticeship.

(3) In relation to Scotland, this Chapter does not apply to a gratuitous contract.

(4) A contract to which this Chapter applies is referred to in this Part as a "contract to supply a service".

(5) The Secretary of State may by order made by statutory instrument provide that a provision of this Chapter does not apply in relation to a service of a description specified in the order.

(6) The power in subsection (5) includes power to provide that a provision of this Chapter does not apply in relation to a service of a description specified in the order in the circumstances so specified.

(7) An order under subsection (5) may contain transitional or transitory provision or savings.

(8) No order may be made under subsection (5) unless a draft of the statutory instrument containing it has been laid before, and approved by a resolution of, each House of Parliament.

What statutory rights are there under a services contract?

Section 49. (1) Every contract to supply a service is to be treated as including a term that the trader must perform the service with reasonable care and skill.

(2) See section 54 for a consumer's rights if the trader is in breach of a term that this section requires to be treated as included in a contract.

Section 50. (1) Every contract to supply a service is to be treated as including as a term of the contract anything that is said or written to the consumer, by or on behalf of the trader, about the trader or the service, if—

(a) it is taken into account by the consumer when deciding to enter into the contract, or

(b) it is taken into account by the consumer when making any decision about the service after entering into the contract.

(2) Anything taken into account by the consumer as mentioned in subsection (1) (a) or (b) is subject to—

(a) anything that qualified it and was said or written to the consumer by the trader on the same occasion, and

(b) any change to it that has been expressly agreed between the consumer and the trader (before entering into the contract or later).

(3) Without prejudice to subsection (1), any information provided by the trader in accordance with regulation 9, 10 or 13 of the Consumer Contracts (Information, Cancellation and Additional Charges) Regulations 2013 (SI 2013/3134) is to be treated as included as a term of the contract.

(4) A change to any of the information mentioned in subsection (3), made before entering into the contract or later, is not effective unless expressly agreed between the consumer and the trader.

(5) See section 54 for a consumer's rights if the trader is in breach of a term that this section requires to be treated as included in a contract.

Section 51. (1) This section applies to a contract to supply a service if—

(a) the consumer has not paid a price or other consideration for the service,

(b) the contract does not expressly fix a price or other consideration, and does not say how it is to be fixed, and

(c) anything that is to be treated under section 50 as included in the contract does not fix a price or other consideration either.

(2) In that case the contract is to be treated as including a term that the consumer must pay a reasonable price for the service, and no more.

(3) What is a reasonable price is a question of fact.

Section 52. (1) This section applies to a contract to supply a service, if—

(a) the contract does not expressly fix the time for the service to be performed, and does not say how it is to be fixed, and

(b) information that is to be treated under section 50 as included in the contract does not fix the time either.

(2) In that case the contract is to be treated as including a term that the trader must perform the service within a reasonable time.

(3) What is a reasonable time is a question of fact.

(4) See section 54 for a consumer's rights if the trader is in breach of a term that this section requires to be treated as included in a contract.

Section 53. (1) Nothing in this Chapter affects any enactment or rule of law that imposes a stricter duty on the trader.

(2) This Chapter is subject to any other enactment which defines or restricts the rights, duties or liabilities arising in connection with a service of any description.

What remedies are there if statutory rights under a services contract are not met?

Section 54. (1) The consumer's rights under this section and sections 55 and 56 do not affect any rights that the contract provides for, if those are not inconsistent.

(2) In this section and section 55 a reference to a service conforming to a contract is a reference to—

(a) the service being performed in accordance with section 49, or

(b) the service conforming to a term that section 50 requires to be treated as included in the contract and that relates to the performance of the service.

(3) If the service does not conform to the contract, the consumer's rights (and the provisions about them and when they are available) are—

(a) the right to require repeat performance (see section 55);

(b) the right to a price reduction (see section 56).

(4) If the trader is in breach of a term that section 50 requires to be treated as included in the contract but that does not relate to the service, the consumer has the right to a price reduction (see section 56 for provisions about that right and when it is available).

(5) If the trader is in breach of what the contract requires under section 52 (performance within a reasonable time), the consumer has the right to a price reduction (see section 56 for provisions about that right and when it is available).

(6) This section and sections 55 and 56 do not prevent the consumer seeking other remedies for a breach of a term to which any of subsections (3) to (5) applies, instead of or in addition to a remedy referred to there (but not so as to recover twice for the same loss).

(7) Those other remedies include any of the following that is open to the consumer in the circumstances—

(a) claiming damages;

(b) seeking to recover money paid where the consideration for payment of the money has failed;

(c) seeking specific performance;

(d) seeking an order for specific implement;

(e) relying on the breach against a claim by the trader under the contract;

(f) exercising a right to treat the contract as at an end.

Section 55. (1) The right to require repeat performance is a right to require the trader to perform the service again, to the extent necessary to complete its performance in conformity with the contract.

(2) If the consumer requires such repeat performance, the trader—

(a) must provide it within a reasonable time and without significant inconvenience to the consumer; and

(b) must bear any necessary costs incurred in doing so (including in particular the cost of any labour or materials).

(3) The consumer cannot require repeat performance if completing performance of the service in conformity with the contract is impossible.

(4) Any question as to what is a reasonable time or significant inconvenience is to be determined taking account of—

(a) the nature of the service, and

(b) the purpose for which the service was to be performed.

Section 56. (1) The right to a price reduction is the right to require the trader to reduce the price to the consumer by an appropriate amount (including the right to receive a refund for anything already paid above the reduced amount).

(2) The amount of the reduction may, where appropriate, be the full amount of the price.

(3) A consumer who has that right and the right to require repeat performance is only entitled to a price reduction in one of these situations—

(a) because of section 55(3) the consumer cannot require repeat performance; or

(b) the consumer has required repeat performance, but the trader is in breach of the requirement of section 55(2) (a) to do it within a reasonable time and without significant inconvenience to the consumer.

(4) A refund under this section must be given without undue delay, and in any event within 14 days beginning with the day on which the trader agrees that the consumer is entitled to a refund.

(5) The trader must give the refund using the same means of payment as the consumer used to pay for the service, unless the consumer expressly agrees otherwise.

(6) The trader must not impose any fee on the consumer in respect of the refund.

Can a trader contract out of statutory rights and remedies under a services contract?

Section 57. (1) A term of a contract to supply services is not binding on the consumer to the extent that it would exclude the trader's liability arising under section 49 (service to be performed with reasonable care and skill).

(2) Subject to section 50(2), a term of a contract to supply services is not binding on the consumer to the extent that it would exclude the trader's liability arising under section 50 (information about trader or service to be binding).

(3) A term of a contract to supply services is not binding on the consumer to the extent that it would restrict the trader's liability arising under any of sections 49 and 50 and, where they apply, sections 51 and 52 (reasonable price and reasonable time), if it would prevent the consumer in an appropriate case from recovering the price paid or the value of any other consideration. (If it would not prevent the consumer from doing so, Part 2 (unfair terms) may apply.)

(4) That also means that a term of a contract to supply services is not binding on the consumer to the extent that it would —

(a) exclude or restrict a right or remedy in respect of a liability under any of sections 49 to 52,

(b) make such a right or remedy or its enforcement subject to a restrictive or onerous condition,

(c) allow a trader to put a person at a disadvantage as a result of pursuing such a right or remedy, or

(d) exclude or restrict rules of evidence or procedure.

(5) The references in subsections (1) to (3) to excluding or restricting a liability also include preventing an obligation or duty arising or limiting its extent.

(6) An agreement in writing to submit present or future differences to arbitration is not to be regarded as excluding or restricting any liability for the purposes of this section.

(7) See Schedule 3 for provision about the enforcement of this section.

Chapter 5. General and Supplementary Provisions

Section 58. (1) In any proceedings in which a remedy is sought by virtue of section 19(3) or (4), 42(2) or 54(3), the court, in addition to any other power it has, may act under this section.
(2) On the application of the consumer the court may make an order requiring specific performance or, in Scotland, specific implement by the trader of any obligation imposed on the trader by virtue of section 23, 43
or 55.
(3) Subsection (4) applies if—

(a) the consumer claims to exercise a right under the relevant remedies provisions, but
(b) the court decides that those provisions have the effect that exercise of another right is appropriate.
(4) The court may proceed as if the consumer had exercised that other right.
(5) If the consumer has claimed to exercise the final right to reject, the court may order that any reimbursement to the consumer is reduced by a deduction for use, to take account of the use the consumer has had of the goods in the period since they were delivered.
(6) Any deduction for use is limited as set out in section 24(9) and (10).
(7) The court may make an order under this section unconditionally or on such terms and conditions as to damages, payment of the price and otherwise as it thinks just.
(8) The "relevant remedies provisions" are—
(a) where Chapter 2 applies, sections 23 and 24;
(b) where Chapter 3 applies, sections 43 and 44;
(c) where Chapter 4 applies, sections 55 and 56.

Section 59. (1) These definitions apply in this Part (as well as the key definitions in section 2) —
"conditional sales contract" has the meaning given in section 5(3);
"Consumer Rights Directive" means Directive 2011/83/EU of the European Parliament and of the Council of 25 October 2011 on consumer rights, amending Council Directive and Directive 1999/44/EC of the European Parliament and of the Council and repealing Council Directive 85/577/EEC and Directive 97/7/EC of the European Parliament and of the Council;
"credit-broker" means a person acting in the course of a business of credit brokerage carried on by that person;
"credit brokerage" means—
(a) introducing individuals who want to obtain credit to persons carrying on any business so far as it relates to the provision of credit,
(b) introducing individuals who want to obtain goods on hire to persons carrying on a business which comprises or relates to supplying goods under a contract for the hire of goods, or
(c) introducing individuals who want to obtain credit, or to obtain goods on hire, to other persons engaged in credit brokerage;
"delivery" means voluntary transfer of possession from one person to another;
"enactment" includes—
(a) an enactment contained in subordinate legislation within the meaning of the Interpretation Act 1978,
(b) an enactment contained in, or in an instrument made under, a Measure or Act of the National Assembly for Wales,
(c) an enactment contained in, or in an instrument made under, an Act of the Scottish Parliament, and
(d) an enactment contained in, or in an instrument made under, Northern Ireland legislation;
"producer", in relation to goods or digital content, means—
(a) the manufacturer,
(b) the importer into the European Economic Area, or
(c) any person who purports to be a producer by placing the person's name, trade mark or other distinctive sign on the goods or using it in connection with the digital content.
(2) References in this Part to treating a contract as at an end are to be read in accordance with section 19(13).

Section 60. Schedule 1 (amendments consequential on this Part) has effect.

Part 2. Unfair Terms

What contracts and notices are covered by this Part?

Section 61. (1) This Part applies to a contract between a trader and a consumer.
(2) This does not include a contract of employment or apprenticeship.

(3) A contract to which this Part applies is referred to in this Part as a "consumer contract".

(4) This Part applies to a notice to the extent that it—

(a) relates to rights or obligations as between a trader and a consumer, or

(b) purports to exclude or restrict a trader's liability to a consumer.

(5) This does not include a notice relating to rights, obligations or liabilities as between an employer and an employee.

(6) It does not matter for the purposes of subsection (4) whether the notice is expressed to apply to a consumer, as long as it is reasonable to assume it is intended to be seen or heard by a consumer.

(7) A notice to which this Part applies is referred to in this Part as a "consumer notice".

(8) In this section "notice" includes an announcement, whether or not in writing, and any other communication or purported communication.

What are the general rules about fairness of contract terms and notices?

Section 62. (1) An unfair term of a consumer contract is not binding on the consumer.

(2) An unfair consumer notice is not binding on the consumer.

(3) This does not prevent the consumer from relying on the term or notice if the consumer chooses to do so.

(4) A term is unfair if, contrary to the requirement of good faith, it causes a significant imbalance in the parties' rights and obligations under the contract to the detriment of the consumer.

(5) Whether a term is fair is to be determined—

(a) taking into account the nature of the subject matter of the contract, and

(b) by reference to all the circumstances existing when the term was agreed and to all of the other terms of the contract or of any other contract on which it depends.

(6) A notice is unfair if, contrary to the requirement of good faith, it causes a significant imbalance in the parties' rights and obligations to the detriment of the consumer.

(7) Whether a notice is fair is to be determined—

(a) taking into account the nature of the subject matter of the notice, and

(b) by reference to all the circumstances existing when the rights or obligations to which it relates arose and to the terms of any contract on which it depends.

(8) This section does not affect the operation of—

(a) section 31 (exclusion of liability: goods contracts),

(b) section 47 (exclusion of liability: digital content contracts),

(c) section 57 (exclusion of liability: services contracts), or

(d) section 65 (exclusion of negligence liability).

Section 63. (1) Part 1 of Schedule 2 contains an indicative and non-exhaustive list of terms of consumer contracts that may be regarded as unfair for the purposes of this Part.

(2) Part 1 of Schedule 2 is subject to Part 2 of that Schedule; but a term listed in Part 2 of that Schedule may nevertheless be assessed for fairness under section 62 unless section 64 or 73 applies to it.

(3) The Secretary of State may by order made by statutory instrument amend Schedule 2 so as to add, modify or remove an entry in Part 1 or Part 2 of that Schedule.

(4) An order under subsection (3) may contain transitional or transitory provision or savings.

(5) No order may be made under subsection (3) unless a draft of the statutory instrument containing it has been laid before, and approved by a resolution of, each House of Parliament.

(6) A term of a consumer contract must be regarded as unfair if it has the effect that the consumer bears the burden of proof with respect to compliance by a distance supplier or an intermediary with an obligation under any enactment or rule implementing the Distance Marketing Directive.

(7) In subsection (6) —

"the Distance Marketing Directive" means Directive 2002/65/EC of the European Parliament and of the Council of 23 September 2002 concerning the distance marketing of consumer financial services and amending Council Directive 90/619/EEC and Directives 97/7/EC and 98/27/EC;

"distance supplier" means—

(a) a supplier under a distance contract within the meaning of the Financial Services (Distance Marketing) Regulations 2004 (SI 2004/2095), or

(b) a supplier of unsolicited financial services within the meaning of regulation 15 of those regulations;

"enactment" includes an enactment contained in subordinate legislation within the meaning of the Interpretation Act 1978;

"intermediary" has the same meaning as in the Financial Services (Distance Marketing) Regulations 2004;

"rule" means a rule made by the Financial Conduct Authority or the Prudential Regulation Authority under the Financial Services and Markets Act 2000 or by a designated professional body within the meaning of section 326(2) of that Act.

Section 64. (1) A term of a consumer contract may not be assessed for fairness under section 62 to the extent that—
(a) it specifies the main subject matter of the contract, or
(b) the assessment is of the appropriateness of the price payable under the contract by comparison with the goods, digital content or services supplied under it.
(2) Subsection (1) excludes a term from an assessment under section 62 only if it is transparent and prominent.
(3) A term is transparent for the purposes of this Part if it is expressed in plain and intelligible language and (in the case of a written term) is legible.
(4) A term is prominent for the purposes of this section if it is brought to the consumer's attention in such a way that an average consumer would be aware of the term.
(5) In subsection (4) "average consumer" means a consumer who is reasonably well-informed, observant and circumspect.
(6) This section does not apply to a term of a contract listed in Part 1 of Schedule 2.

Section 65. (1) A trader cannot by a term of a consumer contract or by a consumer notice exclude or restrict liability for death or personal injury resulting from negligence.
(2) Where a term of a consumer contract, or a consumer notice, purports to exclude or restrict a trader's liability for negligence, a person is not to be taken to have voluntarily accepted any risk merely because the person agreed to or knew about the term or notice.
(3) In this section "personal injury" includes any disease and any impairment of physical or mental condition.
(4) In this section "negligence" means the breach of—
(a) any obligation to take reasonable care or exercise reasonable skill in the performance of a contract where the obligation arises from an express or implied term of the contract,
(b) a common law duty to take reasonable care or exercise reasonable skill,
(c) the common duty of care imposed by the Occupiers' Liability Act 1957 or the Occupiers' Liability Act (Northern Ireland) 1957, or
(d) the duty of reasonable care imposed by section 2(1) of the Occupiers' Liability (Scotland) Act 1960.
(5) It is immaterial for the purposes of subsection (4) —
(a) whether a breach of duty or obligation was inadvertent or intentional, or
(b) whether liability for it arises directly or vicariously.
(6) This section is subject to section 66 (which makes provision about the scope of this section).

Section 66. (1) Section 65 does not apply to—
(a) any contract so far as it is a contract of insurance, including a contract to pay an annuity on human life, or
(b) any contract so far as it relates to the creation or transfer of an interest in land.
(2) Section 65 does not affect the validity of any discharge or indemnity given by a person in consideration of the receipt by that person of compensation in settlement of any claim the person has.
(3) Section 65 does not—
(a) apply to liability which is excluded or discharged as mentioned in section 4(2) (a) (exception to liability to pay damages to relatives) of the Damages (Scotland) Act 2011, or
(b) affect the operation of section 5 (discharge of liability to pay damages: exception for mesothelioma) of that Act.
(4) Section 65 does not apply to the liability of an occupier of premises to a person who obtains access to the premises for recreational purposes if—
(a) the person suffers loss or damage because of the dangerous state of the premises, and
(b) allowing the person access for those purposes is not within the purposes of the occupier's trade, business, craft or profession.

Section 67. Where a term of a consumer contract is not binding on the consumer as a result of this Part, the contract continues, so far as practicable, to have effect in every other respect.

Section 68. (1) A trader must ensure that a written term of a consumer contract, or a consumer notice in writing, is transparent.
(2) A consumer notice is transparent for the purposes of subsection (1) if it is expressed in plain and intelligible language and it is legible.

Section 69. (1) If a term in a consumer contract, or a consumer notice, could have different meanings, the meaning that is most favourable to the consumer is to prevail.

(2) Subsection (1) does not apply to the construction of a term or a notice in proceedings on an application for an injunction or interdict under paragraph 3 of Schedule 3.

How are the general rules enforced?

Section 70. (1) Schedule 3 confers functions on the Competition and Markets Authority and other regulators in relation to the enforcement of this Part.

(2) For provision about the investigatory powers that are available to those regulators for the purposes of that Schedule, see Schedule 5.

Supplementary provisions

Section 71. (1) Subsection (2) applies to proceedings before a court which relate to a term of a consumer contract.

(2) The court must consider whether the term is fair even if none of the parties to the proceedings has raised that issue or indicated that it intends to raise it.

(3) But subsection (2) does not apply unless the court considers that it has before it sufficient legal and factual material to enable it to consider the fairness of the term.

Section 72. (1) This section applies if a term of a contract ("the secondary contract") reduces the rights or remedies or increases the obligations of a person under another contract ("the main contract").

(2) The term is subject to the provisions of this Part that would apply to the term if it were in the main contract.

(3) It does not matter for the purposes of this section—

(a) whether the parties to the secondary contract are the same as the parties to the main contract, or

(b) whether the secondary contract is a consumer contract.

(4) This section does not apply if the secondary contract is a settlement of a claim arising under the main contract.

Section 73. (1) This Part does not apply to a term of a contract, or to a notice, to the extent that it reflects—

(a) mandatory statutory or regulatory provisions, or

(b) the provisions or principles of an international convention to which the United Kingdom or the EU is a party.

(2) In subsection (1) "mandatory statutory or regulatory provisions" includes rules which, according to law, apply between the parties on the basis that no other arrangements have been established.

Section 74. (1) If—

(a) the law of a country or territory other than an EEA State is chosen by the parties to be applicable to a consumer contract, but

(b) the consumer contract has a close connection with the United Kingdom,

this Part applies despite that choice.

(2) For cases where the law applicable has not been chosen or the law of an EEA State is chosen, see Regulation (EC) No. 593/2008 of the European Parliament and of the Council of 17 June 2008 on the law applicable to contractual obligations.

Section 75. Schedule 4 (amendments consequential on this Part) has effect.

Section 76. (1) In this Part—

"consumer contract" has the meaning given by section 61(3);

"consumer notice" has the meaning given by section 61(7);

"transparent" is to be construed in accordance with sections 64(3) and 68(2).

(2) The following have the same meanings in this Part as they have in Part 1—

"trader" (see section 2(2));

"consumer" (see section 2(3));

"goods" (see section 2(8));

"digital content" (see section 2(9)).

(3) Section 2(4) (trader who claims an individual is not a consumer must prove it) applies in relation to this Part as it applies in relation to Part 1.

Part 3. Miscellaneous and General

Chapter 1. Enforcement etc.

Section 77. (1) Schedule 5 (investigatory powers etc) has effect.
(2) Schedule 6 (investigatory powers: consequential amendments) has effect.

Section 78. (1) In the Weights and Measures (Packaged Goods) Regulations 2006 (S.I. 2006/659), Schedule 5 (application to bread) is amended in accordance with subsections (2) and (3).
(2) For paragraph 9 substitute—
"9Regulation 9(1) (b) (ii) (duty to keep records) does not apply to bread which is sold unwrapped or in open packs."
(3) After paragraph 13 insert—

"14Transitional provision
(1) Regulation 9(1) (b) (ii) (duty to keep records) does not apply to a packer who holds a notice of exemption which is in force.
(2) A "notice of exemption" means a notice issued under paragraph 9 as it stood before section 78 of the Consumer Rights Act 2015 came into force."
(4) The use of this Act to make amendments to the Weights and Measures (Packaged Goods) Regulations 2006 has no effect on the availability of any power in the Weights and Measures Act 1985 to amend or revoke those Regulations, including the provision substituted by subsection (2) and that inserted by subsection (3).
(5) In the Weights and Measures (Packaged Goods) Regulations (Northern Ireland) 2011 (SR 2011/331), Schedule 5 (application to bread) is amended in accordance with subsections (6) and (7).
(6) For paragraph 9 substitute—
"9Regulation 9(1) (b) (ii) (duty to keep records) does not apply to bread which is sold unwrapped or in open packets."
(7) After paragraph 13 insert—

"14 Transitional provision
(1) Regulation 9(1) (b) (ii) (duty to keep records) does not apply to a packer who holds a notice of exemption which is in force.
(2) A "notice of exemption" means a notice issued under paragraph 9 as it stood before section 78 of the Consumer Rights Act 2015 came into force."
(8) The use of this Act to make amendments to the Weights and Measures (Packaged Goods) Regulations (Northern Ireland) 2011 has no effect on the availability of any power in the Weights and Measures (Northern Ireland) Order 1981 (SI 1981/231 (NI 10)) to amend or revoke those Regulations, including the provision substituted by subsection (6) and that inserted by subsection (7).

Section 79. (1) Schedule 7 contains amendments of Part 8 of the Enterprise Act 2002 (enforcement of certain consumer legislation).
(2) The amendments have effect only in relation to conduct which occurs, or which is likely to occur, after the commencement of this section.

Section 80. (1) In section 120(3) of the Communications Act 2003 (conditions under section 120 must require compliance with directions given in accordance with an approved code or with an order under section 122) before paragraph (a) insert—
"(za) the provisions of an approved code;".
(2) In section 121(5) of that Act (provision about enforcement that may be made by approved code) after paragraph (a) insert—
"(aa) provision that applies where there is or has been more than one contravention of the code or directions given in accordance with it by a person and which enables—
(i) a single penalty (which does not exceed that maximum penalty) to be imposed on the person in respect of all of those contraventions, or
(ii) separate penalties (each of which does not exceed that maximum penalty) to be imposed on the person in respect of each of those contraventions,
according to whether the person imposing the penalty determines that a single penalty or separate penalties are appropriate and proportionate to those contraventions;".
(3) Section 123 of that Act (enforcement by OFCOM of conditions under section 120) is amended as follows.
(4) After subsection (1) insert—

"(1A) Subsection (1B) applies where a notification under section 94 as applied by this section relates to more than one contravention of—

(a) a code approved under section 121,

(b) directions given in accordance with such a code, or

(c) an order under section 122.

(1B) Section 96(3) as applied by this section enables OFCOM to impose—

(a) a single penalty in respect of all of those contraventions, or

(b) separate penalties in respect of each of those contraventions,

according to whether OFCOM determine that a single penalty or separate penalties are appropriate and proportionate to those contraventions."

(5) In subsection (2) (maximum amount of penalty) for "the penalty" substitute "each penalty ".

Chapter 2. Competition

Section 81. Schedule 8 (private actions in competition law) has effect.

Section 82. (1) In section 12(2) of the Enterprise Act 2002 (constitution of the Competition Appeal Tribunal) after paragraph (a) insert—

"(aa) such judges as are nominated from time to time by the Lord Chief Justice of England and Wales from the High Court of England and Wales;

(ab) such judges as are nominated from time to time by the Lord President of the Court of Session from the judges of the Court of Session;

(ac) such judges as are nominated from time to time by the Lord Chief Justice of Northern Ireland from the High Court in Northern Ireland;".

(2) In section 14 of that Act (constitution of the Competition Appeal Tribunal for particular proceedings and its decisions) —

(a) in subsection (2) after "the President" insert ", a judge within any of paragraphs (aa) to (ac) of section 12(2) ", and

(b) in subsection (3) for "either" substitute " the judges within paragraphs (aa) to (ac) of section 12(2), ".

(3) In Schedule 4 (Tribunal procedure) to that Act, in paragraph 18(3) (b) (consequences of member of Tribunal being unable to continue) after "if that person is not" insert " a judge within any of paragraphs (aa) to (ac) of section 12(2) or ".

Chapter 3. Duty of Letting Agents to Publicise Fees etc

Section 83. (1) A letting agent must, in accordance with this section, publicise details of the agent's relevant fees.

(2) The agent must display a list of the fees—

(a) at each of the agent's premises at which the agent deals face-to-face with persons using or proposing to use services to which the fees relate, and

(b) at a place in each of those premises at which the list is likely to be seen by such persons.

(3) The agent must publish a list of the fees on the agent's website (if it has a website).

(4) A list of fees displayed or published in accordance with subsection (2) or (3) must include—

(a) a description of each fee that is sufficient to enable a person who is liable to pay it to understand the service or cost that is covered by the fee or the purpose for which it is imposed (as the case may be),

(b) in the case of a fee which tenants are liable to pay, an indication of whether the fee relates to each dwelling-house or each tenant under a tenancy of the dwelling-house, and

(c) the amount of each fee inclusive of any applicable tax or, where the amount of a fee cannot reasonably be determined in advance, a description of how that fee is calculated.

(5) Subsections (6) and (7) apply to a letting agent engaging in letting agency or property management work in relation to dwelling-houses in England.

(6) If the agent holds money on behalf of persons to whom the agent provides services as part of that work, the duty imposed on the agent by subsection (2) or (3) includes a duty to display or publish, with the list of fees, a statement of whether the agent is a member of a client money protection scheme.

(7) If the agent is required to be a member of a redress scheme for dealing with complaints in connection with that work, the duty imposed on the agent by subsection (2) or (3) includes a duty to display or publish, with the list of fees, a statement—

(a) that indicates that the agent is a member of a redress scheme, and

(b) that gives the name of the scheme.

(8) The appropriate national authority may by regulations specify—

(a) other ways in which a letting agent must publicise details of the relevant fees charged by the agent or (where applicable) a statement within subsection (6) or (7);

(b) the details that must be given of fees publicised in that way.

(9) In this section—

"client money protection scheme" means a scheme which enables a person on whose behalf a letting agent holds money to be compensated if all or part of that money is not repaid to that person in circumstances where the scheme applies;

"redress scheme" means a redress scheme for which provision is made by order under section 83 or 84 of the Enterprise and Regulatory Reform Act 2013.

Section 84. (1) In this Chapter "letting agent" means a person who engages in letting agency work (whether or not that person engages in other work).

(2) A person is not a letting agent for the purposes of this Chapter if the person engages in letting agency work in the course of that person's employment under a contract of employment.

(3) A person is not a letting agent for the purposes of this Chapter if—

(a) the person is of a description specified in regulations made by the appropriate national authority;

(b) the person engages in work of a description specified in regulations made by the appropriate national authority.

Section 85. (1) In this Chapter "relevant fees", in relation to a letting agent, means the fees, charges or penalties (however expressed) payable to the agent by a landlord or tenant—

(a) in respect of letting agency work carried on by the agent,

(b) in respect of property management work carried on by the agent, or

(c) otherwise in connection with—

(i) an assured tenancy of a dwelling-house, or

(ii) a dwelling-house that is, has been or is proposed to be let under an assured tenancy.

(2) Subsection (1) does not apply to—

(a) the rent payable to a landlord under a tenancy,

(b) any fees, charges or penalties which the letting agent receives from a landlord under a tenancy on behalf of another person,

(c) a tenancy deposit within the meaning of section 212(8) of the Housing Act 2004, or

(d) any fees, charges or penalties of a description specified in regulations made by the appropriate national authority.

Section 86. (1) In this Chapter "letting agency work" means things done by a person in the course of a business in response to instructions received from—

(a) a person ("a prospective landlord") seeking to find another person wishing to rent a dwelling-house under an assured tenancy and, having found such a person, to grant such a tenancy, or

(b) a person ("a prospective tenant") seeking to find a dwelling-house to rent under an assured tenancy and, having found such a dwelling-house, to obtain such a tenancy of it.

(2) But "letting agency work" does not include any of the following things when done by a person who does nothing else within subsection (1) —

(a) publishing advertisements or disseminating information;

(b) providing a means by which a prospective landlord or a prospective tenant can, in response to an advertisement or dissemination of information, make direct contact with a prospective tenant or a prospective landlord;

(c) providing a means by which a prospective landlord and a prospective tenant can communicate directly with each other.

(3) "Letting agency work" also does not include things done by a local authority.

(4) In this Chapter "property management work", in relation to a letting agent, means things done by the agent in the course of a business in response to instructions received from another person where—

(a) that person wishes the agent to arrange services, repairs, maintenance, improvements or insurance in respect of, or to deal with any other aspect of the management of, premises on the person's behalf, and

(b) the premises consist of a dwelling-house let under an assured tenancy.

Section 87. (1) It is the duty of every local weights and measures authority in England and Wales to enforce the provisions of this Chapter in its area.

(2) If a letting agent breaches the duty in section 83(3) (duty to publish list of fees etc on agent's website), that breach is taken to have occurred in each area of a local weights and measures authority

in England and Wales in which a dwelling-house to which the fees relate is located.

(3) Where a local weights and measures authority in England and Wales is satisfied on the balance of probabilities that a letting agent has breached a duty imposed by or under section 83, the authority may impose a financial penalty on the agent in respect of that breach.

(4) A local weights and measures authority in England and Wales may impose a penalty under this section in respect of a breach which occurs in England and Wales but outside that authority's area (as well as in respect of a breach which occurs within that area).

(5) But a local weights and measures authority in England and Wales may impose a penalty in respect of a breach which occurs outside its area and in the area of a local weights and measures authority in Wales only if it has obtained the consent of that authority.

(6) Only one penalty under this section may be imposed on the same letting agent in respect of the same breach.

(7) The amount of a financial penalty imposed under this section—

(a) may be such as the authority imposing it determines, but

(b) must not exceed £5,000.

(8) Schedule 9 (procedure for and appeals against financial penalties) has effect.

(9) A local weights and measures authority in England must have regard to any guidance issued by the Secretary of State about—

(a) compliance by letting agents with duties imposed by or under section 83;

(b) the exercise of its functions under this section or Schedule 9.

(10) A local weights and measures authority in Wales must have regard to any guidance issued by the Welsh Ministers about—

(a) compliance by letting agents with duties imposed by or under section 83;

(b) the exercise of its functions under this section or Schedule 9.

(11) The Secretary of State may by regulations made by statutory instrument—

(a) amend any of the provisions of this section or Schedule 9 in their application in relation to local weights and measures authorities in England;

(b) make consequential amendments to Schedule 5 in its application in relation to such authorities.

(12) The Welsh Ministers may by regulations made by statutory instrument—

(a) amend any of the provisions of this section or Schedule 9 in their application in relation to local weights and measures authorities in Wales;

(b) make consequential amendments to Schedule 5 in its application in relation to such authorities.

Section 88. (1) In this Chapter—

"the appropriate national authority" means—

(a) in relation to England, the Secretary of State, and

(b) in relation to Wales, the Welsh Ministers;

"assured tenancy" means a tenancy which is an assured tenancy for the purposes of the Housing Act 1988 except where—

(a) the landlord is—

(i) a private registered provider of social housing,

(ii) a registered social landlord, or

(iii) a fully mutual housing association, or

(b) the tenancy is a long lease;

"dwelling-house" may be a house or part of a house;

"fully mutual housing association" has the same meaning as in Part 1 of the Housing Associations Act 1985 (see section 1(1) and (2) of that Act);

"landlord" includes a person who proposes to be a landlord under a tenancy and a person who has ceased to be a landlord under a tenancy because the tenancy has come to an end;

"long lease" means a lease which—

(a) is a long lease for the purposes of Chapter 1 of Part 1 of the Leasehold Reform, Housing and Urban Development Act 1993, or

(b) in the case of a shared ownership lease (within the meaning given by section 7(7) of that Act), would be a lease within paragraph (a) of this definition if the tenant's total share (within the meaning given by that section) were 100%;

"registered social landlord" means a body registered as a social landlord under Chapter 1 of Part 1 of the Housing Act 1996;

"tenant" includes a person who proposes to be a tenant under a tenancy and a person who has ceased to be a tenant under a tenancy because the tenancy has come to an end.

(2) In this Chapter "local authority" means—

(a) a county council,

(b) a county borough council,

(c) a district council,

(d) a London borough council,

(e) the Common Council of the City of London in its capacity as local authority, or

(f) the Council of the Isles of Scilly.

(3) References in this Chapter to a tenancy include a proposed tenancy and a tenancy that has come to an end.

(4) References in this Chapter to anything which is payable, or which a person is liable to pay, to a letting agent include anything that the letting agent claims a person is liable to pay, regardless of whether the person is in fact liable to pay it.

(5) Regulations under this Chapter are to be made by statutory instrument.

(6) A statutory instrument containing (whether alone or with other provision) regulations made by the Secretary of State under section 87(11) is not to be made unless a draft of the instrument has been laid before, and approved by a resolution of, each House of Parliament.

(7) A statutory instrument containing (whether alone or with other provision) regulations made by the Welsh Ministers under section 87(12) is not to be made unless a draft of the instrument has been laid before, and approved by a resolution of, the National Assembly for Wales.

(8) A statutory instrument containing regulations made by the Secretary of State under this Chapter other than one to which subsection (6) applies is subject to annulment in pursuance of a resolution of either House of Parliament.

(9) A statutory instrument containing regulations made by the Welsh Ministers under this Chapter other than one to which subsection (7) applies is subject to annulment in pursuance of a resolution of the National Assembly for Wales.

(10) Regulations under this Chapter—

(a) may make different provision for different purposes;

(b) may make provision generally or in relation to specific cases.

(11) Regulations under this Chapter may include incidental, supplementary, consequential, transitional, transitory or saving provision.

Chapter 4. Student Complaints Scheme

Section 89. (1) The Higher Education Act 2004 is amended as follows.

(2) In section 11 (qualifying institutions for the purposes of the student complaints scheme) after paragraph (d) insert—

"(e) an institution (other than one within another paragraph of this section) which provides higher education courses which are designated for the purposes of section 22 of the 1998 Act by or under regulations under that section;

(f) an institution (other than one within another paragraph of this section) whose entitlement to grant awards is conferred by an order under section 76(1) of the 1992 Act."

(3) In section 12 (qualifying complaints for the purposes of the student complaints scheme) —

(a) in subsection (1) for "subsection (2) "substitute "subsections (2) and (3) ", and

(b) after subsection (2) insert—

"(3) The designated operator may determine that a complaint within subsection (1) about an act or omission of a qualifying institution within paragraph (e) or (f) of section 11 is a qualifying complaint only if it is made by a person who is undertaking or has undertaken a particular course or a course of a particular description."

Chapter 5. Secondary Ticketing

Section 90. (1) This section applies where a person ("the seller") re-sells a ticket for a recreational, sporting or cultural event in the United Kingdom through a secondary ticketing facility.

(2) The seller and each operator of the facility must ensure that the person who buys the ticket ("the buyer") is given the information specified in subsection (3), where this is applicable to the ticket.

(3) That information is—

(a) where the ticket is for a particular seat or standing area at the venue for the event, the information necessary to enable the buyer to identify that seat or standing area,

(b) information about any restriction which limits use of the ticket to persons of a particular description, and

(c) the face value of the ticket.

(4) The reference in subsection (3) (a) to information necessary to enable the buyer to identify a seat or standing area at a venue includes, so far as applicable—

(a) the name of the area in the venue in which the seat or standing area is located (for example the name of the stand in which it is located),

(b) information necessary to enable the buyer to identify the part of the area in the venue in which the seat or standing area is located (for example the block of seats in which the seat is located),

(c) the number, letter or other distinguishing mark of the row in which the seat is located,

(d) the number, letter or other distinguishing mark of the seat. ,and

(e) any unique ticket number that may help the buyer to identify the seat or standing area or its location.

(5) The reference in subsection (3) (c) to the face value of the ticket is to the amount stated on the ticket as its price.

(6) The seller and each operator of the facility must ensure that the buyer is given the information specified in subsection (7), where the seller is—

(a) an operator of the secondary ticketing facility,

(b) a person who is a parent undertaking or a subsidiary undertaking in relation to an operator of the secondary ticketing facility,

(c) a person who is employed or engaged by an operator of the secondary ticketing facility,

(d) a person who is acting on behalf of a person within paragraph (c), or

(e) an organiser of the event or a person acting on behalf of an organiser of the event.

(7) That information is a statement that the seller of the ticket is a person within subsection (6) which specifies the ground on which the seller falls within that subsection.

(8) Information required by this section to be given to the buyer must be given—

(a) in a clear and comprehensible manner, and

(b) before the buyer is bound by the contract for the sale of the ticket.

(9) This section applies in relation to the re-sale of a ticket through a secondary ticketing facility only if the ticket is first offered for re-sale through the facility after the coming into force of this section.

Section 91. (1) This section applies where a person ("the seller") re-sells, or offers for re-sale, a ticket for a recreational, sporting or cultural event in the United Kingdom through a secondary ticketing facility.

(2) An organiser of the event must not cancel the ticket merely because the seller has re-sold the ticket or offered it for re-sale unless—

(a) a term of the original contract for the sale of the ticket—

(i) provided for its cancellation if it was re-sold by the buyer under that contract,

(ii) provided for its cancellation if it was offered for re-sale by that buyer, or

(iii) provided as mentioned in sub-paragraph (i) and (ii), and

(b) that term was not unfair for the purposes of Part 2 (unfair terms).

(3) An organiser of the event must not blacklist the seller merely because the seller has re-sold the ticket or offered it for re-sale unless—

(a) a term of the original contract for the sale of the ticket—

(i) provided for the blacklisting of the buyer under that contract if it was re-sold by that buyer,

(ii) provided for the blacklisting of that buyer if it was offered for re-sale by that buyer, or

(iii) provided as mentioned in sub-paragraph (i) and (ii), and

(b) that term was not unfair for the purposes of Part 2 (unfair terms).

(4) In subsections (2) and (3) "the original contract" means the contract for the sale of the ticket by an organiser of the event to a person other than an organiser of the event.

(5) For the purposes of this section an organiser of an event cancels a ticket if the organiser takes steps which result in the holder for the time being of the ticket no longer being entitled to attend that event.

(6) For the purposes of this section an organiser of an event blacklists a person if the organiser takes steps—

(a) to prevent the person from acquiring a ticket for a recreational, sporting or cultural event in the United Kingdom, or

(b) to restrict the person's opportunity to acquire such a ticket.

(7) Part 2 (unfair terms) may apply to a term of a contract which, apart from that Part, would permit the cancellation of a ticket for a recreational, sporting or cultural event in the United Kingdom, or the blacklisting of the seller of such a ticket, in circumstances other than those mentioned in subsection (2) or (3).

(8) Before the coming into force of Part 2, references to that Part in this section are to be read as references to the Unfair Terms in Consumer Contracts Regulations 1999 (SI 1999/2083).

(9) This section applies in relation to a ticket that is re-sold or offered for re-sale before or after the coming into force of this section; but the prohibition in this section applies only to things done after its coming into force.

Section 92. (1) This section applies where—

(a) an operator of a secondary ticketing facility knows that a person has used or is using the facility in such a way that an offence has been or is being committed, and

(b) the offence relates to the re-sale of a ticket for a recreational, sporting or cultural event in the United Kingdom.

(2) The operator must, as soon as the operator becomes aware that a person has used or is using the facility as mentioned in subsection (1), disclose the matters specified in subsection (3) to—

(a) an appropriate person, and

(b) an organiser of the event (subject to subsection (5)).

(3) Those matters are—

(a) the identity of the person mentioned in subsection (1), if this is known to the operator, and

(b) the fact that the operator knows that an offence has been or is being committed as mentioned in that subsection.

(4) The following are appropriate persons for the purposes of this section—

(a) a constable of a police force in England and Wales,

(b) a constable of the police service of Scotland, and

(c) a police officer within the meaning of the Police (Northern Ireland) Act 2000.

(5) This section does not require an operator to make a disclosure to an organiser of an event if the operator has reasonable grounds for believing that to do so will prejudice the investigation of any offence.

(6) References in this section to an offence are to an offence under the law of any part of the United Kingdom.

(7) This section applies only in relation to an offence of which an operator becomes aware after the coming into force of this section.

Section 93. (1) A local weights and measures authority in Great Britain may enforce the provisions of this Chapter in its area.

(2) The Department of Enterprise, Trade and Investment may enforce the provisions of this Chapter in Northern Ireland.

(3) Each of the bodies referred to in subsections (1) and (2) is an "enforcement authority" for the purposes of this Chapter.

(4) Where an enforcement authority is satisfied on the balance of probabilities that a person has breached a duty or prohibition imposed by this Chapter, the authority may impose a financial penalty on the person in respect of that breach.

(5) But in the case of a breach of a duty in section 90 or a prohibition in section 91 an enforcement authority may not impose a financial penalty on a person ("P") if the authority is satisfied on the balance of probabilities that—

(a) the breach was due to—

(i) a mistake,

(ii) reliance on information supplied to P by another person,

(iii) the act or default of another person,

(iv) an accident, or

(v) another cause beyond P's control, and

(b) P took all reasonable precautions and exercised all due diligence to avoid the breach.

(6) A local weights and measures authority in England and Wales may impose a penalty under this section in respect of a breach which occurs in England and Wales but outside that authority's area (as well as in respect of a breach which occurs within that area).

(7) A local weights and measures authority in Scotland may impose a penalty under this section in respect of a breach which occurs in Scotland but outside that authority's area (as well as in respect of a breach which occurs within that area).

(8) Only one penalty under this section may be imposed on the same person in respect of the same breach.

(9) The amount of a financial penalty imposed under this section—

(a) may be such as the enforcement authority imposing it determines, but

(b) must not exceed £5,000.

(10) Schedule 10 (procedure for and appeals against financial penalties) has effect.

(11) References in this section to this Chapter do not include section 94.

Section 94. (1) The Secretary of State must—

(a) review, or arrange for a review of, consumer protection measures applying to the re-sale of tickets for recreational, sporting or cultural events in the United Kingdom through secondary ticketing facilities,

(b) prepare a report on the outcome of the review or arrange for such a report to be prepared, and
(c) publish that report.
(2) The report must be published before the end of the period of 12 months beginning with the day on which this section comes into force.
(3) The Secretary of State must lay the report before Parliament.
(4) In this section "consumer protection measures" includes such legislation, rules of law, codes of practice and guidance as the Secretary of State considers relate to the rights of consumers or the protection of their interests.

Section 95. (1) In this Chapter—
"enforcement authority" has the meaning given by section 93(3);
"operator", in relation to a secondary ticketing facility, means a person who—
(a) exercises control over the operation of the facility, and
(b) receives revenue from the facility,
but this is subject to regulations under subsection (2);
"organiser", in relation to an event, means a person who—
(a) is responsible for organising or managing the event, or
(b) receives some or all of the revenue from the event;
"parent undertaking" has the meaning given by section 1162 of the Companies Act 2006;
"secondary ticketing facility" means an internet-based facility for the re-sale of tickets for recreational, sporting or cultural events;
"subsidiary undertaking" has the meaning given by section 1162 of the Companies Act 2006;
"undertaking" has the meaning given by section 1161(1) of the Companies Act 2006.
(2) The Secretary of State may by regulations provide that a person of a description specified in the regulations is or is not to be treated for the purposes of this Chapter as an operator in relation to a secondary ticketing facility.
(3) Regulations under subsection (2) —
(a) are to be made by statutory instrument;
(b) may make different provision for different purposes;
(c) may include incidental, supplementary, consequential, transitional, transitory or saving provision.
(4) A statutory instrument containing regulations under subsection (2) is not to be made unless a draft of the instrument has been laid before, and approved by a resolution of, each House of Parliament.

Chapter 6. General

Section 96. (1) The Secretary of State may by order made by statutory instrument make provision in consequence of this Act.
(2) The power conferred by subsection (1) includes power—
(a) to amend, repeal, revoke or otherwise modify any provision made by an enactment or an instrument made under an enactment (including an enactment passed or instrument made in the same Session as this Act);
(b) to make transitional, transitory or saving provision.
(3) A statutory instrument containing (whether alone or with other provision) an order under this section which amends, repeals, revokes or otherwise modifies any provision of primary legislation is not to be made unless a draft of the instrument has been laid before, and approved by a resolution of, each House of Parliament.
(4) A statutory instrument containing an order under this section which does not amend, repeal, revoke or otherwise modify any provision of primary legislation is subject to annulment in pursuance of a resolution of either House of Parliament.
(5) In this section—
"enactment" includes an Act of the Scottish Parliament, a Measure or Act of the National Assembly for Wales and Northern Ireland legislation;
"primary legislation" means—
(a) an Act of Parliament,
(b) an Act of the Scottish Parliament,
(c) a Measure or Act of the National Assembly for Wales, and
(d) Northern Ireland legislation.

Section 97. (1) The Secretary of State may by order made by statutory instrument make transitional, transitory or saving provision in connection with the coming into force of any provision of this Act other than the coming into force of Chapter 3 or 4 of this Part in relation to Wales.
(2) The Welsh Ministers may by order made by statutory instrument make transitional, transitory or

saving provision in connection with the coming into force of Chapter 3 or 4 of this Part in relation to Wales.

Section 98. There is to be paid out of money provided by Parliament—
(a) any expenses incurred by a Minister of the Crown or a government department under this Act, and
(b) any increase attributable to this Act in the sums payable under any other Act out of money so provided.

Section 99. (1) The amendment, repeal or revocation of any provision by this Act has the same extent as the provision concerned.
(2) Section 27 extends only to Scotland.
(3) Chapter 3 of this Part extends only to England and Wales.
(4) Subject to that, this Act extends to England and Wales, Scotland and Northern Ireland.

Section 100. (1) The provisions of this Act listed in subsection (2) come into force on the day on which this Act is passed.
(2) Those provisions are—
(a) section 48(5) to (8),
(b) Chapter 3 of this Part in so far as it confer powers to make regulations,
(c) section 88(5) to (11),
(d) this Chapter, and
(e) paragraph 12 of Schedule 5.
(3) Chapters 3 and 4 of this Part come into force—
(a) in relation to England, on such day as the Secretary of State may appoint by order made by statutory instrument;
(b) in relation to Wales, on such day as the Welsh Ministers may appoint by order made by statutory instrument.
(4) Chapter 5 of this Part comes into force at the end of the period of two months beginning with the day on which this Act is passed.
(5) The other provisions of this Act come into force on such day as the Secretary of State may appoint by order made by statutory instrument.
(6) An order under this section may appoint different days for different purposes.

Section 101. This Act may be cited as the Consumer Rights Act 2015.

SCHEDULES

[Schedule 1 is omitted]

Schedule 2. Consumer contract terms which may be regarded as unfair

Part 1. List of Terms

Section 1. A term which has the object or effect of excluding or limiting the trader's liability in the event of the death of or personal injury to the consumer resulting from an act or omission of the trader.

Section 2. A term which has the object or effect of inappropriately excluding or limiting the legal rights of the consumer in relation to the trader or another party in the event of total or partial non-performance or inadequate performance by the trader of any of the contractual obligations, including the option of offsetting a debt owed to the trader against any claim which the consumer may have against the trader.

Section 3. A term which has the object or effect of making an agreement binding on the consumer in a case where the provision of services by the trader is subject to a condition whose realisation depends on the trader's will alone.

Section 4. A term which has the object or effect of permitting the trader to retain sums paid by the consumer where the consumer decides not to conclude or perform the contract, without providing for the consumer to receive compensation of an equivalent amount from the trader where the trader is the party cancelling the contract.

Section 5. A term which has the object or effect of requiring that, where the consumer decides not to conclude or perform the contract, the consumer must pay the trader a disproportionately high sum in compensation or for services which have not been supplied.

Section 6. A term which has the object or effect of requiring a consumer who fails to fulfil his obligations under the contract to pay a disproportionately high sum in compensation.

Section 7. A term which has the object or effect of authorising the trader to dissolve the contract on a discretionary basis where the same facility is not granted to the consumer, or permitting the trader to retain the sums paid for services not yet supplied by the trader where it is the trader who dissolves the contract.

Section 8. A term which has the object or effect of enabling the trader to terminate a contract of indeterminate duration without reasonable notice except where there are serious grounds for doing so.

Section 9. A term which has the object or effect of automatically extending a contract of fixed duration where the consumer does not indicate otherwise, when the deadline fixed for the consumer to express a desire not to extend the contract is unreasonably early.

Section 10. A term which has the object or effect of irrevocably binding the consumer to terms with which the consumer has had no real opportunity of becoming acquainted before the conclusion of the contract.

Section 11. A term which has the object or effect of enabling the trader to alter the terms of the contract unilaterally without a valid reason which is specified in the contract.

Section 12. A term which has the object or effect of permitting the trader to determine the characteristics of the subject matter of the contract after the consumer has become bound by it.

Section 13. A term which has the object or effect of enabling the trader to alter unilaterally without a valid reason any characteristics of the goods, digital content or services to be provided.

Section 14. A term which has the object or effect of giving the trader the discretion to decide the price payable under the contract after the consumer has become bound by it, where no price or method of determining the price is agreed when the consumer becomes bound.

Section 15. A term which has the object or effect of permitting a trader to increase the price of goods, digital content or services without giving the consumer the right to cancel the contract if the final price is too high in relation to the price agreed when the contract was concluded.

Section 16. A term which has the object or effect of giving the trader the right to determine whether the goods, digital content or services supplied are in conformity with the contract, or giving the trader the exclusive right to interpret any term of the contract.

Section 17. A term which has the object or effect of limiting the trader's obligation to respect commitments undertaken by the trader's agents or making the trader's commitments subject to compliance with a particular formality.

Section 18. A term which has the object or effect of obliging the consumer to fulfil all of the consumer's obligations where the trader does not perform the trader's obligations.

Section 19. A term which has the object or effect of allowing the trader to transfer the trader's rights and obligations under the contract, where this may reduce the guarantees for the consumer, without the consumer's agreement.

Section 20. A term which has the object or effect of excluding or hindering the consumer's right to take legal action or exercise any other legal remedy, in particular by—
(a) requiring the consumer to take disputes exclusively to arbitration not covered by legal provisions,
(b) unduly restricting the evidence available to the consumer, or
(c) imposing on the consumer a burden of proof which, according to the applicable law, should lie with another party to the contract.

[Schedules 3-10 are omitted.]

Miscellaneous Private Law Statutes*

Statute of Frauds 1677 (c. 3). Selected provision: S. 4, as last amended by the Law Reform (Enforcement of Contracts) Act 1954 (c. 34). Selected Provision: Section 4.

Section 4. Noe Action shall be brought (…) whereby to charge the Defendant upon any speciall promise to answere for the debt default or miscarriages of another person (…) unlesse the Agreement upon which such Action shall be brought or some Memorandum or Note thereof shall be in Writing and signed by the partie to be charged therewith or some other person thereunto by him lawfully authorized.

Law of Property Act 1925 [An Act to consolidate the enactments relating to conveyancing and the law of property in England and Wales] (c.20), as last amended by the Infrastructure Act 2015 (c. 7). Selected provisions: Sections 1, 2, 11, 12, 52, 54, 101, 136 and 198.

Section 1. (1) The only estates in land which are capable of subsisting or of being conveyed or created at law are—
a) An estate in fee simple absolute in possession;
b) A term of years absolute.
(2) The only interests or charges in or over land which are capable of subsisting or of being conveyed or created at law are—
(a) An easement, right, or privilege in or over land for an interest equivalent to an estate in fee simple absolute in possession or a term of years absolute;
(b) A rentcharge in possession issuing out of or charged on land being either perpetual or for a term of years absolute;
(c) A charge by way of legal mortgage;
(d) and any other similar charge on land which is not created by an instrument;
(e) Rights of entry exercisable over or in respect of a legal term of years absolute, or annexed, for any purpose, to a legal rentcharge.
(3) All other estates, interests, and charges in or over land take effect as equitable interests
(4) The estates, interests, and charges which under this section are authorised to subsist or to be conveyed or created at law are (when subsisting or conveyed or created at law) in this Act referred to as "legal estates," and have the same incidents as legal estates subsisting at the commencement of this Act; and the owner of a legal estate is referred to as "an estate owner" and his legal estate is referred to as his estate.
(5) A legal estate may subsist concurrently with or subject to any other legal estate in the same land in like manner as it could have done before the commencement of this Act.
(6) A legal estate is not capable of subsisting or of being created in an undivided share in land or of being held by an infant.
(7) Every power of appointment over, or power to convey or charge land or any interest therein, whether created by a statute or other instrument or implied by law, and whether created before or after the commencement of this Act (not being a power vested in a legal mortgagee or an estate owner in right of his estate and exercisable by him or by another person in his name and on his behalf), operates only in equity.
(8) Estates, interests, and charges in or over land which are not legal estates are in this Act referred to as "equitable interests," and powers which by this Act are to operate in equity only are in this Act referred to as "equitable powers."
(9) The provisions in any statute or other instrument requiring land to be conveyed to uses shall take effect as directions that the land shall (subject to creating or reserving thereout any legal estate authorised by this Act which may be required) be conveyed to a person of full age upon the requisite trusts.
(10) The repeal of the Statute of Uses (as amended) does not affect the operation thereof in regard to dealings taking effect before the commencement of this Act.

Section 2. (1) A conveyance to a purchaser of a legal estate in land shall overreach any equitable interest or power affecting that estate, whether or not he has notice thereof, if—
(i) the conveyance is made under the powers conferred by the Settled Land Act, 1925, or any

---

*   Arranged by year of enactment.

additional powers conferred by a settlement, and the equitable interest or power is capable of being overreached thereby, and the statutory requirements respecting the payment of capital money arising under the settlement are complied with;

ii) the conveyance is made by trustees of land and the equitable interest or power is at the date of the conveyance capable of being overreached by such trustees under the provisions of subsection (2) of this section or independently of that subsection, and the requirements of section 27 of this Act respecting the payment of capital money arising on such a conveyance are complied with;

(iii) the conveyance is made by a mortgagee or personal representative in the exercise of his paramount powers, and the equitable interest or power is capable of being overreached by such conveyance, and any capital money arising from the transaction is paid to the mortgagee or personal representative;

(iv) the conveyance is made under an order of the court and the equitable interest or power is bound by such order, and any capital money arising from the transaction is paid into, or in accordance with the order of, the court.

(1A) An equitable interest in land subject to a trust of land which remains in, or is to revert to, the settlor shall (subject to any contrary intention) be overreached by the conveyance if it would be so overreached were it an interest under the trust.

(2) Where the legal estate affected is subject to a trust of land, then if at the date of a conveyance made after the commencement of this Act by the trustees, the trustees (whether original or substituted) are either—

(a) two or more individuals approved or appointed by the court or the successors in office of the individuals so approved or appointed; or

(b) a trust corporation,

any equitable interest or power having priority to the trust shall, notwithstanding any stipulation to the contrary, be overreached by the conveyance, and shall, according to its priority, take effect as if created or arising by means of a primary trust affecting the proceeds of sale and the income of the land until sale.

(3) The following equitable interests and powers are excepted from the operation of subsection (2) of this section, namely—

(i) Any equitable interest protected by a deposit of documents relating to the legal estate affected;

(ii) The benefit of any covenant or agreement restrictive of the user of land;

(iii) Any easement, liberty, or privilege over or affecting land and being merely an equitable interest (in this Act referred to as an "equitable easement");

(iv) The benefit of any contract (in this Act referred to as an "estate contract") to convey or create a legal estate, including a contract conferring either expressly or by statutory implication a valid option to purchase, a right of pre-emption, or any other like right;

(v) Any equitable interest protected by registration under the Land Charges Act, 1925, other than—

(a) an annuity within the meaning of Part II. of that Act;

(b) a limited owner's charge or a general equitable charge within the meaning of that Act.

(4) Subject to the protection afforded by this section to the purchaser of a legal estate, nothing contained in this section shall deprive a person entitled to an equitable charge of any of his rights or remedies for enforcing the same.

(5) So far as regards the following interests, created before the commencement of this Act (which accordingly are not within the provisions of the Land Charges Act, 1925), namely—

(a) the benefit of any covenant or agreement restrictive of the user of the land;

(b) any equitable easement;

(c) the interest under a puisne mortgage within the meaning of the Land Charges Act, 1925, unless and until acquired under a transfer made after the commencement of this Act;

(d) the benefit of an estate contract, unless and until the same is acquired under a conveyance made after the commencement of this Act;

a purchaser of a legal estate shall only take subject thereto if he has notice thereof, and the same are not overreached under the provisions contained or in the manner referred to in this section.

Section 11. (1) It shall not be necessary to register a memorial of any instrument made after the commencement of this Act in any local deeds registry unless the instrument operates to transfer or create a legal estate, or to create a charge thereon by way of legal mortgage; nor shall the registration of a memorial of any instrument not required to be registered affect any priority.

(2) Probates and letters of administration shall be treated as instruments capable of transferring a legal estate to personal representatives.

(3) Memorials of all instruments capable of transferring or creating a legal estate or charge by way of legal mortgage, may, when so operating, be registered.

Section 12. Nothing in this Part of this Act affects the operation of any statute, or of the general law for the limitation of actions or proceedings relating to land or with reference to the acquisition of easements or rights over or in respect of land.

Section 52. (1) All conveyances of land or of any interest therein are void for the purpose of conveying or creating a legal estate unless made by deed.
(2) This section does not apply to—
(a) assents by a personal representative;
(b) disclaimers made in accordance with sections 178 to 180 or sections 315 to 319 of the Insolvency Act 1986, or not required to be evidenced in writing;
(c) surrenders by operation of law, including surrenders which may, by law, be effected without writing;
(d) leases or tenancies or other assurances not required by law to be made in writing;
(da) flexible tenancies;
(db) assured tenancies of dwelling-houses in England that are granted by private registered providers of social housing and are not long tenancies or shared ownership leases;
(e) receipts other than those falling within section 115 below;
(f) vesting orders of the court or other competent authority;
(g) conveyances taking effect by operation of law.
(3)In this section—
"assured tenancy" has the same meaning as in Part 1 of the Housing Act 1988;
"dwelling-house" has the same meaning as in Part 1 of the Housing Act 1988;
"flexible tenancy" has the meaning given by section 107A of the Housing Act 1985;
"long tenancy" means a tenancy granted for a term certain of more than 21 years, whether or not it is (or may become) terminable before the end of that term by notice given by the tenant or by re-entry or forfeiture;
"shared ownership lease" means a lease of a dwelling-house—
(a) granted on payment of a premium calculated by reference to a percentage of the value of the dwelling-house or of the cost of providing it, or
(b) under which the lessee (or the lessee's personal representatives) will or may be entitled to a sum calculated by reference, directly or indirectly, to the value of the dwelling-house.

Section 54. (1) All interests in land created by parol and not put in writing and signed by the persons so creating the same, or by their agents thereunto lawfully authorised in writing, have, notwithstanding any consideration having been given for the same, the force and effect of interests at will only.
(2) Nothing in the foregoing provisions of this Part of this Act shall affect the creation by parol of leases taking effect in possession for a term not exceeding three years (whether or not the lessee is given power to extend the term) at the best rent which can be reasonably obtained without taking a fine.

Section 101. (1) A mortgagee, where the mortgage is made by deed, shall, by virtue of this Act, have the following powers, to the like extent as if they had been in terms conferred by the mortgage deed, but not further (namely):
(i) A power, when the mortgage money has become due, to sell, or to concur with any other person in selling, the mortgaged property, or any part thereof, either subject to prior charges or not, and either together or in lots, by public auction or by private contract, subject to such conditions respecting title, or evidence of title, or other matter, as the mortgagee thinks fit, with power to vary any contract for sale, and to buy in at an auction, or to rescind any contract for sale, and to re-sell, without being answerable for any loss occasioned thereby; and
(ii) A power, at any time after the date of the mortgage deed, to insure and keep insured against loss or damage by fire any building, or any effects or property of an insurable nature, whether affixed to the freehold or not, being or forming part of the property which or an estate or interest wherein is mortgaged, and the premiums paid for any such insurance shall be a charge on the mortgaged property or estate or interest, in addition to the mortgage money, and with the same priority, and with interest at the same rate, as the mortgage money; and
(iii) A power, when the mortgage money has become due, to appoint a receiver of the income of the mortgaged property, or any part thereof; or, if the mortgaged property consists of an interest in income, or of a rentcharge or an annual or other periodical sum, a receiver of that property or any part thereof; and
(iv) A power, while the mortgagee is in possession, to cut and sell timber and other trees ripe for

cutting, and not planted or left standing for shelter or ornament, or to contract for any such cutting and sale, to be completed within any time not exceeding twelve months from the making of the contract.

(1A) Subsection (1)(i) is subject to section 21 of the Commonhold and Leasehold Reform Act 2002 (no disposition of part-units)

[Subsections 2 – 6 are omitted.]

Section 136. (1) Any absolute assignment by writing under the hand of the assignor (not purporting to be by way of charge only) of any debt or other legal thing in action, of which express notice in writing has been given to the debtor, trustee or other person from whom the assignor would have been entitled to claim such debt or thing in action, is effectual in law (subject to equities having priority over the right of the assignee) to pass and transfer from the date of such notice-

(a) the legal right to such debt or thing in action;

(b) all legal and other remedies for the same; and

(c) the power to give a good discharge for the same without the concurrence of the assignor:

Provided that, if the debtor, trustee or other person liable in respect of such debt or thing in action has notice-

(a) that the assignment is disputed by the assignor or any person claiming under him; or

(b) of any other opposing or conflicting claims to such debt or thing in action; he may, if he thinks fit, either call upon the persons making claim thereto to interplead concerning the same, or pay the debt or other thing in action into court under the provisions of the Trustee Act, 1925.

[Subsection 2 is omitted.]

(3) The county court has jurisdiction (including power to receive payment of money or securities into court) under the proviso to subsection (1) of this section where the amount or value of the debt or thing in action does not exceed £30,000.

Section 198. (1) The registration of any instrument or matter in any register kept under the Land Charges Act 1972 or the local land charges register, shall be deemed to constitute actual notice of such instrument or matter, and of the fact of such registration, to all persons and for all purposes connected with the land affected, as from the date of registration or other prescribed dates and so long as the registration continues in force.

[Subsection 2 is omitted.]

Occupiers Liability Act 1957. (c. 31) [An Act to amend the law of England and Wales as to the liability of occupiers and others for injury or damage resulting to persons or goods lawfully on any land or other property from dangers due to the state of the property or to things done or omitted to be done there, to make provision as to the operation in relation to the Crown of laws made by the Parliament of Northern Ireland for similar purposes or otherwise amending the law of tort, and for purposes connected therewith.], as last amended by the Countryside and Rights of Way Act 2000 (c. 37).

Section 1. (1) The rules enacted by the two next following sections shall have effect, in place of the rules of the common law, to regulate the duty which an occupier of premises owes to his visitors in respect of dangers due to the state of the premises or to things done or omitted to be done on them.

(2) The rules so enacted shall regulate the nature of the duty imposed by law in consequence of a person's occupation or control of premises and of any invitation or permission he gives (or is to be treated as giving) to another to enter or use the premises, but they shall not alter the rules of the common law as to the persons on whom a duty is so imposed or to whom it is owed; and accordingly for the purpose of the rules so enacted the persons who are to be treated as an occupier and as his visitors are the same (subject to subsection (4) of this section) as the persons who would at common law be treated as an occupier and as his invitees or licensees.

(3) The rules so enacted in relation to an occupier of premises and his visitors shall also apply, in like manner and to the like extent as the principles applicable at common law to an occupier of premises and his invitees or licensees would apply, to regulate—

(a) the obligations of a person occupying or having control over any fixed or moveable structure, including any vessel, vehicle or aircraft; and

(b) the obligations of a person occupying or having control over any premises or structure in respect of damage to property, including the property of persons who are not themselves his visitors.

(4) A person entering any premises in exercise of rights conferred by virtue of—

(a)section 2(1) of the Countryside and Rights of Way Act 2000, or

(b)an access agreement or order under the National Parks and Access to the Countryside Act 1949,

is not, for the purposes of this Act, a visitor of the occupier of the premises.

Section 2. (1) An occupier of premises owes the same duty, the "common duty of care", to all his visitors, except in so far as he is free to and does extend, restrict, modify or exclude his duty to any visitor or visitors by agreement or otherwise.

(2) The common duty of care is a duty to take such care as in all the circumstances of the case is reasonable to see that the visitor will be reasonably safe in using the premises for the purposes for which he is invited or permitted by the occupier to be there.

(3) The circumstances relevant for the present purpose include the degree of care, and of want of care, which would ordinarily be looked for in such a visitor, so that (for example) in proper cases—

(a)an occupier must be prepared for children to be less careful than adults; and

(b)an occupier may expect that a person, in the exercise of his calling, will appreciate and guard against any special risks ordinarily incident to it, so far as the occupier leaves him free to do so.

(4) In determining whether the occupier of premises has discharged the common duty of care to a visitor, regard is to be had to all the circumstances, so that (for example)—

(a)where damage is caused to a visitor by a danger of which he had been warned by the occupier, the warning is not to be treated without more as absolving the occupier from liability, unless in all the circumstances it was enough to enable the visitor to be reasonably safe; and

(b)where damage is caused to a visitor by a danger due to the faulty execution of any work of construction, maintenance or repair by an independent contractor employed by the occupier, the occupier is not to be treated without more as answerable for the danger if in all the circumstances he had acted reasonably in entrusting the work to an independent contractor and had taken such steps (if any) as he reasonably ought in order to satisfy himself that the contractor was competent and that the work had been properly done.

(5) The common duty of care does not impose on an occupier any obligation to a visitor in respect of risks willingly accepted as his by the visitor (the question whether a risk was so accepted to be decided on the same principles as in other cases in which one person owes a duty of care to another).

(6) For the purposes of this section, persons who enter premises for any purpose in the exercise of a right conferred by law are to be treated as permitted by the occupier to be there for that purpose, whether they in fact have his permission or not.

Section 3. (1)Where an occupier of premises is bound by contract to permit persons who are strangers to the contract to enter or use the premises, the duty of care which he owes to them as his visitors cannot be restricted or excluded by that contract, but (subject to any provision of the contract to the contrary) shall include the duty to perform his obligations under the contract, whether undertaken for their protection or not, in so far as those obligations go beyond the obligations otherwise involved in that duty.

(2) A contract shall not by virtue of this section have the effect, unless it expressly so provides, of making an occupier who has taken all reasonable care answerable to strangers to the contract for dangers due to the faulty execution of any work of construction, maintenance or repair or other like operation by persons other than himself, his servants and persons acting under his direction and control.

(3) In this section "stranger to the contract" means a person not for the time being entitled to the benefit of the contract as a party to it or as the successor by assignment or otherwise of a party to it, and accordingly includes a party to the contract who has ceased to be so entitled.

(4) Where by the terms or conditions governing any tenancy (including a statutory tenancy which does not in law amount to a tenancy) either the landlord or the tenant is bound, though not by contract, to permit persons to enter or use premises of which he is the occupier, this section shall apply as if the tenancy were a contract between the landlord and the tenant.

(5)This section, in so far as it prevents the common duty of care from being restricted or excluded, applies to contracts entered into and tenancies created before the commencement of this Act, as well as to those entered into or created after its commencement; but, in so far as it enlarges the duty owed by an occupier beyond the common duty of care, it shall have effect only in relation to obligations which are undertaken after that commencement or which are renewed by agreement (whether express or implied) after that commencement.

Section 4. [Repealed]

Section 5. (1) Where persons enter or use, or bring or send goods to, any premises in exercise of a right conferred by contract with a person occupying or having control of the premises, the duty he owes them in respect of dangers due to the state of the premises or to things done or omitted to be done on them, in so far as the duty depends on a term to be implied in the contract by reason of its conferring that right, shall be the common duty of care.
(2) The foregoing subsection shall apply to fixed and moveable structures as it applies to premises.
(3) This section does not affect the obligations imposed on a person by or by virtue of any contract for the hire of, or for the carriage for reward of persons or goods in, any vehicle, vessel, aircraft or other means of transport, or by or by virtue of any contract of bailment.
(4) This section does not apply to contracts entered into before the commencement of this Act.

Section 6. This Act shall bind the Crown, but as regards the Crown's liability in tort shall not bind the Crown further than the Crown is made liable in tort by the Crown Proceedings Act 1947, and that Act and in particular section two of it shall apply in relation to duties under sections two to four of this Act as statutory duties.

Section 7. The limitation imposed by paragraph (1) of section four of the Government of Ireland Act 1920, precluding the Parliament of Northern Ireland from making laws in respect of the Crown or property of the Crown (including foreshore vested in the Crown) shall not extend to prevent that Parliament from amending the law of tort, or enacting provisions similar to section five of this Act, so as to bind the Crown in common with private persons; but as regards the Crown's liability in tort, no such amendments shall bind the Crown further than the Crown is made liable in tort under the law of Northern Ireland by Orders in Council under section fifty-three of the Crown Proceedings Act 1947.

Section 8. (1) This Act may be cited as the Occupiers' Liability Act 1957.
(2) This Act shall not extend to Scotland, nor to Northern Ireland except in so far as it extends the powers of the Parliament of Northern Ireland.
(3) This Act shall come into force on the first day of January, nineteen hundred and fifty-eight.

Misrepresentation Act 1967 [An Act to amend the law relating to innocent misrepresentations and to amend sections 11 and 35 of the Sale of Goods Act 1893] (c. 7), as last amended by the Consumer Rights Act 2015 (c. 15). Selected provisions: Sections 1 – 3.

Section 1. Where a person has entered into a contract after a misrepresentation has been made to him, and –
(a) the misrepresentation has become a term of the contract; or
(b) the contract has been performed;
or both, then, if otherwise he would be entitled to rescind the contract without alleging fraud, he shall be so entitled, subject to the provisions of this Act, notwithstanding the matters mentioned in paragraphs (a) and (b) of this section.

Section 2. (1) Where a person has entered into a contract after a misrepresentation has been made to him by another party thereto and as a result thereof he has suffered loss, then, if the person making the misrepresentation would be liable to damages in respect thereof had the misrepresentation been made fraudulently, that person shall be so liable notwithstanding that the misrepresentation was not made fraudulently, unless he proves that he had reasonable ground to believe and did believe up to the time the contract was made that the facts represented were true.
(2) Where a person has entered into a contract after a misrepresentation has been made to him otherwise than fraudulently, and he would be entitled, by reason of the misrepresentation, to rescind the contract, then, if it is claimed, in any proceedings arising out of the contract, that the contract ought to be or has been rescinded the court or arbitrator may declare the contract subsisting and award damages in lieu of rescission, if of opinion that it would be equitable to do so, having regard to the nature of the misrepresentation and the loss that would be caused by it if the contract were upheld, as well as to the loss that rescission would cause to the other party.
(3) Damages may be awarded against a person under subsection (2) of this section whether or not he is liable to damages under subsection (1) thereof, but where he is so liable any award under the said subsection (2) shall be taken into account in assessing his liability under the said subsection (1).
(4) This section does not entitle a person to be paid damages in respect of a misrepresentation if the person has a right to redress under Part 4A of the Consumer Protection from Unfair Trading Regulations 2008 (SI 2008/1277) in respect of the conduct constituting the misrepresentation.

(5) Subsection (4) does not prevent a debtor from bringing a claim under section 75(1) of the Consumer Credit Act 1974 against a creditor under a debtor-creditor-supplier agreement in a case where, but for subsection (4), the debtor would have a claim against the supplier in respect of a misrepresentation (and, where section 75 of that Act would otherwise apply, it accordingly applies as if the debtor had a claim against the supplier).

Section 3. (1) If a contract contains a term which would exclude or restrict—
(a) any liability to which a party to a contract may be subject by reason of any misrepresentation made by him before the contract was made; or
(b) any remedy available to another party to the contract by reason of such a misrepresentation, that term shall be of no effect except in so far as it satisfies the requirement of reasonableness as stated in section 11(1) of the Unfair Contract Terms Act 1977; and it is for those claiming that the term satisfies that requirement to show that it does.
(2) This section does not apply to a term in a consumer contract within the meaning of Part 2 of the Consumer Rights Act 2015 (but see the provision made about such contracts in section 62 of that Act).

Animals Act 1971 [An Act to make provision with respect to civil liability for damage done by animals and with respect to the protection of livestock from dogs; and for purposes connected with those matters]. Selected provision : Section 2

Strict liability for damage done by animals

Section 2. (1) Where any damage is caused by an animal which belongs to a dangerous species, any person who is a keeper of the animal is liable for the damage, except as otherwise provided by this Act.
(2) Where damage is caused by an animal which does not belong to a dangerous species, a keeper of the animal is liable for the damage, except as otherwise provided by this Act, if—
(a) the damage is of a kind which the animal, unless restrained, was likely to cause or which, if caused by the animal, was likely to be severe; and
(b) the likelihood of the damage or of its being severe was due to characteristics of the animal which are not normally found in animals of the same species or are not normally so found except at particular times or in particular circumstances; and
(c) those characteristics were known to that keeper or were at any time known to a person who at that time had charge of the animal as that keeper's servant or, where that keeper is the head of a household, were known to another keeper of the animal who is a member of that household and under the age of sixteen.

Consumer Credit Act 1974 (c. 39), as last amended by The Financial Services Act 2012 (Consumer Credit) Order 2013. Selected provision: Sections 60 (1) and (2) and 127.

Section 60. (1) The Treasury shall make regulations as to the form and content of documents embodying regulated agreements, and the regulations shall contain such provisions as appear to them appropriate with a view to ensuring that the debtor or hirer is made aware of—
(a) the rights and duties conferred or imposed on him by the agreement,
(b) the amount and rate of the total charge for credit (in the case of a consumer credit agreement),
(c) the protection and remedies available to him under this Act, and
(d) any other matters which, in the opinion of the Treasury, it is desirable for him to know about in connection with the agreement.
(2) Regulations under subsection (1) may in particular—
(a) require specified information to be included in the prescribed manner in documents, and other specified material to be excluded;
(b) contain requirements to ensure that specified information is clearly brought to the attention of the debtor or hirer, and that one part of a document is not given insufficient or excessive prominence compared with another.
(...)

Section 127. (1) In the case of an application for an enforcement order under —
(za) section 55 (2) (disclosure of information), or

(zb) section 61B (3) (duty to supply copy of overdraft agreement), or

(a) section 65 (1) (improperly executed agreements), or

(b) section 105 (7) (a) or (b) (improperly executed security instruments), or

(c) section 111 (2) (failure to serve copy of notice on surety), or

(d) section 124 (1) or (2) (taking of negotiable instrument in contravention of section 123),

the court shall dismiss the application if, but only if, it considers it just to do so having regard to —

(i) prejudice caused to any person by the contravention in question, and the degree of culpability for it; and

(ii) the powers conferred on the court by subsection (2) and sections 135 and 136.

(2) If it appears to the court just to do so, it may in an enforcement order reduce or discharge any sum payable by the debtor or hirer, or any surety, so as to compensate him for prejudice suffered as a result of the contravention in question.

Fatal Accidents Act 1976 [An Act to consolidate the Fatal Accidents Acts], as last amended by The Damages for Bereavement (Variation of Sum) (England and Wales) Order 2013. Selected Provisions: Sections 1-5.

Section 1. (1) If death is caused by any wrongful act, neglect or default which is such as would (if death had not ensued) have entitled the person injured to maintain an action and recover damages in respect thereof, the person who would have been liable if death had not ensued shall be liable to an action for damages, notwithstanding the death of the person injured.

(2) Subject to section 1A(2) below, every such action shall be for the benefit of the dependants of the person ("the deceased") whose death has been so caused.

(3) In this Act "dependant" means—

(a) the wife or husband or former wife or husband of the deceased;

(aa) the civil partner or former civil partner of the deceased;

(b) any person who—

(i) was living with the deceased in the same household immediately before the date of the death; and

(ii) had been living with the deceased in the same household for at least two years before that date; and

(iii) was living during the whole of that period as the husband or wife or civil partner of the deceased;

(c) any parent or other ascendant of the deceased;

(d) any person who was treated by the deceased as his parent;

(e) any child or other descendant of the deceased;

(f) any person (not being a child of the deceased) who, in the case of any marriage to which the deceased was at any time a party, was treated by the deceased as a child of the family in relation to that marriage;

(fa) any person (not being a child of the deceased) who, in the case of any civil partnership in which the deceased was at any time a civil partner, was treated by the deceased as a child of the family in relation to that civil partnership;

(g) any person who is, or is the issue of, a brother, sister, uncle or aunt of the deceased.

(4) The reference to the former wife or husband of the deceased in subsection (3)(a) above includes a reference to a person whose marriage to the deceased has been annulled or declared void as well as a person whose marriage to the deceased has been dissolved.

(4A) The reference to the former civil partner of the deceased in subsection (3)(aa) above includes a reference to a person whose civil partnership with the deceased has been annulled as well as a person whose civil partnership with the deceased has been dissolved.

(5) In deducing any relationship for the purposes of subsection (3) above—

(a) any relationship by marriage or civil partnership shall be treated as a relationship by consanguinity, any relationship of the half blood as a relationship of the whole blood, and the stepchild of any person as his child, and

(b) an illegitimate person shall be treated as—

(i) the legitimate child of his mother and reputed father, or

(ii) in the case of a person who has a female parent by virtue of section 43 of the Human Fertilisation and Embryology Act 2008, the legitimate child of his mother and that female parent.

(6) Any reference in this Act to injury includes any disease and any impairment of a person's physical or mental condition.

Section 1A. (1) An action under this Act may consist of or include a claim for damages for bereavement.

(2) A claim for damages for bereavement shall only be for the benefit—
(a) of the wife or husband or civil partner of the deceased; and
(b) where the deceased was a minor who was never married or a civil partner—
(i) of his parents, if he was legitimate; and
(ii) of his mother, if he was illegitimate.
(3) Subject to subsection (5) below, the sum to be awarded as damages under this section shall be £12,980.
(4) Where there is a claim for damages under this section for the benefit of both the parents of the deceased, the sum awarded shall be divided equally between them (subject to any deduction falling to be made in respect of costs not recovered from the defendant).
(5) The Lord Chancellor may by order made by statutory instrument, subject to annulment in pursuance of a resolution of either House of Parliament, amend this section by varying the sum for the time being specified in subsection (3) above.

Section 2. (1) The action shall be brought by and in the name of the executor or administrator of the deceased.
(2) If—
(a) there is no executor or administrator of the deceased, or
(b) no action is brought within six months after the death by and in the name of an executor or administrator of the deceased, the action may be brought by and in the name of all or any of the persons for whose benefit an executor or administrator could have brought it.
(3) Not more than one action shall lie for and in respect of the same subject matter of complaint.
(4) The plaintiff in the action shall be required to deliver to the defendant or his solicitor full particulars of the persons for whom and on whose behalf the action is brought and of the nature of the claim in respect of which damages are sought to be recovered.

Section 3. (1) In the action such damages, other than damages for bereavement, may be awarded as are proportioned to the injury resulting from the death to the dependants respectively.
(2) After deducting the costs not recovered from the defendant any amount recovered otherwise than as damages for bereavement shall be divided among the dependants in such shares as may be directed.
(3) In an action under this Act where there fall to be assessed damages payable to a widow in respect of the death of her husband there shall not be taken account the re-marriage of the widow or her prospects of re-marriage.
(4) In an action under this Act where there fall to be assessed damages payable to a person who is a dependant by virtue of section 1(3)(b) above in respect of the death of the person with whom the dependant was living as husband or wife or a civil partner there shall be taken into account (together with any other matter that appears to the court to be relevant to the action) the fact that the dependant had no enforceable right to financial support by the deceased as a result of their living together.
(5) If the dependants have incurred funeral expenses in respect of the deceased, damages may be awarded in respect of those expenses.
(6) Money paid into court in satisfaction of a cause of action under this Act may be in one sum without specifying any person's share.

Section 4. In assessing damages in respect of a person's death in an action under this Act, benefits which have accrued or may accrue to any person from his estate or otherwise as a result of his death shall be disregarded.

Section 5. Where any person dies as the result partly of his own fault and partly of the fault of any other person or persons, and accordingly if an action were brought for the benefit of the estate under the Law Reform (Miscellaneous Provisions) Act 1934 the damages recoverable would be reduced under section 1(1) of the Law Reform (Contributory Negligence) Act 1945, any damages recoverable in an action under this Act shall be reduced to a proportionate extent.

Torts (Interference with Goods) Act 1977 [An Act to amend the law concerning conversion and other torts affecting goods] (c. 32), as last amended by the Crime and Courts Act 2013 (c. 22). Selected provisions: Sections 1 – 11 and 14.

Section 1. In this Act "wrongful interference", or "wrongful interference with goods", means—
(a) conversion of goods (also called trover),

(b) trespass to goods,

(c) negligence so far at it results in damage to goods or to an interest in goods.

(d) subject to section 2, any other tort so far as it results in damage to goods or to an interest in goods.
and references in this Act (however worded) to proceedings for wrongful interference or to a claim or right to a claim for wrongful interference shall include references to proceedings by virtue of Part I of the Consumer Protection Act 1987 or Part II of the Consumer Protection (Northern Ireland) Order 1987 (product liability) in respect of any damage to goods or to an interest in goods or, as the case may be, to a claim or right to claim by virtue of that Part in respect of any such damage.

Section 2. (1) Detinue is abolished.

(2) An action lies in conversion for loss or destruction of goods which a bailee has allowed to happen in breach of his duty to his bailor (that is to say it lies in a case which is not otherwise conversion, but would have been detinue before detinue was abolished).

Section 3. (1) In proceedings for wrongful interference against a person who is in possession or in control of the goods relief may be given in accordance with this section, so far as appropriate.

(2) The relief is—

(a) an order for delivery of the goods, and for payment of any consequential damages, or

(b) an order for delivery of the goods, but giving the defendant the alternative of paying damages by reference to the value of the goods, together in either alternative with payment of any consequential damages, or

(c) damages.

(3) Subject to rules of court—

(a) relief shall be given under only one of paragraphs (a), (b) and (c) of subsection (2),

(b) relief under paragraph (a) of subsection (2) is at the discretion of the court, and the claimant may choose between the others.

(4) If it is shown to the satisfaction of the court that an order under subsection (2)(a) has not been complied with, the court may—

(a) revoke the order, or the relevant part of it, and

(b) make an order for payment of damages by reference to the value of the goods.

(5) Where an order is made under subsection (2)(b) the defendant may satisfy the order by returning the goods at any time before execution of judgment, but without prejudice to liability to pay any consequential damages.

(6) An order for delivery of the goods under subsection (2)(a) or (b) may impose such conditions as may be determined by the court, or pursuant to rules of court, and in particular, where damages by reference to the value of the goods would not be the whole of the value of the goods, may require an allowance to be made by the claimant to reflect the difference.

For example, a bailor's action against the bailee may be one in which the measure of damages is not the full value of the goods, and then the court may order delivery of the goods, but require the bailor to pay the bailee a sum reflecting the difference.

(7) Where under subsection (1) or subsection (2) of section 6 an allowance is to be made in respect of an improvement of the goods, and an order is made under subsection (2)(a) or (b), the court may assess the allowance to be made in respect of the improvement, and by the order require, as a condition for delivery of the goods, that allowance to be made by the claimant.

(8) This section is without prejudice—

(a) to the remedies afforded by section 133 of the Consumer Credit Act 1974, or

(b) to the remedies afforded by sections 35, 42 and 44 of the Hire-Purchase Act 1965, or to those sections of the Hire-Purchase Act (Northern Ireland) 1966 (so long as those sections respectively remain in force), or

(c) to any jurisdiction to afford ancillary or incidental relief.

Section 4. (1) In this section "proceedings" means proceedings for wrongful interference.

(2) On the application of any person in accordance with rules of court, the High Court shall, in such circumstances as may be specified in the rules, have power to make an order providing for the delivery up of any goods which are or may become the subject matter of subsequent proceedings in the court, or as to which any question may arise in proceedings.

(3) Delivery shall be, as the order may provide, to the claimant or to a person appointed by the court for the purpose, and shall be on such terms and conditions as may be specified in the order.

[Subsections 4 and 5 are omitted.]

(6) Subsections (1) to (4) have effect in relation to the county court in England and Wales as they

have effect in relation to the High Court in England and Wales.

(6) Subsections (1) to (4) apply in relation to the family court in England and Wales as they apply in relation to the High Court in England and Wales, but as if references in those subsections to rules of court (including references to rules of court under any particular enactment) were references to Family Procedure Rules.

Section 5. (1) Where damages for wrongful interference are, or would fall to be, assessed on the footing that the claimant is being compensated—

(a) for the whole of his interest in the goods, or

(b) for the whole of his interest in the goods subject to a reduction for contributory negligence, payment of the assessed damages (under all heads), or as the case may be settlement of a claim for damages for the wrong (under all heads), extinguishes the claimant's title to that interest.

[Subsection 2 is omitted.]

(3) It is hereby declared that subsection (1) does not apply where damages are assessed on the footing that the claimant is being compensated for the whole of his interest in the goods, but the damages paid are limited to some lesser amount by virtue of any enactment or rule of law.

(4) Where under section 7(3) the claimant accounts over to another person (the "third party") so as to compensate (under all heads) the third party for the whole of his interest in the goods, the third party's title to that interest is extinguished.

(5) This section has effect subject to any agreement varying the respective rights of the parties to the agreement, and where the claim is made in court proceedings has effect subject to any order of the court.

Section 6. (1) If in proceedings for wrongful interference against a person (the "improver") who has improved the goods, it is shown that the improver acted in the mistaken but honest belief that he had a good title to them, an allowance shall be made for the extent to which, at the time as at which the goods fall to be valued in assessing damages, the value of the goods is attributable to the improvement.

(2) If, in proceedings for wrongful interference against a person ("the purchaser") who has purported to purchase the goods—

(a) from the improver, or

(b) where after such a purported sale the goods passed by a further purported sale on one or more occasions, on any such occasion,

it is shown that the purchaser acted in good faith, an allowance shall be made on the principle set out in subsection (1).

For example, where a person in good faith buys a stolen car from the improver and is sued in conversion by the true owner the damages may be reduced to reflect the improvement, but if the person who bought the stolen car from the improver sues the improver for failure of consideration, and the improver acted in good faith, subsection (3) below will ordinarily make a comparable reduction in the damages he recovers from the improver.

(3) If in a case within subsection (2) the person purporting to sell the goods acted in good faith, then in proceedings by the purchaser for recovery of the purchase price because of failure of consideration, or in any other proceedings founded on that failure of consideration, an allowance shall, where appropriate, be made on the principle set out in subsection (1).

(4) This section applies, with the necessary modifications, to a purported bailment or other disposition of goods as it applies to a purported sale of goods.

Section 7. (1) In this section "double liability" means the double liability of the wrongdoer which can arise—

(a) where one of two or more rights of action for wrongful interference is founded on a possessory title, or

(b) where the measure of damages in an action for wrongful interference founded on a proprietary title is or includes the entire value of the goods, although the interest is one of two or more interests in the goods.

(2) In proceedings to which any two or more claimants are parties, the relief shall be such as to avoid double liability of the wrongdoer as between those claimants.

(3) On satisfaction, in whole or in part, of any claim for an amount exceeding that recoverable if subsection (2) applied, the claimant is liable to account over to the other person having a right to claim to such extent as will avoid double liability.

(4) Where, as the result of enforcement of a double liability, any claimant is unjustly enriched to any

extent, he shall be liable to reimburse the wrongdoer to that extent.

For example, if a converter of goods pays damages first to a finder of the goods, and then to the true owner, the finder is unjustly enriched unless he accounts over to the true owner under subsection (3); and then the true owner is unjustly enriched and becomes liable to reimburse the converter of the goods.

Section 8. (1) The defendant in an action for wrongful interference shall be entitled to show, in accordance with rules of court, that a third party has a better right than the plaintiff as respects all or any part of the interest claimed by the plaintiff, or in right of which he sues, and any rule of law (sometimes called jus tertii) to the contrary is abolished.

(2) Rules of court relating to proceedings for wrongful interference may—

(a) require the plaintiff to give particulars of his title,

(b) require the plaintiff to identify any person who, to his knowledge, has or claims any interest in the goods,

(c) authorise the defendant to apply for directions as to whether any person should be joined with a view to establishing whether he has a better right than the plaintiff, or has a claim as a result of which the defendant might be doubly liable,

(d) where a party fails to appear on an application within paragraph (c), or to comply with any direction given by the court on such an application, authorise the court to deprive him of any right of action against the defendant for the wrong either unconditionally, or subject to such terms or conditions as may be specified.

(3) Subsection (2) is without prejudice to any other power of making rules of court.

Section 9. (1) This section applies where goods are the subject of two or more claims for wrongful interference (whether or not the claims are founded on the same wrongful act, and whether or not any of the claims relates also to other goods).

(2) Where goods are the subject of two or more claims under section 6 this section shall apply as if any claim under section 6(3) were a claim for wrongful interference.

(3) If proceedings have been brought in England and Wales in the county court or in Northern Ireland in a county court on one of those claims, rules of court or county court rules may waive, or allow a court to waive, any limit (financial or territorial) on the jurisdiction of county courts in [the Country Courts Act 1984] or the County Courts [(Northern Ireland) Order 1980] so as to allow another of those claims to be brought in the same county court.

(4) If proceedings are brought on one of the claims in the High Court, and proceedings on any other are brought in England and Wales in the county court or in Northern Ireland in a county court, whether prior to the High Court proceedings or not, the High Court may, on the application of the defendant, after notice has been given to the claimant in the county court proceedings—

(a) order that the county court proceedings be transferred to the High Court, and

(b) order security for costs or impose such other terms as the court thinks fit.

Section 10. (1) Co-ownership is no defence to an action founded on conversion or trespass to goods where the defendant without the authority of the other co-owner—

(a) destroys the goods, or disposes of the goods in a way giving a good title to the entire property in the goods, or otherwise does anything equivalent to the destruction of the other's interest in the goods, or

(b) purports to dispose of the goods in a way which would give a good title to the entire property in the goods if he was acting with the authority of all co-owners of the goods.

(2) Subsection (1) shall not affect the law concerning execution or enforcement of judgments, or concerning any form of distress.

(3) Subsection (1)(a) is by way of restatement of existing law so far as it relates to conversion.

Section 11. (1) Contributory negligence is no defence in proceedings founded on conversion, or on intentional trespass to goods.

(2) Receipt of goods by way of pledge is conversion if the delivery of the goods is conversion.

(3) Denial of title is not of itself conversion.

Section 14. Interpretation

(1) In this Act, unless the context otherwise requires –

[…]

"goods" includes all chattels personal other than things in action and money ...

[The remainder of the section is omitted.]

Limitation Act 1980 [An Act to consolidate the Limitation Acts 1939 to 1980] (c. 58), as last amended by the Land Registration Act 2002 (c. 9). Selected provisions: Sections 3, 5 and 17.

Section 3. (2) Where any such cause of action has accrued to any person and the period prescribed for bringing that action has expired and he [the claimant] has not during that period recovered possession of the chattel, the title of that person to the chattel shall be extinguished.

Section 5. An action founded on simple contract shall not be brought after the expiration of six years from the date on which the cause of action accrued.

Section 17. Subject to –
(a) section 18 of this Act; [...]
at the expiration of the period prescribed by this Act for any person to bring an action to recover land (including a redemption action) the title of that person to the land shall be extinguished.

Occupiers Liability Act 1984. (c. 3) [An Act to amend the law of England and Wales as to the liability of persons as occupiers of premises for injury suffered by persons other than their visitors; and to amend the Unfair Contract Terms Act 1977, as it applies to England and Wales, in relation to persons obtaining access to premises for recreational or educational purposes.], as last amended by the Marine and Coastal Access Act 2009 (c. 23).

Section 1. (1) The rules enacted by this section shall have effect, in place of the rules of the common law, to determine —
(a) whether any duty is owed by a person as occupier of premises to persons other than his visitors in respect of any risk of their suffering injury on the premises by reason of any danger due to the state of the premises or to things done or omitted to be done on them; and
(b) if so, what that duty is.
(2) For the purposes of this section, the persons who are to be treated respectively as an occupier of any premises (which, for those purposes, include any fixed or movable structure) and as his visitors are —
(a) any person who owes in relation to the premises the duty referred to in section 2 of the Occupiers' Liability Act 1957 (the common duty of care), and
(b) those who are his visitors for the purposes of that duty.
(3) An occupier of premises owes a duty to another (not being his visitor) in respect of any such risk as is referred to in subsection (1) above if —
(a) he is aware of the danger or has reasonable grounds to believe that it exists;
(b) he knows or has reasonable grounds to believe that the other is in the vicinity of the danger concerned or that he may come into the vicinity of the danger (in either case, whether the other has lawful authority for being in that vicinity or not); and
(c) the risk is one against which, in all the circumstances of the case, he may reasonably be expected to offer the other some protection.
(4) Where, by virtue of this section, an occupier of premises owes a duty to another in respect of such a risk, the duty is to take such care as is reasonable in all the circumstances of the case to see that he does not suffer injury on the premises by reason of the danger concerned.
(5) Any duty owed by virtue of this section in respect of a risk may, in an appropriate case, be discharged by taking such steps as are reasonable in all the circumstances of the case to give warning of the danger concerned or to discourage persons from incurring the risk.
(6) No duty is owed by virtue of this section to any person in respect of risks willingly accepted as his by that person (the question whether a risk was so accepted to be decided on the same principles as in other cases in which one person owes a duty of care to another).
(6A) At any time when the right conferred by section 2(1) of the Countryside and Rights of Way Act 2000 is exercisable in relation to land which is access land for the purposes of Part I of that Act, an occupier of the land owes (subject to subsection (6C) below) no duty by virtue of this section to any person in respect of—
(a) a risk resulting from the existence of any natural feature of the landscape, or any river, stream, ditch or pond whether or not a natural feature, or
(b) a risk of that person suffering injury when passing over, under or through any wall, fence or gate, except by proper use of the gate or of a stile.
(6AA) Where the land is coastal margin for the purposes of Part 1 of that Act (including any land

treated as coastal margin by virtue of section 16 of that Act), subsection (6A) has effect as if for paragraphs (a) and (b) of that subsection there were substituted " a risk resulting from the existence of any physical feature (whether of the landscape or otherwise). "

(6B) For the purposes of subsection (6A) above, any plant, shrub or tree, of whatever origin, is to be regarded as a natural feature of the landscape.

(6C) Subsection (6A) does not prevent an occupier from owing a duty by virtue of this section in respect of any risk where the danger concerned is due to anything done by the occupier—

(a)with the intention of creating that risk, or

(b)being reckless as to whether that risk is created.

(7) No duty is owed by virtue of this section to persons using the highway, and this section does not affect any duty owed to such persons.

(8) Where a person owes a duty by virtue of this section, he does not, by reason of any breach of the duty, incur any liability in respect of any loss of or damage to property.

(9) In this section —

"highway" means any part of a highway other than a ferry or waterway;

"injury" means anything resulting in death or personal injury, including any disease and any impairment of physical or mental condition; and

"movable structure" includes any vessel, vehicle or aircraft.

Section 1A. In determining whether any, and if so what, duty is owed by virtue of section 1 by an occupier of land at any time when the right conferred by section 2(1) of the Countryside and Rights of Way Act 2000 is exercisable in relation to the land, regard is to be had, in particular, to–

(a)the fact that the existence of that right ought not to place an undue burden (whether financial or otherwise) on the occupier,

(b)the importance of maintaining the character of the countryside, including features of historic, traditional or archaeological interest, and

(c)any relevant guidance given under section 20 of that Act.

Section 2. At the end of section 1(3) of the Unfair Contract Terms Act 1977 (which defines the liability, called "business liability", the exclusion or restriction of which is controlled by virtue of that Act) there is added–

"but liability of an occupier of premises for breach of an obligation or duty towards a person obtaining access to the premises for recreational or educational purposes, being liability for loss or damage suffered by reason of the dangerous state of the premises, is not a business liability of the occupier unless granting that person such access for the purposes concerned falls within the business purposes of the occupier".

Section 3. Section 1 of this Act shall bind the Crown, but as regards the Crown's liability in tort shall not bind the Crown further than the Crown is made liable in tort by the Crown Proceedings Act 1947.

Section 4. (1) This Act may be cited as the Occupiers' Liability Act 19884.

(2) This Act shall come into force at the end of the period of two months beginning with the day on which it is passed.

(3) This Act extends to England and Wales only.

Surrogacy Arrangements Act 1985 (c. 49), as last amended by the Human Fertilisation and Embryology Act 2008 (c. 22). Selected provisions: Sections 1A and 2.

Section 1. (1) The following provisions shall have effect for the interpretation of this Act.

(2) "Surrogate mother" means a woman who carries a child in pursuance of an arrangement—

(a) made before she began to carry the child, and

(b) made with a view to any child carried in pursuance of it being handed over to, and parental responsibility being met (so far as practicable) by, another person or other persons.

(3) An arrangement is a surrogacy arrangement if, were a woman to whom the arrangement relates to carry a child in pursuance of it, she would be a surrogate mother.

(4) In determining whether an arrangement is made with such a view as is mentioned in subsection (2) above regard may be had to the circumstances as a whole (and, in particular, where there is a promise or understanding that any payment will or may be made to the woman or for her benefit in respect of the carrying of any child in pursuance of the arrangement, to that promise or understanding).

(5) An arrangement may be regarded as made with such a view though subject to conditions relating to the handing over of any child.

(6) A woman who carries a child is to be treated for the purposes of subsection (2)(a) above as beginning to carry it at the time of the insemination or of the placing in her of an embryo, of an egg in the process of fertilisation or of sperm and eggs, as the case may be, that results in her carrying the child.

(7) "Body of persons" means a body of persons corporate or unincorporate.

(7A) "Non-profit making body" means a body of persons whose activities are not carried on for profit.

(8) "Payment" means payment in money or money's worth.

(9) This Act applies to arrangements whether or not they are lawful.

Section 1A. No surrogacy arrangement is enforceable by or against any of the persons making it.

Section 2. (1) No person shall on a commercial basis do any of the following acts in the United Kingdom, that is—

(a) initiate any negotiations with a view to the making of a surrogacy arrangement,

(aa) take part in any negotiations with a view to the making of a surrogacy arrangement,

(b) offer or agree to negotiate the making of a surrogacy arrangement, or

(c) compile any information with a view to its use in making, or negotiating the making of, surrogacy arrangements;

and no person shall in the United Kingdom knowingly cause another to do any of those acts on a commercial basis.

(2) A person who contravenes subsection (1) above is guilty of an offence; but it is not a contravention of that subsection—

(a) for a woman, with a view to becoming a surrogate mother herself, to do any act mentioned in that subsection or to cause such an act to be done, or

(b) for any person, with a view to a surrogate mother carrying a child for him, to do such an act or to cause such an act to be done.

(2A) A non-profit making body does not contravene subsection (1) merely because—

(a) the body does an act falling within subsection (1)(a) or (c) in respect of which any reasonable payment is at any time received by it or another, or

(b) it does an act falling within subsection (1)(a) or (c) with a view to any reasonable payment being received by it or another in respect of facilitating the making of any surrogacy arrangement.

(2B) A person who knowingly causes a non-profit making body to do an act falling within subsection (1)(a) or (c) does not contravene subsection (1) merely because—

(a) any reasonable payment is at any time received by the body or another in respect of the body doing the act, or

(b) the body does the act with a view to any reasonable payment being received by it or another person in respect of the body facilitating the making of any surrogacy arrangement.

(2C) Any reference in subsection (2A) or (2B) to a reasonable payment in respect of the doing of an act by a non-profit making body is a reference to a payment not exceeding the body's costs reasonably attributable to the doing of the act.

(3) For the purposes of this section, a person does an act on a commercial basis (subject to subsection (4) below) if—

(a) any payment is at any time received by himself or another in respect of it, or

(b) he does it with a view to any payment being received by himself or another in respect of making, or negotiating or facilitating the making of, any surrogacy arrangement.

In this subsection "payment" does not include payment to or for the benefit of a surrogate mother or prospective surrogate mother.

(4) In proceedings against a person for an offence under subsection (1) above, he is not to be treated as doing an act on a commercial basis by reason of any payment received by another in respect of the act if it is proved that—

(a) in a case where the payment was received before he did the act, he did not do the act knowing or having reasonable cause to suspect that any payment had been received in respect of the act; and

(b) in any other case, he did not do the act with a view to any payment being received in respect of it.

(5) Where—

(a) a person acting on behalf of a body of persons takes any part in negotiating or facilitating the making of a surrogacy arrangement in the United Kingdom, and

(b) negotiating or facilitating the making of surrogacy arrangements is an activity of the body,

then, if the body at any time receives any payment made by or on behalf of—

(i) a woman who carries a child in pursuance of the arrangement,

(ii) the person or persons for whom she carries it, or

(iii) any person connected with the woman or with that person or those persons,

the body is guilty of an offence.

For the purposes of this subsection, a payment received by a person connected with a body is to be treated as received by the body.

(5A) A non-profit making body is not guilty of an offence under subsection (5), in respect of the receipt of any payment described in that subsection, merely because a person acting on behalf of the body takes part in facilitating the making of a surrogacy arrangement.

(6) In proceedings against a body for an offence under subsection (5) above, it is a defence to prove that the payment concerned was not made in respect of the arrangement mentioned in paragraph (a) of that subsection.

(7) A person who in the United Kingdom takes part in the management or control—

(a) of any body of persons, or

(b) of any of the activities of any body of persons,

is guilty of an offence if the activity described in subsection (8) below is an activity of the body concerned.

(8) The activity referred to in subsection (7) above is negotiating or facilitating the making of surrogacy arrangements in the United Kingdom, being—

(a) arrangements the making of which is negotiated or facilitated on a commercial basis, or

(b) arrangements in the case of which payments are received (or treated for the purposes of subsection (5) above as received) by the body concerned in contravention of subsection (5) above.

(8A) A person is not guilty of an offence under subsection (7) if—

(a) the body of persons referred to in that subsection is a non-profit making body, and

(b) the only activity of that body which falls within subsection (8) is facilitating the making of surrogacy arrangements in the United Kingdom.

(8B) In subsection (8A)(b) "facilitating the making of surrogacy arrangements " is to be construed in accordance with subsection (8).

(9) In proceedings against a person for an offence under subsection (7) above, it is a defence to prove that he neither knew nor had reasonable cause to suspect that the activity described in subsection (8) above was an activity of the body concerned; and for the purposes of such proceedings any arrangement falling within subsection (8) (b) above shall be disregarded if it is proved that the payment concerned was not made in respect of the arrangement.

Insolvency Act 1986

[An Act to consolidate the enactments relating to company insolvency and winding up (including the winding up of companies that are not insolvent, and of unregistered companies); enactments relating to the insolvency and bankruptcy of individuals; and other enactments bearing on those two subject matters, including the functions and qualification of insolvency practitioners, the public administration of insolvency, the penalisation and redress of malpractice and wrongdoing, and the avoidance of certain transactions at an undervalue] (c. 45). Selected provision: Sections 213, 214 and 283.

Section 213. (1) If in the course of the winding up of a company it appears that any business of the company has been carried on with intent to defraud creditors of the company or creditors of any other person, or for any fraudulent purpose, the following has effect.

(2) The court, on the application of the liquidator may declare that any persons who were knowingly parties to the carrying on of the business in the manner above-mentioned are to be liable to make such contributions (if any) to the company's assets as the court thinks proper.

Section 214. (1) Subject to subsection (3) below, if in the course of the winding up of a company it appears that subsection (2) of this section applies in relation to a person who is or has been a director of the company, the court, on the application of the liquidator, may declare that that person is to be liable to make such contribution (if any) to the company's assets as the court thinks proper.

(2) This subsection applies in relation to a person if—

(a) the company has gone into insolvent liquidation,

(b) at some time before the commencement of the winding up of the company, that person knew or ought to have concluded that there was no reasonable prospect that the company would avoid going into insolvent liquidation, and

(c) that person was a director of the company at that time;

but the court shall not make a declaration under this section in any case where the time mentioned in paragraph (b) above was before 28th April 1986.

(3) The court shall not make a declaration under this section with respect to any person if it is satisfied that after the condition specified in subsection (2)(b) was first satisfied in relation to him that person took every step with a view to minimising the potential loss to the company's creditors as (assuming him to have known that there was no reasonable prospect that the company would avoid going into solvent liquidation) he ought to have taken.

(4) For the purposes of subsections (2) and (3), the facts which a director of a company ought to know or ascertain, the conclusions which he ought to reach and the steps which he ought to take are those which would be known or ascertained, or reached or taken, by a reasonably diligent person having both—

(a) the general knowledge, skill and experience that may reasonably be expected of a person carrying out the same functions as are carried out by that director in relation to the company, and

(b) the general knowledge, skill and experience that that director has.

(5) The reference in subsection (4) to the functions carried out in relation to a company by a director of the company includes any functions which he does not carry out but which have been entrusted to him.

(6) For the purposes of this section a company goes into insolvent liquidation if it goes into liquidation at a time when its assets are insufficient for the payment of its debts and other liabilities and the expenses of the winding up.

(7) In this section "director" includes a shadow director.

(8) This section is without prejudice to section 213.

Section 283. (1) Subject as follows, a bankrupt's estate for the purposes of any of this Group of Parts comprises –

(a) all property belonging to or vested in the bankrupt at the commencement of the bankruptcy, and

(b) any property which by virtue of any of the following provisions of this Part is comprised in that estate or is treated as falling within the preceding paragraph.

(2) Subsection (1) does not apply to –

(a) such tools, books, vehicles and other items of equipment as are necessary to the bankrupt for use personally by him in his employment, business or vocation;

(b) such clothing, bedding, furniture, household equipment and provisions as are necessary for satisfying the basic domestic needs of the bankrupt and his family. ...

(3) Subsection (1) does not apply to –

(a) property held by the bankrupt on trust for any other person, or

(b) the right of nomination to a vacant ecclesiastical benefice.

Minors' Contracts Act 1987 [An Act to amend the law relating to minors' contracts] (c. 13). Selected provisions: Sections 2 and 3.

Section 2. Where—

(a) a guarantee is given in respect of an obligation of a party to a contract made after the commencement of this Act, and

(b) the obligation is unenforceable against him (or he repudiates the contract) because he was a minor when the contract was made,

the guarantee shall not for that reason alone be unenforceable against the guarantor.

Section 3. (1) Where—

(a) a person ("the plaintiff") has after the commencement of this Act entered into a contract with another ("the defendant"), and

(b) the contract is unenforceable against the defendant (or he repudiates it) because he was a minor when the contract was made,

the court may, if it is just and equitable to do so, require the defendant to transfer to the plaintiff any property acquired by the defendant under the contract, or any property representing it.

(2) Nothing in this section shall be taken to prejudice any other remedy available to the plaintiff.

Consumer Protection Act 1987 (c. 43), as last amended by the Consumer Protection Act 1987 (Product Liability) (Modification) Order 2000. Selected Provisions: Sections 1-9

Part 1. Product Liability

Section 1. This Part shall have effect for the purpose of making such provision as is necessary in order to comply with the product liability Directive and shall be construed accordingly.

(2) In this Part, except in so far as the context otherwise requires—

"dependant" and "relative" have the same meaning as they have in, respectively, the Fatal Accidents Act 1976 and the Damages (Scotland) Act 2011;

"producer", in relation to a product, means—

(a) the person who manufactured it;

(b) in the case of a substance which has not been manufactured but has been won or abstracted, the person who won or abstracted it;

(c)in the case of a product which has not been manufactured, won or abstracted but essential characteristics of which are attributable to an industrial or other process having been carried out (for example, in relation to agricultural produce), the person who carried out that process;

"product" means any goods or electricity and (subject to subsection (3) below) includes a product which is comprised in another product, whether by virtue of being a component part or raw material or otherwise; and

"the product liability Directive" means the Directive of the Council of the European Union, dated 25th July 1985, (No. 85/374/EEC) on the approximation of the laws, regulations and administrative provisions of the member States concerning liability for defective products.

(3) For the purposes of this Part a person who supplies any product in which products are comprised, whether by virtue of being component parts or raw materials or otherwise, shall not be treated by reason only of his supply of that product as supplying any of the products so comprised.

Section 2. (1) Subject to the following provisions of this Part, where any damage is caused wholly or partly by a defect in a product, every person to whom subsection (2) below applies shall be liable for the damage.

(2) This subsection applies to—

(a) the producer of the product;

(b) any person who, by putting his name on the product or using a trade mark or other distinguishing mark in relation to the product, has held himself out to be the producer of the product;

(c) any person who has imported the product into a member State from a place outside the member States in order, in the course of any business of his, to supply it to another.

(3) Subject as aforesaid, where any damage is caused wholly or partly by a defect in a product, any person who supplied the product (whether to the person who suffered the damage, to the producer of any product in which the product in question is comprised or to any other person) shall be liable for the damage if—

(a) the person who suffered the damage requests the supplier to identify one or more of the persons (whether still in existence or not) to whom subsection (2) above applies in relation to the product;

(b) that request is made within a reasonable period after the damage occurs and at a time when it is not reasonably practicable for the person making the request to identify all those persons; and

(c) the supplier fails, within a reasonable period after receiving the request, either to comply with the request or to identify the person who supplied the product to him.

(4) (Repealed.)

(5) Where two or more persons are liable by virtue of this Part for the same damage, their liability shall be joint and several.

(6) This section shall be without prejudice to any liability arising otherwise than by virtue of this Part.

Section 3. (1) Subject to the following provisions of this section, there is a defect in a product for the purposes of this Part if the safety of the product is not such as persons generally are entitled to expect; and for those purposes "safety", in relation to a product, shall include safety with respect to products comprised in that product and safety in the context of risks of damage to property, as well as in the context of risks of death or personal injury.

(2) In determining for the purposes of subsection (1) above what persons generally are entitled to expect in relation to a product all the circumstances shall be taken into account, including—

(a) the manner in which, and purposes for which, the product has been marketed, its get-up, the use of any mark in relation to the product and any instructions for, or warnings with respect to, doing or refraining from doing anything with or in relation to the product;

(b) what might reasonably be expected to be done with or in relation to the product; and

(c) the time when the product was supplied by its producer to another;

and nothing in this section shall require a defect to be inferred from the fact alone that the safety of a product which is supplied after that time is greater than the safety of the product in question.

Section 4. (1) In any civil proceedings by virtue of this Part against any person ("the person proceeded against") in respect of a defect in a product it shall be a defence for him to show—
(a) that the defect is attributable to compliance with any requirement imposed by or under any enactment or with any EU; or
(b) that the person proceeded against did not at any time supply the product to another; or
(c) that the following conditions are satisfied, that is to say—
(i) that the only supply of the product to another by the person proceeded against was otherwise than in the course of a business of that person's; and
(ii) that section 2(2) above does not apply to that person or applies to him by virtue only of things done otherwise than with a view to profit; or
(d) that the defect did not exist in the product at the relevant time; or
(e) that the state of scientific and technical knowledge at the relevant time was not such that a producer of products of the same description as the product in question might be expected to have discovered the defect if it had existed in his products while they were under his control; or
(f)that the defect—
(i) constituted a defect in a product ("the subsequent product") in which the product in question had been comprised; and
(ii) was wholly attributable to the design of the subsequent product or to compliance by the producer of the product in question with instructions given by the producer of the subsequent product.
(2) In this section "the relevant time", in relation to electricity, means the time at which it was generated, being a time before it was transmitted or distributed, and in relation to any other product, means—
(a) if the person proceeded against is a person to whom subsection (2) of section 2 above applies in relation to the product, the time when he supplied the product to another;
(b) if that subsection does not apply to that person in relation to the product, the time when the product was last supplied by a person to whom that subsection does apply in relation to the product.

Section 5. (1) Subject to the following provisions of this section, in this Part "damage" means death or personal injury or any loss of or damage to any property (including land).
(2) A person shall not be liable under section 2 above in respect of any defect in a product for the loss of or any damage to the product itself or for the loss of or any damage to the whole or any part of any product which has been supplied with the product in question comprised in it.
(3) A person shall not be liable under section 2 above for any loss of or damage to any property which, at the time it is lost or damaged, is not—
(a)of a description of property ordinarily intended for private use, occupation or consumption; and
(b)intended by the person suffering the loss or damage mainly for his own private use, occupation or consumption.
(4) No damages shall be awarded to any person by virtue of this Part in respect of any loss of or damage to any property if the amount which would fall to be so awarded to that person, apart from this subsection and any liability for interest, does not exceed £275.
(5) In determining for the purposes of this Part who has suffered any loss of or damage to property and when any such loss or damage occurred, the loss or damage shall be regarded as having occurred at the earliest time at which a person with an interest in the property had knowledge of the material facts about the loss or damage.
(6) For the purposes of subsection (5) above the material facts about any loss of or damage to any property are such facts about the loss or damage as would lead a reasonable person with an interest in the property to consider the loss or damage sufficiently serious to justify his instituting proceedings for damages against a defendant who did not dispute liability and was able to satisfy a judgment.
(7) For the purposes of subsection (5) above a person's knowledge includes knowledge which he might reasonably have been expected to acquire—
(a) from facts observable or ascertainable by him; or
(b) from facts ascertainable by him with the help of appropriate expert advice which it is reasonable for him to seek;
but a person shall not be taken by virtue of this subsection to have knowledge of a fact ascertainable by him only with the help of expert advice unless he has failed to take all reasonable steps to obtain (and, where appropriate, to act on) that advice.
(8) Subsections (5) to (7) above shall not extend to Scotland.

Section 6. (1) Any damage for which a person is liable under section 2 above shall be deemed to have been caused–

(a) for the purposes of the Fatal Accidents Act 1976, by that person's wrongful act, neglect or default;

(b) for the purposes of section 3 of the Law Reform (Miscellaneous Provisions) (Scotland) Act 1940 (contribution among joint wrongdoers), by that person's wrongful act or negligent act or omission;

(c)for the purposes of sections 3 to 6 of the Damages (Scotland) Act 2011(rights of relatives of a deceased), by that person's act or omission; and

(d) for the purposes of Part II of the Administration of Justice Act 1982 (damages for personal injuries, etc.—Scotland), by an act or omission giving rise to liability in that person to pay damages.

(2) Where—

(a) a person's death is caused wholly or partly by a defect in a product, or a person dies after suffering damage which has been so caused;

(b) a request such as mentioned in paragraph (a) of subsection (3) of section 2 above is made to a supplier of the product by that person's personal representatives or, in the case of a person whose death is caused wholly or partly by the defect, by any dependant or relative of that person; and

(c) the conditions specified in paragraphs (b) and (c) of that subsection are satisfied in relation to that request,

this Part shall have effect for the purposes of the Law Reform (Miscellaneous Provisions) Act 1934, the Fatal Accidents Act 1976 and the Damages (Scotland) Act 2011 as if liability of the supplier to that person under that subsection did not depend on that person having requested the supplier to identify certain persons or on the said conditions having been satisfied in relation to a request made by that person.

(3) Section 1 of the Congenital Disabilities (Civil Liability) Act 1976 shall have effect for the purposes of this Part as if—

(a) a person were answerable to a child in respect of an occurrence caused wholly or partly by a defect in a product if he is or has been liable under section 2 above in respect of any effect of the occurrence on a parent of the child, or would be so liable if the occurrence caused a parent of the child to suffer damage;

(b)the provisions of this Part relating to liability under section 2 above applied in relation to liability by virtue of paragraph (a) above under the said section 1; and

(c) subsection (6) of the said section 1 (exclusion of liability) were omitted.

(4) Where any damage is caused partly by a defect in a product and partly by the fault of the person suffering the damage, the Law Reform (Contributory Negligence) Act 1945 and section 5 of the Fatal Accidents Act 1976 (contributory negligence) shall have effect as if the defect were the fault of every person liable by virtue of this Part for the damage caused by the defect.

(5) In subsection (4) above "fault" has the same meaning as in the said Act of 1945.

(6) Schedule 1 to this Act shall have effect for the purpose of amending the Limitation Act 1980 and the Prescription and Limitation (Scotland) Act 1973 in their application in relation to the bringing of actions by virtue of this Part.

(7) It is hereby declared that liability by virtue of this Part is to be treated as liability in tort for the purposes of any enactment conferring jurisdiction on any court with respect to any matter.

(8) Nothing in this Part shall prejudice the operation of section 12 of the Nuclear Installations Act 1965 (rights to compensation for certain breaches of duties confined to rights under that Act).

Section 7. The liability of a person by virtue of this Part to a person who has suffered damage caused wholly or partly by a defect in a product, or to a dependant or relative of such a person, shall not be limited or excluded by any contract term, by any notice or by any other provision.

Section 8. (1) Her Majesty may by Order in Council make such modifications of this Part and of any other enactment (including an enactment contained in the following Parts of this Act, or in an Act passed after this Act) as appear to Her Majesty in Council to be necessary or expedient in consequence of any modification of the product liability Directive which is made at any time after the passing of this Act.

(2) An Order in Council under subsection (1) above shall not be submitted to Her Majesty in Council unless a draft of the Order has been laid before, and approved by a resolution of, each House of Parliament.

Section 9. (1) Subject to subsection (2) below, this Part shall bind the Crown.

(2) The Crown shall not, as regards the Crown's liability by virtue of this Part, be bound by this Part further than the Crown is made liable in tort or in reparation under the Crown Proceedings Act 1947, as that Act has effect from time to time.

Law of Property (Miscellaneous Provisions) Act 1989 [An Act to make new provision with respect to deeds and their execution and contracts for the sale or other disposition of interests in land; and to abolish the rule of law known as the rule in Bain v. Fothergill] (c. 34), as last amended by The Financial Services and Markets Act 2000 (Regulated Activities) (Amendment) Order 2009. Selected Provisions: Sections 1 and 2.

Section 1. (1) Any rule of law which—
(a) restricts the substances on which a deed may be written;
(b) requires a seal for the valid execution of an instrument as a deed by an individual; or
(c) requires authority by one person to another to deliver an instrument as a deed on his behalf to be given by deed, is abolished.
(2) An instrument shall not be a deed unless—
(a) it makes it clear on its face that it is intended to be a deed by the person making it or, as the case may be, by the parties to it (whether by describing itself as a deed or expressing itself to be executed or signed as a deed or otherwise); and
(b) it is validly executed as a deed by that person or, as the case may be, one or more of those parties.
(2A) For the purposes of subsection (2)(a) above, an instrument shall not be taken to make it clear on its face that it is intended to be a deed merely because it is executed under seal.
(3) An instrument is validly executed as a deed by an individual if, and only if—
(a) it is signed—
(i) by him in the presence of a witness who attests the signature; or
(ii) at his direction and in his presence and the presence of two witnesses who each attest the signature; and
(b) it is delivered as a deed.
(4) In subsections (2) and (3) above "sign", in relation to an instrument, includes making one's mark on the instrument and "signature" is to be construed accordingly.
(4A) Subsection (3) above applies in the case of an instrument executed by an individual in the name or on behalf of another person whether or not that person is also an individual.
(5) Where a relevant lawyer, or an agent or employee of a relevant lawyer, in the course of or in connection with a transaction, purports to deliver an instrument as a deed on behalf of a party to the instrument, it shall be conclusively presumed in favour of a purchaser that he is authorised so to deliver the instrument.
(6) In subsection (5) above—
"purchaser" has the same meaning as in the [1925 c. 20.] Law of Property Act 1925;
"relevant lawyer" means a person who, for the purposes of the Legal Services Act 2007, is an authorised person in relation to an activity which constitutes a reserved instrument activity (within the meaning of that Act).
(7) Where an instrument under seal that constitutes a deed is required for the purposes of an Act passed before this section comes into force, this section shall have effect as to signing, sealing or delivery of an instrument by an individual in place of any provision of that Act as to signing, sealing or delivery.

[Subsections 8 – 11 are omitted.]

Section 2. (1) A contract for the sale or other disposition of an interest in land can only be made in writing and only by incorporating all the terms which the parties have expressly agreed in one document or, where contracts are exchanged, in each.
(2) The terms may be incorporated in a document either by being set out in it or by reference to some other document.
(3) The document incorporating the terms or, where contracts are exchanged, one of the documents incorporating them (but not necessarily the same one) must be signed by or on behalf of each party to the contract.
(4) Where a contract for the sale or other disposition of an interest in land satisfies the conditions of this section by reason only of the rectification of one or more documents in pursuance of an order of a court, the contract shall come into being, or be deemed to have come into being, at such time as may be specified in the order.
(5) This section does not apply in relation to—
(a) a contract to grant such a lease as is mentioned in section 54(2) of the [1925 c. 20.] Law of Property Act 1925 (short leases);
(b) a contract made in the course of a public auction; or

(c) a contract regulated under the Financial Services and Markets Act 2000, other than a regulated mortgage contract a regulated home reversion plan, a regulated home purchase plan or a regulated sale and rent back agreement;
and nothing in this section affects the creation or operation of resulting, implied or constructive trusts.
(6) In this section—
"disposition" has the same meaning as in the Law of Property Act 1925;
"interest in land" means any estate, interest or charge in or over land or in or over the proceeds of sale of land.
"regulated mortgage contract", "regulated home reversion plan", "regulated home purchase plan" and "regulated sale and rent back agreement" must be read with—
(a) section 22 of the Financial Services and Markets Act 2000,
(b) any relevant order under that section, and
(c) Schedule 2 to that Act.
[Subsections 7 – 8 are omitted.]

Contracts (Rights of Third Parties) Act 1999. Selected provision: Section 1.

Section 1 (1) Subject to the provisions of this Act, a person who is not a party to a contract (a 'third party') may in his own right enforce a term of the contract if –
(a) the contract expressly provides that he may, or
(b) subject to subsection (2), the term purports to confer a benefit on him.
(2) Subsection (1)(b) does not apply if on a proper construction of the contract it appears that the parties did not intend the term to be enforceable by the third party.
(3) The third party must be expressly identified in the contract by name, as a member of a class or as answering a particular description but need not be in existence when the contract is entered into.
(4) This section does not confer a right on a third party to enforce a term of a contract otherwise than subject to and in accordance with any other relevant terms of the contract.
(5) For the purpose of exercising his right to enforce a term of the contract, there shall be available to the third party any remedy that would have been available to him in an action for breach of contract if he had been a party to the contract (and the rules relating to damages, injunctions, specific performance and other relief shall apply accordingly).
(6) Where a term of a contract excludes or limits liability in relation to any matter references in this Act to the third party enforcing the term shall be construed as references to his availing himself of the exclusion or limitation.
(7) In this Act, in relation to a term of a contract which is enforceable by a third party —
"the promisor" means the party to the contract against whom the term is enforceable by the third party, and
"the promisee" means the party to the contract by whom the term is enforceable against the promisor.

Land Registration Act 2002 [An Act to make provision about land registration; and for connected purposes] (c. 9), as last amended by the Localism Act 2011 (c. 20). Selected provisions: Schedule 1.

Schedule 1. Unregistered interests which override first registration
1. A leasehold estate in land granted for a term not exceeding seven years from the date of the grant, except for a lease the grant of which falls within section 4(1) (d), (e) or (f).
1A. A leasehold estate in land under a relevant social housing tenancy.
2. An interest belonging to a person in actual occupation, so far as relating to land of which he is in actual occupation, except for an interest under a settlement und the Settled Land Act 1925.
3. A legal easement or profit a prendre.
4. A customary right.
5. A public right.
6. A local land charge

[Paragraphs 7 – 9 are omitted.]

10. A franchise.
11. A manorial right.
12. A right to rent which was reserved to the Crown on the granting of any freehold estate (whether or not the right is still vested in the Crown).

13. A non-statutory right in respect of an embankment or sea or river wall.

14. A right to payment in lieu of tithe.

16. A right in respect of the repair of a church chancel.

Mental Capacity Act 2005 [An Act to make new provision relating to persons who lack capacity; to establish a superior court of record called the Court of Protection in place of the office of the Supreme Court called by that name; to make provision in connection with the Convention on the International Protection of Adults signed at the Hague on 13th January 2000; and for connected purposes] (c. 9). Selected provisions: Sections 1 – 4 and 7.

Part I Persons Who Lack Capacity

Preliminary

Section 1. (1) The following principles apply for the purposes of this Act.

(2) A person must be assumed to have capacity unless it is established that he lacks capacity.

(3) A person is not to be treated as unable to make a decision unless all practicable steps to help him to do so have been taken without success.

(4) A person is not to be treated as unable to make a decision merely because he makes an unwise decision.

(5) An act done, or decision made, under this Act for or on behalf of a person who lacks capacity must be done, or made, in his best interests.

(6) Before the act is done, or the decision is made, regard must be had to whether the purpose for which it is needed can be as effectively achieved in a way that is less restrictive of the person's rights and freedom of action.

Section 2. (1) For the purposes of this Act, a person lacks capacity in relation to a matter if at the material time he is unable to make a decision for himself in relation to the matter because of an impairment of, or a disturbance in the functioning of, the mind or brain.

(2) It does not matter whether the impairment or disturbance is permanent or temporary.

(3) A lack of capacity cannot be established merely by reference to—

(a) a person's age or appearance, or

(b) a condition of his, or an aspect of his behaviour, which might lead others to make unjustified assumptions about his capacity.

(4) In proceedings under this Act or any other enactment, any question whether a person lacks capacity within the meaning of this Act must be decided on the balance of probabilities.

(5) No power which a person ("D") may exercise under this Act—

(a) in relation to a person who lacks capacity, or

(b) where D reasonably thinks that a person lacks capacity,

is exercisable in relation to a person under 16.

(6) Subsection (5) is subject to section 18(3).

Section 3. (1) For the purposes of section 2, a person is unable to make a decision for himself if he is unable—

(a) to understand the information relevant to the decision,

(b) to retain that information,

(c) to use or weigh that information as part of the process of making the decision, or

(d) to communicate his decision (whether by talking, using sign language or any other means).

(2) A person is not to be regarded as unable to understand the information relevant to a decision if he is able to understand an explanation of it given to him in a way that is appropriate to his circumstances (using simple language, visual aids or any other means).

(3) The fact that a person is able to retain the information relevant to a decision for a short period only does not prevent him from being regarded as able to make the decision.

(4) The information relevant to a decision includes information about the reasonably foreseeable consequences of—

(a) deciding one way or another, or

(b) failing to make the decision.

Section 4. (1) In determining for the purposes of this Act what is in a person's best interests, the person making the determination must not make it merely on the basis of—

(a) the person's age or appearance, or

(b) a condition of his, or an aspect of his behaviour, which might lead others to make unjustified assumptions about what might be in his best interests.

(2) The person making the determination must consider all the relevant circumstances and, in particular, take the following steps.

(3) He must consider—

(a) whether it is likely that the person will at some time have capacity in relation to the matter in question, and

(b) if it appears likely that he will, when that is likely to be.

(4) He must, so far as reasonably practicable, permit and encourage the person to participate, or to improve his ability to participate, as fully as possible in any act done for him and any decision affecting him.

(5) Where the determination relates to life-sustaining treatment he must not, in considering whether the treatment is in the best interests of the person concerned, be motivated by a desire to bring about his death.

(6) He must consider, so far as is reasonably ascertainable—

(a) the person's past and present wishes and feelings (and, in particular, any relevant written statement made by him when he had capacity),

(b) the beliefs and values that would be likely to influence his decision if he had capacity, and

(c) the other factors that he would be likely to consider if he were able to do so.

(7) He must take into account, if it is practicable and appropriate to consult them, the views of—

(a) anyone named by the person as someone to be consulted on the matter in question or on matters of that kind,

(b) anyone engaged in caring for the person or interested in his welfare,

(c) any donee of a lasting power of attorney granted by the person, and

(d) any deputy appointed for the person by the court,

as to what would be in the person's best interests and, in particular, as to the matters mentioned in subsection (6).

(8) The duties imposed by subsections (1) to (7) also apply in relation to the exercise of any powers which—

(a) are exercisable under a lasting power of attorney, or

(b) are exercisable by a person under this Act where he reasonably believes that another person lacks capacity.

(9) In the case of an act done, or a decision made, by a person other than the court, there is sufficient compliance with this section if (having complied with the requirements of subsections (1) to (7)) he reasonably believes that what he does or decides is in the best interests of the person concerned.

(10) "Life-sustaining treatment" means treatment which in the view of a person providing health care for the person concerned is necessary to sustain life.

(11) "Relevant circumstances" are those—

(a) of which the person making the determination is aware, and

(b) which it would be reasonable to regard as relevant.

Section 7. (1) If necessary goods or services are supplied to a person who lacks capacity to contract for the supply, he must pay a reasonable price for them.

(2) "Necessary" means suitable to a person's condition in life and to his actual requirements at the time when the goods or services are supplied.

Companies Act 2006 [An Act to reform company law and restate the greater part of the enactments relating to companies; to make other provision relating to companies and other forms of business organisation; to make provision about directors' disqualification, business names, auditors and actuaries; to amend Part 9 of the Enterprise Act 2002; and for connected purposes.] (c.46), as last amended by the Small Business, Enterprise and Employment Act 2015 (c. 26). Selected provisions: Sections 40, 170-178 and 260.

Part 4. A company's capacity and related matters

Section 40. (1) In favour of a person dealing with a company in good faith, the power of the directors to bind the company, or authorise others to do so, is deemed to be free of any limitation under the company's constitution.

(2) For this purpose—

(a) a person "deals with" a company if he is a party to any transaction or other act to which the company is a party,

(b) a person dealing with a company—
(i) is not bound to enquire as to any limitation on the powers of the directors to bind the company or authorise others to do so,
(ii) is presumed to have acted in good faith unless the contrary is proved, and
(iii) is not to be regarded as acting in bad faith by reason only of his knowing that an act is beyond the powers of the directors under the company's constitution.
(3) The references above to limitations on the directors' powers under the company's constitution include limitations deriving—
(a) from a resolution of the company or of any class of shareholders, or
(b) from any agreement between the members of the company or of any class of shareholders.
(4) This section does not affect any right of a member of the company to bring proceedings to restrain the doing of an action that is beyond the powers of the directors.
But no such proceedings lie in respect of an act to be done in fulfilment of a legal obligation arising from a previous act of the company.
(5) This section does not affect any liability incurred by the directors, or any other person, by reason of the directors' exceeding their powers.
(6) This section has effect subject to—
section 41 (transactions with directors or their associates), and
section 42 (companies that are charities).

Part 10. A company's directors

Chapter 2. General duties of directors

Section 170. (1) The general duties specified in sections 171 to 177 are owed by a director of a company to the company.
(2) A person who ceases to be a director continues to be subject—
(a) to the duty in section 175 (duty to avoid conflicts of interest) as regards the exploitation of any property, information or opportunity of which he became aware at a time when he was a director, and
(b) to the duty in section 176 (duty not to accept benefits from third parties) as regards things done or omitted by him before he ceased to be a director.
To that extent those duties apply to a former director as to a director, subject to any necessary adaptations.
(3) The general duties are based on certain common law rules and equitable principles as they apply in relation to directors and have effect in place of those rules and principles as regards the duties owed to a company by a director.
(4) The general duties shall be interpreted and applied in the same way as common law rules or equitable principles, and regard shall be had to the corresponding common law rules and equitable principles in interpreting and applying the general duties.
(5) The general duties apply to a shadow director of a company where and to the extent that they are capable of so applying.

Section 171. A director of a company must—
(a) act in accordance with the company's constitution, and
(b) only exercise powers for the purposes for which they are conferred.

Section 172. (1) A director of a company must act in the way he considers, in good faith, would be most likely to promote the success of the company for the benefit of its members as a whole, and in doing so have regard (amongst other matters) to—
(a) the likely consequences of any decision in the long term,
(b) the interests of the company's employees,
(c) the need to foster the company's business relationships with suppliers, customers and others,
(d) the impact of the company's operations on the community and the environment,
(e) the desirability of the company maintaining a reputation for high standards of business conduct, and
(f) the need to act fairly as between members of the company.
(2) Where or to the extent that the purposes of the company consist of or include purposes other than the benefit of its members, subsection (1) has effect as if
the reference to promoting the success of the company for the benefit of its members were to achieving those purposes.
(3) The duty imposed by this section has effect subject to any enactment or rule of law requiring directors, in certain circumstances, to consider or act in the interests of creditors of the company.

Section 173. (1) A director of a company must exercise independent judgment.
(2) This duty is not infringed by his acting—
(a) in accordance with an agreement duly entered into by the company that restricts the future exercise of discretion by its directors, or
(b) in a way authorised by the company's constitution.

Section 174. (1) A director of a company must exercise reasonable care, skill and diligence.
(2) This means the care, skill and diligence that would be exercised by a reasonably diligent person with—
(a) the general knowledge, skill and experience that may reasonably be expected of a person carrying out the functions carried out by the director in relation to the company, and
(b) the general knowledge, skill and experience that the director has.

Section 175. (1) A director of a company must avoid a situation in which he has, or can have, a direct or indirect interest that conflicts, or possibly may conflict, with the interests of the company.
(2) This applies in particular to the exploitation of any property, information or opportunity (and it is immaterial whether the company could take advantage of the property, information or opportunity).
(3) This duty does not apply to a conflict of interest arising in relation to a transaction or arrangement with the company.
(4) This duty is not infringed—
(a) if the situation cannot reasonably be regarded as likely to give rise to a conflict of interest; or
(b) if the matter has been authorised by the directors.
(5) Authorisation may be given by the directors—
(a) where the company is a private company and nothing in the company's constitution invalidates such authorisation, by the matter being proposed to and authorised by the directors; or
(b) where the company is a public company and its constitution includes provision enabling the directors to authorise the matter, by the matter being proposed to and authorised by them in accordance with the constitution.
(6) The authorisation is effective only if—
(a) any requirement as to the quorum at the meeting at which the matter is considered is met without counting the director in question or any other interested director, and
(b) the matter was agreed to without their voting or would have been agreed to if their votes had not been counted.
(7) Any reference in this section to a conflict of interest includes a conflict of interest and duty and a conflict of duties.

Section 176. (1) A director of a company must not accept a benefit from a third party conferred by reason of—
(a) his being a director, or
(b) his doing (or not doing) anything as director.
(2) A "third party" means a person other than the company, an associated body corporate or a person acting on behalf of the company or an associated body corporate.
(3) Benefits received by a director from a person by whom his services (as a director or otherwise) are provided to the company are not regarded as conferred by a third party.
(4) This duty is not infringed if the acceptance of the benefit cannot reasonably be regarded as likely to give rise to a conflict of interest.
(5) Any reference in this section to a conflict of interest includes a conflict of interest and duty and a conflict of duties.

Section 177. (1) If a director of a company is in any way, directly or indirectly, interested in a proposed transaction or arrangement with the company, he must declare the nature and extent of that interest to the other directors.
(2) The declaration may (but need not) be made—
(a) at a meeting of the directors, or
(b) by notice to the directors in accordance with—
(i) section 184 (notice in writing), or
(ii) section 185 (general notice).
(3) If a declaration of interest under this section proves to be, or becomes, inaccurate or incomplete, a further declaration must be made.
(4) Any declaration required by this section must be made before the company enters into the transaction or arrangement.
(5) This section does not require a declaration of an interest of which the director is not aware or

where the director is not aware of the transaction or arrangement in question.

For this purpose a director is treated as being aware of matters of which he ought reasonably to be aware.

(6) A director need not declare an interest—

(a) if it cannot reasonably be regarded as likely to give rise to a conflict of interest;

(b) if, or to the extent that, the other directors are already aware of it (and

for this purpose the other directors are treated as aware of anything of which they ought reasonably to be aware); or

(c) if, or to the extent that, it concerns terms of his service contract that have been or are to be considered—

(i) by a meeting of the directors, or

(ii) by a committee of the directors appointed for the purpose under the company's constitution.

Section 178. (1) The consequences of breach (or threatened breach) of sections 171 to 177 are the same as would apply if the corresponding common law rule or equitable principle applied.

(2) The duties in those sections (with the exception of section 174 (duty to exercise reasonable care, skill and diligence)) are, accordingly, enforceable in the same way as any other fiduciary duty owed to a company by its directors.

Part 11. Derivative claims and proceedings by members

Chapter 1. Derivative claims in England and Wales or Northern Ireland

Section 260. (1) This Chapter applies to proceedings in England and Wales or Northern Ireland by a member of a company—

(a) in respect of a cause of action vested in the company, and

(b) seeking relief on behalf of the company.

This is referred to in this Chapter as a "derivative claim".

(2) A derivative claim may only be brought—

(a) under this Chapter, or

(b) in pursuance of an order of the court in proceedings under section 994 (proceedings for protection of members against unfair prejudice).

(3) A derivative claim under this Chapter may be brought only in respect of a cause of action arising from an actual or proposed act or omission involving negligence, default, breach of duty or breach of trust by a director of the company.

The cause of action may be against the director or another person (or both).

(4) It is immaterial whether the cause of action arose before or after the person seeking to bring or continue the derivative claim became a member of the company.

(5) For the purposes of this Chapter—

(a) "director" includes a former director;

(b) a shadow director is treated as a director; and

(c) references to a member of a company include a person who is not a member but to whom shares in the company have been transferred or transmitted by operation of law.

The Consumer Contracts (Information, Cancellation and Additional Charges) Regulations 2013, No. 3134 Selected provisions: Regulations 7 – 10, 13 – 14, 27, 29-31.

Part 2. Information Requirements

7. (1) This Part applies to on-premises, off-premises and distance contracts, subject to paragraphs (2), (3) and (4) and regulation 6. (…)

8. For the purposes of this Part, something is made available to a consumer only if the consumer can reasonably be expected to know how to access it.

Information to be provided before making an on-premises contract

9. (1) Before the consumer is bound by an on-premises contract, the trader must give or make available to the consumer the information described in Schedule 1 in a clear and comprehensible manner, if that information is not already apparent from the context.

(2) Paragraph (1) does not apply to a contract which involves a day-to-day transaction and is performed immediately at the time when the contract is entered into.

(3) Any information that the trader gives the consumer as required by this regulation is to be treated as included as a term of the contract.

(4) A change to any of that information, made before entering into the contract or later, is not effective unless expressly agreed between the consumer and the trader.

Information to be provided before making an off-premises contract

10. (1) Before the consumer is bound by an off-premises contract, the trader —
(a) must give the consumer the information listed in Schedule 2 in a clear and comprehensible manner, and
(b) if a right to cancel exists, must give the consumer a cancellation form as set out in part B of Schedule 3.
(2) The information and any cancellation form must be given on paper or, if the consumer agrees, on another durable medium and must be legible.
(3) The information referred to in paragraphs (l), (m) and (n) of Schedule 2 may be provided by means of the model instructions on cancellation set out in part A of Schedule 3; and a trader who has supplied those instructions to the consumer, correctly filled in, is to be treated as having complied with paragraph (1) in respect of those paragraphs.
(4) If the trader has not complied with paragraph (1) in respect of paragraph (g), (h) or (m) of Schedule 2, the consumer is not to bear the charges or costs referred to in those paragraphs.
(5) Any information that the trader gives the consumer as required by this regulation is to be treated as included as a term of the contract.
(6) A change to any of that information, made before entering into the contract or later, is not effective unless expressly agreed between the consumer and the trader.
(7) This regulation is subject to regulation 11.

Information to be provided before making a distance contract

13. (1) Before the consumer is bound by a distance contract, the trader —
(a) must give or make available to the consumer the information listed in Schedule 2 in a clear and comprehensible manner, and in a way appropriate to the means of distance communication used, and
(b) if a right to cancel exists, must give or make available to the consumer a cancellation form as set out in part B of Schedule 3.
(2) In so far as the information is provided on a durable medium, it must be legible.
(3) The information referred to in paragraphs (l), (m) and (n) of Schedule 2 may be provided by means of the model instructions on cancellation set out in part A of Schedule 3; and a trader who has supplied those instructions to the consumer, correctly filled in, is to be treated as having complied with paragraph (1) in respect of those paragraphs.
(4) Where a distance contract is concluded through a means of distance communication which allows limited space or time to display the information —
(a) the information listed in paragraphs (a), (b), (f), (g), (h), (l) and (s) of Schedule 2 must be provided on that means of communication in accordance with paragraphs (1) and (2), but
(b) the other information required by paragraph (1) may be provided in another appropriate way.
(5) If the trader has not complied with paragraph (1) in respect of paragraph (g), (h) or (m) of Schedule 2, the consumer is not to bear the charges or costs referred to in those paragraphs.
(6) Any information that the trader gives the consumer as required by this regulation is to be treated as included as a term of the contract.
(7) A change to any of that information, made before entering into the contract or later, is not effective unless expressly agreed between the consumer and the trader.
Requirements for distance contracts concluded by electronic means
14. (1) This regulation applies where a distance contract is concluded by electronic means.
(2) If the contract places the consumer under an obligation to pay, the trader must make the consumer aware in a clear and prominent manner, and directly before the consumer places the order, of the information listed in paragraphs (a), (f), (g), (h), (s) and (t) of Schedule 2.
(3) The trader must ensure that the consumer, when placing the order, explicitly acknowledges that the order implies an obligation to pay.
(4) If placing an order entails activating a button or a similar function, the trader must ensure that the button or similar function is labelled in an easily legible manner only with the words 'order with obligation to pay' or a corresponding unambiguous formulation indicating that placing the order entails an obligation to pay the trader.
(5) If the trader has not complied with paragraphs (3) and (4), the consumer is not bound by the contract or order.
(6) The trader must ensure that any trading website through which the contract is concluded indicates clearly and legibly, at the latest at the beginning of the ordering process, whether any delivery restrictions apply and which means of payment are accepted.

Part 3. Right to Cancel

Application of Part 3

27. (1) This Part applies to distance and off-premises contracts between a trader and a consumer, subject to paragraphs (2) and (3) and regulations 6 and 28.
(...)

Right to cancel

29. (1) The consumer may cancel a distance or off-premises contract at any time in the cancellation period without giving any reason, and without incurring any liability except under these provisions —

(a) regulation 34(3) (where enhanced delivery chosen by consumer);
(b) regulation 34(9) (where value of goods diminished by consumer handling);
(c) regulation 35(5) (where goods returned by consumer);
(d) regulation 36(4) (where consumer requests early supply of service).
(2) The cancellation period begins when the contract is entered into and ends in accordance with regulation 30 or 31.
(3) Paragraph (1) does not affect the consumer's right to withdraw an offer made by the consumer to enter into a distance or off-premises contract, at any time before the contract is entered into, without giving any reason and without incurring any liability.

Normal cancellation period

30. (1) The cancellation period ends as follows, unless regulation 31 applies.
(2) If the contract is —
(a) a service contract, or
(b) a contract for the supply of digital content which is not supplied on a tangible medium, the cancellation period ends at the end of 14 days after the day on which the contract is entered into.
(3) If the contract is a sales contract and none of paragraphs (4) to (6) applies, the cancellation period ends at the end of 14 days after the day on which the goods come into the physical possession of —
(a) the consumer, or
(b) a person, other than the carrier, identified by the consumer to take possession of them.
(...)

Cancellation period extended for breach of information requirement

31. (1) This regulation applies if the trader does not provide the consumer with the information on the right to cancel required by paragraph (l) of Schedule 2, in accordance with Part 2.
(2) If the trader provides the consumer with that information in the period of 12 months beginning with the first day of the 14 days mentioned in regulation 30(2) to (6), but otherwise in accordance with Part 2, the cancellation period ends at the end of 14 days after the consumer receives the information.
(3) Otherwise the cancellation period ends at the end of 12 months after the day on which it would have ended under regulation 3.